Econometrics and data analysis for developing countries

D0139988

Econometrics and Data Analysis for Developing Countries provides a rigorous but accessible foundation to modern data analysis and econometric practice. The book contains many examples and exercises with data from developing countries, available for immediate use on the floppy disk provided.

Distinctive features include:

- teaching regression by example using data from actual development experiences
- a wide range of detailed information from Latin America, Africa and South Asia
- extensive use of regression graphics as a complementary diagnostic tool of applied regression
- opportunities for readers to gain hands-on experience in empirical research
- hundreds of useful statistical examples from developing countries on computer disk

Econometrics and Data Analysis for Developing Countries is designed as a course consisting both of lecture and of computer-assisted practical workshops. It is a unique resource for students and researchers in development economics, quantitative development studies and policy analysis.

Chandan Mukherjee is the Director of the Centre for Development Studies, Trivandrum, India. He has over twenty years' experience of teaching quantitative methods to economics students.

Howard White is Senior Lecturer in Applied Quantitative Economics at the Institute of Social Studies, The Hague, The Netherlands. He has published widely on development economics and other subjects.

Marc Wuyts is Professor in Applied Quantitative Economics at the Institute of Social Studies, The Hague, The Netherlands. He has extensive experience as a teacher in statistics, econometrics and development economics.

Priorities for development economics
Series Editor: Paul Mosley
University of Reading

Development economics deals with the most fundamental problems of economics – poverty, famine, population growth, structural change, indus- trialisation, debt, international finance, the relations between state and market, the gap between rich and poor countries. Partly because of this, its subject matter has fluctuated abruptly over time in response to polit- ical currents in a way which sometimes causes the main issues to be obscured; at the same time it is being constantly added to and modified in every developed and developing country. The present series confronts these problems. Each contribution will begin with a dispassionate review of the literature worldwide and will use this as a springboard to argue the author's own original point of view. In this way the reader will both be brought up to date with the latest advances in a particular field of study and encounter a distinctive approach to that area.

Econometrics and data analysis for developing countries

Chandan Mukherjee, Howard White and Marc Wuyts

London and New York

First published 1998 by Routledge
11 New Fetter Lane, London EC4P 4EE

Simultaneously published in the USA and Canada
by Routledge
29 West 35th Street, New York, NY 10001

Typeset in Times by Florencetype Ltd, Stoodleigh, Devon
Printed and bound in Great Britain by TJ International Ltd, Padstow, Cornwall

British Library Cataloguing in Publication Data
A catalogue record for this book is available from the British Library.

Library of Congress Cataloging in Publication Data
A catalogue record for this book has been requested.

ISBN 0–415–09399–6 (hbk)
ISBN 0–415–09400–3 (pbk)

Contents

Figures

Tables

Boxes

Preface

This book grew out of our frustration as teachers of data analysis and econometrics to post-graduate students in development economics and in population and development at the Centre of Development Studies (CDS, Trivandrum, India) and the Institute of Social Studies (ISS, The Hague, The Netherlands). Our main aim in both institutions was to develop a course which puts the emphasis squarely on data analysis and econometrics as a research tool in the analysis of development issues. But while many good texts exist on statistical and econometric theory, only a few of them deal explicitly with the practice of data analysis in research, and hardly any do so with data relating to the specific problems of developing countries. The purpose of this book is to fill this gap.

This book would not have come about but for the successive cohorts of students at both CDS and ISS who sat through lectures and computer-assisted workshops based upon the successive drafts which accompanied its development. They provided us with both encouragement and invaluable feedback needed to develop a book of this nature. This feedback was particularly important to improve the design of the exercises with real data which constitute an important element of this book. Our sincere thanks to all these students. The development of this book also benefited from the involvement of two of its authors (during 1991–2) in the design and write up of the courses in econometrics and in research methods for the MSc in Financial Economics, the external programme in economics of the School of Oriental and African Studies. Some of the materials and exercises found in this book were initially developed for this programme. Our thanks go to SOAS (and to SIDA, the funding agency) for giving us this opportunity to participate in the development of long-distance courses which included both conventional study materials and computer-assisted exercises. The feedback from course readers, tutors and students was of great help in the subsequent development of this book.

Its writing was made possible by the close collaboration between the Population and Development programmes and CDS and ISS within the framework of the Global Planning Programme in Population and

Development of the UNFPA. Our thanks to UNFPA for creating the opportunity and facility for this collaboration between the two institutions.

We are grateful to Lucia Hanmer and Niek de Jong, ISS colleagues, and to PhD students Hari Kurup, Suresh Babu and Saikat Sinha at CDS and Philomen Harrison and Alemayehu Geda Fole at ISS for their valuable comments on various drafts of the book and their willingness to check for errors and inconsistencies. We thank Philomen Harrison also for her assistance in setting up some of the data sets used here. Furthermore, the comments of three anonymous reviewers and of Professor N. Krishnaji (Centre for Economic and Social Studies, Hyderabad, India) were much appreciated as they greatly helped us to improve the final version of the book. Thanks also to Paul Mosley, the series editor, and to Alison Kirk, the economics editor of Routledge, for their patience and advice during the gestation period. Finally, we would like to express our special appreciation and thanks to Annamarie Voorvelt at ISS who worked tirelessly to turn our various drafts and notes into a finished manuscript.

Centre for Development Studies, Trivandrum   CHANDAN MUKHERJEE
Institute of Social Studies, The Hague   HOWARD WHITE
MARC WUYTS

Introduction

THE PURPOSE OF THIS BOOK

This book provides an introduction to data analysis in the context of econometric practice. More specifically, this book deals with regression analysis as a research tool in development studies. It is a second course in statistics and data analysis for economists and other social scientists working on the problems of the economy and society of developing countries. We assume that you already have done at least one basic course in statistics for economists or for social scientists, and possibly a basic course in econometrics as well. Hence, in this book we assume a basic familiarity with descriptive statistics, with probability theory, random variables and probability distributions, with statistical inference (estimation and hypothesis testing) in the univariate case, and with correlation and regression analysis, bivariate and multiple.

This book is not meant to be a specialised text for econometricians. Instead, it seeks to equip students in development economics in particular, and in development studies in general, with a solid but accessible foundation in the practice of regression analysis in empirical research. This is what lends this book the following distinctive characteristics:

1 it teaches regression analysis by example by making ample use of examples and exercises with real data (available in data files on diskette) drawn from the experience of developing countries;
2 it pays extensive attention not just to statistical inference, but especially to model specification in applied regression analysis – a problem of main concern to applied researchers who are often at a loss as to which model best suits the concrete problem at hand;
3 it draws upon modern approaches to data analysis: exploratory data analysis, misspecification testing, specification searches, and model selection through general to specific modelling;
4 it makes extensive use of graphical methods in data analysis which, along with hypothesis testing, constitute powerful diagnostic tools of applied regression analysis;

5   it deals with specific problems associated with the analysis of survey data (heteroscedasticity; the analysis with categorical variables; logit regression) and with regression analysis of time series data (deterministic versus stochastic trends; cointegration; error correction models).

6   it discusses the simultaneous equation bias, shows how to test for its presence, and deals with the problem of the identification and estimation of simultaneous equation models.

In dealing with these topics we choose to be selective and not encyclopedic in scope. That is, while the book covers a wide range of techniques and methods, it is not our aim here to provide an encyclopedic introduction to all the latest techniques in the practice of econometrics and data analysis. Instead, this book puts the emphasis on explaining the underlying principles of data analysis in applied research, and shows with a selection of specific methods and techniques how these principles inform the practice of data analysis and econometrics without, however, being exhaustive in coverage.

The book is an intermediate text which can be used to teach the practice of econometrics and data analysis to final-year undergraduates or to master-level students. Its mathematical level is not high because the book is not concerned with mathematical derivations and formal proofs of statistical and econometric theory. There are many excellent introductory and intermediate textbooks on statistics for economists and on econometric theory at different levels of mathematical threshold. It is not the purpose of this book to substitute for such texts. It can nevertheless be read and studied independently since it reviews the basic assumptions and properties of classical regression analysis; most statistical and econometric results, however, are stated without proof.

This does not mean that this book relegates statistical and econometric theory to a secondary position. On the contrary, the argument of the book is that theory matters a great deal in applied work. It argues that it is not sufficient to know that certain estimators or tests possess desirable statistical properties given a set of assumptions, since, in applied work, assumptions can never be taken for granted. It is important, therefore, to verify whether they are reasonably satisfied in practice and to know what to do if this is not the case. This book aims to introduce you to the practice of applying statistical and econometric methods in a world of messy data where nothing can be taken for granted.

In statistical theory, we assume that the statistical model is correctly specified and subsequently derive the properties of the estimators and of the hypothesis tests based upon them. The applied researcher, however, more often than not is mainly concerned with finding an appropriate model for the problem at hand. A major theme running through this book, therefore, is that, in applied research, it is important not just to test ideas against data, but also to get ideas from data. Data help you to confirm (or falsify) ideas you hold, but they often also provide clues and hints which point towards other, perhaps more powerful, ideas. Indeed, applied workers are often as much concerned with model creation as with model estimation.

To get ideas from data it is important to look at the data. This is the reason why this book draws heavily upon modern data analysis (in particular, exploratory data analysis) and makes extensive use of modern graphical methods in regression analysis. Indeed, the most distinctive characteristic of statistical data is their variability. No summary statistic such as an average or a regression line can do justice to the full range of variation in data. Graphical methods allow us to look at patterns within the data without ignoring its total variation and, in particular, the exceptions to the rule. In fact, 'exceptions are the rule' (Levine, 1993), or, as Stephen Jay Gould (1996: 40) put it, 'we are still suffering from a legacy as old as Plato, a tendency to abstract a single ideal or average as the "essence" of a system, and to devalue or ignore, variation among the individuals that constitute the whole population'. Graphical methods allow us to see our abstractions in the context of the full range of variation, and to assess whether further clues and hints can be gleaned from the data which may suggest novel ideas or things we overlooked in our analysis.

This book, we hope, may help to guard against the mechanical use of regression analysis in applied research where a model is simply imposed on the data without checking whether its assumptions are reasonably valid in practice or whether it is the most appropriate model for the problem at hand. It also guards against the all too common practice of running a string of regressions in the hope of hitting upon one which looks good and, hence, is singled out as the preferred model while the other results find their way into the waste basket. To do so is data mining, a practice rightly vilified in the literature. Specification searches and data analysis employ similar techniques, but with a very different philosophy. Good data analysis, we argue, involves a theory-inspired dialogue in which data play an active part in the process of arriving at an appropriate specification of a model, and not just in its testing. It is no use to force the data into a straitjacket and ignore the signs which tell us that our model is clearly inadequate, nor should we just discard bad results in the waste basket without asking the obvious question whether the data can help us find out why the results obtained ran counter to our expectations. In the next section we illustrate these points with a simple example of a multiple regression.

THE APPROACH OF THIS BOOK: AN EXAMPLE

This section uses an example to show that seemingly good results in regression analysis may turn out to be quite questionable if we care to scrutinise our data in greater depth. It shows that the mechanical application of regression analysis can lead us astray. And it further illustrates how graphical methods in particular provide us with powerful diagnostic tools which tell us what is wrong with the model and often guide us towards a better way of modelling our data. The example, therefore, aims to give you an initial flavour of the approach to data analysis we seek to develop in this book.

It is not necessary for you to be familiar with all the techniques or graphs used in this example to grasp the main points it makes concerning the approach adopted in this book. In subsequent chapters we shall deal in detail with the methods illustrated in this example. To keep the example simple, however, we shall confine our analysis to a three-variable regression model. In developing this example we shall first adopt a more mechanical approach to regression analysis; subsequently, we shall take a closer look at the seemingly good results obtained with this regression; and finally, we shall explore how the clues and hints obtained from data analysis allow us to arrive at a better model.

Initial model specification and estimation, with some diagnostic testing

Suppose, then, that we intend to explain the variations in the birth rate across countries in terms of the variations in the gross national product per capita and in infant mortality. The birth rate of a country measures the ratio of the number of births in a year over the population in the mid-year, expressed per 1,000 population. It is a fairly crude measure of fertility since it relates total births to the total population without taking account of the age and sex structure of the population. GNP per capita measures the value added per capita accruing to residents of a particular country. Infant mortality is an (inverse) indicator of the health of a nation and measures the ratio of the number of deaths of infants under age one in a year over the number of live births in that year, expressed per 1,000 live births.

Why would fertility depend on these two variables? Fertility may depend on the level of income per capita for a variety of reasons (see, for example, Dasgupta, 1993: 343–76). The conventional argument is that the ratio of costs and benefits of children vary with the level of development of a country. Bearing and rearing children costs time (which falls predominantly on women) and material resources. In many agrarian societies these costs are often spread among kith and kin, while in industrialised and urbanised societies these costs mainly fall on the nuclear family or a single mother. The costs of education, both in terms of time and material resources, varies widely between countries, and tends to be much higher in higher-income countries. Conversely, in terms of benefits, in poor countries children often matter a great deal in terms of the income they generate through paid labour or the contribution they render to the household through unpaid labour, and as potential providers of old-age security for their parents. Taking all these factors, and others, into account, it is usually argued that, *ceteris paribus*, there would appear to be a negative relation between fertility and income (Dasgupta, 1993: 345). In contrast, we would expect fertility to vary positively with infant mortality. Under conditions of poverty and ill-health, where infant mortality is high, it is the expected number of surviving children – that is, children who survive into adulthood – which guides fertility decisions.

Assuming the regression model to be linear, we arrive at the following specification of the regression model (using convenient abbreviations to denote the three variables in play):

$$Birth_i = \alpha_1 + \alpha_2 Y_{i_i} + \alpha_3 IMR_{i_i} + \epsilon_i$$

where birth is the birth rate, Y income per capita, IMR the infant mortality rate, $i = 1, \ldots, n$, where n is the sample size. The error terms, the ϵ_is in the model, are assumed to be each normally distributed with zero mean and constant variance, and to have zero covariances. Following our discussion above, our *a priori* expectations as to the signs of the coefficients are as follows: $\alpha_2 < 0$ and $\alpha_3 > 0$. Hence, the slope coefficient of the income variable is expected to be negative and that of infant mortality to be positive.

Having specified our statistical model, we can now proceed with its estimation. To do this, we use a sample of observations for 109 countries in the year 1985, taken from the World Bank tables. The data can be found in the file BIRTH on the data diskette which accompanies this book. The least squares estimators of the regression model yield the following results (*t*-statistics in brackets):

$$\hat{Birth}_i = 18.8 - 0.00039\ Y_i + 0.22\ IMR_i \quad R^2 = 0.79$$
$$(11.65) \quad (-2.23) \quad (14.04) \quad n = 109$$

At first sight, these results look good. The coefficient of determination, R^2, tells us that the regression explains 79 per cent of the total variation in the crude birth rate. This is a good result given that we are working with cross-section data and a relatively large sample size. Moreover, both slope coefficients have the expected sign and are statistically significant at 5 per cent significance level. The near zero value of the slope coefficient of GNP per capita should not worry you. Why? The reason that this coefficient turns out to be so small is due to the fact that GNP per capita, measured in dollars, varies over a much wider range than the crude birth rate, measured as the number of births per 1,000 population. Consequently, the slope coefficient which measures the impact of a $1 change in GNP per capita on the crude birth rate is bound to be very small, but its overall effect is nevertheless substantive because of the large variations in GNP per capita across countries.

Given that the evidence obtained from the regression confirms our initial hypothesis, many researchers may be inclined to stop the data analysis at this point. This is unwise, however, since the statistical properties of the regression results depend on the assumptions of the regression model being reasonably satisfied in practice. This calls for diagnostic testing of the validity of the assumptions of the regression model. In our example, of particular importance is the normality assumption of the error term which underscores statistical inference (e.g. the *t*- or *F*-statistics), and, since we are dealing with cross-section data, the assumption that the error term has a constant variance.

To test whether the normality assumption is reasonably satisfied in practice we use Jarque–Bera's skewness–kurtosis test (which will be explained in detail in Chapter 3). The basic idea behind this test is to verify whether the higher moments of an empirical distribution conform with those that would be obtained if the distribution were normal. A normal distribution has zero skew and a kurtosis equal to 3. The Jarque–Bera statistic, therefore, tests whether we can accept the joint null-hypothesis that a given empirical distribution (of, say, the residuals of a regression) has zero skew and kurtosis equal to 3. This implies the use of a chi-square test with two degrees of freedom. In this example, the probability value of this test applied to the residuals of our multiple regression yields a value of 0.0574, or 5.74 per cent. At 5 per cent significance level, therefore, we would accept the hypothesis that the residuals are drawn from a normal distribution, although we should not overlook the fact that the probability value is only just above the cut-off point of 5 per cent.

To test whether the error terms have a constant variance we shall use the Goldfeld–Quandt test (which will be explained in detail in Chapter 7). The idea behind this test is fairly simple. The practice of data analysis shows that the variance of the error term often tends to increase (decrease) with the level of one (or more) of the explanatory variables. That is, for example, in a regression of Y on X, the variance of the error term increases (decreases) as X increases. This is particularly common with cross-section data. The test involves sorting the data in ascending order of each explanatory variable in turn, and running two separate regressions with equal sample size for the lower and upper parts of the data, while deleting about a quarter of the observations in the middle. If the error variance is homoscedastic (that is, equal variances prevail), the sums of squared residuals of both sets of residuals will be roughly equal in size. The relevant test features an *F*-statistic which involves the ratio of the larger to the lower sums of squared residuals of both regressions. If we do this test for our example by first sorting the data by GNP per capita and subsequently by infant mortality, we find that we can accept the null-hypothesis that the error variance is homoscedastic in both cases.

This preliminary analysis may lead us to conclude that the available evidence supports our initial model. Indeed, the coefficients of the model have the expected signs and are statistically significant, and the coefficient of determination indicates that the regression explains 79 per cent of the total variation in the birth rate across countries. Moreover, subsequent diagnostic testing shows that the normality assumption is acceptable (at the 5 per cent significance level) and that the error terms are homoscedastic. Our results, therefore, give strong evidence for our hypothesis. But how sound are they really?

Exploring data with graphical methods

Did you notice that we never actually looked at the data when arriving at these results? Similarly, did it strike you that the main purpose in the analysis above was to check whether the evidence supports our hypothesis without much concern about whether there is more that could be learned from the data? The argument of this book is that data analysis can be made more productive and more lively if we care to look at our data. But how do we do this?

The first important lesson of data analysis is that, as Hamilton (1992: 1–2) put it, it is always preferable to proceed from the ground up by first carefully study each variable in turn, and then in pairs, before proceeding to more complex analyses. This is the main reason why this book features two chapters on univariate analysis before moving on to regression analysis. But why is this so important?

The main aim of regression analysis is to explain the total variation in a dependent variable by breaking it down into the explained variation due to the explanatory variables included in the model and the residual variation. It is useful, therefore, to have a good preliminary look at the nature of the variation (of the dependent variable) to be explained and to compare it with the character of the variations in the explanatory variables. To do this, we look at the empirical distribution of the data of each of the variables in play. Figure 1 uses histograms to capture the variation in each of the variables in our model.

The most striking feature about Figure 1 is that the three histograms differ radically in shape. While the crude birth rate appears to be vaguely rectangular in shape, GNP per capita is strongly skewed to the right, and infant mortality is moderately skewed to the right. In general, regressions between variables which differ significantly in shape do not perform well. Ideally, with non-experimental data, we would like our variables to be similar in shape. Why? The econometrician Granger (1990: 12) gives us the following important principle as a possible reason: 'if a variable being explained by a model, the dependent variable, has some dominant features, a minimum condition for the model to be satisfied is that the explanatory variables should be capable of explaining this feature.' And, undoubtedly, the shape of the distribution of the dependent variable is one of its most important features, and, hence, it is important to verify the shapes of the distributions of the variables in the model. Furthermore, regression theory suggests that we would like our variables to be at least

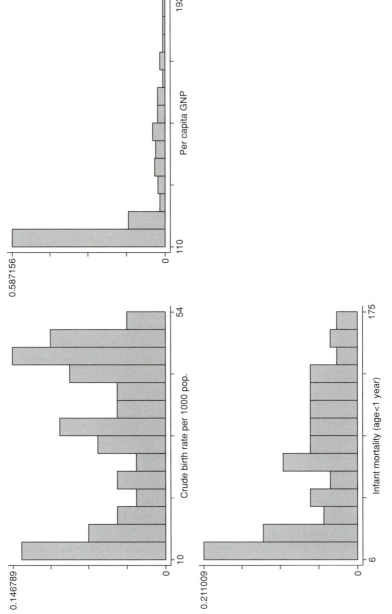

Figure 1 Histogram of the three variables

more or less symmetrical in shape, preferably bell-shaped. In our example, this is not the case. This brief glance, therefore, at the univariate distributions of the data gives us a warning that regression analysis with these data may not be without problems.

Let us go one step further, while still proceeding from the ground upwards, by looking at the bivariate relations between the variables in play. This can best be done by using the simple but powerful device of the scatter plot matrix as shown in Figure 2.

The scatter plot matrix is the graphical equivalent of a correlation matrix and features the pairwise scatter plots of the variables included in a multiple regression. Hence, for example, the plot in the first row and second column features the scatter plot of GNP per capita against infant mortality, while the plot in the second row and first column shows the same plot with the axes reversed (infant mortality against GNP per capita), and so on. The diagonal plots are omitted because they merely involve plotting a variable against itself. The third row features the plots of the dependent variable against each of the explanatory variables.

All the plots are non-linear in shape. This is particularly clear in the plot of the birth rate against GNP per capita (third row, first column) and in the plot of infant mortality against GNP per capita (second row, first column), but also, to a lesser extent, in the plot of the birth rate against infant mortality (third row, second column). This should not surprise you, given the marked skewness in the distributions of the explanatory variables as distinct from that of the dependent variable. Furthermore, some of the plots also reveal the presence of outliers: points which do not fit the general patterns inherent in their scatters.

But undoubtedly the main features of the data are the pervasive presence of skewness in the explanatory variables and the presence of non-linearities in the pairwise scatter plots. As we shall show in subsequent chapters, this calls for appropriate transformations of the explanatory variables aimed at eliminating the effects of the skewness in our data. Not uncommonly, this type of transformation also helps us to correct the non-linearities in the scatter plots. The application of Tukey's ladder of transformations (explained in Chapter 3) led us to the decision to use the logarithms of GNP per capita and the square root of infant mortality, while leaving the birth rate unchanged. Figure 3 shows the corresponding histograms of the variables thus transformed.

As can be seen from these histograms, the shape of the distributions of the new variables, while still different, are now quite similar as far as symmetry is concerned. There is no longer any pronounced skewness in any of these distributions. In fact, the empirical distributions above all appear more rectangular in shape.

Figure 4 shows the corresponding scatter plot matrix. It can be seen from this that the non-linear patterns which dominated the scatter plot matrix with the raw data (depicted in Figure 2) have largely disappeared.

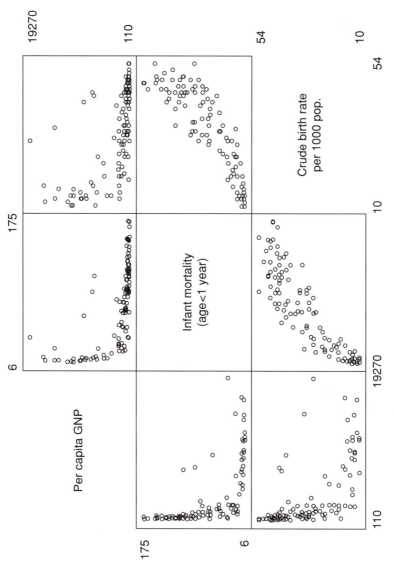

Figure 2 The scatter plot matrix of the variables

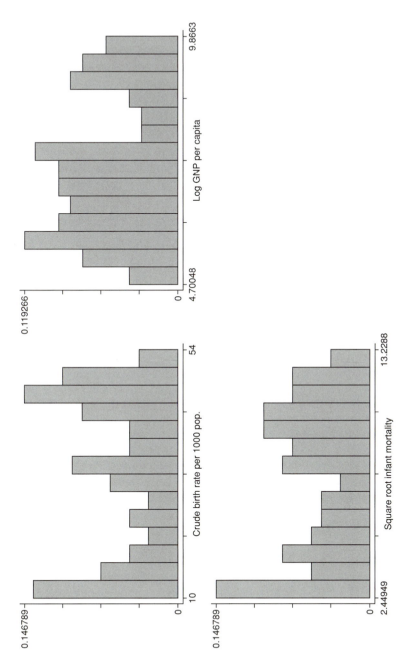

Figure 3 Histograms with transformed data

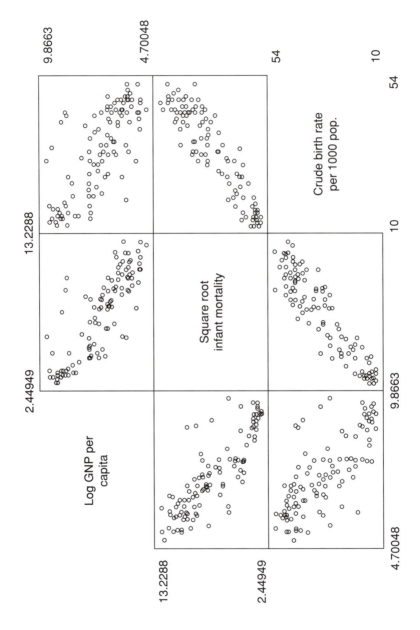

Figure 4 The scatter plot matrix of the transformed variables

Each of the scatter plots now displays a linear pattern, although some still reveal the presence of outliers. More specifically, the plots featuring GNP per capita on one of their axes contain outliers both above and below the main pattern in the data. For example, the plot of the birth rate against GNP per capita shows that, on average, as GNP per capita increases, the birth rate declines, but some points do not conform with this general pattern. Some countries (about four) show a high birth rate given their GNP per capita, while two countries in particular have a low birth rate given their GNP per capita.

In data analysis, these type of clues and hints given by the data can be invaluable to push the analysis further. In this case, for example, the two outliers which lie significantly beneath the main pattern in the data are China and Sri Lanka: both countries have a low birth rate given their GNP per capita (and, similarly, both countries have a low infant mortality rate given their GNP per capita). The countries which lie significantly above the main pattern of the data are mainly fairly rich oil-producing countries with high GNP per capita, high birth rates, and also high infant mortality. These outliers show that it is not always true that a higher (lower) income per capita implies a lower (higher) birth rate (or lower (higher) infant mortality). They are the exceptions to the rule which can give us deeper insights into the problem at hand. Note, however, that the scatter plot of the birth rate against the (square root of) infant mortality does not show the presence of any outliers. This is an important point which can help us to model our data better.

The graphical analysis of the shape of the distributions of each of the variables and of their pairwise scatter plots suggests that it may be preferable to try out a regression with the transformed explanatory variables. It is to this that we turn to next.

A regression model with transformed explanatory variables

The graphical analysis above prompts us to reformulate the specification of our model of the birth rate as follows:

$$Birth_i = \alpha_1 + \alpha_2 \log(Y)_i + \alpha_3 \sqrt{IMR_i} + \epsilon_i$$

The estimation with least squares of this model yields the following results (*t*-statistics in brackets):

$$\hat{Birth_i} = -2.59 + 0.63 \log(Y)_i + 4.06 \sqrt{IMR_i} \qquad R^2 = 0.85$$
$$\quad\;\; (-0.38) \;\; (0.925) \qquad\qquad (13.78) \qquad\qquad n = 109$$

The first thing to note about this new regression is that its coefficient of determination is now about 85 per cent, as against 79 per cent in our earlier regression. Since both regressions feature the same dependent variable, the crude birth rate, their R^2s are comparable because they are both ratios of the same total sum of squares (i.e. the total sums of squares of the crude birth rate). Note, however, that the slope coefficient of the logarithm of GNP per capita no longer has the expected sign, nor is it statistically significant at the 5 per cent significance level.

This lack of significance suggests that the income variable should be dropped from the equation altogether. It is possible to check this proposition graphically using a partial regression plot (as we shall show in Chapter 5). Here we just report the regression results obtained by dropping the income variable (*t*-statistic in brackets):

$$\hat{Birth} = 3.61 + 3.83 \sqrt{IMR_i} \qquad R^2 = 0.85$$
$$(2.75) \quad (24.17) \qquad\qquad n = 109$$

This simple regression confirms that dropping the income variable from the equation hardly affects the coefficient of determination. This regression, therefore, yields a better result than the multiple regression of the birth rate on both GNP per capita and infant mortality.

But perhaps you may be inclined to think that the loss of importance of the income variable, GNP per capita, is solely due to the use of the logarithmic transformation which may have been inappropriate in this case. But the results of the following regression of the birth rate on GNP per capita and on the square root of infant mortality (*t*-statistics in brackets) shows that this is not the case:

$$\hat{Birth}_i = 3.31 + 0.00003 \, y_i + 3.86 \sqrt{IMR_i} \qquad R^2 = 0.85$$
$$(1.56) \quad (0.185) \qquad\qquad (17.61) \qquad\qquad n = 109$$

Clearly, GNP per capita is not statistically significant and, hence, can be dropped from the equation without any significant change in the coefficient of determination. The simple regression of the birth rate on the square root of infant mortality, therefore, is superior to any regression model which also includes GNP per capita or its logarithm.

As can be seen from Figure 3, the distributions of the birth rate and the square root of infant mortality are quite similar: both tend to be rectangular in shape. Furthermore, Figure 4 shows that the scatter plot of the crude birth rate against the square root of infant mortality (third row, second column), unlike the other scatter plots in this matrix, does not feature any outliers.

Further testing also shows that the residuals of the simple regression of the birth rate on the square root of infant mortality lead us to accept the hypothesis that they are drawn from a normal distribution. In this case, the probability value of the Jarque–Bera skewness-kurtosis test equals 0.165, or 16.5 per cent, which is well above the cut-off point of 5 per cent. The scatter plot of the birth rate against the root of infant mortality reveals a very slight tendency towards heteroscedasticity, but this is unlikely to be very significant. In fact, the application of the Goldfeld-Quandt test leads us to accept the null-hypothesis of homogeneous error variances.

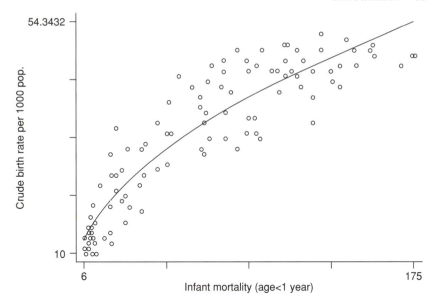

Figure 5 Scatter plot of birth against infant mortality with regression curve (regression of birth against square root of infant mortality)

Figure 5 shows the scatter plot of the birth rate against infant mortality (untransformed) along with the predicted regression curve obtained by regressing the birth rate on the square root of infant mortality. As can be seen from this figure, the slope of this regression curve declines as infant mortality increases. That is, at higher levels of infant mortality it requires a much greater reduction in infant mortality to reduce the birth rate by a given amount than it does at lower levels of infant mortality. Intuitively, this makes sense. If parents' decisions on fertility are determined by their concern with the number of children who survive into adulthood, changes in infant mortality when its level is already low is likely to have a much bigger impact on the birth rate than similar changes when the level of infant mortality is high. Indeed, in the latter case, infant mortality still remains high (even if it declines somewhat) and, hence, the risk of children not surviving still remains considerable. This might explain why the square root of infant mortality performs better as an explanatory variable than infant mortality itself.

This example showed that the transformation of the explanatory variables led us to adopt a simpler model which no longer features GNP per capita as an explanatory variable. This may have come as a bit of a surprise since, clearly, the level of income would appear to be an important factor in explaining the variations in the birth rate. Our results, however, do not imply that the level of income does not matter at all. What they say is that GNP per capita has nothing to add in terms of explaining the variation in the birth rate once we have already taken account of the influence of infant mortality on the birth rate. But clearly the health of a nation in part depends on its wealth in general, and on its average income in particular. A quick glance back at the scatter plot of infant mortality against GNP per capita (or, better still, of the square root of infant mortality against the logarithm of GNP per capita) tells us that both are clearly related. But these plots also reveal that some countries (in particular, China and Sri Lanka) have low infant mortality despite their low GNP per capita, while other countries (such as some of the richer oil-producing countries) have a high infant mortality despite their high GNP per capita. In these exceptional cases, the variation in the birth rate tallies with the variation in infant mortality, and not with that in GNP per capita. Hence, health appears to matter more than wealth in explaining fertility, yet clearly the health of a nation depends to a great extent on its wealth.

Exercise

The data set SOCECON (available on the data diskette) which features a set of socioeconomic data for a sample of countries for the year 1990, contains observations for the birth rate, GNP per capita, and infant mortality. Use these data to repeat the analysis carried in this section (which was done with data for the year 1985) and verify whether you obtain similar results for 1990.

Conclusion

The example in this section shows that we cannot always take our initial model and the numerical results obtained from it at face value. Results which look good at first sight may be riddled with problems if we care to look at our data more carefully. Many of the problems which emerge at the level of multivariate analysis can often be traced back to particularities of the data we encounter in studying their univariate distributions and their pairwise scatter plots. And, as shown in this book, even when we move to multivariate analysis it is still possible to combine diagnostic testing with the use of various simple yet powerful graphical methods (such as, for example, partial regression plots) which allow us to look in depth at the results of multiple regressions. Graphical methods of data analysis and careful diagnostic testing are indeed the principal tools which allow data to play an active part in model specification and evaluation, and as such are invaluable instruments in applied research.

THE STRUCTURE OF THE BOOK

The book is divided into five parts. Part I lays the foundations for the practice of regression analysis. Chapter 1 contrasts traditional and modern approaches to model specification. It argues that, while traditionally (in theory at least) data were not supposed to play any role in model specification, modern approaches recognise the importance of data analysis in model creation, and not just in model estimation and testing. The chapter also briefly discusses the specific problems associated with modelling cross-section as against time-series data. Chapters 2 and 3 deal with the analysis of univariate data. Chapter 2 discusses the centrality of the normality assumption in statistical analysis and shows that if data are drawn from a normal distribution, the mean is the most powerful estimator of the average of the distribution. In practice, however, socioeconomic data are seldom normal in shape. Chapter 3 goes on to see what happens if an empirical distribution cannot reasonably be approximated by a normal distribution, and shows that the mean, which is a least squares estimator, rapidly loses its desirable properties. More specifically, it shows that skewness and the prevalence of outliers in an empirical distribution often render the mean a highly misleading average. The chapter shows how to test for normality and, if needed, how to correct for skewness using appropriate power transformations so as to render the empirical distribution symmetrical and preferably bell-shaped. Finally, the chapter shows why it is that, with most socioeconomic data, it is the median, rather than the mean, which provides us with a more reliable estimator of the average of a distribution.

Part II deals with the practice of applied regression analysis and constitutes the core of the book. Chapter 4 discusses simple regression, while Chapters 5 and 6 deal with its extension to multiple regression. As a point of departure, this part briefly reviews the assumptions and properties of the classical linear regression model (first simple, then multiple regression) and the standard statistical inferences (estimation and hypothesis testing) based upon it. But, as argued in the chapters of this part, we can never take the assumptions of the model we use in practice for granted, nor do we always know *a priori* whether our model is correctly specified. The problem is further complicated by the fact that, in development research (as in socioeconomic analysis in general), we work almost exclusively with non-experimental data which are often highly collinear in nature and, hence, render the interpretation of results difficult. The novelty of the material discussed in this part, therefore, concerns the treatment of the practice of regression analysis when it is uncertain what the most appropriate model is and whether its assumptions are likely to be satisfied in practice, and when the interpretation of the resulting regression coefficients is often obscured due to the prevalence of collinear regressors in socioeconomic research. This explains the importance devoted in this book to residual analysis and influence diagnostics; to transformations towards normality and linearity; to the interpretation of regression coefficients, using partial regression and partial regression plots, in situations where nothing is held constant; to the sensitivity of regression coefficients to alternative neighbouring specifications with collinear regressors; to the practical problems associated with the potential trade-off between the misspecification bias and the precision of an estimator; and to the practice of testing down by imposing linear restrictions on a general model to arrive at a more specific specification.

Part III then turns to particular problems of regression and data analysis which are mainly (but not exclusively) associated with the use of cross-section data. Chapter 7 deals with heteroscedasticity: how to detect it (using both graphical methods and diagnostic tests) and how to correct for it, either through the use of an appropriate transformation of the data or through the use of weighted least squares. Chapter 8 deals with the use of categorical data in regression analysis. This is particularly important in development research where survey data (in which categories and counts are often prominent) occupy an important role in applied research. Apart from the use of categorical data in regression analysis by means of dummy variables, this chapter also discusses the analysis of contingency tables and test of independence between categorical variables. Finally, Chapter 9 looks at the problem when the dependent variable is categorical and dichotomous in nature, and discusses the use of logit modelling and regression in applied research. Specific attention is paid in this chapter to the logit as a convenient transformation of counts of a binary categorical variable, and to residual analysis and influence diagnostics in logit regression.

Part IV deals with some of the problems associated with regression analysis with time series data. Chapter 10 discusses why the problem of spurious correlation is so prevalent with trended time series data. It introduces the concepts of stationarity and of deterministic and stochastic trends in time series, and shows how to test for stationarity. Chapter 11 deals with autocorrelation as a problem of model misspecification and shows how to test for its presence and what lessons can be learned from it in terms of model specification. Finally, Chapter 12 gives an introduction to the analysis and application of cointegration and of error correction models in applied research.

Finally, Part V deals briefly with the implication of simultaneity in economic models for empirical analysis. Chapter 13 discusses the problem of the simultaneous equation bias and shows how to test for the exogeneity of the explanatory variables in a model, and subsequently deals with the identification of a simultaneous equation model. Chapter 14 then discusses single equation methods for estimating an equation in a simultaneous model.

USING THE DATA SETS WITH THIS BOOK

This book puts the emphasis squarely on data analysis in econometric practice as applied to problems of developing countries. As stated above, our aim in this book is not to provide specialised training in advanced econometrics, but rather to provide applied researchers and students of development problems with a solid foundation in the practice of empirical research. Our experience as teachers in econometrics, data analysis and development has taught us that this can best be done by giving students ample opportunity to practice with real data drawn from problems of developing countries. For this reason, the data sets used in the major examples and in the various exercises of this book are included in the diskette with the book.

Appendix A, on the data sets, lists the definitions and sources of the variables used in each of the data sets provided on diskette and used in the examples and exercises of this book. These sets contain both cross-section and time-series data. Some of the data sets contain comparative data for a sample of countries, some are secondary data relating to one country only, and the remainder feature primary survey data drawn from micro studies of specific problems. All data sets relate to problems of developing countries, a focus which is generally not found in textbooks on econometrics and data analysis. Taken together, these data sets provide teachers with many examples and students with ample opportunity to gain hands-on experience with real data. In the main text of this book each data set is identified by its file name without extension. The data diskette then contains the data sets both as LOTUS and ASCII files. Hence, in the text of this book, the file BIRTH refers to the data used in the example of this introduction; on the data diskette, the corresponding data can be found as BIRTH.WK1 in a LOTUS file and as BIRTH.TXT in an ASCII file.

To be able to carry out the exercises in this book or to redo its examples, students should have access to a computer. Many of the exercises of the book can be done with a spreadsheet program; in teaching we find that first introducing examples through a spreadsheet encourages students to better understand the basic concepts. Even though most spreadsheets do not calculate statistics such as the Durbin–Watson statistic, such output may be fairly readily constructed. However, in more advanced applications the use of a spreadsheet can become quite tedious. Hence it is preferable to be equipped with an appropriate statistical and/or econometric software package. We found it quite useful to rely on both a statistical package and an econometric package: the examples in this book were worked out with either STATA or TSP, depending on which was most convenient to use (although STATA is not so common, few other packages have its range of data analysis tools). The use of the data sets in this book, however, in no way depends on the use of any particular statistical or econometric package, although obviously some packages lend themselves more easily to the approach adopted here.

In general, a statistical package equipped with good analytical graphical methods of modern exploratory data analysis lends itself best to teaching regression applications, particularly when coupled with univariate analysis. They are also useful for teaching cross-section analysis, particularly when it involves the extensive use of categorical data. Econometrics packages, in contrast, have a clear advantage with time series data. Hence, the analysis of stochastic or deterministic trends, the use of lagged variables in regression models, and, more specifically, the analysis of cointegration and of error correction models, can best be done with econometric software. As a general rule, however, the approach of this book favours the use of statistical or econometric packages which are equipped with good analytical graphics.

Part I
Foundations of data analysis

1 Model specification and applied research

1.1 INTRODUCTION

In development research, most research questions typically involve relations between two or more variables. Regression provides a powerful tool to investigate such relations empirically. This book deals with applied regression as a research tool. Applied regression is about modelling data, a complex process of the evolving specification, estimation, evaluation and interpretation of a model (Granger, 1990: 1). Good modelling requires an active dialogue between theoretical reflection and empirical evidence to arrive at a model which presents an adequate, yet parsimonious, approximation of the underlying mechanisms helping to bring about the phenomena to be explained.

You may find the task of modelling data rather daunting notwithstanding the fact that you may have received prior basic training in statistical or econometric principles. Working with real data always turns out to be less straightforward and definitely more messy than conventional textbooks make it out to be. Part of the problem is that good modelling is both an art as well as a science and, hence, a good grounding in statistical and econometric theory is necessary but not sufficient. But it is equally true that traditional textbooks in statistics or econometrics do not always address the type of concerns which are foremost in the mind of applied researchers. They often pay undue attention to estimation and hypothesis testing within the confines of a given model, but have little to say about the difficulties involved in arriving at an appropriate model specification in the first place. In other words, traditional texts tend to assume that a researcher is fully equipped with a correctly specified model which he or she seeks to estimate or test against data specifically sampled for that purpose. In applied work, however, we cannot make this assumption so easily. In fact, model creation or selection is often the most creative and exciting but also frustrating aspect of doing research. The search for an appropriate model which answers the research question of an empirical study is more often than not the main preoccupation of an applied researcher. But, unfortunately, traditional textbooks in statistics and econometrics remain rather silent on this issue. This book puts the emphasis squarely on modelling data by applied regression analysis. Obviously, to do this we shall make extensive use of regression theory within the context of formal statistical inference. But, while reviewing the basics of regression theory, our point of view will consistently be that of an applied researcher who seeks to put to use what he or she has learned in statistics or econometrics courses in a context where he or she is preoccupied with finding out what the appropriate model is that best answers the research question which guides empirical work. It is this viewpoint which gives this book its particular flavour.

This chapter addresses the question of the role that data play in model specification. This is not an easy question nor is there agreement as to its possible answers. It is, however, a question of great practical significance. The way you answer this question will shape the modelling strategies you are likely to adopt or consider permissible, although it is not uncommon for a researcher to profess one answer in principle, yet behave quite differently in practice. The key issue is whether data have a role to play in model creation or whether they should only be used to test a given model or estimate its unknown parameters. In other words, do we only test ideas against the data or do we also get ideas from analysing data? This is a highly contentious issue which underlies debates on modelling strategies in applied research. Section 1.2 gives a simple framework to clarify the connection between statistical inference (model estimation and testing), on the one hand, and model specification, on the other. Section 1.3 then discusses traditional econometric modelling in which data were not meant to play any role in model specification, although in applied work *ad hoc* modifications were made to improve a model. In modern parlance, as a result of mounting criticism against this approach, this type of modelling is known as specific-to-general modelling or the average economic regression. Section 1.4 discusses three modern approaches to modelling: general-to-specific modelling, exploratory data analysis, and fragility analysis (known, more technically, as extreme bounds analysis). Finally, section 1.5 briefly discusses the distinction between cross-section and time-series data in the light of the problems they pose in terms of modelling data.

1.2 MODEL SPECIFICATION AND STATISTICAL INFERENCE

In development research, our interest is to investigate relations between two or more variables. The types of relations we are talking about seldom concern exact relationships between variables unless we are dealing with identities in a context of accounting frameworks. Typically, our problem is to come to grips with relations between variables in non-deterministic situations in which regularity of data goes hand in hand with considerable random error fluctuations. For example, Engel's law, which postulates that the share of food expenditures in total household expenditure falls as household income rises, does not imply that two households with equal income will spend an equal amount of money on food. On the contrary, Engel's law at most refers to an average relation. Hence, most of the relations we investigate in applied work tend to be blurred due to unaccountable erratic variation in the data. The types of relations we deal with, therefore, are essentially imperfect.

This is the reason why we rely on statistical modelling to analyse relations between economic variables. Typically, statistical data display two distinctive features: a regularity of some kind coupled with erratic variation. A statistical model based on probability theory seeks to capture both these components (regularity and error variation) in a single specification, a model, of the way the data behave. This theoretical stochastic specification, therefore, embraces both a systematic structural component (which can be a simple average or a more complex average relation between several variables) and a random component, which taken together account for the total variation in the dependent variable.

The easiest way to think about this distinction between regularity and residual random variations is to reflect on the difference between sound and noise. If you listen to a badly tuned radio, you will have difficulties in distilling the meaningful message (the sound) in the midst of the interfering noise. Statistical modelling tries to do something similar when analysing variability in data. The aim is to extract a meaningful message (the systematic component) in the midst of erratic variations (the noise element). A well-specified model, then, conveys a clear message (sound) surrounded by unexplained and irreducible error variation (noise). What matters is not just that the structural part of the model is theoretically meaningful and incisive, but also that the noise component no longer contains any significant messages. Perhaps paradoxically, therefore, to check whether an estimated model is reasonably adequate we need to take a good look at the residual variation it leaves unexplained to see whether it no longer contains hidden messages which signal that the model is probably misspecified. Put differently, to test for model adequacy we do not just look at the message its structural component conveys, but we also scrutinise its residual variation to check whether it leaves things unsaid.

A statistical model, therefore, is an abstraction we use to characterise and explain the variability in real data. It is a theoretical construction in a double sense. First, to model the data we draw upon substantive theory (e.g. economics, population studies, social analysis), and second, we also rely on probability and statistical theory to model the stochastic nature of the relations between variables. Both sources of theoretical inspiration – substantive theory and statistical theory – do not join together, however, in an additive fashion. As we shall see repeatedly in this book, modelling does not just involve tagging on a random component after the substantive analysis has been completed. The choice of the random component, the error term, is itself an important part of the modelling exercise.

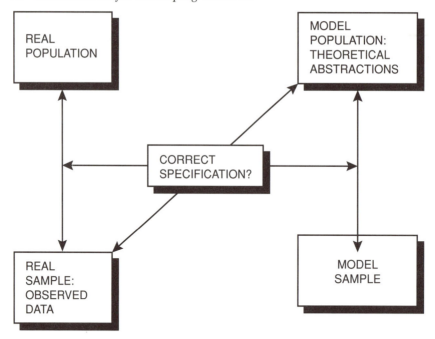

Figure 1.1   The elements of a statistical study
Source: Adapted from Giere, 1991: 126–8.

An empirical study involves a dialogue between theory and empirical evidence so as to arrive at an explanation which provides an adequate answer to our research question. This dialogue implies a confrontation between abstract theory-inspired models and the data, in a process which is generally interactive. Figure 1.1 provides a schematic overview based on Giere (1991: 126–8). It has a simple but powerful message.

Giere makes a distinction between the four components of a statistical study: the real population, the real sample, the model population and the model sample. To start with, in statistical analysis we sample data from a real population so as to be able to make valid inferences from the real sample about its population. In other words, we seek to generalise our conclusions derived from a sample beyond the confines of the sample. To do this, however, we need to make explicit assumptions about the character of the real population and about the nature of the sampling procedure. This is where theoretical abstractions come into play. The model population is a hypothetical theoretical construction (a model) which depicts our assumptions about the character of the real population. It is, therefore, a theoretical population which behaves exactly in accordance with our assumptions. Finally, a model sample is a hypothetical sample drawn from the model population in accordance with our assumptions about the sampling procedures.

The theory of statistical inference allows us to make valid inferences about the model population from the model sample. It deals with estimation and hypothesis testing in a context where the data behave exactly as our assumptions would have them behave. If our assumptions are reasonably valid in practice, the real sample will more or less behave as a model sample would do, and, hence, we can reasonably safely proceed by making inferences from the real sample about its population as characterised by the model population. Our inferences, therefore, proceed from real sample to model population, as indicated by the diagonal line in Figure 1.1.

Hence, to be able to generalise conclusions drawn from a real sample we always need to make explicit assumptions about the character of the real population. But for these inferences to be valid in practice, our theoretical model has to be a reasonably adequate specification of the character of the population and of the nature of the sampling procedure. Otherwise, any conclusions we draw from our sample are invalid notwithstanding the outward sophistication of models and techniques we use.

This is what the art of modelling is all about. It is very important, therefore, that we should never confuse the real data with the abstractions we use to model them. There are two reasons for this. First, it would lead us to accept models at face value without investigating whether they are reasonably good approximations of the patterns inherent in the data. In other words, as Leamer (1978: 4) put it, in applied work we cannot take the 'axiom of correct specification' for granted. That is, we cannot just assume that our model correctly specifies the character of a real population and of the sampling procedures used to obtain the observed data. Part of the exercise of modelling is the need to verify whether the assumptions we make are reasonably valid in practice. But, second, even if this is the case, we should never forget that real data never behave exactly as the theoretical variables we use to represent them.

To see this latter point, consider a simple hypothetical example of a modelling exercise with only one variable. Suppose we have a sample of observations on daily wages of casual workers (paid on a piece-rate basis), randomly drawn from a wider population of daily wages paid out over a given period in time. As we shall see in Chapters 2 and 3, we might consider modelling the data by assuming that they were independently sampled from a normal distribution with unknown mean and variance. This assumption now defines a theoretical stochastic variable which depicts the assumed behaviour of our real data on daily wages. If the real data display a typical bell-shaped empirical distribution (without major outliers), we can safely base our inferences on this assumption and proceed, for example, by estimating the mean and variance of this distribution using the sample data.

But daily wages cannot be negative nor can they exceed some definite upper limit. In contrast, a theoretically normally distributed variable ranges over a domain from minus to plus infinity. Given a big enough sample, it is always possible to show that the real data diverge from our theoretical assumptions (Chambers *et al.*, 1983: 192). Real data can never come from a genuine normal distribution with its exact shape, infinite precision and range. What matters in practice, however, is whether this theoretical bell-shaped curve provides a reasonable approximation of the empirical distribution of the real population. What do we mean by reasonable? If our aim is to make inferences from a sample about a population with certain precision and confidence, a reasonable approximation means that the actual departures of the data from the theoretical assumptions do not seriously affect the inferences we draw from that data. Fortunately, most commonly used statistical techniques tend to be fairly robust with respect to minor discrepancies between data and the theoretical distribution used to model them, but they are by no means insensitive to major departures from the assumptions. For example, if daily wages display a skewed distribution or reveal the presence of significant outliers, inferences based on the assumption of normality can be seriously misleading.

Hence, in order to make valid inferences from a sample about its population it is necessary that the assumptions we make in modelling the population are reasonably valid in practice. But this raises a thorny issue. Do we not rely in part on the data to verify whether our assumptions are valid in practice? If so, do we not adapt models in the light of hints, clues or tests derived from the data so as to end up with a better specification? But does this approach not entail the danger of getting caught up in a circle: using our data to improve a model and, subsequently, using the model to make inferences from the data? There is, therefore, a potential tension between the two roles that data can play in analysis: testing models against data and getting ideas from data to improve our models. As we shall see, this tension is inherent in the practice of modelling data. As such, it is a major preoccupation for any practitioner engaged in data analysis.

To avoid confusion, however, let us make clear from the outset that model specification inevitably involves abstraction and, hence, is always theory-inspired. Nobody argues that facts speak for themselves. Theory is the driving force in the process of modelling. But this raises two interrelated questions. First, how much guidance do we expect from theory in model development or creation? Second, at which point, if at all, do data enter the scene? Both questions underlie the debates on the approaches to modelling.

What guidance do we expect from theory? Here is an interesting quotation from two economists-turned-anthropologists on this issue:

> Theories can stimulate new ideas, facilitate the posing of novel, interesting questions and generally guide fieldwork. However, they can also overdetermine field research and be a barrier to the development of

understanding. Discovering the fine line between theoretical guidance and theoretical overdetermination – between pre-formulated questions and pre-formulated answers – is no easy task.

(Gregory and Altman, 1989: 20)

Hence, in this view, good theoretical groundwork can open up opportunities in developing new ideas but it can also act as a barrier. Or, as the anthropologist Malinowski put it more vividly, 'preconceived ideas are pernicious in any scientific work, but foreshadowed problems are the main endowment of a scientific thinker' (cited in ibid.: 11). This is a nice way of stating a key problem that a researcher typically confronts in empirical work, but it still begs many questions when discussing approaches to modelling. Few methodologists would disagree with Gregory and Altman that theoretical guidance is a good thing, while theoretical overdetermination can act as a hindrance. Nobody prides themselves that they engage in research equipped with preconceived ideas. The problem remains as to what we mean by appropriate theoretical guidance. How much is too much? Indeed, what some consider as well-structured guidance, others may dismiss as gross overdetermination. So, when does theoretical guidance turn into overdetermination?

To dig deeper into this question it is necessary to take a closer look at what we mean by doing theoretical groundwork for research. Sound research requires an applied worker to be familiar with the theoretical debates surrounding his or her research question. Theories differ because they derive from competing schools of thought or because they present different positions within a given paradigm. Whichever is the case, solid research requires that a researcher comes to grips with rival theories which address his or her research question. The question now arises as to the role data play in choosing among competing rival explanations. Should a researcher be committed to a particular hypothesis, cast it in a well-specified model, and subsequently test this model in isolation against the data? Or should a researcher approach the data in a more open-ended fashion, allowing the data to play a role in choosing among competing rival explanations, so as to end up with a preferred model which appears most plausible in the light of the evidence? Which of these two approaches should guide the practice of research? In the next section we look at how traditional modelling strategies approached this question, while in section 1.4 we turn to modern approaches to modelling data.

1.3 THE ROLE OF DATA IN MODEL SPECIFICATION: TRADITIONAL MODELLING

Traditional econometric modelling (as well as classical statistics) unconditionally opted for the first variant: models are to be tested in isolation against data specifically sampled for that purpose. Consequently, theory reigns supreme in the business of model specification. This tradition in econometrics came of age in the wake of the Haavelmo–Cowles research programme initiated in the 1940s, and reached its heyday in the 1960s, after which it came under increasing methodological attack in the 1970s (Morgan, 1990).

In this view, model specification was the exclusive preserve of theoretical groundwork. Data entered the scene to test whether a model stood up to scrutiny and to estimate its unknown coefficients. If a model failed the test, a researcher had to go back to the drawing board, reassess the core theory of the model or its auxiliary premises, and come up with a new conjecture – a new model – to be tested against a fresh set of data. Data could reject or validate a model and estimate its coefficients, but they should never be allowed to suggest new or better models. Data analysis, therefore, was confined to what the philosopher R. W. Miller (1987: 173) called 'a lonely encounter of hypothesis with evidence'. Any attempt to allow data to play a role in model specification was dismissed as non-rigorous and methodologically unsound (Heckman, 1992: 884). This amounted to data mining, which was the greatest sin any researcher could commit.

So much for the principles laid down by this approach. But where did it leave an applied researcher? In theory, at least, the tension inherent in the dual role of data was settled by denying data any role in model specification. Applied econometrics, as Mary Morgan (1990: 263) put it, was reduced to a mere statistical complement of theoretical discourse. But applied econometricians found it hard to conform with this principle, even when they agreed with it in theory. Real data always prove to be unruly when a model is first tested against them. A relation assumed to exist between two or more variables may turn out to be weak or non-existent; the estimated coefficients of a model may have the wrong signs or take on implausible values; or the residual variation of the estimated model may signal that the assumptions about the error term are by no means satisfied. A researcher adopting the traditional strategy to modelling should in principle discard the data set, think again and come up with a new model to be tested against a fresh sample of data. But data are hard to come by: there is only one set of national accounts for a particular country over a given period; a household budget survey is normally done only once every five or ten years. Researchers who collect their own data are equally aware of the costs and time involved in sampling a fresh set of data. In practice, therefore, the option of starting anew when a model fails to perform well is rather limited. So how did applied workers resolve this problem?

Actual practice involved a process of trial and error in which data inevitably played a role in model specification. Typically, a researcher would start by trying out a preferred specification against the available data. If things went well – that is, the results were in line with theoretical expectations and the estimated relation came out strong – the process could stop there. But more commonly things did not go smoothly on the first trial. In this case, it was common to assume that the core idea of the model was still correct, but further complications needed to be taken into account to bring out the assumed relation in full view. A researcher would try out a range of *ad hoc* modifications to the model: perhaps add another variable, change the functional form of the equation, or incorporate a more complex specification of the random component. This process is not unlike the way a cook tries out a given recipe, tastes it and, depending on the taste, decides to add a few more ingredients to improve its aroma or appearance.

This approach to modelling is still very widespread in applied work today. You might be inclined to argue that cooks who proceed in this trial and error fashion often make dishes worth eating. This is undoubtedly true. Similarly, many data analysts often come up with interesting models arrived at by *ad hoc* modifications of an initial simpler version. But this approach also has its pitfalls. To understand this, remember that traditional econometric modelling requires a researcher to make a firm commitment to a particular model specification. The model is subsequently tested against the data in isolation from possible rival models. Most commonly the model chosen by a researcher is his or her pet theory. Trial and error through *ad hoc* modifications will then result in a model specification which generally retains the main thrust of the researcher's preferred theory. But this entails the real danger that applied work merely boils down to 'an unstinting collection of evidence in support of one's ruling theoretical position' (Pelto and Pelto, 1978: 283). At no point is any attention given to the possibility that rival theories or models may explain the phenomenon in question just as well, or even better, without perhaps requiring as many *ad hoc* alterations in model specification as were necessary to get one's pet theory into shape.

Hence, the real problem with this approach is not that it is unable to come up with interesting models. The problem is that it concentrates exclusively on one theoretical explanation in isolation from its possible rivals. But should empirical analysis just boil down to a lonely encounter of a hypothesis with its evidence? Or is genuine analysis comparative in nature? It is perfectly possible that a particular explanation looks plausible in the light of its evidence, yet another rival explanation may do just as well, if not better. What matters in applied analysis, therefore, is that empirical analysis enables us to discriminate between rival explanations. One philosopher put this point as follows:

> No encounter with data is a step towards genuine confirmation unless the hypothesis does a better job of coping with the data than some natural rival ... What strengthens a hypothesis, here, is a victory that is, at the same time, a defeat for a plausible rival.
>
> (Miller, 1987: 176)

The underlying principle here is that the strength of an idea, or of a model, shows itself only when compared with rival ideas or models, and not when analysed in isolation.

In conclusion, traditional econometric modelling requires a researcher to make a firm commitment to a particular model which subsequently is to be tested against data. In this view, therefore, theoretical guidance means that model specification is the exclusive preserve of theory. In practice, however, *ad hoc* modifications are made to the initial specification in the light of trial and error testing against a given data set. Data mining, while condemned in principle, was (and continues to be) rampant in practice. Models emerge after an iterative process in which data play a role in deciding on the final specification. Throughout the process, the model remains insulated from rival explanations and is fortified by a battery of *ad hoc* alterations to fit its evidence better. While this process can undoubtedly produce challenging and interesting models, it lacks the real essence of genuine testing of a theory which inevitably involves taking account of competing theories. Because of this critical weakness, this approach came under increased attack, particularly from the 1970s onwards. The traditional approach subsequently became known as what Leamer called the 'average economic regression' or what Hendry labelled 'specific to general modelling'. Let us now look at some modern modelling strategies.

1.4   THE ROLE OF DATA IN MODEL SPECIFICATION: MODERN APPROACHES

Modern modelling strategies all share the common characteristic that they tend to be more data-centred, meaning that they allow data to play a more prominent role in model specification. While traditional modelling practices saw model specification as the exclusive domain of theory and, therefore, outside the reach of data analysis, modern approaches to modelling include specification searches, guided by theory, as an integral part of data analysis. More specifically, a common feature of the more modern approaches to modelling is that they are far more comparative in nature. Data are made to play an active part in choosing among rival specifications. In other respects, however, these approaches differ markedly from one another and, as such, they do not represent a unified strategy for modelling data.

It is not our intention here, however, to provide an exhaustive survey of modelling strategies in statistics and econometrics nor to compare different methodologies in any great detail (see, for example, Diaconis, 1985; Granger, 1990; Kennedy, 1992: 73–90; 278–89). Instead, in this section we shall briefly discuss some leading ideas and principles of three main variants of modern approaches to data analysis: (a) general to specific modelling based on model selection through hypothesis testing; (b) exploratory data analysis as a tool to detect meaningful patterns in the data; and (c) fragility (or sensitivity) analysis which checks how sensitive particular results of model estimation and testing are with respect to neighbouring (competing) model specifications.

General to specific modelling

The principle of testing downwards rather than adjusting upwards seeks to make the problem of model selection an integral part of statistical inference. It arose in opposition to the established practice in traditional econometric modelling which, as we discussed in the previous section, proceeded by making *ad hoc* alterations whenever needed to an initial preferred (and simpler) version of a model. The problem with adjusting upwards is that subsequent statistical inferences (estimation and hypothesis testing) lose precision because the model has been adapted to fit the data against which testing and estimation takes place. General to specific modelling, in contrast, proceeds by testing downwards inasmuch as it requires a researcher to start with a broadly specified overarching model which contains within it several feasible specifications that depict rival explanations of the phenomenon in question. It is akin to fitting a loose dress to a person – a dress which could fit several candidates – and, subsequently, tailoring it down to size. Hence, the process involves two steps.

First, a researcher formulates a model which encompasses rival explanations deemed relevant in the light of theoretical research. The task is to make sure that the initial broader model is itself an adequate specification of the data-generating process. Hence, before testing downwards can start, it is necessary to subject the general model to a battery of misspecification tests which seek to verify that the noise component of the general model no longer conveys hidden messages. To prevent this happening, researchers are advised to make the initial general model sufficiently broad so as to avoid leaving out relevant factors. The obvious implication is that the initial specification will inevitably carry a lot of extra baggage.

Second, the researcher then attempts to simplify the general model by imposing restrictions on it, the validity of which can be formally tested. In this way, a researcher hopes to arrive at a simpler model which is acceptable in the light of the empirical evidence. Hypothesis testing against data plays an active role in model selection which involves a choice among rival models. Testing downwards, therefore, implies general to specific modelling through vigorous sequential hypothesis testing which enables a researcher to weed out rivals which do not stand up to the empirical evidence and to zoom in on a model which appears plausible in the light of the data.

Consider a simple example. A researcher postulates a model which involves a simple relation between Y and X along with a noise element (the error term). A rival theory, however, suggests that a third variable, Z, is also important in explaining the variation in Y. Traditional econometric modelling proceeds by first trying out the simple relation between Y and X. If the results look good, our researcher will stop there. General to specific modelling, however, requires that the researcher starts with the broader model – Y is explained by both X and Z along with an error term – and subsequently the researcher should test formally whether Z can be dropped from the equation. Hence, our researcher should formally test the restriction that the coefficient of Z equals zero against the data. The simple model is only selected if the data allow this restriction to be imposed on the more general model.

This approach of general to specific modelling puts great emphasis on rigorous testing: misspecification testing of an initial general model followed by further model selection based on sequential testing of various restrictions imposed on the general model. For this reason, this approach (which is associated with work carried out by Professor Hendry at the London School of Economics in the 1970s and 1980s) is often referred to as the test-test-test approach to modelling because of its insistence on rigorous testing (see for example, Gilbert, 1990; Spanos, 1990; Charemza and Deadman, 1992; Kennedy, 1992: 73–90). The approach has been developed mostly in the context of dynamic models involving time series analysis, but the general principle of model selection by testing downwards is obviously equally applicable to cross-section data.

How does this approach address the tension between learning from data and testing ideas against data? To resolve this tension, general to specific modelling integrates model selection within the realm of statistical inference. To learn from data which model to choose, it is necessary to select between models through formal hypothesis testing. As we shall show repeatedly in this book, this approach to modelling is a handy and powerful tool for applied workers. Whenever possible, it is always preferable to test downwards rather than adjust upwards so as to check the validity of the assumptions underlying a particular model.

But as is the case with all methodological approaches, the method of general to specific modelling also has its weaknesses, apart from its considerable strengths as a guide to data analysis. Two problems are worth mentioning in this context.

First, the particular path taken in testing downwards from a general specification to a specific model may determine the final outcome. In other words, two researchers using the same general model with the same data will not necessary arrive at the same restricted version of the model. A given set of data may well admit quite different theoretical explanations. This in itself should not surprise us; empirical evidence does not always allow us to discriminate clearly between rival explanations. Part of the problem is that, by its nature, a general model carries a lot of extra baggage. With non-experimental data, it is quite common that the different variables in an equation end up blurring each other messages because they tend to overlap in various ways. As Leamer (1978) argued, much of the testing downwards exercises undertaken in applied work have a lot to do with making sense of blurred messages and involve interpretative or simplification searches rather than clear-cut hypothesis testing between well-defined rival explanations. That is, restrictions are imposed on the general model to ease the economic interpretation of the results (because the data do not allow for greater complexity). In such circumstances testing downwards may well be more a matter of convenience – the hope of arriving at a restricted version which makes good sense – than of a conscious choice between rival explanations.

Second, the method of model selection by testing downwards starts with the proposition that, as Heckman (1992: 883) put it, 'a wide class of models can be, or has been, enumerated in advance of looking at the data and that empirical work consists in picking one element in a fixed set'. In other words, the theoretical groundwork prior to data analysis is supposed to come up with a comprehensive account of all rival theories deemed relevant to the research question and to cast them within the confines of a testable overarching model which allows data analysis to play its part in the process of selection between this fixed set of rivals. But, with Heckman, we can argue that 'more often, empirical work suggests rich new classes of models that could not have been anticipated before the data are analysed' (ibid.). The point is that data analysis can enrich theory, not just pick a rival explanation among a predetermined list.

This second point is highly relevant for development economists. If our interest is to estimate a demand function for food, for example, we can rely on demand theory and a wide range of empirical examples to guide our work. In this context it is preferable to make sure that we start with a general specification which includes all variables deemed relevant and, subsequently, proceed by testing downwards. In this case our aim is well defined (estimating a demand function) and economic theory provides us with strong guidance. But what if we embark on a study of the effects of structural adjustment on informal sector manufacturing in a developing country? In this case we may find that our initial theoretical preparation does not give us such firm handles that we can integrate into a model which embraces all relevant rival explanations. Theory will provide guidance, but more in the shape of a set of vague ideas – avenues to be explored – rather than a set of fully fledged rival hypotheses. Research of this nature will almost certainly involve exploratory empirical work of a type which falls outside the reach of formal statistical inference. This brings us to exploratory data analysis (EDA) as a second approach to modelling data.

Exploratory data analysis (EDA)

The set of techniques initiated by Tukey (1977) and Mosteller and Tukey (1977) rapidly evolved into a novel approach to data analysis. EDA puts the emphasis squarely on learning from data so as to arrive at an explanation which appears plausible in the light of the evidence. At first sight it may appear that this approach simply advocates facts speaking for themselves and, hence, that it is sufficient to scrutinise data to distil an explanation out of empirical evidence. This is not the case. Data by themselves do not tell you anything unless you engage with data in a dialogue which is theory-inspired. It is necessary for you to fire questions at the data so as to get hints and clues from them. In exploratory data analysis, this process of questioning the data has two distinct features.

First, EDA insists that data should be approached from different angles by analysing them in several different ways through an interactive process informed by theoretical reflection (Hamilton, 1992: viii). The point is to try out a particular avenue, reflect on it, perhaps follow up any clues or hints, and plan what to do next. It involves, therefore, a trial and error process inspired by theoretical preparation and subsequent reflection. The process will obviously be richer, the more a researcher incorporates the perspectives of rival theories in the analysis of data so as to weed out theories which appear implausible in the light of the evidence and to follow up more promising avenues.

Second, in pursuing a given question, EDA proceeds by fitting patterns readily detectable in the data so as to be able to focus on the remaining residuals obtained by removing the fit from the data. Hence,

$$DATA = FIT + RESIDUALS$$

where the FIT is a preliminary model employed to remove key patterns from the data so as to be able to look more carefully at the residual variation. In EDA, a researcher does not assume that the residuals no longer contain meaningful messages and, hence, they cannot be put aside as pure noise.

The latter point is important. In traditional econometric analysis, residuals played only a relatively minor role. At most, a few tests were routinely performed with residuals to check whether it was necessary to make specific *ad hoc* modifications to the original specification. In this view, residual analysis allowed a researcher to detect the symptoms of a few known specification illnesses which could readily be cured by applying appropriate corrections. Modern approaches to modelling do not operate in this way. If residuals behave contrary to model assumptions, modern approaches to data analysis will see this as a general sign of model misspecification. This is the reason why general to specific modelling, based on the principle of test-test-test, always starts with a battery of misspecification tests to check whether the general model is data admissible. EDA, in contrast, uses residuals to look for further meaningful patterns in the data so as to come up with novel discoveries as to which other factors should also be taken into account. Hence, in EDA, the basic premise is that it is necessary first to remove patterns which are obviously present in the data so as to bring out more hidden factors at play. To put it simply, while traditional modelling often finds the residual variation a nuisance (particularly when it fails to behave as pure noise), exploratory data analysts treat residuals of earlier fits as a rich source from which to extract clues and hints as to further avenues of inquiry. In this way they hope to be able to come up with new models which could not conceived before the data are analysed.

To find the unexpected, it is necessary to look for it. This is the reason why EDA, unlike traditional modelling approaches, makes extensive use of analytical graphics along with numerical summaries. As Kennedy (1992: 284) put it:

> EDA, exploratory data analysis, is an approach to statistics which emphasizes that a researcher should begin his or her analysis by looking at the data, on grounds that the more familiar one is with one's data the more effective they can be used to develop, test, and refine theory. Econometricians are often accused of never actually looking at their data. Exploratory data analysts believe in the inter-ocular trauma test: keep looking at the data until the answer hits you between the eyes!

EDA, therefore, allows us to get clues and hints from data which, after further theoretical reflections, may lead us to new ideas and models. In terms of the inherent tension between learning from data and testing against data, EDA is explicitly concerned with the former. This is its strength, but also its weakness. In situations where our knowledge is as yet vague and no firm hypotheses exist, EDA can be of great help to dig deeper into a problem. At times, due to lack of data availability, this may imply that we cannot do more than arrive at a model which seems plausible in the light of the evidence without being able to test it independently against a fresh set of data. But at times it is possible that ideas obtained through data exploration in one part of the research lead us to interesting follow-ups which can then be formally tested against the data. In actual research exploratory and confirmatory data analysis interact in ways which are neither purely rigorous hypothesis testing nor mere post-data model construction.

Fragility or sensitivity analysis

How sensitive are the key results of model estimation to minor changes in model specification? This is a question which guides a third approach to modelling rooted in fragility or sensitivity analysis. This approach is associated with the work of Leamer (1978, 1983); a similar notion can also be found in Mosteller and Tukey (1977) in their discussion on all-subset regression and on the woes of regression coefficients. The basic principle, as Leamer (1983; Granger, 1990) put it, is that an inference is not believable if it is fragile, i.e. if it can be reversed by minor changes in assumptions. The point is that often researchers are mainly interested in the value or the sign of one coefficient in a model. For example, a researcher may wish to know whether the demand for a particular commodity is price elastic or not. Alternatively, the interest of a researcher may be to investigate whether public investment crowds out private investment. Or you may wish to test Griffin's famous hypothesis that foreign aid displaces domestic saving. In all such cases, the attention of the analyst centres on the value or sign of the coefficient of what Leamer referred to as the focus variable in the model. But the models actually employed to obtain these estimates will generally include more variables, the coefficients of which are of lesser immediate concern. If, however, minor changes in model specification lead to major changes in the coefficient of the focus variable, we have good reason to doubt the conclusions drawn from any such particular specification which proves to be highly fragile.

Leamer's methodology is Bayesian in approach and hence, by its very nature, more comparative in scope than classical statistical inference. Leamer's particular brand of fragility analysis, or what he called extreme bounds analysis, is highly complex. The 'extreme bounds' refer to the upper and lower boundaries of the range within which a coefficient varies with respect to alternative model specifications. Leamer's specific approach is well beyond the scope of this book, but we shall nevertheless retain the general idea of fragility analysis: the necessity to investigate the bounds within which a coefficient varies as a result of minor changes in model specification.

The basic idea, therefore, is that key results of a model should be subjected to sensitivity analysis with respect to a neighbouring range of alternative specifications which differ from one another by the inclusion or exclusion of a number of doubtful variables (variables which the researcher is not fully confident should be included or not in a specification), apart from key variables (one or more of which can be focus variables) which feature in all specifications. If the inferences from the coefficients of focus variables prove to be highly fragile with respect to the inclusion or exclusion of doubtful variables, not much confidence can be placed in the conclusions derived from such inferences. This approach to modelling, therefore, seeks to assess how fragile the inferences we make are with respect to minor changes in model specification. To do this, we seek to find the bounds in the variation of one or more key coefficients across a range of alternative neighbouring specifications so as to judge the robustness of our results to minor changes in model specification.

Summary

In this section we reviewed three distinct sets of ideas on the role of data in model specification. These three methodologies share in common that they assign an active role for data in model choice, development or selection. Obviously, as shown above, each approach has its distinctive flavour which corresponds to a particular methodological outlook. But we would also argue that each approach has its own strengths and weaknesses which differ depending on the particular context of research. If, for example, your particular interest is to show that public investment crowds out private investment, it is not very sensible to settle on one specification which happens to produce the required negative coefficient if minor alterations to this preferred specification render this result insignificant or even reverse its sign (we shall see an example of this in Chapter 6). If you are dealing with a problem of model choice in which economic theory provides you with forceful handles that allow you to nest rival models inside a more general specification, hypothesis testing in the context of general to specific modelling seems to be a logical choice of modelling strategy. But if, in contrast, your research question is still rather vague and theory can do no more than indicate plausible avenues of inquiry, a researcher may well have to rely on extensive data exploration to arrive at a firmer hypothesis. In actual practice, from the start of a piece of applied analysis to its conclusion you may well find yourself drawing on a combination of the three approaches.

Hence, while each of these approaches is rooted in distinctive methodological outlooks, it seems fair to say that each approach will prove its strengths or reveal its weaknesses, depending also on the specific context of the research. Therefore, in this book, we do not seek to rally your support in favour of one of these approaches, but instead our aim is to draw upon each of these methodologies and show their usefulness in different research contexts so as to enhance your own ability to employ data actively in the process of model specification. Indeed, the three approaches are complements rather than substitutes, all rooted in the same basic philosophy that data have a role to play in model specification.

1.5 THE TIME DIMENSION IN DATA

The data we use in development studies always have a time dimension. Time enters in a double sense depending on (a) how we measure our variables, and (b) whether our interest is to study evolution over time or to make comparisons at a particular point or period in time.

As to measurement, it is useful to distinguish clearly between stock and flow variables. A stock is measured at a particular point in time; a flow is measured for a particular period (say, a month or a year) in time. The consumer price index, for example, is a stock variable since it measures the level of prices at a point in time. The rate of inflation, in contrast, is a flow variable defined over a period in time. Similarly, population is a stock variable, while births, deaths and migration are flow variables. These examples also show that changes in stock variables are themselves flow variables. Investment, for example, is a flow variable which adds to the stock of capital.

Time series depict evolution over time; cross-section data make comparisons at a particular point or period in time. National income accounts, trade data, industrial production statistics and price series are examples of time-series data. A household budget survey, a population survey, an industrial survey, employment and labour market surveys are typical examples of published cross-section data. Both types of data are commonly used in development research, although modern-day econometrics tends to give greater prominence to the analysis of time series data.

Cross-section data generally consist of surveys and, hence, involve random sampling from a wider population. Regression theory is based on the assumption that the sample is drawn randomly from the population, and so survey data normally conform with this requirement. In contrast, however, time-series data seldom do, and therefore they pose special problems.

Indeed, a time series can best be seen as one observation of a particular historical process over a number of years, rather than as a collection of independent observations of unconnected occurrences. This year's price of a commodity bears some relation to last year's price. GDP growth, stagnation or decline takes place in discernible trends, reversals or cycles. Time-series data, therefore, reflect an inherent momentum which can often continue over long periods of time. This is the reason why conventional time-series analysis (Box and Jenkins, 1970) sought to forecast the future evolution of a variable solely in terms of its own past. In sum, time series seldom behave as a set of data randomly sampled without any connection between successive observations. Instead, they reflect the underlying history of an economy or society.

But this leads us to a second problem inherent in working with time series: the danger of interpreting spurious correlations as evidence for the existence of causal connections between two or more variables. What is a spurious correlation? At its simplest it may mean that two or more variables are causally unrelated but, by chance, a correlation exists between them. But in time-series analysis we are likely to observe spurious correlations for another reason. Consider a simple example. Two persons, unconnected in any way, walk side by side along the same street in the direction of a bus stop to catch the same bus. We observe their movements but are unaware of their respective purposes. We might be tempted to infer that they belong together. This is a spurious correlation. In fact, each intends to catch the bus, never mind what the other does, and neither influences the behaviour of the other. Yet they walk together at the same time in the same direction. Time series often 'walk together' in this way: both may be following a deterministic trend or what is called a random walk. Hence the fact that many socioeconomic variables seem to move together should not lead us to infer that such variables are necessarily causally linked in a direct manner. The history of econometric practice, however, has shown that all too often such causal inferences are made.

But all is not bad news as far as working with time series is concerned. Time series also offer opportunities in analysis precisely because of their time dimension. They allow us to investigate the structure of determination between variables over time by linking the past history of some

variables to the future evolution of others. For example, we could investigate whether, in a cash-crop-producing economy constrained by foreign
exchange availability, income earned from last year's sale of export crops
limits expenditures on imports in the current year. Put differently, time
series allow us to specify equations which include lagged variables so as
to capture dynamic interactions between variables over time. Furthermore,
the inclusion of lags in the dependent variable allows us to distinguish
between long-run equilibrium relations and short-run dynamic disequilibrium behaviour. This explains why time series play such a prominent
role in econometrics.

Recent developments in econometric theory and practice have been
particularly concerned with these special challenges posed by time series
in applied work. The danger of spurious correlations has led to more
attention being given to modelling trends (particularly, stochastic trends)
in time series. In fact, as we shall see, many economic time series tend
to behave as random walks. This has led to the development of cointegration analysis (Granger and Newbold, 1974, 1977) which seeks to
investigate long-run relations between economic variables without falling
prey to spurious correlations. Furthermore, error-correction models (for
a recent and comprehensive reference, see, for example, Banerjee *et al.*,
1993) seek to incorporate short-run disequilibrium behaviour along with
long-run tendencies in econometric modelling.

A word of warning is, however, in order with respect to empirical
analysis with time series. In econometric models, time generally enters as
a subscript of variables in an equation. That is, time enters as logical time,
not chronological or historical time. A useful way to see how time is dealt
with in econometric studies is to consider an analogy with experiments in
physics. Suppose we heat a container with a fixed volume of water and
graph the rise in the temperature of the water against time (measured,
say, in seconds). We can repeat this experiment several times under identical conditions to produce the same graph over and over again. Time *t*
in the graph refers to logical time, not historical time. Development
research, however, is a historical science. Time is more than a mere
subscript in an equation. Economies and societies evolve and transform
over time. Events unfold over time and produce irreversible change. For
example, South Africa in the 1990s is qualitatively different from what
it was in the 1960s. We can analyse history but we cannot replay it.
Econometric models often aim to come to grips with structural interactions between variables which characterise the basic momentum of an
economy over a prolonged period in time. In so doing, we abstract from
the more historically specific events which marked this particular period,
but obviously we cannot abstract from the broader historical context
to which the model refers. The point of it all is to model some key
features which capture the interactions between variables inherent in the
momentum of the economy in the period concerned. Note, however, that

data exploration of time series can help to bring out specific historical features which matter in modelling the dynamic character of a particular economy in a particular period.

1.6   SUMMARY OF MAIN POINTS

1   Modelling data is not just a question of model estimation and hypothesis testing; it also involves model specification. Traditional textbooks in statistics and econometrics tended to emphasise the former, but applied researchers are often more concerned with the task of finding an appropriate model which best answers the research question.

2   A statistical or econometric model seeks to come to grips with relations between variables in non-deterministic situations in which regularity in data (an average or an average relation) goes hand in hand with considerable residual random variations. A model specification, therefore, has both a structural component (sound) as well as a residual error component (noise), both of which together seek to capture the variation in the data. Modelling data, therefore, requires that we rely both on substantive (development economics) and statistical (probability) theory.

3   The validity of statistical inferences (estimation and hypothesis testing) depends on whether the assumptions behind the models we use to analyse the data are reasonably valid in practice. Before making any inferences, therefore, it is necessary to check whether the assumptions of our model are reasonable, given the problem at hand.

4   There is a potential tension between the dual roles data can play in analysis: (a) testing ideas against data within the confines of a given model, and (b) getting ideas from data to develop or improve a model or to choose between rival models. Modelling strategies differ, depending on the way they handle this tension.

5   Traditional modelling approaches sought to resolve this tension by denying that data had a role to play in model specification. Theory reigned supreme in the business of model specification. Data entered to test a model in isolation from its rivals or to estimate its coefficients. In practice, however, applied work generally involved making *ad hoc* modifications to a model in the light of the initial results of model estimation and testing. Data mining, while condemned in principle, turned out to be rampant in practice.

6   Modern approaches to modelling give data a greater role to play in model specification: (a) general to specific modelling allows data to choose between rival models through formal hypothesis testing. Model selection takes place by testing downwards within a general model which allows for different interpretations depending on the nature of the restrictions imposed on it; (b) exploratory data analysis seeks to obtain hints and clues from data by looking carefully at the (residual)

patterns within the data. Its main object is to learn from data, rather than to test ideas against data; (c) fragility analysis investigates how sensitive the results of model estimation and hypothesis testing are with respect to minor changes in model specification. The basic idea behind this approach to modelling is that not much confidence can be placed in fragile inferences which can be reversed by minor changes in the model.

7 In data analysis it is useful to distinguish between stock and flow variables. The former are measured at a point in time and the latter are measured over a period in time. Stock and flow variables can feature in both cross-section and time-series analysis. Cross-section data make comparisons at a given point or in a given period in time, while time-series data depict evolution over time. The latter are specifically suited to analysing the dynamic interplay between variables but pose the problem that they are prone to spurious correlations.

2 Modelling an average

2.1 INTRODUCTION

This chapter and Chapter 3 deal with the problem of modelling a simple average of a single variable. But why bother with univariate analysis if, in development research, our main interest is to study empirical relations between two or more variables? Why not jump straight to regression analysis? We can think of three reasons why it is best to start with uni-variate analysis.

First, we should always be aware that specific features we may come across in univariate analysis, such as the presence of an outlier or of pronounced skewness in the distribution of a variable, invariably have multivariate implications. Unexpected or puzzling results in regression analysis can often only be properly understood if we look at the distributions of its variables. Failure to do this often leads to nonsense regressions. For this reason, it is best to proceed from the ground up: study each variable in turn before embarking on investigating relations between them (Hamilton, 1992: 1–2). Starting in this way also gives you an excellent opportunity to become familiar with basic techniques of EDA (exploratory data analysis) which teach you how to look carefully at a batch of data. Second, residuals play a key role in the process of modelling data with regression analysis, particularly in the context of modern modelling strategies. To verify whether the assumptions of the models we use are valid in practice, it is important to look carefully for hidden messages in the residuals. To do this, we treat the residuals of a regression as an observed variable in its own right. Univariate analysis helps us to look for patterns within residuals or to test the distributional assumptions we make about the random error term in a regression. Finally, regression analysis involves averaging of a complex nature. In empirical analysis, when we say that Y is a function of X, we mean to say that the average value of Y is a function of X (Goldberger, 1991: 5). In other words, in regression analysis we deal with conditional means of Y for given values of X. Consequently, common errors we make when dealing with a simple average often crop up again in more complex forms when we subsequently move from univariate to multivariate analysis.

Data analysis embraces both the problem of finding an appropriate model (model specification), on the one hand, and model estimation and testing, on the other. This chapter only deals with the latter aspect: estimation and hypothesis testing within the confines of a model which we assume to be correct. It further assumes that a univariate sample is drawn from a normal distribution. Why do we make this assumption? One reason could be that most data we encounter in practice are approximately normal. Hence, if normality is the rule, it makes good sense to start with this assumption. Unfortunately, while in some sciences data often behave in this way, most social or economic data are not (approximately) normally distributed. As we shall see, it is hard to find examples of social or economic data which display the typical bell-shaped, normal distribution. More often than not, social and economic data are skewed. Another reason could be that the normal distribution is ideal for obtaining meaningful averages and, hence, serves as a useful example for the problem of averaging. This is indeed the case and explains why we take the normality assumption as a point of our departure. A final reason is that it is often possible to find an appropriate mathematical transformation which eliminates skewness in the distribution of a variable, and makes the normality assumption acceptable.

In section 2.2, we show intuitively that normality in data renders it easier to make sense of averages. Section 2.3 then reviews the assumptions of the classical model for estimating the mean of a univariate distribution. Section 2.4 shows that, given these assumptions, the arithmetic mean of the sample data is the best, linear, unbiased estimator of the population mean. Subsequently, section 2.5 introduces the principle of maximum likelihood and shows that the sample mean is also a maximum likelihood estimator if the population distribution is normal. Section 2.6 then deals with estimation and hypothesis testing with respect to the population mean. Finally, section 2.7 summarises the main points of this chapter. What to do if the normality assumption is not valid in practice will be dealt with in Chapter 3.

2.2 KINDS OF AVERAGES

In data analysis, we use theoretical abstractions – probability distributions – to analyse real data. Model specification, therefore, should capture the main features of the data. An average is one such feature: it gives us the location parameter of a distribution (Rosenberger and Gasko, 1983: 297). To model an average, it is useful to reflect on the kinds of averages we use when dealing with real data, and what each of these averages tell us about the data. This type of reflection should help us to gain insights into the problem of modelling an average.

In descriptive analysis, three kinds of averages are frequently used: the mean, the median and the mode. To obtain the mean of a sample, we sum the data and divide the result by the number of observations. The median is the middle value of the ordered list of the data: half of the observations lie below the median and half above it. The mode is the most frequently observed value of the data. In a theoretical distribution, the mean and median give us respectively the centre of gravity (i.e. the balance point: the point at which a distribution would balance if it were made of a solid substance) and the centre of probability (middle value) of a distribution, while the mode is its peak. If a distribution has several peaks (not necessarily of equal height) we say that it is multimodal.

An average, taken alone, tells us very little about the data. To interpret an average we need to have a good idea about the shape of the empirical distribution of the data which shows the pattern of variability in the data. To look at shape, we shall make use of the familiar histogram. Generally, the questions we are interested in are the following: (a) are the data unimodal, or multimodal? (b) are the data symmetrically distributed around the average, or are they skewed? (c) does the empirical distribution have a main body together with fat, thin or no tails? and (d) if unimodal and symmetric, does the distribution display a typical bell-shaped curve?

These questions help us to search for key features of an empirical distribution and allow us to assess the relative usefulness of different kinds of averages. If, say, a distribution turns out to be bimodal, a median or a mean will be of little use. In this case, it is preferable to look at each mode in turn. More often than not, bimodal (or multimodal) empirical distributions give us a clear signal that we have lumped together two (or more) sets of data which should have been kept separate. For example, if women are paid less than men, income data for a given level of education or skill may turn out to be bimodal. In general, whenever a distribution shows clear multimodal patterns, sit back, think hard, and try to find the factor(s) which may account for the multiple modes. In this way, the data can often be split up in distinct sets of unimodal data (which are always far easier to analyse).

But even if our data are (roughly) unimodal, shape continues to matter when looking at the practical relevance of different kinds of averages. In general, symmetry in the data makes life easier for a data analyst. If, furthermore, the data turn out to be bell-shaped, the notion of an average becomes even more meaningful. To see this, take a look at Figure 2.1. The top panel depicts the daily demand (in terms of number of workers) for casual (manual) labour in Maputo harbour, from March 1980 to June 1981 (a total of 485 observations); the bottom panel gives the distribution of actual recruitment of these workers for the same period. The data for this example are in the data file MAPUTO. Both distributions are reasonably symmetric and bell-shaped (with the data on recruitment showing a slight skew to the left). For this reason, we superimposed a normal distribution (with the same mean and standard deviation as the data) on each of the histograms. The vertical lines depict the means of both distributions.

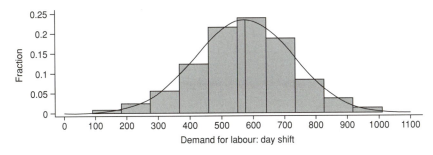

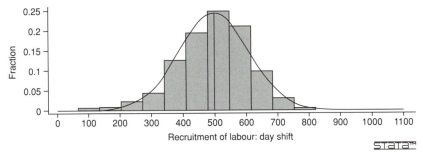

Figure 2.1 The demand for and recruitment of casual labour, Maputo harbour

Table 2.1 lists the means, medians and modes, along with the standard deviations, for both sets of data. Since the mode is the midpoint of the group with the highest frequency (fraction) of the data, computation of its location is sensitive to the number of groupings used to construct the histogram. As we can see, in each case the mean, median and mode are virtually equal to each other. Hence, for descriptive purposes, it does not matter much which one we use. They all tell the same story.

In sum, this type of bell-shaped distribution has the following characteristics:

1   The average (mean, median or mode) is unambiguously located in the centre of the distribution. Symmetry assures that the two halves left and right of the average are mirror images.
2   The greater the distance from the average, the lower the frequency: the mass of the distribution is concentrated in the neighbourhood of the average.
3   The smaller the variance, the more representative the average becomes for the data as a whole.

Table 2.1   Averaging the demand for and recruitment of labour at Maputo harbour

	Mean	*Median*	*Mode*	*Standard deviation*
Demand	574	571	Similar	155
Recruitment	500	503	Similar	109

In our example, average recruitment is considerably lower than the average demand for labour. Furthermore, the variation in recruitment clearly does not match the much greater variation in the demand for labour. In this case, therefore, the supply of labour appears to have been insufficient and relatively inflexible with respect to the larger variations in demand. Both examples show us that the average of a bell-shaped distribution is easy to interpret. This ease of interpretation is due to the essential symmetry of the data.

Note, however, that symmetrically distributed data are not always bell-shaped. For example, the distribution of rounding errors (say, when we round up aggregate data to the nearest million) has a typical rectangular shape – a distribution with a body but no tails. We can best describe this distribution by its range (the difference between the two extremes) since its average (mean, median or mode) is nothing but the middle value of this range.

Now, take a look at Figure 2.2 which depicts a skewed empirical distribution. It is the distribution of weekly overtime payments for casual labour on the day-shift in Maputo harbour in the period from March 1980 to June 1981. During this period, wage rates were constant, but obviously weekly earnings will differ due to variations in recruitment and in access to overtime work. The data were obtained by taking a random sample of the weekly earnings of 45 workers over 13 weeks randomly selected within this period, and subsequently selecting those observations (368 in total) which pertained to the day-shift (as distinct from the night-shift). The vertical lines in the graph show, from left to right, the locations of the mode, median and mean of the distribution. Table 2.2 lists their

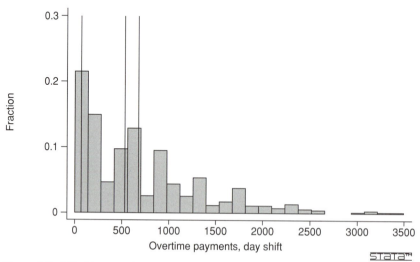

Figure 2.2   Weekly overtime payments

Table 2.2   Averaging overtime payments

	Mean	Median	Mode	Standard deviation
Overtime payments	674	525	±80	629

numerical values, along with the value of the standard deviation. As can be seen from Figure 2.2, these three kinds of averages do not tell the same story. In this case, therefore, the usefulness of an average is much more ambiguous.

In fact, the mean, median and, particularly, the mode are far apart. Each of these 'averages' tells a different story. The mode is the peak of the distribution, the median its middle value, and the mean its balance point. This example shows that, for a unimodal distribution which is skewed to the right (i.e. its tail is on the right), the mode will be smaller than the median which, in turn, will be smaller than the mean. Conversely, the mode of a unimodal distribution skewed to the left will be greater than its median which, in turn, is greater than the mean. The lack of symmetry, therefore, results in no clear centre of the distribution. In fact, in this example, the most distinctive feature of the distribution is its virtual exponential decline from left to right, ending up in a long tail.

In sum, when an empirical distribution is unimodal, symmetric and (preferably) bell-shaped, the concept of an average is fairly straightforward. The peak of the distribution, its middle value and its balance point all coincide. Symmetry ensures that both halves left and right of the average are mirror images. The bell-shaped distribution implies that the frequency declines as the distance from the average increases. By contrast, the average of a unimodal skewed distribution is far more ambiguous: the location of the mean, the median and the mode depends on the distribution of the data between its peak and its tail.

Let us now return to the question of modelling data. The lesson we can learn from these examples with real data is that modelling an average invariably requires us to make assumptions about the shape of the distribution. In this chapter we shall assume that the population distribution is symmetrical and bell-shaped. More precisely, we shall assume that the relevant model is the normal distribution. In this case, the population mean (the first uncentred moment of the distribution), the median and the mode all coincide in one unambiguous 'average'. Furthermore, the normal distribution is characterised by its thin tails. In fact, there is only a 5 per cent chance that an observation drawn from a normal distribution is more than 2 standard deviations away from its mean; the probability of encountering an observation which is more than 3 standard deviations distant from the mean is as low as 0.3 per cent. Finally, as we shall see, if data are distributed (approximately) normally, the mean and the standard deviation tell us all we need to know about the data.

Exercise 2.1

Using the data file SOCECON (with world socioeconomic data for 1990) on the diskette, make histograms and compute means, medians and modes for the following variables:

1   GNP (gross national product) per capita;
2   HDI (human development index);
3   FERT (fertility rate);
4   LEXPM and LEXPF (male and female life expectancy);
5   POPGRWTH (population growth rate).

In each case, discuss the different averages in the light of the shape of the empirical distribution. Would you say that any of the distributions is reasonably symmetrical and bell-shaped? (If you do not know how to compute a median, jump ahead to Box 3.1 in Chapter 3.)

2.3   THE ASSUMPTIONS OF THE MODEL

A statistical model is an analytical construct which helps us to come to grips with non-deterministic situations in which regularity in the data can only be understood in a context of considerable random fluctuations. Perhaps the simplest statistical model is one where its systematic component merely states that the variable fluctuates around a constant population mean, μ:

$$Y_i = \mu + \epsilon_i \qquad i = 1 \ldots n \tag{2.1}$$

where ϵ_i is a random variable which depicts the random fluctuations of the data around its constant mean. In statistical language, this random variable is referred to as the error term or the disturbance term of the model. If we intend to use this specification in practice, the first task we have to confront is to check whether the assumption of a constant mean is reasonable.

For example, the assumption of a constant mean does not seem far-fetched in the case of the day-to-day fluctuations in the demand for labour in Maputo harbour, at least in the period specified. But take a look at Figure 2.3, which plots real manufacturing GDP of Tanzania against time over the period 1964–73. It is obvious that it would make little sense to average manufacturing output over that period. The reason is that the variable in question clearly grows over time and, hence, the assumption of a constant mean for all observations is simply not valid. Consequently, the systematic component in equation (2.1) is clearly misspecified in this case. A more appropriate specification would be:

$$Y_t = \mu_t + \epsilon_t \tag{2.2}$$

where $t = 1964 \ldots 1973$. In fact, the systematic component, μ_t, of the model could conceivably be depicted by a linear trend, as follows:

$$\mu_t = \alpha + \beta t \tag{2.3}$$

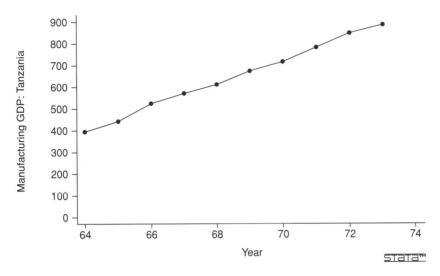

Figure 2.3 Real manufacturing GDP, Tanzania

The model now becomes,

$$Y_t = \alpha + \beta t + \epsilon_t \qquad (2.4)$$

an alternative specification which allows for the mean of Y_t to vary linearly with time. But now we are jumping ahead into bivariate analysis, a topic we shall further explore in Chapter 4. The point we want to make here, however, is that there are many instances in which we cannot assume that a constant mean prevails for all observations in the sample. This assumption is questionable in many time-series applications, as it may be with some applications with cross-section data.

Exercise 2.2

Can you think of a few concrete examples with cross-section data where the assumption of a constant population mean for all observations in the sample is clearly inappropriate?

In fact, we have come across one example already. If women are paid less than men for equal levels of education or skills, equation (2.1) would be inappropriate to model the fluctuations of income of both men and women with similar education and skills. In this case, it would be more correct to apply the model separately to incomes of, respectively, men and women. Similarly, mortality levels may differ between urban and rural populations, or among social classes. Averaging across these categories may well give us misleading results since we assume a single population when, in fact, several distinct populations should be considered.

But let us assume that we are dealing with a situation where the assumption of a constant mean is valid in practice. The model as specified in equation (2.1), however, is still incomplete. The reason is that we need to specify the stochastic nature of the error term. In classical statistics, at least three assumptions are made with respect to the behaviour of the error term:

$$E(\epsilon_i) = 0 \tag{2.5}$$

$$E(\epsilon_i^2) = \sigma^2 \tag{2.6}$$

$$E(\epsilon_i \epsilon_j) = 0 \text{ for all } i \neq j \tag{2.7}$$

The first assumption is obvious: the error term has zero mean. This ensures that μ is indeed the population mean of the variable Y_i, since,

$$E(Y_i) = \mu + E(\epsilon_i) \tag{2.8}$$
$$= \mu$$

Assumption (2.6) states that the error term is homoscedastic. That is, it has a constant variance. When we say that the error term has a constant variance, we do not mean to say that all error terms will have the same size. What it means is that each error is drawn from a population with the same variance. Since the probability distribution of Y_i and ϵ_i are identical but for their respective means, it follows that Y_i also has the same constant variance:

$$E(Y_i - \mu)^2 = E(\epsilon_i^2) = \sigma^2 \tag{2.9}$$

The systematic component, μ, does not explain the variation in Y, but only its average level. Consequently, the total variation in Y_i equals the variation in the error term.

The assumption in equation (2.7) states that the various error terms (ϵ_i; $i = 1, \ldots, n$) are statistically independent of one another. For example, the fact that the error term of observation i was large should not influence the size of any prior or successive error terms. We assume, therefore, that the data have been generated through random sampling. This assumption is not always valid in practice. For example, if our sample is a time series, the error terms may well be autocorrelated; that is:

$$E(\epsilon_i \epsilon_j) \neq 0 \text{ for all } i \neq j \tag{2.10}$$

Consequently, the data generating process does not conform to our assumption that the data were randomly sampled.

As yet, we made no assumption about the shape of the population distribution. However, as we have seen in the previous section, shape matters when assessing the usefulness of different kinds of averages. So, do we not make any assumption about the shape of the distribution of the error term? In fact, in classical statistics, we certainly do. More specifically, we add the assumption that the error term derives from a normal distribution. This assumption, together with equations (2.5) and (2.6), can be written as follows:

$$\epsilon_i \sim N(0,\sigma^2) \tag{2.11}$$

which states that the error terms are normally distributed with mean 0 and a constant variance.

This is a strong assumption which in practice we should never take for granted without scrutinising the data first. For example, the normality assumption appears to be quite reasonable for the data on the demand for and recruitment of casual labour in Maputo harbour as shown in Figure 2.1. (Recall that we can judge the variance of ϵ_i from the graph of Y_i since, provided our model of the mean is correct, the two variables have the same variance.) It would be far-fetched, however, to assume that overtime payments to manual workers in the harbour are also distributed normally. Figure 2.2 throws serious doubt on such an assumption.

Let us now look at the properties of the sample mean as an estimator of the population mean, subject to assumptions (2.1) and (2.5)–(2.7). Thereafter, we shall add the normality assumption which sets the stage for statistical inference about the population mean.

2.4   THE SAMPLE MEAN AS BEST LINEAR UNBIASED ESTIMATOR (BLUE)

To judge whether an estimator is good or bad, we need to be clear on what we mean by the concept of an estimator and how it differs from that of an estimate. The short answer is that an estimator is a formula we use to calculate an estimate. An estimate is a numerical value based on a sample. For example, the generic formula of the sample mean as defined in equation (2.12) is an estimator:

$$\bar{Y} = \frac{1}{n} (Y_1 + Y_2 + \ldots + Y_n) \tag{2.12}$$

$$= \frac{1}{n} \sum_{i=1}^{n} Y_i$$

Once a sample is drawn, we can compute the sample mean by applying this formula to the data. This computed value of the sample mean is an estimate of the population mean.

The estimate produced by an estimator depends on the particular sample we happen to use. It will vary from sample to sample, giving rise to a distribution of the estimator. The sampling distribution is the probability distribution of the estimator which, unlike any particular estimate, is a random variable. Its outcome is unknown until we draw a particular sample which allows us to calculate the particular estimate. Each sample will yield another estimate. The sampling distribution tells us how such estimates are likely to vary from sample to sample. For this reason, the sampling distribution is a fundamental concept of classical statistical theory, but unfortunately it is not always well understood. The difficulty with this concept arises because we normally have only one sample at our disposal and hence our main concern is whether the estimate based on this particular sample is good or bad. In classical statistics, however, we do not ask whether the estimate is good or bad but, rather, whether the estimate was made by a good or bad estimator. To judge whether an estimator is good or bad, we look at its sampling distribution in general, and its average and variance in particular.

If the centre of the sampling distribution of an estimator is exactly equal to the population mean, we say that the estimator is unbiased. That is, the estimator does not have a systematic tendency to produce estimates away from the population mean. Obviously, unbiasedness is a desirable property that we like our estimators to have. The variation around the centre has implications for the margin of error (precision) in estimation. The wider the variation around the centre, the larger will be the margin of error and, hence, the less precise the estimator will be. While an estimator is either unbiased or not, its precision is generally defined in comparative terms. An unbiased estimator is more precise than a rival unbiased estimator if its sampling distribution has a smaller variance. An estimator is best if it can be shown to have the lowest variance among a class of estimators (say, among all linear estimators).

Unbiasedness and precision are criteria we use to assess the quality of an estimator and to make comparisons among estimators. As we have seen, they refer to the sampling distribution of the estimator which is the distribution of all possible estimates that can be produced by the estimator, given the sampling procedure. But does this mean that we have to enumerate all the possible samples we can draw from a particular population? To do this, we would need to know all the elements of the real population and, subsequently, enumerate all the possible samples we can draw from this population. This is obviously not feasible in a real-life situation.

Instead, usually we derive the moments of the sampling distribution mathematically from the assumptions of the statistical model (i.e. the assumptions about the model population and about the sampling procedure). To do this, we make use of the standard properties of the mathematical expectations and variances of random variables shown in Appendix 2.1. The bias of an estimator is measured by the difference between the mean of the theoretical sampling distribution and the population mean we seek to estimate. Hence, in the case of the sample mean the bias will be given by:

$$\text{BIAS} = E(\bar{X}) - \mu \tag{2.13}$$

If the bias equals zero, that is the mathematical expectation of the estimator equals the population mean, we say that the estimator is unbiased. Similarly, precision is measured by the variance or, equivalently, the standard deviation of the sampling distribution. This standard deviation is called the standard error of the estimator. It gives us an idea about the possible margin of error involved in estimating the population mean.

Unbiasedness of the sample mean

Given the assumptions of the statistical model (2.1), it can be shown mathematically that the sample mean is an unbiased estimator of the population mean. In other words:

$$E(\bar{Y}) = \mu \qquad (2.14)$$

Let us take a real-life example to illustrate this property of the sample mean more vividly. Take another look at the top panel of Figure 2.1, which depicts the daily demand for casual labour in Maputo harbour during the period from March 1980 to June 1981. For illustrative purposes, let us consider this set of data as our real population. If we now draw, say, 1,000 random samples, each with 15 observations, from this larger population, the sample mean will obviously vary from sample to sample. The histogram of the empirical distribution of these sample means gives us a good approximation of the sampling distribution of the sample mean

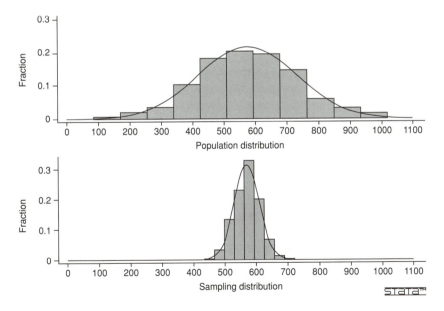

Figure 2.4 Comparing the sampling and population distributions of labour demand

Table 2.3   Means and standard deviations: sampling versus population
distribution

	Population distribution	*Sampling distribution*
Mean	574	574
Standard deviation	155	40

in this case. Figure 2.4 compares this histogram of sample means of 1,000
samples (bottom panel) with the histogram of its population distribution.
As shown in Table 2.3, this (approximate) sampling distribution has exactly
the same mean as the population distribution, which illustrates the fact
that the sample mean is an unbiased estimator. Note, however, that the
standard deviation of the sampling distribution is much smaller than that
of the population distribution, for reasons we shall now explain.

Minimum variance property of the sample mean

The sample mean is a linear combination of the sample values, hence, it
is called a linear estimator of the population mean. The variance of this
estimator is obtained as follows:

$$V(\bar{Y}) = V\left(\frac{1}{n}\sum_{i=1}^{n}Y_i\right)$$

(2.15)

$$= \frac{1}{n^2}\sum_{i=1}^{n}V(Y)_i + \frac{1}{n^2}\sum_{i\neq j}\text{Cov}(Y_i\ Y_j)$$

But the assumption that the error term is not autocorrelated means that
the covariances of each pair of Y_i and Y_j will be zero. Thus equation (2.15)
can be reduced to the following expression:

$$V(\bar{Y}) = \frac{\sigma^2}{n}$$

(2.16)

Take another look at Table 2.3. It shows that the standard deviation of
the sampling distribution is significantly smaller than that of the population distribution. Equation (2.16) tells us why this is the case. The
difference between the sample and population variance depends on the
sample size. It is easy to verify that the calculated standard deviation of
the sampling distribution, 40, approximately equals the standard deviation of the population distribution, 155, divided by the square root of
the sample size, 15. Other things being equal, the larger the sample, the
smaller the margin of error of our estimates.

It can be shown that the variance of any linear estimator of the population mean, say U, will be greater than or equal to the variance of the sample mean. That is,

$$V(U) \geqslant \frac{\sigma^2}{n} = V(\bar{Y}) \tag{2.17}$$

The sample mean, therefore, has the property of least variance among all linear estimators of the population mean.

Hence, the sample mean is the best linear unbiased estimator (BLUE) of the population mean. This result depends on the assumptions of the model. It is useful to reflect carefully on how each assumption was used to prove that the sample mean is BLUE:

1   We assumed that all sample units Y_i come from the same population – i.e. they have the same mean and variance. The assumption of an equal population mean is critical to proving that the sample mean is unbiased.
2   In addition, we assumed that all the sample units are independent of each other – i.e. our sample is an independent random sample. This assumption is crucial for the sample mean to have the minimum variance property. If the sample units are not independent of each other, the sample mean will not necessarily have the minimum variance property, though it will still be unbiased. As a result, the precision of the estimator will be in doubt.

Perhaps we can best end with a final word of warning. We have shown that to prove that the sample mean is BLUE, no assumption was needed with respect to the shape of the population distribution. But this should not lead us to believe that shape does not matter. In section 2.2 we saw that a mean is not always that meaningful. Indeed, if a distribution is symmetric and preferably bell-shaped, the mean is at its centre. But if a distribution is strongly skewed the mean is no more than a balance point with little further interpretative value. As we shall see in Chapter 3, the sample mean loses much of its power if the distribution of the variable in question is strongly skewed or riddled with outliers. The validity of the normality assumption, therefore, is not a luxury, but quite essential to ensure the power of the sample mean as an estimator.

Exercise 2.3

This exercise can best be done in the context of a classroom workshop. The aim is to get a better grip on the concept of a sampling distribution. To do this, take a particular set of data on a variable such as one of the variables listed in Exercise 2.1. Consider the data as the real population for illustrative purposes, and draw a number of random samples of equal size (say, $n = 10$, or 15, or 25) from this population. (If doing the exercise in the classroom each student can draw his or her own sample.) Now:

1 draw a histogram of the population distribution and calculate its mean and standard deviation;
2 calculate the mean and standard deviation for each sample drawn from this population;
3 draw a histogram of all sample means and calculate its mean and standard deviation;
4 check the relation between the mean and standard deviation of the population and those of the distribution of sample means;
5 comment on the respective shapes of the distribution.

The latter point is particularly instructive if the population distribution from which samples are taken is strongly skewed. The histogram of sample means (an approximation of the shape of the sampling distribution) will tend to be bell-shaped. This tendency derives from what is called the central limit theorem in statistics. In short, the sampling distribution of the sample mean will tend to the normal distribution as the sample size increases, notwithstanding the shape of the population distribution from which the data were sampled.

(*A note on sampling* To do this exercise well, it is advisable to use a reasonably large number of samples. To prevent the exercise becoming tedious, especially if doing it on an individual basis, it is best to use a software package which allows you to (a) generate a random variable; (b) sort the database by ordering any variable; (c) calculate summary statistics (means and standard deviations) for any subset of the data; and (d) draw histograms. If one is available, proceed as follows, assuming Y is the variable which defines the population distribution: (a) generate a random variable, R; (b) sort the database with respect to R; (c) select the first n (= sample size) observations of Y which will be a random sample of the wider population; (d) calculate the mean and standard deviation of this sample of Y values; (e) delete R and start again at (a) to generate the next sample.)

2.5 NORMALITY AND THE MAXIMUM LIKELIHOOD PRINCIPLE

Let us now introduce the normality assumption. If Y is a normally distributed variable, its density function, say $f(Y)$, is specified as follows:

$$f(Y) = \frac{1}{\sigma\sqrt{2\pi}} e^{-\frac{1}{2}\left(\frac{Y-\mu}{\sigma}\right)^2} \qquad ; -\infty \leqslant Y \leqslant +\infty \tag{2.18}$$

Notation: $Y \sim N(\mu, \sigma^2)$

This distribution has two parameters, μ and σ^2, which are, respectively, its mean and its variance. In other words, if we know its mean and its variance, we have all the information necessary to define a normal distribution.

If a sample is drawn at random from a normal distribution then the probability that the sample value Y will be between limits α and β is given by the area under the density curve over the interval (α, β) of the range of Y, as given by:

$$P(\alpha < Y \leqslant \beta) = \int_{\alpha}^{\beta} f(Y)dY \qquad (2.19)$$

Given μ, σ^2, and α, β, it is possible to compute the numerical value of the probability by evaluating this integral numerically. The results of such computations for $\alpha = -\infty$ and various values of β are routinely available for the standard normal distribution with zero mean and unit variance: $\mu = 0$ and $\sigma^2 = 1$. The table for distribution $N(0,1)$, or 'the z table' is included amongst the statistical tables to this book (see p. 463). The reader should verify that 95 per cent of the distribution lies in the range –1.96 to 1.96. The probabilities for other normal distributions can be obtained from this standard normal distribution table by means of a linear transformation which we shall discuss later when dealing with statistical inference based on the model.

Maximum likelihood function

For theoretical exercises, we can use the density function to express the necessary probabilities. If Y_i; $i = 1, 2, 3, \ldots n$, is the ith sample unit in an independent random sample of size n, then because of independence, the probability of obtaining such a sample is the product of individual probabilities for each of the sample units. This is the joint probability of the sample, i.e. all sample units considered together. If the mean and the variance of the parent distribution are unknown, the joint probability of the observed sample Y, where $Y = (Y_1, Y_2, Y_3, \ldots Y_n)$, is obtained as a function L equal to the product of the probabilities of each of the sample units as follows:

$$L(Y \mid \mu, \sigma^2) = f(Y_1 \mid \mu, \sigma^2) \, f(Y_2 \mid \mu, \sigma^2) \ldots f(Y_n \mid \mu, \sigma^2) \qquad (2.20)$$

where $f(Y \mid \mu, \sigma^2)$ is given by equation (2.18).

The function L is the likelihood function of the sample. It expresses the probability of obtaining the sample Y, given that it is drawn from a normal distribution with mean μ and variance σ^2. This likelihood function allows us to derive an estimator for the population mean μ. To do this, we ask what the value of μ is that assigns the highest probability to obtain the sample we actually have in hand. This principle of estimation is called the maximum likelihood principle. Statistical theory shows that maximum likelihood (ML) estimators are minimum variance estimators among all estimators. The sample mean is the maximum likelihood estimator of the population mean and is, therefore, the least variance estimator if the normality assumption is reasonably valid.

The relative efficiency of mean versus median

To illustrate the superiority of the mean when the population distribution is normal, let us compare its performance with that of the median. It can be shown that, if the population distribution is normal, the sample median is also an unbiased estimator, but it will have a larger standard error than the sample mean. In other words, the sample median is a less precise estimator of the population mean of a normally distributed variable. In fact, for large samples from normal distributions, the sample median has a variance which is approximately 1.57 ($= \pi/2$) times larger than that of the mean (Mosteller and Tukey, 1977: 17). This implies that the standard error of the median will be approximately 1.25 times larger than that of the mean.

Let us again use our example of the daily demand for labour in Maputo harbour to compare the relative performance of the mean and the median as estimators of the population mean. Figure 2.5 compares the (earlier) histogram of the sample means of 1,000 samples with 15 observations each, with the histogram of the medians of these samples. Both distributions have the same mean, 574, which is equal to the population mean, but different standard errors: 40 for the mean and 50 for the median. Although the sample size is small, the standard error of the median is exactly 25 per cent larger than that of the mean. The mean, therefore, is clearly the better estimator, as you can readily verify if you compare both histograms in Figure 2.5.

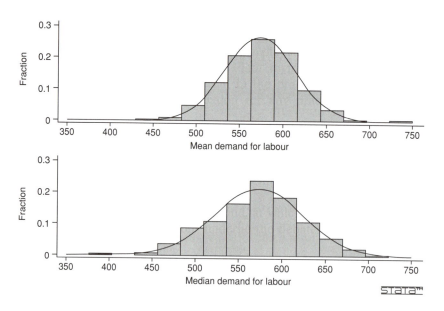

Figure 2.5 Comparing the sampling distributions of mean and median: demand for labour

Exercise 2.4

This exercise is an extension of Exercise 2.3. Before you calculated the mean of each sample, now obtain its median as well. Compare the histograms of the sample means and sample median and comment on their relative efficiency. If the population distribution is not approximately normal, you should find that the mean does not necessarily perform better than the median.

To sum up, if the normality assumption is reasonably valid in practice, the sample mean is unbeatable as an estimator of the population mean. It is not only BLUE, but is also the minimum variance estimator among all possible estimators. Furthermore, as we have seen in section 2.2, a symmetric and bell-shaped distribution with thin tails has a clear centre around which the mass of points concentrates. Mean, median and mode all coincide and, hence, the centre of the distribution lends itself to easy interpretation. In this case, therefore, the mean is a powerful tool for the data analyst. Given these theoretical properties of the mean, it is not surprising that the mean is so prominent in data analysis. But the power of the sample mean as an estimator relies on the normality assumption being reasonably valid in practice for the problem at hand. As we shall see in Chapter 3, if this is not the case, the mean loses much of its power and may even yield misleading results.

2.6 INFERENCE FROM A SAMPLE OF A NORMAL DISTRIBUTION

Standard normal distribution and the distribution of the sample mean

The normality assumption not only gives substance to the choice of the sample mean as the estimator of the population mean, but it also opens up the possibility for measuring the degree of confidence we have in making inferences about the population mean from the sample. In applied work, the problem we confront is that we generally have only one sample at our disposal on the basis of which we can calculate a sample mean. But how close is the sample mean to the population mean? Of course, it is not possible to give an exact answer to this question. But, given that the parent distribution is normal, we can state the probability that the estimator produces outcomes within a specified distance from the population mean. To do this, we resort to probability theory.

Probability theory tells us that a linear function of a set of variables, each of which has a normal distribution, also is distributed normally. Hence, since the sample mean is a linear function of Y_i, $i = 1, 2, 3, \ldots n$, where each Y_i has a normal distribution, it follows that the sample mean as an estimator is also normally distributed. To see this more vividly, take another look at Figure 2.4. The top panel shows that the distribution of the daily demand for labour in Maputo harbour is approximately normal in shape; the bottom panel shows that the histogram which depicts the sampling distribution of the sample mean also displays a typical normal shape, but with a much smaller variance than that of the parent population. As we have seen, the sampling distribution of the sample mean when an independent random sample of size n is drawn from a normal distribution is normally distributed with mean μ and variance σ^2/n.

Now, the probabilities corresponding to any arbitrary normal distribution can be derived from the standard normal distribution by means of a simple linear transformation. The transformation is given as follows:

$$Z = \left(\frac{\bar{Y} - \mu}{\sigma/\sqrt{n}}\right) \tag{2.21}$$

Since Z is a linear function of $Y_1, Y_2, Y_3, \ldots, Y_n$, each of which is normally distributed, it follows that Z is also distributed normally. This transformed variable Z is called a standardised variable. The advantage is that it has zero mean and unit variance which can be shown as follows:

$$E\left(\frac{\bar{Y} - \mu}{\sigma/\sqrt{n}}\right) = \frac{\sqrt{n}}{\sigma} E\left(\bar{Y} - \mu\right) = 0 \tag{2.22}$$

$$V\left(\frac{\bar{Y} - \mu}{\sigma/\sqrt{n}}\right) = \frac{n}{\sigma^2} . V(\bar{Y} - \mu) = \frac{n}{\sigma^2} . V(Y) = 1 \tag{2.23}$$

consequently, Z has a standard normal distribution.

Now, from the density curve of the standard normal distribution we know that there is 95 per cent probability that a random observation will be within the range -1.96 and $+1.96$. We can, therefore, write:

$$P\left(-1.96 \leqslant \frac{\bar{Y} - \mu}{\sigma/\sqrt{n}} \leqslant 1.96\right) = 0.95 \tag{2.24}$$

Multiplying all terms in this inequality by $\sigma/\sqrt{n}$ and adding μ yields:

$$P\left(\mu - 1.96 \frac{\sigma}{\sqrt{n}} \leqslant \bar{Y} \leqslant \mu + 1.96 \frac{\sigma}{\sqrt{n}}\right) = 0.95 \tag{2.25}$$

What this means is that, under conditions of repeated sampling, the probability of the sample mean falling within a distance of ($\pm 1.96\ \sigma/\sqrt{n}$) of the unknown population mean is 95 per cent, given the population distribution is normal with mean μ and variance σ^2.

Confidence intervals

Our main interest, however, is to make inferences about the population mean based on the sample mean. Now, if the sample mean is, with 95 per cent probability, within a certain distance of the unknown population mean, it follows that the unknown population mean is within a certain distance of the sample mean. That is, inequality (2.25) can be rearranged as follows:

$$P(\bar{Y} - 1.96 \, \frac{\sigma}{\sqrt{n}} \leqslant \mu \leqslant \bar{Y} + 1.96 \, \frac{\sigma}{\sqrt{n}}) = 0.95 \qquad (2.26)$$

which gives us a probability statement about the location of the population mean: under conditions of repeated sampling, there is 95 per cent chance that the unknown population mean lies within the boundaries of $\pm 1.96\sigma/\sqrt{n}$ of the sample mean. Strictly speaking, this statement pertains to the sample mean as an estimator, and not to any specific estimate obtained from a given sample. However, we use these boundaries to construct what is called a confidence interval. A confidence interval gives us an interval estimate as distinct from a point estimate (i.e. the calculated value of the sample mean). The advantage of an interval estimate is that, unlike a point estimate, it gives us a sense of the margin of error involved in estimation.

It is not correct, however, to say that the population mean lies with 95 per cent probability within the boundaries of a calculated confidence interval. Indeed, for any given estimate, the population mean lies either within or outside the boundaries of its confidence interval. There is nothing probable about this, although in real-life situations we do not know which is the case. A probability statement about confidence intervals, therefore, relates to the estimator, not to the estimate. It states that the estimator we use has, in conditions of repeated sampling, 95 per cent probability of producing confidence intervals which include the population mean.

To see this point, let us perform a simple experiment. Suppose, once more, that the empirical distribution of the daily demand for labour in Maputo harbour over the period from March 1980 to June 1981 is the relevant real population with mean 574 and standard deviation 155. Figure 2.6 gives us, respectively, the sample means and their 95 per cent confidence intervals for the first 20 samples (of 15 observations each) that we generated to produce the histogram of sample mean in Figure 2.4. The horizontal line in Figure 2.6 depicts the position of the population mean (= 574). As you can see, all but one (the tenth sample) of the 95 per cent confidence intervals include the population mean and, hence, 1 in 20 samples (or 5 per cent) misfired. Obviously, if we were to do this experiment again, the number of samples out of 20 which contain the true population mean would vary from none, to one, to a few. Under conditions of repeated sampling, 95 per cent of the samples will include the population mean. Any given sample, however, produces a confidence interval which either includes the population mean, or does not. It would be wrong, therefore, to say that there is 95 per cent probability that a particular confidence interval includes the population mean.

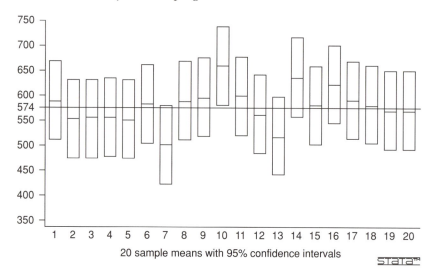

Figure 2.6   Confidence intervals of sample means: demand for labour, Maputo harbour

A striking feature of this graph is that different samples drawn from the same distribution can give quite different results in term of the estimates they yield. Admittedly, in this case our samples were very small (only 15 observations), but we should not forget that these samples were drawn from a population which behaved approximately as a normal distribution. In general, therefore, sampling conditions were favourable for obtaining good results. While most of the samples produce a sample mean close to the population mean, we should not overlook the fact that a significant minority of samples nevertheless give us a different picture. Obviously, sample 10 is an exception, but samples 7, 13, 14 and 16 also do not perform all that well. In practice, however, we only have one sample at our disposal and, unfortunately, we do not have the benefit of knowing the 'true' population mean.

There is, then, inevitably quite a lot of uncertainty about what inferences we can validly make. This conclusion may be a bit disappointing at first sight. But, in fact, it is a good thing (instead of a bad thing) to be warned of the inevitable vagaries of random fluctuations. If you despair about this, never forget that many people are inclined to jump to general conclusions based on a single sample without ever having the slightest notion of how day-to-day chance variations may affect the inferences they make. It is always better to be forewarned than not to have any clue about whether there is a problem at all. Statistical reasoning at least warns you to take randomness (chance variations) seriously. This, in itself, is a positive (not a negative) thing.

Estimating the population variance

In practice, we cannot use inequality (2.26) to produce a confidence interval because we generally do not know the population variance, σ^2, and therefore we need to estimate it in order to compute a confidence interval for a given sample. How do we obtain an estimator for the population variance? We could again resort to the maximum likelihood principle to find the formula for σ^2 which maximises the likelihood function. It can be shown that the resulting ML estimator of the population variance becomes:

$$\frac{1}{n} \sum (Y_i - \bar{Y})^2 \text{ where } \bar{Y} = \frac{1}{n} \sum Y_i \tag{2.27}$$

But it can be shown that this sample variance turns out to be a biased estimator of the population variance. The ML sample variance tends to underestimate the population variance since the bias involves a factor, $(n-1)/n$, which is less than 1. Consequently, an unbiased estimator of the population variance is obtained by multiplying the ML sample variance by $n/(n-1)$, as follows:

$$s^2 = \frac{1}{n-1} \sum (Y_i - \bar{Y})^2 \tag{2.28}$$

where s^2, the sample variance, is an unbiased estimator of population variance σ^2. As the sample size increases, the factor $n/(n-1)$ will tend to 1 and the sample variance and the ML variance yield similar results. In other words, the bias inherent in the ML variance will disappear as the sample size increases. This is typical for many other ML estimators as well.

The *t*-distribution

Substituting s for σ in equation (2.21) yields a new variable t, as follows:

$$t = \left(\frac{\bar{Y} - \mu}{s/\sqrt{n}} \right) \tag{2.29}$$

The variable t is no longer a linear function of the sample mean since the formula for s^2 includes the square of the sample mean. Consequently, the variable t does not have a normal distribution. This implies we cannot simply replace σ with s in inequality (2.26) which defines the confidence interval, and proceed as if nothing has changed. In inequality (2.26), the boundaries of the confidence interval were obtained by using the critical values (i.e. ±1.96) of a standard normal distribution. Hence, that statement was based on the premise that Z is distributed normally. As shown in Appendix 2.2, the variable t has its own distribution, a *t*-distribution, which is a symmetric bell-shaped density curve with somewhat fatter tails than the normal distribution. The *t*-distribution model has only one parameter, its degrees of freedom (df), equal to $n-1$ in this case. But why are there $n-1$ degrees of freedom, and not n, the sample size?

In this case, the degrees of freedom refer to the number of independent observations in a sum of squares. Note that the definition of t in equation (2.29) involves the square root of the sample variance as given by (2.28). The definition of the sample variance itself features a sum of n squared deviations from the sample mean. However, although this sum has n components, only $n-1$ of these can vary freely because, as we shall see in Chapter 3, the deviations from the sample mean sum to zero. In other words, given $n-1$ components of this sum of squares, the last component is no longer free to vary. This explains why there are only $n-1$, not n, degrees of freedom.

Statistical tables list the critical values of the t-distribution for different degrees of freedom. Following the same procedure as we did in the case of a standard normal variable, the confidence interval for the population mean, with unknown population variance, can then be obtained as follows:

$$\left(\bar{Y} - t_{0.95}\frac{s}{\sqrt{n}} , \bar{Y} + t_{0.95}\frac{s}{\sqrt{n}} \right) \tag{2.30}$$

where $t_{0.95}$ is the critical value of the relevant t-distribution with $n-1$ degrees of freedom. Note, however, that, as sample size grows, the t-distribution converges to the standard normal distribution; hence, for larger samples (say, with $n > 100$) we can safely resort to the standard normal distribution, even when the population variance is unknown.

Hypothesis testing

A statistical hypothesis is a statement about the value of a parameter of the statistical model (in this case, about the population mean). The difference between a confidence interval and a test of a hypothesis is that in the former we are trying get an idea about the range of likely values of the unknown population mean, given a particular sample, while in the latter we are trying to see how likely the sample is for a given hypothesised value of the population mean. In hypothesis testing, we always consider two complementary hypotheses which do not overlap but, between them, exhaust all possible values that the relevant parameter can take. Why do we need two hypotheses? The reason is that hypothesis testing involves making a decision on whether or not to reject a particular hypothesis which we denote by H_0, the null hypothesis. If H_0 is rejected, it means that we effectively accept the alternative hypothesis, called H_1, which contains all other possible values apart from the particular value specified in H_0. Hence, H_1 is always very vague in contrast with the precise nature of H_0: H_1 simply tells us that any other value is possible apart from the one hypothesised in H_0.

For example, the summary statistics in Table 2.1 tell us that daily recruitment of casual labour in Maputo harbour fluctuated around 500 in the early 1980s. Suppose that, in a subsequent period, we draw a sample of observations on daily recruitment and seek to test whether a recruitment level of 500 continues to be the average. Our two complementary hypotheses will then look as follows:

$$H_0: \mu = 500 \text{ and } H_1: \mu \neq 500 \qquad (2.31)$$

The basic idea then is to test the null hypothesis that the sample is drawn from a population with mean 500. In this case, the alternative hypothesis specifies that the population mean can be either greater than or less than 500. This is what is called a two-tailed test.

But suppose we know that transport activity in Maputo harbour dropped significantly after the early 1980s and, hence, we do not expect recruitment levels to average as much as 500 per day. In this case, we specify the complementary hypotheses as follows:

$$H_0: \mu = 500 \text{ and } H_1: \mu < 500 \qquad (2.32)$$

Note that H_0 and H_1 continue to exhaust all possible values for the population mean, since the possibility of $\mu > 500$ has been ruled out. This is a one-tailed test. If we now replace μ by 500 in the expression for t in (2.29), it follows that our null hypothesis implies that T has a t-distribution with population mean 500, i.e.:

$$t = \frac{\overline{Y} - 500}{s/\sqrt{n}} \sim t_{(n-1)} \text{ if } H_0 \text{ is true} \qquad (2.33)$$

since H_0 specifies that $\mu = 500$. How then do we carry out the test? We have already noted that hypothesis testing involves making a decision as to whether or not to accept the null hypothesis. This decision will never be foolproof. The reason is that we make such decision under uncertainty due to the random nature of the error term. Our decisions, therefore, will involve probability statements, not absolute certainties. Table 2.4 lists the two types of errors which we may encounter when making this type of decision.

A type I error involves rejecting the null hypothesis when in fact it is true. The probability of making a type I error, α, is called the level of significance of a test. We always specify this level of significance clearly before we do the test. It is customary to allow for a 5 per cent probability

Table 2.4 Types of errors in hypothesis testing

		Decision with respect to H_0	
	True	Correct	Type I error
H_0 is actually		Probability = $(1 - \alpha)$	Level of significance = α
	False	Type II error	Correct
		Probability = β	Power of the test = $(1 - \beta)$

of making a type I error. A type II error involves accepting the null hypothesis when in fact it is not true. The power of a test is given by the probability of correctly rejecting the null hypothesis and, hence, equals (1–β), where β is the probability of making a type II error. In most cases, it is difficult to calculate this latter probability precisely since this would require the alternative hypothesis to be very precise (equal to a particular value), rather than vague. However, it is important to choose the most powerful test for any given level of significance. For example, if the alternative hypothesis is such that a one-tailed test is feasible, then this test will have higher power than one using a two-tailed procedure. Finally, other things being equal (the inherent randomness of the data; sample size), setting a higher level of significance will increase the risk of wrongly accepting H_0 to be true when in fact H_1 is true.

Box 2.1 reviews the step-by-step procedure required to carry out a test of hypothesis. To illustrate the procedure, consider our earlier example of recruitment of casual labour in Maputo harbour. In 1980–81, recruitment levels fluctuated in a typical bell-shaped fashion around an average level of 500. Thereafter, the activity at the harbour fell dramatically. We would expect, therefore, daily recruitment to decline equally. Suppose

---

Box 2.1   Step-by-step procedure of hypothesis testing

1   Formulate the null-hypothesis, H_0.
2   Formulate the alternative hypothesis, H_1, in such a way that the rejection of H_0 implies the acceptance of H_1; the specification of the alternative hypothesis determines whether we are dealing with a one-tailed or a two-tailed test.
3   Specify the level of significance, α, of the test (usually, 5 per cent).
4   Specify the appropriate test statistic (which requires that the underlying assumptions are reasonably valid in practice).
5   Find the appropriate critical value of the test statistic from the relevant statistical tables, taking account of whether the test is one- or two-tailed.
6   Calculate the value of the test statistic on the basis of the sample.
7   Compare the calculated value of the test statistic with the critical value(s) obtained from the statistical tables and accept/reject the null hypothesis depending on whether or not the calculated value of the test statistic lies outside the critical boundary. As a general rule for all statistical tests, if the absolute value of the calculated value of the test statistic exceeds the absolute value of the critical value given in the tables then we reject the null hypothesis.

now that we have a random sample of 30 observations on daily recruitment, drawn in the mid-1980s, which gives us a sample mean of 450 with a sample standard deviation equal to 90. Is this enough evidence to conclude that recruitment levels have fallen? Let us proceed step by step to test this hypothesis.

1 Our null hypothesis is straightforward: H_0: $\mu = 500$.
2 Since we have strong reasons to believe that recruitment levels remained at most the same and probably declined, a one-tailed test appears to be appropriate: H_1: $\mu < 500$.
3 We shall use the conventional 5 per cent level of significance.
4 Assuming that the population distribution is approximately normal with unknown standard deviation, the appropriate test statistic under the null hypothesis is the t-statistic as given in equation (2.29).
5 The critical value $t_{0.95}$ with 29 ($= 30 - 1$) degrees of freedom in a one-tailed test with 5 per cent significance equals -1.699, a negative value since we are dealing with the left tail of the distribution.
6 Using equation (2.29), we find that $t = -3.04$.
7 Since the calculated t value lies in the tail ($-3.04 < -1.70$), we reject the null hypothesis, H_0: $\mu = 500$, and accept the alternative hypothesis that the population mean is less than 500. Applying the general rule, the absolute value of the calculated t-statistic (3.04) is greater than the absolute value of the critical value (1.70).

The t-test outlined above is fairly robust, which means that it remains reliable even if the assumptions of the model are not fully satisfied. But this does not mean that anything goes. In general, if the data are reasonably symmetrical or near-symmetrical, the t-test will perform adequately. But, obviously, if the data are strongly skewed or the danger of outliers is great, the t-test cannot be relied upon to make a valid inference about the population mean.

Exercise 2.5

The population distribution of the demand for labour in Maputo harbour is assumed to be (approximately) normal, with population mean 574. Five random samples of the daily demand for labour were drawn, with 15 observations each. The resulting sample means and standard deviations

Table 2.5 Samples of daily demand for labour

Sample	Mean	Standard deviation
1	589	173
2	636	168
3	473	195
4	561	123
5	664	163

are listed in Table 2.5. For each sample test the hypothesis $H_0 : \mu = 574$, assuming (a) that the population variance is known to be 155; and (b) that the population variance is unknown. (Use the seven steps outlined in the box to carry out each test.)

Statistical versus substantive significance

Testing a hypothesis means that we assess its validity in the light of often considerable uncertainty due to chance variations in the sample. The level of significance of a test specifies this degree of uncertainty or risk involved in making decisions of this nature. Remember, however, that the term significance here is used in a statistical sense, and not in any substantive sense. As we have seen, the level of significance of a test only refers to the risk of rejecting a true hypothesis.

There is, however, a tendency in applied work to confuse statistical with substantive significance or importance. All that is meant by a high statistical significance of a test is that there is very little risk in rejecting the null hypothesis wrongly. But this does not say anything about the substantive significance of the test. In our example of daily recruitment of casual labour, given a big enough sample, we might reject the null hypothesis that the population mean equals 500 on the basis of a sample with sample mean 490. In statistical jargon we say that the sample mean is significantly different (given the level of significance of the test) from the postulated value and, hence, we reject the null hypothesis. But, substantively, does it matter all that much if the population mean only declined marginally? Suppose the population mean has indeed declined from 500 to 495. We may be able to spot the difference statistically, given a big enough sample which yields greater precision. But the plight of these casual labourers in terms of access to daily work is unlikely to be very much affected by such a slight decline. Hence, a difference which turns out to be statistically significant may not be all that important.

Conversely, suppose we only have a very small sample at our disposal with mean 420 and a large standard deviation. In this case, lack of statistical precision may not allow us to reject the null hypothesis that the population mean is 500. The difference between the sample mean and the postulated population mean, therefore, is not statistically significant in this case. But we may still be left with the worry that a substantive decline in average recruitment may have taken place which our data, due to the lack of precision, fail to confirm. Indeed, a possible drop in average recruitment from 500 to somewhere in the region of 420 will affect the plight of workers significantly (in the substantive sense).

This bring us to a second point. We never accept a hypothesis in the literal sense. A statistical test only leads to an inference as to whether or not a hypothesis is consistent with the sample data. In the former case we say that the hypothesis is maintained, while in the latter it is rejected.

Therefore, if the hypothesis $\mu = 500$ is maintained, it does not necessarily mean that we accept $\mu = 500$ to be correct. All we can say is that this hypothesis is consistent with the data. Only rejection by a statistical test, therefore, is a conclusive inference, given the level of significance, about a hypothesis.

To sum up, hypothesis testing is an important tool in data analysis, which should, however, be used with caution. This section has shown, first, that it is important to check whether the assumptions of the model are (approximately) valid in practice. A test is as good as the assumptions upon which it is based. If the latter are not satisfied, the test is meaningless, even if it 'looks good'. Second, never confuse substantive significance with statistical significance. The latter tells us something about the confidence we have in the inferences we make, but this does not necessarily mean that these inferences are substantively important. Obviously, a good data analyst always seeks to obtain significant statistical results on issues which matter substantively. But at times our data are insufficient to establish conclusive proof which allows us to dismiss a hypothesis. The fact that we maintain such a hypothesis does not mean it is correct. Conversely, with a large sample we may be able to detect small differences and render them statistically significant, although substantively it may well make little difference one way or the other. Hypothesis analysis, therefore, should not be used blindly but to help us to draw inferences on issues which matter substantively.

2.7 SUMMARY OF MAIN POINTS

1 Modelling an average requires us to make assumptions about the shape of the population distribution. That is, an average, on its own, tells us very little unless we have a good idea about the shape of a distribution.

2 In empirical work, three kinds of averages are commonly used: the mean, the median and the mode. If the distribution is unimodal and symmetric, all three measures coincide. If, furthermore, the distribution is bell-shaped with thin tails, the mass of the distribution is concentrated around this typical value. Consequently, if the normality assumption is reasonably valid in practice, the average (mean, median or mode) gives us the unambiguous centre of the distribution. The classical way of modelling a population mean is based on this assumption that the variable is distributed normally.

3 Unimodal skewed distributions are much harder to interpret as far as their average is concerned. Each kind of average highlights a different aspect of the distribution: the mode yields its maximum, the mean its balance point, and the median its middle value. But none of these measures depicts an unambiguous centre of the distribution due to its lack of symmetry. In Chapter 3 we shall discuss what to do if our data derive from a skewed population distribution.

4   To model an average we assume that the data fluctuate randomly around a constant population mean. The random fluctuations around this mean are given by the error terms corresponding to the different observations in a sample. We assume that each error term has zero mean and a constant variance, and that the various error terms are statistically independent of one another (i.e. the data are generated through random sampling). Finally, we also assume that each error term has a normal distribution.

5   Given the assumptions of a constant mean with homoscedastic and statistically independent errors, the sample mean is the best linear unbiased estimator. Unbiasedness implies that, under conditions of repeated sampling, the mean of the sampling distribution of the sample mean equals the population mean. An estimator is best if it has the smallest standard error (greatest precision) within its class of estimators (in this case, linear estimators). If, furthermore, the normality assumption prevails, the sample mean is the ML (maximum likelihood) estimator which is the minimum variance estimator among all estimators. In general, if the population distribution is normal, the sample mean is unbeatable as an estimator of the population mean.

6   As an example, we have shown that, if the population distribution is normal, the sample mean will be more efficient (precise) than the median. In fact, the variance of the sampling distribution of the sample median will be approximately 1.57 ($= \pi/2$) times larger than that of the sample mean.

7   The normality assumption lays the basis for statistical inference. If the population variance is known, we can construct confidence intervals or test hypotheses using the normal distribution. If not, we use the *t*-distribution which requires us to estimate the standard deviation of the population from the sample. Confidence intervals and hypothesis testing involve statements about the value of a parameter of the model: in this case, about the population mean. The difference between a confidence interval and a test of a hypothesis is that, in the former, we try to get an idea about the range of likely values of the unknown population mean, while, in the latter, we try to see how likely the sample is for a given value (hypothesised) of the population mean.

8   Never confuse statistical with substantive significance or importance. The former refers to the fact that the decision whether to accept or reject a statistical hypothesis always entails the risk or uncertainty of rejecting a hypothesis when in fact (but unknown to us) it is correct. All that is meant by a result being highly statistically significant is that there is little risk of rejecting the null hypothesis when in fact it is true. But a result which is statistically significant may not be significant in any substantive sense. In hypothesis testing, what matters is to obtain statistically significant results concerning issues of substantive importance.

APPENDIX 2.1: PROPERTIES OF MEAN AND VARIANCE

Suppose X, Y are variables, and a, b are constants. Then the following relationships hold:

$E(X)$ = Expectation (theoretical mean) of variable X

$V(X)$ = Variance of variable X
$$= E[X - E(X)]^2 = E(X^2) - [E(X)]^2$$

$SD(X)$ = Standard deviation of $X = \sqrt{V(X)}$

$E(aX) = aE(X)$

$V(aX) = a^2V(X)$

$E(X + Y) = E(X) + E(Y)$

$Cov(X,Y)$ = Covariance of variables X and Y
$$= E\{[X - E(X)] [Y - E(Y)]\} = E(XY) - E(X)E(Y)$$

$Cov(X,Y) = 0$ if X and Y are independent

Therefore $E(XY) = E(X)E(Y)$ if X and Y are independent

$V(X \pm Y) = V(X) + V(Y) \pm 2Cov(X,Y)$
$$= V(X) + V(Y) \text{ if } X \text{ and } Y \text{ are independent}$$

$E(aX + bY) = aE(X) + bE(Y)$

$V(aX + bY) = a^2V(X) + b^2V(Y) + 2abCov(X,Y)$

$Cov(aX,bY) = abCov(X,Y)$

APPENDIX 2.2: STANDARD SAMPLING DISTRIBUTIONS

Given the distribution of a random variable Y, the distribution of $g(Y)$, where g is a function of Y with certain properties, can be found by using probability calculus. If $Y_1, Y_2, Y_3, \ldots Y_n$ constitute a simple random sample from a population, then each Y_i has the same distribution as the distribution of the population, and they are independent of one another. They are called independently and identically distributed (iid) random variables. Based on the assumption of normal distribution of the population, distributions of various functions of the sample $(Y_1, Y_2, Y_3, \ldots Y_n)$ have been worked out. The distribution of any function of the sample, such as sample mean, sample variance, is called the sampling distribution. A selection of these standard sampling distributions is given below:

1　Let Y be a standard normal distribution (zero mean and unit variance). The distribution of Y^2 can be worked out to be what is called a chi-square distribution with one degree of freedom. The degree of freedom is the only parameter of the chi-square distribution in this case:

$$Y \sim N(1,0) \text{ then } Y^2 \sim \chi^2_{(1)} \tag{A.2.1}$$

It is a positively skewed distribution, i.e. it has a long tail on the right-hand side.

2　Let $Y_1, Y_2, Y_3, \ldots Y_n$ be independent variables and each have a standard normal distribution (a simple random sample from a normal population), then:

$$Y = \sum Y_i^2 \sim \chi^2_{(n)} \tag{A.2.2}$$

i.e. Y has a chi-square distribution with n degrees of freedom.

3　Let $Y_1, Y_2, Y_3, \ldots Y_n$ be a random sample from a normal distribution with mean μ and variance σ^2. The sample mean is:

$$\bar{Y} = \frac{1}{n} \sum Y_i \tag{A.2.3}$$

The sample variance is:

$$s^2 = \frac{1}{n-1} \sum (Y_i - \bar{Y})^2 \tag{A.2.4}$$

and it can be shown that (a) sample mean and sample variance are independent, and (b) the random variable

$$\frac{(n-1)\ s^2}{\sigma^2} \tag{A.2.5}$$

has a chi-square distribution with $(n-1)$ degrees of freedom.

4　Let Z have a standard normal distribution, S have a chi-square distribution with k degrees of freedom, and Z and S be independent. Then:

$$T = \frac{Z}{\sqrt{S/k}} \tag{A.2.6}$$

has a t-distribution with k degrees of freedom. The t-distribution is symmetric around zero.

5　It follows from (A.2.2), (A.2.3) and (A.2.4) above that:

$$T = \frac{\bar{Y} - \mu}{s/\sqrt{n}} \tag{A.2.7}$$

has a t-distribution with $(n-1)$ degrees of freedom.

3 Outliers, skewness and data transformations

3.1 INTRODUCTION

In Chapter 2, we saw that the sample mean is a powerful estimator of the population mean if the parent distribution from which the data are randomly sampled behaves (approximately) as a normal distribution: symmetric, bell-shaped and thin-tailed. In this case, the sample mean is not only the best linear unbiased estimator (BLUE) but, as maximum likelihood estimator, it also has the minimum variance property (among all estimators). But the sample mean rapidly loses its superiority if the normality assumption is invalid in practice: particularly, when the parent distribution is strongly skewed or has heavier than normal tails which implies that it is prone to produce samples riddled with outliers. This chapter discusses ways to deal with skewness and outliers in data.

The chapter is structured as follows. Section 3.2 starts from the result that the sample mean is a least squares summary of the location (centre) of the data. This is, in fact, a further reason for its popularity. But least squares estimators are not resistant summaries, meaning that they are sensitive to the presence of outliers in a sample. Section 3.3 compares mean-based with order-based summary statistics and argues that the latter, unlike the former, are resistant summaries. This explains why exploratory data analysis (EDA) favours the use of order-based statistics when dealing with data for which the underlying conditions are unknown. In this section we shall introduce some basic tools to analyse skewness and outliers in data: the coefficients of skewness and kurtosis as mean-based summaries on the one hand, and EDA's five-number summary and box plot, on the other. The section ends with an example which highlights the importance of paying attention to outliers when examining the difference between female and male life expectancies for different groups of developing countries (low, lower-middle and upper-middle income countries). In fact, the presence of outliers in this example throws some light on the question whether or not there exists a sex bias against women in some low-income developing countries.

Section 3.4 turns to the important issue of how to check whether the normality assumption is reasonably valid in practice. We review two practical procedures: a quick and dirty exploratory device which involves comparing mean-based with order-based statistics, and a formal test using mean-based statistics (the skewness–kurtosis test). These procedures point in two directions as to what to do when the normality assumption is invalid. First, the data may be reasonably symmetric and bell-shaped, but have heavier tails than a normal distribution. Second, the data may reflect a strong unimodal skew. To deal with the first problem, this section argues that it is preferable to use a robust estimator such as the median instead of the mean to estimate the centre of the parent distribution. A robust estimator is an estimator which is likely to perform well for a variety of underlying conditions (i.e. deviations from normality), particularly the presence of fat tails. Section 3.5 shows how simple non-linear transformations of the data often enable us to eliminate skewness in the data. Consequently, data transformations allow us to get more mileage out of the classical model for estimating a population mean based on the normality assumption. The basic principle is that, if the assumptions of the model do not apply to the raw data, they may well be valid for the transformed data. But then we also need to translate the results of our analysis with transformed data back to the realm of the raw data. We show that to do so gives us interesting insights as to the question of choosing an appropriate average when dealing with skewed (raw) data. Finally, section 3.6 summarises the main points of this chapter.

3.2. THE LEAST SQUARES PRINCIPLE AND THE CONCEPT OF RESISTANCE

In Chapter 2, we discussed the statistical properties of the sample mean, given the assumption of the model. In this section we look instead at its mathematical properties as a numerical summary of the location (centre) of a batch of data. A numerical summary always involves fitting a pattern to the data, leaving residuals in its wake. Hence, in the case of the sample mean, the residuals, e_i, are the deviations of the sample values from their mean:

$$Y_i = \bar{Y} + e_i \tag{3.1}$$

Never confuse the residuals of numerical summaries with the error terms in our models: the latter are theoretical constructs (random variables) used to model the data, while the former are the leftovers of the numerical summaries we try out on the data. Given the nature of a fit, the residuals will obey certain mathematical properties.

Mathematical properties of the sample mean

Two properties of the residuals of a sample mean matter a great deal in practice: (a) the zero-sum property, and (b) the least squares property.

The first property merely states that the sum of the deviations from the mean equals zero. The proof is straightforward:

$$\sum e_i = \sum (Y_i - \bar{Y}) = \sum Y_i - \sum \bar{Y} = n\bar{Y} - n\bar{Y} = 0 \qquad (3.2)$$

which shows that positive and negative residuals cancel each other out. The fact that the sum of the mean deviations for any variable equals zero is a useful result to remember for the algebra of least squares regression.

Exercise 3.1

Table 3.1 lists GNP per capita (in $) for a small sample of seven African countries in 1990. Using these data:

1 calculate the mean and median of the sample;
2 calculate the residuals of the sample mean and check whether they sum to zero.

The least squares property tells us that the sum of squared deviations of the sample values from the sample mean will always be less than the sum of squared deviations from any other arbitrarily chosen value, say c. Mathematically stated, this means:

$$\sum (Y_i - \bar{Y})^2 \leqslant \sum (Y_i - c)^2 \text{ for any } c \qquad (3.3)$$

In other words:

$$c_{minimum} = \bar{Y} \qquad (3.4)$$

Figure 3.1 illustrates this least squares property in the case of our sample on GNP per capita for seven African countries (Table 3.1). As you can see, the sum of squared deviations of sample values from different values for c reaches a minimum when c equals the sample mean.

Exercise 3.2

Calculate the sum of squared residuals for the sample in Table 3.1.

Table 3.1 GNP per capita: seven African economies, 1990

Country	GNP per capita
Tanzania	110
Chad	190
Malawi	200
Kenya	370
Guinea	440
Lesotho	530
Zimbabwe	640

Source: World Development Report 1992

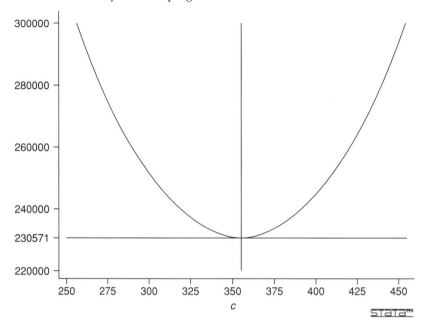

Figure 3.1 The least squares property

Least squares summaries are commonly used in applied work. In fact, the principle of least squares has a long track record in statistics. It was first formulated in 1805 by the French mathematician Legendre and refined by the famous German mathematician Gauss (Stigler, 1986: 145–6). The mean is the simplest application of the least squares principle. In subsequent chapters we shall see that one of the most common methods to derive a regression line is also based on the least squares principle. Like the sample mean, other least squares estimators are also BLUE subject to a similar set of assumptions of the model.

Given this least squares property, it should then not surprise us that the most commonly used measure of the spread, the variance, is derived from this minimal sum of squared deviations from the mean:

$$s^2 = \frac{1}{n-1} \sum (Y_i - \bar{Y})^2 \tag{3.5}$$

where s, the square root of the variance, is the sample standard deviation.

The concept of resistant summaries

These mean-based statistics, the mean itself and the standard deviation, have become so popular that we no longer question their usefulness as numerical summaries. But are least squares estimators such as the mean and standard deviation appropriate in all circumstances? In fact, they are not. The reason is that least squares summaries tend to be very sensitive to the presence of outliers in the data. Another way of saying this is that least squares summaries are generally not resistant summaries. What does this mean? The property of resistance can be defined as follows:

> Resistance is a property we would like summary statistics to have. If changing a small part of the body of data, perhaps drastically, can change the value of the summary substantially, the summary is not resistant. Conversely, if a change of a small part of the data, no matter what part or how substantially, fails to change the summary substantially, the summary is said to be resistant.
>
> (Mosteller and Tukey, 1977: 2)

In other words, a resistant summary is unaffected by erratic extreme values in the sample. To illustrate this property of resistance, consider once more our simple example of the GNP per capita of seven African countries. Let us see what happens to the sample mean if, for example, we include in the sample Botswana, which has a GNP per capita of $2,040, instead of Lesotho's $530.

Table 3.2 gives the picture: the mean reacted quite dramatically, from $354 to $570, but the median remained unchanged. The standard deviation more than tripled: from $196 to $673!

Exercise 3.3

Repeat exercises 3.1 and 3.2 with the data for sample 2 in Table 3.2:

1   check how big the residual of Botswana is in relation to the other residuals;
2   check the relative size of the squared residual of Botswana in the total sum of squared residuals.

What do you conclude from this exercise?

Table 3.2   Resistance of mean versus median

Country	GNP per capita	
	Sample 1	*Sample 2*
Tanzania	110	110
Chad	190	190
Malawi	200	200
Kenya	370	370
Guinea	440	440
Lesotho	530	–
Zimbabwe	640	640
Botswana	–	2040
Mean	354	570
Median	370	370
Standard deviation	196	673

The example shows that the mean is a much less resistant summary than the median. The reason why the mean is so sensitive to outliers directly follows from the least squares principle itself (the concept of an outlier is defined more formally below; for now, think of it as an observation far removed from the body of the data). Squaring each deviation to calculate the total sum of squares means that large deviations acquire a disproportionate weight in the total sum. Since the mean minimises this sum of squares, an outlier will tend to pull the mean in its direction. Note, for example, that the mean in sample 2 (Table 3.2) has become more distant from its median. It has been pulled in the direction of the outlier (Botswana) to minimise the weight exerted by the outlier's large deviation. In contrast, the median is not subject to this kind of pull since it is merely the middle value in the ordered sample and hence insensitive to the distance of values in its tails.

The least-squares property also explains why the mean is sensitive to skewness in the empirical distribution of the data. The one-sided long tail of such a distribution will exert undue weight on the total sum of squared deviations and therefore pull the mean in its direction. Hence, the mean will exceed the median when the distribution is positively skewed (i.e. skewed towards higher values), and conversely, the mean will be less than the median when the distribution is negatively skewed. The tail-end of a skewed distribution runs over a larger distance and so will exert a stronger pull on the location of the mean.

In applied work, we like our summaries to be resistant to avoid one or more outliers dominating the scene and leading us astray. This is particularly true if we are unsure about the actual shape of the population distribution from which our data are drawn. A single large outlier can exert great influence on the location of the sample mean and, hence, can be misleading. For example, sample 2 in Table 3.2 might lead us to conclude that African countries, on average, nearly qualify as lower-middle income countries (which, in 1990, had incomes above $600 per capita), just because Botswana happened to be in the sample. The median, in contrast, shows that this is not the case and, moreover, reveals more clearly that Botswana is the exception.

3.3   MEAN-BASED VERSUS ORDER-BASED SAMPLE STATISTICS

When analysing an empirical distribution we are interested in its centre (location), spread and shape. As to the latter, two characteristics matter a great deal: symmetry and the presence or absence of heavy tails. To describe a distribution, therefore, we rely on descriptive measures for each of these characteristics. Traditionally, this was done using mainly mean-based statistics, but more recently EDA has stressed the importance of the more resistant order-based statistics to describe and picture empirical distributions. Let us look at each in turn.

Mean-based statistics

You are probably most familiar with mean-based statistics. To describe a distribution, mean-based statistics rely on four measures: the mean itself (centre), the standard deviation (spread), the coefficient of skewness (skewness/symmetry), and the coefficient of kurtosis (heavy or thin tails). All these measures either are, or are derived from, moments of the distribution. Each of these measures can be defined for a theoretical distribution or calculated on the basis of a sample (computed for an empirical distribution).

The mean is the first uncentred moment of a distribution. As you know already, the population and sample means are given respectively by:

$$\mu = E(Y) \tag{3.6}$$

$$\bar{Y} = \frac{1}{n} \sum Y_i \tag{3.7}$$

The spread of a distribution is measured by its standard deviation, the square root of the variance which is the second centred (around the mean) moment of the distribution. The population and sample variances are respectively given by:

$$\sigma^2 = E (Y - \mu)^2 \tag{3.8}$$

$$s^2 = \frac{1}{n-1} \sum (Y_i - \bar{Y})^2 \tag{3.9}$$

Another measure of the variation of a probability distribution is its coefficient of variation, *CV*. This is a relative measure defined as the ratio of its standard deviation to its mean, as follows:

$$CV = \sigma/\mu \tag{3.10}$$

while the corresponding sample estimate is given by:

$$cv = s / \bar{Y} \tag{3.11}$$

We now come to the measures of shape – the coefficients of skewness and kurtosis – with which you may be less familiar. These are derived from the higher centred moments of a distribution. Let us start with the coefficient of skewness. For a theoretical probability distribution, this coefficient, α_3, is derived from its third centred moment (hence, the subscript 3), as follows:

$$\alpha_3 = \frac{\mu_3}{\sigma^3} = \frac{E(Y - \mu)^3}{\sigma^3} \tag{3.12}$$

where $\alpha_3 = 0$ if the distribution is symmetric. A distribution is skewed to the right (meaning its long tail is to the right) if $\alpha_3 > 0$, and to the left if $\alpha_3 < 0$. This explains why we say that a distribution is positively or negatively skewed. To see this, take another look at equation (3.12). Its numerator features cubic powers of the deviations of Y values from the population mean. Cubic powers preserve the sign of an expression but inflate the larger deviations proportionally much more than smaller deviations. If the distribution is symmetrical, negative and positive cubic powers will cancel each other out. If the distribution is skewed, however, the long tail will dominate the overall sign of the expression. The cubic power of the standard deviation in the denominator is used to standardise the measure and so remove the dimension (i.e. it will not depend on the units in which the variable is measured).

With sample data, we compute the sample coefficients of skewness, a_3, as follows:

$$a_3 = \frac{\frac{1}{n} \sum_{i=1}^{n} (Y_i - \overline{Y})^3}{s^3} \tag{3.13}$$

The coefficient of kurtosis, α_4, of a theoretical distribution is derived from its fourth centred moment (hence the subscript 4) and defined as follows:

$$\alpha_4 = \frac{\mu_4}{\sigma^4} = \frac{E(Y - \mu)^4}{\sigma^4} \tag{3.14}$$

an expression which measures the 'heaviness' of the tails of the distribution. The fourth power of the standard deviation in the denominator standardises the measure and renders it dimensionless. Why does this coefficient give us a measure of the heaviness of the tails of a distribution? To see this, note that fourth powers make each sign positive but inflate large deviations even more than cubic powers or squares would do. The presence of heavy tails, therefore, will tend to inflate the numerator proportionally more than denominator. The fatter the tails, therefore, the higher the kurtosis. But what is a high or low value of the kurtosis?

Here the normal distribution with its thin tails serves as a benchmark. As you know, a normal distribution has two parameters, its mean and its variance, which jointly define the distribution. All normal distributions are symmetrical (hence their skewness equals 0) and have a kurtosis equal to 3. A symmetric distribution with $\alpha_4 > 3$ has heavier tails than a normal distribution. For example, the t-distribution we came across in Chapter 2 has heavier tails than the normal distribution and hence its kurtosis exceeds 3 (the exact size depending on the number of degrees of freedom). In contrast, a rectangular distribution which has a body but no tails has a kurtosis $\alpha_4 = 1.8$ which is markedly smaller than that of a normal distribution.

The sample coefficient of kurtosis, a_4, is obtained as follows:

$$a_4 = \frac{\frac{1}{n} \sum (Y_i - \overline{Y})^4}{s^4} \tag{3.15}$$

In practice, the main purpose of calculating the sample kurtosis is to check whether a symmetric distribution behaves approximately as a normal distribution. There is not much point, therefore, in calculating a kurtosis of a skewed distribution. A unimodal bell-shaped empirical distribution with skewness close to 0 and a sample kurtosis close to 3 can be taken to behave similar to a normal distribution. For example, in Chapter 2 we made frequent use of the empirical distribution of the demand for casual labour on the day-shift in Maputo harbour during the early 1980s. The skewness and kurtosis of this empirical distribution are, respectively, $a_3 = -0.013$ and $a_4 = 3.007$. Not surprisingly, therefore, this distribution behaves very similarly to a normal distribution. An empirical distribution with a_3 roughly equal to zero and $a_4 > 3$ has heavier tails than a normal distribution would have, while $a_4 < 3$ indicates thinner tails than normal.

Exercise 3.4

For samples 1 and 2 in Table 3.2 compute, respectively, the sample coefficients of skewness and of kurtosis. How does the presence of an outlier in sample 2 affect both measures?

Exercise 3.5

In exercise 2.1 you were asked to compute means, medians and modes for a set of socioeconomic variables. For each of these variables:

1 compute the coefficients of skewness and kurtosis;
2 comment whether the distribution can be taken to be symmetrical or not;
3 if so, whether is has normal tails or not.

What do your results tell you about whether the mean is a good summary of the data?

Order-based statistics

The order statistics of a sample of observations Y_i ($i = 1, 2, \ldots n$) are obtained by rearranging the observations in order of increasing magnitude. We denote the resulting ordered sample as $Y_{(i)}$ ($i = 1, 2, \ldots n$) such that $Y_{(1)} < Y_{(2)} < \ldots < Y_{(n)}$, where the bracketed subscripts refer to the position of each observation in the ordered list. Suppose, for example, that we have the following sample of five observations: 4, 0, –3, 5 and –2. These are the Y_i values, $i = 1, \ldots 5$. The ordered sample is obtained as follows: –3, –2, 0, 4, and 5. This ordered list contains the $Y_{(i)}$ values. Hence, while $Y_2 = 0$, $Y_{(2)} = -2$, since –2 is the second value in the ordered list.

The median, Md, is the middle value of the ordered sample, $Y_{(i)}$ ($i = 1, \ldots n$), and, hence, splits the ordered list into two halves; that is, half the observations $Y_{(I)}$ lie below the median, and the other half above it. Box 3.1 explains how to obtain the median of a sample. For a theoretical probability distribution the median is the centre of probability of the distribution: 50 per cent of the probability mass lie below it, and 50 per cent above it.

Box 3.1   Computing the median and quartiles

Let Y_i ($i = 1, \ldots, n$) be the ordered list of sample observations arranged in ascending order. To obtain the median and the quartiles of the sample, proceed as follows:

Median

The location of the median depends on whether the sample size, n, is even or odd. First, compute the median depth = $(n + 1)/2$:

1   If the resulting value is an integer and, hence, the sample size is odd, the position of the median is given by $(n + 1)/2$. For example, if $n = 5$ and, hence, $(n + 1)/2 = 3$, the median is Y_3, the third value in the ordered list.
2   If the resulting value contains a fraction (0.5) and, hence, the sample size is even, the median is obtained by calculating the arithmetic mean of $Y_{n/2}$ and $Y_{(n/2)+1}$. For example, if $n = 6$, $(n + 1)/2 = 3.5$, the median is obtained by taking the mean of Y_3 and Y_4. Note that positions 3 and 4 are the nearest integers on either side of 3.5.

Note that the median depth indicates how far we have to count inwards to encounter the median. This concept of depth is also used to pinpoint the position of an observation in an ordered list with reference to the median. Hence, the depth of Y_i is obtained by counting its position upwards from the lowest value if Y_i lies below the median, and downwards from the highest value if it lies above the median.

Upper and lower quartiles

To find the depth of the quartiles on either side of the median, first obtain the truncated median depth by dropping the fraction 0.5, if present, from the median depth. Then, compute the quartile depth = (truncated median depth + 1)/2

1   If the resulting value is an integer, it indicates the depth of the quartiles on either side of the median. For example, if $n = 10$, the median depth will be $(n + 1)/2 = 11/2 = 5.5$. The truncated median depth is 5. The depth of the quartiles, therefore, equals $(5 + 1)/2 = 3$. To obtain the lower quartile, count upwards starting

with Y_1, the lowest value in the sample. To obtain the upper quartile, count downwards starting with Y_n, the highest value in the sample. In our example, the lower quartile will be the third value from the bottom of the ordered list; the upper quartile is the third value from the top.

2 If the resulting value contains a fraction (0.5), the quartiles can be obtained by averaging the two values whose depths are the integers adjacent to the computed quartile depth. To find the lower quartile, start from the bottom of the list; to find the upper quartile, start from the top. For example, if $n = 7$, the median depth will be 4 (which equals the truncated median depth because it does not contain a fraction). The quartile depth then equals (truncated median depth + 1)/2 = (4 + 1)/2 = 2.5. The lower quartile, therefore, is obtained by taking the average of the second and third values in the ordered list: $Q_L = (Y_2 + Y_3)/2$. Similarly, the upper quartile is found by averaging the second and third values from the top of the list: $Q_U = (Y_5 + Y_6)/2$.

Source: Hoaglin (1983)

Quartiles divide an ordered sample into quarters. Box 3.1 explains how to do this. The median itself is the second quartile. Apart from the median, we have the lower, Q_L, and upper, Q_U, quartiles. The interquartile range, IQR $= Q_U - Q_L$, is the most commonly used measure of spread for order statistics. It gives us the range of the middle 50 per cent of the data. The range of the data is another order-based measure of spread and involves computing the difference between the extreme values, respectively X_U and X_L, of the sample, where $X_U = Y_{(n)}$ and $X_L = Y_{(1)}$. Unlike the IQR, however, the range $(X_U - X_L)$ is not a resistant summary of spread.

Exercise 3.6

Using Table 3.2, find the median and the upper and lower quartiles for the following samples:

1 sample 1;
2 sample 1 without Zimbabwe;
3 sample 2;
4 the sample of GNP per capita for all eight countries listed.

(Between them, these four cases cover all possibilities listed in Box 3.1.)

Exercise 3.7

Using the variables selected in exercises 2.1 and 3.5, for each variable find the median and the upper and lower quartiles.

To look at the shape of an empirical distribution EDA starts from what is called the five-number summary of the data: the median, Md, the lower and upper quartiles, Q_L and Q_U, and the two extreme values, X_L and X_U. The box plot, a graphical display of this five-number summary, shows us the basic structure of the data: more specifically, it shows the location, spread, skewness, tail length and outliers of a batch of data (Emerson and Strenio, 1983: 58). To see how to construct a box plot it is best to look at an example. Figure 3.2 compares the two box plots corresponding to the two seven-country samples of GNP per capita of African countries listed in Table 3.2.

First, take a look at the box plot of sample 1. The plot is constructed with the aid of the five-number summary. A box plot consists of a box and two tails. The box gives the variation of the middle 50 per cent of the data: its upper and lower boundaries are, respectively, the upper and lower quartiles. The horizontal line inside the box indicates the position of the median. The tails (line segments up and down the box) run to the most extreme data values which do not qualify as outliers. Box 3.2 gives a simple procedure to determine which data points can be considered as outliers. In sample 1 there are no outliers and, hence, the tails run up to both extreme values of the sample. In contrast, sample 2 features an outlier, the high GNP per capita of Botswana. To highlight its status as an outlier, we plot it as an isolated point.

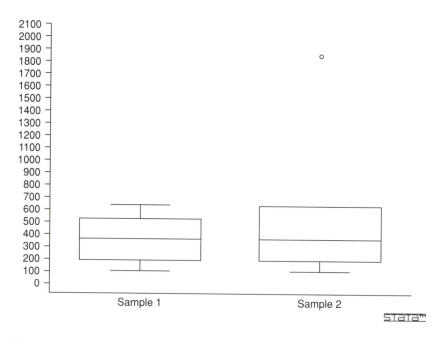

Figure 3.2   Box plots of GNP per capita (two samples of seven African countries)

Box 3.2   The definition of an outlier

Intuitively, an outlier is a data point which is distant from the main body (say, the middle 50 per cent) of the data. To measure distance, EDA uses the IQR, the range of this middle 50 per cent of the data. A data point Y_o is considered to be an outlier if:

$$Y_o < Q_L - 1.5 \text{ IQR} \text{ or } Y_o > Q_U + 1.5 \text{ IQR}$$

respectively, lower and upper outliers.

A data point is a far-outlier if:

$$Y_o < Q_L - 3.0 \text{ IQR} \text{ or } Y_o > Q_U + 3.0 \text{ IQR}$$

Source: Hoaglin (1983).

Detecting outliers: the sex bias against women

This section has aimed to equip you with tools to analyse skewness and the presence of outliers in data: the coefficients of skewness and kurtosis, on the one hand, and the five-number summary and box plot, on the other. Let us now put these tools to work in a concrete case by investigating the relation between the difference in life expectancy between women and men, on the one hand, and the wealth of nations (measured by income per capita), on the other. Since our concern here is with univariate analysis only, we shall investigate this relation between two variables by comparing the distributions of female–male differences in life expectancy for three groups of countries: low, lower-middle and upper-middle income countries.

On average, women live longer than men. However, the discrepancy in life expectancy between women and men varies with the wealth of nations as measured by GNP per capita. More specifically, as wealth increases, women outlive men longer. Table 3.3 summarises the data.

EDA teaches us that we should never look at summary statistics in isolation. Indeed, EDA's approach to data analysis is based on the premise that data should be organised in ways which help you to detect key features and see the unexpected. Therefore, always use numerical summaries in conjunction with visual (graphical) displays of the data so that you are able to look at the data and see the relevance of particular summaries. In this case, as shown in Figure 3.3, comparative box plots prove to be powerful devices that enable us to look carefully at the structure of the data while interpreting summary statistics.

At this point, we suggest that you attempt exercise 3.8 before reading on. This will allow you to compare your observations on the data with ours.

Table 3.3   Difference (female – male) in life expectancy by level of wealth
(GNP per capita groupings), 99 developing countries, 1990

	Low	*Lower-middle*	*Upper-middle*
Sample size	42	40	
Order statistics			
X_L	–3	0	3
Q_L	2	3	5
Median	3	4	6
Q_U	4	5	7
X_U	5	8	8
IQR	2	2	2
Outliers			
India/Nepal	(-2)	0	0
Bhutan	(-3)		
Near-outliers			
Pakistan, Bangladesh	(-1)		
Mean-based statistics			
Mean	2.600	4.230	5.650
s	1.940	1.760	1.460
cv	0.750	0.410	0.260
a_3	–1.400	0.023	–0.500
a_4	4.250	3.20	2.330

Source: World Socioeconomic Data (SOCECON data file)

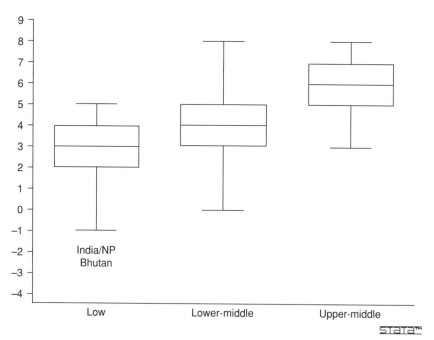

Figure 3.3   Comparative box plots of gender differences in life expectancy

Exercise 3.8

Take a careful look at both Table 3.3 and Figure 3.3. Write down your general comments. More specifically, comment on the following questions:

1   Is there a relation between gender differences in life expectancy and the wealth of nations?
2   How do these three distributions differ with respect to spread?
3   Are the distributions similar in shape, or not?
4   What does the little cluster of outliers in the distribution of low income countries tell you?
5   What did you learn from this exercise in terms of the relative usefulness of mean-based versus order-based statistics?

Clearly, as wealth increases so does the difference between female and male life expectancy: the median difference doubles from three years for low income countries to six years for upper-middle income countries, a result which confirms that women outlive men longer as wealth increases. The means also indicate this basic pattern, but the respective positions of the means are more strongly influenced by the presence of outliers.

In terms of spread, the IQR is resistant to what happens in the tails and, hence, picks up the variation of the middle 50 per cent of the data across samples. An interesting feature of the data is that the IQR remains remarkably stable as we move from low to upper-middle income countries. Moreover, in all three cases, the medians are situated exactly in the middle of the box plots. This result normally indicates that the middle body of the data is symmetrically distributed. In general, this would be an appropriate conclusion to draw, but we need to be a bit careful here. Why? The reason why we should not jump too quickly to this conclusion is that the published data on life expectancy are rounded to the nearest integer (for example, 65 or 66, but never 65.5). Consequently, the difference between female and male life expectancy is always a (relatively small) integer (1, 2, 3, or –2), never a fraction. Did you notice in Table 3.3 that all order statistics were small integers? There are no data points between any two adjoining integers, but only gaps. But with IQR = 2, a data point within the box will be equal to either the median or the lower quartile or the upper quartile. There is no reason, however, to expect that the lower quartile will have an equal number of observations as the upper quartile.

This does not mean, however, that the constancy of the IQR from sample to sample does not convey a real message. Indeed, it is remarkable that the spread of the data does not increase as the level (i.e. the average difference between female and male life expectancies) increases from sample to sample. This is interesting because level and spread often do move together across comparative samples. The decline in the coefficients of variation from sample to sample confirms that here the increase in level does not go hand in hand with the increase in spread. Note, however, that the standard deviations (and, hence, the coefficients of variation) are far more sensitive to the tails of the distributions. This fact is most obvious in the case of low income countries. It should not surprise us, therefore, that its standard deviation is the highest among the three samples.

But undoubtedly, in substantive terms, the most striking feature of the data is the unusual cluster of negative outliers in the distribution for low income countries. Three countries, India, Nepal and Bhutan, along with two borderline cases (in so far as the definition of outliers is concerned), Pakistan and Bangladesh, all have in common that the life expectancy of men exceeds that of women, contrary to the dominant pattern across the world. This finding has led to an extensive debate in the development literature as to whether there is a sex bias against women in these countries (see, for example, Wheeler, 1984; Sen and Sengupta, 1983; Sen, 1985, and Harriss, 1990).

The lesson we want to draw from this example is that we can get much more mileage out of the data if we use mean-based statistics jointly with order statistics and their graphical display. For example, it is much easier to see why the sample of low income countries has a much higher kurtosis than the other samples once we have taken note of the cluster of outliers in its lower tail. The kurtosis does not by itself explain this feature in the data. Similarly, a quick look at the standard deviations of the three samples may lead us to overlook the remarkable constancy of the spread of the middle 50 per cent of the data, the IQR, as we move from sample to sample. Level increases from sample to sample, but the mid spread does not. More importantly, however, merely to calculate the means and standard deviations of the three samples may cause us to overlook the outliers in the sample of low income countries. The point here, however, is to explain the outliers, not to hide them. This is where comparative box plots show their power as analytical tools of exploratory data analysis. They draw our attention both to regular patterns within the data as well as to the unusual or exceptional. In this case, a set of three to five countries clearly does not fit the overall pattern. This calls for an explanation as to why the life expectancy of women is less than that of men in these countries. Or, more vividly, as Sen put it, where are the missing millions of women in these countries?

3.4   DETECTING NON-NORMALITY IN DATA

If the normality assumption is reasonably valid in practice, the sample mean is unbeatable as an estimator of the population mean. But how do we detect non-normality in sample data? This section discusses two procedures to do this: a quick exploratory check and a formal test. Before doing either of these, always take a good look at the data first. You can do this with a histogram or a box plot. In many cases it will be plainly obvious that the normality assumption is invalid. Take, for example, another look at the histogram in Figure 2.2. It does not require a formal test to see that this sample does not derive from a normal distribution. Similarly, in Figure 3.3, the box plot of the difference between female and male life expectancy for low income countries reveals a heavy lower tail which clearly violates the normality assumption, although the middle 50 per cent of the data are quite symmetric. As a rule, use numerical summaries and graphical displays to get a good grip on your data. This in itself allows you to weed out cases which clearly violate the normality assumption. If further scrutiny is required, apply the procedures we shall now discuss.

An exploratory check for normality in data

This two-step procedure is a simple application of the tools developed in the previous section. It involves comparing mean-based with order-based statistics to check for normality in data. The procedure involves two steps. First, we check whether the data are reasonably symmetric and, if so, subsequently verify whether the tails of the sample distribution are sufficiently thin to warrant the normality assumption.

Step 1: Checking skewness

The first step involves comparing the sample median, a resistant summary, with the sample mean which is non-resistant. The absence or presence of skewness is deduced from the location of the mean relative to the median, as follows:

1 positive skewness   mean > median
2 approximate symmetry   mean $\cong$ median
3 negative skewness   mean < median

To judge whether the mean is approximately equal to the median, it is useful to compare the distance between them with the IQR. A graphical variant of this is to draw the position of the mean in the box plot of the data. Figure 3.4 gives an example: it features the box plot of the distribution of GNP per capita for 111 countries in 1990 (from data file SOCECON). The mean (depicted by the horizontal line) is close to the upper quartile of the data, while the median is close to the lower quartile. If the mean and median differ significantly because of the systematic skewness in the data, it is best to try out a power transformation of the data to eliminate skewness. We shall show how to do this in section 3.5.

A word of warning is necessary here. It is possible to come across data where the mean and median differ sufficiently for us to be inclined to try out a transformation, yet none is called for because the discrepancy between mean and median is solely due to the behaviour in one of the tails of the distribution. In fact, our example on the differences between female and male life expectancy for low income countries is such a case.

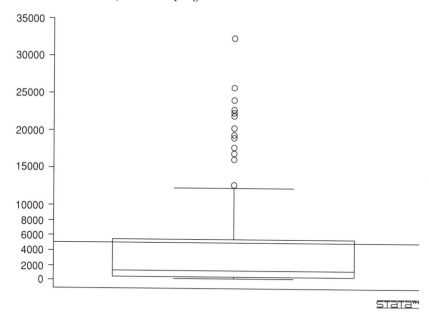

Figure 3.4 Mean versus median: GNP per capita

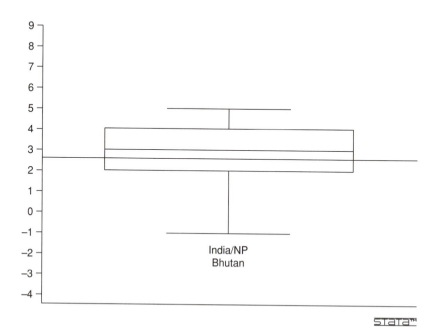

Figure 3.5 Symmetric but unusual tail: female–male life expectancy

Figure 3.5 reproduces the box plot along with the position of the mean. The reasonably significant discrepancy between the mean and the median may lead us to decide to transform the data. But if we do this, we overlook the fact that the middle body of the data is symmetric, as indicated by the position of the median which cuts the box in halves. As discussed above, the problem here is not skewness, but the presence of a cluster of outliers in the lower tail.

To avoid failing to distinguish between genuine skewness in data and unusual behaviour (outliers) in one of the tails (both of which lead to the divergence between the mean and the median), always observe whether the middle 50 per cent of the data also manifest skewness. If they do, a transformation is called for; if not, our attention should go to the unusual behaviour in the tail. To make this distinction you can use a box plot to check the location of the median in relation to the quartiles. Symmetry requires that the median (approximately) divides the box into halves. Alternatively, you may use Bowley's coefficient of skewness, b_s, which is a resistant measure of skewness defined as follows:

$$b_s = (Q_U + Q_L - 2 \text{ Md}) / \text{IQR} \qquad (3.18)$$

where b_s lies within the range -1 and $+1$. You can easily verify that if the median is situated in the middle of the upper and lower quartiles, b_s equals 0, indicating symmetry in the middle body of the data. If $b_s < 0$, the middle 50 per cent of the data is skewed to the left (negative skew), and if $b_s > 0$, it is skewed to the right (positive skewness).

To sum up, step 1 checks whether or not the distribution is skewed. To do this, compare the mean with the median to see whether they diverge significantly. Compute b_s, Bowley's resistant measure of skewness, to verify whether the middle 50 per cent of the data confirm your conclusion. If the distribution is genuinely skewed, you may decide to try out a transformation of the data to see whether it is possible to eliminate skewness. If the data are approximately symmetrical (or manifest only slight skewness), you can proceed with step 2.

Step 2: Checking for heavy tails

To detect whether the sample data display thinner or fatter tails than those of a normal distribution, we may be inclined to compare the standard deviation, s, which is non-resistant, with the IQR, a resistant measure of spread. However, unlike the mean and median, the standard deviation and the IQR do not measure the same thing even if the underlying distribution is symmetric and undisturbed by outliers. Indeed, the IQR measures the range of the middle 50 per cent of the (ordered) data, while the standard deviation is a measure of spread derived from the least squares property. Consequently, the two measures are not directly comparable. But we can nevertheless make use of the property that, for a normal distribution, a definite relation exists between its interquartile range (IQR) and its standard deviation σ:

$$\sigma = \frac{\text{IQR}}{1.35} \qquad (3.19)$$

Using this theoretical relation of a normal distribution, we can now define an alternative resistant measure of spread, the pseudo standard deviation (s_p), based on the IQR and comparable with a standard deviation, as follows (Hoaglin, 1985: 426–7):

$$s_p = \frac{\text{IQR}}{1.35} \qquad (3.20)$$

Now, if a symmetrical empirical distribution approximately has normal tails, its pseudo standard deviation will be very similar to its standard deviation. If not, the two values will diverge. More specifically, we get:

1 $s_p < s$ implies heavier than normal tails;
2 $s_p \cong s$ implies (approximately) normal tails;
3 $s_p > s$ implies thinner than normal tails.

Consider two examples. First, take once more the data on the demand for casual labour in Maputo harbour, as depicted in the histogram of Figure 2.1. As you know by now, these data behave very much like a normal distribution. So let us see how they stand up to our simple test. In this case, $s = 155$ and IQR $= (Q_U - Q_L) = (677 - 476) = 201$. Consequently, $s_p = 201/1.35 = 149$, which is only slightly less than the standard deviation. For practical purposes, therefore, this distribution can be taken to behave as a normal distribution (since, as you already know, its mean and median are close together).

Second, consider the data on the difference between female and male life expectancy for low income countries. We have seen that this distribution is symmetric in the middle, but its mean deviates significantly from its median due to the unusual behaviour of its lower tail. How does it perform on our simple test? Table 3.3 gives us the relevant information: IQR $= 2$; hence, $s_p = 1.48 < s = 1.94$. In other words, the tails of this distribution are much heavier than those of a normal distribution with a similar IQR. Consequently, we reject the normality assumption in this case.

In conclusion, if a sample of data passes both tests (steps 1 and 2), we can safely conclude that the data are drawn from a parent distribution which is approximately normally distributed.

The skewness–kurtosis (Jarque–Bera) test for normality

It is also possible to test more formally, using the mean-based coefficients of skewness and kurtosis, whether data are approximately normal in shape. It can be shown that:

$$Z_3 = \frac{a_3 \cdot \sqrt{n}}{\sqrt{6}} \text{ and } Z_4 = \frac{(a_4 - 3) \cdot \sqrt{n}}{\sqrt{24}} \tag{3.21}$$

where both have a standard normal distribution in large samples. The skewness–kurtosis (Jarque–Bera) test for normality tests the joint hypothesis that $\alpha_3 = 0$ and $\alpha_4 = 3$ (i.e. the values of α_3 and α_4 for a normal distribution). The relevant test-statistic is $(Z_3^2 + Z_4^2)$ which follows a chi-square distribution with two degrees of freedom. Hence,

H_0: $\alpha_3 = 0$ and $\alpha_4 = 3$

H_1: $\alpha_3 \neq 0$ or $\alpha_4 \neq 3$ or both $\tag{3.22}$

$Z_3^2 + Z_4^2 = a_3^2 \cdot (n/6) + (a_4 - 3)^2 \cdot (n/24) \sim \chi_{(2)}$

where the critical value of the chi-square statistic with two degrees of freedom equals 5.99 at the 5 per cent level of significance. Strictly speaking, this test is only valid for (very) large sample sizes: $n > 1,000$. The reason is that Z_3 and Z_4 cannot be taken to be independent if the sample size is smaller than 1,000 and, therefore, the use of the chi-square distribution as the sampling distribution of $(Z_3^2 + Z_4^2)$ is not strictly valid. However, the test is still worthwhile as an indicative exercise if our sample size happens to be smaller, which will often be the case in applied work.

More specifically, if the test rejects the normality assumption, you can be reasonably assured that the data are not derived from a normal distribution. But if the test does not reject the null hypothesis, you still need to be careful about its interpretation. It is possible that the test has missed out one or another indication of non-normality. This apparent ambiguity should not trouble you too much. The mechanical application of techniques or tests by themselves is never fruitful. Applied data analysis invariably involves informed judgement along with technical expertise. It is always useful to look at data in different ways to assess the reasonableness of the assumptions involved in modelling. In this case, use the skewness–kurtosis test in conjunction with the more informal exploratory checks obtained by comparing resistant and non-resistant measures of level and spread to judge whether the normality assumption is likely to be valid in practice.

Exercise 3.9

Using the variables selected in exercise 2.1, 3.5 and 3.7, for each variable:

1 summarise mean-based and order-based statistics;
2 find the outliers, if any, in the sample;
3 produce the relevant box plot;
4 test the normality assumption by (a) using the two-step exploratory check and (b) using the skewness–kurtosis test.

Heavy tails: mean versus median revisited

So what do we do if our data are skewed or have heavy tails? If the data are skewed, a transformation of the data may help. We discuss how to do this in section 3.5. But what to do if the data are reasonably symmetric but have heavier than normal tails? Should we continue to use the sample mean as the preferred estimator of the population mean?

In section 2.5 we showed that the mean is the superior estimator if the normality assumption prevails. In those circumstances the mean clearly outperforms the median: the standard deviation of the sampling distribution of the median will be about 25 per cent larger than that of the mean. But what if the underlying conditions of the parent distribution are unknown and, in particular, if it is likely to have heavy tails? In such cases, an estimator which performs well under very restrictive circumstances but does not do so well under a variety of different conditions is not much use. It is then preferable to use a robust estimator such as the median. Indeed:

> In non normal distributions with long tails, the relative efficiency of the median to the mean rises and may become larger than 1. We can now define more specifically what is meant by a robust estimate – namely, one whose efficiency relative to competitors is high (i.e. seldom much less than 1) over a wide range of parent populations. The median is more robust as well as more resistant to erratic extreme observations, although it is inferior to the mean with symmetrical distributions not far from normal.
>
> (Snedecor and Cochran, 1989: 136)

Hence, in cases where the empirical distribution is reasonably symmetrical but s_p is significantly larger than s (or a_4 is well above 3), it is preferable by far to use the median as the estimator of the population mean (which, for a symmetrical distribution, is also equal to the population median).

If we rely on the sample median as our estimator, it is possible to construct a conservative confidence interval for the population median that is valid for any continuous distribution, as follows (ibid.: 136–7). Two values in the ordered list of sample values serve as the lower and upper confidence limits. To obtain a 95 per cent confidence interval, we obtain the positions for the confidence interval by first calculating the values of, respectively, $[(n + 1)/2 - \sqrt{n}]$ and $[(n + 1)/2 + \sqrt{n}]$, subsequently rounding down the lower value and rounding up the upper value to the nearest integers.

To illustrate this procedure, suppose we have an ordered sample of the following 15 observations:

Sample: 1, 2, 3, 6, 8, 10, 12, 14, 16, 17, 19, 20, 27, 32, 34
Median: 14

To obtain 95 per cent confidence interval, we calculate the position of the approximate limits as follows:

$(n + 1)/2 - \sqrt{n} = (15 + 1)/2 - \sqrt{15} = 4.3$, which rounds down to 4

$(n + 1)/2 + \sqrt{n} = (15 + 1)/2 + \sqrt{15} = 11.87$ which rounds up to 12

giving us the positions of the lower and upper confidence limits. Hence, the lower limit of the 95 per cent confidence interval is 6, the fourth value in the ordered list, and the upper limit is 24, the twelfth value in the list. Note that the distance of the lower limit of this confidence interval to the median is not necessarily equal to the distance from the median to the upper limit. This will only be approximately the case if the data are fairly symmetrically distributed. Indeed, since the confidence interval is based on order statistics, its limits depend on the shape of the distribution.

3.5 DATA TRANSFORMATIONS TO ELIMINATE SKEWNESS

Many socioeconomic data, when unimodal, are strongly skewed: usually, but not always, to the right. One reason is that most socioeconomic data have a clear floor but no definite ceiling. For example, production cannot be negative, but enterprises differ widely in the level of their output. Another reason is that socioeconomic data reflect inequalities in the economy and society. Income distribution, for example, is usually heavily skewed to the right: most people have relatively low and modest incomes while fewer and fewer persons have ever larger incomes. Similarly, a time series which grows at roughly a constant rate of growth will produce a set of data points which are skewed to the right because the increment between successive points increases as the level goes up, due to the constancy of the growth rate.

Skewness in data is a major problem when modelling an average. First, as we have seen, a skewed distribution has no clear centre. The mean, its centre of gravity, will differ from the median, its centre of probability. Second, the sample mean is no longer an attractive estimator of the population mean since the normality assumption is not satisfied. It appears, therefore, that the model discussed in Chapter 2 is of no use here. Or is it? Fortunately, it is often still possible to use the powerful properties of the classical model based on the normality assumption even when working with data which derive from a skewed distribution. We do this by changing the shape of the underlying distribution using a non-linear transformation of the data. This section shows how to do this.

A transformation is a conversion of the data by mathematical means. The conversion of degrees Celsius into Fahrenheit is an example of a linear transformation. A linear transformation only changes the scale and the location of the data, not its shape. To change the shape of the distribution of the data, we need non-linear transformations, for example, a power, a square root or a logarithm. The latter, the logarithmic transformation, is highly popular in applied data analysis. So let us start with this transformation.

The logarithmic transformation

Logarithms have the property of shrinking the distance between two or more values which are greater than 1. Take a look at Table 3.4 which lists the GNP per capita of three African countries. The raw data show that the GNP per capita of Zimbabwe is relatively close to that of Tanzania, while Botswana's is clearly way out. Using logarithms, however, shows a different picture. The position of Zimbabwe is now closer to that of Botswana than to that of Tanzania. Why is this? The reason is that logarithms shrink larger numbers more dramatically than they do smaller numbers, as is evident from Table 3.4. Consequently, in terms of logarithms, Botswana is no longer an outlier. This simple example suggests that we can use the logarithmic transformation to shrink the right tail of a positively skewed distribution proportionally much more than any of the smaller values in its main body or its left tail. In this way, a skewed distribution may be rendered more symmetrical.

Let us try out this idea with a larger sample of data. Figure 3.6 shows the histogram of the distribution of per capita household income for a sample of 197 households in Hebei province of China, obtained from the World Fertility Survey, 1985. The data are available in the CHINA file. As you can see, this distribution is strongly skewed to the right. What happens if we make a histogram of the logarithms of per capita household incomes? Figure 3.7 shows the picture. As you can see, the skewness of the distribution of household income is drastically reduced after the transformation.

Exercise 3.10

Table 3.5 gives you selected summary statistics for both distributions depicted in Figures 3.6 and 3.7: respectively, per capita household income and the logarithm thereof. Check whether either or both distribution approximately satisfies the normality assumption, using: (a) the two-step procedure involving the comparison of mean-based and order-based statistics; and (b) the skewness–kurtosis test for normality.

Table 3.4 The shrinking effect of logarithms

Country	Per capita GNP (US$)	Difference from previous country	$Log_e(GNP)$	Difference from previous country
Tanzania	110	–	4.70	–
Zimbabwe	640	530	6.46	1.76
Botswana	2040	1400	7.62	1.16

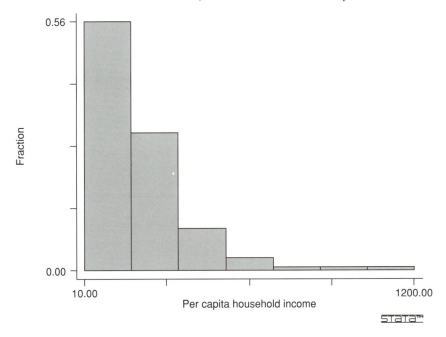

Figure 3.6   Household income data

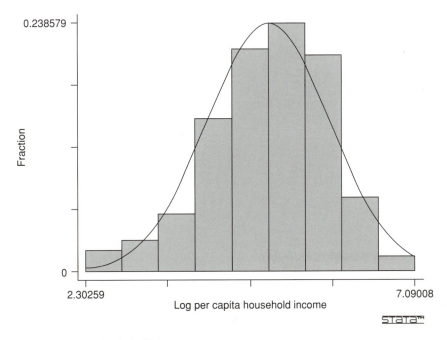

Figure 3.7   Log household income

Table 3.5　Summary statistics of per capita household income

Summary statistics	Per capita household income	Logarithm of per capita household income
Median	153.33	5.03
Mean	198.25	4.95
IQR	166.67	1.10
Standard deviation	170.65	0.89
Skewness (a_3)	2.25	−0.48
Kurtosis (a_4)	10.88	3.17
Sample size	197	197

You will have noted that the logarithmic transformation somewhat over-corrected the skewness in the original data. Indeed, the transformed data show a slight but significant skew to the left. Strong positive skewness in the raw data, therefore, has been turned into mild negative skewness with the transformed data. This is the main reason why the skewness–kurtosis test, at 5 per cent significance level, rejects the null hypothesis that the data are derived from a normal distribution.

As far as the problem of fat tails is concerned, our log transformation did a splendid job. You will have found that the resulting pseudo standard deviation is slightly less than the standard deviation, while the coefficient of kurtosis is slightly above 3. For all practical purposes, the log transformed data have thin tails. Given these results – slight but significant negative skew and thin tails – you might rightly be inclined to decide that the log transformation did a satisfactory job. The parent distribution may not be wholly normal, but this does not mean that the classical model based on the sample mean as estimator is likely to perform badly. In other words, the underlying distribution of the log transformed data is unlikely to be so far away from the normal distribution as to affect seriously the relative efficiency of the sample mean. Furthermore, for reasons which will become more apparent throughout this book, the logarithmic transformation is very attractive and, if it is likely to perform reasonably well, you may feel inclined to stick with it. But, alternatively, you may want to search for a better transformation which corrects for positive skewness in the data without overdoing it. Which other types of transformations can we use?

The ladder of power transformation

In fact, EDA uses a graduated family of transformations, the power transformations, to convert a range of unimodal distributions. These transformations can change both the direction (negative or positive) and the extent of skewness in the data. Table 3.6 illustrates the hierarchy of these power transformations and their impact on the skewness in the data.

Table 3.6 Ladder of powers to reduce skewness

Power p	Transformation	Effect on skewness
3	Y^3	Reduces extreme negative skewness
2	Y^2	Reduces negative skewness
1	Y	Leaves data unchanged
0	$\log_e(Y)$	Reduces positive skewness
−1	$-Y^{-1}$	Reduces extreme positive skewness

In general, the power transformation is of the form Y^p, where p is a non-zero real number. The choice of the power p depends on the nature of skewness in the original distribution. The higher the value of p above unity, the greater is the impact of transformation in reducing negative skewness. Similarly, the lower the value of p below unity, the greater its impact in reducing positive skewness, except when p is exactly zero. If $p = 0$, $Y^p = 1$ for any non-zero value of Y. Obviously, this type of transformation does not serve any purpose since all the information about Y would be lost. But it so happens, however, that the logarithmic transformation fits nicely into this position of the ladder of transformations and so, by convention, $p = 0$ is the log transformation. The reason is that it reduces positive skewness less than a negative power ($p < 0$) would do, but more than any power p, such that $1 < p < 0$. Thus we obtain a hierarchy of powers, p, in terms of its effects on reducing skewness. This hierarchy is depicted in the so-called ladder of powers as shown in Table 3.6.

The power used in transformation need not be only an integer but can contain fractions as well. Hence, for example, it is possible to use a square root ($p = 0.5$) which corrects for milder positive skewness in data. However, the idea is not that you should try to find the exact power, correct to so many places of decimal, like 0.627 or some such number, to get a perfect symmetry. In practice, a suitable rounded power such as 0.25 or 0.75 will suffice as long a reasonable symmetry is achieved.

Let us now go back to our example of per capita incomes of Chinese households, depicted in Figures 3.6 and 3.7. The effect of the logarithmic transformation was somewhat stronger than necessary, resulting in a mild negative skewness in the transformed data. To avoid over-correcting skewness in the original data, we need to move up the ladder a bit: some power in between 0 and 1 should do the trick. For example, we could try a square root, $p = 0.5$, or a fourth root, $p = 0.25$. With a bit of trial and error we settle on the fourth root: $p = 0.25$. Table 3.7 gives us the summary statistics and Figure 3.8 shows the histogram.

Table 3.7 Fourth root transformation of per capita household income data

Power transformation	Median	Mean	IQR	Standard deviation	Skewness a_3	Kurtosis a_4
Fourth root	3.52	3.53	0.95	0.75	0.15	2.98

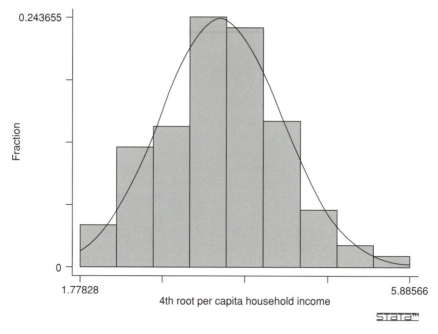

Figure 3.8   Fourth root transformation

Exercise 3.11

As in exercise 3.10, check whether the underlying distribution of the fourth root transformation of the data on household income per capita can be taken to be approximately normal in shape.

You should find that the fourth root transformation brings the data in line with the normality assumption. In this case, the fourth root is a superior transformation to the logarithmic one. But for reasons which will become clear in subsequent chapters, economists often find it easier to work with a variable $\log(Y)$ in an equation rather than with $Y^{0.25}$. Hence, the choice of an appropriate transformation often involves a trade-off between one which is ideal for the purposes of data analysis and one which performs reasonably well on this count but also has the advantage that it lends itself to a more straightforward interpretation (in substantive terms) of the results.

Modelling with transformed data

So what have we achieved now in terms of modelling? Clearly, the classical model of inference about the population mean:

$$Y_i = \mu + \epsilon_i \tag{3.23}$$

where the error term is assumed to be distributed normally, is inappropriate to model the population mean of the distribution of per capita incomes of Chinese households. But what about modelling the transformed data? Our analysis suggests two models which are likely to perform well, namely:

$$Y_i^{1/4} = \mu' + \epsilon_i \qquad (3.24)$$

and

$$\ln(Y_i) = \mu'' + \epsilon_i \qquad (3.25)$$

where, respectively, μ' is the population mean of $Y_i^{1/4}$ (i.e. $\mu' = E(Y_i^{1/4})$) and μ'' is the population mean of $\ln(Y_i)$ (i.e. $\mu'' = E(\ln Y_i)$). The fourth root specification is most appropriate, given the normality assumption of the classical model. The logarithmic specification is likely to perform reasonably well inasmuch as the deviations from the normality assumption are unlikely to affect the relative efficiency of the sample mean (*vis à vis*, for example, the median) too adversely. Hence, in both cases, we can take advantage of the attractive properties of the sample mean as an estimator.

At this point you may be inclined to ask what good it does if the fourth power or logarithmic transformations render our statistical analysis more amenable. After all, what interpretation are we to give to the fourth power of household income, or to its logarithm? The question now arises of how we go back to the original data. In other words, how does this μ' and μ'' relate to the average of the original data of per capita household income?

The answer lies in the nature of transformation itself. To go back to the original data, we use the inverse transformation. Let us illustrate this point with the logarithmic transformation. For example, if 4.70 is the natural logarithm of per capita GNP of Tanzania, the original income value is obtained by simply raising 4.70 to the power of e: that is, $e^{4.70} = 110$. Hence, in the case of the logarithmic transformation we get:

Logarithmic transformation of Y to W: $W = \log_e(Y)$
Inverse transformation of W to Y: $Y = e^W$

This application of the inverse transformation of the transformed data therefore takes us back to the original data. The implication is that no information is lost in the process of transformation but the point is to interpret it correctly. If we estimate the mean of log transformed data, what does this say about the location of the centre of the distribution of the original data?

To answer this question, let us proceed step by step. First, keep in mind that if the logarithmic transformation proves to be successful in eliminating skewness, the distribution of the log transformed data will be (near-)symmetric. Hence, given the (near) symmetry of the distribution, the mean of the transformed data will be close to its median.

Second, the logarithmic transformation alters the shape but not the order of the data (the latter property is the definition of a monotonic transformation). More formally:

$$\text{If } Y_i > Y_j \text{ then } \log_e (Y_i) > \log_e (Y_j) \tag{3.26}$$

It follows that the sample unit which is the median of the transformed data will also be the median in the original data. Obviously, if the sample size is even and, hence, the median is obtained by taking the arithmetic mean of the two middle values, the inverse transformation (i.e. the antilogarithm) of the median of the transformed data will diverge somewhat from the calculated median of the original. In conclusion, the antilogarithm of the median of the transformed data will be equal to (if the sample size, n, is odd) or near to (if n is even) the median of the original data. Consequently, since the sample mean and median of the transformed data will be approximately equal, it follows that the antilogarithm of the sample mean of the transformed data will be equal to (or very close to) the sample median of the raw data.

Third, while the sample mean of the transformed data is an estimator of the population mean of the transformed data, its antilogarithm is an estimator of the population median of the original data. Hence, in conclusion, when estimating the population mean of the distribution of the log transformed data, the inverse transformation of our estimate will give us an estimate of the median of the distribution of the original data.

Exercise 3.12

Figure 3.4 shows the distribution of GNP per capita (in the file SOCECON), a distribution which is skewed to the right. Using the data in the data file:

1   take the logarithms of the GNP per capita data;
2   calculate the mean-based and order-based statistics of GNP per capita and of log(GNP per capita);
3   check whether log(GNP per capita) is reasonably symmetric and thin tailed;
4   compute the antilogarithm of the sample mean of the log(GNP per capita) and compare it with the mean and median of the original data (GNP per capita).

What do you conclude?

The same argument can be applied to the whole family of power transformations since all these transformations preserve the order of the data. The inverse transformation of the sample mean of the transformed data gives us an estimate of the population median of the original raw data. For example, the median per capita household income of the data on China is 153.3. The mean of the fourth root of the data is 3.526. The fourth power of 3.526, which is the appropriate inverse transformation in this case, is 154.5, which is very close to the median of the original data.

What applies to the point estimate also applies to the interval estimate (the confidence interval). Hence, after estimating the sample mean of the transformed data and calculating its confidence limits, we can then take the inverse transformation of this sample mean and of its confidence limits to obtain an interval estimate of the population median of the original data. It is not valid, however, to calculate the inverse transformation of the standard error of the sample mean of the transformed data because the reverse transformation changes the nature of the sampling distribution of the estimator obtained by reverse transformation.

Once more: mean versus median

The mean is the centre of gravity of a distribution and the median its centre of probability. If the distribution is symmetrical, the mean and median will coincide and both measure the centre of symmetry of a distribution. In Chapter 2 we sung the praise of the sample mean as an estimator of the population mean if the normality assumption is approximately valid in practice. Under these conditions, the sample mean is indeed unbeatable as an estimator of the population mean (which is also its median as well as its mode). The classical model is a powerful tool and whenever possible we seek to apply it, provided we can be assured that deviations from the normality assumption do not invalidate its power.

If the parent distribution of a sample is symmetric but not normal, inasmuch as its tails are too heavy, we have seen that the mean ceases to be the best estimator since its lacks resistance to outliers as well as robustness to underlying conditions which deviate too much from the normality assumption. In such cases, it is preferable to estimate the population mean with the median, a more robust estimator.

If the parent distribution is skewed but unimodal, it is often, but not always, possible to render it symmetric and, hopefully, normal by applying a simple transformation taken from the ladder of transformations. If the transformation works well, we can again rely on the classical model and use the sample mean of the transformed data as a powerful estimator of its population mean (which, given the symmetry of the distribution, is also its median). After estimation, however, we have to go back to the original data characterised by a skewed distribution. For the latter distribution, there is no centre of symmetry and consequently its centre of gravity (the mean) will diverge from its centre of probability (the median). The inverse transformation of the sample mean of the transformed data then gives us an estimate of the population median of the original data, not of its population mean.

3.6   SUMMARY OF MAIN POINTS

1   The sample mean is a least squares estimator. In general, least squares estimators have desirable properties if the normality assumption is satisfied. But the least squares property also accounts for the lack of resistance of the sample mean to outliers and skewness in the sample.

2   To analyse the shape of a distribution (particularly skewness and the heaviness of its tails) we can use both mean-based and order-based statistics: respectively, the coefficients of skewness and kurtosis, on the one hand, and the five-number summary and box plots (along with the definition of outliers), on the other. The latter, unlike the former, are resistant summaries which are more appropriate when analysing data the underlying conditions of which are largely unknown. These measures are summarised in Table 3.8.

3   To check whether the normality assumption is reasonably valid in practice, we suggested two procedures. The first procedure is based on a comparison of mean-based and order-based statistics and involves two steps. First, check for skewness in the data, by comparing the mean and the median of the sample. To avoid skewness being due only to outliers in the tail, Bowley's resistant coefficient of skewness can be used to check whether the middle 50 per cent of the data are skewed. Second, to check whether the data display heavier tails than a normal distribution, compare the pseudo standard deviation, a resistant measure of spread based on the IQR, with the standard deviation of the sample. The second procedure involves a formal test – the skewness–kurtosis test – which verifies whether the data are drawn from a normal distribution (for which the coefficient of skewness equals 0 and kurtosis equals 3).

4   If the data are reasonably symmetrical but have heavier than normal tails, the sample mean may not be the best estimator due to its lack of resistance and robustness. Robustness of an estimator is the property

Table 3.8   Moment-based characteristics of a distribution

	Population	Sample	Measure of	Value for population $Y \sim N(0,1)$
First moment	$E(Y) = \mu$	$\frac{1}{n} \Sigma\, X_i = \bar{X}$	Centre	0
Second moment	$E(Y - \mu)^2 = \sigma^2$	$\frac{1}{n-1} \Sigma\, (X_i - \bar{X})^2 = s^2$	Spread	1
Third moment	$\frac{1}{\sigma^3} E\,(Y - \mu)^3 = \alpha_3$	$\frac{1}{ns^3} \Sigma\, (X_i - \bar{X})^3 = a_3$	Skewness (outliers)	0
Fourth moment	$\frac{1}{\sigma^4} E\,(Y - \mu)^4 = \alpha_4$	$\frac{1}{ns^4} \Sigma\, (X_i - \bar{X})^4 = a_4$	Kurtosis (heavy tails)	3

Note: First moment is given as first moment around zero, whereas the remaining are moments around the mean, or derived from the latter.

of the estimator to perform well (relative to competitors) over a range of different underlying conditions. While the sample mean is superior when the data are drawn from a normal distribution, the sample median is the more robust estimator and, hence, preferable when the underlying conditions are unknown.

5 If the data are unimodal but skewed, a data transformation is called for to correct for the skewness in the data. To do this we rely on the ladder of power transformations which enable us to correct for differences in the direction of skewness (positive or negative) and in its strength. Often, but not always, a transformation renders the transformed data symmetric and, hopefully, also more normal in shape. If so, the classical model of inference about the population mean using the sample mean as estimator can again be used.

6 After analysis with transformed data it is necessary to translate the results back to the original data. If the transformation was successful and, hence, the transformed data are near symmetrical, the inverse transformation of the sample mean (and of its confidence interval) yields a point (and interval) estimate of the population median of the original data, and not of its population mean. Yet the estimate is obtained by applying the classical model based on the superiority of the sample mean as an estimator when the normality assumption is satisfied, to the transformed data.

ADDITIONAL EXERCISES

Exercise 3.13

Demonstrate algebraically that adding observation X_{n+1} to a sample of n observations will: (a) leave the sample mean unchanged when X_{n+1} equals the sample mean for the first n observations; and (b) increase/decrease the sample mean when X_{n+1} is greater/less than the sample mean for the first n observations.

Exercise 3.14

Using your results from Exercise 3.9, choose appropriate transformations for each of your selected variables. Test for normality in each of the transformed data series and comment on your results.

Part II
Regression and data analysis

4   Data analysis and simple regression

4.1   INTRODUCTION

The model of an average discussed in Chapter 2 depicts data as being composed of a systematic component (the mean) and random variation around it (the error term). The study of relationships between variables extends this idea of an average as the systematic component of a statistical model by making the average of the dependent variable conditional upon the values of the explanatory variables. Hence, in this case we do not have only one average (i.e. the unconditional average), but a line or curve of averages of Y, the dependent variable, for different values of the explanatory variables. This line or curve of averages is called the regression of Y on the explanatory variables. Put differently, the systematic component of our statistical model now becomes a function of the explanatory variables. Fortunately, as we shall see, many of the principles and properties encountered when dealing with a simple average can be applied to regression analysis. Hence, the least squares principle can be logically extended to obtain BLUE estimators of the population parameters of the regression line and, similarly, the normality assumption of the error terms lays the foundations of statistical inference (estimation and hypothesis testing) in regression analysis as well as extending the application of the maximum likelihood principle with its desirable properties.

Simple regression means that we only consider one explanatory variable, X. This chapter deals with simple regression as a tool of data analysis: more precisely, it deals with simple linear regression, which means that the conditional means of Y for given values of X are situated on a straight line. As we shall see below, in many cases data transformations make it possible to extend the reach of simple linear regression to deal with non-linear relations between variables. But why consider two variables only? In fact, most commonly, a variable is deemed to be affected by a score of other variables. The study of relations between variables, therefore, typically involves more than two variables. However, our basic principle is to proceed from the ground upwards. Later, we shall show that multiple regression which models the relationship of one variable with a set of others is essentially arrived at through a hierarchy of several simple regressions. An examination of the relationship of one variable with a set of others, therefore, requires that we have a good understanding of simple regression. Many of the problems encountered in the practice of multiple regression analysis can be understood and resolved through the examination of the component simple regressions.

This chapter is structured as follows. Section 4.2 introduces the concept of regression as a line or curve of conditional means of Y for given values of X. Section 4.3 deals with the classical linear regression model and reviews the properties of the least squares regression line as an estimator of the population regression. Section 4.5 considers a simple regression in practice and argues for the need to check carefully whether the assumptions of the model are reasonably valid in practice since least squares regression, like the sample mean, is not resistant. Although it is not our purpose in this book to deal with resistant and robust regression, we shall nevertheless briefly discuss exploratory band regression as a quick median-based method to obtain a resistant regression curve. We then discuss a set of simple analytical graphs which help us to detect problems with the assumptions of the model. Section 4.6 is an interlude: it deals with the special case of regression through the origin. Section 4.7 discusses the important concepts of outliers, leverage and influential points in linear regression. Section 4.8 shows how data transformations can help to linearise non-linear relations between variables, thus extending the reach of linear regression analysis. Finally, section 4.9 summarises the main points of this chapter.

4.2   MODELLING SIMPLE REGRESSION

In mathematics, the equation $Y = a + b X$ implies that there is one and only one value of Y for a given value of X. In data analysis, however, the relation between two variables is imperfect in the above sense – there is generally more than one value of Y for a given value of X (Mosteller and Tukey, 1977: 262). Consider, for example, Engel's famous empirical law of consumer behaviour. Using a household budget survey of Belgian working class families carefully collected by the Belgian statistician Ducpetiaux in 1855, Engel (a German economist and statistician) observed that the share of household expenditure on food in total expenditure (i.e. the Y variable) was a declining function of household income (i.e. the X variable) (Barten, 1985). This is what one would expect: poorer families spend a higher proportion of their income on food in comparison with better-off families. But this relationship is not perfect. Families with identical income do not necessarily spend an equal proportion of their income on food. Differences in the demographic composition of families and in consumption habits and tastes will account for differences in food expenditures. In fact, actual budget studies reveal considerable variation within

Table 4.1   Share of food in total expenditure

Income group ('000 Shs)	Average proportion of food expenditure (%)
Below 1.0	66.6
1.0–1.9	61.5
2.0–3.9	50.4
4.0–5.9	45.2
6.0–7.9	38.0
8.0–9.9	25.6
10.0–24.9	25.5
Above 24.9	18.2
All	50.0

each income class with respect to the proportion of household expenditure spent on food. However, on average, the proportion of food expenditure in income declines as income increases. Table 4.1 shows this inverse relation based on data obtained from the household budget survey of Tanzania in 1969.

This average inverse relation between the share of food in household expenditures, on the one hand, and income, on the other, is the regression line or curve. This is an average relation inasmuch as most of the data points will not be situated on the regression line/curve. Regression analysis, therefore, aims to establish statistical regularities amidst a great many erratic variations. The regression line, therefore, depicts the systematic component of a statistical model which also includes an error term that accounts for the (often considerable) random variations around the line.

In general, we can write the regression of Y on X as follows:

$$Y = \mu(X) + \epsilon_x \tag{4.1}$$

where, $\mu(X)$ is the average of Y for a given value of X such the average share of food expenditure in household expenditures, in other words, the conditional average, ϵ_X is the corresponding error term, and $E(\epsilon_X) = 0$.

Modelling the regression of Y on X, therefore, implies two steps. First, we need to consider the question of the specification of $\mu(X)$. The regression of Y on X is nothing but the locus of $\mu(X)$ over the range of X. This locus can take various shapes depending on the nature of the relation between Y and X. In practice, with the exception of exploratory band regression (see section 4.5), we try to describe this locus of conditional means by a suitable mathematical function: say, a straight line or a non-linear function which can easily be linearised by applying simple data transformations. This has two advantages: (a) it facilitates statistical analysis of the model such as the derivation of estimation procedures or the examination of the properties of the estimators of the parameters of such functional forms (as, for example, the intercept and slope of a line), and (b) it allows us to give meaningful economic interpretations to the coefficients (parameters) of these functions. Our main purpose is not so much to find the most accurate description of the locus of the regression points, but rather, to find a function which yields an adequate approximation of this locus of conditional means.

At times, the choice of the functional form of the regression may be suggested by theory. For example, theory suggests that the average costs of a firm vary inversely with capacity utilisation. More often, theory does not give us guidance on the precise functional form of a relation but may allow us to narrow down the range of feasible alternatives. But frequently a researcher will pick a particular functional form because its coefficients lend themselves to convenient economic interpretation, such as, for example, a marginal or average propensity, an elasticity or a growth rate. Another approach is to let the data decide on the best specification of the functional form of $\mu(X)$. In this case, a data analyst has to resort to hints and clues obtained from sample data to arrive at a judgement about the best shape of the population regression $\mu(X)$. These approaches, theory-guided versus data-instigated choices, are not incompatible, but often complement each other. We generally start with hints and clues provided by theory as to the shape of the population regression, perhaps taking account as well of convenience in terms of the economic interpretation of the coefficients of alternative specifications, and subsequently we check whether the sample data support our hunches as to the preferred functional form. Hence, the choice of the population regression $\mu(X)$ requires us to find a satisfactory description for the average relation of Y on X on the basis of the sample data. We call this the sample regression.

But modelling a regression curve is not just a question of choosing an appropriate functional form for $\mu(X)$ in equation (4.1). The second task in modelling the regression of Y on X is to specify the stochastic nature of ϵ_x. As we shall see, we do this in much the same way as in the case of modelling a simple (unconditional) average. The assumptions we make about the error term lay the basis for statistical inference, i.e. drawing conclusions from the sample about the population regression.

4.3   LINEAR REGRESSION AND THE LEAST SQUARES PRINCIPLE

Finding a sample regression consists of fitting a line or curve to the sample data. This implies that we make an explicit assumption about the shape of the curve – a straight line, an exponential curve, a quadratic function, or whatever – that seems reasonable from the point of view of *a priori* information, if any, and of the sample data. Subsequently, we fit the curve or line using one or another statistical method. In regression, the most commonly used method is derived from the least squares principle. The simplest shape is of course a straight line which can be readily estimated using the least squares principle. The two coefficients of a straight line, the intercept and slope, are easy to interpret. A straight line may not be the most appropriate summary of the relation between Y and X. However, by starting with this simple shape, we often detect its inadequacies from the data and are, therefore, in a position to move towards a better specification. As was the case with the sample mean, the least squares regression line is an attractive (and, in fact, unbeatable) estimator if certain conditions prevail: that is, if certain model assumptions are reasonably valid in practice. The model which renders least squares regression powerful as an estimator of the population regression is the classical (normal) linear regression model.

The classical linear regression model

In classical linear regression we assume that the population regression is a straight line within the context of the following set of model assumptions:

$$Y = \beta_1 + \beta_2 X + \epsilon_x \quad \text{where } E(\epsilon_x) = 0; \; V(\epsilon_x) = \sigma^2 \qquad (4.2)$$

The move from the general specification in the previous section to the classical linear model above, therefore, involved two steps. First, $\mu(X)$ is specified as a linear function of X. Hence, once we know the actual values of β_1 and β_2 we can compute the average Y for any given X by using the linear function $(\beta_1 + \beta_2 X)$. Second, $V(\epsilon_X)$ is assumed to be the same, irrespective of the value of X. Hence, we assume that the error term is homoscedastic. In applied terms, this assumption of homoscedasticity in the context of regression means that the variation around average relationship is assumed to be similar across the range of X: it neither increases nor decreases with increasing X.

The parameters of the model β_1, β_2 and σ^2, therefore, specify the nature of the average relation between Y and X and the error variation around it. The analogous sample regression can be written as follows:

$$Y_i = b_1 + b_2 X_i + e_i \qquad (4.3)$$

where $i = 1, \ldots n$ (where n = sample size); b_1 is the estimator of β_1; b_2 the estimator of β_2; e are the residuals. The residual, e, is the sample equivalent of the population error term, ϵ. In fact, e can be seen as the estimator of ϵ_x, the error term of the population regression model in (4.2). However, you should not confuse the residual and the error: they are not the same thing. The general convention adopted in this text is thus to use Greek letters to denote population values and lower case to denote the corresponding sample estimate (the mean is an exception to this rule). Other texts may use a 'hat' (ˆ) to denote sample estimates.

To be able to make valid inferences from the sample about the population, in addition to the assumptions about population, we also need to specify the nature of the sampling procedure. We assume that the sample is obtained through independent random sampling of Y for a given set of fixed values of X. Note that X is assumed to be non-stochastic: there is no chance variation involved in the X values. This is a strong assumption which implies that X is controlled by the researcher. This assumption is often quite appropriate for data obtained through experimentation, but not when our data result from observational programmes. In development research we generally observe (but do not control) the variation in Y and X, both of which are subject to chance variations. For the time being, however, let us remain with this assumption. Later in this chapter, we discuss what happens if X is a stochastic variable. If X is non-stochastic, it follows that X and ϵ must be uncorrelated since only the latter is stochastic.

To sum up, if we have a set of paired observations of sample values (Y_i, X_i), $i = 1 \ldots n$, randomly sampled from a wider population, the classical linear regression model is based on the following assumptions:

1. the population regression is adequately represented by a straight line:
   $E(Y_i) = \mu(X_i) = \beta_1 + \beta_2 X_i;$ (4.4)
2. the error terms have zero mean: $E(\epsilon_i) = 0,$ (4.5)
3. a constant variance (homoscedasticity): $V(\epsilon_i) = \sigma^2,$ (4.6)
4. and zero covariances (no autocorrelation): $E(\epsilon_i, \epsilon_j) = 0,$
   for all $i \neq j;$ (4.7)
5. and X is non-stochastic, implying that $E(X_i\,\epsilon_i) = 0.$ (4.8)

Nothing has been said as yet about the shape of the distribution of the error term ϵ_i. In the classical normal linear regression model we shall make the further assumption that:

6. the error term follows a normal distribution: $\epsilon_i \sim N(0, \sigma^2)$ (4.9)

As we shall see, these assumptions make the point that least squares regression has attractive statistical properties as well as providing the foundations for statistical inference based on the least squares regression line. But before we discuss these properties and the inferences to which they give rise in greater detail, let us first have a look at the sample regression line itself.

Least squares estimation

Given the sample regression (4.3), its least squares estimators b_1 and b_2 are obtained by minimising the sum of squared residuals with respect to b_1 and b_2: where:

$$\Sigma e_i^2 = \Sigma (y_i - b_1 - b_2 X_i)^2$$

The resulting estimators of b_1 and b_2 are then given by:

$$b_1 = \bar{Y} - b_1 \bar{X} \tag{4.11}$$

$$b_2 = \frac{\Sigma(X_i - \bar{X})(Y_i - \bar{Y})}{\Sigma(X_i - \bar{X})^2} \tag{4.12}$$

where

$$\bar{Y} = \frac{1}{n} \sum Y_i \text{ and } \bar{X} = \frac{1}{n} \sum X_i \qquad (4.13)$$

are, respectively, the sample means of Y and X.

Mathematical properties of the least squares regression line

The least squares regression line obeys certain mathematical properties which are useful to know in practice. The following properties can be established algebraically:

1 The least squares regression line passes through the point of sample means of Y and X. This can be easily seen from (4.11) which can be rewritten as follows:

$$\bar{Y} = b_1 + b_2 \bar{X} \qquad (4.14)$$

2 The mean of the fitted (predicted) values of Y is equal to the mean of the Y values:

$$\text{Let } \hat{Y}_i = b_1 + b_2 X_i \text{ then we have } \bar{\hat{Y}} = \bar{Y} \qquad (4.15)$$

3 The residuals of the regression line sum to zero:

$$\frac{1}{n} \sum e_i = \frac{1}{n} \sum (Y_i - \hat{Y}_i) = \bar{Y} - \bar{\hat{Y}} = 0 \qquad (4.16)$$

4 The residuals e_i are uncorrelated with the X_i values, i.e.:

$$\sum e_i X_i = 0 \qquad (4.17)$$

5 The residuals e_i are uncorrelated with the fitted values Y_i. This property follows logically from the previous one since each fitted value of Y_i is a linear function of the corresponding X_i value.

6 The least squares regression splits the variation in the Y variable into two components – the explained variation due to the variation in X_i and the residual variation:

$$\text{TSS} = \text{RSS} + \text{ESS} \qquad (4.18)$$

where

$$\text{TSS} = \sum (Y_i - \bar{Y})^2$$

$$\text{ESS} = \sum (\hat{Y}_i - \bar{Y})^2$$

$$\text{RSS} = \sum e_i^2 = \sum (Y_i - \hat{Y}_i)^2$$

TSS is the total variation observed in the dependent variable Y. It is called the total sum of squares. ESS, the explained sum of squares, is the variation of the predicted values $(b_1 + b_2.X)$. This is the variation in Y accounted for by the variation in the explanatory variable X. What is left is the RSS, the residual sum of squares. The reason why the ESS and RSS neatly add up to the TSS is that the residuals are uncorrelated with the fitted Y values and, hence, there is no term with the sum of covariances.

This last property suggests a useful way to measure the goodness of fit of the estimated sample regression. This is done as follows:

$$R^2 = \text{ESS/TSS} \qquad (4.19)$$

where R^2, called R-squared, is the coefficient of determination. It gives us the proportion of the total sum of squares of the dependent variable explained by the variation in the explanatory variable. In fact, R^2 equals the square of the linear correlation coefficient between the observed and the predicted values of the dependent variable Y, computed as follows:

$$r = \frac{\text{Cov}(Y, \hat{Y})}{\sqrt{[V(Y)\,V(\hat{Y})]}} = \frac{\Sigma(Y_i - \overline{Y})(\hat{Y}_i - \overline{\hat{Y}})}{\sqrt{[\Sigma(Y_i - \overline{Y})^2\,\Sigma(\hat{Y}_i - \overline{\hat{Y}})^2}} \qquad (4.20)$$

A correlation coefficient measures the degree of linear association between two variables. Note, however, that if the underlying relation between the variables is non-linear, the correlation coefficient may perform poorly, notwithstanding the fact that a strong non-linear association exists between two variables.

Association versus causality

Regression analysis allows us to investigate the statistical association between two (or more) variables. Association merely means that two variables covary together, but in itself says nothing about any causal link between them. The terminology we use in empirical work often suggests the contrary. Hence, we talk about the dependent and the independent variables, which suggests that the former depends on the latter. This usually indicates more than the direction of association: it implies causality as well. Similarly, we often talk about X as the explanatory variable, which clearly implies that X is seen as a causal factor of Y. A more neutral but less vivid terminology consists of referring to the variable X as the regressor and Y as the regressand. Whatever your preference with regard to terminology, never forget that a regression model only depicts statistical association between two variables, but in itself it cannot establish the direction of causality between them. Whether a causal link exists between two variables and which way the causality runs is a matter which can only be settled by sound theoretical reflection. This fact should be borne in mind, although there are various econometric tests of causality (discussed in Chapter 13).

Exercise 4.1

The file TPEASANT on the diskette contains data (based on a survey of 600 Tanzanian peasant households) on, respectively, the average size of agricultural landholdings, L, and the average household size, H, for eight groupings by size of land holdings. Use these data to:

1 regress L on H and compute the R^2;
2 check whether the mathematical properties listed above hold for this regression;
3 regress H on L and compute its R^2.
4 Why does the regression of L on H differ from that of H on L?
5 In your opinion, which regression best depicts the direction of causality?

The Gauss-Markov theorem: least squares estimators as BLUE

Like the sample mean, the least squares estimators have desirable properties subject to the assumptions of the classical linear regression model (i.e. not including the normality assumption). First of all, note that the least squares estimators b_1 and b_2 can be shown to be linear functions of the sample values of Y, just like the sample average.

The Gauss-Markov theorem states that the least squares estimators are best among the class of all linear unbiased estimators, i.e.:

$$E(b_1) = \beta_1 \text{ and } E(b_2) = \beta_2 \qquad (4.21)$$

$$V(b_1) \text{ and } V(b_2) \text{ have minimum variances among}$$
$$\text{all unbiased linear estimators of } \beta_1 \text{ and } \beta_2 \qquad (4.22)$$

In fact, the sample mean is a special case of the Gauss-Markov theorem. Suffice it to say, however, that the assumptions of homoscedasticity and lack of correlation of the errors ϵ_i are crucial to establish the validity of the minimum variance property of b_1 and b_2.

Maximum likelihood and the normality assumption

If we now make the further assumption that the distribution of the error term ϵ has a normal distribution:

$$\epsilon \sim N(0, \sigma^2) \qquad (4.23)$$

we can again show that the least squares estimators derived above also happen to be the maximum likelihood estimators. Hence, apart from being BLUE, the least squares estimators turn out to have the minimum variance property among all unbiased estimators. As was the case for the sample mean, the least squares estimators of the regression coefficients are unbeatable if the assumptions of the classical normal linear model are reasonably valid in practice. But, as we shall see below, these least squares estimators are neither resistant nor robust to a wider range of different underlying conditions. Least squares estimators, therefore, are high-class performers under ideal conditions when the normality assumption is reasonably valid in practice. The normality assumption also allows us to construct confidence intervals and to test hypotheses. This is the issue to which we now turn.

4.4   INFERENCE FROM CLASSICAL NORMAL LINEAR REGRESSION MODEL

The treatment of inference in the classical normal linear regression model is very similar to our discussion of the classical model for estimating a sample mean. Consequently, in this section we briefly review the main points without much further elaboration, apart from a few specific points which concern regression only.

Standard errors

Given the assumptions of the classical linear regression model, the variances of the least squares estimators are given by:

$$\text{var}\,(b_1) = \sigma^2 \left(\frac{1}{n} + \frac{\overline{X}^2}{\Sigma(X_i - \overline{X})^2} \right) \qquad (4.24)$$

$$\text{var}\,(b_2) = \frac{\sigma^2}{\Sigma(X_i - \overline{X})^2} \qquad (4.25)$$

Furthermore, an unbiased estimator of σ^2 is given by s^2 as follows:

$$s^2 = \frac{\Sigma(Y_i - b_1 - b_2 X_i)^2}{n - 2} = \frac{\text{RSS}}{n - 2} \qquad (4.26)$$

where s is called the standard error of regression. Replacing σ^2 by s^2 in (4.24) and in (4.25), we get unbiased estimates of the variances of b_1 and b_2. Obviously, the estimated standard errors are the square roots of these variances.

The total sum of squares of X, $\Sigma\,(X_i - \overline{X})^2$, which features in the denominator of the variances of the intercept and slope coefficients, is a measure of the total variation in the X values. Thus, other things being equal, the higher the variation in the X values, the lower will be the variances of the estimators, which implies higher precision in estimation. In other words, the range of observed X plays a crucial role in the reliability of the estimates. Think about this. It would indeed be difficult to measure the response of Y on X if X hardly varied at all. The greater the range over which X varies, the easier it is to capture its impact on the variation in Y.

Sampling distributions

To construct the confidence intervals and to perform tests of hypotheses we need the probability distribution of the errors, which implies that we use the normality assumption of the error terms. Under this assumption, the least squares estimators b_1 and b_2 each follow a normal distribution. However, since we generally do not know the variance of the error term, we cannot make use of the normal distribution directly. Instead, we use the t-distribution defined as follows in the case of b_2:

$$t = \frac{b_2 - H_0(\beta_2)}{se(b_2)} \sim t_{(n-2)} \tag{4.27}$$

where $H_0(\beta_2)$ is the hypothesised value of β and $se(b_2)$ is the standard error of b_2, given by:

$$se(b_2) = \frac{s}{[\Sigma(X_i - \overline{X})^2]^{1/2}} \tag{4.28}$$

using (4.25) and (4.26). The statistic, $t_{(n-2)}$, denotes the Student's t-distribution with $(n - 2)$ degrees of freedom. The reason we now have only $(n - 2)$ degrees of freedom is that, in simple regression, we use the sample data to estimate two coefficients: the slope and the intercept of the line. In the case of the sample mean, in contrast, we only estimated one parameter (the mean itself) from the sample.

Similarly, for b_1, we get:

$$t = \frac{b_1 - H_0(\beta_1)}{se(b_1)} \sim t_{(n-2)} \tag{4.29}$$

where $se(b_1)$, the standard error of b_1, is given by:

$$se(b_1) = s\left[\frac{1}{n} + \frac{\overline{X}^2}{\Sigma(X_i - \overline{X}^2)}\right]^{1/2} \tag{4.30}$$

Confidence intervals for the parameters β_1 and β_2

The confidence limits for β_2 and β_1 with $(1 - \alpha)$ per cent confidence co-efficient (say, 95 per cent, in which case $\alpha = 0.05$) are given by:

$$b_2 \pm t\left(n-2, \frac{\alpha}{2}\right) se(b_2) \tag{4.31}$$

$$b_1 \pm t\left(n-2, \frac{\alpha}{2}\right) se(b_1) \tag{4.32}$$

respectively, where $t(n - 2, \alpha/2)$ is the $(1 - \alpha/2)$ percentile of a t-distribution with $(n - 2)$ degrees of freedom, and $se(b_2)$ and $se(b_1)$ are given by (4.28) and (4.29) respectively.

Confidence interval for the conditional mean of Y

At times, we may be interested to construct a confidence interval for the conditional mean. For example, after fitting a regression of household savings on income, we may want to construct a confidence interval for average savings, given the level of income, in order to assess the savings potential of a certain type of households. Suppose:

$$\mu_0 = \beta_1 + \beta_2 X_0 \tag{4.33}$$

i.e. μ_0 is the conditional mean of Y given $X = X_0$. The point estimate of μ_0 is given by:

$$b_1 + b_2 X_0$$

while its $(1 - \alpha)$ per cent confidence interval can be obtained as follows:

$$\mu_0 \pm t\left(n-2, \frac{\alpha}{2}\right) se(\mu_0) \tag{4.34}$$

where its standard error is given by:

$$se(\mu_0) = s\left[\frac{1}{n} + \frac{(X_0 - \bar{X})^2}{\Sigma(X_i - \bar{X})^2}\right]^{1/2} \tag{4.35}$$

Confidence interval for the predicted Y values

There are other occasions when we might be interested in the uncertainty of prediction on the basis of the estimated regression. For example, when estimating a regression of paddy yield (physical output per unit area) on annual rainfall, we may want to predict next year's yield given the anticipated rainfall. In this case, our interest is not to obtain a confidence interval of the conditional mean of the yield, i.e. the mean yield at a given level of rainfall. Rather, we want to find a confidence interval for the yield (Y_0) itself, given the rainfall (X_0). In this case:

$$Y_0 = \beta_1 + \beta_2 X_0 + \epsilon = \mu_0 + \epsilon \tag{4.36}$$

where μ_0 is given by (4.31). The $(1 - \alpha)$ per cent confidence interval for Y_0 given $X = X_0$ is then obtained as follows:

$$Y_0 = t\left(n-2, \frac{\alpha}{2}\right) se(Y_0) \tag{4.37}$$

where

$$se(Y_0) = s\left[1 + \frac{1}{n} + \frac{(X_0 - \bar{X})^2}{\Sigma(X_i - \bar{X})^2}\right]^{1/2} \tag{4.38}$$

In this case, therefore, the standard error of Y_0 is larger than that of μ_0, since the latter corresponds to the conditional mean of the yield for a given level of rainfall, while the former corresponds to the predicted value of the yield. In both cases, (4.33) and (4.36), the confidence intervals will be larger the further away the X value is from its mean in the sample.

Standard error of a residual

Finally, the residuals e_i are the estimators of errors ϵ_i. The standard error of e_i is obtained as follows:

$$se(e_i) = s\sqrt{(1 - h_i)} \text{ where } \quad h_i = \frac{1}{n} + \frac{(X_i - \overline{X})^2}{\Sigma(X_i - \overline{X})^2} \quad (4.39)$$

where s is given by (4.26). Note that while the standard deviation of the error term is assumed to be homoscedastic, equation (4.37) shows that the residuals of the regression line are heteroscedastic in nature. The standard error of each residual depends on the value of h_i.

The statistic h_i is called the hat statistic: h_i will be larger, the greater the distance of X_i from its mean. A value of X that is far away from its mean (such as an outlier in the univariate analysis of X) will produce a large hat statistic which, as we shall see in section 4.7, can exert undue influence on the location of a regression line. A data point with a large hat statistic is said to exert leverage on the least squares regression line, the importance of which will also be shown in section 4.7.

Hypothesis testing

The sampling distributions given in (4.27) and in (4.29) can be used for tests of hypotheses regarding the intercept and the slope of the population regression in much the same way as we did in the case of hypothesis testing concerning the population mean of a univariate normal distribution. Remember, however, that in this case the t-distribution has $(n - 2)$ degrees of freedom instead of $(n - 1)$. We shall illustrate the use of the t-test in the exercises with section 4.5.

What if X is stochastic?

The inferences we make from the sample regression about the parameters of the population regression are contingent upon the assumptions of the classical normal linear regression model. One of these assumptions states that X is non-stochastic but a given set of values. As we pointed out above, this is perhaps a plausible assumption when regression analysis is done in the context of experiments in which the researcher has control over the values of X. But in development research our data derive from observational programmes where neither Y nor X is subject to control. Consequently, in most cases, both Y and X have to be considered as stochastic variables.

How does this influence the validity of our inferences? If X is stochastic, the critical question turns out to be whether X_i and ϵ_i are statistically independent from one another, and consequently do not covary. If:

$$E(X_i, \epsilon_i) = 0, \text{ for } i = 1, \ldots n \tag{4.40}$$

it can be shown that the least squares estimators retain their property of unbiasedness and, furthermore, the variances of the estimators, the confidence intervals and the tests of hypotheses that we derived in this section remain valid conditional upon the realised values of X. In other words, provided X is independent of the error term, once a sample is drawn (and hence the observed values of X are known), our inferences are valid contingent upon these 'given' X values.

This may appear rather restrictive. However, if we make the additional assumption that Y and X are jointly distributed as a bivariate normal distribution, all formulae derived above with regard to the estimators of the population regression coefficients, their standard errors, the confidence intervals and the tests of hypotheses are all valid. In this book, we shall not go into detail about the bivariate (or, for that matter, multivariate) normal distribution. Suffice it to say that if Y and X jointly follow a bivariate normal distribution, both the marginal and conditional distributions will be normal, and, importantly, the regression of Y on X is linear. However, the converse is not true. If we find that Y and X each follow a normal distribution, this does not imply that they are jointly normally distributed (see, for example, Maddala, 1992: 104–5; Goldberger, 1991: 68–79).

This completes our brief review of statistical inference in the classical normal linear regression model. You will undoubtedly have noted the similarities with the problem of inference about the population mean of a univariate normal distribution. The latter is in fact a special case of the general regression model. As with the sample mean, the least squares regression line turns out to be a powerful tool of analysis if the assumptions of the classical normal linear regression model are approximately valid in practice or if Y and X are jointly normally distributed. But if the assumptions of the model are likely to be invalid in practice, the least squares line, like the sample mean, rapidly loses its superiority as an estimator of the population regression. Hence, before embarking on statistical inferences based on the least squares line, it is important to check carefully the validity of the assumptions of the model in practice. This is the issue to which we now turn.

4.5 REGRESSION WITH GRAPHICS: CHECKING THE MODEL ASSUMPTIONS

The strength of a statistical model, however powerful it may appear on paper, rests upon its assumptions being reasonably valid in practice. The least squares regression model is a powerful research tool but, as with most sophisticated tools, when applied inappropriately it easily leads to nonsensical results being brandished about as deep insights or truths based on hard facts. This danger is particularly acute now that we have easy access to powerful computers which allow us to run a multitude of regressions at virtually no cost at all. Unfortunately, many researchers appear to switch their heads off when turning the computer on. Often the aim is to arrive through trial and error at a regression which looks good on paper, never mind its fragile foundations. Good data analysis, however, requires that we take modelling and the assumptions upon which it rests seriously.

In simple regression, the kind of questions we want to investigate so as to check whether the model assumptions are reasonably valid in practice are as follows:

1   Does the relation between Y and X follow a linear pattern?
2   Are the residuals reasonably homoscedastic?
3   Are the residuals autocorrelated?
4   Are the residuals approximately normally distributed?
5   Do all data points contribute roughly equally to determine the position of the line (i.e. its intercept and its slope), or do some points exert undue influence on the outcome?
6   Are there any outlying data points which clearly do not fit the general pattern?

To answer these types of question, EDA teaches us that it is preferable to combine numerical summaries with graphical displays which focus our attention on both the regularity of data as well as their unusual, often unexpected, features. As to graphics, in bivariate analysis, a simple but powerful tool is the scatter plot which displays either (a) the raw data themselves (i.e. a plot of Y against X), or (b) quantities derived from the data (such as, for example, a plot of the residuals against the X values or against the predicted values of Y). As to numerical summaries, EDA prefers the use of resistant summaries when the underlying conditions of the population regression are unknown since the least squares regression estimators, like the sample mean, lack resistance, as we shall see in section 4.7. In this book, however, we shall deal mainly with least squares regression, and therefore we do not discuss median-based resistant methods of estimating a regression line (see, for example, Hoaglin *et al.*, 1983). But we shall nevertheless make use of exploratory band regression (Hamilton, 1992: 146–7): a simple, but powerful median-based graphical method of obtaining a regression curve without imposing any functional form on the shape of the regression. We do not use this method as an alternative to least squares regression, but as a diagnostic tool to verify whether our least squares simple regression is a reasonable summary of the data. The method of exploratory band regression is based on the concept of regression as a conditional average of Y for given X. Let us use a simple example to illustrate its usefulness in applied work.

Exploratory band regression

Take another look at Figure 2.1 (p. 47) which depicts the empirical distributions of, respectively, the demand (D) for and recruitment (R) of casual labour on the day shift in Maputo harbour during the early 1980s. Both distributions are approximately normal in shape. Obviously, the two variables are not unrelated. More specifically, we expect recruitment to depend on demand. In fact, it is tempting to assume that both variables are distributed jointly as a bivariate normal distribution since each of the variables is approximately normal. Suppose we jump to this conclusion and estimate the regression line of R on D, which yields the following results (standard errors in brackets):

$$R = 184 + 0.55\,D \qquad R^2 = 0.61 \qquad (4.41)$$
$$(12)\ \ (0.02)$$

As a numerical summary, this result looks quite good: the standard errors are small and the R^2 indicates that 61 per cent of the total variation in recruitment can be explained by variations in the demand for daily labour. But take a look at the scatter plot in Figure 4.1 which shows the data along with the estimated regression line. You will see a band of observations lying along a straight line. This line is the 45° line, and so represents those days on which recruitment equalled demand.

The scatter plot reveals two problems: heteroscedasticity and non-linearity. Moreover, this example clearly shows that we cannot assume that two related variables, each of which are approximately normally distributed, will of necessity jointly follow a bivariate normal distribution. What went wrong with our initial hunch?

A moment's reflection reveals the problem. In Chapter 2, we saw that mean recruitment is well below mean demand and, moreover, the standard deviation of recruitment is significantly lower than that of demand. At that point, we hinted that it appeared as if the port experiences a shortage of labour on its day shift when demand is high. This seems to be the problem. When demand is low, the scatter in Figure 4.1 clearly shows that recruitment equals demand. However, as demand increases, recruitment progressively but erratically falls short of demand, indicating supply shortages. This explains why the plot is heteroscedastic as well as non-linear.

So what about exploratory band regression? Exploratory band regression is a simple technique which starts by dividing the scatter plot into a series of equal vertical bands; subsequently, within each band we find the point of medians of Y and X; and finally, we connect these points of medians with straight line segments (Hamilton, 1992: 166). The line

Figure 4.1 Regressing *D* on *R*

segments which connect these points of medians of the successive bands trace a curve which approximates the regression of *Y* on *X* without imposing any *a priori* shape on this curve. Figure 4.2 gives the exploratory band regression of *R* on *D* using four bands. The curve connecting the points of medians of these four bands clearly reveals that the underlying regression is non-linear: as *D* increases, the slope of the curve, while remaining positive, declines significantly.

As a diagnostic tool, exploratory band regression helps us to trace the nature of the non-linear relation between *Y* and *X*. Furthermore, it is resistant to the pull of data points which, because of their location, may exert influence on the regression line. The resistance of the exploratory band regression follows from the fact that it is based on medians, and not on means. As explained above, exploratory band regression is not really an alternative to least squares regression since it does not involve fitting any particular functional form to the data. In fact, the curve it traces by connecting successive medians depends on the number of bands we care to consider. As such, exploratory band regression does not give us a set of coefficients which allow for straightforward economic interpretation. In this sense, therefore, exploratory band regression is a diagnostic tool and not an alternative to fitting a line to the data. But it helps us to choose which line to fit.

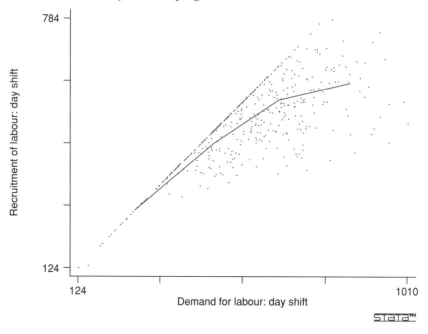

Figure 4.2   Exploratory band regression: *D* on *R*

Scatter plots and residuals plots

Apart from exploratory band regression, other graphical displays, along with numerical summaries, can be of help in investigating whether the assumptions of classical normal linear regression are reasonably valid in practice. These are scatter plots of the raw data along with the regression line, on the one hand, and residual plots, on the other. To illustrate their use in practice, let us use another concrete example with Tanzanian data (in file TANZANIA) on the annual growth rates of, respectively, recurrent expenditures (*RE*) and recurrent revenue (*RR*), both deflated by the consumer price index, of the government budget in Tanzania during the 1970s and 1980s. Our interest is to examine to what extent the growth in recurrent expenditure was constrained by the growth in recurrent revenue. Before you read on, we suggest that you work out exercise 4.2 which is based on these data. This way, you can compare your analysis with ours.

Exercise 4.2

Using the data file TANZANIA, compute the growth rates of government recurrent expenditures and revenues and then answer the following questions:

1 regress *RE* on *RR*, computing the regression coefficients, their standard errors, the R^2, the residuals, and the fitted values of *RE*;
2 graph *RE* against *RR* with the regression line;
3 graph the residuals against the predicted values of *RE*;
4 plot the residuals against time, *t*;
5 fit a three-band exploratory band regression;
6 check whether the residuals behave as a sample of a normal distribution.

Is this a satisfactory regression? Explain your answer.

The regression of *RE* on *RR* yields the following results (standard errors in brackets):

$$RE = 0.0086 + 0.924\ RR \qquad R^2 = 0.78 \qquad (4.42)$$
$$(0.1036)\ (0.114)$$

Before we can make any inferences from this sample regression, however, we need to check that the data do not violate our model assumptions. Let us do this step by step. First and foremost, let is see whether the data support the linearity assumption. Figure 4.3 gives us the scatter plot of *RE* on *RR* along with the estimated regression line. A scatter plot with regression line is a powerful analytical graph which combines, at a glance, the scatter of the data points with the fitted line. It allows us, therefore, to see whether the regression line is reasonably supported by the scatter as a whole without there being any systematic deviations of data points away from the regression line. At first glance, our estimated regression seems quite satisfactory in this sense. However, a closer look reveals that there are relatively more points below than above the regression line. Note also that there is one point at the left of the scatter which has a relatively large positive residual; we may expect that this point will exert a slight pull upwards on the regression line.

To enable us to take a closer look at the residual variation after fitting the regression line we use a plot of residuals against predicted values. This type of plot is akin to Sherlock Holmes's magnifying glass: it blows up the residuals to enable us to detect abnormal behaviour. Remember that the residuals have zero mean, hence, ideally most residuals will be distributed linearly and evenly with roughly equal spread around this zero mean. If a residual plot shows some curvature in the scatter of the residuals around its mean zero, this indicates that the relation between *Y* and *X* may not be linear. If the spread of residuals widens, or narrows, with increasing values of the fitted *Y*s, this indicates the presence of heteroscedasticity. Unusually large residuals will show up because of their distant location (as compared with other residuals) from the zero mean.

Figure 4.4 plots the residuals of the regression of *RE* against *RR* against the predicted values of *RE*. The horizontal line in the plot shows the

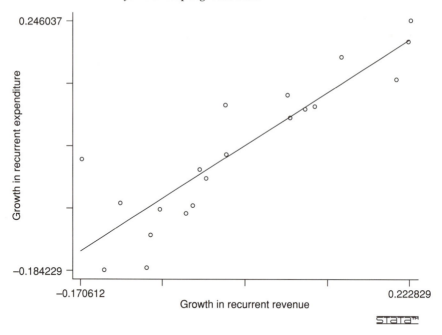

Figure 4.3   Scatter plot with regression line: *RE* on *RR*

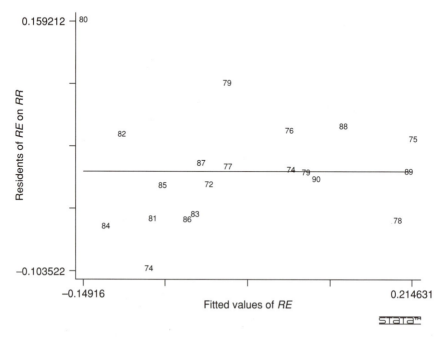

Figure 4.4   Residuals versus fitted values

position of the zero mean. For convenience, each data point is identified by the year to which it refers: hence, the growth rate from 1979 to 1980 is indicated by the label 80. In this way, it is easy to identify unusually large residuals, such as the year 1980. In this year, recurrent revenue fell dramatically while recurrent expenditure still registered mild positive growth. It appears as if the Tanzanian government was caught unaware in 1980 when government revenue clearly collapsed with the onset of the economic crisis of the early 1980s. Apart from this unusually large residual, most other residuals are reasonably evenly spread around the zero mean. Hence, the plot does not show strong evidence of heteroscedasticity. Note, however, that the majority of points on the left-hand side of the scatter slope slightly upwards towards the horizontal (zero mean) line, indicating mild non-linearity.

To verify this last point, let us try out a simple three-band exploratory band regression. Figure 4.5. shows the picture. To enhance this plot, we drew the vertical and horizontal axes corresponding to zero growth rates for each of the variables. The exploratory band regression shows a slight non-linearity of the underlying relationship between *RE* and *RR*, indicating that recurrent expenditure responded slightly more strongly to a fall in recurrent revenue than to its positive growth. This slight non-linearity is so mild, however, that it does not seriously invalidate the linearity assumption.

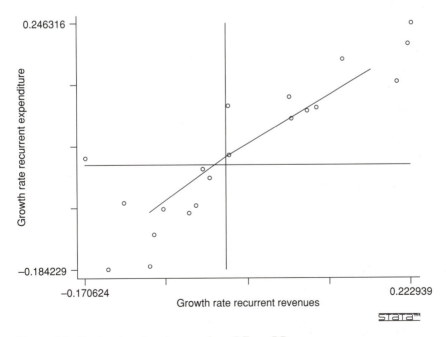

Figure 4.5 Exploratory band regression: *RE* on *RR*

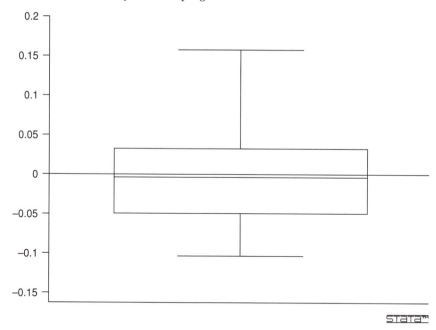

Figure 4.6   Box plot of residuals: *RE* on *RR*

To check whether the residuals behave approximately as a normal distribution, we use the methods outlined in section 3.4 of Chapter 3. Figure 4.6 gives the box plot of the residuals of the regression of *RE* on *RR*, while Table 4.2 gives the relevant summary statistics. The box plot shows that the residuals are fairly symmetrical but with a somewhat longer upper tail due to the large residual for 1980 which does not quite qualify as an outlier. The median and mean are close together and, similarly, Bowley's measure of skewness does not indicate the presence of skewness as far as the middle 50 per cent of the residuals are concerned. The pseudo standard deviation is somewhat larger than the standard deviation, indicating that the tails of the distribution are heavier than those from a normal distribution, but not particularly so. The computed value of the skewness-kurtosis test statistic turns out to be 5.62 which is not significant at the 5 per cent level. In other words, the hypothesis of normal distribution of the error term ϵ cannot be rejected at the 5 per cent level of significance.

When dealing with time series, it is important to check for the presence of autocorrelation. We shall discuss how to do this in far more detail in Part IV of this book. However, a plot of the residuals versus time is a useful diagnostic tool to provide us with a rough check whether or not the residuals are autocorrelated. When plotting residuals against time, it

Table 4.2   Numerical summaries of the residuals

Order-based statistics		Mean-based statistics	
Median	−0.0026	Mean	−0.0000
IQR	0.0836		
Pseudo-standard deviation (S_p)	0.0619	Standard deviation	0.0586
Skewness Bowley's measure (b_8)	−0.1100	Skewness (a_3)	0.8500
		Kurtosis (a_4)	4.1200

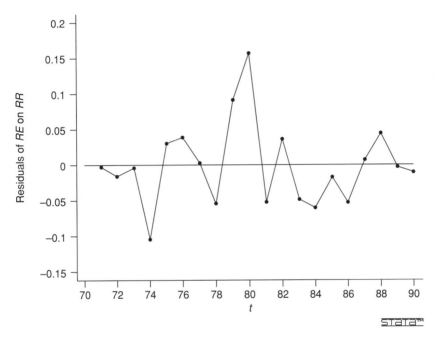

Figure 4.7   Residuals against time

is useful (a) to draw a horizontal line indicating the zero mean, and (b) to connect successive points with line segments. Figure 4.7 uses our example to show you how to do this. If errors in successive years tend to move in the same direction, this type of residual plot will show the presence of runs of positive or of negative residuals (respectively, strings of points above or below the line). If successive residuals are relatively uncorrelated, the curve of connected residuals will cross the line in a similar way as flipping a coin switches from a run of heads to a run of tails. If, however, successive residuals are negatively correlated, a positive residual will probably be followed by a negative residual and, hence, the curve will be very jagged (crossing the zero line almost continuously). In our case, the curve connecting successive residuals shows a series of runs up and down the zero mean, not unlike the type of runs you get by flipping a coin. Hence, this quick check seems to indicate that the residuals show little evidence of autocorrelation.

It appears, therefore, that in our example the assumptions of the classical normal linear simple regression model are reasonably satisfied. This sets the stage for statistical inference based on the sample regression line. Exercise 4.3 suggests some questions of statistical inference applied to this simple example.

Exercise 4.3

Using the regression results listed in 4.40:

1 What economic interpretation would you give to the slope coefficient of this regression?
2 What does its intercept tell you?
3 Formally test the hypothesis that the slope coefficient equals 1.
4 Formally test the hypothesis that the intercept term equals 0.
5 Construct confidence intervals for (a) the conditional mean of RE, and (b) the predicted value of RE for, respectively, $RR = -0.10$; $RR = 0.0$, and $RR = 0.15$.
6 Compute the hat statistics and the standard errors for each of the residuals of the regression.

The slope coefficient measures the absolute change in the dependent variable, the growth rate of recurrent expenditures, in response to a unit change in the regressor, the growth rate of recurrent revenue. In this case, the estimated slope coefficient turns out to be very close to 1 and, in fact, the hypothesis that this coefficient equals 1 is quite acceptable from the sample regression as can readily be seen if you do the relevant *t*-test (if you remain unsure how to perform the *t*-test look at Box 4.1). Hence, a unit change in the growth rate of recurrent revenue leads to a unit change in the growth rate of recurrent expenditures as well. Furthermore, we note that the intercept is close to zero. If, using a *t*-test, you formally test the hypothesis that the intercept is zero, you will have found that this hypothesis is also maintained. It appears, therefore, that the assumption that the regression line goes through the origin is quite plausible in this case, meaning that the growth rate in recurrent expenditures varies proportionally with the growth rate in recurrent revenue, thus indicating a constant elasticity between both variables. But how do we estimate a regression through the origin? This is the question we turn to next.

Box 4.1   Performing the *t*-test in regression analysis

The formula to use is:

$$t\text{-stat} = \frac{b_2 - H_0(\beta_2)}{se(b_2)}$$

Let us first test if the intercept is zero; i.e.:

$$H_0: b_1 = 0 \quad H_1: b_1 \neq 0$$

When the null hypothesis value of the coefficient is zero the calculated *t*-statistic simplifies to the ratio of the estimate to its standard error. So in this case:

$$t\text{-stat} = \frac{0.0086}{0.0136} = 0.63$$

There are 20 observations, so there are 18 (= 20 – 2) degrees of freedom. The critical value of the t-statistic at the 5 per cent level is 2.101; i.e. if the null hypothesis is true then 95 per cent of all sample estimates are expected to produce *t*-stats of between –2.101 and 2.101. The calculated value falls within this band (or, to put the same thing another way, the absolute value of the calculated value is less than the critical value), so we accept the null hypothesis.

To test if the slope coefficient is significantly different from zero we set up the hypotheses:

$$H_0: b_2 = 0 \quad H_1: b_2 \neq 0$$

and the corresponding *t*-statistic is

$$t\text{-stat} = \frac{0.924}{0.114} = 8.11$$

The same critical value applies so in this case we reject the null hypothesis; i.e. the slope coefficient is significant. When we say a coefficient is 'significant', it is short-hand for 'significantly different from zero at a given (most usually 5 per cent) level'.

Suppose now we wish to test if the slope coefficient is significantly different from unity. In this case the null and alternate are:

$$H_0: b_2 = 1 \quad H_1: b_2 \neq 1$$

and so the test-statistic is:

$$t\text{-stat} = \frac{0.924 - 1}{0.114} = -0.67$$

The critical value is again the same and we are unable to reject the null; that is, the slope coefficient is insignificantly different from one.

4.6   REGRESSION THROUGH THE ORIGIN

A regression with zero intercept, $\beta_1 = 0$, is called a regression through the origin since it passes through the point (0,0). We often have *a priori* reasons why a regression should go through the origin. For example, when specifying the regression of *RE* on *RR* we might have had strong reasons to believe that this regression will go through the origin. However, this should not lead us to try out a regression through the origin before formally testing whether the hypothesis $\beta_1 = 0$ is in fact data admissible.

Why should we test first? The reason is that the restricted model (without constant term) does not tell you how much worse or better it is in comparison with the unrestricted model (with the intercept included). To see whether the intercept can be dropped, we should first estimate the regression with the intercept and subsequently test whether the constant term can be dropped from the equation. This is a very rudimentary application of the principle of general to specific modelling. Never jump to the specific (restricted) model before testing whether the restriction (in this case, dropping the constant term) is in fact data admissible. Dropping a constant term from an equation may appear trivial but, as we shall show in Chapter 6, if inappropriate, it can lead to serious misspecification of the underlying relation.

Without intercept, the relevant regression model becomes:

$$Y = \beta_2 X + \epsilon \tag{4.43}$$

with all the usual assumptions of the classical model about ϵ and the sampling process. The sample regression will obviously feature only one coefficient b_2, as $b_1 = 0$. In this case, the least squares solution is as follows:

$$b_2 = \frac{\Sigma Y_i X_i}{\Sigma X_i^2} \tag{4.44}$$

This regression through the origin, unlike the general model with slope and intercept, does not adjust for the sample means. In other words, all the formulae for the relevant statistics in this case can be derived simply by taking the corresponding formulae for simple regression with a slope and intercept and replacing all sample means by zero. The test statistics and confidence intervals can also be derived in this way.

The R^2 statistic of a regression through the origin, however, loses much of its usefulness as a measure of goodness of fit. It is not comparable with the R^2 of the corresponding regression with intercept and slope. It is furthermore possible to come across a negative R^2 in a regression through the origin. This can occur when the intercept should not have been dropped and the resulting residual sums of squares turns out to be higher than the total sums of squares.

Our example yields the following regression through the origin:

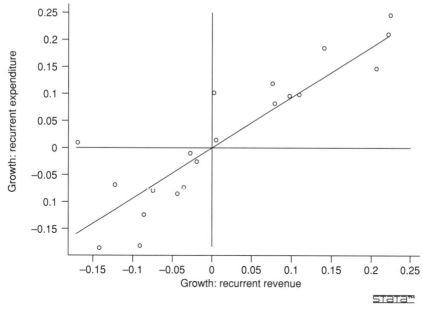

Figure 4.8 Regression through the origin: *RE* on *RR*

$$RE = 0.934RR \qquad R^2 = 0.788 \qquad (4.45)$$
$$(0.111)$$

Exercise 4.4

Using the regression results in equation 4.45:

1 Formally test the hypothesis $\beta_2 = 1$.
2 What economic interpretation can you give to this unitary slope coefficient? Why might we think it valid on theoretical grounds to exclude the intercept from this regression?

4.7 OUTLIERS, LEVERAGE AND INFLUENCE

As in univariate analysis, you should always beware of points which do not fit the general pattern or exert undue influence on the outcome of our numerical summaries. In univariate analysis, we only had to deal with the problem of outliers. In regression analysis, however, the problems we can encounter with unruly data points are more complex. Consequently, we need to sharpen our concepts to be able to spot the unusual and to single out data points which exert undue pressure on our results. This is particularly important when we rely on least squares regression since, as we know, the least squares principle does not give us resistant nor robust summaries. In regression analysis, there are three types of data points which should concern us. These are: an outlier, a point of high leverage, and an influential point. It is important to get a good intuitive grasp of these concepts in order to be able to use them effectively in applied work. Let us explain them one by one.

To start with, An outlier in a regression is a data point which has a large residual. Large in this context does not refer to the absolute size of a residual but to its size relative to most of the other residuals in the regression. In Chapter 3, you saw how to identify outliers in a univariate empirical distribution. The same techniques can be used to analyse residuals of a regression. Note, however, an important distinction. When we say a point is an outlier in univariate analysis, it is so defined with reference to its own mean (i.e. unconditional mean). When a point is an outlier in bivariate analysis it has a large residual, i.e. Y value, far removed from its fitted value (i.e. its conditional mean). But in general, a large residual is easy to spot since it usually sticks out in a residual plot.

A point of high leverage is a different matter and its effect on a regression is more complex. It can be defined thus: 'A data point has a high leverage if it is extreme in the X-direction; i.e. it is a disproportionate distance away from the middle range of the X-values' (Myers, 1990: 250).

Note the difference between outliers and points of high leverage. In regression, the concept of an outlier refers to a residual. That is, an outlier is defined as an exceptionally large vertical distance of a data point from the regression line. The definition of leverage does not involve the regression line at all. High leverage simply refers to a data point which is disproportionately distant from the other data points in the X-direction: that is, its X-coordinate deviates considerably from the X-coordinates of the (majority of) the other data points. In other words, a point of (very) high leverage in a regression of Y by X is an outlier in the univariate distribution of X.

But why does leverage matter if its definition does not involve the regression line at all? The reason is that points of high leverage can exert undue influence on the outcome of a least squares regression line. That is, points with high leverage are capable of exerting a strong pull on the slope of the regression line. Whether they do so or not is another matter. The point is that they have the potential to do so.

This brings us to the concept of an influential point. 'A data point is influential if removing it from the sample would markedly change the position of the least squares regression line' (Moore and McCabe, 1989: 185). Hence, influential data points pull the regression line in their direction. Note that influential data points do not necessarily produce large residuals: that is, they are not always outliers as well, although they can be. It is precisely because they draw the regression line toward themselves that they may end up with small residuals. Conversely, an outlier is not necessarily an influential point, particularly when it is a point with little leverage (see exercise 4.10).

The concepts of outlier, leverage and influence matter a great deal in applied work. The reason is that the least squares regression line (like its cousin, the sample mean) is neither resistant nor robust. In other words, least squares performs well under ideal circumstances, but not when the assumptions of classical normal linear regression are seriously violated in practice. The presence of outliers or of influential points often gives us a clear signal that our model is probably misspecified. For example, a cluster of outliers or influential points may indicate that we wrongly applied our model to a set of points which do not derive from the same (homogeneous) population. A single exceptional point may signal that a typing error was made when recording its value or it may point us towards variables which we failed to account for in our model.

Exercise 4.5

Look carefully at the four plots in Figure 4.9 (overleaf). For each plot write down whether any of the points is: an outlier, a point of high leverage, an influential point, or some combination of these.

You will have noticed that each plot contains only one point which qualifies for discussion. Obviously, with real data the situation can be more complex. Table 4.3 shows our quick summary. In general we note:

1 outliers are not necessarily influential   (Plot 4)
2 but they can be so (depending on leverage)   (Plot 3)
3 yet high leverage points are not always influential (Plot 1)
4 and influential points are not necessarily outliers (Plot 2)

In terms of visual displays, outliers can best be spotted with residual plots (but they are also visible in a scatter plot especially if the fitted line is shown), while influential points require us to look at scatter plots since they do not show themselves on residual plots if they do not have large residuals. Just running regression without looking at any plots leads you to ignore influential points and makes spotting outliers more tedious. This is the simple but powerful lesson of this exercise.

As shown above, graphical displays can be of great help in spotting outliers and influential points. Apart from these graphical methods,

Table 4.3   Plot summary

Plots	Outlier	High Leverage	Influence
Plot 1	No	Yes	No
Plot 2	No	Yes	Yes
Plot 3	Yes	Yes	Yes
Plot 4	Yes	No	No

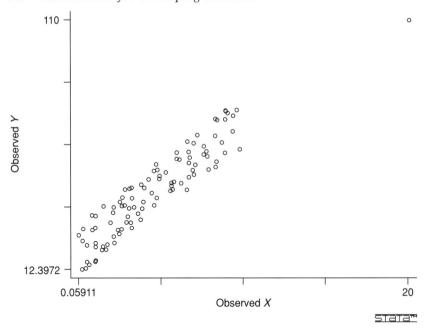

Plot 1

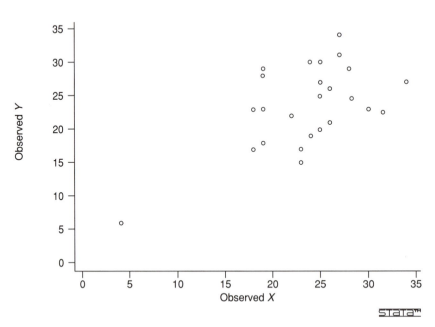

Plot 2

Figure 4.9   Graph for exercise 4.5

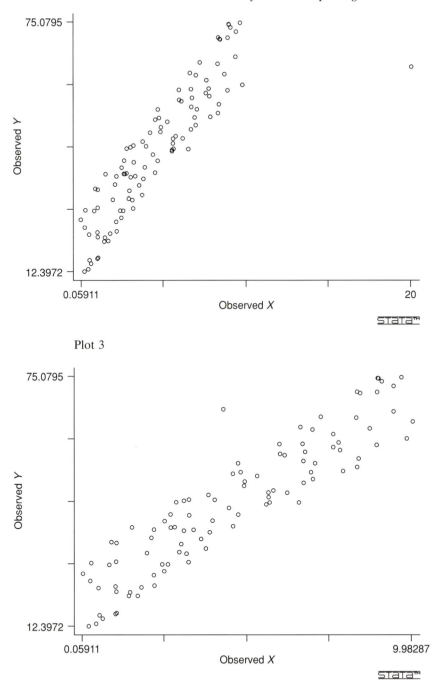

Plot 3

Plot 4

Figure 4.9 (continued) Graph for exercise 4.5

however, we can also rely on special statistics designed to detect outliers, leverage and influence. Here we shall look at three such statistics: student-ised residuals to detect outliers, the hat statistics to measure leverage, and DFBETA statistics to measure influence.

Studentised residuals

In order to make the outliers conspicuous in relation to rest of the resid-uals, it is useful to consider them in the context of the overall residual variation. One way in which this can be done is to calculate the stan-dardised residual, which is simply the residual divided by the standard error of the estimate (i.e. standardised residual $= e_i/s$). However, the problem with this measure is that if there is an outlier in the data set it will inflate the standard error of the regression. This problem is catered for by using instead $s_{(i)}$ where the (i) subscript denotes a statistic calcu-lated having dropped the ith observation from the sample. Be careful not to be confused by this notation; for example h_i is the hat statistic for observation i (see below), whereas $b_{2(i)}$ is the slope coefficient having dropped the ith observation from the sample.

Making this adjustment, we define the studentised residuals (t_i):

$$t_i = \frac{e_i}{s_{(i)}\sqrt{(1 - h_i)}} \tag{4.46}$$

where $s_{(i)}$ is the standard error estimate of the regression (defined in equa-tion (4.26)) fitted after deleting the ith observation, and h_i is a measure of leverage as defined in equation (4.39). The additional term in the numerator, $\sqrt{(1 - h_i)}$, is necessary since the variance of the residuals is not constant. With this adjustment, we get a t-statistic which tests whether the ith residual is significantly different from 0 and, hence, signals an outlier which does not really fit the overall pattern. (In fact the studentised residual may be interpreted as a test of influence on intercept, but we pursue this interpretation in Chapter 6.) It is possible to obtain formally derived critical values (which are larger than those from the usual t-table) against which to compare the calculated value, but we recommend that the studentised residual be used as an exploratory tool, as in the example below.

Take another look at Figure 4.6 which depicts the box plot of the resid-uals of the regression of *RE* on *RR*. This plot does not reveal the presence of outliers, although its upper tail is somewhat more prolonged than its lower tail. The box plot of the studentised residuals shown in Figure 4.10, however, tells a different story: the data point for the year 1980 now appears as an outlier. Studentised residuals, therefore, are much better than the usual residuals at spotting outliers. The reason is that each studentised residual is obtained by dividing the least squares residual by its standard error (hence, a t-value) where the standard error of the

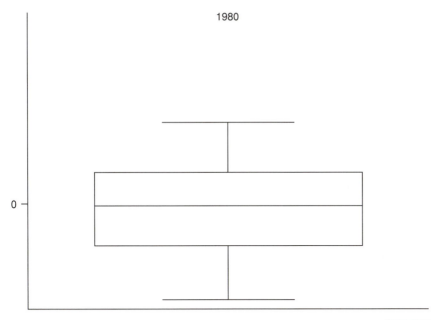

Figure 4.10 Studentised residual *RE*

regression is estimated by deleting the *i*th data point. If the *i*th data point is an outlier, the standard error of the regression after deleting the *i*th observation will be significantly lower than the standard error of the regression with all points included. This explains why the studentised residual is better at bringing out outlying points.

The hat statistic

We already defined the statistic h$_i$ in equation 4.39 as follows:

$$h_i = \frac{1}{n} + \frac{(X_i - \overline{X})^2}{\Sigma(X_i - \overline{X})^2} \qquad (4.47)$$

which serves as a measure of leverage of the *i*th data point. It measures leverage because its numerator is the squared distance of the *i*th data point from its mean in the *X* direction, while its denominator is a measure of overall variability of the data points along the *X*-axis. The statistic h_i, therefore, measures the distance of a data point in relation to the overall variation in the *X* direction. Therefore, the higher the value of h_i the higher is the leverage of the *i*th data point.

Theoretically, as can be seen from equation (4.47), leverage can range from 1/*n* to 1. If the *X* value of a data point is exactly equal to the mean of X values, the point has no leverage and h_i is equal to $1/n$. The statistic h_i approaches 1 as a point has very high leverage. Such a point will dominate the scene completely and control the location of the regression line. Obviously, this would be an extreme case. But when is leverage high such that it can pose a problem? Huber (1981, see also Hamilton, 1992: 130–1) suggests the following guidelines based on the maximum observed $h_i = \max(h_i)$:

$\max(h_i) < 0.2$ little to worry about
$0.2 < \max(h_i) < 0.5$ risky
$0.5 < \max(h_i)$ too much leverage

Figure 4.11 graphs the hat statistics against the values of the regressor in our regression of *RE* on *RR*. The graph clearly shows that leverage increases as the X values are more distant from their mean. Hence, $\max(h_i)$ is slightly above 0.20, but it corresponds to a point which presents little danger in our regression. As such, there is little to worry about as far as leverage is concerned.

Why do we refer to the h_i values as hat statistics? To see this point, recall that the least squares estimators are linear functions of the observed Y values. Consequently, the predicted values of Y, called Y-hat, are also

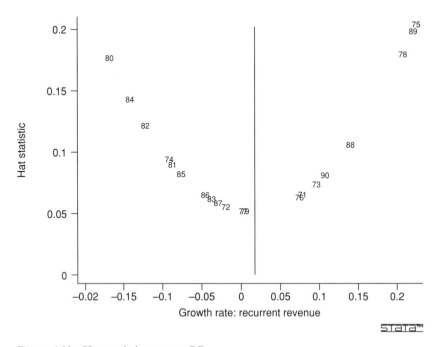

Figure 4.11   Hat statistics versus *RR*

linear functions of the observed Y values. The hat statistic, h_i is nothing other than the coefficient of the observed Y_i in the linear equation which expresses the predicted value Y_i as a linear function of all observed Y_is. This explains why they are called hat statistics.

DFBETA statistics

The DFBETA statistic is defined as:

$$\text{DFBETA}_i = \frac{b_2 - b_{2(i)}}{se(b_2)_{(i)}} \tag{4.48}$$

where $b_{2(i)}$ and $se(b_2)_{(i)}$ are the slope coefficient and standard error of the estimate of the slope from regression estimated, having dropped the ith data point from the sample. The DFBETAs measure the sensitivity of the slope coefficient to the deletion of the ith data point. If the deletion of this point leads to a drastic change in the slope coefficient, it follows that the ith data point is influential. In other words, a large value of the DFBETA statistic for a given data point indicates that this observation has a sizeable impact on the slope coefficient of the regression. DFBETA may also be calculated for the intercept, although this is not a common practice. (In Figure 4.9, plot 4, the outlier will influence the intercept, though not the slope coefficient.)

But how big does a DFBETA statistic have to be to be considered large? The DFBETA is not a formal test statistic like, say, the t-test. Therefore we do not have critical values derived from statistical theory. But we can use some rules of thumb. In general, if DFBETA > 2, the corresponding data point is unquestionably an influential point. This is a general criterion. It is also possible to relate the cut-off value of the DFBETAs to the sample size, n. If DFBETA $> 2/\sqrt{n}$, the corresponding data point may be deemed influential (Myers, 1990: 261; though some sources suggest $3/\sqrt{n}$). As a rule, it is useful to make a box plot of the DFBETA statistics and check whether there are any outliers. Figure 4.12 shows the box plot of the DFBETA statistics of the regression of *RE* against *RR*. As we can see, none of the data points has a DFBETA statistic which exceeds 2, while only the data point 80 (corresponding to the growth rate from 1979 to 1980) exceeds $2/\sqrt{20} = 0.447$. This confirms our earlier hunch that this point exerted a slight pull on the regression line without, however, causing any major distortion of the results.

A final point: DFBETA statistics are obtained by deleting each data point in turn and checking the effect of doing so on the slope coefficient of the regression line. It is possible, however, that a number of influential points may cluster together and jointly pull the regression line in their direction. In such a case, deleting data points one by one may not reveal the pull exerted by this influential cluster of points. This is why you should never rely solely on DFBETA statistics to check for influence, but also take

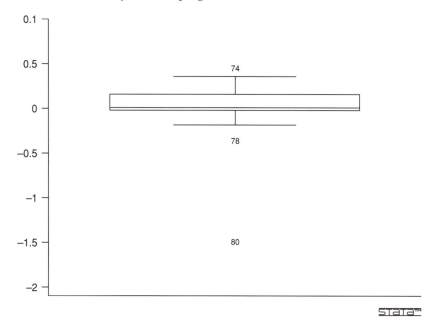

Figure 4.12   Box plot of DFBETA statistics

a good look at the scatter plot of Y against X to see whether there are any clusters of influential points. The formula for DFBETA may be just as easily applied by dropping two or three points from the regression. At times, several clusters exist which may pull the regression line in similar or opposite directions. But if you find you have many 'influential points' you can be sure that the problem is one of model misspecification.

Exercise 4.6

In section 3.3 of Chapter 3 we investigated the relation between the difference between female and male life expectancy, L, of developing countries, on the one hand, and GNP per capita, Y, on the other. In doing so, we grouped the data into three income categories: low, lower-middle and upper-middle income countries. Here we look at the same relation without prior grouping of countries in income categories. Using the data file SOCECON:

1   regress L on Y;
2   check whether this regression is likely to satisfy the model assumption;
3   try an exploratory band regression;
4   check graphically whether there are outliers, points of high leverage, or influential points;

Table 4.4 Summary measures of outliers, influence and leverage

Statistic	Formula	Use	Critical value
Studentised residual (t_i)	$t_i = \dfrac{e_i}{s_{(i)}\sqrt{(1-h_i)}}$	Outliers	Critical values available (higher than usual t-test), but recommend use studentised residual as an exploratory tool
Hat statistic (h)	$h = \dfrac{1}{n} + \dfrac{(X_i - \overline{X})^2}{\Sigma(X_i - \overline{X})^2}$	Leverage	Bounded by $1/n$ (no leverage) and 1 (extreme leverage); values above 0.5 indicate excessive leverage and values over 0.2 indicate that the observation may give problems.
DFBETA	$\text{DFBETA}_i = \dfrac{b_2 - b_{2(i)}}{se(b_2)_{(i)}}$	Influence	Under $2/\sqrt{n}$ the point has no influence; over $3/\sqrt{n}$ the point is influential and strongly so if DFBETA exceeds 2.

Note: n is the sample size; k is the number of regressors; the subscript (i) (i.e. with parentheses) indicates an estimate from the sample omitting observation i. In each case you should use the absolute value of the calculated statistic.

5   compute the studentised residuals, the hat statistics, and the DFBETAs
    for the data points. Is this regression a good summary of the data?
    Note that the computation of studentised residuals, hat statistics and
    DFBETAs is cumbersome unless you have access to a statistical pack-
    age which routinely provides these diagnostic statistics. Unfortunately,
    most econometric packages do not provide these statistics. For this
    reason, it is useful to familiarise yourself with a statistical package (for
    example, STATA) which incorporates residual analysis and influence
    diagnostics in its statistical routines.

4.8   TRANSFORMATION TOWARDS LINEARITY

In Chapter 3 we saw that simple data transformations help us to extend
the reach of the classical model to make inferences around the population mean of a normal distribution. There we used transformations to
alter the shape of the distribution of our observed variables. The main
purpose, therefore, was to transform our data towards normality. In a
similar fashion, data transformation can be used to extend the reach of
regression analysis. Here, however, our aim is to transform the bivariate
data towards linearity. Indeed, ordinary least squares is based on the
assumption that the regression line is linear. But at times data transformations allow us to extend the reach of simple linear regression to handle
a wide variety of curvilinear relationships between Y and X.

In fact, there is an important principle here in statistical analysis which
is often overlooked. In statistics, we generally start with simple models
which perform well if a rather restrictive set of ideal conditions (usually
involving the normality assumption) are satisfied. Obviously, there are
many situations in which this restrictive model will not be appropriate.
But this does not mean that we immediately discard the model. Instead,
the basic idea is to get as much mileage as possible out of these simple
but powerful models. In Chapter 3 we showed how data transformation
towards normality extends the reach of the classical normal model for
making inferences about the population mean. In this section we show
how to extend simple regression analysis through transformations towards
linearity.

If we transform either X or Y, or both, to achieve linearity of the regression line, we should not forget that, in the process, we also transformed
the distributions of Y or X. Hence, while here our main aim is to achieve
linearity, we should not set aside the lessons we learned in Chapter 3 as
to how data transformations alter the shape of the distributions of the
variables. In practice, a useful rule of thumb is to keep in mind that linear
regression tends to work best when both variables are similarly (preferably symmetrically) shaped (Hamilton, 1992: 148). The reason this is so
is straightforward. If, for example, X is skewed while Y is more or less
normally distributed, it is hard to expect that the regression of Y on X

will leave an error component which is normally distributed. However, the converse is not true. Y and X may be associated with one another and similarly shaped, but this does not mean that the regression between them will be linear. To see this point, take another look at Figures 4.1 and 4.2, which depict the relation between the recruitment of and the demand for casual labour on the day-shift in Maputo harbour in the early 1980s. Both variables are approximately normally distributed, but the regression line is non-linear as well as heteroscedastic.

In econometric practice, the logarithmic transformation is very popular. One reason is that functions which can be linearised with the aid of logarithms have coefficients which lend themselves to meaningful economic interpretations, such as an elasticity or a growth rate. Another reason is that the logarithmic transformation frequently, but not always, does the trick with socioeconomic data which are often skewed to the right. In this section, therefore, we shall discuss several functional forms which can easily be rendered linear by using the logarithmic transformation.

The double-log transformation

A commonly used function in mathematical economics takes the following form:

$$Y = A \ X^{\beta_2} \tag{4.49}$$

This is a function with a constant elasticity given by β_2. That is:

$$\frac{dY}{dX} \frac{X}{Y} = \beta_2 \tag{4.50}$$

Taking logarithms of both sides of equation (4.49) yields:

$$\ln Y = \beta_1 + \beta_2 \ln X \tag{4.51}$$

where

$$\beta_1 = \ln A \tag{4.52}$$

As we can see, this double-log equation is linear with respect to its transformed variables. Linear regression, therefore, is feasible, but what assumptions do we make about the error term?

The normal procedure is to add an error term to the double-log specification and to assume that it satisfies the usual assumptions of the linear regression model. Hence, we get:

$$\ln Y = \beta_1 + \beta_2 \ln X + \epsilon \tag{4.53}$$

Taking anti-logarithms of both sides yields:

$$Y = AX^{\beta_2} \epsilon' \tag{4.54}$$

where

$$\epsilon' = e^{\epsilon} \tag{4.55}$$

which shows that the error term in the original model is multiplicative rather than additive in nature. If we assume that the error term in the double-log specification is normally distributed, it follows that the error term in the original model will have a lognormal distribution (see Box 4.2). An error term which is lognormal in nature and which enters the specification in a multiplicative fashion is bound to affect the variation in the dependent variable due to the behaviour of outlying values in its tail. If, instead, we assume that the error term in the original equation is additive rather than multiplicative, the resulting model specification becomes:

$$Y = AX^{\beta_2} + \epsilon' \tag{4.56}$$

which can no longer be linearised by taking logarithms of both sides of the equation and, hence, we need to apply non-linear regression, a topic which is beyond the scope of this book.

Box 4.2   A lognormal variable

A variable has a lognormal distribution if the logarithm of the variable is distributed normally. The lognormal distribution is skewed to the right and takes only positive values. It rises rather steeply to a maximum and subsequently declines smoothly into a long right tail which grows thinner and thinner as it reaches towards higher and higher values.

But, in fact, the assumption of a multiplicative error term in specification (4.54) is quite appropriate in many practical application, as we shall now illustrate with a simple example. The top panel in Figure 4.13 depicts the scatter plot of energy consumption per capita against GNP per capita for low, lower-middle and upper-middle countries for which data are in the file SOCECON. We enhanced the scatter plot with simple box plots for each variable (the horizontal box plot depicts the shape of the regressor, GNP/capita, and the vertical box plot that of the regressand, energy consumption per capita). As you can see, both variables are fairly strongly skewed to the right. In fact, most of the data points are huddled together in the bottom-left corner of the scatter plot. Moreover, the scatter clearly is heteroscedastic. A careful look at the plot also reveals that the scatter of points bends upwards from left to right. A linear regression, therefore, does not appear to be appropriate.

The bottom panel of Figure 4.13 shows what happens if we plot the logarithms of both variables against each other. The double-log transformation worked remarkably well. The scatter of points is now homoscedastic and more evenly spread out. What matters even more is that the data points trace a reasonable linear relation between both transformed variables. As

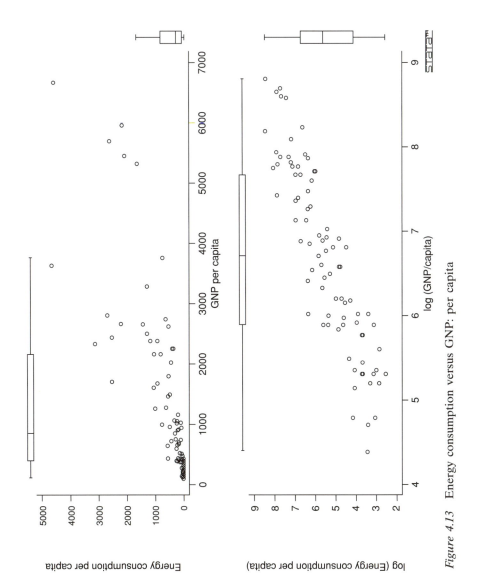

Figure 4.13 Energy consumption versus GNP: per capita

we can see, the double-log transformation appears to have solved three problems at once: non-linearity, heteroscedasticity and unequal density of the original scatter. In Chapter 7, on heteroscedasticity, we shall return to this property of power transformations to render residuals homoscedastic in cases where one or both of the variables is skewed. Note that, after transformation, both variables have become reasonably symmetric in shape. But our main point here is that the double-log scatter now is more linear in shape and, hence, allows us to extend the reach of linear regression to a curvilinear relationship.

Exercise 4.7

Use the data on energy consumption per capita, E, and GNP per capita, Y, from the data file SOCECON for all countries with a GNP per capita of less than \$10,000. These are the low, lower-middle and upper-middle income countries. Answer the following questions:

1 Regress E on Y, and $\log(E)$ on $\log(Y)$.
2 In each case, check whether the normality assumption is reasonably satisfied, whether the residuals are homoscedastic, and whether there are any outliers or influential points.
3 Which, do you think, is the better regression, and why?

Perhaps you were inclined to base your judgement on a comparison of the R^2s of both regressions? If so, keep in mind that such a comparison is invalid since the dependent variable is not the same in both cases: the linear specification features energy consumption per capita as the dependent variable while the double-log specification has the logarithm of energy consumption per capita as regressand. To be able to compare two R^2s, we have to compare like with like: both should be expressed as a share of the total variation in the same dependent variable. If the dependent variables differ across specifications, so will their total sums of squares and, hence, comparisons between shares of different things will be meaningless.

But, more importantly, to choose between specifications it is far more important to look carefully to see which specification best satisfies the assumptions of the regression model rather than mechanically picking out the one which features the highest R^2. In this case, the double-log regression is more in line with the assumptions of the classical regression model. Note that the linear fit with the transformed data yields a non-linear relationship if we return to the original raw data. Figure 4.14 compares the simple regression of energy consumption per capita on GNP per capita with the non-linear fit obtained from the double-log regression. While not immediately obvious from the graph, the non-linear curve fits the large number of data points huddled in the bottom-left corner far better than the linear specification. The reason is that the double-log curve gives

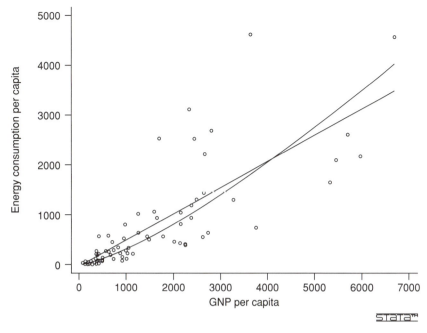

Figure 4.14   *E* on *Y* versus log(*E*) on log(*Y*)

roughly equal weight to all data points, unlike the linear regression, the location of which is mainly determined by the influential points on the right-hand side of the scatter.

More formally, there is a procedure which may be followed to compare the R^2s for regressions with transformed dependent variables. The method is as follows:

1 Carry out the regression with the transformed dependent variable and calculate the fitted values.
2 Convert these fitted values back to the original data units (for example, if you have made a log transformation, then take the exponential of the fitted values).
3 Calculate the correlation coefficient between the converted fitted values from step 2 and the actual values of the dependent variable. The square of this correlation coefficient may be directly compared with the R^2 from the regression with the untransformed dependent variable.

Semi-logarithmic transformations

Semi-logarithmic transformations involve equations which can be linearised by a logarithmic transformation of either the dependent or the independent variable. There are two variants. The first is given by:

$$Y = Ae^{\beta_2 X}\epsilon'$$ (4.57)

This specification, like the double-log specification, involves a multiplicative error term. Taking logarithms of both sides yields:

$$\ln Y = \beta_1 + \beta_2 X + \epsilon$$ (4.58)

where

$$\beta_1 = \ln A$$ (4.59)

The slope coefficient of this specification can be expressed as follows:

$$\beta_2 = \frac{d \ln Y}{dX} = \frac{dY}{Y}\frac{1}{dX}$$ (4.60)

which shows that the slope coefficient depicts the relative change in Y per unit change in X.

To illustrate this semi-log model, let us take another example with data from the file SOCECON. The top panel of Figure 4.15 shows the scatter plot of energy consumption per capita, E, against the urban population as a percentage of the total population, U, for low, lower-middle and upper-middle income countries. As you can see, the scatter plot reveals that the underlying relationship is non-linear. Note, furthermore, that the distribution of the regressor, U, is fairly symmetric in shape, while that of the regressand, as we know already, is skewed to the right. The lower panel of Figure 4.15 plots $\log(E)$ against U. Once more, the transformation solved more than one problem: the scatter shows a linear pattern and is no longer heteroscedastic. Consequently, the regression of $\log(E)$ against U, unlike that of E against U, is likely to satisfy the assumptions of the classical linear model. We leave it to you as an exercise to verify this. Figure 4.16 compares the linear regression line with the non-linear curve estimated by the semi-log model.

An interesting case of this semi-log model arises if its regressor is a variable denoting time, t. For example, if t denotes continuous time the semi-log model depicts an exponential trend with a constant (instantaneous) rate of growth given by its slope coefficient.

It is more common, however, to measure time in discrete intervals (say, a year). In this case, we can best modify the specification as follows:

$$Y_t = Y_0(1 + r)^t\epsilon'$$ (4.61)

where r is the constant (yearly) growth rate implied by the trend. Taking logarithms of both sides of the equation yields:

$$\ln Y_t = \beta_1 + \beta_2 t + \epsilon$$ (4.62)

where

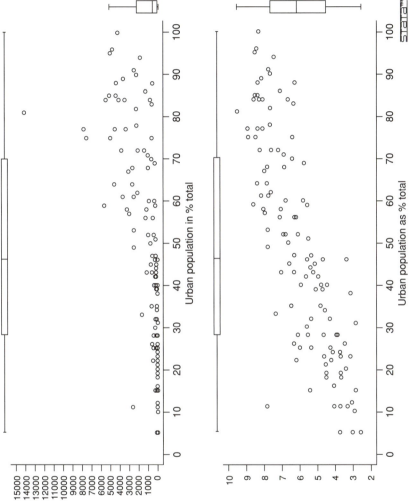

Figure 4.15 Energy consumption versus urban population as percentage of total population

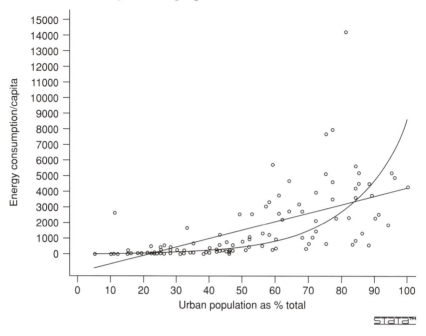

Figure 4.16   E on U versus log(E) on U

$$\beta_1 = \ln Y_0 \quad \beta_2 = \ln (1 + r) \tag{4.63}$$

In summary, the slope coefficient obtained by regressing log(Y) against t gives us an estimate of either the instantaneous rate of growth or, after taking the anti-logarithm and subtracting 1, the period rate of growth, depending on whether time is seen as a continuous or a discrete variable. Note however that $\ln(1 + r) \simeq r$ for small r so that the growth rate will be approximately the same by either interpretation under these circumstances.

The second variant of the semi-logarithmic model only involves the log transformation of the regressor, as follows:

$$Y = \beta_1 + \beta_2 \ln X + \epsilon \tag{4.64}$$

Note that this model does not involve a transformation of the dependent variable and hence the error term enters the equation in its usual additive fashion. The slope coefficient of the model is given by:

$$\beta_2 = \frac{dY}{d \ln X} = \frac{dY}{dX / X} \tag{4.65}$$

which, less formally, depicts the absolute change in Y per unit relative change in X.

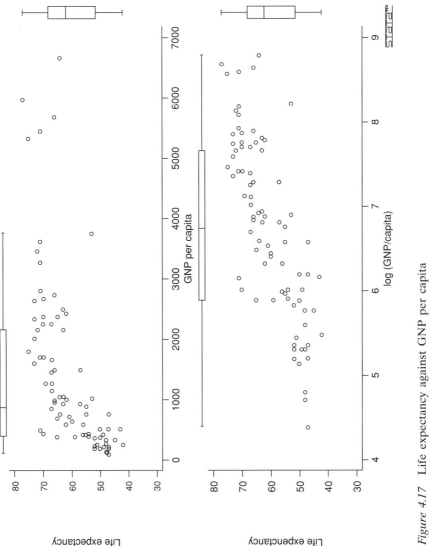

Figure 4.17 Life expectancy against GNP per capita

Let us consider an example which depicts a regression of Y against $\log(X)$. The example, as before, is drawn from the file SOCECON to enable you to follow it up as an exercise. The top panel of Figure 4.17 depicts the scatter plot of life expectancy, L, against GNP per capita, Y, a simple plot of the relation between the health and the wealth of nations. In this case, the data clearly are curvilinear in shape. The scatter of L against $\log(Y)$ shown in the bottom panel of Figure 4.17 goes a long way towards unbending the curve in the raw data. It appears, therefore, that in this case the semi-log model, L against $\log(Y)$, is more in line with the assumptions of classical linear regression. Figure 4.18 compares the linear regression with the non-linear curve produced by the semi-log model.

This particular functional form, which features the raw data as dependent variable and the log transformed data as regressor, is appropriate in the analysis of Engel curves with household budget data. Engel's law postulates that 'the proportion of total expenditures that is devoted to food tends to decrease exactly in arithmetic progression as total expenditure increases in geometric progression' (Working, 1943, quoted in Barten, 1985: 462). In the regression of Y on $\log(X)$, the slope coefficient measures the absolute change (arithmetic progression) of Y against relative chance (geometric progression) of X. This explains why this specification is so commonly used to estimate Engel curves. In fact, this

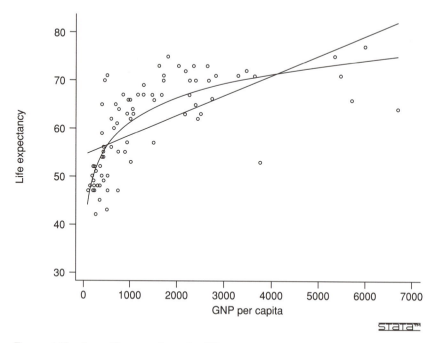

Figure 4.18 L on Y versus L on $\log(Y)$

specification would have been most appropriate to model the data in Table 4.1 on food expenditures as a percentage of total household expenditures as a function of total household income in Tanzania in 1969.

Exercise 4.8

Do exercise 4.6 again, regressing L (the difference between female and male life expectancy) on Log(Y) rather than on Y (GNP per capita). Are there any outliers or (clusters of) influential points left. If so, how do you suggest tackling the problem?

In conclusion, data transformations can help us to get more mileage out of the simple linear regression model since they make it possible to linearise curvilinear relationships. The logarithmic transformation is particularly popular on this count. They often do the trick and, furthermore, the slope coefficients of models involving log transformations lend themselves to easy, straightforward interpretations such as an elasticity or a growth rate. Other power transformations can also be used. Regressing Y on $1/X$, for example, allows Y to grow or decline towards a limiting value given by the intercept of the model. A regression of Y on X^2 depicts a simple quadratic relation which can come in handy when X is skewed to the left while Y is reasonably symmetric. Power transformations, therefore, extend the reach of the regression model. Moreover, as we shall discuss in Chapter 7, power transformations often allow us to eliminate heteroscedasticity of the residuals, as illustrated by our examples in this section.

4.9 SUMMARY OF MAIN POINTS

1   The simple regression of Y on X is the line or curve of conditional means of Y for given values of X. Simple linear regression assumes that the conditional mean of Y is a linear function of X.
2   The most commonly used method to derive the sample regression is based on the least squares principle. Given the assumption of classical linear regression, the least squares estimators of the coefficients of the regression line are BLUE. If, furthermore, the error term is distributed normally, the least squares estimators will be minimum variance estimators.
3   The least squares regression line splits the total variation of the dependent variable, Y, into two components: the explained variation due to the variation in X and the residual variation. The R^2, a measure of goodness of fit, is the proportion of the explained variation in the total variation of Y.
4   Inference in regression analysis is based on the assumptions of the classical normal linear regression model – in particular, on the normality assumption of the error terms. The treatment of estimation,

confidence intervals and hypothesis testing is very similar to that of the classical model of estimating a population mean.

5   The least squares regression line, like the sample mean, is a powerful tool of analysis if the assumptions of classical normal linear regression are reasonably satisfied in practice. If not, the least squares regression line rapidly loses its superiority. For this reason, it is important to check whether the assumptions of the model are valid in practice. Regression graphics – exploratory band regression, scatter plot with regression line and residual plots – are important tools to check the approximate validity of the assumptions.

6   A regression through the origin involves dropping the intercept from the model. Always test first whether the data admit this type of model restriction and keep in mind that the R^2s of the models with and without the intercept are not comparable.

7   Outliers, leverage and influential points can lead us astray when making inferences from a sample regression about the population. Outliers are data points with an exceptionally large residual, while influential points pull the regression line in their direction. Leverage – a property of the X dimension – indicates whether a data point lies nearer the edges of the scatter or in the middle as far as the X direction is concerned.

8   Hat statistics measure leverage. Studentised residuals and DFBETAs help us to detect the presence of, respectively, outliers and influential points. The latter two are deletion statistics inasmuch as their calculation involves deleting each data point in turn from the sample. (These measures are summarised in Table 4.4.) DFBETAs should always be used in conjunction with diagnostic regression graphics. It is always possible that a cluster of points is exerting influence rather than a single data point.

9   Data transformations can help to achieve linearity. In this respect, the logarithmic transformation is most frequently used. Three basic specifications are possible depending on whether we transform Y or X or both. Always check how the data transformation affects the shape of the distributions of the variables concerned.

ADDITIONAL EXERCISES

Exercise 4.9

Use the data in data files INDONA and SRINA to estimate a consumption function for Indonesia and Sri Lanka respectively. Repeat the estimation excluding the intercept in each case, and comment on your findings.

Exercise 4.10

Demonstrate algebraically that adding a point (X_{n+1}, Y_{n+1}) to a sample of n observations will (a) not influence the slope coefficient of the regression of Y on X if X_{n+1} is equal to the sample mean for X of the n observations; (b) that the intercept from the regression will probably change even if Y_{n+1} is equal to the sample mean for Y of the n observations; and (c) that if X_{n+1}, Y_{n+1} lies at the point of means of the sample of observations, then the regression line is unchanged. Generate a numerical example to illustrate your findings.

Exercise 4.11

Use the data in the data file TOT to regress the terms of trade on a constant and a time trend where the trend is defined as (a) $t = 1, 2, \ldots$ 39; and (b) $t = 1950, 1951 \ldots 1988$. Compare the estimated coefficients. Derive algebraically the general result which is verified by your terms-of-trade regression.

Exercise 4.12

Using the data in the data file TOT, regress the terms-of-trade index and its log on a time trend. How do you interpret these two sets of results, and which regression model has the more appropriate specification?

Exercise 4.13

Prove that the least squares estimate of the slope coefficient in the simple regression model is an unbiased estimator. State clearly any assumptions you make.

Exercise 4.14

Draw a scatter plot of consumption against income using the data in data file SRINA. Plot on this graph (a) the fitted values of consumption from the consumption function; and (b) the upper and lower limits of the confidence interval for the fitted values. Comment on the shape of each of the curves you have plotted.

Exercise 4.15

Figure 4.19 shows a data set with a clear point of high leverage. Also shown are the regression line with and without this observation included in the sample. When the observation is excluded, the regression line seems to fit nicely through the points. However, for the full sample the regression

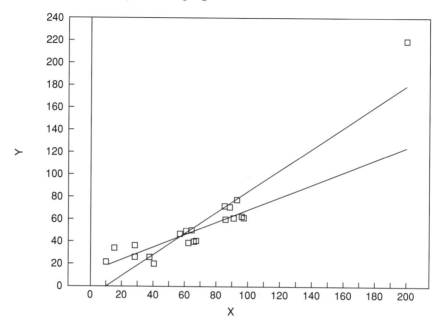

Figure 4.19   Graph for exercise 4.15

line not only misses the point of high leverage but seems also to fit less well to the other points. However, the R^2 from the full sample regression is 0.85, compared to 0.78 when the point of high leverage is excluded. How can this result be explained and what important lessons can you draw from this example?

5   Partial regression: interpreting multiple regression coefficients

5.1   INTRODUCTION

This chapter and Chapter 6 extend our analysis of regression to models with more than one explanatory variable. This is a major advance since in applied work we usually are concerned with relations which involve several explanatory variables. The good news is that not much additional statistical theory is required when moving from simple to multiple regression. First, the least square line is derived in much the same way as we did in simple regression. Second, the Gauss-Markov theorem extends to multiple regression with minor modifications in the assumptions, and, similarly, the least squares estimators turn out to be maximum likelihood estimators and hence have minimum variances if the assumption that the error terms are distributed normally is valid. Third, statistical inference in multiple regression is a natural extension of earlier theory. At first glance, therefore, multiple regression poses few new problems. But this is not wholly true. In applied work, multiple regression poses new challenges and raises new problems. The main reason is that we now are dealing with several explanatory variables at once.

But this raises the thorny question of variable selection – which variables to include in a regression? This is where modelling strategies come into full play. With non-experimental data (that is, when we do not control the explanatory variables), regression results differ, often markedly, depending on the number of regressors we choose to include in the model. In other words, the regression coefficient of an explanatory variable X will, in general, differ depending on whether we regress Y, the dependent variable, on X alone, on X and W, on X, W and Z, and so on. Theory often offers a range of competing explanations which leave us still with a great deal of specification uncertainty as to which variables really matter. Furthermore, theoretical arguments mostly involve postulating relations between two or more variables, assuming other things to be equal. In empirical research, we cannot make such an assumption because we cannot hold other things constant. Our problem, therefore, is to disentangle the separate effect of each explanatory variable on the dependent variable in a context where we are not quite sure which variables to include and where we cannot hold any of them constant.

Traditional textbooks offer little assistance on this count in as much as they generally assume that the model is correctly specified and, subsequently, go on to show that, under the by now familiar assumptions, least squares estimators will be BLUE as well as minimum variance estimators. These texts also teach us what happens to the properties of our estimators if we omit a relevant variable from the model or if we include superfluous variables, but generally have little else to say about data analysis in the context of specification uncertainty. But in applied work with non-experimental data, variable selection – finding out which variables to include – is more often than not the name of the game. To come to grips with this issue is our main concern in this chapter and the next.

This does not mean, however, that we shall not discuss the multiple regression model, its assumptions and its properties. On the contrary, the question of specification uncertainty arises precisely because of our awareness that models are as good as the assumptions upon which they are based. Misspecification matters because it leads us to make shaky or invalid inferences from our data. Hence, a good understanding of the statistical foundations of the models we use to approach data is essential. Our concern here, however, is with understanding the assumptions and the properties which follow from them, not with formal proofs and theorems. Our aim is to focus on modelling strategies in applied work. It is this emphasis which gives this chapter and the next their particular flavour as well as structure.

This chapter is structured as follows. In section 5.2 we use an example to show how we can move from simple to multiple regression through partial regression, which involves a hierarchical sequence of simple regressions. Partial regression shows that a multiple regression coefficient for a particular regressor, X, is arrived at by sweeping out the linear influence of the other regressors included in the model on both the dependent variable, Y, and the particular regressor in question. In this example we investigate the effect of changes in the price of basic foodstuffs on the demand for manufacturing goods in India. Section 5.3 deals with the application of the least squares principle to derive the sample multiple regression line and discusses its mathematical properties. Section 5.4 returns to the concept of partial regression to show its formal equivalence with multiple regression and discusses the coefficient of partial correlation. The main purpose of this section, however, is to introduce you to EDA's partial regression plot (also called the added variable plot), a powerful graphical diagnostic tool which allows us to look carefully at a bivariate scatter plot for any slope coefficient in a multiple regression.

Section 5.5 discusses the classical multiple linear regression model, its assumptions and its properties. Section 5.6 reviews the use of the *t*-test in multiple regression and shows how it can be put to work, through re-parameterisation of the model specification, to test more complex hypotheses which involve linear combinations of regression coefficients. Subsequently, section 5.7 introduces you to a simple variant of fragility analysis in multiple regression. The basic idea is to find the bounds within which a particular regression coefficient varies across a range of plausible rival neighbouring specifications (which differ with respect to the choice of variables included in the model) so as to judge the robustness of co-efficient estimates to changes in model specification. As usual, the final section summarises the main points of this chapter.

This chapter, therefore, concentrates on the interpretation of regression coefficients in the context of rival model specifications. As to modelling, it teaches you how multiple regression seeks to disentangle the separate effect of a particular regressor on the dependent variable when other regressors are also included in the model. It shows how you can look care-fully at how well the data support an individual regression coefficient in a multiple regression. And, finally, it teaches you how to check the fragility of a regression coefficient to neighbouring plausible alternative specifi-cations of the model. In the next chapter, we turn to 'general to specific modelling' in multiple regression as an alternative data-based approach to modelling which involves model selection through testing down to see which variables to include. There we shall make use of the *F*-test as an important analytical tool to allow us to test linear restrictions on the coef-ficients of a general model so as to arrive at a simpler model.

5.2 THE PRICE OF FOOD AND THE DEMAND FOR MANUFACTURED GOODS IN INDIA

Much of the economic literature on India concerns the analysis of the interplay of agriculture and industry in economic development. Here we shall investigate one particular contribution to this wider set of issues: namely, Krishnaji's (1992: 96) argument concerning the perceived narrow-ness of the market base for manufactured goods in the context of wide-spread poverty. Krishnaji argued that 'other things remaining the same, rising cereal prices depress the demand for manufactures' (ibid.: 105). It is this hypothesis we seek to test in this section with Krishnaji's data (avail-able on diskette in the data file KRISHNAJI). However, we shall use a somewhat different specification from that employed by Krishnaji.

In its most general form, our model consists of a constant elasticity function which features the per capita demand for manufactured consumer goods (M) as dependent variable as a function of nominal disposable income per capita (Y), the price index of manufactured goods (P_m) and the price index of cereals (P_f). Our model specification thus becomes:

$$M = AY^{\beta_2}P_f^{\beta_3}P_m^{\beta_4}e^\epsilon \qquad (5.1)$$

where ϵ is the error term subject to the usual set of assumptions of the classical normal linear regression model.

Taking logarithms of both sides yields:

$$\log M = \beta_1 + \beta_2 \log Y + \beta_3 \log P_f + \beta_4 \log P_m + \epsilon \qquad (5.2)$$

where $\beta_1 = \log A$.

Economic theory suggests that $\beta_2 > 0$ and $\beta_4 < 0$: that is, the income elasticity is positive while the own price elasticity is negative. As to the expected sign of β_3, the coefficient of the price of food, Krishnaji (1992: 106) argues that this coefficient will be negative for the following reason:

> if, as seems to be the case, food consumption levels are either inadequate for survival (as among the poor) or unsatiated (whether in quantity or quality, as among some above the poverty line), what determines the allocation process for the majority of the population is not the total but the 'residual income': that part of income which is left over after food articles have been bought.

Consequently, if Krishnaji's hypothesis is correct, we expect that $\beta_3 < 0$: the rise in the price of food will adversely affect the demand for manufactured goods.

Furthermore, unlike Krishnaji, we assume there is no 'money illusion' – that is, if nominal income and both price indices rise proportionally, the demand for manufactured goods remains unchanged. Hence, our assumption – which we shall not formally verify at this juncture – requires that the slope coefficients in equation (5.2) add up to zero (see Box 5.1). That is, we assume that equation (5.2) is homogeneous of degree zero, hence:

$$\beta_2 + \beta_3 + \beta_4 = 0 \qquad (5.3)$$

or

$$\beta_4 = -\beta_2 - \beta_3 \qquad (5.4)$$

Box 5.1　Money illusion in the demand function

Suppose that income and all prices increase by a constant multiple k. The demand for manufactures becomes:

$$\log M' = \beta_1 + \beta_2 \log (kY) + \beta_3 \log (kP_f) + \beta_4 \log (kP_m) + \epsilon$$

$$= \log M + (\beta_2 + \beta_3 + \beta_4) \log k$$

The absence of money illusion means that the equiproportionate rise in income and prices leaves demand unchanged, i.e. $M' = M$. It is readily apparent that for this condition to be met it must be the case that $\beta_2 + \beta_3 + \beta_4 = 0$.

Substituting equations (5.4) into equation (5.2), yields:

$$\log M = \beta_1 + \beta_2(\log Y - \log P_m) + \beta_3(\log P_f - \log P_m) + \epsilon$$

or, alternatively:

$$\log M = \beta_1 + \beta_2 \log \left(\frac{Y}{P_m} \right) + \beta_3 \log \left(\frac{P_f}{P_m} \right) \tag{5.5}$$

which conveniently reduces our initial four-variables model to a three-variable case. In section 5.6 we shall investigate whether the assumption of no money illusion is valid for these data.

Ignoring the income variable: simple regression

Our main concern is the sign of the coefficient of the relative price of food *vis à vis* manufactured goods. Should we then start by ignoring the income variable and simply regress the demand for manufactured goods on this relative price variable? If we do this, we obtain the following results for the period from 1960–1 to 1980–1 (standard errors in brackets):

$$\log M = 4.59 + 0.266 \log \left(\frac{P_f}{P_m} \right) \tag{5.6}$$

$$(0.36) \quad (0.195)$$

$$R^2 = 0.09, \ TSS = 0.4158, \ RSS = 0.3788, \ ESS = 0.0037$$

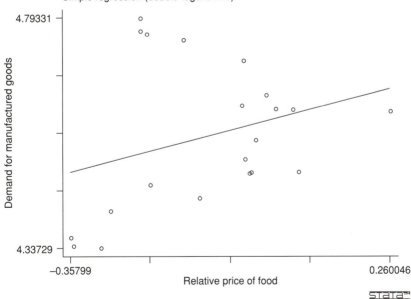

Figure 5.1 Manufacturing demand versus relative food price

For reasons explained below we shall give detailed information about the total, the residual and the explained sums of squares of all regressions in this section. The scatter plot along with the resulting regression is depicted in Figure 5.1. To say the least, the results are rather disappointing: the slope coefficient is insignificant and has the wrong sign, and the coefficient of determination is disappointingly low. It appears, therefore, that the relative price of food is of little significance in the demand for manufactured goods. But the problem with this regression is that we did not really test Krishnaji's hypothesis at all. His argument was that, other things being equal, the demand for manufactured consumer goods varies inversely with the price of food. But, in this case, other things did not remain constant: in particular, our real income variable, Y/P_m varied from year to year. In development research, we do not control the variation of the different variables and we cannot hold some of them constant while investigating the effect of one explanatory variable on the dependent variable. So how do we deal with this problem?

Removing the linear influence of the income variable: partial regression

To investigate the relation between the demand for manufactured consumer goods and the relative price of food we need to find a method which allows us to account for the influence exerted by the other explanatory variable – the real income variable. How can we do this? The trick is to remove the linear influence of our real income variable on both variables under study. In other words, if we cannot control real income, at least we can try to account for its influence by removing the effect of its linear covariation with both other variables.

To do this, we run two regressions which both feature the real income variable as the explanatory variable:

$$\log M = \begin{array}{cc} 3.3 & + \ 0.74 \end{array} \log\left(\frac{Y}{P_m}\right) + e_{12} \tag{5.7}$$
$$ (0.14) \quad (0.08)$$

$$R^2 = 0.82, \ TSS = 0.4158, \ RSS = 0.0750, \ ESS = 0.3408$$

where e_{12} refers to the residual obtained by regressing the dependent variable (denoted with subscript 1 since it is the first variable to appear in model specification (5.5)) with the real income variable (the second variable in the model; hence, subscript 2). The second regression becomes:

$$\log\left(\frac{P_f}{P_m}\right) = \begin{array}{cc} - \ 1.06 & + \ 0.57 \end{array} \log\left(\frac{Y}{P_m}\right) + e_{32} \tag{5.8}$$
$$\phantom{\log\left(\frac{P_f}{P_m}\right) = } (0.28) \quad (0.166)$$

$$R^2 = 0.38, \ TSS = 0.5228, \ RSS = 0.3227, \ ESS = 0.2001$$

where e_{32} are the residuals obtained by regressing the relative price variable (the third variable to appear in model specification (5.5): hence, subscript 3) on the second variable, the real income variable. This last regression is called an auxiliary regression in as much as it regresses one explanatory variable on the other.

The residuals e_{12} and e_{32} represent, respectively, the variation in the demand variable (M), on the one hand, and in the relative price variable (P_f/P_m), on the other, after removing the linear influence of the real income variable (Y/P_m) from both these variables. What happens if we now regress e_{12} on e_{32}? This is called the partial regression of log(M) on log(P_f/P_m) after taking account of the linear influence of log(Y/P_m). A partial regression, therefore, is a simple regression which features the residuals of prior regressions as its variables.

The partial regression now gives us the following results:

$$\hat{e}_{12} = -0.38\ e_{32}$$
$$(0.067) \tag{5.9}$$

$$R^2 = 0.61,\ TSS = 0.0750,\ RSS = 0.0288,\ ESS = 0.0462$$

This regression does not feature a constant term. Why is this? The reason is easy to understand: the point of means is always on the simple regression line, and, in the case of a partial regression, both variables are residuals which have zero means. Consequently, the partial regression line goes through the origin which is its point of means.

Interestingly, the slope coefficient in the regression (5.9) now turns out to be negative and is statistically significantly different from zero. This is what we would expect, given our initial hypothesis that there exists an inverse relation between the demand for manufactured goods and the price of food, other things being equal. But, in fact, we did not hold anything constant while estimating this inverse relation. Instead, what we did was to remove the linear influence of the income variable on both the demand variable and the relative price variable. In this way we managed to bring out a relation which was hidden deep in the structure of our data.

The partial regression plot

The partial regression (5.9) also provides us with a powerful analytical graph – a partial regression plot – which enables us to look at what lies behind a multiple regression coefficient. We do this simply by plotting e_{12} against e_{32}, along with the simple regression line between them, as shown in Figure 5.2. Take a good look at this graph and compare it with the earlier simple scatter plot in Figure 5.1. The simple scatter plot does not show any relation between the demand variable and the food price variable. Obviously, the reason is that money incomes also varied during the period shown. The partial regression plot is more revealing, however, since it depicts the relation between demand and the price of food after removing the linear influence of the income variable. Hence, if food prices

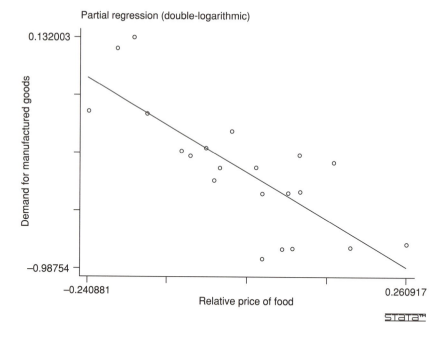

Figure 5.2   Partial regression plot of demand on food price

went up, but so did money incomes, the partial regression plot would remove this covariation between both explanatory variables and only depict movements in the price variables over and above changes in the income variable. In the process, nothing is held constant, but nevertheless the linear influence of the income variable is removed from the stage to allow us to look deeper into the patterns of covariation.

Lessons: partial versus multiple regression

Let us now jump ahead a bit and ask the obvious question. How does this partial regression relate to the multiple regression of the three variables? In section 5.3 we shall discuss how such a regression can be obtained using the least squares principle. But at this juncture let us compare our partial regression with the multiple regression. If we apply the least squares principle to the model specification (5.5), we get the following results, the interpretation of which are analogous to those of simple regression:

$$\log M = \underset{(0.11)}{2.89} + \underset{(0.06)}{0.95} \log\left(\frac{Y}{P_m}\right) - \underset{(0.065)}{0.38} \log\left(\frac{P_f}{P_m}\right) \qquad (5.10)$$

$$R^2 = 0.93, \ TSS = 0.4158, \ RSS = 0.02877, \ ESS = 0.3870$$

Note that the slope coefficient of the relative price variable in the multiple regression is exactly the same as the slope coefficient obtained in the partial regression (5.9). This gives us insight into the way multiple regression coefficients single out the separate effect of each explanatory variable on the dependent variable in a context where we cannot hold other things equal. In regression analysis, therefore, we investigate relations between two variables by removing the linear influence of third variables deemed important. In this way we account for the influence of the latter without, however, keeping them constant. A multiple (or partial) regression coefficient, therefore, cannot be interpreted as the impact of the explanatory variable in question on the dependent variables, other things being equal, but instead measures its impact after accounting for (i.e. removing) the (linear) influence of the third variables.

Decomposing the sums of squares across regressions

Finally, it is instructive to see how the multiple coefficient of determination, the R^2 in equation (5.10), can be derived from the sequence of simple and partial regressions. To see this, take another look at equation (5.7) which depicts the simple regression of $\log(M)$ on $\text{Log}(Y/P_m)$. In this case, the total sum of squares can be decomposed as follows:

$$TSS_s = ESS_s + RSS_s$$
$$0.4158 = 0.3408 + 0.0750$$

where the subscript s refers to the simple regression. The residuals of this simple regression then feature as a dependent variable in the partial regression (given by equation (5.9)) with the following breakdown of its total sum of squares:

$$TSS_p = ESS_p + RSS_p$$
$$0.0750 = 0.0462 + 0.0288$$

where the subscript p refers to the partial regression. Note that $RSS_s = TSS_p$, which must be so since the residuals of the simple regression feature as the dependent variable in the partial regression. Consequently, the residual sum of squares of the simple regression will be equal to the total sum of squares of the partial regression.

Now, ESS_s is the explained variation in $\log M$ due to the inclusion of the income variable only, and ESS_p gives us the added explained variation due to the further inclusion of the price variable (after removing the linear influence of the income variable). We obtain the explained variation due to the influence of both explanatory variables by adding both these explained sums of squares as follows:

$$ESS_m = ESS_s + ESS_p$$
$$= 0.3408 + 0.0462$$
$$= 0.387$$

where the subscript m refers to the multiple regression. Indeed, as you can easily verify, the *ESS* of the multiple regression 5.10 equals $(TSS_m - RSS_m) = (0.4158 - 0.02877) = 0.387$.

The multiple coefficient of determination can now be calculated as follows:

$$R^2_m = ESS_m \,/\, TSS$$
$$= 0.387 \,/\, 0.4158$$
$$= 0.93$$

which, as can you can see, equals the value of R^2 of the multiple regression (5.10). In sum, while the simple R^2 gives us the goodness of fit due to a single explanatory variable, the multiple R^2 gives the goodness of fit due to two (or more) explanatory variables. The simple and the multiple R^2s are directly comparable because the respective regressions feature the same dependent variable. Hence, in this case, we say that the goodness of fit increases from 0.82 to 0.93 as we move from the simple to the multiple regression.

But what is the meaning of the R^2 in the partial regression (5.9)? This R^2 is not comparable with either the simple or the multiple R^2s because it does not feature the same dependent variable. Its dependent variable is the residuals obtained by removing the linear influence of the income variable on the demand variable. This R^2 is the partial coefficient of determination which measures the contribution of the relative price variable in explaining the variation in the demand variable after removing the linear influence of the income variable from both these variables. In other words, it gives us the added contribution of the price variable to the multiple regression over and above the influence already exerted by the income variable.

In our example, the simple R^2 in equation (5.6) equals 0.09, which tells us that, taken on its own, the price variable contributes little towards explaining the variation in the demand variable. This is not surprising since the influence of a price variable on demand can hardly be meaningfully assessed without taking account of income variation. In contrast, the partial R^2 equals 0.61 (as obtained in equation (5.9)). This tells us that once the variations in income are accounted for, the price variable proves to be important in explaining the remaining variation in the demand variable.

Sweeping out

This section has introduced you to a powerful concept, partial regression, which allows you to look deep into the structure of data so as to bring to the surface patterns within the data which are not immediately obvious but indicative of deeper relations among variables. Partial regression uses residuals of prior regressions with the raw data. For this reason we used terms such as 'accounting for the influence of other variables' or 'removing the linear influence of other variables'. Or, equivalently, we say that we 'control for other variables' while looking at the relation between any two variables. These expressions are quite cumbersome to use. Perhaps you will agree with us that EDA's more colourful expression of sweeping out makes the point more vividly (Emerson and Hoaglin, 1985). Hence, when we return to these important concepts of partial regression, partial correlation and partial regression plot in section 5.3, we shall frequently say that we look at the relation between Y and X, while sweeping out Z, meaning that we control for the linear influence of Z on both Y and X.

Exercise 5.1

From SOCECON, select the variables Birth (B, the birth rate), the logarithm of GNP per capita (log Y), and Urban (U, the urban as percentage of total population). Compare the partial regression of B or log Y, sweeping out U, with the simple regression of B or log Y. Next, look at the partial regression of B or U, sweeping out log Y and compare it with the simple regression of B on U. What do you conclude?

5.3 LEAST SQUARES AND THE SAMPLE MULTIPLE REGRESSION LINE

As in simple regression, the least squares principle can be applied to derive an average relation between Y and a number of explanatory variables, $X_j, j = 1 \ldots k$ (on notation, see Box 5.2). To start with, let us consider the case of three-variables: a dependent variable Y and two regressors, X_2 and X_3. The three-variable case is instructive since it provides us with all the flavour of multiple regression without the excessive strain of cumbersome mathematical expressions when using summation signs. The results can subsequently be extended easily to the k-variable case.

In the three-variable case, the sample multiple regression can be written as follows:

$$Y_i = b_1 + b_2 X_{2i} + b_3 X_{3i} + e_i \; ; \; i = 1, 2, \ldots, n \qquad (5.11)$$

where b_1, b_2, b_3 are the regression coefficients and the e_is are the residuals. Following the least squares principle, the estimates of the regression coefficients are obtained by minimising the sum of squared residuals:

$$\Sigma \, e_i^2 = \Sigma \, (Y_i - b_1 - b_2 X_{2i} - b_3 X_{3i})^2$$

with respect to b_1, b_2, b_3.

The first-order conditions yield the following normal equations:

$$\Sigma \, Y_i = n b_1 + b_2 \Sigma \, X_{2i} + b_3 \Sigma \, X_{3i} \qquad (5.12)$$

$$\Sigma \, Y_i X_{2i} = b_1 \Sigma \, X_{2i} + b_2 \Sigma \, X_{2i}^2 + b_3 \Sigma \, X_{2i} X_{3i} \qquad (5.13)$$

$$\Sigma \, Y_i X_{3i} = b_1 \Sigma \, X_{3i} + b_2 \Sigma \, X_{2i} X_{3i} + b_3 \Sigma \, X_{3i}^2 \qquad (5.14)$$

Box 5.2 A note on notation

In this text, we denote explanatory variables by X_j: $j = 2 \ldots k$. We number the explanatory variables from subscript 2 onwards. One reason for this notation is that it allows us to refer to the dependent variable as the first variable in the equation. Alternatively, we can consider $X_{1i} = 1$, for all $i = 1, 2, 3, \ldots, n$, as the variable representing the constant term.

Hence, when we refer to a three-variable regression, we mean a regression between Y and two explanatory variables, X_2 and X_3, with slope coefficients b_2 and b_3, respectively. The coefficient b_1 refers to the intercept.

In some applications, however, we also need a subscript for the dependent variable. In general, when the dependent variable is denoted by Y, we prefer to use the subscript Y as well. In examples, however, the dependent variable is often denoted with a different symbol (such as M in our earlier example), in which case we use subscript 1 to refer to the dependent variable.

Before deriving the estimators by solving these three equations for b_1, b_2 and b_3, let us first take a closer look at each equation in turn because each reveals some important properties of the estimated regression.

The mathematical properties of the least squares regression line

Equation (5.12) can be rewritten in two different ways, each of which highlights a different property of the least squares line. First, dividing both sides by the number of observations, n, yields the following result:

$$\bar{Y}_i = b_1 + b_2 \bar{X}_2 + b_3 \bar{X}_3 \tag{5.12a}$$

which tells us that the point of means satisfies the least squares regression equation. In other words, the least squares regression line passes through the point of means, a result which is familiar from simple regression.

Second, rewriting the normal equation (5.12) as follows:

$$\Sigma (Y_i - b_1 - b_2 X_{2i} - b_3 X_{3i}) = \Sigma e_i = 0 \tag{5.12b}$$

gives us the familiar zero-mean property of the least squares residuals.

Third, the normal equations (5.13) and (5.14) can be rearranged as follows:

$$\Sigma X_{2i} (Y_i - b_1 - b_2 X_{2i} - b_3 X_{3i}) = \Sigma X_{2i} e_i = 0 \tag{5.13a}$$

and

$$\Sigma \, X_{3i}(Y_i - b_1 - b_2 \, X_{2i} - b_3 \, X_{3i}) = \Sigma \, X_{3i} \, e_i = 0 \qquad (5.14a)$$

which show that the least squares residuals are uncorrelated with each of the regressors, a result which is again familiar from simple regression analysis.

Fourth, the least squares regression is a plane in the three-dimensional space, though it is often referred to as the 'regression line' by analogy with the case of simple regression. The resulting regression line which yields the average relation of Y for given X_2 and X_3 is written as:

$$\hat{Y}_i = b_1 + b_2 \, X_{2i} + b_3 \, X_{3i} \qquad (5.15)$$

Now, equations (5.13a) and (5.14a) imply that the predicted (or fitted) Y values are uncorrelated with the residuals. This can be shown as follows:

$$\Sigma \, e_i.\hat{Y}_i = b_1 \, \Sigma \, e_i + b_2 \, \Sigma \, X_{2i}.e_i + b_3 \, \Sigma \, X_{3i}.e_i = 0 \qquad (5.16)$$

Hence, the mathematical properties of the least squares regression line in multiple regression are a simple extension of the properties of the simple regression line.

Multiple regression coefficients

The solutions of the simultaneous normal equations for the sample regression coefficients yield the least squares estimators for b_1, b_2 and b_3. Since the resulting formulae become somewhat cumbersome, it is useful to simplify the algebraic expressions by using the following notational conventions:

$$S_{YY} = \Sigma \, Y_i^2 - n\bar{Y}_i^2 \qquad\qquad S_{Y2} = \Sigma \, Y_i X_{2i} - n \, \bar{Y} \bar{X}_2$$

$$S_{22} = \Sigma \, X_{2i}^2 - n\bar{X}_2^2 \qquad\qquad S_{Y3} = \Sigma \, Y_i X_{3i} - n \, \bar{Y} \bar{X}_3$$

$$S_{33} = \Sigma \, X_{3i}^2 - n\bar{X}_3^2 \qquad\qquad S_{23} = \Sigma \, X_{2i} X_{3i} - n \bar{X}_2 \bar{X}_3$$

First, the intercept, b_1, can be obtained from equation (5.12a) which specifies that the regression line goes through the point of means, as follows:

$$b_1 = \bar{Y}_i - b_2 \bar{X}_{2i} + b_3 \bar{X}_{3i} \qquad (5.17)$$

The coefficient b_2 is given by,

$$b_2 = \frac{S_{33}S_{Y2} - S_{3Y}S_{23}}{S_{22}S_{33} - (S_{23})^2} \qquad (5.18)$$

It is important to note that b_2 depends not only on X_2 but also on the other explanatory variable X_3 since the formula in equation (5.19) also includes the terms S_{33} and S_{23} which depend on the sample values of X_3.

It is instructive to divide both the numerator and the denominator in (5.18) by the product term $(S_{22}.S_{33})$ in order to obtain the following alternative expressions for b_2:

$$b_2 = \frac{b_{Y2} - b_{Y3}b_{32}}{1 - b_{23}b_{32}} = \frac{r_{Y2} - r_{Y3}r_{23}}{1 - r_{23}^2}\frac{s_Y}{s_2} \tag{5.18a}$$

where, b_{Yj} = the slope coefficient of the simple regressions of Y on X_j, for $j = 2,3$; b_{ij} = the slope coefficients of the simple regression of X_i on X_j, $i,j = 2,3$, $i \neq j$; r_{ij} = the simple correlation coefficients among Y, X_2 and X_3, for $i,j = Y,2,3$; s_i = the sample standard deviations of Y, X_2 and X_3, for $i = Y,2,3$.

Similarly, the corresponding formulae for the coefficient b_3 are as follows:

$$b_2 = \frac{S_{22}S_{Y3} - S_{2Y}S_{23}}{S_{22}S_{33} - (S_{23})^2} \tag{5.18}$$

$$b_3 = \frac{b_{Y3} - b_{Y2}b_{23}}{1 - b_{23}b_{32}} = \frac{r_{Y3} - r_{12}r_{23}}{1 - r_{23}^2}\frac{s_Y}{s_3} \tag{5.19a}$$

Expressions (5.18) and (5.18a) reveal that b_2 depends not only on the slope coefficient of the simple regression of Y on X_2, but also on the slopes of the simple regressions of, respectively, Y on X_3 and X_2 on X_3 (the auxiliary regression). A similar argument can be made for b_3. Hence, in general, simple and multiple regression do not yield the same estimates of slope coefficients of simple and multiple regressions. There are, however, two exceptions to this general rule, about both of which it is instructive to know. To see what these exceptions are, we suggest you attempt exercise 5.2 before reading on.

Exercise 5.2

Using equations (5.18) or (5.18a) and (5.19) or (5.19a), show that the slope coefficient of X_2 will be the same in the simple regression of Y on X_2 and in the multiple regression of Y on X_2 and X_3, if (a) X_2 and X_3 are uncorrelated with each other; and (b) b_3, the multiple regression coefficient of X_3, equals 0. Generate a data set to illustrate both of these special cases.

The proofs are simple and straightforward. Each case, however, gives us some interesting insights into the question as to how multiple regression seeks to disentangle the separate effects of different explanatory variables on the dependent variable. We discuss each case in turn.

Orthogonality and perfect collinearity of regressors

If X_2 and X_3 are uncorrelated, b_{23}, b_{32} and r_{23} all equal 0, and, hence, the simple regression coefficient of Y on X_2 equals the slope coefficient of X_2 in the multiple regression of Y on X_2 and X_3: that is, $b_2 = b_{Y2}$. In this case we say that the regressors X_2 and X_3 are orthogonal.

Intuitively, this result makes sense. If the explanatory variables in a multiple regression do not covary linearly with one another, it follows that multiple regression analysis allows us to distinguish clearly between their separate effects on the dependent variable. Multiple regression, therefore, becomes the simple addition of the constituent simple regressions. Sweeping out is unnecessary because the explanatory variables do not overlap.

The opposite of orthogonality occurs when a perfect linear relation exists between X_2 and X_3, that is, $X_2 = a + b.X_3$, where a and b are non-zero constants. In this case, $r_{23} = 1$: we say that both regressors are perfectly collinear. From equation (5.19) it follows that b_2 will be inde-terminate because the denominator in the formula will be zero: we can either regress Y on X_2 or Y on X_3 but not Y on both X_2 and X_3 together. In many regression packages you may get a message such as 'singular' or 'near singular matrix' when attempting to perform a regression. This message means that some of your regressors have a strong linear rela-tionship with one another and so, since it involves a division by zero, the computer cannot complete the calculation.

Adding a superfluous variable

If $b_3 = 0$, dropping X_3 from the multiple regression will not affect the slope coefficient of X_2. That is, $b_2 = b_{Y2}$. The proof is straightforward: if $b_3 = 0$, and X_2 and X_3 are not perfectly collinear, it follows that the numer-ator in equation (5.19) (or (5.19a)) equals zero, which then yields an expression which can be substituted into equation (5.18) (or (5.18a)) to show that $b_2 = b_{Y2}$. Intuitively, this makes sense as well. If the addition of X_3 does not add anything in terms of explaining the variation in Y, dropping X_3 from the regression model should not affect our results. In this case, X_3 is a superfluous variable: it contributes nothing once we have already taken account of the influence of X_2.

Note, however, that $b_3 = 0$ does not mean that $b_{Y3} = 0$ as well. Taken on its own, X_3 may covary with Y and, hence, the slope coefficient, b_{Y3}, in the simple regression is not necessarily equal to zero. Once X_2 enters the scene, however, X_3 is effectively eclipsed by the introduction of this new variable and, hence, its influence dwindles to zero. This teaches us an important lesson. Whether, in a multiple regression, an explanatory variable turns out to be superfluous or not cannot be deduced from its performance in its simple regression with the dependent variable; a vari-able which plays no role at all in the true model may appear significant if we begin from a more specific, incorrectly specified model.

Extension to the *k*-variable case

The analysis above can easily be extended to the *k*-variable case. The normal equations obtained by minimising the sum of squared residuals have a similar structure to the one shown in the case of three variables. In this case, however, the solution for the b_j $(j = 1, 2, 3, \ldots k)$ in terms of the Y_i and X_{ji} values becomes cumbersome when using summation signs once we consider the case of $k > 3$. The use of matrix algebra is more appropriate to derive the general solution for this system of equations. In practice, of course, we rely on computer software to solve the system of equations involved. Our interest here, however, is with the general properties of the least squares solution. Box 5.3 provides a summary of these properties.

Box 5.3   The properties of the least square line

1   The least squares line passes through the point of means.
2   The least squares residuals have zero mean.
3   The least squares residuals are uncorrelated with and, hence, orthogonal to each of regressors.
4   The least squares residuals are uncorrelated with and, consequently, orthogonal to the fitted values of the dependent variable.

The concepts of orthogonality and perfect collinearity can equally be extended to the *k*-variable case. The case of orthogonality is straightforward: X_j is said to be orthogonal to all other explanatory variables if it is uncorrelated with each of the other regressors included in the model. In this case, the simple regression coefficient of Y on X_j will be the same as the slope coefficient of X_j in the multiple regression of Y on X_j with all other regressors included in the model.

As far as the question of collinearity is concerned, its generalisation to the *k*-variable case is somewhat more complex. If a set of constants a_j $(j = 1, 2, 3, \ldots k)$, not all equal to zero, can be found such that

$$a_1 + a_2 X_2 + a_3 X_3 + \ldots + a_k X_k = 0 \qquad (5.20)$$

then X_1 (i.e. the constant term: $X_{1i} = 1$, for all i), X_2, X_3, $\ldots$, X_k are said to be perfectly multicollinear because, in this case, any of the X_js can be expressed as a linear function of the remaining regressors. As in the three-variable case, it will then not be possible to solve the system of normal equations and, hence, multiple regression breaks down.

The question of superfluous variables extends equally to the *k*-variable case in multiple regression. If we find that $b_j = 0$, dropping X_j from the regression model will not affect the other coefficients in the model. But this does not mean that this variable X_j will yield zero coefficients in regressions (simple and multiple) which involve subsets of the initial broader model. In other words, if regressing Y on X, Z and W yields a zero coefficient for X, it does not necessarily imply that the slope coefficients for X will also be zero in the simple regression of Y on X, in the regression of Y on X and Z, or in the regression of Y on X and W.

Orthogonality or perfect collinearity as well as slope coefficients which yield exact zero values are in fact extreme situations. With respect to collinearity, as far as regression is concerned, life is simplest when regressors are orthogonal and it is impossible when perfect collinearity prevails. Most socioeconomic data, however, fall somewhere in between these two extremes: regressors derived from non-experimental data tend to covary with one another but not in an exact linear fashion. However, more often than not the strength of the correlation between regressors tends to be very high, which makes it difficult to distinguish clearly between their separate effects on the dependent variable. Moreover, due to the presence of collinearity, a variable may perform well in either simple or multiple regressions until some other variable takes the stage and renders it superfluous.

Interpreting multiple regressions, therefore, is a complex problem since the presence of imperfectly collinear regressors blurs the picture when dealing with non-experimental data. The main lesson we learn from looking at the algebra of least squares is that the inclusion or deletion of one or more explanatory variable(s) from a regression will generally not leave the regression coefficients of the other regressors included in the model unchanged. In other words, when interpreting the slope coefficient of a particular regressor, X_j, it usually matters which other regressors are also included in the model. That is, the estimated coefficient of any regressor can change quite dramatically across a range of specifications which differ depending on which other variables are included in or excluded from the model. We shall return to this issue in section 5.7.

The coefficient of determination

The coefficient of determination, the square of the multiple correlation coefficient, measures the strength or goodness of fit of the combined influence of all regressors on the dependent variable. It is defined as the ratio *ESS/RSS* – the proportion of total variation in Y explained by the set of the explanatory variables X_j ($j = 2, 3, \ldots, k$). In multiple regression, these sums of squares are obtained as follows:

$$TSS = S_{YY} = ESS + RSS$$

where

$$ESS = \text{explained sum of squares} = \sum_j b_j S_{Yj}$$

$$RSS = \text{residual sum of squares} = \sum_i e_i^2 \tag{5.21}$$

$$\text{where } S_{Yj} = \sum_i Y_i X_{ji} - n\bar{Y}\bar{X}_j \,; j = 2, 3, \ldots, k$$

As with simple linear regression, therefore, the total sums of squares, *TSS*, can be divided up into two components: the explained sum of squares, *ESS*, which gives the variation in *Y* explained by the variation in all regressors included in the model, and the residual sum of squares, *RSS*. The coefficient of determination is then obtained as follows,

$$R^2 = ESS/TSS \qquad (5.22)$$

which measures the goodness of fit for the multiple regression as a whole. The R^2 can also be obtained by computing the square of the simple coefficient of correlation between Y_i and its predicted values derived from the multiple regression. As explained above, the R^2 of a multiple regression measures the explained variation in *Y* due to all explanatory variables included in the model as a proportion of the total variation in *Y*. In general, however, it is not possible to disentangle the *ESS* with respect to the contribution of each of the regressors. In other words, the *ESS* of a multiple regression is not a simple addition of the R^2s of the set of simple regressions of the dependent variable with each of the regressors in the model. The reason is that, in general, regressors covary with one another and, hence, they overlap in terms of explaining the variation in *Y*. Our example in section 5.2 showed this point very clearly.

If, however, the regressors in a multiple regression are orthogonal, the R^2 of the multiple regression is the simple addition of the R^2s of the corresponding simple regressions. In practice, exact orthogonality seldom occurs, but if regressors are near-orthogonal, the sum of the simple R^2s will not be much larger than the multiple R^2. If, in contrast, a variable X_j turns out to be totally superfluous in a multiple regression and hence $b_j = 0$, dropping it from the model will not affect the *ESS* and so the R^2 will also be unchanged. We seldom get b_j exactly equal to zero, but a regressor can be said to be redundant for practical purposes if dropping it from the regression hardly affects the *ESS*.

5.4   PARTIAL REGRESSION AND PARTIAL CORRELATION

We now take a closer look at partial regression – the technique of sweeping out the influence of other regressors when analysing the relation between the dependent variable and one specific explanatory variable. In the three-variable case, the partial regression of *Y* on X_2 is the simple regression of the residuals of, respectively, *Y* on X_3 and X_2 on X_3.

Partial and multiple regression coefficients

To avoid an overdose of cumbersome notation, let y, x_2 and x_3 denote the deviations of, respectively, *Y*, X_2 and X_3 from their respective means. Consequently, the slope of the partial regression of *Y* on X_2 which we denote here as $b_2{}^p$ is given as follows (ignoring subscripts *i*),

$$b_2^p = \frac{\sum(y - b_{13}x_3)(x_2 - b_{23}x_3)}{\sum(x_2 - b_{23}x_3)^2} = \frac{\sum y(x_2 - b_{23}x_3)}{\sum(x_2 - b_{23}x_3)^2} \qquad (5.23)$$

since x_3 is uncorrelated with the residuals $(x_2 - b_{23}x_3)$. Substituting the formula for b_{23} into equation (5.23) yields:

$$b_2^p = \frac{\sum yx_2 \sum x_3^2 - \sum yx_3 \sum x_2x_3}{\sum x_2^2 \sum x_3^2 - (\sum x_2x_3)^2} = b_2$$

which is identical to the slope coefficient of X_2 in the multiple regression of Y on X_2 and X_3 as given by equation (5.18).

Similarly, b_3 can be shown to be equal to the slope of the partial regression of Y on X_3, after sweeping out X_2. Hence, partial regressions yield exactly the same slope coefficients as the corresponding coefficients in the multiple regression. This explains why the regression coefficients in the multiple regression are most commonly referred to as partial regression coefficients.

The coefficient of partial correlation

The coefficient of correlation between $(y - b_{y3}\,x_3)$ and $(x_2 - b_{23}\,x_3)$, the residuals from the regressions of Y on X_3 and of X_2 on X_3, is called the coefficient of partial correlation. We shall denote this partial correlation as $r_{Y2.3}$: the subscripts before the dot '.' indicate the two variables under consideration and the number after the '.' indicates the other regressor the linear influence of which has been removed. The coefficient of partial correlation, therefore, can be expressed as follows:

$$r_{Y2.3} = \frac{\sum(y - b_{Y3}x_3)(x_2 - b_{23}x_3)}{\sqrt{\left(\sum(y - b_{Y3}x_3)^2\right)}\sqrt{\left(\sum(x_2 - b_{23}x_3)^2\right)}} \qquad (5.24)$$

which, after some manipulation, can be simplified as follows:

$$r_{Y2.3} = \frac{r_{Y2} - r_{Y3}r_{23}}{\sqrt{\left[1 - r_{Y3}^2\right]}\sqrt{\left[1 - r_{23}^2\right]}} \qquad (5.25)$$

In other words, the partial correlation between Y and X_2 is nothing but the simple correlation between both variables net of the correlations between Y and X_3, and X_2 and X_3. In a similar fashion, the partial correlation between Y and X_3 is obtained as follows:

$$r_{Y3.2} = \frac{r_{Y3} - r_{Y2}r_{23}}{\sqrt{\left[1 - r_{Y2}^2\right]}\sqrt{\left[1 - r_{23}^2\right]}} \tag{5.26}$$

Partial regression and correlation in the *k*-variable case

The concept of partial regression can easily be extended to the general case of *k* variables. The partial regression between the dependent variable and any of the explanatory variables involves sweeping out the combined influence of all other regressors in the model, which is done by regressing *Y* and the explanatory variable in question on all other regressors so as to obtain two sets of residuals which then feature as the variables in the partial regression. The auxiliary regressions are thus multiple regressions (see Box 5.4). As in the three-variables case, the slope coefficient of this partial regression will be equal to the corresponding slope coefficient in the multiple regression.

As far as the concept of partial correlation is concerned, it is useful to consider the notion of the 'order of partial correlation'. A partial correlation which involves sweeping out only one regressor (as was the case of

---

Box 5.4   The concept of auxiliary regressions

1   Auxiliary regressions involve regressions between two or more explanatory variables.

2   In the multiple regression of *Y* on X_2 and X_3, the auxiliary regressions are the simple regressions of X_2 on X_3 and of X_3 on X_2. These regressions are useful for two purposes: first, in partial regression analysis they allow us to sweep out the linear influence of each regressor on the other, and, second, they show the extent to which both regressors are collinear or not.

3   In the *k*-variable case ($k > 3$), the auxiliary regressions are multiple regressions since here we regress each explanatory variable on all the other regressors included in the model. Again these regressions are useful for two purposes. First, they allow us to sweep out the linear influence of all other regressors on the remaining one. Second, they reveal the extent of multicollinearity among the regressors. The reason is that pairwise simple regressions and correlations between regressors are not sufficient to check for the presence of multicollinearity. There is indeed the possibility that three or more variables covary in a pattern which is not revealed by simple correlations between any pair of these regressors.

$r_{Y2.3}$ above) is called a first-order partial correlation. Similarly, a partial correlation obtained after sweeping out two regressors is called a second-order partial correlation, and so on. The simple correlation between any two variables – for example, r_{Yj}, $j = 2, 3, \ldots, k$, can be then looked upon as a special case of a zero-order partial correlation. Obviously, in the k-variable case (which involves a dependent variable and $k - 1$ explanatory variables) we are most commonly interested in the partial correlations of order $k - 2$ which give us the individual contributions of each regressor in terms of reducing the residual sum of squares obtained by regression Y on all other regressors.

The partial regression plot

The partial regression plot – also called the added-variable plot – is a simple yet powerful graphical tool of analysis which allows us to look carefully at the scatter plot that underscores a particular regression coefficient in a multiple regression. As we saw above, a partial regression plot is a scatter plot featuring residuals on its axes rather than the original variables. In the k-variable case, there are $k - 1$ partial regression plots each of which throws a different light on the structure of the data.

It is customary to plot the residuals along with the partial regression line which goes through the origin, since residuals have zero mean. The plot, therefore, shows how well a slope coefficient of a multiple regression is supported by the data. Partial regression plots can be interpreted in much the same way as you would look at a simple scatter plot (see Chapter 3). They allow you to look for non-linearity, heteroscedasticity, outliers and influential points. There is, however, an important difference: partial regression plots depict residuals and, hence, they allow you to look deep into the structure of the data by controlling for the combined influence exerted by other regressors. Consequently, a partial regression plot depends on the other regressors taken into consideration and so the plot will differ depending on which other regressors are included in the model and on any transformations applied to the variables in it.

Exercise 5.3

In section 5.2, we studied the effect of the price of food on the demand for manufacturing goods in India in the context of a three-variable model arrived by imposing the assumption of 'no money illusion' on the general model given by equation (5.2). In this exercise, you are requested to drop this assumption and to use model specification (5.2) instead to work out the following questions:

1 Regress $\log(M)$ on $\log(Y)$, $\log(P_f)$ and $\log(P_m)$.
2 Compute the three partial regressions and their coefficients of partial correlation.

3   Compare the partial regression plots with the corresponding simple scatter plots.
4   How would you interpret, respectively, the simple, partial and multiple coefficients of determination?
5   Show how the multiple R^2 can be derived from the *ESS*s of a hierarchy of simple regressions involving the raw data as well as residuals from prior regressions.
6   Compare the results of the four-variable model with those of the three-variable model based on the assumption of 'no money illusion'.
7   In your opinion, do you think the assumption of 'no money illusion' is warranted? Why?

5.5   THE LINEAR REGRESSION MODEL

Up to this point we have dealt with the sample regression line which in the k-variable case can be formulated as follows:

$$Y_i = b_1 + b_2 X_{2i} + b_3 X_{3i} + b_4 X_{4i} + \ldots + b_k X_{ki} + e_i \qquad (5.27)$$

where the b_j ($j = 1, \ldots k$) are the least squares estimators of the coefficients β_j ($j = 1, \ldots k$) of the population regression model which is:

$$Y_i = \beta_1 + \beta_2 X_{2i} + \beta_3 X_{3i} + \ldots + \beta_k X_{ki} + \epsilon_i \ ; \ i = 1,2, \ldots,n \qquad (5.27)$$

where the ϵs denote the error terms of the population regression line as distinct from the es which are the residuals obtained from the estimated sample regression.

Model assumptions

The classical model is subject to the following usual assumptions:

1   The population regression is adequately represented by a linear function of the k variables included in the model: $E(Y_i) = \beta_1 + \beta_2 X_{2i} + \beta_3 X_{3i} \ldots + \beta_j X_{ji}$;
2   the error terms have zero mean: $E(\epsilon_i) = 0$;
3   constant variances: $V(\epsilon_i) = \sigma^2$, for all i;
4   and zero covariances: ϵ_i and ϵ_j are uncorrelated for $i \neq j$;
5   the error term and the X_js have zero covariances: $E(\epsilon_i, X_{ji}) = 0$, for all i and j;
6   there is no perfect collinearity between regressors: no exact linear relation exists between the X_{ji}s, $j = 1, 2, 3, \ldots k$, where $X_{1i} = 1$ for all i (i.e. the constant term).

Apart from the last one, all assumptions are exactly the same as with simple regression. An added assumption is needed to ensure that least squares will yield a solution for the coefficients of the model. The classical normal multiple regression model requires that we add the familiar normality assumption:

7   the error terms have identical normal distributions: $\epsilon_i \sim N(0,\sigma^2)$, $i = 1 \ldots n$.

Statistical properties

Given the assumptions of classical multiple linear regression, the Gauss-Markov theorem can be extended to the k-variable case to prove that, as in the simple regression model, the least squares estimators of β_j are BLUE – best, linear and unbiased estimators. Furthermore, if the normality assumption is valid, the least squares estimators will also be ML (maximum likelihood) estimators and, hence, have the property that they have minimum variance among all estimators. As with the sample mean and the least squares simple regression line, the least squares estimators are unbeatable if the assumptions of classical normal multiple regression are satisfied in practice. As before, the normality assumption lays the basis for statistical inference in the linear regression model.

The variances of the sampling distribution of the b_js

Given these assumptions, the least squares estimators, b_j ($j = 1, \ldots k$), are also normally distributed since they are linear functions of the Y_is. Furthermore, $E(b_j) = \beta_j$, since the least squares estimators are unbiased. The standard errors of the b_js are given by:

$$V(\beta_1) = \frac{\sigma^2}{n} + \sum_{i=2}^{k} \sum_{j=2}^{k} \overline{X_i}\overline{X_j} \, \text{Cov}\,(\beta_i, \beta_j) \tag{5.29}$$

where

$$\text{Cov}\,(\beta_i, \beta_j) = \frac{-\sigma^2 r_{ij}}{S_{ij}(1 - r_{ij}^2)} \, ; S_{ij} = \sum_{p=1}^{n} X_{jp}X_{ip} - n\overline{X_i}\overline{X_j}$$

for the constant term, and, similarly, for the slope coefficients, we get:

$$V(\beta_j) = \frac{\sigma^2}{S_{jj}(1 - R_j^2)} \, ; j = 2,3,\ldots,k \tag{5.30}$$

where, $R_j^2 =$ the coefficient of determination of the auxiliary regression of X_j on all other regressors included in the model.

Equation (5.30) shows that the variance of the slope coefficient of any of the regressors, X_j, depends on three factors: (a) the variance of the error term; (b) the sampling variance of the regressor of X_j; and (c) the coefficient of determination (R_j^2) of the auxiliary regression of regressor j on all other regressors included in the model. Consequently, other things being equal, the variance of the regression coefficients will be smallest in the absence of multicollinearity. To see this, we can rewrite (5.30) as follows:

$$V(\beta_j) = \frac{\sigma^2}{S_{jj}} \frac{1}{(1 - R_j^2)} ; j = 2,3,\ldots,k \tag{5.31}$$

or

$$V(\beta_j) = \frac{\sigma^2}{S_{jj}} \cdot VIF_j ; j = 2,3,\ldots,k \tag{5.32}$$

where

$$VIF_j = \frac{1}{1 - R_j^2} ; j = 1,2,3,\ldots,k \P \tag{5.33}$$

are called the variance inflation factors of the coefficients of the regression model. The VIF_js measure the degree of multicollinearity among regressors with reference to the ideal situation where all explanatory variables are uncorrelated ($R_j^2 = 0$ implies $VIF_j = 1$, for all $j = 2, \ldots k$). If, however, R_j^2 is positive but smaller than 1, $VIF_j > 1$, approaching infinity when R_j^2 approaches 1. If we obtain high values of the R_j^2s, however, we should not conclude that our regression coefficients will also have high variances. Much depends on other factors, namely, the sampling variances of the regressors and the error variance. For example, a small error variance coupled with a relatively high degree of multicollinearity can still produce acceptable sampling variances of our estimates.

Conversely, the prevalence of large estimated standard errors for the coefficients of the regression model cannot always be ascribed to the problem of multicollinearity. It is indeed equally possible that our model was badly specified and, hence, does not capture the real determinants of the dependent variable in question. Consequently, our error variance will tend to be large. Alternatively, our X variables may vary too little to get meaningful precision in estimation.

The estimator of the error variance

In practice, we do not know the value of the variance of the error term, but, as in the case of simple regression, we use the ratio of the sum of squared residuals of the estimated model to the number of degrees of freedom (i.e. sample size minus the number of estimated coefficients) as an estimator for the error variance. Hence:

$$s^2 = RSS/(n - k) \tag{5.34}$$

where, n = the sample size, and k = the number of coefficients in the regression line. This expression gives us an unbiased estimator for the variance of the error term, the square root of which is the standard error of the regression. The value is substituted into equations (5.29) and (5.30) to obtain estimators for the variances (and standard errors) of the least squares regression coefficients, allowing statistical inference in multiple regression. Before turning to the latter issue, it is important to stress that the inferences we make from, and the properties we ascribe to, the least squares estimators are only valid if the assumptions of the classical normal linear multiple regression model are reasonably valid in practice.

Checking the assumptions of the regression model

As with simple regression, it is useful to make use of analytical graphs along with numerical summaries as diagnostic tools to check whether the model assumptions are reasonably satisfied in practice. To check model assumptions, it is a good strategy to start from the ground upwards; that is, first take a good look at the empirical distributions of each of the variables in play. Next, take a look at the two-by-two scatter plots of all variables. This can best be done with a scatter matrix which arranges all possible two-way scatter plots between the variables in matrix form. You have already come across an example how to do this in the introduction to this book where we looked at the relation between the crude birth rate as a dependent variable and GNP per capita and infant mortality as explanatory variables. In this example, we first looked at the individual empirical distributions of each of these variables and at their two-way scatter plots before arriving at our preferred multiple regression. In the exercise in the introduction you were asked to redo this example with data from the file SOCECON. Suppose that we now bring two more explanatory variables in play: say, the human development index and the degree of urbanisation as measured by the percentage of the population living in urban areas. A quick graphical check (not done here) of their empirical distributions tells you that the latter variable is reasonably symmetrical in nature but, interestingly, the human development index is skewed to the left. Figure 5.3 shows the corresponding scatter plot matrix with the raw data on all the variables in the analysis (GNP per capita, infant mortality, human development index, the degree of urbanisation, and the crude birth rate).

The scatter plot matrix is a powerful graphical tool of analysis which allows you, at a glance, to detect the presence of non-linearities, heteroscedasticity and outliers or influential points across the range of two-way scatter plots. These two-way plots do not reveal the patterns inherent in multiple regression since this involves sweeping out the influence of third variables on the interplay between the dependent variable and a particular explanatory variable; but the simple scatter plots are nevertheless useful since they often warn us against problems which may crop up again in multivariate analysis. In this enlarged example we found

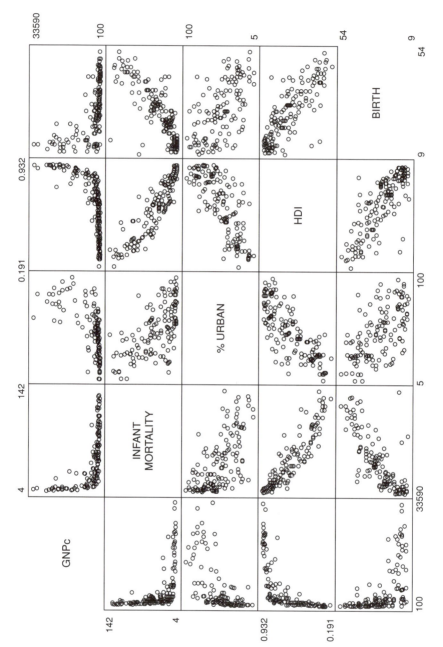

Figure 5.3 Scatter plot matrix with untransformed data

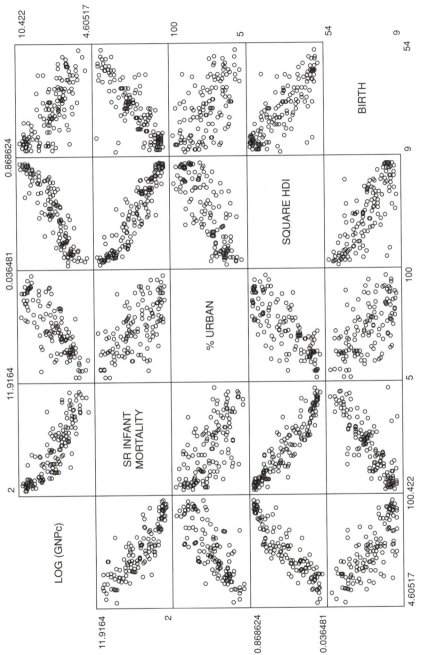

Figure 5.4 Scatter plot matrix with transformed data

it useful to try out the following transformations: the logarithm of GNP per capita, the square root of infant mortality, and the square of the human development index, leaving the other variables (the birth rate and the degree of urbanisation) unchanged. This yields the scatter plot matrix depicted in Figure 5.4. which no longer shows major non-linearities in the two-ways plots. This scatter plot matrix shows that the problem of non-linearities has been largely removed from the two-way plots. This is usually a good indication that it is also better to work with these transformed variables in multiple regression.

To look specifically at the performance of each regressor in a multiple regression we use partial regression plots. These are powerful graphical tools of analysis which help us to assess how well the data points support the slope of a multiple regression coefficient. To do this you look at each partial regression plot in turn in much the same way as you would look at simple scatter plots. These partial regression plots help you to detect non-linearities, heteroscedasticity and the presence of outliers, leverage and influential points. Figure 5.5, for example, shows the matrix of partial regression plots of the regression of the crude birth rate on the logarithm of GNP per capita, the square root of infant mortality, the square of the human development index, and the degree of urbanisation. It is clear from these plots that the logarithm of GNP per capita and the degree of urban-isation appear to be of little relevance. While infant mortality and the development index perform better, the partial regression plots reveal that the results are undoubtedly affected by the presence of influential points and outliers.

Residual plots can also be used in much the same way as we used them in simple regression analysis. Hence, we can plot residuals against the predicted values of Y. Alternatively, we may also choose to plot the residuals against each of the regressors. If the residuals are heteroscedastic, the latter type of plots can be useful to check whether the heteroscedasticity of the residuals is linked with any one of the regressors. For example, in a regression of household expenditures on manufactured consumer goods as the dependent variable and, respectively, household income and household size as independent variables, we often find that residuals are heteroscedastic. This heteroscedasticity, however, is usually related to the income variable, and not to the demographic variable. Rich households not only consume more manufactured goods but also have more varia-tion in their expenditures patterns. A plot of residuals against the income variable will reveal how the level and spread of such expenditures both increase with higher incomes.

Studentised residuals, hat statistics and DFBETAs can easily be extended to multiple regression along with careful scrutiny of partial regression plots. The formula for the hat statistics becomes more complex since we are now dealing with several explanatory variables at once (see, for example, Hamilton, 1990: 130). However, the basic principle for its

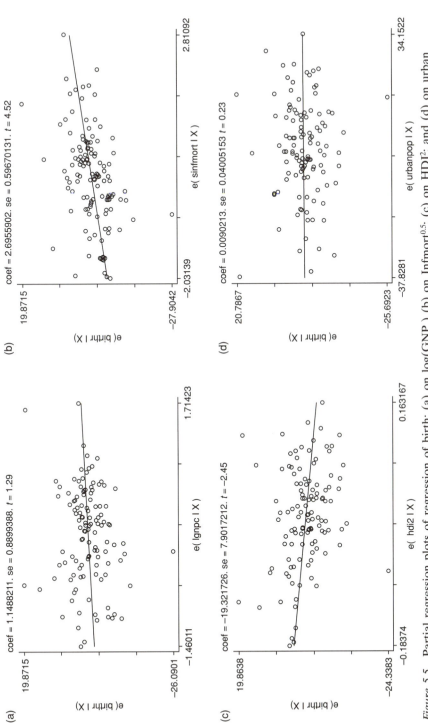

Figure 5.5 Partial regression plots of regression of birth: (a) on log(GNP$_c$) (b) on Infmort$^{0.5}$; (c) on HDI^2; and (d) on urban

derivation remains the same. Since the least squares estimators are linear functions of the Y_is, it follows that the predicted Y_is are also linear functions of the Y_is. The hat statistic h_{ii} is the coefficient of Y_i in the function which expresses the predicted Y_i as a linear combination of the observed Y_is. It can be shown that this statistic measures the distance a particular configuration of X values corresponding to data point i lies in relation to the main body of the X data. Hence, h_{ii} measures leverage as a result of the position of various X_js in combination. The studentised residuals as well as the DFBETAs are calculated analogously to the case of simple regression. Note, however, that in multiple regression we have a set of k DFBETAs, one for each coefficient in the regression. In a three-variable case, for example, a particular data point may exert influence on the slope coefficient of X_2 without affecting the slope of X_3.

Obviously, a critical assumption of the classical linear regression model is that all relevant variables have been included in the model. Much of our concern in the remainder of this chapter as well as in Chapter 6 is to come to terms with this assumption. How do we know whether our model is adequate inasmuch as it includes the main variables? As we shall see, there is no easy answer to this. At this juncture, suffice it to say that if our model is reasonably adequate, our error terms should behave as noise (i.e. a normally distributed random variable with mean zero and a constant variance). If, however, the residuals of the estimated model show signs that something has been left out, we should conclude that our model is misspecified, although we may be unaware of the exact nature of the problem. In fact, partial regression is built on this principle inasmuch as it uses the residuals of a regression which include explanatory variables deemed relevant to check whether another variable adds anything further in terms of making a significant contribution towards explaining the variation in Y.

5.6 THE *t*-TEST IN MULTIPLE REGRESSION

Statistical inference through hypothesis testing becomes definitely more interesting, varied and challenging as we move from simple to multiple regression. The presence of several explanatory variables in the regression model invites us to explore more complex hypotheses. As in simple regression, we may want to ask questions about the specific values a coefficient can take. But in the case of multiple regression we are also interested to see whether definite relations exists between two or more regression coefficients. This section deals with the use of the *t*-test in multiple regression analysis. The next chapter deals with the more versatile *F*-test, which allows us to test for a whole range of linear restrictions among regression coefficients. But this does not mean that the *t*-test is of little use. This section shows that the *t*-test is a useful research tool in applied analysis.

The *t*-statistic and the coefficient of partial correlation

The generalization of the use of the *t*-test to multiple regression analysis is quite straightforward. Given the assumptions of the linear model and adding the assumption that the error terms are normally distributed, it can be shown that the least squares estimators $b_1, b_2 \ldots b_k$ are also normally distributed. Analogous to the results obtained in simple regression it can then be shown that the variables

$$t_j = \frac{b - \beta_j}{se(b_j)}; j = 1,2,3, \ldots, k \tag{5.35}$$

each has a *t*-distribution with $(n - k)$ degrees of freedom, where n is the sample size and k the number of regression coefficients in the model.

The calculated *t*-statistics which are generally included in any software package on regression or econometrics formally tests the hypothesis H_0: $\beta_j = 0$, and hence involve computing the respective values of $b_j/se(b_j)$ for each regressor X_j. This test is used to see whether a single variable can be dropped from the equation. In a sense, therefore, this test checks whether or not a given variable contributes to explaining the variation in the dependent variable.

This suggests that a relation should exist between a regressor's *t*-value, thus calculated, and its partial coefficient of determination as defined in section 5.4. This relation, stated without proof, is:

$$r_{Yj}^2 = \frac{t_j^2}{t_j^2 + (n - k)} \tag{5.36}$$

or

$$r_{Yj}^2 = \frac{t_j^2}{t_j^2 + \text{degrees of freedom}} \tag{5.37}$$

where r_{Yj} is the partial coefficient of correlation of regressor X_j with the dependent variable Y, and t_j is its calculated *t*-value under the hypothesis H_0: $\beta_j = 0$. Consequently, it is always possible to calculate the partial correlation coefficients corresponding to each regressor from the results of a multiple regression analysis.

The implication of (5.36) (or (5.37)) is that the multiple regression line contains all relevant information about the partial regressions for each of its explanatory variables. The partial regression coefficient equals the corresponding slope coefficient of the multiple regression line and the coefficient of partial correlation can be obtained directly from the calculated *t*-statistic of the corresponding slope coefficient in the multiple regression. There is no need, therefore, to sweep out the other regressors in order to arrive at a partial regression. However, the concept of sweeping out is important since it teaches us how a multiple regression coefficient is arrived at by controlling for the linear influence of the other regressors also included in the model. Moreover, to construct a partial regression plot we need to be familiar with the method of partial regression. Let us now illustrate the various uses of the *t*-test in multiple regression. Many researchers only use the *t*-test to check the hypothesis whether a particular regressor has coefficient zero and, hence, should be dropped from the equation. Obviously, this is an important application of the *t*-test. But the *t*-statistic is more versatile in its use. For this reason, let us illustrate varied applications of the *t*-test using our example of section 5.2 concerning the demand for manufactured consumer goods in India.

Testing for a unitary elasticity

Starting with model specification (5.5), let us test whether we can simplify the model by assuming a unitary income elasticity of the demand for manufactured goods. Hence, our null hypothesis is:

$$H_o : \beta_2 = 1 \; ; H_1 : \beta_2 \neq 1 \tag{5.38}$$

consequently, the resulting *t*-value is:

$$t = \frac{0.959 - 1}{0.0648} = -0.63 \tag{5.39}$$

At 5 per cent level of significance, the critical value of the *t*-distribution with 18 ($= 21 - 3$) degrees of freedom is $t_{0.05} = -2.1$. The absolute value of the calculated t-statistic is well below that for the critical value. Consequently, the data allow us to maintain the null hypothesis of a unitary elasticity.

We can now simplify the regression by imposing this unit elasticity on the model. How do we do this? The general specification of the model is given by equation (5.5). Imposing the assumption that $\beta_2 = 1$, our model becomes:

$$\log M = \beta_1 + \log \left(\frac{Y}{P_m} \right) + \beta_3 \log \left(\frac{P_f}{P_m} \right) + \epsilon \tag{5.40}$$

which, after rearranging terms, gives us the following specification:

$$\log M - \log \left(\frac{Y}{P_m} \right) = \beta_1 + \beta_3 \log \left(\frac{P_f}{P_m} \right) + e \tag{5.41}$$

which reduces our model to a simple regression model. We can re-estimate the model with least squares, obtaining the following results:

$$\left[\log M - \log \left(\frac{Y}{P_m} \right) \right] = \underset{(0.01)}{2.82} - \underset{(0.054)}{0.406} \log \left(\frac{P_f}{P_m} \right) \tag{5.42}$$

$$R^2 = 0.75, \; TSS = 0.1155; \; RSS = 0.0294$$

This equation may look quite cumbersome, but if you take anti-logarithms of both sides, you will obtain a neat average summary equation, as follows:

$$\frac{P_m M}{Y} = e^{2.82} \left(\frac{P_f}{P_m}\right)^{-0.41}$$

$$= 16.8 \left(\frac{P_f}{P_m}\right)^{-0.41} \tag{5.43}$$

which tells us that the share of manufactured goods consumption in income is inversely related to the relative price of food.

You may have noticed that the R^2 in regression (5.42) is much lower than the R^2 obtained in regression (5.10). This should not give you cause for concern, since the R^2s are *not* comparable as the regressions do not feature the same dependent variable. However, the residual sums of squares of both regression can be compared directly. Note that the *RSS* hardly increased as a result of imposing the assumption that the income variable has a unitary elasticity. We shall see in the next chapter that a comparison of the *RSS* from restricted and unrestricted regressions is the basis for the F-test.

Exercise 5.4

Using model specification (5.3) which you estimated in exercise 5.2, test the following hypotheses:

1 H_0: $\beta_2 = 1$;
2 H_0: $\beta_3 = 0$;
3 H_0: $\beta_4 = -1$.

In each case, specify clearly what you consider to be the relevant alternative hypothesis. Explain the economic meaning of each of these hypotheses.

Testing for a linear combination between regression coefficients

Our final equation (5.43), which depicts the interplay between the demand for manufactured goods and the relative price of food, was arrived at by simplifying model specification (5.5) which, however, is itself a restricted version of the broader model (5.2). So far we have assumed that there is no money illusion; an assumption which allowed us to move from a four-variable to a three-variable case. But are the data really comfortable with this assumption? We should test whether the assumption:

$$\beta_2 + \beta_3 + \beta_4 = 0 \tag{5.44}$$

is in fact data-admissible. To test this assumption with a *t*-test, we need to reparameterise the coefficients of our general model as given in equation (5.2): that is, we need to rearrange the terms in equation (5.2) in such a way that the sum of the slope coefficients in the original specification now features as a single slope coefficient. To do this, add and subtract the term $(\beta_2 + \beta_3)\log P_m$ to the left-hand side of equation 5.2, leaving the overall expression unchanged, as follows:

$$\text{Log}M = \beta_1 + \beta_2\log Y + \beta_3\text{Log}P_f + (\beta_2 + \beta_3 + \beta_4)\log P_m$$
$$- \beta_2\log P_m - \beta_3\log P_m + \epsilon$$

and, collecting all terms with the same coefficients, we get:

$$\log M = \beta_1 + \beta_2 \log\left(\frac{Y}{P_m}\right) + \beta_3 \log\left(\frac{P_f}{P_m}\right) + (\beta_2 + \beta_3 + \beta_4) \log P_m + \epsilon$$

$$(5.45)$$

which yields a specification which now features income deflated by industrial prices, the relative price of food, and the price of manufactured goods, all in logarithms, as explanatory variables. Importantly, the slope coefficient of the latter variable equals the sum of the coefficients β_2, β_3 and β_4. This enables us to test formally the homogeneity condition based on the assumption of 'no money illusion'.

Exercise 5.5

Using specification 5.45, formally test H_0: $\beta_2 + \beta_3 + \beta_4 = 0$.

If you did the test, you will find that the data reject the null hypothesis. This result may come as a surprise since the assumption that no money illusion prevails appears quite reasonable in the light of demand theory. But, as explained by Krishnaji (1992), our data are in fact highly aggregated time series. As such, serious problems may emerge. For example, the effect of rising average income per capita on the demand for manufactured goods depends on how the increase in average income is distributed across households. If, as Krishnaji argues, rising average income goes hand in hand with a worsening income distribution, the growth of the demand for manufactured goods may conceivably be depressed accordingly. Similarly, a rise in the price index does not mean that all prices go up at the same rate. Differential price rises can have different consequences for incomes and demand patterns. With aggregate data, therefore, the homogeneity assumption is not as straightforward as it appears at first.

In exercise 5.4, you tested the hypothesis H_0: $\beta_2 = 1$ in model specification (5.2) and found that the data reject the null hypothesis that the income variable has an unitary elasticity. In other words, the demand for manufactured goods grows less than proportionally with income. Krishnaji's explanation for this low income elasticity is that the worsening distribution of income limits the expansion of the home market for manufactured goods. But in fact Krishnaji did not use a double-log specification to estimate the demand curve. Instead, in his specification he tried explicitly to take account of the dampening effect of rising incomes with worsening distribution on the demand for manufactured goods. He modelled the demand for manufactured goods as a linear function of the price variables, P_f and P_m, and a quadratic function of income.

Testing for a quadratic term

Why this quadratic function? To see the point, it is instructive to start with a linear specification in all variables:

$$M = \beta_1 + \beta_2 P_f + \beta_3 P_m + \alpha Y + \epsilon \qquad (5.46)$$

Now, Krishnaji's argument is that, given the pattern of income growth and its worsening distribution during the period concerned, the coefficient of income cannot be assumed to be constant. Instead, he argued that this coefficient is likely to fall as income per capita grows due to a worsening income distribution. This requires that we model this coefficient as a function of the income variable itself. The simplest way to do this is by assuming a linear function as follows:

$$\alpha = \beta_4 + \beta_5 Y \qquad (5.47)$$

Substituting equation (5.47) into equation (5.46) yields a quadratic term income in the specification of the demand for manufactured goods, as follows:

$$M = \beta_1 + \beta_2 P_f + \beta_3 P_m + \beta_4 Y + \beta_5 Y^2 + \epsilon \qquad (5.48)$$

which gives us Krishnaji's chosen specification.

Exercise 5.6

Using model specification (5.48):

1 Estimate the regression coefficients of the model.
2 Estimate the partial regression of M and Y^2.
3 Construct the partial regression plot of M and Y^2.
4 Estimate the partial regression of M and Y.
5 Construct the partial regression plot of M and Y.
6 Formally test the hypothesis H_0: $\beta_5 = 0$.
7 Formally test the hypothesis H_0: $\beta_3 = 0$.
8 Explain the economic significance of each of these hypotheses.
9 What does each partial regression plot (respectively, M on Y and M on Y^2) tell you?

This section illustrates various uses of the t-test in multiple regression. We have shown that the t-test can be used as a versatile instrument not only to test hypotheses pertaining to one coefficient, but also those which involve linear combinations between a subset of coefficients. In the next chapter we show the use of the *F*-test, which is even more flexible to test for linear restrictions on regression coefficients – a characteristic which makes it highly useful in the context of general to specific modelling.

5.7   FRAGILITY ANALYSIS: MAKING SENSE OF REGRESSION COEFFICIENTS

An important conclusion from this chapter is that the estimate of the effect of one variable (say, X_j) on Y, depends on the range of other explanatory variables taken into consideration. Only in the case where X_j is orthogonal to all other regressors in the model can we safely assess the influence of X_j on Y independently of the exact specification used in estimating the coefficients. But orthogonality of regressors is rather rare in applied socioeconomic analysis where we work with non-experimental data. The special problem caused by multicollinearity is therefore largely unavoidable with this type of data.

The problem is that collinear data provide 'weak evidence' (Leamer, 1978: 171) on the specific contribution of one or more individual regressors. Typically, we end up with a very untidy regression: the R^2 may be high but many coefficients of variables we believe to be important have the wrong sign, take on an implausible value, or end up being statistically insignificant due to their large standard errors. Furthermore, the subsequent exclusion or inclusion of a subset of regressors to the model can often radically alter the estimated values of the regression coefficients in the model. Hence, applied data analysis is often a messy business.

It is useful, therefore, to be aware how sensitive regression coefficients can be across neighbouring specifications which involve different combinations of collinear regressors. Much can be learned from looking carefully at the behaviour of regression coefficients across alternative specifications. To see this, let us look at a five-variable regression which is riddled with multicollinearity.

Comparing regression coefficients across neighbouring specifications

Our interest is to investigate the socioeconomic determinants of fertility levels across nations. Our dependent variable, therefore, is the total fertility rate, *TFR*. The total fertility rate is a demographic measure of the average number of children born to a woman, using age-specific fertility rates for a given year. This measure, unlike the crude birth rate, is independent of the age distribution of the population and hence lends itself better for cross-country comparisons. To explain the variation in the *TFR*, we consider three sets of regressors. The first, a single regressor, is an index of the strength of family planning programmes, *FP*. We would indeed expect that fertility depends, in part, on differences in family planning efforts across countries. But, second, it is also reasonable to assume that fertility also depends on the general socioeconomic context in which people are born, live, work and die. It is difficult to find appropriate proxy variables to capture this social context. In our simple model, we shall use the logarithm of gross national income per capita, $\log(GNP_c)$, and child mortality, *CM* (re-scaled per 100, instead of the usual 1,000, live births), as indicators of, respectively, the income and the health of nations. Third, and finally, fertility will obviously depend on the position of women in society – in particular, the extent to which they can control their own fertility. This is not easy to measure. We shall use female literacy, *FL*, as a very rough indicator of the position of women in society (see, however, Sen, 1993, who uses age at marriage as an alternative proxy to denote women's autonomy in society).

Our regression model, including all five variables becomes:

$$TFR = \beta_1 + \beta_2 FP + \beta_3 \log(GNP_c) + \beta_4 FL + \beta_5 CM + \epsilon \qquad (5.49)$$

subject to the usual assumptions of classical normal linear regression. To estimate this broader model or any models which involve possible subsets of these regressors, we use the cross-section data on 64 countries given in the data file FERTILITY.

Specification bounds on regression coefficients

How sensitive are regression coefficients to alternative model specifications? In our example, we have four regressors. Let us first see what happens to their coefficients if we combine them in different ways across a range of specifications. How many different specifications are possible with four regressors? Box 5.5 gives some simple rules on how to determine the number of various combinations of possible specifications to be used in a sensitivity analysis.

In this example, we have four regressors and, hence, 15 ($= 2^4 - 1$) possible regressions. Table 5.2 records all possible regressions with these four variables. Before discussing the results, it is useful to take a closer look at the structure of the table. Three aspects are worth noting. First, the alternative regressions are grouped with respect to the number of explanatory variables included in the regression: starting with all simple regressions and ending with the five-variable case. Second, within each group we follow a lexicographic order. Setting up the table in this way prevents us overlooking one or other combination of regressors. Third, each regressor features eight ($= 2^3$) times in the set of alternative regressions.

If we look at the regression results listed in Table 5.1, we note that there is quite considerable variation in regression coefficients across different specifications. You can see this by running your eye down each column, showing how the regression coefficient of a particular regressor varies across the eight specifications in which this regressor is included.

Table 5.1   All regressions with four regressors: the determinants of the total fertility rate (TFR)

Dependent Variable: TFR	FP: family planning	LG: log GNP per capita	FL: female literacy	CM: child mortality	R^2
1	–0.042	–	–	–	0.57
2	–	–0.568	–	–	0.16
3	–	–	–0.036	–	0.39
4	–	–	–	0.133	0.45
5	–0.040	–0.453	–	–	0.67
6	–0.033	–	–0.022	–	0.69
7	–0.031	–	–	0.076	0.67
8	–	–0.038	–0.035	–	0.39
9	–	0.237	–	0.157	0.46
10	–	–	–0.013	0.096	0.47
11	–0.035	–0.234	–0.016	–	0.70
12	–0.034	–0.228	–	0.047	0.68
13	–0.031	–	–0.015	0.033	0.69
14	–	0.255	–0.014	0.119	0.48
15	–0.034	–0.212	–0.015	0.008	0.70

Box 5.5   Counting the number of alternative specifications

1   If there are $(k - 1)$ regressors, the number of alternative regressions we can run equals $2^{(k-1)} - 1$. Why? Each regressor is either included or not in any specific specification: hence, there are two possibilities here. But we have $(k - 1)$ regressors, each of which is either included or not in any given specification, and, hence, to arrive at all possible ways of combining these regressors in alternative specifications we multiply the number of possibilities of the inclusion/exclusion for each regressor $(k - 1)$ times since there are $(k - 1)$ regressors. We thus arrive at $2^{(k-1)}$ possibilities in total. But this includes the case where none of the regressors are included in the model. Subtracting this uninteresting case, we arrive at $2^{(k-1)} - 1$ alternative specifications.

2   In practice, however, we do not always want to investigate all possible alternative specifications given the number of regressors. Often we are confident that some key regressors should always feature in our regressions but we doubt the inclusion or exclusion of the remaining candidate regressors. Hence, if there are $(k - 1)$ regressors of which k' are considered doubtful, we need to consider $2^{k'}$ alternative specifications. Note that, in this case, the specifications which do not include the doubtful regressors is also important: this is why there are $2^{k'}$ cases and not $2^{k'} - 1$.

Table 5.2 Minimum and maximum bounds of estimated regression coefficient

Bounds	FP	LG	FL	CM
Maximum	−0.031	0.255	−0.013	0.157
Minimum	−0.042	−0.568	−0.036	0.001

Clearly, some regressors have more stable coefficients across alternative specifications than others. A quick summary can be obtained by listing the minimum and maximum bounds for each coefficient across its alternative specifications, as shown in Table 5.2.

Alternatively, we can also use techniques of exploratory data analysis to look at the variation of the coefficients across specifications. Of particular relevance here is the use of single and comparative box plots. These box plots reveal at a glance the average level of the point estimates, their spread, skewness as well as possible outliers. Figure 5.6 shows the comparative box plot for our coefficient estimates. Note that, to construct this plot, we standardised each coefficient estimate by dividing it by the absolute value of its mean across the different specifications which include that coefficient.

The plot shows that the estimates of the family planning variable are remarkably stable across specifications. The estimates fluctuate within very narrow bounds. In contrast, the coefficient of the income variable is much

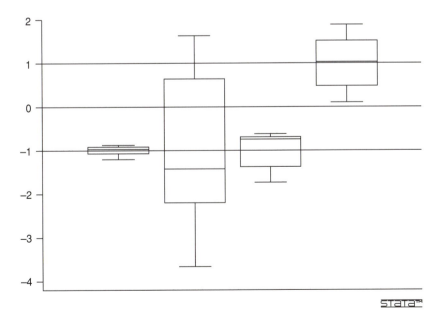

Figure 5.6 Variation in regression coefficients across specifications
Note: From left to right: *FP*; log(GNP$_c$); *FL*; and *CM*

more fragile with respect to alternative specifications, occasionally even producing the wrong sign. The coefficients of child mortality and female literacy vary significantly across specifications without, however, producing the wrong sign in any of them. Obviously, there is a fair amount of multi-collinearity among regressors. To see this, take a good look at the last column in Table 5.1. None of the multiple regressions have an R^2 which is anywhere near the sum of R^2s of the simple regressions featuring their corresponding regressors. The table also reveals some cases of the presence of superfluous variables. In specification 15, for example, the coefficient of child mortality dwindled almost to zero and, hence, dropping this variable from the regression hardly affects the regression coefficients of the other regressors, as can be seen from specification 11. Similarly, in specification 8, the coefficient of the income variable is exceptionally close to zero; dropping it from the regression hardly affects the regression coefficient of the other regressor, *FL*, as can be seen from specification 3.

Conditional bounds on regression coefficients

Up to this point we have looked at the maximum and minimum bounds for each coefficient across all possible combinations of regressors in the model. This procedure can be useful to pick out coefficients which are remarkably stable across various specifications, but it may at times be misleading. Indeed, some regressors will only have meaningful coefficients if they feature in the model along with other regressors. In a demand equation, for example, the inclusion of a price variable is unlikely to give good results if the income variable is not included in the model. Hence, in most applications we are not interested in the maximum and minimum bounds of regression coefficients across all possible specifications, but instead we are likely to narrow down the range to a subset of reasonable specifications. Obviously, it is always important to explain clearly what you consider to be the relevant set of specifications to be taken into consideration.

Let us try this idea with our example. First, a closer look at the table with alternative specifications shows that, if we include either female literacy or child mortality in the regression, the bounds of the family planning variable become even more proximate to each other: the coefficient values now lie within the range –0.31 to –0.35! The fact that this range narrows down once we include any one of these social indicators should not surprise us: family planning is not isolated from the general socio-economic context and from the position of women in society. It is sensible, therefore, to remove the influence of general social conditions in order to assess the separate effects of family planning.

Similarly, it is clear that the family planning variable should not be discarded from a serious analysis and, hence, we should only consider the conditional bounds of the coefficients of the other regressors in those

Table 5.3 Conditional bounds of coefficients of *FL* and *CM*: *FP* included

Bounds	Female literacy	Child mortality	Income per capita
Maximum	−0.015	−0.076	−0.212
Minimum	−0.022	−0.008	−0.453

regressions which include the family planning variable. Table 5.3 gives us the conditional bounds of the coefficients of *FL* and of *CM* in regressions which include the family planning variable. As you can see, the bounds have now become considerably closer. Undoubtedly, the female literacy variable is less fragile in the sense that its point estimate is much less sensitive to the range of specifications under consideration. The income variable retains a relatively large fluctuation in its coefficient, but the bond is also narrowed and all values have the 'right sign'.

The question of competing proxy variables

A closer look at Table 5.3 reveals that the joint presence of *FL* and *CM* in the model invariably affects the coefficient estimate and the statistical significance of either one of these variables. It appears, therefore, that both variables compete for attention as rival proxies for a similar underlying variable. Yet clearly the female literacy variable performs best.

A plausible explanation is the following. Both variables are in fact social indicators and, as such, are proxies for general underlying social conditions. But the female literacy variable captures something in addition to this: it also functions as a rough proxy for women's autonomy or status in society. In fact, you could convincingly argue that female literacy goes more to the heart of the matter since it is indicative of conditions which may be equally important in explaining child mortality as well as fertility behaviour. It is not surprising, therefore, that female literacy proves to be a more robust regressor in the model.

In view of our discussion above, it seems sensible to conclude that model specification 6 (in Table 5.1) which features the regression with two explanatory variables – family planning effort and female literacy – is probably the most suitable for our purposes, given the initial specification from which we started. Little or nothing is gained by adding the other two explanatory variables.

Lessons

This example shows that sensitivity analysis can be a great help in guarding against making fragile inferences. Looking carefully at the behaviour of regression coefficients across alternative specifications often gives us useful insights. When one or more coefficients prove to be highly robust with respect to alternative specifications we may feel more confident about the inferences we make about the influence exerted by such variables. But this does not mean that we should look at other variables with suspicion. Indeed, quite often one or another coefficient of a regressor only becomes reasonably stable once one or more other regressors are already included in the model. In fact, in any regression there are usually some variables we feel confident should always feature in the regression model. However, it is always important to check how stable such coefficients are once we include or exclude other variables which we consider to be doubtful, superfluous or of minor importance. Finally, our example also taught us that some of the regressors we take into consideration when searching for an appropriate specification may in fact be different proxy variables of a deeper variable which may be hard to measure directly. The joint presence of such related proxy variables often renders their coefficients unstable or insignificant, or both. Sensitivity analysis may help to spot such problems and help us to select the proxy which seems most appropriate.

Other things being equal?

Can we interpret a regression coefficient as the marginal impact of its regressor on the dependent variable, other things being equal, when in fact we know other things were not at all equal? This is a tricky question which requires careful reflection. One thing is certain: it is important to avoid giving a mechanical interpretation to any regression coefficient. Given a model such as:

$$Y = \beta_1 + \beta_2 X_2 + \beta_3 X_3 + \epsilon \tag{5.50}$$

it has become far too common to interpret the coefficient of X_2 as the marginal impact of X_2 on Y, other things being equal (i.e. holding X_3 constant). This interpretation is most definitely not always valid (Mosteller and Tukey, 1977: 300). Consider, for example, the following regression model:

$$Y = \beta_1 + \beta_2 t + \beta_3 t^2 + \epsilon \tag{5.51}$$

which expresses a quadratic trend line. It is clearly wrong to interpret β_2 as the marginal impact of time on Y holding t^2 constant. In this case the error we make is obvious since the same variable appears twice in the regression line: once linearly and once as a quadratic term. But often we find regressors jointly in a model which are either related to one another or serve as alternative proxies for the same deeper variable we cannot hope to measure accurately. For example, can we really argue that the coefficient of female literacy in our model gives us the effect of a unit change in female literacy holding other things (including child mortality) constant? In fact, as we argued above, female literacy may well be a determinant of both child mortality and fertility behaviour. Regression allows us to come to grips with the separate influence of a regressor on the dependent variable over and above the combined influence exerted by other regressors. But this does not necessarily mean that this reflects the effect of this regressor on the dependent variable, holding other things constant.

Hence, the interpretation of regression coefficients always requires careful reflection. In some cases it may be plausible to interpret the coefficient as if other things were held constant. But we should never jump too quickly to conclusions. For example, we may rashly assume that, other things being equal, a proportional increase in income per capita and in prices will leave demand for manufactured goods unchanged. But with real data, as we have seen, changes in the distribution of income may well render our estimates of the coefficients in the model contingent on the actually prevailing conditions where things are never equal. The elasticities we measure in such a case are rather complex and composite measures which reflect that other things are changing all the time, for example, the distribution of incomes.

The mechanical interpretation of regression coefficients, therefore, can lead us astray in many ways, particularly if we intend to base policy conclusions upon the premise that a single coefficient of a regression measures the impact of its variable on the dependent variable, other things being equal. Other things are never equal, and often the pattern of covariation between regressors is part of the fabric which structures the phenomenon in question. Overlooking this fact can lead to simplistic conclusions being drawn from the application of sophisticated statistical techniques.

Exercise 5.7

Model specification (5.2) is, in fact, a restricted version of a more elaborate model which include, apart from the income variable, Y, the price variables, P_f (the price of cereals) and P_m, two more price variables: namely, P_{of}, a price index of other food products, and P_s, a price index of consumer services. These data are in the data file KRISHNAJI. Including the last two variables into the double-log model specification yields a six-variable regression.

1   Construct a table with the results of all possible regressions which at least include the income variable (why?)
2   Construct comparative box plots of the variation in the slope coefficient of each regressor in the model.
3   Judging from your table, check whether there is much evidence of multicollinearity.
4   Check whether any variables in any of the specifications appear superfluous.
5   How robust is the income elasticity across alternative specifications?
6   In your opinion, which price variables appear to be most relevant in the model?

5.8 SUMMARY OF MAIN POINTS

1 Multiple regression is nothing more than a hierarchy of simple regressions involving regressions between the dependent variable and each of the regressors, auxiliary regressions between regressors, and regressions featuring as its variables residuals of prior regressions.

2 The regression coefficient of an explanatory variable in a multiple regression equals that of the partial regression arrived at by sweeping out the linear influence of the other regressors included in the model from both the dependent variable and the explanatory variable in question. This procedure yields a partial regression which allows us to control for the influence of other variables while investigating the relation between the dependent variable and an explanatory variable in a context where other things are not equal.

3 The coefficient of partial correlation is the square root of the coefficient of determination of the partial regression. It is the coefficient of correlation between the dependent variable and the added regressor after sweeping out the influence of the other regressors in the model.

4 A partial regression plot (or added-variable plot) is a scatter plot between two sets of residuals obtained by removing the linear influence of the other regressors from both the dependent variable and the added regressor. A partial regression plot allows us to look at a multiple regression coefficient by means of a two-dimensional scatter plot. It is a powerful diagnostic tool to detect deviations from model assumptions.

5 The extension of the least squares principle to multiple regression is quite straightforward and yields mathematical properties which are similar to those of simple regression. The main difference is that there is now more than one explanatory variable, and with non-experimental data, these variables often display a fair amount of multicollinearity. Perfect collinearity implies that an exact linear relation exists between the regressors (including the constant term), in which case linear regression breaks down. Orthogonality of regressors implies that they are uncorrelated with one another, a situation which is ideal for regression but seldom satisfied in practice.

6 Due to the presence of collinearity, the slope coefficient of a given regressor in relation to the dependent variable depends on the other regressors included in the model. Consequently, the slope coefficient varies with model specification as a result of the inclusion or exclusion of other regressors. Only if all regressors are orthogonal on each other will simple regression yield the same slope coefficients as multiple regressions.

7 A superfluous variable in a regression is one which adds nothing to the explained variation once the effect of other regressors have been taken into account. Strictly speaking, its slope coefficient in the multiple

regression will be zero, but it may well be non-zero in subset regressions drawn from this broader model. Dropping a superfluous variable from the regression does not alter the slope coefficients of the other regressors.

8 Given the usual assumptions of classical linear regression jointly with the added assumption that regressors are not exactly collinear, the least squares estimators turn out the be BLUE. If we add the normality assumption, the least squares estimators are also ML estimators and, therefore, have minimum variances among all estimators. Given these assumptions, the least square line is unbeatable as an estimator of the population regression.

9 The *t*-statistic allows us not only to test hypotheses concerning individual values of the coefficients, but also hypotheses which involve linear combinations of coefficients provided we can suitably reparameterise the model.

10 It is a useful exercise to investigate the sensitivity of regression coefficients across plausible neighbouring specifications to check the fragility of the inferences we make on the basis of any one specification with respect to specification uncertainty as to which variables to include.

11 An important conclusion of this chapter is that we should not to readily be led to assume that a slope coefficient in a multiple regression measures the marginal impact of its regressor on the dependent variable, other things being equal. With non-experimental data, other things are never equal and hence our estimation and hypothesis testing always takes place in a context where the covariation between regressors is part of the picture. Regression only allows us to remove the linear influence of other regressors when looking at the bivariate relation between *Y* and a particular regressor, but this is by no means the same as holding the other regressors constant. Whether or not such an inference can be made requires careful reflection, not a leap of faith or blind trust.

6 Model selection and misspecification in multiple regression

6.1 INTRODUCTION

In the last chapter we saw that any particular slope coefficient of a regressor generally depends on the other regressors included in the model. Hence, even if we are interested in the impact of only one of the regressors, it is important that we include all relevant variables in the regression equation. In this chapter we take this point further and show that if we omit a relevant variable from the model, least squares will no longer give us unbiased estimators of the coefficients of the population regression. The problem is misspecification due to the omitted variable bias. That is, unless all relevant variables are included in the regression equation, then none of the estimated parameters will be unbiased (except in a special case shown below). However, this result should not lead to a strategy of including every conceivable variable one can think off in a regression since, with collinear data, regression results are likely to yield foggy messages due to inflated standard errors of the coefficients. Variable selection in model specification is, therefore, a challenging task in applied research and has serious consequences for the validity of the inferences we make from our data.

This chapter deals with hypothesis testing in the context of model selection and hence introduces you to some of the basic principles of general to specific modelling. In section 6.2, we begin this chapter with an example of misspecification: Griffin's well-known argument that aid displaces savings. We show how, according to his own theory, Griffin's equation was misspecified. Next, in section 6.3, we examine the theory behind omitted variable bias as well as the implications of omitting relevant variables or adding irrelevant variables for the standard errors of regression coefficients, and relate this discussion to our examination of Griffin's model. Excluding variables from a model is a form of restriction being imposed on a more general model which includes these variables. This point is explained in section 6.4, where the use of F- and t-tests in specification searches is explored.

The F-test can be used to test any linear restrictions we place on a model: not just testing for the exclusion of certain variables (zero restrictions), but also testing for particular linear relations between regression coefficients (non-zero restrictions) and for pooling data from different samples (including different time periods). These issues are discussed in sections 6.5 and 6.6. Even if it is not valid to pool the data in a particular sample, it may still be possible to estimate a single equation by the use of dummy variables to allow some variation in coefficients between sub-samples, this application is explored in section 6.7. Section 6.8 summarises the main points from this chapter.

6.2   GRIFFIN'S AID VERSUS SAVINGS MODEL: THE OMITTED VARIABLE BIAS

During the 1960s there was a very optimistic view of aid's role in economic growth. Aid would supplement domestic savings, allowing higher investment which (through a Harrod–Domar equation) would result in higher growth (see Box 6.1). By the end of the decade a greater pessimism was developing and doubts began to be expressed about aid's effectiveness in increasing growth. Theoretical backing for these doubts was given by Griffin (1970; see also Griffin and Enos, 1971) who argued that aid would not simply supplement domestic savings, as had been hitherto expected, but rather displace at least some part of them. The rise in investment resulting from higher aid would thus be rather less than the one-to-one increment assumed in the optimistic 1960s growth models.

In a response to criticisms of his original paper, Griffin (1971) re-presented his argument in the following model. Consumption is given by:

$$C = \alpha + \beta \, (Y + A) \qquad (6.1)$$

where C is consumption, Y is income and A aid. Since savings (S) are given by:

$$S = Y - C \qquad (6.2)$$

it follows that:

$$S = -\alpha + (1 - \beta) \, Y - \beta A \qquad (6.3)$$

demonstrating the negative relationship between aid and savings. Griffin then, in his own words, 'suppresses' (i.e. ignores) the constant term and, dividing through by Y, gets a model to be estimated of the form:

$$\left(\frac{S}{Y}\right)_i = \beta_1 + \beta_2 \left(\frac{A}{Y}\right)_i + \varepsilon_i \qquad (6.4)$$

where his theory would suggest that $\beta_2 < 0$.

In his 1970 paper, Griffin presented four estimates of equation (6.4), in which the slope coefficient ranged from –0.67 to –0.84. We re-estimated the equation using 1987 data for 66 developing countries. These data, which are used throughout this chapter, are given in the file AIDSAV on the diskette. Estimation of equation (6.4) gives (standard errors in parentheses):

Box 6.1   Aid in the Harrod–Domer Model

The Harrod–Domer equation is an identity which relates the rate of growth of output (Y) to the level of investment:

$$g = \frac{1}{k} \, \frac{I}{Y}$$

where I/Y is the investment rate and k is the incremental capital–output ratio (ICOR). This identity becomes a theory of growth if we assume capital to be the critical constraint on output, i.e. higher investment is a necessary and sufficient condition for increased output. Investment is given by the accounting identity:

$$I = S + A$$

where S is gross domestic savings and A foreign savings (i.e. capital inflows, which are largely aid for many developing countries). This identity may be expressed as a percentage of GDP (Y):

$$\frac{I}{Y} = \frac{S}{Y} + \frac{A}{Y}$$

It is evident that higher aid (A/Y) will increase I/Y and hence growth. Suppose initially there is no aid and the domestic savings rate is 9 per cent. An ICOR of 3 will translate these savings to a growth rate of 3 per cent. Suppose now that the country receives aid equivalent to 6 per cent of GDP. The investment rate rises from 9 to 15 per cent and growth increases to 5 per cent.

Griffin contested this view, arguing that aid would displace savings so that the investment rate would rise by less than the increase in A/Y.

$$\frac{\hat{S}}{Y} = 19.14 - 0.87 \, \frac{A}{Y} \qquad R^2 = 0.33 \qquad (6.5)$$
$$\quad\;\; (2.06) \quad (0.16) \qquad\;\; RSS = 10{,}358$$

The coefficient of –0.87, which is not very different from Griffin's results, is significant at the 1 per cent level and appears to confirm the argument that aid will displace savings. But we saw above that the estimated model should not be equation (6.4) at all, since to get it Griffin ignored the intercept term in equation (6.3). As the estimated equation is divided through by income, the 'true model' should also include the reciprocal of income on the right-hand side, that is:

$$\left(\frac{S}{Y}\right)_i = \beta_1 + \beta_2 \left(\frac{A}{Y}\right)_i + \beta_3 \left(\frac{1}{Y}\right)_i + \varepsilon_i \qquad (6.6)$$

Estimation of equation (6.6) yields:

$$\frac{\hat{S}}{Y} = 20.90 - 0.40 \frac{A}{Y} - 17375 \frac{1}{Y} \qquad R^2 = 0.57$$
$$\qquad (1.69) \quad (0.15) \qquad (2923) \qquad RSS = 6{,}637 \tag{6.7}$$

The magnitude of the negative relationship between aid and savings is halved by estimating the correct equation derived from Griffin's model, vividly illustrating the point made in the last chapter that the value of an estimated coefficient depends on the other regressors included in the model. Before we go on to look at the theory behind this omitted variable bias, it is useful to pause and consider what we have done above.

Encompassing in empirical research

There are many unresolved debates in the social sciences, and development research is no exception. Empirical research often seems to further confuse, rather than resolve, these debates. The encompassing approach seeks to isolate one such source of confusion, by first analysing if different results are simply the results of different data sets. Many issues have been analysed using a range of different data sets. Therefore different conclusions may be put down to different data. In the case of the aid-savings debate, Riddell wrote that the: 'negative relationship between capital inflow and domestic savings was confirmed by Landau for 18 Latin American countries. However, Gupta's 1970 results for 31 countries indicate the foreign capital inflow has had little effect on domestic savings ratios' (Riddell, 1987: 118). But if the researchers are using both different data and different models there really is no basis of comparison for their results. For some problems – say those for a specific country – it would be helpful if the same data set were used, and some authors publish their data to facilitate replication of their results. This practice is a very helpful one.

In the case of Griffin's analysis his data set was not available to us. But, as a next best thing, we estimated his model using our data. We found that we reproduced (or replicated) his result fairly closely. Such replication is a very important stage of empirical research: it means that differences between our conclusions and those of previous researchers do not arise out of differences in the data. Therefore, it would be wrong to say that 'using 1960s data Griffin found a displacement effect of up to –0.82, whereas with more recent data a smaller effect of only –0.40 was found'. This conclusion might be valid if we had not first replicated Griffin's result. Our estimated slope coefficient of –0.40, however, is not a product of the data, but of our model specification.

Our example shows that inadvertently dropping a relevant variable from the model can lead to significant changes in our coefficient estimates. In section 6.4, we shall try to test whether or not Griffin's equation (6.4) is an invalid restriction of the correct model as specified in equation

(6.6). But before we do so, we need to equip ourselves with some more theoretical tools concerning the omitted variable bias. This we do first in the next section.

Exercise 6.1

Use the data in the file MALTA (Maltese exports demand and supply) to estimate the following demand equation for exports, X:

$$\ln(X_t) = \beta_1 + \beta_2 \ln(WY_t) + \epsilon_{1,i}$$

where WY is a variable measuring (world) income: the income of Malta's main trading partners.

1   How would you interpret the slope coefficient from this regression? Next, estimate the equation:

$$\ln(X_t) = \beta_1 + \beta_2 \ln(WY_t) + \beta_3 \ln(PX_t) + \epsilon_{2,i}$$

where PX is an index of export prices.

2   How do these results alter your conclusions from the simple regression?

6.3   OMITTED VARIABLE BIAS: THE THEORY

What are the implications of erroneously omitting a relevant variable from a model? To tackle this question, let us first use the three-variable case. Suppose that the 'correct model,' also known as the data generation process (DGP), is as follows:

$$Y_i = \beta_1 + \beta_2 X_{2i} + \beta_3 X_{3i} + \epsilon_i \tag{6.8}$$

but that, overlooking the importance of X_3, we wrongly specify the model as:

$$Y_i = \beta_1 + \beta_2 X_{2i} + \epsilon_i' \tag{6.9}$$

What then are the implications of omitting X_3 for our estimate of the slope coefficient of X_2?

You will recall from Chapter 4 that the OLS estimator of β_2, b_{Y2}, in the simple regression (6.9) is given by:

$$b_{Y2} = \frac{\sum_{i=1}^{n} (X_{2i} - \bar{X})Y_i}{\sum_{i=1}^{n} (X_{2i} - \bar{X})^2} \tag{6.10}$$

If model (6.9) were correct, b_{Y2} will be an unbiased estimator of β_2. However, by assumption, we know the correct model is given by equation (6.8). Substituting the correct expression for Y_i into equation (6.10), yields:

$$b_2 = \frac{\sum_{i=1}^{n} (X_{2i} - \overline{X})(\beta_1 + \beta_2 X_{2i} + \beta_2 X_{2i} + \varepsilon_i)}{\sum_{i=1}^{n} (X_{2i} - \overline{X})^2} \tag{6.11}$$

If we work out the product in the numerator, we shall see that the first term disappears since the sum of deviations from the mean of X equals zero. The second term will reduce to β_2, as its numerator and denominator are equal.

Taking expectations of both sides of equation (6.11) then yields:

$$E(b_2) = \beta_2 + \beta_3 + \frac{\sum_{i=1}^{n} (X_{2i} - \overline{X})X_{3i}}{\sum_{i=1}^{n} (X_{2i} - \overline{X})^2} \tag{6.12}$$

since the X-variables are given and, hence, non-stochastic, and $E(\epsilon_i) = 0$. Equation (6.12) shows that b_{Y2} yields a biased estimator of β_2. This bias is the product of two terms. The first term, β_3, is the population slope coefficient which measures the impact of the wrongly omitted variable on the regressand. The second term is the estimate, c_2, of the slope coefficient of the following auxiliary regression:

$$Y_{3i} = \gamma_1 + \gamma_2 X_{2i} + \epsilon_i \tag{6.13}$$

Hence, equation (6.12) can also be rewritten as:

$$E(b_2) = \beta_2 + \beta_3 c_2 \tag{6.14}$$

Equation (6.14) allows us to determine the direction of the bias. If the relationship between the omitted variable and the regressand (X_3 and Y) and the correlation between the omitted and included variables (X_3 and X_2) have the same sign (i.e. both are positive or both negative), then their product is positive and there is an upward bias. If the two expressions have different signs, their product is negative and there is a downward bias.

The exceptions: orthogonal regressors and irrelevant variables

This last expression of the bias allows us to see when omitting a variable does not lead to any bias in the estimates of the slope coefficients of the other regressors. More specifically, there will be no omitted variable bias if, either (a) $\beta_3 = 0$, which would indicate that X_3 is in fact an irrelevant variable in the model, and hence, can conveniently be dropped (in which case equation (6.9) gives us a correct specification), or (b) X_3 happens to be uncorrelated (orthogonal) with X_2 in the sample and, hence, the slope coefficient in the auxiliary regression of X_3 on X_2 is zero.

You will have noted the striking similarities of these formal results with our discussion in Chapter 5 on the behaviour of regression coefficients across different specifications which involve the inclusion/exclusion of other regressors. The case of orthogonality is exactly the same as before. If regressors are orthogonal, no omitted variable bias will occur and, similarly, simple regression estimates yield the same slope coefficients as multiple regressions. This is an ideal situation which, unfortunately, is seldom found when working with real data.

The case of the inclusion of irrelevant variables is similar to, but not identical with, that of what we called superfluous variables. A variable X_j is irrelevant if its slope coefficient of the population regression equals zero: i.e. $\beta_j = 0$. A variable is superfluous in a particular regression, however, if its estimated (sample) slope coefficient equals zero: $b_j = 0$. These are not equivalent statements. It is perfectly possible that a relevant variable yields a zero slope estimate in a particular sample, perhaps due to excessive multicollinearity or unfortunate sampling. Similarly, the fact that a variable is irrelevant does not mean that it may not produce a non-zero (or even significant) slope estimate in a particular regression. Obviously, under conditions of repeated sampling, an irrelevant variable will produce coefficient estimates which, on average, equal zero.

Assessing the direction of the bias

Let us now return to Griffin's model. We found that our estimation of his restricted model led to a downward pull on the estimate (from –0.40 to –0.87). In fact, this is what we should expect to happen. Why is this? As we have just seen, the direction of the bias depends on the sign of the product of two terms: (a) the sign of the slope coefficient of the omitted variable in the population regression of the correct model; and (b) the sign of the correlation coefficient between the omitted and included regressors (the correlation coefficient between two variables has the same sign as the regression coefficient). Equation (6.3) shows that the first of these should be negative. But what about the correlation between $1/Y$ and A/Y? The omitted variable, $1/Y$, will be small for two reasons: if a country is either big or rich. Small countries are known, on average, to receive disproportionately more aid than large ones. Also rich countries may expect to receive less aid than poor ones. For both these reasons, as income rises (so $1/Y$ falls) the aid ratio (A/Y) will also fall. The correlation between $1/Y$ and A/Y is therefore positive and the sign of the omitted variable bias (the product of a negative and a positive) is negative.

Equation (6.12) can also be used to estimate the value of the bias. We do not know β_2, but we estimated it to be –17,375, as shown in equation (6.7). We also need to know the coefficient from regressing $1/Y$ on A/Y, which yields a coefficient of 0.000026 (small, but significant: the t-statistic is 4.98). The product of these two is –0.47: which is exactly equal to the difference between the estimates of this slope coefficient obtained from equations (6.5) and (6.7): respectively, –0.87 and –0.40

Exercise 6.2

Using Exercise 6.1, assess the direction of the bias obtained by estimating the simple regression if, in fact, the three-variable model is the correct specification. Is your theoretical analysis verified by your empirical results?

Omitted variable bias in the *k*-variable case

The extension of the omitted variable bias to the k-variable case is quite straightforward. In the case where our estimated model includes $(k - 2)$ explanatory variables, $X_2, \ldots, X_{k-1}$, but the correct model also includes the relevant variable X_k, the omitted variable bias of the slope coefficient of the included regressor X_j is obtained as follows:

$$E(b_j) = \beta_j + \beta_k\, c_{kj}\,; j = 2,3, \ldots, (k - 1) \tag{6.15}$$

where c_{kj} is the slope coefficient of X_j in the auxiliary multiple regression of X_k, the omitted variable, on all the regressors included in the model. As you can see, equation (6.13) is a special case of this equation.

What happens if we omit more than one relevant variable from the model? Suppose our estimated model included $(k' - 1)$ regressors, $X_2, \ldots, X_{k'}$, and omitted $(k - k')$ regressors, $X_{k' + 1}, \ldots, X_k$, from the correct model. In this case, the omitted variable bias for the slope coefficient of X_j is given by:

$$E(b_j) = \beta_j + \sum_{l=k'+1}^{k} (\beta_l c_{lj}); \ j = 2,3, \ldots, k'; \ l = (k'+1), \ldots, k \tag{6.16}$$

where c_{lj} is the slope coefficient of X_j in the auxiliary multiple regression of X_l, an omitted variable, on all regressors included in the model. Equation (6.15) gives us the most general case of the omitted variable bias. Obviously, the more complex the situation in terms of the number of variables included and excluded from the model, the more difficult it becomes to make any *a priori* statements about the likely sign of the bias. But as you can easily verify, the slope coefficient of X_j, a variable included in the model, will not be affected by any omitted variables bias if (a) the omitted variables are all orthogonal on X_j, or (b) if they all happen to be irrelevant and, hence, can rightfully be omitted from the equation.

What about the standard errors of the regression coefficients?

We have seen that omitting one or more relevant variable from a regression renders the least squares estimators of the coefficients of the model biased. Hence, the mean of the sampling distribution of a regression coefficient will no longer equal the corresponding population parameter. But what about the variance of this sampling distribution? How is this affected by omitting a relevant variable from the model? In this case, the outcome is more ambiguous.

To see this, recall from Chapter 5 that the variance of the least squares estimator of a slope coefficient of a multiple regression is given by:

$$V(\beta_j) = \frac{\sigma^2}{S_{jj}} \cdot VIF_j ; \quad j = 2,3, \ldots, k \qquad (6.17)$$

Where VIF_j is the variance inflation factor of the slope coefficient of regressor X_j, and S_{jj} is the sum of squared deviation of X_j from its mean. $VIF_j = 1/(1 - R_j^2)$, where R_j^2 is the coefficient of determination of the auxiliary regression of X_j with all other regressors included in the model. The variance of the estimator of the slope coefficient of a regressor X_j, therefore, depends on the three factors: the error variance, the total sum of squares of X_j, and its variance inflation factor.

Now, it can be shown that if we omit one or more relevant variables from the model, the variance of the estimator of the slope coefficient of regressor X_j in the model which omits one or more relevant variables is also given by equation (6.17) with the exception that its VIF_j is now derived from the auxiliary regression of X_j with the smaller set of regressors included in this simpler model. Now, since the simpler model features less regressors than the larger model, it follows that the variance inflation factor of the former will be less than (or at most equal to) that of the latter. The reason is that the more variables we include in the model, the greater the multicollinearity, and, hence, the greater the R^2 of the auxiliary regressions, unless the omitted variables happen to be orthogonal to the regressors included in the simpler model. The crux of the matter is that the simpler model which omits relevant variables produces biased estimates but with smaller variances! Consequently, there appears to be a trade-off between bias and precision.

But the story does not end here. Equation (6.17) features the variance of the error term which in practice is unknown to us. To estimate the standard errors of the regression coefficients we estimate this variance using the residual sums of squares of the estimated model as shown in equation (5.34) in the previous chapter; that is:

$$s^2 = RSS/(n - k) \qquad (6.18)$$

But this estimate will differ depending upon the number of regressors included in the model. To see this, let us see what happens to, respectively, the numerator and to the denominator of s^2 if we include omitted variables. As to the numerator in (6.18), the RSS of the larger model will generally be less than that of the model which omits relevant variables. In particular, when we omit an important relevant variable, the gain in terms of reducing the residual sums of squares obtained by including it in the model is likely to be considerable. As to the denominator, given the sample size, smaller models have more degrees of freedom. In sum, whether the inclusion of omitted variables in the model leads to a reduction in s^2, the estimated standard error of the regression, depends on whether the *RSS* falls sufficiently to offset the loss in degrees of freedom. In general, if our omitted variables play an important role in explaining the variation in the dependent variable, we would expect the estimated error variance to fall with the inclusion of the omitted variables in the regression, unless the sample size is very small. This last point is obvious, but often overlooked. There is not much point, for example, in estimating a regression with five or more variables if we have only a handful of observations.

So what will happen to the estimated standard errors of regression coefficients if we add omitted variables to the model? Our discussion above shows that two opposite tendencies are at work: adding relevant variables to the model generally reduces the estimated error variance, s^2 (unless the loss in degrees of freedom offsets the gain in the reduction in the *RSS*), but increases the *VIF*s, the variance inflation factors of the slope coefficients due to multicollinearity. The net outcome cannot be stated *a priori*. It differs from case to case. If the reduction in the estimated error variance dominates the scene, the standard errors of the regression coefficients will decrease with the introduction of the omitted variables in the model, and vice versa if the variance inflation factor gains the upper hand.

What practical lessons can we learn from this discussion on bias and precision due to omitting relevant variables? First, omitting an important variable which has a strong impact on the dependent variable produces a bias as well as larger standard errors for the regression coefficients. In this case, in practical terms, there is no real trade-off: omitting the variable worsens both bias and precision. For example, this generally happens when the income variable in a demand equation is omitted: the resulting regression will not make much sense. Second, if we omit a relevant variable which has a more limited impact on the dependent variable and which correlates strongly with other regressors already included in the model, the trade-off between bias and precision may well be very real. The reduction in bias is likely to be bought at the price of less precision. For example, in a demand equation, the inclusion of a minor price variable of a more distant substitute may well make matters worse even if there are sound theoretical reasons for the variable to play a role, although not a major one. In such cases, we often end up with a large R^2 and a large number of insignificant coefficients (as was the case with the example in exercise 5.7). Finally, if we only have a small sample at hand, we cannot hope to include all relevant variables and still get reasonably precise results. The smaller the sample size, the more the loss in degrees of freedom due to the inclusion of added variables matters in terms of precision. Regressions with many variables and few data points are unlikely to produce firm inferences.

The problem of irrelevant variables

This analysis of the trade-off between bias and precision leads us to an important but often neglected point: a regression is not a sack into which we can throw any variable we can think of. Even with relevant variables we often have to decide whether the reduction in bias is worth the loss in precision. Not surprisingly, the problem gets worse if we take a lot of irrelevant variables on board as well. Hence, the bad news is that irrelevant variables boost the variance inflation factors of regression coefficients without yielding any gain in terms of reducing the estimated standard error of the regression. The greater the collinearity between variables, the greater the loss in precision will be. But the good news is that, as you would expect, the inclusion of irrelevant variables does not affect the unbiasedness of our estimators (if the model is otherwise correctly specified).

A final point: often the problem is not so much that we attempt to burden a regression with a number of irrelevant variables, but rather that our stock of potential regressors includes one or more subsets of proxy variables which, within each set, essentially seek to measure the same thing. We came across an example when discussing the determinant of fertility levels across countries in Chapter 5. Our point is not that we should not try out various proxies. Indeed, proxy variable specification searches are important in many regression applications. Instead, our point is that we should always keep in mind that some of the variables we select for consideration are chosen to serve as proxies for some deeper underlying variables which we cannot measure. The danger is, however, that once these variables enter a regression, we no longer see them as rival proxies, but treat them as separate variables in their own right.

Exercise 6.3

This exercise requires that you generate a set of artificial data to check on the implications of adding irrelevant variables to a model. Start with the assumption that the correct specification involves a simple regression model: $Y = 10 + 0.6 X_2 + \epsilon$. Set your sample size equal to 30, and generate, respectively, X_2 as a normally distributed variable with mean 10 and variance 25, and ϵ as a normally distributed error term with mean 0 and variance 16. The Y values are then obtained from the postulated regression model. Next, generate two more variables, X_3 and X_4, which, by construction, bear no relation to Y whatsoever. To do this, generate X_3 as a normally distributed random variable with mean 5 and variance 16, while X_4 has mean 15 and variance 36. Given these artificial data, regress (a) Y on X_2, and (b) Y on X_2, X_3 and X_4. You know that, by design, the latter regression carries a lot of extra baggage due to the inclusion of two irrelevant variables. Carefully check how the introduction of irrelevant variables affects the standard errors and coefficient estimates of the regression coefficient of the relevant variable. What do you conclude about the effect of including irrelevant variables on the precision of the estimates of the relevant variable?

Conclusion

This section discussed the implications of omitting relevant variables or adding irrelevant ones in terms of bias and precision of regression results. The resulting message is quite complicated. On the one hand, it is important that we take seriously the implications of omitting a relevant variable because it can lead to misleading conclusions as a result of the bias it introduces. But, on the other hand, with collinear variables, adding regressors to a model has a cost in term of the precision of our estimates due to the variance inflation factor of the collinear regressor. If a regressor matters a great deal, the gain obtained by adding it far outweighs the cost of omitting it from the regression. The question of including regressors which are relevant but less vital in terms of their effect on the dependent variable is more tricky: the gain in the reduction in bias needs to be balanced against the loss in precision, particularly when the sample size is relatively small. The presence of rival proxy variables often amplifies the problem. Irrelevant variables merely blur the picture, but we do not always know which variables are irrelevant. The task of variable selection, therefore, is quite daunting. Let us now see how hypothesis testing can help once we have decided upon a set of variables to include in our general model.

6.4   TESTING ZERO RESTRICTIONS

It is a poor strategy to start with a regression which only includes a few variables of direct interest and sets aside other variables which also matter. In empirical research we cannot assume that other things are equal and, hence, we cannot set aside important variables merely because they are not of immediate interest to us. Nor can we discard variables for which there are strong reasons to include them, although we may doubt whether they matter a great deal. If you doubt whether one or more of such variables should be added to a model along with the regressors already included, the best strategy is to include them right from the start. Indeed, if we begin by estimating the simpler model which does not include the doubtful variables, our subsequent testing will not tell us whether or not the model is correctly specified. The *t*-statistics, for example, are calculated on the assumption that the model is correct and, therefore they cannot help us to discover if in fact it is not. As we saw above, Griffin found a strong and significant negative statistical relationship between aid and savings. But his results cannot tell us whether his model is, in fact, correctly specified. To see whether a simpler model is valid, therefore, it is preferable to start with the general model and try to see which variables may be dropped through formal hypothesis testing. How do we do this?

Suppose, as in the previous section, we have a model with two regressors:

$$Y_i = \beta_1 + \beta_2 X_{2i} + \beta_3 X_{3i} + \epsilon_i \qquad (6.19)$$

but we doubt whether X_3 affects Y. That is, we have good reasons to believe the model to be:

$$Y_i = \beta_1 + \beta_2 X_{2i} + \epsilon'_i \qquad (6.20)$$

obtained by imposing a linear restriction on the general model: namely, $\beta_3 = 0$. Hence, omitting a variable results from imposing a zero restriction on its coefficient in the general, unrestricted model. Hypothesis testing then involves that we test the hypothesis H_0: $\beta_3 = 0$ against the H_1: $\beta_3 \neq 0$. In this case, you already know how to do this with the t-test. However, here we shall introduce you to the F-test which is more versatile in its use.

The *F*-test

The F-test is a powerful tool in specification testing since it enables us to test a whole range of linear restrictions. The versatility of the F-test, unlike the t-test, is due to the fact that it does not rely on the standard errors of individual coefficients, but operates on the residual sums of squares of the regression as a whole. In other words, the F-test checks whether the imposition of a linear restriction on a model significantly increases its residual sums of squares. To do this, the F-statistic takes account of the degrees of freedom of, respectively, the unrestricted (i.e. without imposing the restriction) and restricted versions of the model. The general formula for the F-test is as follows:

$$F_{(m,n-k_U)} = \frac{RSS_R - RSS_U}{RSS_U} \frac{n - k_U}{m} \qquad (6.21)$$

where $RSS_{U,R}$ = the residual sums of squares of, respectively, the unrestricted and the restricted model estimations; n = sample size; k_U = number of estimated coefficients in the unrestricted model; m = number of linear restrictions imposed on the model.

The different parts of this formula need some explanation. Note that if we add one or more regressors to an equation, the RSS cannot possibly increase. If the added variable has any explanatory power at all, it will reduce the RSS. Consequently, dropping one or more variables from a model will increase the RSS (unless the estimated slope coefficients of the deleted variables are exactly equal to zero). More generally, the imposition of a linear restriction on the model can never reduce the RSS when the restricted model is estimated. The numerator of the first term in the formula shows the difference between these two residual sums of squares, and dividing this by RSS_U gives the proportional increase in the RSS from imposing the restriction. How big does an increase have to be to make it significant?

Box 6.2   The *F*-distribution

The *F*-distribution is the distribution of a ratio of two independent chi-square variables (say, *W* and *Z*), each divided by their own degrees of freedom (say, v_1 and v_2). In turn, a chi-square distribution with v degrees of freedom is the sum of squares of v independent random variables with a standard normal distribution. Hence:

$$F = \frac{W/v_1}{Z/v_2}$$

follows an *F*-distribution with v_1 and v_2 degrees of freedom (of, respectively, the numerator and the denominator).

Fortunately, it is easy to test whether or not the increase in the *RSS* caused by imposing the restrictions is significant, since if we divide the numerator and denominator of the first term by their respective degrees of freedom the resulting statistic follows an *F*-distribution (see Box 6.1) under the assumption of the null hypothesis. As you know from Chapter 5, the degrees of freedom for RSS_U is $(n - k_U)$. Similarly, the degrees of freedom of RSS_R is $(n - k_R)$ since it contains fewer coefficients to estimate.

Therefore, the degrees of freedom of the difference term, ($RSS_R - RSS_U$), is given by:

$$(n - k_R) - (n - k_U) = k_U - k_R = m \tag{6.22}$$

and, hence, the increase in the residual sums of squares as a result of imposing *m* zero restrictions on the model will have *m* degrees of freedom. More generally, if we impose *m* linear restrictions on the model, whatever their form, the increase in the residual sum of squares will have *m* degrees of freedom since the imposition of the restrictions will reduce the number of coefficients in the model by that number. The resulting *F*-statistic is distributed with $m, n - k_U$ degrees of freedom.

Exercise 6.3

If the restrictions we impose on a model concern dropping one or more explanatory variables, both the restricted and unrestricted versions of the model will feature the same dependent variable. Now, given that $R^2 = ESS/TSS = (1 - RSS/TSS)$ show how the *F*-test in equation 6.16 can be re-expressed using R^2s rather than *RSS*s of the restricted and unrestricted regressions. To do this, express *RSS* as a function of *TSS* and the R^2, and substitute this solution into equation (6.21).

If you completed exercise 6.3, you will have found that the F-test can also be formulated as:

$$F_{(m,n-k_U)} = \frac{R_U^2 - R_R^2}{1 - R_U^2} \frac{n - k_U}{m} \tag{6.23}$$

Note that in the R^2 version of the F-test, it is the statistic of the unrestricted model which appears first in the numerator. This is what we would expect, since R_U^2 will be greater than R_R^2. Note that expression (6.21) is generally applicable, whatever the form of linear restrictions we impose on the model, while (6.23) can only be used if both the restricted and unrestricted version of the model feature the same dependent variable.

Dropping a regressor from the model: the F-test and t-test compared

But let us now return to our example in section 6.2 and test formally whether the variable $1/Y$ can be dropped from the model. We already have all the information we require to apply the F-test to Griffin's restriction imposed on the 'correct' savings model. Griffin imposed the restriction that $\beta_3 = 0$, and, hence, $k_U = 3$ and $k_R = 2$, so that $m = 1$. The sample size, n, is 66 and we have $RSS_R = 10{,}358$ and $RSS_U = 6{,}637$. The restricted RSS is indeed considerably greater than the unrestricted. But is the difference significant? We test this with the F-test:

$$F_{(1,63)} = \frac{10{,}358 - 6{,}637}{6{,}637} \frac{66 - 3}{1} = 35.3$$

This calculated figure compares with a critical value of just under 4.0 at the 5 per cent level. Since the calculated value is greater than the critical value, we can reject the null that $\beta_3 = 0$, in favour of the alternate hypothesis that it is non-zero: Griffin's restriction is invalid. We leave it to you to verify that the R^2 version of the F-test will yield the same result.

You may think that all this is much ado about nothing. If we wish to test the null hypothesis that $\beta_3 = 0$, why not just look at the t-statistic? As can be calculated from the results in equation (6.7), $t = 5.92$, and, hence, we reject the null hypothesis at the 5 per cent significance level. In this case, the t-test is indeed easier, but it is only valid as a test of a single zero restriction. If we want to impose two or more zero restrictions, we can no longer rely on separate t-tests, but we must use an F-test. In other words, we cannot test the hypothesis that two or more coefficients in a multiple regression are both zero by looking at their respective t-statistics; we must do a joint test with the F-test. The reason that combining individual t-tests is insufficient to test whether we can drop two or more variables from a model is because, in general, the sampling distributions of these coefficients are not independent of one another: in the three-variable case, for example, as shown in equation (5.29), the covariance of the least squares slope coefficients is generally not zero, unless the corresponding regressors are orthogonal. The knowledge that one coefficient is zero, therefore, will generally affect the probability of the other being zero as well, and hence a joint test is required.

If our restriction involves dropping only one variable, it does not matter whether we use the t- or F-tests: both tests are equivalent. In fact, it can be shown that $t^2 = F$. In our example $t^2 = 5.92^2 = 35.1$, which, allowing for rounding errors, is acceptably close to the calculated F-statistic of 35.3. But, to repeat, if we wish to restrict more than one variable, we must apply the F-test.

Testing several zero restrictions at once

A recurrent debate among macroeconomists is whether government expenditures (particularly government investment) increase or decrease private investment: i.e. crowding in versus crowding out. We explore this question for the case of Sri Lanka, using the data file SRINA. To start with, Figure 6.1 gives the scatter plot of private investment (I_p) against government investment (I_g) along with the fitted line which is (t-statistics in parentheses):

$$\hat{I}_p = -648 + 1.04I_g \quad R^2 = 0.723 \qquad (6.24)$$
$$\phantom{\hat{I}_p = }(-0.24) \quad (6.84)$$

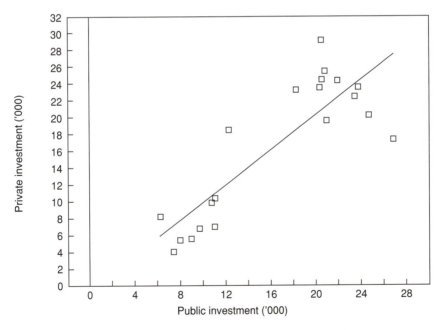

Figure 6.1 Private versus public investment: Sri Lanka, 1970–89

At first sight, it appears that, over this period, there was strong crowding-in: each rupee increase in public investment led to an equivalent rise in private investment (the coefficient of 1.04 is insignificantly different from one).

But not so fast. We saw above that if we omit any important variables from our equation, then our parameter estimates will be biased. Surely private investment depends on variables other than the level of government investment? Our data set includes two further potential determinants of private investment: the real interest rate (r) and imports (M).

The importance of imported capital to sustaining investment in developing countries underpins the foreign exchange constraint in the two-gap model (see Chenery and Strout, 1966): higher levels of imports should permit higher levels of investment. In Sri Lanka prior to 1977 this constraint was compounded by quantity restrictions on imports. We use here total imports, although it may be desirable to exclude consumer imports from this figure.

The role of the interest rate is more ambiguous. In the standard investment function a higher real interest rate (cost of capital) results in reduced investment: this view motivated subsidised interest rates in favoured sectors in many developing countries for many years. The contrary position, associated with McKinnon (1973) and Shaw (1973) (see also Fry, 1988), is that investment is constrained by lack of investible resources, savings being discouraged by low interest rates: higher interest rates thus lead to higher investment. Which position is correct is an empirical matter, so the sign on the real interest rate in our regression is also of interest.

We thus formulate the general model as follows:

$$I_{p,t} = \beta_0 + \beta_1 I_{g,t} + \beta_2 M_t + \beta_3 r_t + \epsilon_t \tag{6.25}$$

which yields the following estimates:

$$\hat{I}_p = -12{,}147 - 0.33 I_g + 0.61 M - 17{,}970 r$$
$$\quad\;\; (-4.31)\;\; (-1.17)\quad (5.26)\quad (-1.54) \tag{6.26}$$

$$R^2 = 0.898 \quad RSS = 1.33 \times 10^8$$

We can see that the coefficient on I_g is now insignificantly different from zero (at the 5 per cent level): there is neither crowding in or out, a result which contrasts markedly with our earlier conclusion from the simple regression.

Which equation should we use to decide on the relationship between public and private investment? Clearly, equation (6.25) is a general model of which the simple regression is a restricted version. If these restrictions are valid we may proceed to test the crowding-in hypothesis on the basis of the simple regression estimates. But if the restrictions are invalid then these estimates may not be used. What are these restrictions and how do we test them? The simple regression omits the variables M and r; that is, it imposes the restriction: $\beta_2 = \beta_3 = 0$. We may use an F-test to test whether or not both these restrictions are jointly valid. First we lay out the hypothesis being tested, as follows:

$$H_0: \beta_2 = \beta_3 = 0$$
$$H_1: \text{at least one of the coefficients, } \beta_2 \text{ or } \beta_3, \text{ is non-zero}$$

The unrestricted equation is given by equation (6.25), so that $k_U = 4$, while the restricted version is the simple regression with $k_R = 2$. Therefore, $m = 2$ (as can be seen from H_0). Let us use the R^2 version of the F-test. To do so we make sure to specify the R^2 values up to three decimal places to avoid excessive rounding errors (which can be quite substantial). The F-statistic then becomes:

$$F_{(2,16)} = \frac{0.898 - 0.723}{1 - 0.898} \times \frac{16}{2} = 13.73$$

which compares with a critical value of 3.63 at the 5 per cent level. Therefore, we must reject the null hypothesis that the simple regression of private investment on public investment is a valid model of the determinants of private investment. We conclude that there appears to be neither crowding in nor crowding out in the Sri Lankan case. We shall return to this example, however, in section 6.7.

At this juncture, we should stress an important point. In both examples discussed above, Griffin's aid-savings relation and the crowding-in hypothesis, we started with a simpler model and then showed how the results changed dramatically when additional variables were introduced to the regression. This order of presentation was a pedagogical device to illustrate the importance of not jumping to conclusions on the basis of oversimplified regressions. If we had been presenting these regressions as results from research there would have been no call to report the simple regression results as they are statistically meaningless (though we may choose to report that we tested whether the simpler model were a valid restriction of the data and found it not to be so).

Restricting all the slope coefficients to zero: testing the significance of the R^2

We can also use the F-test to test whether all regressors can be dropped jointly from the regression. If this restriction is acceptable, then none of the variables matters in explaining the variation in the dependent variable. In this case, the test can best be done using the R^2 variant of the F-statistic. The reason is that a model without any explanatory variables apart from the constant term has an *ESS* equal to 0. Consequently, $R_R^2 = 0$, a result which reduces equation (6.23) to:

$$F_{(m,n-k_U)} = \frac{R_U^2}{1 - R_U^2} \frac{n - k_U}{m}$$

(6.27)

There is, however, generally no need to calculate this *F*-value since most software packages list its value as the *F*-statistic of the regression.

Exercise 6.4

With the results of exercise 6.1, formally test whether (a) both explanatory variables and (b) the price variable only can be dropped from the three-variable model. In the latter case, use both the *t*- and the F-tests and check the relation between them.

A word of warning: checking model assumptions

Before we engage in variable selection through testing downwards, however, we should always carefully investigate whether our starting point, the general model itself, reasonably satisfies the assumptions of classical normal regression. In other words, we should not take our general model for granted. The reason is that statistical inferences are only valid if the model assumptions are reasonably satisfied in practice. For this reason, we should always subject our general model to diagnostic

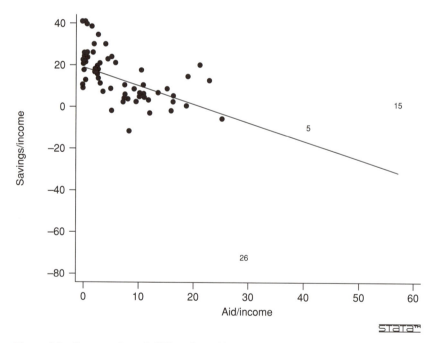

Figure 6.2   Scatter plot of *S/Y* against *A/Y*

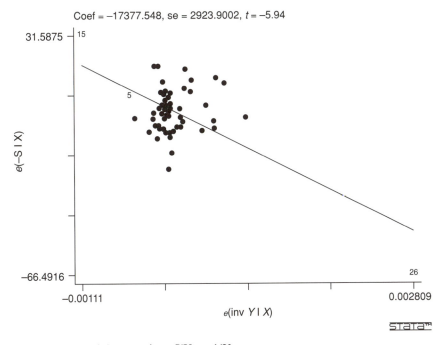

Figure 6.3 Partial regression: *S*/*Y* on 1/*Y*

misspecification checks and test. There is indeed a real danger that we may take our general model too easily for granted and jump straight into hypothesis testing. In fact, as you may have noticed, this is precisely what we did in the case of Griffin's hypothesis. But we never really checked whether his general model reasonably satisfies the assumptions of classical normal linear regression. We make such an analysis by looking at the various plots (scatter plots, box plots and residual plots).

How does Griffin's model fare? In fact, there are quite serious problems with the model due to the presence of influential points and outliers. A glance at the scatter plot of *S*/*Y* against *A*/*Y* in Figure 6.2 reveals that the simple regression of both variables is not a good fit at all. In fact, three data points – respectively, points 5, 15 and 26 – dominate the scene.

But our major concern is whether the assumptions of the general model as given by specification (6.6) and estimated in equation (6.7) are reasonably satisfied in practice. A simple scatter plot of *S*/*Y* on *A*/*Y* does not tell us how well the coefficients of the multiple regression are supported by the data. Figure 6.3 shows the partial regression plot for the slope coefficient of *I*/*Y* in the estimated general model. This plot reveals that the coefficient estimate of 1/*Y* is extremely shaky and depends essentially on two data points only! These happen to be points 15 and 26 which already proved troublesome in the simple scatter plot.

The implication of this discovery, however, is that our earlier *F*-test (or, for that matter, *t*-test) whether the variable 1/*Y* could be dropped from the general model rests upon very fragile foundations. Based on this test, we concluded that the slope coefficient of this variable was significantly different from zero, but we now see that the result we obtained is solely based on the position of two data points. In fact, if we remove these two points from the sample, the *t*-statistic of 1/*Y* becomes insignificant. The implication is, therefore, that the test we did earlier to see whether Griffin's general model could be simplified was largely meaningless. Given that the assumptions of classical normal linear least squares are clearly violated in this case, our estimations do not allow us to make meaningful inferences. The fact, however, that the removal of two data points render the coefficient of 1/*Y* insignificantly different from zero should not lead us to conclude that we might as well use the simpler model. A quick glance at Figure 6.2 shows that the simple regression is not better in terms of satisfying the assumptions of least squares.

Perhaps this comes as a bit of a surprise. But think how often we accept hypothesis tests presented in papers, articles or books at face value because we take it for granted that the assumptions of the model are satisfied. The problem is that often the authors may have done exactly the same, testing hypotheses based on the normality assumption without first checking whether this assumption prevails in practice. This type of hypothesis testing may look good on paper but, if the assumptions are not reasonably valid in practice, the result of the test is also not valid.

Exercise 6.5

Rework the example of Griffin's hypothesis and systematically check the assumptions of the model using diagnostic graphs, normality checks, studentised residuals and DFBETAs.

If you tried out studentised residuals and DFBETAs, you will have seen that they also confirm the presence of outliers and influence in the regression: the studentised residuals for data points 15 and 26 are, respectively, 2.3 and –6.73, and data point 26 gives a DFBETA value of –2.97 for the slope coefficient of 1/*Y*. These statistics, therefore, also confirm that outliers and influential points are prevalent and are likely to distort the inferences we make.

An important lesson we learn from this example is that we should never forget that the presence of serious outliers and influential points is a sign of misspecification. It tells us that the error term of the model still contains a lot of meaningful information which we have not as yet grasped. Jumping ahead into hypothesis testing without carefully checking the assumptions of the model is a poor strategy in data analysis. Superficially, it may look good on paper. But many of these inferences may prove worthless if you care to check your assumptions. Before drawing conclusions from a model make sure its foundations are sound so that you can assert them with some confidence.

In this section we have seen how to use an *F*-test as a means of testing zero restrictions, so we can test a specific model against a more general one. But the example we have just seen shows that you must also check the specification of the general model. If the 'general model' still has omitted variables then this problem will quite possibly show up in the residuals – possibly as influential points as in the example just discussed. But omitted variables can also produce problems of heteroscedasticity (see Chapter 7) and serial correlation (see Chapter 11). Hence a key message of this text is borne out here: always look at the residuals for clues as to possible misspecification.

6.5 TESTING NON-ZERO LINEAR RESTRICTIONS

Imposing zero restrictions on a model implies that we seek to drop one or more variables from the regression. Non-zero linear restrictions are of a different nature. Their purpose is not to drop a regressor, but to check whether one or more coefficients of the model obey some linear condition. Why would we do this? The best way to answer this is to consider a few examples.

A common example of such a non-zero restriction is to test for constant returns to scale in a Cobb–Douglas production function:

$$Q_i = AL_i^{\beta_2}K_i^{\beta_3}X_{3i}\epsilon'_i \tag{6.28}$$

where Q is output, K capital, L labour and ϵ' a multiplicative error term. OLS estimation requires linearisation of the equation by taking logs of both sides:

$$\ln Q_i = \beta_1 + \beta_2\ln L_i + \beta_3\ln K_i + \epsilon_i \tag{6.29}$$

where β_1 is the logarithm of A and ϵ the logarithm of ϵ'.

Now, suppose we want to test the hypothesis that there are indeed constant returns to scale, i.e. to test the null hypothesis that $\beta_2 + \beta_3 = 1$. This is a non-zero linear restriction. How do we impose this restriction on the model? To do this, re-write the null hypothesis as $\beta_2 = 1 - \beta_3$ and substitute this expression into the unrestricted model, as follows:

$$\ln Q_i = \beta_1 + (1 - \beta_3)\ln L_i + \beta_3\ln K_i + \epsilon_i \tag{6.30}$$
$$= \beta_1 + \ln L_i + \beta_3(\ln K_i - \ln L_i) + \epsilon_i$$

and, after rearranging terms, we get:

$$\ln(Q_i/L_i) = \ln\beta_1 + \beta_3\ln(K_i/L_i) + \epsilon_i \tag{6.31}$$

Take a good look at this restricted version of the model. Two things are noticeable. First, the restricted model now has only two coefficients

---

Box 6.3   Constant returns to scale

Constant returns to scale (CRS) means that an increase in all the factors of production by a factor m increases output by the same proportion. Thus if:

$$Q = AL^{\beta_2} K^{\beta_3}$$

then output with increased factors of production (Q') is given by

$$Q' = A(mL)^{\beta_2} (mK)^{\beta_3}$$

$$= Qm^{\beta_2 + \beta_3}$$

Thus $Q' = mQ$ (i.e. there are constant returns to scale) if $\beta_2 + \beta_3 = 1$. If $Q' < mQ$ there are decreasing returns to scale and increasing returns if $Q' > mQ$.

---

instead of three in the unrestricted version. The imposition of the linear restriction, therefore, has reduced the number of model parameters by one. Second, the dependent variable in the restricted model is different from that in the unrestricted model. The latter features the logarithm of output as the dependent variable; the former the logarithm of the output to labour ratio. Hence, if we test this restriction with real data we cannot use the R^2 variant of the F-test, but must use the RSS variant instead.

Exercise 6.6

The data file PRODFUN contains data from a developing country business survey covering two manufacturing sectors. Estimate specifications (6.29) and (6.31) using the data in this file, and formally test the hypothesis whether there are constant returns.

Exercise 6.7

Using the data set KRISHNAJI (food price and manufacturing demand in India), estimate equations (5.5) and (5.41), which differ inasmuch as the latter imposes the restriction of a unitary income elasticity on the demand for manufacturing goods: that is, $\beta_2 = 1$, which is a non-zero linear restriction. Note that the unrestricted (equation 5.5) and restricted (equation 5.41) versions of the model do not feature the same dependent variable.

1   Use (6.31) to calculate the F-statistic to test the restriction of a unitary elasticity.

2   Check what would happen if you had calculated the *F*-statistic with formula (6.23).

Another common example in economics which involves non-zero restrictions is the assumption of no money illusion in demand equations (i.e. demand depends on real not nominal income). We came across such a case in the previous chapter when discussing the demand for manufacturing goods in India. A further example involves testing for parameter stability across different samples. This is the issue we shall turn to in the next section.

Exercise 6.8

Khan and Reinhart (1990) argue that the productivities of public and private capital are different, the latter being more productive. To test this they first regressed growth (y) on aggregate investment (I), growth of the labour force (L), growth of exports (X) and a constant. They then repeated the regression with investment desegregated into public (I_g) and private (I_p). Using cross-section data for 24 countries they achieved the following results:

$$\hat{y} = 1.085 + 0.119I + 0.427L + 0.212X \qquad\qquad R^2 = 0.660$$
$$\quad\;\;(0.81)\quad(2.36)\quad\;(1.33)\quad\;\;(4.97)$$

$$\hat{y} = 2.145 + 0.158I_p - 0.108I_g + 0.573L + 0.163X \quad R^2 = 0.737$$
$$\quad\;\;(1.66)\quad(3.27)\quad\quad(1.02)\quad\quad(1.94)\quad\;\;(3.75)$$

Show how you would use these results to test the hypothesis that the productivities of public and private capital are the same.

6.6   TESTS OF PARAMETER STABILITY

When we run a regression with sample data we assume that the data are sampled from the same population to which the population regression line applies. But what if our sample lumps together data which do not really belong together inasmuch as the same model does not apply to them? It is often useful, therefore, to test for parameter instability across different samples before we decide to pool them. Once more, this test can be done with the help of linear restrictions.

Pooling data

In Chapter 4, we discussed the relation between using the data file SOCECON. Our model, therefore, is as follows

$$LE_i = \beta_1 + \beta_2 \log(Y_i) + \epsilon_{1i} \qquad\qquad (6.32)$$

This model assumes, however, that the values of β_1 and β_2 are the same

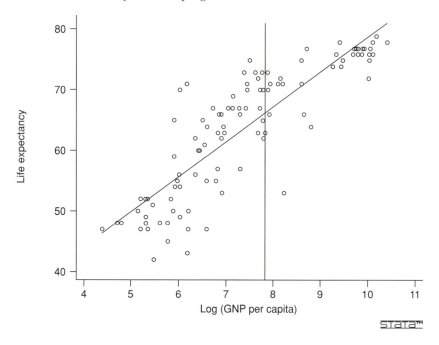

Figure 6.4 Scatter plot of life expectancy against log(GNP$_c$)

for all observations. Figure 6.4, which depicts the scatter plot of the data using all available countries, shows there are actually two sets of relationships: the scatter is steeper on the left-hand side (left of the vertical line indicating incomes below $2,500), and flatter for countries with higher incomes. This result is not very surprising, since there is a physiological limit on life expectancy.

The result of these underlying data patterns is that if we fit the regression line to all observations, it does not capture the relationship at all well, as is clear from Figure 6.4. The resulting regression line is as follows:

$$\hat{LE}_i = 20.96 + 5.80\log(Y_i) \quad R^2 = 0.75 \tag{6.33}$$
$$(2.41) \ (0.32) \qquad RSS = 3125.8$$

Looking at the scatter suggests that the relationship between income and life expectancy is different for high and low income countries. That is, we should have two separate regressions:

$$\text{For } Y_i \leq \$2,500 \quad LE_i = \alpha_1 + \alpha_2 \log(Y_i) + \epsilon_{2i} \tag{6.34}$$

$$\text{For } Y_i > \$2,500 \quad LE_i = \gamma_1 + \gamma_2 \log(Y_i) + \epsilon_{3i} \tag{6.35}$$

Running a single regression means that we pool the data: that is, we assume an identical intercept and slope for the two sets of observations.

More formally this can be stated as the null hypothesis:

$$H_0: \alpha_1 = \gamma_1 \quad \alpha_2 = \gamma_2$$

where the alternate hypothesis entails that at least one of these equalities does not hold.

This null hypothesis may be tested by the application of the usual F-test. In this case the unrestricted model consists of the two separate equations (6.34) and (6.35). Hence, the unrestricted residual sum of squares, RSS_U, is the sum of the residual sums of squares from the two regressions: i.e. $RSS_U = RSS_1 + RSS_2$, where RSS_1 and RSS_2 are the residual sums of squares from the two sub-sample regressions. This version of the F-test is sometimes called the 'Chow test' (or first Chow test). The R^2 version of the F-test cannot be used for testing parameter stability.

The number of regressors in the unrestricted model, k_U, is the total number of regressors in the two equations: in this case $k_U = 4$. The sub-sample regressions are:

$$\text{For } Y_i \leqslant \$2,500 \; \hat{LR}_i \; = \; 7.96 \; + \; 7.89 \; \log(Y_i) \qquad R^2 = 0.63 \qquad (6.36)$$
$$(4.64) \quad (0.72) \qquad RSS_1 = 2217.6$$

$$\text{For } Y_i > \$2,500 \; \hat{LE}_i = \; 37.3 \; + \; 3.94 \; \log(Y_i) \qquad R^2 = 0.42 \qquad (6.37)$$
$$(7.25) \quad (0.78) \qquad RSS_2 = 529.0$$

Hence, we calculate $RSS_U = 2{,}217.6 + 529.0 = 2{,}746.6$. Consequently, the F-statistic may be calculated as:

$$F_{(2,106)} = \frac{3125.8 - 2746.6}{2746.6} , \; \frac{111 - 4}{2} = 7.39 \qquad (6.38)$$

This calculated value is much greater than the critical value of a little over 3.07 at the 5 per cent level, so we reject the null hypothesis that it is valid to pool our data.

Testing for the validity of pooling is often not done in published research. Yet a glance at the scatter plot shows in this case that it is improbable that the data may be pooled for a linear regression. This is thus yet a further example where preliminary data analysis – such as looking at the scatter plots – can yield useful information about specification (and warnings about possible misspecification) of your model. What we can do once the data has rejected pooling is discussed in section 6.7 below. First we show how a similar test may be used to test parameter stability across time.

Exercise 6.9

White (1992) presents results listed in Table 6.1 for the regression of real GDP growth on a constant, savings, exports, grants and other capital inflows for three developing regions: Africa, Asia, and Latin America and

Table 6.1　Results of growth regressions

	Savings	Exports	Grants	Capital inflows	RSS
Africa	0.08	–0.02	0.15	0.08	26,401
	(0.02)	(0.02)	(0.03)	(0.08)	
Asia	0.09	0.03	0.07	–0.17	3,150
	(0.03)	(0.01)	(0.07)	(0.08)	
LAC	0.18	–0.09	0.08	–0.10	10,290
	(0.03)	(0.02)	(0.04)	(0.11)	
All regions	0.11	–0.03	0.13	0.01	41,717
	(0.11)	(0.01)	(0.02)	(0.05)	

Note:　Absolute values of *t*-statistics are listed within brackets.

Caribbean. He also gives the results from pooling the data across the three regions. What assumption is being made in running the pooled regression? Test this assumption by means of an *F*-test, stating clearly your null hypothesis. (The size of the pooled sample is 1,334 observations.)

Parameter stability across time

If we estimate an equation using time-series data we assume that the parameters of the model remain constant over time. That is, we are pooling data from different time periods. Whether or not this is a valid procedure may be tested in precisely the same way as we tested pooling data above.

A well-known example of a time-series regression is that of the terms of trade of developing countries against time. Prebisch and Singer maintained that these were declining over time. There are a number of theoretical and measurement issues that are important to this debate which we shall not discuss here (see Sproas, 1980; Sapsford, 1985; Grilli and Yang, 1988). The data file TOT gives the ratio of an index of the price of non-fuel primary commodities to that of an index of export unit values for manufactured goods from industrial countries. A log-linear regression using these data gives the following result (standard errors in parentheses) for the period from 1950 to 1986:

$$\widehat{\ln(TOT)}_i = 0.163 - 0.007t \qquad R^2 = 0.31 \qquad (6.39)$$
$$(0.039)\ (0.002)$$

The R^2 of 0.31 is not particularly good. A glance at Figure 6.5 tells us why this poor result is obtained. The data appears to have a break in the early 1970s. If there are good reasons to believe why a break would occur at that point, we can refer to it as a structural break. If, however, there are no good reasons for a break in the trend, the relevant conclusion is that the pattern we seek to impose on the data is not an adequate fit. In this case, there are good reasons why the trend would have changed around this time: the oil price boom in 1973–4 was accompanied by a

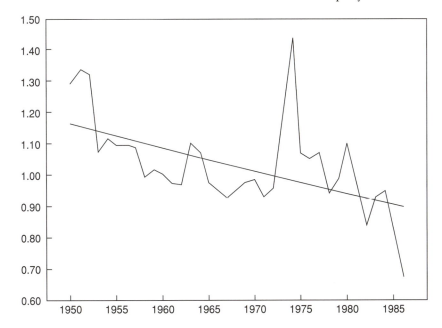

Figure 6.5 Terms of trade of developing countries over time

marked increase in the prices of many other primary commodities. We really should have looked at the graph of the data before estimating equation (6.39), since it seems that we need two equations, not one. Let us split the sample into two sub-samples, 1950–72 and 1973–86.

The model therefore becomes:

$$\ln(TOT)_t = \alpha_1 + \alpha_2 t + \epsilon_{1t} \quad \text{for } t = 1950 \ldots 1972 \tag{6.40}$$

$$\ln(TOT)_t = \gamma_1 + \gamma_2 t + \epsilon_{2t} \quad \text{for } t = 1973 \ldots 1986 \tag{6.41}$$

The single regression we estimated above (equation (6.39)) imposes the restriction on the data that:

$$H_0: \alpha_1 = \gamma_1 \quad \alpha_2 = \gamma_2$$

This restriction is exactly the same as the one we encountered in testing the validity of pooling the data. And so, as before, we test this null (against the alternative that at least one of the equalities does not hold) with the *F*-test where the unrestricted residual sum of squares is the sum of the *RSS*s from the two sub-sample regressions. Estimating equations (6.40) and (6.41) gives the two residual sums of squares as:

$$RSS_1 = 0.083 \quad RSS_2 = 0.121$$

These results may be used to derive a calculated *F*-statistic of 22.0, which is greater than the critical value of $F_{(2,33)}$ (just under 3.32) at the 5 per cent level, so we reject the null hypothesis that it is valid to pool the data.

Chow's second test and predictive failure

It may happen that the supposed structural break occurs late in the time series. Especially where we have a large number of regressors it is possible that we have too few observations to estimate the equation for the second sub-sample. In this case, Chow suggested an alternative test (also based on the F-statistic) which is:

$$F_{(m,n-k_R-m)} = \frac{RSS_R - RSS_1}{RSS_1} \frac{n - k_R - m}{m} \tag{6.42}$$

where RSS_R is, as before, the RSS from the estimated equation for the whole sample period, RSS_1 is the RSS from the estimated equation for the first sub-sample, k_R is the number of regressors (including the constant) in the restricted equation, and n is the number of observations in the full sample. That is all as before. However, m is no longer the number of restrictions, but is now the number of omitted observations (i.e. the number of observations is the smaller of the two sub-samples). The null hypothesis is as before.

Chow's second test can be used as a predictive failure test and is a very useful diagnostic tool in testing for misspecification. In fact, in small samples it is often not so difficult to find a reasonably good fit. More demanding than getting a high R^2 is to be able to predict out-of-sample values. If the model really is the data generation process, then it should be able to do this (subject to error fluctuations). A useful test, therefore, is to withhold observations (one or two will suffice, though up to four is preferred if possible) from the data set when estimating and then compare actual with predicted values. The relevant test statistic is the F-statistic calculated by the formula in equation (6.42).

Whilst the discussion of Chow's second test has been illustrated in the context of time-series data, there is no reason why it cannot be applied to cross-section data. In the latter case, make sure that the observations to be omitted appear at the end of the data file.

Exercise 6.10

Repeat the test for a structural break in the developing country terms of trade putting the break at 1974, rather than at 1973 as is done in the text. Which is the more appropriate break point?

Exercise 6.11

Population figures for Kenya for the period 1968–88 were regressed on a constant and a trend. The residual sum of squares (RSS) from this regression was 8.77. The same equation was re-estimated for the sub-sample 1968–85, from which the *RSS* was 3.89. Use a Chow test to determine the stability of the parameters.

6.7 THE USE OF DUMMY VARIABLES

Take another look at our regression of the terms of trade against time. We found that they declined at 0.7 per cent per annum over the full sample period, yet we established that the parameters are not stable. As we can see from Figure 6.5, the effect of the jump in 1973–74 is to 'level out' the fitted line – the slope coefficients from the two sub-samples suggested a much more rapid decline. Can we model this structural break in the early 1970s in a single equation? Yes, we can. Dummy variables allow us to vary either the intercept or slope coefficients between sub-samples. Let us first illustrate the use of intercept dummies.

Intercept dummies

An intercept dummy is a variable which takes the value one for a specific sub-sample and zero for the rest of the sample. In our example on the decline in the terms of trade, we shall distinguish the periods 1950–72, for which years the variable *DUM* takes the value zero, and the remaining years (1973–86) for which it takes the value 1. The regression equation becomes:

$$\ln(TOT)_t = \beta_1 + \beta_2 DUM_t + \beta_3 t + \epsilon_t \tag{6.43}$$

Note that *DUM* must also be given a time subscript since it is a variable. Now, when $DUM = 0$, the estimated regression line is given by:

$$\widehat{\ln(TOT)}_t = \beta_1 + \beta_3 t \tag{6.44}$$

But when $DUM = 1$, the line is:

$$\widehat{\ln(TOT)}_t = (b_1 + b_2) + b_3 t \tag{6.45}$$

The coefficient b_2 is the differential intercept – that is, the shift in the intercept for those observations for which $DUM = 1$. Do not interpret b_2 as the intercept for the second sub-sample – this is not what it is. The intercept for the second sub-sample is given by $b_1 + b_2$.

Estimating equation (6.43) using the terms of trade data set yields:

$$\widehat{\ln(TOT)}_t = 0.254 + 0.262 DUM - 0.017t \qquad R^2 = 0.57 \tag{6.46}$$
$$\phantom{\widehat{\ln(TOT)}_t =} (0.038) \ (0.059) \qquad (0.003) \qquad RSS = 0.299$$

The slope coefficient now shows an annual deterioration in the terms of trade of 1.7 per cent – two and a half times more than before! Excluding the intercept dummy resulted in omitted variable bias, giving an underestimate

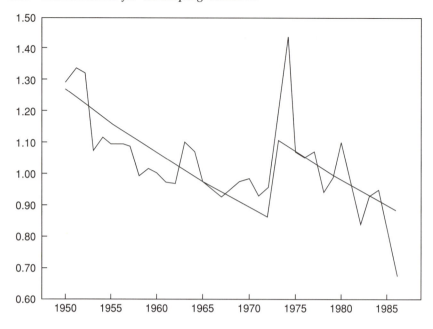

Figure 6.6   Fitted line of terms of trade with intercept dummy

of the true slope coefficient. Figure 6.6 shows the fitted lines from equation (6.46). You will have observed that we have here assumed that the slope is constant between sub-samples, but that the intercept can vary. So we are still imposing a restriction on the unrestricted (two-equation) model. It is left to you as an exercise to test this restriction. You will find that it is not valid.

The intercept dummy interpretation of a studentised residual

What happens if we construct a dummy such that it selects one only observation in the sample? Hence, the dummy will equal 1 for this data point only and zero otherwise. This is a very special case of an intercept dummy: we divide the data into two sub-samples, one of which has only one observation in it. Why do we do this?

If we include this type of one-point dummy in a regression, the residual for this data point will be zero. The reason is simple: the estimated coefficient of the dummy variable will make sure that the point 'fits' the regression. Consequently, this data point will not play any role in determining the other coefficients of the model. Hence, using a one-point dummy is equivalent to deleting the point from the regression and estimating the coefficients of the model with the remaining data points. The slope coefficient of the dummy is nothing else but the vertical deviation of its data point from the regression line estimated with the other points in the sample. The

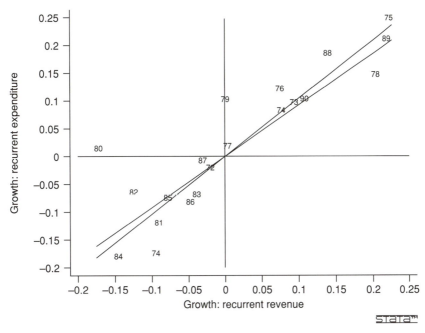

Figure 6.7 Regressions of *RE* on *RR* with and without data point 1980

Table 6.2 Regressions with and without intercept dummy for 1980 (*t*-statistics in brackets)

RE on	RR	D80	RSS	R^2
1 All observations	0.934 (8.405)	–	0.0667	0.788
2 All except1980	1.047 (12.05)	–	0.0347	0.890
3 All observations	1.047 (12.05)	0.189 (4.077)	0.0347	0.890

estimated coefficient of the dummy, therefore, is a deletion residual.

The studentised residual then is nothing else but the *t*-statistic of the coefficient of the dummy variable. It tests whether the distance of the data point from the regression line estimated without including it is significantly different from zero. If so, it would indicate that this data point might be an outlier. This explains why, in Chapter 4, we hinted that studentised residuals were in fact *t*-statistics.

To illustrate the point, consider once more our example in Chapter 4 on the relation between the growth rates of recurrent expenditures (*RE*) and revenues (*RR*) in Tanzania, 1970–90. There we noted that the year 1980 was quite exceptional because it signalled the onset of a major economic crisis. In this year, the Tanzanian government appears to have been caught unaware when trying to maintain government expenditures while its revenues collapsed as a result of the crisis. Consequently, as we saw in Chapter 4, the data point for 1980 (corresponding to the growth rates from 1979 to 1980) was both an outlier and an influential point. Let us see how we can obtain the standardised residual for this data point using an intercept dummy, D80. Hence, D80 = 1 in 1980, and zero otherwise. Table 6.2 gives us three regressions, all without constant term: (a) *RE* on *RR* with all data points; (b) RE on RR with all data points except 1980; and (c) *RE* on *RR* and D80. Figure 6.7 shows the scatter plot along with the regression lines corresponding to regressions 1 and 2 in Table 6.2.

Take a careful look at this table. First, the second and third regression have identical values for, respectively, the slope coefficients of *RR*, its *t*-values, the *RSS*s (residual sums of squares), and the R^2s. This shows that including an intercept dummy which selects one observation from the sample is equivalent to running the regression which does not include the data point. Hence, the slope coefficient of the dummy in the third regression ensures that the residual for 1980 equals zero. Consequently, the slope of the dummy measures the vertical distance of the data point for 1980 with respect to the regression line estimated without including 1980 in the sample (regression 2). The *t*-statistic for this slope coefficient is the studentised residual of the simple regression of *RE* on *RR*. If this slope turns out to be significantly different from zero, it indicates that the corresponding data point (1980) is an outlier. In this case, the *t*-value of 4.077 is well above the critical limit and, hence, leads us to reject the hypothesis that the population value of the dummy's slope equals zero. The test confirms that 1980 was an exceptional year inasmuch as it signalled the onset of Tanzania's economic crisis of the early 1980s.

Note that the data point for 1980 is not just an outlier but also exerts some influence on the regression line. This explains why the slope coefficient in regression 1 is less than that in the other two regressions. As you can see from the graph, the point 1980 pulls the line slightly in its direction. Table 6.2 also shows that the *RSS* of regression 1 is nearly double the *RSS* of the other regressions which shows that the outlier has quite a heavy weight in the residual sum of squares.

In this example we expected beforehand that the data point for 1980 might give us problems and, hence, we formally tested this by including the intercept dummy for that particular year. But in many applications we do not have any *a priori* reason to believe that any point is an outlier. Generally, we compute all studentised residuals and see if any of them is exceptional. In this case, however, we cannot just use the normal 5 per cent significance level to pick the critical value of the *t*-statistic. Why not?

The reason is quite simple, but not immediately obvious. Take an example. If the probability of success in any given trial of a game is 5 per cent, the probability of encountering one success in ten successive (independent) trials will not be 5 per cent. Similarly, if we seek to test whether one and only one data point is an outlier, the 5 per cent significance level is appropriate for the corresponding *t*-test. But if we look at a string of *n* residuals at once to test whether there is an outlier among them, we cannot use the critical *t*-value corresponding to a significance level of 5 per cent on a single trial. Indeed, in this case, *n* different *t*-tests are essentially being made. These multiple tests cannot be treated formally as if they were separate tests, but instead, in order to end up with a significance level of no larger than 5 per cent for the test that one of these residuals is an outlier, we need to use the *t*-test with a significance level of 5 per cent divided by *n*, the sample size (Myers, 1990: 225). In our example, the relevant critical *t*-value is 4.29 for 20 observations with two coefficients in the model. Given the small probabilities involved, most tabulations of *t*-tables do not give us critical values to do this type of outlier test (see, however, Myers, 1990: Appendix C). However, you should not worry if you do not have access to a detailed *t*-table. In Chapter 4 we argued that studentised residuals can best be used as exploratory diagnostic tools. The point we want to make here is that you should not use the normal 5 per cent critical *t*-values to pick out seemingly large studentised residuals since there is nothing exceptional about having a relatively large value now and then in a bigger sample.

Slope dummies

An intercept dummy allows us to vary the intercept across sub-samples while keeping the slopes of the regressors constant. But at times we want to be able to vary the slopes. This requires the use of slope dummies. To see how we can construct these, let us continue for a while with this example of the simple regression of Tanzania recurrent expenditures against recurrent revenues. Recall that, in Chapter 4, the exploratory band regression of *RE* on *RR* noted a mild non-linearity of the regression curve. More particularly, with the exception of the outlier 1980, it appeared as if the slope coefficient was lower when the growth rates in recurrent revenues were positive than when they were negative. Let us see how we can use a slope dummy to check whether this is true.

To obtain a slope dummy, we first construct an intercept dummy, *DNEG*, such that *DNEG* = 1 if *RR* < 0 , and 0 otherwise. The dummy DNEG, therefore, picks out all observations for which the growth in recurrent revenue was negative. The slope dummy, *DRR*, is then obtained as follows: *DRR* = *DNEG.RR*. Hence, *DRR* = *RR* when *RR* < 0; otherwise, *DRR* = 0. We now formulate our regression model as follows:

$$RE_t = \beta_2 RR_t + \beta_3 DRR_t + \beta_4 D80_t + \epsilon \qquad (6.47)$$

As before, the regression model features no constant term. Now, if *DRR* = 0, the slope of the regression will be β_2, but if *DRR* = *RR* (when *RR* < 0), the slope coefficient will be ($\beta_2 + \beta_3$).

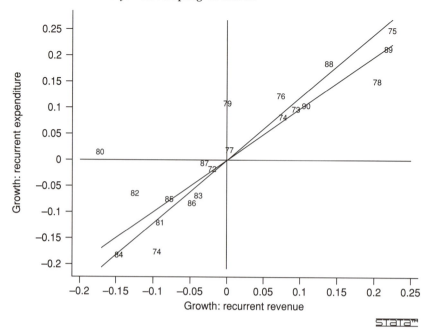

Figure 6.8 Scatter plot of expenditure against revenue

Estimating equation (6.48) yields the following results (*t*-statistics in brackets):

$$\hat{RE}_t = 0.994RR_t + 0.217DRR_t + 0.217D80_t \; ; \; R^2 = 0.90 \qquad (6.48)$$
$$\quad (9.99) \qquad (1.08) \qquad\quad (4.1) \qquad\quad RSS = 0.0325$$

which yield two regressions, both through the origin (i.e. they have the same intercept), as shown in Figure 6.8. As you can see, the slope of the line when *RR* is positive is 0.993 (about 1), while it is (0.993 + 0.217), or 1.21, when *RR* is negative. Hence, at first sight, there is a marked difference between both slopes. However, in Chapter 4 we suggested that this kink in the regression line did not appear to invalidate the linearity assumption for the data as a whole (with the exception of the outlier year 1980). Does our regression confirm this view?

The advantage of using dummies is that we can use the familiar *t*-test to see whether the same regression applies to all data points or not. In this case, the *t*-value of the slope dummy is 1.08, a value which does not lead us to accept the alternative hypothesis that the population coefficient of slope dummy is significantly different from 0. Hence, there appears to be no reason to split the sample for negative and positive values of the growth rate of government revenue. The overall regression (excluding the outlier year 1980) through the origin appears to be a good enough summary of the data.

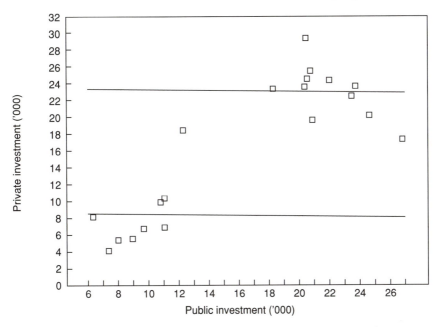

Figure 6.9 Sri Lankan investment function with intercept dummy only

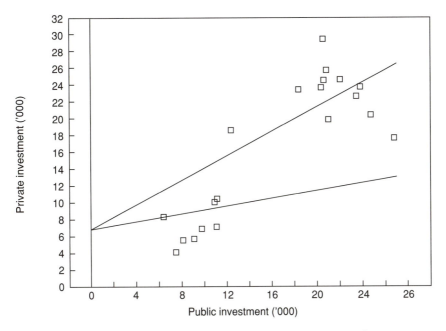

Figure 6.10 Sri Lankan investment function with slope dummy only

Combining intercept and slope dummies: the Sri Lankan investment function

Let us now return to the Sri Lankan investment function and see how intercept and slope dummies can be combined to throw more light on the crowding-in or crowding-out issue. Take another look at Figure 6.3: government investment appears to fall into two distinct sub-samples – one set to the right in excess of Rs 16,000 million and another of lower value in the bottom-left of the graph. Looking at the data set (or adding data-labels to our graph if it has this facility) we can see that the former, higher values all correspond to the years 1979–89 and the latter to 1970–8. The Sri Lankan government embarked on a liberalisation programme late in 1977 and on an investment boom in 1978–9. This suggests that we could use dummy variables to distinguish between periods with different policy regimes. The question then is whether there was a structural break in our investment function between these two periods? The scatter plot suggests there was such a break: with crowding in during the earlier period, but crowding out later on – so the coefficient on government investment should be positive in the first period and negative later on.

For pedagogical reasons, let us compare the effects of three different uses of dummies: Figures 6.9, 6.10 and 6.11 show the fitted lines from introducing, respectively, an intercept dummy, a slope dummy and both slope and intercept dummies into the simple regression. If we use an inter-

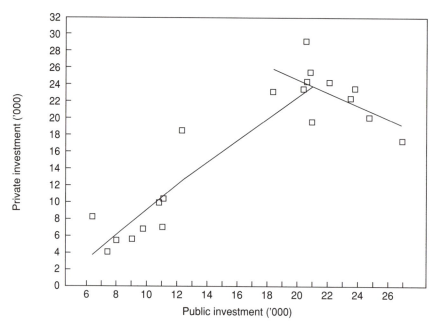

Figure 6.11   Sri Lankan investment function with intercept and slope dummies

cept dummy only, there is neither crowding in or out in either period (Figure 6.9). The problem is that, in this figure, we are constraining the slope coefficient to be the same in each period. In the case in which we allow the slope to vary (Figure 6.10), we find crowding in to be stronger in the second period than the first. Here we are imposing the constraint that the intercept must be the same for the two sub-samples. The result is that both regression lines look awkward.

As shown in Figure 6.11, it is only when we allow both slope and intercept to vary that we get a clearer picture: the fitted lines now conform to the patterns apparent in the scatter. This example allows us to draw an important conclusion: the difference in the slope coefficient between the two sub-samples will only reveal itself if we also introduce an intercept dummy. The intercept dummy is clearly necessary since it is not possible to have a negatively sloped line through the 1979–89 sub-sample of data points that has the same intercept as a line with a positive slope through the 1970–8 data points. The intercept dummy, therefore, is necessary to accommodate the difference in slope. This is, in fact, nothing more than a specific example of omitted variable bias.

When we include both slope and intercept dummies then both coefficients vary between sample periods. That is, including a dummy for all regressors yields the same coefficients as estimating separate sub-sample regressions. We may therefore test the validity of pooling data either by the Chow test presented earlier or by an *F*-test of the restriction that the coefficients on all dummy variables are jointly zero. These two tests are equivalent, i.e. they yield exactly the same result. You are asked to verify this equivalence in exercise 6.13.

This should not lead us, however, to interpret the intercept dummy as reflective of a higher level of 'autonomous' private investment in the later period. In general, in the presence of a slope dummy, an intercept dummy should be interpreted as accommodating the change in slope.

Exercise 6.12

Using the example of the regression of life expectancy on the logarithm of GNP per capita, re-estimate the model using intercept and slope dummies combined. Compare your results with those obtained earlier with two separate regressions. Test formally whether either one or both of the dummies can be dropped from the model. Do your results confirm the conclusions reached earlier?

Exercise 6.13

Test whether it is valid to pool the data for the regression of I_p on I_g using the data in the file SRINA by (a) running separate sub-sample regressions for 1970–8 and 1979–89; and (b) using dummy variables. Compare the estimated coefficients and restricted and unrestricted *RSS*s from the two methods, and comment on your results.

6.8   SUMMARY OF MAIN POINTS

1   Omitting relevant variables from a model will bias the estimates of all the coefficients in the equation. Its impact on the standard errors of the regression coefficients is more ambiguous: the theoretical standard errors will be less in the simpler model if the omitted variables are collinear with the regressors included in the model, but the estimated standard errors will generally be less in the larger model if the omitted variables have a sizeable impact on the dependent variable and if the sample size is not very small. Hence, at times a trade-off exists between bias and precision when dealing with omitted variables.

2   The inclusion of irrelevant variables does not result in bias, but affects the precision of all the model's estimates adversely.

3   Conventional hypothesis testing (*t*- or *F*-tests) is based on the assumption of correct specification and, hence, does not help us discover whether important variables have been left out of the picture. The results may look good, therefore, but coefficient estimates may be seriously biased. This fact provides the rationale for testing downwards, i.e. general to specific modelling. If you seek to prove that a simpler model is an adequate representation of the data, start by estimating the more general model and test down to see whether your assertion is justified. Merely estimating the simple model will not prove your point, even if the results look good.

4   Before testing downwards, always check whether the general model satisfies the assumptions of classical linear normal regression. If not, your inferences drawn from testing downwards may not be valid. Always remember that statistical inferences are as sound as the foundations upon which they rest.

5   In combining numerical summaries and diagnostic plots (particularly partial regression plots), use residual analysis and influence diagnostics to subject your general model to serious scrutiny.

6   Linear restrictions on a general model can be tested with an *F*-test. Common restrictions are (a) excluding variables (zero restrictions); (b) non-zero restrictions (e.g. equality of two parameters); and (c) parameter stability.

7   The use of the *F*-test to test for parameter stability is often called the Chow test. Chow also provided an alternative specification of the *F*-test to apply in the case when one sub-sample has too few observations to be estimated.

8   Dummy variables, both intercept and slope dummies, may also be used to model parameter instability. If a dummy is included for every coefficient, then the *F*-test on the null hypothesis that the coefficients on

the dummies are jointly zero is equivalent to the Chow test. Dummies allow us to estimate a single equation which differentiates regression results with respect to different sub-samples. Subsequent testing allows us to check whether parameter instability across sub-samples applies to all coefficients alike.

9 Studentised residuals are nothing but *t*-statistics of dummy variables which, each in turn, pick out a single observation from the sample. This is a special application of an intercept dummy.

ADDITIONAL EXERCISES

Exercise 6.14

Using the data in data files INDONA and SRINA test whether it is valid to estimate a pooled consumption function for the two countries and comment on your findings.

Exercise 6.15

In section 6.7 we found a structural break in the simple private investment function for Sri Lanka. But in section 6.4 we found the simple regression to be misspecified owing to omitted variables. Using the data in the file SRINA:

1 Construct partial scatter plots of I_p against each of I_g, M and r.
2 Use your scatter plots to judge if there is a structural break in any of these relationships.
3 Hence, define a general investment function which regresses I_p on I_g, M and r and any appropriate dummy variables.
4 Try to obtain a more specific model but testing restriction on the coefficients of the general model.

How do you interpret your findings?

Exercise 6.16

Mosley *et al.* (1991) are concerned to examine the impact of adjustment policies on a range of macroeconomic performance variables (such as growth of GDP and exports). They estimate a number of equations in which the main regressors are current and lagged adjustment-related financial flows and measures of compliance with conditionality. A small number of other variables are included (all unlagged). The authors argue that:

> The equations represent somewhat crude hypotheses regarding the determinants of the five dependent variables. There are many other independent variables which could have been included as explanatory

variables in the equations. In addition, lags could have been introduced to more of the independent variables . . . However, since it is specifically the impact of Bank finance and policy conditions which we wish to quantify, we have refrained from more complex specification of the equations.

(Mosley *et al.* 1991: 210)

Comment on their argument.

Exercise 6.17

Given the following estimates of the consumption function, both calculated from the same data set of 20 cross-country observations, what would you expect to be the sign of the correlation coefficient between income and the real interest rate:

$$C = 0.14 + 0.82 \ Y - 0.04r$$

$$C = 0.05 + 0.83 \ Y$$

where C is consumption, Y income and r the real interest rate? Explain your answer.

Exercise 6.18

Suppose that the true model of private investment (I_p) is:

$$I_{p,t} = \beta_1 + \beta_2 I_{g,t} + \beta_3 M_t + \epsilon_t$$

but that you estimate

$$I_{p,t} = \beta_1 + \beta_2 I_{g,t} + \epsilon'_t$$

What would you expect to be the direction of the bias in the coefficient on I_g in the simple regression of I_p on I_g? Use the data for Sri Lanka (SRINA) to verify your answer.

Exercise 6.19

Using the data in data file PRODFUN estimate a separate production function for each sector. Is it valid to pool the data from the two sub-sectors? How do your results affect your answer to exercise 6.6?

Part III
Analysing cross-section data

7 Dealing with heteroscedasticity

7.1 INTRODUCTION

Real data do not conform to the idealised conditions of the classical linear regression model. As we pointed out in Chapter 4, you are likely to encounter heteroscedasticity frequently in economic data, particularly with cross-section data. The reason is that the variation in the dependent variable seldom remains constant when the level of one (or more) explanatory variable(s) increases or decreases. For example, not only is the level of consumption of the rich much higher than that of the poor, but it is also more varied. The poor have few options but to spend their income on the basic essentials of life; the rich enjoy the privilege of making choices. Similarly, there tends to be much less variation in output or expenditure levels among small enterprises than among large firms. The implication for statistical analysis is that you will not be able to apply the regression model to the data straight away. But fortunately, the techniques of transformation make the application of the model possible in very many situations in practice. In Chapter 4, we showed how a well-chosen transformation can help to convert a non-linear relationship into a linear one. Like non-linearity, heteroscedasticity is also often due to the skewness in the distribution of the variables under study. As a result, a suitable transformation can make the heteroscedasticity disappear while making the average relationship linear at the same time. However, you may not always be able to do this. There are also cases where the relationship will look clearly linear but the scatter plot indicates heteroscedastic errors.

If all the other assumptions of the regression model, i.e. the assumptions of linearity of the regression, independence and zero expectation of the error term, are valid, then it can be shown that heteroscedastic errors do not affect the unbiasedness of the least squares estimates of the regression coefficients. But the precision in estimation of the coefficients is no more the best. In other words, the least squares estimators are not best linear unbiased estimators (BLUE) but only linear unbiased estimators. Further, the standard formulae for the standard errors will not be valid, since they are based on the assumption of homoscedasticity. Consequently, it is not possible to perform the t-tests and F-tests under heteroscedasticity. Thus, in order to make reliable inferences from the heteroscedastic data on the basis of the linear regression model, we seek to eliminate heteroscedasticity by means of a suitable transformation. Incorrect functional form is the type of model misspecification most likely to account for heteroscedasticity in the residuals; but it may also be a symptom of omitted variables.

There is a very important point here, one on which we depart from many traditional textbooks. Heteroscedasticity (and autocorrelation, dealt with in Chapter 11) is a violation of our assumptions about the error term, which has adverse implications for least squares estimation. But we do not know the errors, but proxy them with the residuals. The residuals are a function of our model specifications. Hence 'problems' which appear in the residuals, such as heteroscedasticity, are just as likely to be a result of a misspecified model as they are of a genuinely heteroscedastic error in the true model. When coming across a problem in the residuals the first course of action must always be to check the model specification. Only once you are sure that the model is correctly specified should you turn to one of the traditional 'cures' for residual heteroscedasticity.

In Chapter 4, we showed how the residual versus predicted plot can be used to check for heteroscedasticity. In this chapter, in section 7.2 we discuss two other plots which are useful in the visual examination for heteroscedasticity. Next, in section 7.3, we introduce a selection of statistical tests for heteroscedasticity. Section 7.4 discusses how to explore suitable transformations for elimination of heteroscedasticity in order to obtain the best estimators. Section 7.5 shows how weighted least squares regression can sometimes be used to make inferences when the error term is heteroscedastic. We show that weighted least squares can also be done by a linear regression with suitably transformed variables. Finally, section 7.6 gives a summary of the main points.

7.2   DIAGNOSTIC PLOTS: LOOKING FOR HETEROSCEDASTICITY

Under heteroscedastic conditions, the simple linear regression model of Y on X is given by:

$$Y = \beta_1 + \beta_2 X + \epsilon_x \tag{7.1}$$

where $V(\epsilon_x) = \sigma_x^2$, the conditional variance of ϵ_x given X, varies with X, with all other assumptions of the classical model remaining the same. The best way to spot the presence of heteroscedasticity is to look for it using visual displays. The basic principles to construct such displays are:

1   Suppose σ_x^2 increases with X.
2   Then, for $i > j$ we will have $\sigma_i^2 > \sigma_j^2$.
3   Now, the variance σ_x^2 is the average squared deviations of the errors from its own mean at a given value of X.

4 Consequently, $\sigma_i^2 > \sigma_j^2$ implies that, on average, the deviations of errors from its own mean will be larger at $X = X_i$ than at $X = X_j$. But since mean of the errors ϵ_x is zero at every given X, the errors themselves are the deviations.

5 Therefore, $\sigma_i^2 > \sigma_j^2$ implies that the magnitude of the errors ϵ_is will be larger than ϵ_js.

6 Thus, if σ_x^2 increases with X then the magnitude of the errors will tend to increase with X.

7 However, the errors ϵ_x are unobservable, but the residuals e_x from the fitted regression serve as estimates of the errors ϵ_x.

8 We can, therefore, expect that the plot of the residuals against the corresponding values of X will indicate an increasing spread of the residuals if σ_x^2 increases with X.

9 Further, since the fitted Y values are linear functions of X, the same pattern of increasing spread of the residuals should be discernible in the plot of the residuals against the predicted values of Y from the fitted regression.

The above is the basis of the residual versus predicted value plot. But since the magnitude of the residuals increases with predicted Y, it follows that the squared and the absolute residuals will also increase with predicted Y. In general, if σ_x^2 varies with X then the scatter plots of the raw, squared and absolute residuals against the predicted values of Y will all reveal a pattern of heteroscedasticity. At times, however, one of them is more revealing than the other. It is useful, therefore, to examine all three plots separately. Let us illustrate their utility.

In the case of the simple regression, the plots of residuals (raw, squared or absolute) against the X values and the predicted Y values are equivalent. In the case of the multiple regression, however, the situation is more complex. As a rule, you should first look at the plot of the residuals against the predicted values for any indication of heteroscedasticity. If there is any such indication then you should try the plot of residuals against each of the explanatory variables to find out which of the regressors accounts for the heteroscedasticity. Generally, there is only one such explanatory variable. However, in rare situations, heteroscedasticity may be related to more than one explanatory variable, which makes the life of an empirical analyst more difficult.

An example: urban weekly earnings against the age of workers

The file INDIA contains data on weekly earnings of 261 workers along with their age, obtained from a survey of workers' households in an industrial town in southern India. The estimated regression of weekly wage income on age is given below (standard error in brackets),

$$\text{Income} = 8.65 + 4.88 \text{ Age} \qquad R^2 = 0.20 \qquad (7.2)$$
$$(21.13) \ (0.61)$$

Figure 7.1 presents the residual versus predicted plot. The points spread vertically wider and wider with the increase in the predicted value of weekly wage income, indicating heteroscedasticity.

Figures 7.2 and 7.3 are the plots of squared and absolute residuals against the predicted values, respectively. Both these plots exhibit similar patterns to those observed in Figure 7.1. However, in this example, the increasing spread of the points is much more clearly discernible in Figures 7.1 and 7.3 than in Figure 7.2. This is because of the presence of one outlier which is easily identifiable in all three plots. This outlier makes the magnitude of its squared residual so large compared to the rest of the residuals that the latter points are pressed down to the horizontal axis in Figure 7.2. It is always useful to look at all three plots, as it is possible that one of them many fail to bring out the pattern of heteroscedasticity, if any, in a given situation. In this case, plot 7.2 mainly draws our attention to the presence of an outlier (which, incidentally, is a good way to spot outliers).

The plots of absolute and squared residuals against predicted values of Y are not just useful to spot the presence of heteroscedasticity, but, as we shall see, they also provide valuable clues to the possible form of transformations which may enable us to cope with heteroscedastic situations. Before we do this, we discuss in the next section how these visual techniques can be complemented by formal testing for heteroscedasticity.

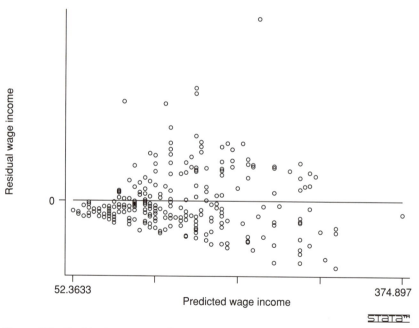

Figure 7.1   Residual versus predicted plot

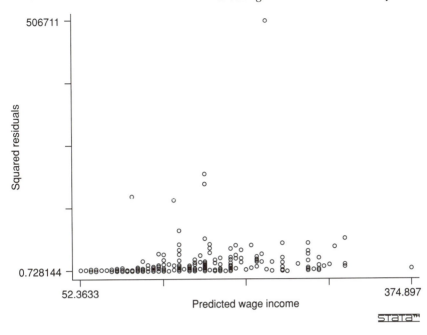

Figure 7.2   Squared residuals versus predicted

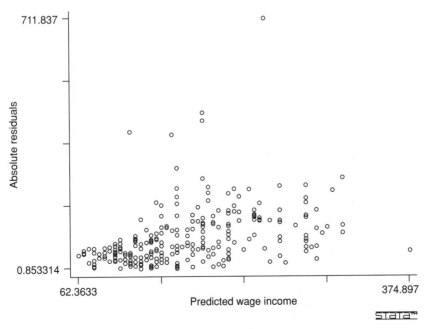

Figure 7.3   Absolute residuals versus predicted

Exercise 7.1

In Chapter 4, while discussing transformations towards linearity, we used three examples with data taken from the data file SOCECON: respectively, the relation between energy consumption (E) and GNP (Y), both per capita; between energy consumption (E) and the degree of urbanisation as measured by the percentage of the population living in urban areas (U); and, finally, between life expectancy (L) and GNP per capita (Y). For each of these simple regressions between the raw data, compare the plots of raw, absolute and squared residuals against the predicted values of the dependent variable or against the regressor. In each case, check which plot is most revealing in terms of detecting heteroscedasticity.

Exercise 7.2

Use the INDIA data set to estimate the regression line between the logarithm of wage income and the age of the worker, compute the residuals, and plot the raw, absolute and squared residuals against the predicted values of wage income and against the age of workers. What do you conclude about the presence or absence of heteroscedasticity?

7.3   TESTING FOR HETEROSCEDASTICITY

There are a number of tests available in the literature which help us to detect the presence of heteroscedasticity. We shall not review these tests exhaustively. What follows is an illustration of a selection of commonly used tests. However, none is foolproof in detecting heteroscedasticity. Detection of heteroscedasticity really requires a blend of visual and confirmatory (i.e. hypothesis testing) analysis.

There are two distinct approaches to testing for heteroscedasticity. One approach is to try to detect heteroscedasticity by comparing the conditional variances across different ranges of the explanatory variable(s). Bartlett's test and the Goldfeld-Quandt test illustrated below are examples of this approach. While Bartlett's test is a general test for equality of variances between groups which can be adopted for the purpose of testing for heteroscedasticity, the Goldfeld-Quandt test is specifically developed for this purpose. The other approach is based on the formalisation of the graphical checks outlined above: the idea is to explore if there is any systematic relation between the residuals and any one of the explanatory variables. White's test and the Glejser test illustrated below fall in this category. Let us have a look at each in turn.

Bartlett's test

Bartlett's test can be applied to check for the equality of the variances of the dependent variable across groups defined by an explanatory variable.

The conditional variance of Y given X is the same as the conditional variance of the error term, σ_x^2. Indeed, using equation (7.1), we get:

$$V(Y) = V(\beta_1 + \beta_2 X + \epsilon_x)$$

but, since X is given, ϵ_x is uncorrelated with X, i.e. $\text{Cov}(\epsilon_x, X) = 0$, and the variance of $(\beta_1 + \beta_2 X)$ is zero for any given X, we have (see Appendix 2.1 in Chapter 2):

$$V(Y) = V(\beta_1 + \beta_2 X) + V(\epsilon_x) = V(\epsilon_x) = \sigma_x^2$$

Hence, one way of checking for heteroscedasticity is to test for the stability of the conditional variance of Y across the range of X in the sample data. In practical situations, we generally do not have multiple observations of Y for a given X. The application of Bartlett's test, therefore, involves that we first sort the data in ascending order of the explanatory variable which is suspected to be the cause of the heteroscedastic pattern of the error term, and divide the sample into several groups, say k groups (classes), based on this explanatory variable, after which we subsequently test the hypothesis of homogeneous variances across the groups.

If σ_i^2 is the variance of Y in the ith class, the null hypothesis we seek to test can then be stated as

$$H_0: \sigma_1^2 = \sigma_2^2 = \sigma_3^2 = \ldots = \sigma_k^2 = \sigma^2$$

Now let $Y_{ij} = j$th Y value in the ith class; $n_i = $ the number of observations in ith class; and $f_i = (n_i - 1)$; $f = \Sigma f_i$. The test is then performed as follows:

1   Compute the sample variance for each group i:

$$s_i^2 = \frac{1}{n_i - 1} \sum_{j=1}^{n_i} (Y_{ij} - \bar{Y}_i)^2$$

where

$$\bar{Y}_i = \frac{1}{n_i} \sum_{j=1}^{n_i} Y_{ij}$$

s_i^2 is the estimator of σ_i^2, $i = 1, 2, 3, \ldots, k$.

2   Compute the pooled sample variance of all the groups together:

$$s^2 = \frac{\sum_{i=1}^{k} f_i s_i^2}{\sum_{i=1}^{k} f_i} = \frac{\sum_{i=1}^{k} f_i s_i^2}{f}$$

s^2 is the estimator of σ^2 under H_0.

3   Under the null hypothesis the ratio A/B has approximately a chi-square distribution with $(k - 1)$ degrees of freedom, where:

$$A = f \cdot \ln (s^2) - \sum_{i=1}^{k} f_i \cdot \ln (s_i^2)$$

$$B = 1 + \frac{1}{3(k - 1)} \left[\sum_{i=1}^{k} \left(\frac{1}{f_i} \right) - \frac{1}{f} \right]$$

(7.3)

In our example, we first sort the sample of 261 workers in ascending order of age, divide it into three groups of 87 workers each, and compute the means and sample variance s_i^2 of weekly wage income for each group (these calculations are summarised in Table 7.1). The computation of s^2, A and B are all calculated in accordance with the formulae stated above. The larger the computed value of the statistic A/B, the more suspect the null hypothesis of homogeneity of variances across the three classes will be. Thus, the test consists in comparing the computed chi-square value with the 5 per cent or 1 per cent critical value of the chi-square distribution for the corresponding degrees of freedom ($2 = 3 - 1$). The null hypothesis is rejected if the ratio A/B exceeds the critical value. Most statistical software provide the means to use Bartlett's test, or it can be done on spreadsheet (see, for example, Table 7.1). The test statistic computed for wage income was 47.8 which is significant at 5 per cent level. Consequently, we reject the null hypothesis.

Note, however, that Bartlett's test is only valid under the assumption that the dependent variable is distributed normally, which is not the case with wage income. Not surprisingly, the distribution of weekly wage income data is highly skewed. Bartlett's test, therefore, is not valid for this reason. But its utility lies in exploring transformations which can

Table 7.1   Calculation of Bartlett's test for income data

	Sample	*Income*	*Logged income*
Mean	1	88.0	4.2
	2	179.6	4.9
	3	232.1	5.2
s_i^2	1	4734	0.49
	2	16676	0.52
	3	22096	0.61
$\ln(s_i^2)$	1	8.46	−0.72
	2	9.72	−0.66
	3	10.00	−0.50
s^2		14502	0.54
$\ln(s^2)$		9.58203	−0.62223
A		48.05	1.15
B		1.01	1.01
Bartlett's		47.81	1.15

remove heteroscedasticity. Following the ladder of power transformations discussed in Chapter 3, we perform the logarithmic transformation of the weekly wage income, and the transformed distribution turns out to be approximately symmetrical according to the exploratory checks illustrated in Chapter 3. The skewness-kurtosis test for normality of the logarithms of wage income also turns out to be insignificant at the 5 per cent level. Hence, we can apply Bartlett's test to the transformed data (log weekly wage income), following the same steps explained above. The only difference this time is that we compute the sample variances of log income for the different groups instead of those of income itself. The computed test statistic now works out to be 1.15, which is insignificant at the 5 per cent level. The test is valid this time as the hypothesis of normality of the distribution of log income could not be rejected by the skewness-kurtosis test. We can, therefore, conclude that log transformation successfully removes the heteroscedasticity observed in the raw data.

How do we divide the observations across the different groupings? In this example, arriving at the number 87 to divide the sample into three groups was easy because 261 is divisible by 3. If the sample size is not divisible by 3, take the next highest integer of the quotient, say n, and divide the sample so that the bottom and the top groups have n units each, and put the remainder of the data in the middle group. For example, if the sample size were 250, then 250/3 = 83.33 is rounded to 84, and the sample could be divided into 84 + 82 + 84. Here, we used three groups as a matter of convenience. The point is to choose a suitable number of groups (minimum of two) depending on the total sample size. Too many groups with too few data points in each groups will not lead to reliable conclusions. If heteroscedasticity is present and increasing (or decreasing) with one of the explanatory variables, this will show up if you use a few (preferably three or more) sizeable groupings. Two groupings is not so advisable because they border each other and, hence, they will have similar variation where they meet. Only use two groups when your sample size is rather small.

Goldfeld-Quandt test

Bartlett's test was used to check for homogeneity in the conditional variances of Y, the dependent variable. The Goldfeld-Quandt test checks for homogeneity in the conditional error variances. Hence, with Bartlett's test, you group Y with reference to the ascending order of one of the X variables, but you do not run groupwise regressions. The test is performed using the computed conditional variances of Y. As we shall see, the Goldfeld-Quandt test also implies that you group the data with reference to the order of one of the X variables, but in this case you run groupwise regressions to obtain sets of within-group residuals. The test is commonly used when the heteroscedastic variance σ^2_x is suspected to vary monotonically (i.e. consistently increasing or decreasing) with one of the explanatory variables in the regression model. The procedure is based on dividing the sample into three groups in ascending order of one of the explanatory variables, and testing for the difference in the error variance between the bottom and the top groups. Hence, the middle group is not considered in the test. Its only function is to prevent the extreme groups bordering on each other.

The test involves the following steps:

1   Arrange the data in ascending order of the explanatory variable suspected to be related to the error variance.
2   Drop a number of the middle observations, say c, so that $(n - c)$ is divisible by 2, hence n' = $(n - c)/2$ is the subsample size. A rule of thumb is to drop about 1/4 of the total observations from the middle.
3   Estimate two separate regressions for the bottom and the top group of observations, and compute the corresponding residual sums of squares – respectively, RSS_1 and RSS_2.
4   Compute the ratio of the higher to the lower residual sums of squares. This ratio has an F-distribution with $[d, d]$ degrees of freedom where

$$d = \frac{n - c}{2} - k = n' - k$$

k = No. of estimated coefficients

under the hypothesis that the error distribution within each group is normal, and that the error variances are the same. The higher the computed ratio, the less likely it is for the hypothesis to be true.
5   Compare the computed ratio with the critical value of the relevant F-distribution. If the computed exceeds the critical value, then the hypothesis of homoscedasticity is rejected.

Let us use our sample data of 261 workers again to illustrate this test step by step:

1   Since there is only one explanatory variable, age, we arrange the data in ascending order of age.
2   The total number of observations is 261. One-fourth of 261 is 65.25. Now $(261 - 65)$ is an even number and, hence, we drop the middle 65 observations. This leaves us with 98 (i.e. $(261 - 65)/2$) observations each in the bottom and top groups. The bottom group corresponds to lower values of the age variable and the top group to the higher values.
3   Bottom group (observations 1 to 98): RSS_1 = 382,302
    Top group (observations 164 to 261): RSS_2 = 2,207,120
4   $F_{calculated} = RSS_2/RSS_1$ = 5.63.

5   The computed value of 5.63 is higher than the critical value in the *F*-distribution with [96, 96] degrees of freedom at 5 per cent level of significance. Hence, we reject the null hypothesis of homoscedasticity.

Again, this test is not strictly valid because of the non-normality of the distribution of wage income. If we repeat this test with log income, this time the test is valid, and the corresponding calculated value much lower (1.96), though not insignificant.

It is not necessarily the case that the different tests for heteroscedasticity will lead to the same conclusion. These tests depend on the way in which we divide the data into groups, hence, different groupings may yield different results. We shall come back to this point later.

White's test

The basis for this test is to check whether there is any systematic relation between the squared residuals and the explanatory variables. This is achieved by regressing the squared residuals e_i^2 on all the explanatory variables and on their squares and cross products. Thus, if X_1 and X_2 are the explanatory variables, then White's test involves regressing e^2 on X_1, X_2, X_1^2, X_2^2 and $X_1.X_2$, and using the overall *F*-test to check if the regression is significant or not. This test (and others like it) is in fact a general regression specification error test (RESET) and not solely a test for heteroscedastic errors (see Box 7.1).

In our example of the regression of wage income on the age of the worker, the only explanatory variable, we regress the squared residuals e^2 from the fitted regression in (7.2) on *AGE* and AGE^2, which yields an *F*-statistic of 6.58. This calculated value should be compared with the critical value $F_{(2,258)}$. The calculated *F*-statistic is significant at the 1 per cent level and, hence, we reject the hypothesis that there is no relationship between squared residuals and age and age squared. By implication, we reject the hypothesis of homoscedasticity.

Glejser's test

Like White's test, Glejser's test also checks whether a systematic relation exists between the residuals and the explanatory variables. However, Glejser approaches the problem in a different way. The test involves regressing absolute residuals separately on X, X^{-1} and $X^{1/2}$, and uses *t*-tests for the slope coefficients to be zero. If there is more than one explanatory variable then this exercise is to be repeated for each of the explanatory variables. The hypothesis of homoscedasticity is rejected if any of the slope coefficients turns out to be significantly different from zero. The difference with White's test, therefore, is that Glejser's

---

Box 7.1   White's test as RESET (regression specification error test)

The presence of heteroscedastic residuals can result from heteroscedastic error terms in a model which is otherwise correctly specified. However, heteroscedastic residuals can also occur because of
misspecification of the regression model itself: in particular, because
one or more relevant variables have been omitted from the regression or because of non-linearity of the regression curve.

Heteroscedastic residuals due to omitted variables

If a variable has been incorrectly omitted from a regression model,
the residuals of the estimated model will incorporate the effect of
this omitted variable. In so far as the omitted variable varies (in
whichever way) with one or more of the regressors included in the
model, heteroscedastic residuals may result. For example, if an
omitted variable Z varies strongly with regressor X, the variation in
the observed residuals is likely to reflect this covariation (whatever
its form: linear, quadratic, etc.) between Z and X. White's test, which
involves regressing squared residuals on the regressors, their squares
and their cross-products, is likely to pick up this effect of omitting
a relevant variable.

Heteroscedasticity and non-linearity

Similarly, misspecification due to non-linearity can lead to heteroscedastic errors. For example, in a simple regression of Y on X,
fitting a straight line to a scatter which reflects a typical quadratic
shape will produce U-shaped residuals, the variation in which is
determined by X.

White's test, therefore, is rather indiscriminate in its scope. It tells
you when things are wrong but does not necessarily point the direction to look for the cause. In this sense, it is a general misspecification test which prompts you to see what the problem could be. It does
not allow you, however, to jump to an immediate conclusion.

---

test selectively investigates which explanatory variable accounts for the
heteroscedasticity as well as the form it takes. White's test, in contrast, is
akin to a broad-spectrum diagnostic device aimed at checking whether
something is wrong. Let us try out Glejser's tests on the income–age data.
The results are as follows (standard errors in parentheses):

$$|\hat{e}| = 4.52 + 2.55 \; AGE$$
$$(0.39)$$

Table 7.2 Summary of tests for heteroscedasticity with values for various regressions

Statistic	Definition	Test statistic	Income on age	Log income on age	Log income on age, education and sex
Bartlett's	$$\dfrac{f \cdot \ln(s^2) - \sum_{i=1}^{k} f_i \cdot \ln(s_i^2)}{1 + \dfrac{1}{3(k-1)}\left[\sum_{i=1}^{k}\left(\dfrac{1}{f_i}\right) - \dfrac{1}{f}\right]}$$	χ^2	47.81	1.15	Age: 1.15 Edu: 1.77
Goldfeld–Quandt	$\dfrac{RSS_1}{RSS_2}$	F	5.63	1.96	1.42
White's	F-test on null hypothesis that $R^2 = 0$ in regression of squared residuals on regressors, their squares and cross-products	F	6.58	1.93	1.47[a]
Glejser[b]	Test of significance of slope coefficient from separate regressions of absolute residual on regressor, its inverse and its square root	t	Age: 6.5 1/Age: 6.4 $\sqrt{\text{Age}}$: 4.5	Age: 1.9 1/Age: 1.4 $\sqrt{\text{Age}}$: 1.9	Age: 1.8 1/Age: 0.8 $\sqrt{\text{Age}}$: 1.6

Notes:
[a] Sex squared omitted from White's test for multiple regression owing to multicollinearity in the test equation.
[b] t-statistics for Glejser test are absolute values.

$$|\hat{e}| = 163.97 - 2159.0 \; \frac{1}{AGE}$$
$$(335.5)$$

$$|\hat{e}| = -81.74 + 30.18 \; \sqrt{AGE}$$
$$(6.69)$$

The two-sided t-tests for the slope coefficients equal to zero are significant at the 1 per cent level in all three regressions above (see Table 7.2). Thus, Glejser's test also rejects the hypothesis of homoscedasticity.

It is quite possible that not all the four tests – Bartlett's, Goldfeld-Quandt, White's and Glejser's – produce the same results in terms of either rejecting or accepting the hypothesis of homoscedasticity. If all the tests fail to reject homoscedasticity then we are on firm ground to proceed with the initial model. If at least one test rejects homoscedasticity then we should examine carefully the nature of heteroscedasticity by means of the graphs discussed earlier and proceed according to the principles which we shall discuss in the next section.

Exercise 7.3

Using the cases listed in exercise 7.1, try out all four tests discussed in this section to test for heteroscedasticity.

Exercise 7.4

Continuing with exercise 7.2, do the tests for heteroscedasticity with the model featuring the logarithms of income versus the age of Indian workers.

7.4   TRANSFORMATIONS TOWARDS HOMOSCEDASTICITY

Heteroscedasticity of the error term implies that we cannot use the estimates of the standard errors of the regression coefficients computed on the basis of the standard formulae derived from the classical regression model. Furthermore, the least squares estimators are inefficient, but unbiased. Consider, for example, our income–age relationship: we can use the estimated regression (7.2) for predicting the average weekly wage income of the workers of a given age without falling prey to a statistical bias. But this prediction is not the most reliable (since it is inefficient) among all linear predictions and we cannot make any statement about the uncertainty (confidence interval, hypothesis tests) of the predictions based on the standard errors computed according to the formulae under the assumption of homoscedasticity.

Why not modify the formulae accordingly to allow for heteroscedastic errors? In principle, this is possible. But to do so we need to be able to state the nature of the heteroscedasticity of the error term. This is exactly what we try to do, but not necessarily by forsaking the advantages of the normal linear regression model. As we shall now see, transformations often do the trick by eliminating heteroscedasticity in the residuals, indicating that our model may well have had the wrong functional form. Indeed, we find that in very many situations in practice transformations help us to get rid of heteroscedasticity.

Finding an appropriate transformation

One of the most common reasons for heteroscedasticity is the skewness of the distribution of one or more variables involved in a regression model with socioeconomic data. In such cases, a power transformation – and, in particular, the logarithmic transformation – often eliminates the skewness in the data. How do we find the appropriate transformation to eliminate heteroscedasticity? As we have seen, heteroscedasticity implies that the conditional variance of the dependent variable Y or the error term ϵ varies with the conditional mean of Y. Now, 'if the functional relationship between the variance and the mean is known, a transformation exists which will make the variance (approximately) constant' (Rawlings, 1988: 309); and one such general functional relationship between the conditional variance of the dependent variable and its conditional mean is commonly applied in practice which allows us to use power transformations to eliminate heteroscedasticity. That is, if:

$$\sigma_Y^2 = A^2 \, \mu_Y^k \tag{7.4}$$

or, alternatively:

$$\sigma_Y = A \, \mu_Y^k \tag{7.5}$$

which we can conveniently re-express as a double-log equation as follows:

$$\ln(\sigma_Y) = A + k\ln(\mu_Y) \tag{7.6}$$

where, $\sigma_Y^2 = $ the conditional variance of Y; $\mu_Y = $ the conditional mean of Y; and, A and k are constants. That is, if the standard deviation of Y is proportional to some power k of its conditional mean, then the power transformation Y^{1-k} when k is not unity and the log transformation when $k = 1$, will (approximately) eliminate heteroscedasticity (ibid.). Thus, if $k = 1$ and, hence, the standard deviation is proportional to the mean, the logarithmic transformation will do. If, however, the variance (and not the standard deviation) is proportional to the mean and, hence, $2k = 1$, the square root transformation will do the trick.

But, typically, σ_Y and μ_Y are unknown. So how do we find the appropriate value for k? What we can do is to substitute the absolute residuals $|e|$ for σ_Y and the predicted Y_p for μ_Y in equation (7.6) and use the data to estimate its slope coefficient, k, with least squares. In our example of

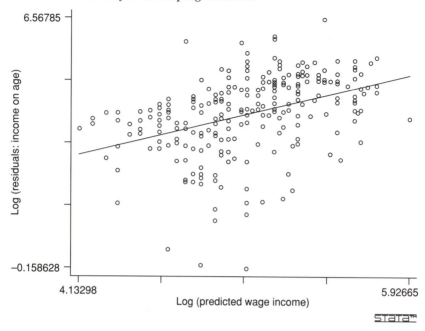

Figure 7.4 Log $|e|$ versus predicted *Y*

the income–age data the corresponding scatter plot with regression line
is depicted in Figure 7.4.

The plot indicates a linear relationship between $\ln(|e|)$ and the $\ln(Y_p)$,
where Y_p is the predicted *Y*. The corresponding fitted regression is given
as follows:

$$\ln(|e|) = -2.0930 + 1.2108 \ln(Y_p)$$
$$(0.1691)$$

which reveals that the slope coefficient is reasonably close to unity.

Exercise 7.5

Test formally whether the slope coefficient in equation (7.7) is significantly
different from one, using the 5 per cent significance level. What do you
conclude from this test?

You will have found from the two-sided *t*-test that the slope coefficient is
insignificantly different from one at the 5 per cent significance level.
Hence, it seems a good idea to try out the logarithmic transformation to
see whether it helps us to eliminate heteroscedasticity. The regression of
$\ln(Y)$ on AGE yields the following results (*t*-statistics in brackets):

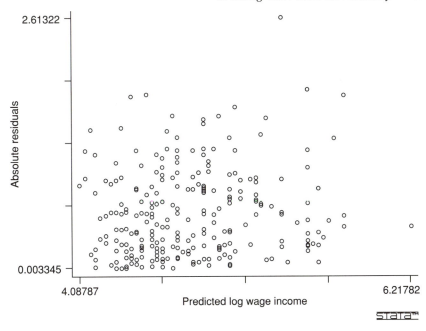

Figure 7.5 Scatter plot of absolute residuals versus predicted

$$\ln(Y) = 3.72 + 0.03AGE \qquad R^2 = 0.23$$
$$(28.9) \quad (8.89)$$

Figure 7.5 plots the absolute residuals of this regression against its predicted log income. As you can see, this scatter plot no longer shows a heteroscedastic pattern and, hence, our transformation proved to be quite successful.

The plots (not shown here) of the residuals and the squared residuals against the predicted values also confirm that there is no longer any systematic pattern in the scatter. This should not surprise us: our earlier application of Bartlett's test to the log transformed income data led us to conclude that the hypothesis of homogeneous variances of the log income data is acceptable. All other tests (Goldfeld-Quandt test, White's test and Glejser's test) come to a more or less similar conclusion. We can now be reasonably confident, therefore, that our transformation resolved the problem of heteroscedasticity.

Exercise 7.6

Using the data in INDIA, perform Bartlett's, Goldfeld-Quandt, Glejser's and White's test for the regression of log income on age. Comment on your results.

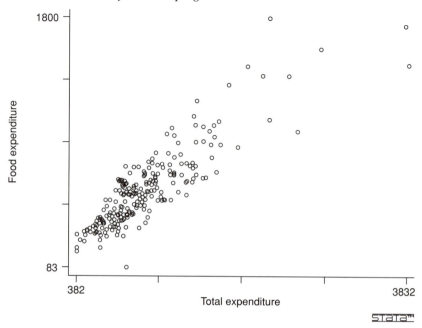

Figure 7.6   Food and total expenditure

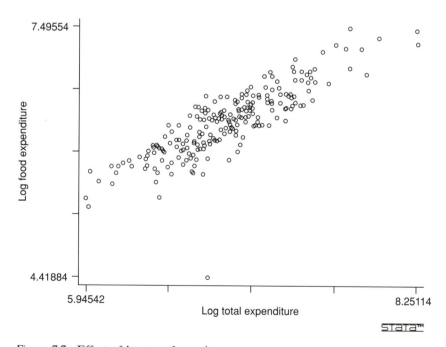

Figure 7.7   Effect of log transformation

The results you should achieve are summarised in Table 7.2 Compared with the regression of untransformed income on age, a dramatic reduction in each of the calculated test statistics can be observed. It therefore does seem, as observed in the previous paragraph, that the log transformation of income has removed the problem of heteroscedasticity (though we return to this point below).

The versatility of the logarithmic transformation

Once more, the logarithmic transformation has shown its versatility to rectify problems to do with skewed distributions. Let us conclude this section with a final graphical example of the use of logarithms.

Figure 7.6 presents the scatter plot of household food expenditure against total expenditure. The data (in the file INDFOOD) were obtained from a household sample survey of a selection of villages in India. The sample size is 217 households. The skewness in both the distributions is clearly evident from the scatter plot. So is the inherent pattern of heteroscedasticity, although a straight line seems to be an appropriate description of the average relationship. The effect of log transformation of both the variables is shown in Figure 7.7. As you can see, skewness has been removed from both these distributions and the scatter plot no longer indicates any sign of heteroscedasticity.

Heteroscedasticity as a symptom of omitted variable bias

In the example so far we have examined the impact of age on earnings. But after our analysis in Chapter 6, we may well expect that this equation suffers from misspecification due to omitted variables. Surely other factors, such as education, affect earnings. The data file INDIA also includes data on the age and sex (a dummy variable) of the workers.

Exercise 7.7

Using the data in INDIA, regress log income on age, education and sex. Test the hypothesis that education and sex may be dropped from the equation. Perform Bartlett's, Goldfeld-Quandt, Glejser and White's tests. Comment on your results.

The results you should achieve for exercise 7.7 are shown in Table 7.2. All the calculated test statistics, except Bartlett's, have fallen still further and the null hypothesis may now be accepted in the case of the Goldfeld-Quandt test. This example shows that residual heteroscedasticity may well result from omitted variable bias, and the inclusion of incorrectly omitted variables will reduce evidence of heteroscedasticity.

The statistic for Bartlett's test did not change since it is calculated with reference to the dependent variable. It is therefore unchanged by changes in the functional form of the regressor rather than regressand. Except White's test, all the tests are calculated with respect to a single regressor (age in the example here). If there are more regressors, then the data should be sorted by each regressor in turn and the test recalculated for Bartlett's (as shown in Table 7.2) and the Goldfeld-Quandt tests, and the absolute residual regressed on each regressor (and transformations thereof) in turn for the Glejser test. These steps are not necessary if there is some good reason to believe that the heteroscedasticity is related to one specific regressor.

7.5   DEALING WITH GENUINE HETEROSCEDASTICITY: WEIGHTED LEAST SQUARES AND HETEROSCEDASTIC STANDARD ERRORS

The previous section showed that the presence of heteroscedasticity in the residuals is probably a result of model misspecification. The example we used of Indian workers showed how changing functional form and adding incorrectly omitted variables reduced the evidence of heteroscedasticity. However, it can also happen that heteroscedasticity remains a problem even when we are sure that the model is correctly specified, which could be the case for the consumption function in which richer people enjoy more variation in their consumption than those who are less well off. In such cases we must try to cure the problem. The traditional solution is weighted least squares, which permits BLUE estimates to be obtained from ordinary least squares. However, weighted least squares is not always appropriate, in which case we may use heteroscedastic consistent standard errors. We consider each of these possibilities in turn.

There are occasions when we can model the heteroscedastic error variance of the population regression (7.1) in the following form:

$$\sigma_i^2 = w_i^2 \, \sigma^2 \tag{7.9}$$

where $i = 1, \ldots, n$, the sample observations; σ_i = the error variance for observation i; w_i = the weight for observation i; σ = a constant variance. Hence, the specific error variance for observation i can be obtained by multiplying a constant variance, σ, by the corresponding weight of observation i. As we shall see, if the set of weights are known or if their values can be easily hypothesised, it is possible to obtain efficient estimators of the coefficients of the regression model and make valid statistical inferences. A typical case where we can do so is when we have grouped data. So let us first consider this case.

Table 7.3 Grouped household expenditure

Per capita average expenditure class	Per capita average total expenditure	Per capita average food expenditures
Below 175	145.67	83.39
175–225	199.42	115.96
225–275	247.36	143.95
275–350	301.92	165.86
Above 350	437.93	206.70

Working with grouped data

In development research we often deal with published data which are typically presented in the tabular form of group means. Table 7.2 is an example of such data. The table lists per capita total and food expenditures by per capita expenditure groups for the data depicted in Figure 7.6.

Suppose the correct model is given as follows:

$$Y = \beta_1 + \beta_2 X + \epsilon \qquad (7.10)$$

where ϵ is homoscedastic with variance σ^2. This model applies to the data on individual households. However, the data as listed in Table 7.3 are grouped and, hence, model specification (7.10) will not be appropriate. In general, if there are k grouped means, then the appropriate model for the data can be written as follows:

$$\bar{Y}_i = \beta_1 + \beta_2 \bar{X}_i + \bar{\epsilon}_i \qquad i = 1,2,3,\ldots,k \qquad (7.11)$$

where the bars on the variables Y, X and ϵ denote the corresponding group means.

But, in this case, due to the grouping of the data, we get:

$$V(\bar{\epsilon}_i) = \frac{\sigma^2}{n_i} \qquad i = 1,2,3,\ldots,k \qquad (7.12)$$

and, hence, the model for grouped data has heteroscedastic error terms. But note that the error variance is of the form as specified in (7.9) with $w_i^2 = (1/n_i)$.

Weighted least squares

When the weights are known, as in the case of grouped data, a simple transformation of the variables in the model provides us with a way to apply the classical model. In general, if the heteroscedastic model is given as follows:

$$Y_i = \beta_1 + \beta_2 X_i + \epsilon_i \qquad (7.13)$$

where $V(\epsilon_i) = \sigma_i^2 = w_i^2\,\sigma^2$, we can divide equation 7.13 by w_i so as to get the following model:

$$\frac{Y_i}{w_i} = \beta_1\frac{1}{w_i} + \beta_2\frac{X_i}{w_i} + \frac{\epsilon_i}{w_i} \tag{7.14}$$

This transformed regression has no constant term. The variance of the error term in the new specification is homoscedastic because

$$V\!\left(\frac{\epsilon_i}{w_i}\right) = \frac{1}{w_i^2}V(\epsilon_i) = \frac{1}{w_i^2}w_i^2\,\sigma^2 = \sigma^2 \tag{7.15}$$

Therefore, if we regress (Y_i/w_i) on $(1/w_i)$ and (X_i/w_i) without a constant term, the least squares estimators of β_1 and β_2 will have the BLUE properties. This procedure of estimation of the regression coefficients subject to the additional assumption (7.9) is called the weighted least squares method of estimation.

So much for the method in theoretical terms. The crucial issue in practice is to check whether the specification (7.9) of the error variance is correct and to find the appropriate weights, w_i. If we are dealing with grouped data such as shown in Table 7.3, then $w_i = 1/n_i$. However, we shall have to be reasonably sure that the regression model (7.10) is valid in order to use model (7.11). This is important. If, for example, the regression of per capita food expenditure on total expenditure has a double-log form, then the model (7.11) can no longer be validly applied to the grouped data since the group averages are calculated from the original values and not the log-transformed values.

Exercise 7.8

Using the data in the file TPEASANT (farm size and household size in Tanzania), estimate the regression of landholding size on household size with weighted least squares. Do you think that the resulting regression satisfies the assumptions of classical linear regression?

When X_i is an appropriate weight

There are other situations where assumption (7.9) seems to be appropriate. One special case is when the X variable can serve as the relevant weight:

$$\sigma_i^2 = X_i^2\,\sigma^2 \tag{7.16}$$

and, hence:

$$w_i = X_i \tag{7.17}$$

which states that the error variance is proportional to the square of (one of) the explanatory variable(s). This case is commonly applicable. With economic data, for example, the variance of Y often tends to increase with X. If the relationship of the variance with X can be adequately described by equation (7.16), then we can use a transformed regression equation specified as follows:

$$\frac{Y_i}{X_i} = \beta_1 \frac{1}{X_i} + \beta_2 + \epsilon_i^1 \qquad (7.18)$$

The interesting aspect of this specification is that the intercept and slope coefficients in the model (7.13) have interchanged their places in the new specification (7.18): β_1 is now the slope coefficient in the transformed equation and β_2 is its intercept. Let us try this special case with the example of the data on household total expenditure and food expenditure used in Figure 7.6. We showed in Figure 7.7 that the logarithmic transformation of both food and total expenditure removes the heteroscedasticity. Therefore, the double log transformation gives us one way to model the data. But let us try a different avenue of modelling the same data.

To do this, we examine the residuals from the fitted regression of food (F) on total expenditures (T). The estimated regression is given below (standard errors in brackets) as:

$$\hat{F} = 88.51 + 0.47T \qquad (7.19)$$
$$(21.61) \quad (0.02)$$

The standard errors are not usable due to heteroscedasticity, as is evident in Figure 7.8 which plots the residuals against the predicted values. Figure 7.9 present the plots of the absolute residuals of regression (7.19) against total household expenditures. A linear relationship between $|e|$ and T is discernible in Figure 7.9, which implies that a quadratic relationship between e^2 and T^2 seems plausible. In other words, it seems that assumption (7.9) is worth a try in this case.

The estimated transformed regression is:

$$\widehat{(F/T)} = 0.50 + 56.49\ (1/T)$$
$$(0.02) \quad (17.80) \qquad (7.20)$$

Figure 7.10 presents the scatter plot of the absolute residuals of this regression against $(1/T)$. The pattern that we observed in Figure 7.9 has now disappeared in Figure 7.10, indicating that the error term of the transformed model is homoscedastic. The other two plots of the raw residuals and the squared residuals (not shown here) also show the same absence of any heteroscedastic pattern. The tests for heteroscedasticity all yield insignificant results. Exploratory checks as well as the skewness- kurtosis test for normality indicate that there is no evidence of deviation from the normal distribution of the error term of the transformed model. We can, therefore, accept the transformed model as adequate in the sense that the standard assumptions of the classical normal linear regression model hold in the case of the transformed model.

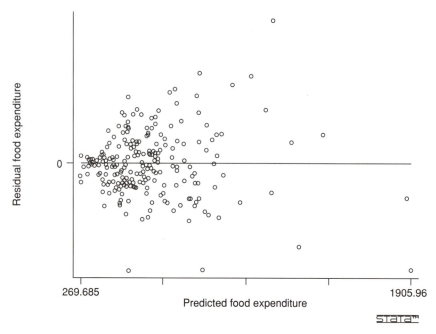

Figure 7.8   Residual versus predicted plot

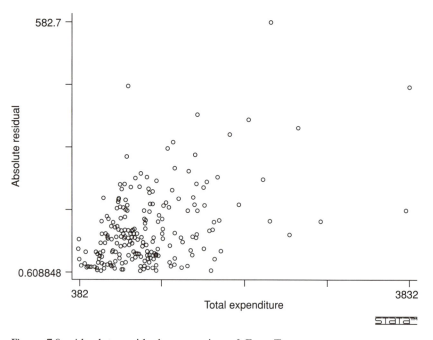

Figure 7.9   Absolute residuals: regression of *F* on *T*

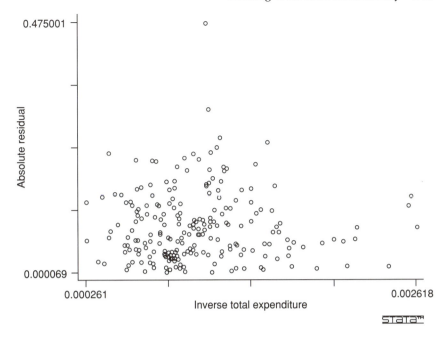

Figure 7.10 Absolute residuals: regression of *F/T* on 1/*T*

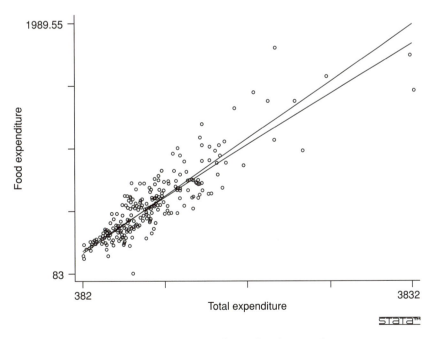

Figure 7.11 Comparing double-log and linear fitted regressions

Let us now compare the estimates we obtained from regressions (7.19) and (7.20), before and after transformation. The estimates of β_2 are fairly close: 0.47 and 0.50. But, the estimates of β_1 differ substantially: 88.51 and 56.49. The estimates of the standard error of the coefficients are not very different but higher in the transformed model. Given that the transformed model conforms to the assumptions of the classical normal linear regression model, the latter estimates can be used to make inferences from the sample data. The R^2 values are not comparable between (7.19) and (7.20) which explains why we did not bother to report them.

This leaves us with an interesting question. We have seen that the double-log model allows us to model these data in an acceptable way. Similarly, the linear model, suitably adapted to deal with heteroscedastic errors, also gives us a viable way to model the same data. So which model should we use? This is impossible to sort out, at least in the present state of statistical theory. The point is that we are resorting to *ad hoc* transformations to find an adequate description of the data. The problem arises because two different models may be equally data admissible. You may find this surprising, but the reason is easy to see if, as shown in Figure 7.11, you compare the fitted regression line and the curve produced by both models. On statistical grounds, therefore, both models perform equally satisfactorily and, hence, there is no reason to prefer one to the other. But we might decide on substantive grounds. The double-log specification gives us a constant elasticity of food expenditure with respect to the total expenditure whereas the slope coefficient in the linear model (which is the intercept in regression (7.20)) is a marginal propensity. Hence, much depends on which measure you find more appropriate to use.

White's heteroscedastic consistent standard errors (HCSEs)

Whilst weighted least squares allows us to obtain BLUE estimates from ordinary least squares we have seen that it is not without its problems. Specifically, we need a model of the heteroscedasticity, and even then the procedure may not be appropriate if the correct functional form of the regression differs from the functional form of the relationship between regressor and error term. For these reasons much current practice favours the use of heteroscedastic consistent standard errors.

In the two-variable case we saw that:

$$\text{Var} (b_2) = \frac{\sigma^2}{\Sigma (X_i - \overline{X})^2} \tag{7.21}$$

where the formula is simplified using the assumption that $E(\epsilon_i^2) = \sigma^2$ for all i. Where this assumption is not valid (i.e. the errors are heteroscedastic) then:

$$\text{Var}(b_2) = \frac{\sum (X_i - \overline{X})^2 \, \sigma_i^2}{\sum (X_i - \overline{X})^2} \qquad (7.22)$$

White (1980) showed that substituting the squared residuals (e_i^2) into equation (7.22) yields a consistent estimate of the standard errors (this result generalises to the k variable case). However, unlike with weighted least squares, these are not the minimum variances.

Inspection of equation (7.22) shows that if the errors are homoscedastic then the expression simplifies to that in equation (7.21). That is, the heteroscedastic consistent standard errors and those usually reported will be the same if there is no heteroscedasticity. A divergence between these two sets of standard errors is thus a rough test for the presence of heteroscedasticity.

7.6 SUMMARY OF MAIN POINTS

1   Heteroscedasticity is a non-constant error variance across the sample. The presence of heteroscedasticity renders least squares estimators inefficient, but they remain unbiased. In other words, they are linear unbiased estimators, not best linear unbiased estimators. Moreover, the standard formulae for the standard errors of the coefficients no longer apply and, hence, statistical inferences based on the *t*-test or *F*-test are not valid.

2   To detect heteroscedasticity we can use visual diagnostic tools: more specifically, we use the plots of raw, absolute and squared residuals against the predicted values of the dependent variable or against each regressor in turn.

3   Tests for heteroscedasticity fall into two categories. The first involves grouping the data with respect to different ranges of one of the explanatory variables and testing whether the conditional variances of the dependent variable or of the error term are the same. The second approach tests whether any systematic relation exists between the error term and any of the explanatory variables. Bartlett's and Goldfeld-Quandt's tests are examples of the former, while White's and Glejser's tests apply the latter principle.

4   White's test also serves as a general regression specification error test (RESET). As such, it is a broad-spectrum diagnostic test, which tells you when something is wrong but not necessarily what is wrong. The problem can be heteroscedastic errors, omitted variables or non-linearity of the regression curve.

5   Heteroscedasticity may be detected as a symptom of model misspecification (either incorrect functional form or omitted variables) rather than a genuine problem in the residuals of the true model. Hence model respecification is the first course of action to take in the presence of heteroscedastic residuals.

6   Power transformations often remove the problem of heteroscedasticity. A plot of the logarithms of the absolute residuals against the logarithms of the predicted values of the dependent variable allows us to judge whether a transformation is likely to solve the problem of heteroscedasticity. The slope coefficient of the corresponding regression tells us which transformation may be most appropriate.

7   If we believe we are dealing with a case of genuine heteroscedasticity then, in some cases, the method of weighted least squares allows us to derive efficient estimators of a regression model with heteroscedastic errors and to make valid inferences. Two cases are common in this respect: regressions with grouped data and situations where the error variance varies proportionally with one of the regressors.

8   If weighted least squares is not possible, then unbiased, though not the most efficient, standard errors may be calculated using White's heteroscedastic consistent standard errors (HCSEs).

ADDITIONAL EXERCISES

Exercise 7.9

Use the data in data file INDFOOD to test for heteroscedasticity in the regression of household food expenditure on total expenditure. Repeat the tests using the log of both variables. Comment on your findings.

Exercise 7.10

Using the data in data file LEACCESS, regress life expectancy on (a) income per capita; (b) logged income per capita; and (c) logged income per capita and access to health. Test for heteroscedasticity in each regression equation. Comment on your results.

8 Categories, counts and measurements

8.1 INTRODUCTION

Categories matter a great deal in empirical analysis. The reason is that the average level of a numerical variable or relations between variables may differ quite markedly across different categories. For example, rural or urban location affects consumption and production patterns of households. Similarly, wage and salary earnings may differ between men and women, even for the same level of education and years of experience. Occupational status affects both the health (for example, mortality rates) and the wealth of people. Categorical variables allow us to classify our data into a set of mutually exclusive categories with respect to some qualitative criterion: for example, men/women; rural/urban; occupation; region, countries or continents; policy regimes. In practice, this type of variable is inevitably discrete in nature inasmuch as we only consider a definite (usually limited) number of categories. For example, the gender variable has only two categories (male/female), while a variable on occupational status usually distinguishes among eight to ten categories. The distinctive nature of these variables, therefore, is that they do not measure anything, but assign a quality to our data (i.e. they are qualitative not quantitative). Hence, we cannot compute an average for this type of variable, but we can count (frequencies) how many observations in our data set fall in a group defined by a qualitative categorical variable. This chapter deals with ways in which these variables can be employed in empirical analysis to look deeper into the structure of our data. In particular, this chapter shows that the use of categorical variables helps us to guard against making unwarranted generalisations based on the assumption that homogeneity prevails when, in fact, we are lumping things together which should be kept separate. We have already come across categorical variables in Chapter 6, when we introduced dummy variables. In this chapter, we take this analysis further and look at the categories behind the dummies.

Throughout this chapter we shall use one extended example concerning the effects of education and gender on weekly wage earnings for the sample of 261 workers in an industrial town of southern India (data set INDIA) to illustrate our argument on categorical variables. Section 8.2 deals with the analysis of the relation between a numerical dependent variable and a categorical explanatory variable, which involves comparing averages between categories and, hence, is a natural extension of the principle of regression. We show that dummy variables can be used to depict categories of a categorical variable, a technique which allows us to extend the reach of regression analysis to deal with qualitative explanatory variables. Section 8.3 shows how to analyse the association between two (or more) categorical variables in the context of a contingency table. This technique allows us to test whether two (or more) categorical variables are statistically independent or not, using a chi-square statistic, thus laying the groundwork for discussing the regression between a quantitative dependent variable and two (or more) categorical variables in section 8.4. Here we meet again the by now familiar concept of partial association which we came across in Chapter 5. But we also introduce you to interaction effects which result when two or more categorical variables interact in unison to affect the outcome of the dependent variable. As usual, the last section 8.5 summarises the main points of this chapter. Perhaps you are wondering whether certain problems involve the use of a dependent qualitative (categorical) variable. They do, but they will be dealt with in the next chapter.

8.2 REGRESSION ON A CATEGORICAL VARIABLE: USING DUMMY VARIABLES

Take a look at Table 8.1. On the left, workers are classified by gender; on the right, weekly earnings are tabulated by weekly wage income groupings. Gender is a typical nominal categorical variable inasmuch as it defines two categories (and, hence, it is dichotomous) which are named but imply no ordering. While the frequency distribution of weekly income (in Indian rupees) is obtained by first defining income groups and then counting the number of workers in the sample that fall into each group, the frequency distribution of gender is obtained simply by counting the number of male and female workers. Obviously, we cannot talk about the mean or median of a categorical variable as we do about income. But, as we shall see in this and the next chapter, we can still analyse the proportions based on counts in various ways.

Categorical variables can also be based on a measurement variable. For example, it is generally quite difficult, if not impossible, to get the exact figure for the monthly or annual income of households in a survey. This is particularly true of developing countries because of the informal nature of various sources of income which are hardly recorded, officially or otherwise. One can, however, manage to get a rough figure of the income of a household by using a combination of direct and indirect means. Naturally, it will not be always very meaningful to use such shaky income figures in a regression and, hence, it may be more useful to categorise

Table 8.1 Frequency distributions of a categorical variable and a measurement variable

Distribution of workers by gender			Distribution of workers by weekly wage		
Gender	Frequency	Per cent	Income	Frequency	Per cent
Male	206	78.9	Up to 70	64	24.5
Female	55	21.1	70–150	94	36.0
			151–300	54	20.7
			Over 300	49	18.8
Total	261	100.0	Total	261	100.0

households into a few income categories such as low, middle and high income earners. This gives rise to income as an ordinal categorical variable. We use the term 'ordinal' because the three categories involve an ordering. In a similar way, a rainfall variable classified by low, medium and high rainfall is also an ordinal variable. Another such variable, and one we shall use in this example, is educational achievement: below primary, primary, secondary and higher education. The latter example shows that an ordinal variable is not necessarily derived from a measurement variable. Years of schooling is a quantitative variable but educational achievement is not exactly the same: it indicates that certain standards have been reached and successfully accomplished.

Exercise 8.1

Using the data set SOCECON, construct an ordinal income variable by grouping developing countries into low, lower-middle and upper-middle income countries as measured by GNP per capita. To do so, use the following cut-off points: low income countries, $600 or below; lower-middle income countries: above $600 and up to $2,500; upper-middle income countries: above $2,500 and up to $9,000. (Exercise 8.4 will require you to analyse life expectancy by these categories, so be sure to sort these data by the income categories when doing this exercise.)

Do men earn more than women? To answer this question with our data we need to analyse the association between weekly earnings, a quantitative variable, and a dichotomous qualitative variable. To do this, we need to tabulate earnings by gender. This is done in Table 8.2. The income differences between male and female workers come out quite sharply from these two columns: almost 78 per cent of the female workers earned less than Rs 150 while the corresponding proportion among their male counterparts was about 56 per cent. These differences are reflected in the average earnings of male and female workers, shown in the last row of Table 8.2. Gender as a category, in this case, thus identifies heterogeneity with respect to wage earnings in the population: women earn less than men; hence, averaging across male and female workers is incorrect.

Table 8.2 Distribution of weekly wage earnings (per cent by gender in each income group)

Weekly wage earnings (Indian Rs) (1)	Gender Male (2)	Female (3)	Total (4)
Up to 70	16.5	54.6	24.5
71–150	39.3	23.6	36.0
151–300	22.8	12.7	20.7
300 +	21.4	9.1	18.8
Total	100.0	100.0	100.0
Average weekly income	182.9	102.0	165.9

Recall that regression is the loci of conditional means or averages of the dependent variable for given values of the explanatory variable(s). The last row in Table 8.2 is, therefore, the sample regression of wage income on gender as it gives the conditional average of wage income given the gender category; that is:

$$\text{Average } (W \mid G = \text{Male}) = 182.94$$
$$\text{Average } (W \mid G = \text{Female}) = 101.99 \qquad (8.1)$$

where, W = weekly wage income; G = gender.

In Chapter 4, we discussed the regression of a measurement (numerical) variable on another similar variable. Consequently, we could talk about a regression line or a curve which depicts the average of the dependent variable at each point in the continuous range of the explanatory variable. If the regressor is a categorical variable, however, we can only consider averages for each category: a series of distinct conditional averages. But the point to note is that we are essentially talking about the same thing: the locus of conditional averages, either in the form of a continuous line or a curve if the explanatory variable is numerical and continuous, or in the form of a discrete series when the explanatory variable is categorical.

The latter type of a discrete regression is not only applicable to categorical variables. A discrete numerical explanatory variable such as family size will produce a similar result: we shall have average per capita income, for example, at each discrete point of family size. But, in this case, we can talk of increasing or decreasing conditional averages with increasing values of the explanatory variable – a positive or a negative relationship. By contrast, categories cannot always be ordered, for example, for the gender variable (a nominal categorical variable). Here, we can only analyse the differences in conditional averages to answer questions such as whether, on average, men earn more than women. Obviously, when our categorical variable can be ordered, for example, educational achievement, it is possible to speak of positive or negative association: income rises with higher education achievement.

How do we use categorical variables as regressors in our familiar linear regression model? To do this, we make use of dummy variables, with which you are familiar from Chapter 6. In the case of our example of the relation between weekly wage income and gender we construct a numerical variable, say D, so that:

$$D = 0 \quad \text{if} \quad G = \text{male}$$
$$D = 1 \quad \text{if} \quad G = \text{female} \tag{8.2}$$

where D is a dummy variable denoting the categorical variable gender, G. The difference between D and G is that the latter names two distinct categories while the former is numerical in nature. In other words, we can add up D or multiply it with some other number, but we cannot do the same with G. As far as G is concerned, we can only count the number of observations in each category. In fact, in this case, adding up D yields the same result as counting the number of women within the sample. We can now write the sample regression as follows:

$$\text{Average } (W \mid G) = \text{average } (W \mid D)$$
$$= b_1 + b_2 D$$

which implies:

$$\text{Average } (W \mid G = \text{Male}) = \text{Average } (W \mid D = 0)$$
$$= b_1 + b_2 0 = b_1$$
$$\text{Average } (W \mid G = \text{Female}) = \text{Average } (W \mid D = 1)$$
$$= b_1 + b_2 1 = b_1 + b_2$$

In other words, b_1 is the average wage income of the male workers, i.e. $b_1 = 182.94$, and b_2 is the difference between average female and male wage incomes: $b_2 = 101.99 - 182.94 = -80.95$. This result may be proved more formally (see exercise 8.8). Note that we are talking about sample averages (or, more precisely, sample means). The regression model, therefore, can be written as follows:

$$W = \beta_1 + \beta_2 D + \epsilon \tag{8.3}$$

where β_1 and β_2 are the population parameters of the model: respectively, the mean earnings of male workers and the mean difference in earnings between female and male workers.

However, not surprisingly, the distribution of weekly wage earnings of the 261 workers is skewed, as can be seen from Table 8.2. The skew in the distribution is clearly discernible – while the average weekly income is about Rs 166 (given in the last row), more than 60 per cent of the workers earned below Rs 150. The standard assumptions about ϵ in the classical regression model are obviously not applicable here. Therefore, a transformation of the dependent variables is called for: once more, the logarithmic transformation of W does the trick. Hence, we rewrite the model (8.3) as:

$$\ln(W) = \beta_1 + \beta_2 D + \epsilon \tag{8.4}$$

As explained earlier, in regression model (8.4) the constant term, β_1, gives us mean log earnings of male workers while the slope coefficient, β_2, states the mean difference in log earnings between female and male workers. This is typical of modelling categorical variables with dummy variables: one of the categories is used as the benchmark represented by the constant term, and the other categories are then compared (through differencing) with this reference category by means of their corresponding slopes. Box 8.1 tells you why this is the best way to use dummy variables in regression

---

Box 8.1   Dummies and the constant term

In principle, there are two ways in which dummies can be made to represent a categorical variable with a given number of mutually exclusive categories. One way is to use a dummy variable for each category. Hence, in the case of the gender variable, we could use a dummy, D_M, denoting men ($D_M = 1$ if the person is male; 0 otherwise) and another dummy, D_F, denoting women ($D_F = 1$ if the person is female; 0 otherwise). The other way is to use one fewer dummy than the number of categories because, if all dummies equal 0, the remainder category which depicts the benchmark will be selected.

Which method is preferable? Clearly, the latter method saves us from defining an additional, rather redundant, dummy variable. This in itself is a good enough reason to use $(C - 1)$ dummies when there are C categories. But there is a further reason to use $(C - 1)$ dummies for C categories. This has to do with their use in regression analysis. To see this, consider again the example of the gender variable. Suppose we prefer to use two dummies, D_M and D_F, and decide to feature them both in a regression line along with a constant term. As a result, the regressors (including the constant term) will now be orthogonal. Indeed, you can easily verify that $D_{Mi} + D_{Fi} = 1$, for all $i = 1, 2, 3, \ldots n$, where n is the sample size. Now, since the constant term is a variable X_1 such that $X_{1i} = 1$ for all i, it follows that a perfect linear relation exists between the dummies and the constant term: $X_{1i} - (D_{Mi} + D_{Fi}) = 0$. Hence, if you want to use two dummies in this case, you need to drop the constant term from the model.

It is generally less cumbersome to use $(C - 1)$ dummies to depict C categories as it avoids falling into the trap of rendering the regressors orthogonal as a result of including the constant term in the regression. The benchmark then depicts the category when all $(C - 1)$ dummies equal 0. In the case of an ordinal variable it is often useful to select the lowest (or highest) category as the benchmark.

Table 8.3 Regression of $\log_e(W)$ on D

	Coefficient	Standard errors	t-statistic
D	−0.703	0.119	−5.906
Intercept	4.941	0.055	90.383

Number of observations = 261; R^2 = 0.12

to denote categorical variables. Table 8.3 presents the results obtained by estimating the log-linear model in equation (8.4).

Hence, b_1, the estimate of β_1, equals 4.942, the antilogarithm of which equals 140 (rounded). As you know from Chapter 3, this is not an estimate of the population mean of average weekly earnings of male workers, but of its population median (and, incidentally, also of its geometric mean). Table 8.2 shows that the mean of 183 (rounded) is well above this median value, which shows that the data are indeed skewed to the right. To obtain the median weekly earning of female workers we first have to compute $(b_1 + b_2) = (4.94 − 0.70) = 4.24$, the antilogarithm of which is 69.28, the estimate of the median weekly earnings of female workers. This median is also significantly below the mean of 102, again showing that these data are also skewed to the right.

Exercise 8.2

Using Table 8.3, formally test the hypothesis $b_2 = 0$. Does your conclusion confirm that gender matters in terms of explaining earning differences?

The categorical variable for gender is a dichotomous variable, which implies that there are only two categories: male and female. As a result, a single dummy variable is sufficient to represent this categorical variable. If our categorical variables have more than two categories (say, a total number of C categories), we need $(C − 1)$ dummies, as explained in Box 8.1. For example, education achievement of the workers in our data set has four categories: below primary, primary, secondary, and post-secondary education. A regression between log income (W) and education (E), therefore, requires three dummy variables defined as follows:

$$D_2 = 1 \text{ if } E = \text{primary}, D_2 = 0 \text{ otherwise}$$
$$D_3 = 1 \text{ if } E = \text{secondary}, D_3 = 0 \text{ otherwise}$$
$$D_4 = 1 \text{ if } E = \text{post-secondary}, D_4 = 0 \text{ otherwise}. \tag{8.5}$$

The matrix in Table 8.4 shows how the three dummy variables D_2, D_3, D_4 together represent the four categories of education. Each category of education is represented by a unique combination of zeros and ones. In the case of 'below primary' education all dummy variables are zero. Thus, 'below primary' education serves as the reference category, the benchmark, to which other educational categories are compared.

Table 8.4   Categories of education

Educational achievement	D_2	D_3	D_4
Below primary	0	0	0
Primary	1	0	0
Secondary	0	1	0
Above secondary	0	0	1

Table 8.5   Regression of log(W) on educational levels

	Coefficient	Standard error	t-statistic
D2	0.081	0.134	0.604
D3	0.531	0.129	4.107
D4	0.827	0.204	4.059
Intercept	4.622	0.066	70.491

Number of observations = 261; $R^2 = 0.10$

The regression model of income on education is specified as:

$$\ln W = \beta_1 + \beta_2 D_2 + \beta_3 D_3 + \beta_4 D_4 + \epsilon \qquad (8.6)$$

where, β_1 = average log income of workers with below primary education; β_2 = difference of average log income of workers with primary education from β_1; β_3 = difference of average log income of workers with secondary education from β_1; β_4 = difference of average log income of workers with post-secondary education from β_1. Hence:

$$
\begin{aligned}
\text{Mean } \ln(W) &= \beta_1 && \text{if } E = \text{below primary} \\
&= \beta_1 + \beta_2 && \text{if } E = \text{primary} \\
&= \beta_1 + \beta_3 && \text{if } E = \text{secondary} \\
&= \beta_1 + \beta_4 && \text{if } E = \text{post-secondary}
\end{aligned}
$$

The results of estimation of this model are given in Table 8.5.

Exercise 8.3

Using Table 8.5, formally test the hypotheses $\beta_j = 0$, for $j = 2, 3, 4$. What do you conclude in terms of the importance of educational level on weekly earnings?

You should have found that there does not appear to be a significant difference between average earnings of workers with primary and below primary education, but both secondary and post-secondary education clearly matter.

Exercise 8.4

In exercise 8.1 you were requested to construct a categorical variable to depict income per capita categories for different countries. Select life expectancy as an additional (numerical) variable from the data set SOCECON and:

1 compare mean- and order-based statistics of life expectancy for each category of the income variable and construct the corresponding comparative box plots;
2 construct dummy variables to represent this categorical income variable;
3 regress life expectancy as dependent variable on the dummies thus constructed.

How does your analysis under (1) compare with your regression results obtained in 3?

8.3 CONTINGENCY TABLES: ASSOCIATION BETWEEN CATEGORICAL VARIABLES

We can now begin to put gender and education together to analyse their joint influence on wage income. In other words, let us now consider a multiple regression of a measurement variable such as income on the dummy variable representations of the categorical variables gender and education. But before we do so we need to do some more groundwork and develop ways to examine the association between two categorical variables. As an example, we ask whether educational achievement is itself associated with gender.

Contingency tables

First, we take up the issue of association between gender and education which, if it exists, will play a role in the partial associations with income (recall Chapter 5). To do this we use a contingency table. A two-way contingency table presents a joint frequency distribution of two categorical variables. Table 8.6 is the contingency table of gender and education, listing frequencies (or counts) of 261 workers jointly by gender and by education. A contingency table such as is given in Table 8.6 is used to examine whether or not two categorical variables are stochastically (statistically) independent (see Box 8.2). We need a table of cross-tabulations because, with categorical variables, we cannot compute numerical summaries like a covariance or a coefficient of correlation straight away. But we can use the frequencies to compute fractions of counts or proportions which, as we shall see, serve as estimates of the corresponding probabilities.

To say that two categorical variables are stochastically dependent does not imply any statement about causation. It merely states that they are associated with one another. Hence, when investigating stochastic

---

Box 8.2   Stochastic independence

Two events *A* and *B* are stochastically independent if

$$P(A \mid B) = P(A) \text{ or } P(B \mid A) = P(B)$$

In other words, *A* and *B* are stochastically independent if occurrence of one of the events does not change the probability of occurrence of the other event.

Thus, gender and education of a worker are stochastically independent if the probability of a certain level of education achievements of a randomly selected worker (event *A*) remains the same irrespective of whether the worker is male or female (event *B*). Or, equivalently, the probability that a randomly selected worker is male or female is the same irrespective of the educational category from which the worker is selected.

The definition of conditional probability implies:

$$P(A \mid B) = P(A \text{ and } B)/P(B)$$

or

$$P(A \text{ and } B) = P(A \mid B) \cdot P(B) \{ = P(B \mid A) \cdot P(A) \}$$

Therefore, if *A* and *B* are independent: $P(A \mid B) = P(A)$, it follows that:

$$P(A \text{ and } B) = P(A) \cdot P(B)$$

In other words, if gender and education are independent then:

$$P(G = g \text{ and } E = e) = P(G = g) \cdot P(E = e)$$

for all combinations of *g* and *e*, where *G* = Gender (*g* = male or female); *E* = education (*e* = below primary, primary, secondary, or post-secondary).

Table 8.6   Contingency table of gender education

Gender	Below primary	Primary	Secondary	Above secondary	Total
Male	111	40	44	11	206
	(42.5)	(15.3)	(16.9)	(4.2)	(78.9)
Female	36	6	7	6	55
	(13.8)	(2.3)	(2.7)	(2.3)	(21.1)
Total	147	46	51	17	261
	(56.3)	(17.6)	(19.5)	(6.5)	(100.0)

Education spans the columns Below primary, Primary, Secondary, Above secondary.

Note: Figures in parentheses indicate cell counts as per cent of total counts (= 261).

dependence between two (or more) categorical variables we do not necessarily imply any direction of causation. If we have good reason to believe that one variable depends causally on the other, it is preferable to model the data likewise by making explicit that one variable depends on the other(s). This we shall do in the context of logit modelling in the next chapter. Here, our interest is to see whether two categorical variables 'covary' in the sense that they are not statistically independent.

The test of independence that we develop is based on a comparison of the observed counts or frequencies of the contingency table with what would be the expected frequencies if the two variables were independent. To work out what are the expected frequencies under the hypothesis of independence requires that we make use of the property that $P(A$ and $B) = P(A) \cdot P(B)$ if A and B are stochastically independent in the context of the binomial distribution.

The binomial distribution

The binomial probability distribution is concerned with modelling a dichotomous variable whose outcome in a single trial can be one of two possibilities only. The common analogy used for discussing the binomial distribution is that of tossing a coin which results in either a 'head' or a 'tail'. A practical example is our sample worker being male or female. Let p be the probability that a randomly selected worker is female and, hence, $(1 - p)$ is the probability that a randomly selected worker is male. The binomial distribution model gives us the probabilities of the number of women, F, in an independent random sample of size n. The value of F can be anywhere between zero (no women in the sample), and n (all sample workers are women). Hence, F can assume any of the values $(0, 1, 2, \ldots n)$. The variable F is called a binomial variable, and the probability p is called the binomial probability.

To express the probability that $F = f$ (in a sample of size n) we proceed as follows. The probabilities of sampling f female workers and $(n - f)$ male workers in a particular sample are, respectively, p^f and $(1 - p)^{n-f}$, and, hence, $p^f(1 - p)^{n-f}$ is the probability associated with this sample. But there are several ways of getting this type of sample. For example, in a sample of size three (i.e. $n = 3$), one can get two women ($F = 2$) and one man in three different ways: (male, female, female), (female, male, female) or (female, female, male). Each of these samples has a probability of $p^2(1 - p)^{3-2}$. Thus, the probability of $F = 2$ in a sample of 3 equals $3 p^2(1 - p)^{3-2}$. In general, the number of ways one can get f women and $(n - f)$ men in a sample is given by the following convenient algebraic formula:

$$C_f^n = \text{number of ways } f \text{ women and } (n - f) \text{ men can}$$
$$\text{be obtained in a sample of size } n$$

$$= n!/\{ f! \, (n - f)! \} \text{ where } k! = k(k - 1)(k - 2) \ldots 2.1;$$

and, hence, the probability distribution of F can be written as:

$$P\ (F = f) = C_f^n\ p^f\ (1 - p)^{n-f} \qquad f = 0,1,2,\ldots, n \qquad (8.7)$$

which is the well-known binomial distribution, denoted by $B(n,p)$, where n, the sample size, and p, the binomial probability, are the parameters of the distribution. Thus, if F has a binomial distribution $B(n,p)$, then its probabilities for $F = 0,1,2,\ldots, n$ are given by the expression above. The theoretical mean and variance of a binomial distribution is given as follows:

$$F \sim B(n,p) \qquad\qquad\qquad\qquad\qquad (8.8)$$
$$E(F) = n\ p; \qquad V(F) = n\ p\ (1-p)$$

Hence, the mean of a binomial distribution with parameters n and p is the product of the two parameters: its sample size multiplied by the binomial probability. Now, it can be shown that the sample proportion is an unbiased and minimum variance estimator of the probability p, a property we can use to work out the expected frequencies under the hypothesis of independence.

Contingency chi-square test of independence

Let us return to our contingency table (Table 8.6). Each cell in Table 8.6 corresponds to a specific gender and education category. Let us consider a particular cell – male and below primary. Hence, only if a worker is male and has below primary education will he be counted in this cell; otherwise, not. This is obviously a dichotomous situation. Now, recall that the sample of workers is independently and randomly selected. Therefore, we have 261 randomly selected workers each of whom either falls into this specific cell or does not. The situation is similar to that of a binomial distribution discussed above: that is, the cell frequency can be modelled by a binomial distribution. Hence, we can treat the cell frequency as a binomial variable with binomial probability equal to $P(G$ = male and E = below primary). The observed frequency (OBS) in the cell is 111; its expected frequency (EXP) will, according to equation (8.8) be equal to $n\ P(G$ = male and E = below primary). Now, under the hypothesis of independence, we get $P(G$ = male and E = below primary) = $P(G$ = male)$\cdot P(E$ = below primary) and, hence:

$$EXP(G = \text{male and } E = \text{below primary}) \quad = n\ P(G = \text{male and}$$
$$E = \text{below primary})$$

$$= 261\ P(G = \text{male })$$
$$\cdot P(E = \text{below primary})$$

$P(G$ = male) and $P(E$ = below primary) are also binomial probabilities corresponding to binomial variables: respectively, the number of male

Table 8.7 Computation of contingency chi-square statistic

Observed cell frequency (O)	Estimated probability (P)	Expected cell frequency (261.P)	Relative squared deviations (O – E)^2/E
111	(206/261)·(147/261)	116.02	0.218
40	(206/261)·(46/261)	36.31	0.378
44	(206/261)·(51/261)	40.25	0.349
11	(206/261)·(17/261)	13.42	0.436
36	(55/261)·(147/261)	30.98	0.814
6	(55/261)·(46/261)	9.69	1.407
7	(55/261)·(51/261)	10.75	1.307
6	(55/261)·(17/261)	3.58	1.632
261			6.538

workers and the number of 'below primary' workers. Since the sample proportions are good estimators of the corresponding binomial probabilities, we can use the corresponding sample proportions of male workers (206/261) and 'below primary' workers (147/261) as estimators of these probabilities. Hence, the estimated expected cell frequency for (G = male and E = below primary), under the hypothesis of stochastic independence, is equal to 261 (206/261)·(147/261) = 116.02, which compares with an observed frequency of 111. The same steps can be repeated for the rest of the cells of the contingency table to obtain the estimated expected frequencies under the hypothesis of independence. The third column in Table 8.7 lists all estimated expected cell frequencies.

If the hypothesis of independence is correct, then these expected frequencies should be very close to the actually observed frequencies in the sample, i.e. the first and the third column of Table 8.7 will be very close to each other. The more the third column deviates from the first column, the less likely it is that both variables are indeed stochastically independent. What we need, therefore, is a numerical tool to summarise the deviations of the expected frequencies (*EXP*) from the observed frequencies (*OBS*). This is done as follows:

$$\chi^2 = \sum \left[\frac{(OBS - EXP)^2}{EXP} \right] \tag{8.9}$$

where the summation is over all the cells in the contingency table.

The resulting measure is called the contingency chi-square statistic. It is easy to see that the more the expected frequencies deviate from the observed frequencies, the larger will be the value of the statistic since it is based on the squared differences between the two sets of frequencies. The larger the value of the statistic, therefore, the more the hypothesis of independence is suspected. But how large a value of this statistic is large enough to reject the hypothesis of independence? Such a judgement is based on how unlikely (in the probability sense) is the large value of the statistic. Now, the sampling distribution of this statistic is a chi-square distribution with degrees of freedom equal to $d = (c - 1)(r - 1)$, where c is the number of columns and r the number of rows in the contingency table. This explains the name of the summary measure in equation (8.9).

So all we need next is to find the cut-off points (critical values) in the corresponding chi-square distribution at which there is only 5 per cent or 1 per cent probability (level of significance) for the statistic to have a larger value. If the computed value of the statistic is larger than the critical value, then we reject the hypothesis of independence at the corresponding level of significance. Note that computer software often provides the upper-tail probability of the computed value, i.e. the probability of the statistic being larger than the computed value. In that case, we reject the hypothesis of independence if the upper-tail probability is less than 5 per cent or 1 per cent. This procedure to test the hypothesis of independence of two categorical variables is called the contingency chi-square test of independence.

In our present example, the value of the test statistic computed at the bottom of the fourth column is 6.54. The degrees of freedom are $(4 - 1) \cdot (2 - 1) = 3$. The critical value of a chi-square distribution with three degrees of freedom is 7.81 at 5 per cent level of significance. Since the computed test statistic of 6.54 is below the critical value we cannot reject the hypothesis of independence between gender and education of workers at the 5 per cent level of significance.

The test of independence described above checks for the existence of association. The larger the value of the test statistic, the greater is the evidence of association. The same chi-square statistic can also be used to develop a measure of association. One such measure is given by Cramer's V, defined as follows:

$$V = \sqrt{\frac{(OBS - EXP)^2}{EXP} \cdot \frac{1}{n \cdot (k - 1)}} \tag{8.10}$$

where n is the total frequency and k is the minimum of the number of rows and columns. The value of V lies between 0 and 1, both inclusive. In our case, Cramer's V measure of association between gender and education is equal to $[6.5375/\{261.(2 - 1)\}]^{\frac{1}{2}} = 0.16$, which indicates that the association is rather weak.

Exercise 8.5

Using exercises 8.1 and 8.4 and the data set SOCECON (world socio-economic data), define a categorical variable which picks out the countries of Sub-Saharan Africa from among the developing countries. Investigate whether this variable and the categorical income variable are statistically independent or not, using both the contingency chi-square test of independence and Cramer's V statistic.

8.4 PARTIAL ASSOCIATION AND INTERACTION

In our example we found that both gender and education are related to wage income. To distinguish between their separate effects on wage income, we shall make use of the familiar concept of partial association. But we also need another concept which, initially, is a little difficult to understand but matters a great deal when working with categorical variables. This is the concept of interaction between two (or more) categorical variables in their effects on a measurement variable: for example, the differences in partial associations of income with education across the gender categories.

Let us start with the question of the partial associations of income with gender and education. For convenience of exposition, we collapse the four categories of education into two categories – 'below secondary', and 'secondary and above'. The partial association between weekly wage income and education is the association between these two variables, keeping the third variable, gender, fixed at a specific category. For example, consider the contingency table of income groups and educational categories for male workers in Table 8.8(a). The degree of association in this contingency table is the association between income and education for male workers. Therefore, it is a partial association between income and education.

Similarly, the degree of association between income and education in the contingency table for female workers, Table 8.8(b), is also a partial association. The chi-square statistics indicate that the hypothesis of independence between income and education can be rejected at the 1 per cent

Table 8.8 Partial associations of weekly wage income and education

Weekly wage income	*Below secondary education*	*To or above secondary education*	*Total*
(a) Male workers			
Up to 70	29	5	34
71–150	68	13	81
151–300	30	17	47
Over 300	24	20	44
Total	151	55	206
Chi-square (3 df) = 17.26			
Upper tail probability = 0.001			
Cramer's V = 0.29			
(b) Female workers			
Up to 70	28	2	30
71–150	7	6	13
151–300	5	2	7
Over 300	2	3	5
Total	42	13	55
Chi-square (3 df) = 12.20			
Upper tail probability = 0.007			
Cramer's V = 0.47			

level of significance for both male and female workers. In other words, there is evidence of association in both cases, which is not at all surprising. Higher education is likely to bring better-paid jobs. What is more interesting is that the sample association between income and education is comparatively stronger among female workers than among male workers as indicated by Cramer's V measures of association. In other words, the partial association between income and education varies with gender. Hence, the way in which education relates to income depends on whether we are dealing with men or women: we say that education and gender interact with each other in their respective association with income.

Take a look at Table 8.9, which presents the average log income of workers by education and gender. The entries in the table are the conditional averages of the logarithm of weekly earnings for given gender and education categories. The rows in the table are the partial regressions of log income on education, because each row presents average log income by education, keeping gender fixed. Similarly, the columns present the partial regressions of log income on gender, keeping education fixed. The interaction effect shows up in the way the partial regressions differ. For example, male workers with secondary or above education fetch 0.5 (= 5.31 – 4.81) higher average log income as compared with other male workers with 'below secondary' education, while for female workers the similar difference is 0.84 (= 4.88 – 4.04). In other words, the effect of higher education is different between males and females. The interaction effect can also be seen the other way, that is, how the average log income differs between gender groups within each educational category. The differences are 0.77 (= 4.81 – 4.04) and 0.43 (= 5.31 – 4.88) for lower and higher education categories, respectively; that is, the gender differences in average log income is less among workers with higher education. In the absence of interaction effects these differences in average log income, between gender or between education, would be the same.

Exercise 8.6

Using the data set SOCECON, investigate the partial associations and the interaction effects of the categorical income variable and the variable denoting Sub-Saharan African countries on life expectancy. In each case, explain carefully what each of these concepts measures in this concrete example.

Table 8.9 Average log wage income by gender and by education

	Below secondary education	*To or above secondary education*
Male	4.81	5.31
Female	4.04	4.88

8.5 MULTIPLE REGRESSION ON CATEGORICAL VARIABLES

Our next step is to develop an appropriate multiple regression model in order to study the relationship of weekly wage income with gender and education such that we capture both the separate influence of each of these explanatory variables net of the other and their interaction effect on income. To be able to use the regression model we need to construct dummy variables since our explanatory variables are categorical in nature. Let DG and DE be the dummy variables for gender and education.

$$DG \quad = 0 \text{ if gender } = \text{ male}$$
$$= 1 \text{ if gender } = \text{ female} \qquad (8.11)$$

$$DE \quad = 0 \text{ if education } < \text{ secondary}$$
$$= 1 \text{ if education } \geq \text{ secondary} \qquad (8.12)$$

$$DGE = DG \cdot DE$$
$$= 1 \text{ if gender } = \text{ female and education } \geq \text{ secondary}$$
$$= 0 \text{ otherwise} \qquad (8.13)$$

where DGE is the interaction dummy between gender and education.

The multiple regression model can now be specified as follows:

$$\widehat{\ln(W)} = \beta_1 + \beta_2 DG + \beta_3 DE + \beta_4 DGE \qquad (8.14)$$

where, β_1 = average log income for men with 'below secondary' education which is the benchmark category; $\beta_1 + \beta_2$ = average log income for women with 'below secondary' education; $\beta_1 + \beta_3$ = average log income for men with 'above-secondary' education; $\beta_1 + \beta_2 + \beta_3 + \beta_4$ = average log income for women with 'above-secondary education.

We could now proceed by estimating this model with least squares regression. However, before we do this, it is instructive to show how the regression can be deduced from Table 8.9 by taking row and column differences. This is done in Table 8.10.

The row and column differences in Table 8.10 clearly show how the interaction effect comes into play. Note, in particular, that the difference of the differences (right-hand bottom corner) gives us the interaction

Table 8.10 Breakdown of average log income into components

	Below secondary education	*At or above secondary education*	*Difference*	
Male	4.81 ($= \beta_1$)	5.31	= 0.50	($= \beta_3$)
Female	4.04	4.88	= 0.84	= 0.50 + 0.34 ($= \beta_3 + \beta_4$)
Difference	= −0.77 ($= \beta_2$)	= −0.43 = −0.77 + 0.34 ($= \beta_2 + \beta_4$)	= −0.34	($= \beta_4$)

Table 8.11   Regressing log income on gender and education

	Coefficient	Standard error	t-statistic
DG	–0.77	0.13	–5.92
DE	0.50	0.12	4.63
DGE	0.34	0.26	1.29
Intercept	4.81	0.06	79.37

Number of observations = 261; R^2 = 0.21

effect directly. Therefore, if there is no interaction, column and row differences add up to zero. In this case, there is some interaction. To see whether it is significantly different from zero or not, it is best to turn to the estimation of model (8.14) with least squares regression. This is done in Table 8.11.

The regression results reproduce the results obtained in Table 8.10. Take some time to verify this by carefully comparing these regressions with the column and row margins (depicting differences) of Table 8.10. The regression model, therefore, does not add much except for the fact that you can carry out the tests of significance more easily. Note that the interaction dummy turns out not to be significantly different from zero at the 5 per cent significance level.

As we have already seen in Table 8.10, the regression coefficients can be easily read out from Table 8.9. This is only possible, however, when the explanatory variables are all categorical.

What makes the regression modelling by means of dummy variables particularly useful is that it allows us to combine measurement variables along with categorical variables in the same model. For example, up to now we have not yet considered the age of the workers in analysing their weekly earnings. But age obviously matters. To the extent that workers earn more with age as they acquire skills or experiences, variations in the age of the workers must be at least part of the reason for the variations in the earnings. Let us, therefore, incorporate the age as a variable in our model:

$$\ln W = \beta_1 + \beta_2 \cdot DG + \beta_3 \cdot DE + \beta_4 \cdot DGE + \beta_5 \cdot AGE + \epsilon \qquad (8.15)$$

The estimated regression is given in Table 8.12. This model fits quite well. The residuals behave approximately normal: the skewness-kurtosis test turns out to be insignificant at the 5 per cent level (results not presented here). By all indications, the regression model in (8.15), therefore, appears to be a satisfactory specification.

Interestingly, the interaction coefficient turns out to be significantly different from zero at the 5 per cent level and, moreover, it takes on a higher value of 0.52 as compared to 0.34 before we included age into the model! All other coefficients are also significant at the 5 per cent level. Obviously, omitting the age factor blurred the interaction effect. What we

Table 8.12 Regression of log income on gender, education and age

	Coefficient	Standard error	t-statistic
DG	–0.75	0.11	–6.90
DE	0.50	0.10	5.06
DGE	0.52	0.22	2.33
AGE	0.03	0.01	10.38
Intercept	3.72	0.11	31.93

Number of observations = 261; R^2 = 0.45

have achieved in the final regression analysis in this section is first to remove the impact of age variation among the workers on the variation in weekly wage earnings, and then to look deeper into the variation by identifying heterogeneity among the workers with respect to gender and income. The R^2 value indicates that about 45 per cent of the variation in weekly wage earnings is explained by age, education and gender. Significantly, we found that there was no evidence of association between gender and education (recall the result of the contingency chi-square test). This is probably not so much indicative of women having the same access to education as men, but rather that men also have limited access to education because of the socioeconomic handicap suffered by working-class households which, in turn, reduces the gender gap in education. The negative coefficient of the gender dummy shows that female workers earn less than male workers irrespective of education. But a redeeming feature is the positive coefficient of the dummy for the interaction between gender and education: the incremental earnings of female workers with higher education is higher than that of the male workers. In other words, the earning benefits of higher education is higher for women. But this only means that the gender gap in earnings reduces with higher education: on average, women still earn less.

The introduction of the age variable changed the picture quite dramatically with regard to the interaction dummy between gender and education. This illustrates the argument we made in Chapter 6 that we should beware of omitting an important relevant variable from the model since our coefficient estimates will end up being biased as well as less precise. In fact, this example illustrates how the introduction of an important relevant variable increases the precision of the estimates of the variables already included in the model. Note how introduction of the age variable improved the *t*-statistics of all dummy variables included in the model. Compare Table 8.12 with Table 8.11. Furthermore, we also note that the bias produced by omitting the age variable mainly affected the interaction variable *DGE*, the coefficient of which increases markedly. The other slope coefficients, however, hardly changed at all.

Obviously, we should have known all along that age matters. In fact, in Chapter 7 we discussed the regression of the logarithm of wage income on the age of workers. But the structure of the argument in this chapter reflects pedagogical concerns, not research priorities. Hence, we started step by step, introducing our categorical variables one by one, moving on to multiple regression with two dummy variables, and ending up with a regression which features dummies along with a measurement variable as regressors in the model. In actual research we would have started with a general model which included the age variable from the beginning along with a string of dummy variables and subsequently we would have checked whether any of the variables could be dropped from the equation.

What about the interaction between a categorical variable and a quantitative variable? Is this possible? Yes, it is and, in fact, we already dealt with such interaction in Chapter 6. Note, for example, that our specification (8.15) only includes intercept dummies, although one of them is an interaction term. The interaction between a categorical variable and a quantitative variable is done with the slope dummy. In general, the technique consists in introducing relevant product terms between the dummy variable and the quantitative variable in question. For example, a model of multiple regression of Y on X and D (respectively, a measurement variable and a dummy variable) along with the interaction effect of X and D can be specified as follows:

$$Y = \beta_1 + \beta_2 X + \beta_3 D + \beta_4 X \cdot D + \epsilon \qquad (8.16)$$

where β_4 captures the interaction effect. There is no need to give examples here since Chapter 6 showed you how to do this. What is useful, however, is to go back to Chapter 6 and see how each of the dummies used reflect categorical variables (policy regimes; time periods; heterogeneous sub-samples).

Exercise 8.7

Show how regression analysis can be used to investigate the relation between life expectancy as dependent variable and the categorical income per capita variable and the Sub-Saharan Africa identification variable as explanatory variables. Check whether your results conform with those obtained in exercise 8.6.

8.6 SUMMARY OF MAIN POINTS

1   Categorical variables allow us to classify our data with respect to some qualitative criterion in a set of mutually exclusive categories. A qualitative variable is dichotomous if it contains only two mutually exclusive categories. We cannot measure a categorical variable, but we can count how many observations fall into a particular category. This allows us to perform quantitative calculations with respect to frequencies of qualitative variables.

2   To include qualitative variables into regression analysis as explanatory variables we make use of dummies. In general, we use $(C - 1)$ dichotomous dummies to represent a categorical variable with C categories. Each dummy takes on the value 1 if the observation belongs to its category, and zero otherwise. The category without a corresponding dummy variable is the benchmark or reference category which is selected when all dummies equal zero.

3   A contingency table allows us to study the association between two (or more) categorical variables. This is done by verifying whether the variables are statistically independent from each other. The test consists in comparing observed with expected counts (i.e. frequencies), where the expected counts are derived with the aid of the binomial distribution, assuming randomly sampled observations. The relevant test is the contingency chi-square test of independence. A derived measure of association is Cramer's V which lies between zero and one.

4   When looking at the relation between a quantitative dependent variable Y and two (or more) categorical variables, W and Z, we take account of partial associations and interaction effects. The partial association between Y and W is the association between them, keeping Z fixed within a given category. If such partial associations between Y and W varies for different categories of Z, we say that there is interaction between W and Z in their effects on Y.

5   The use of dummy variables associated with two or more categorical variables allows us to study partial association and interaction effects in the context of multiple regression. Interaction dummies are obtained by multiplying dummies corresponding to different categorical variables. This procedure allows us to test formally whether interaction is present or not using the familiar t-test (or an F-test if we want to drop more than one interaction term from the regression).

6   A slope dummy is nothing else but an interaction variable between a dummy variable and a quantitative variable. Its slope measures the interaction effect and its t-statistic shows whether it is significant or not.

ADDITIONAL EXERCISES

Exercise 8.8

Consider the regression model

$$Y = \beta_1 + \beta_2 D + \epsilon$$

where Y is income and D a dummy variable for gender ($D = 1$ for female and $D = 0$ for male). Use the formulae for the least squares estimators to show that

$$b_1 = \bar{Y}_m \text{ and } b_2 = \bar{Y}_f - \bar{Y}_m$$

where the m and f subscripts denote male and female respectively. (The solution to this exercise is given as Appendix 8.1.)

Exercise 8.9

Repeat your analysis of life expectancy carried out in this chapter but now including dummy variables to separately identify Sub-Saharan Africa, Asia, North Africa and the Middle East, Eastern Europe and developed countries. Compare your results with those obtained earlier.

Exercise 8.10

Using the data in the PRODFUN file, calculate labour productivity and classify firms as having low, medium and high productivity. Is the level of labour productivity independent from the sector in which a firm operates?

APPENDIX 8.1: SOLUTION TO EXERCISE 8.8

The model is

$$Y = \beta_1 + \beta_2 D + \epsilon \tag{A.8.1}$$

We know that

$$b_2 = \frac{\Sigma(D - \bar{D})Y}{\Sigma(D - \bar{D})^2} \tag{A.8.2}$$

Now

$$\bar{D} = \frac{1}{n} \sum_{i=1}^{n} D_i = \frac{n_f}{n}$$

$$\therefore D - \bar{D} = \frac{n_m}{n} \text{ if } D = 1$$

$$= -\frac{n_f}{n} \text{ if } D = 0 \tag{A.8.3}$$

where n_f and n_m are the number of women and men respectively. The denominator in equation (A.8.2) is therefore given by:

$$\sum_{i=1}^{n}(D - \bar{D})^2 = \sum_{i=1}^{n_m}(D_i - \bar{D})^2 + \sum_{i=1}^{n_f}(D_i - \bar{D})^2$$

$$= n_m\left(\frac{-n_f}{n}\right)^2 + n_f\left(\frac{n_m}{n}\right)^2 = \frac{n_m n_f}{n} \tag{A.8.4}$$

The numerator is:

$$\sum_{i=1}^{n} (D - \overline{D})Y_i = \sum_{i=1}^{n_m} (D_i - \overline{D})Y_i + \sum_{i=1}^{n_f} (D_i - \overline{D})Y_i$$

$$= -\frac{n_f}{n} \sum_{i=1}^{n_m} Y_i + \frac{n_m}{n} \sum_{i=1}^{n_f} Y_i \qquad (A.8.5)$$

Substituting equations (A.8.4) and (A.8.5) into (A.8.2):

$$b_2 = -\frac{1}{n_m} \sum_{i=1}^{n_m} Y_i + \frac{1}{n_f} \sum_{i=1}^{n_f} Y_i$$

$$= \overline{Y}_f - \overline{Y}_m \qquad (A.8.6)$$

the intercept is given by:

$$b_1 = \overline{Y} - b_2 \overline{D}$$

$$= \overline{Y} - \frac{n_m}{n} \left[\overline{Y}_f - \overline{Y}_m \right]$$

$$= \frac{1}{n} \sum_{i=1}^{n} Y_i - \frac{1}{n} \sum_{i=1}^{n_f} Y_i + \frac{n_m}{n\,n_m} \sum_{i=1}^{n_m} Y_i$$

$$= \frac{1}{n_m} \sum_{i=1}^{n_m} Y_i = \overline{Y}_m \qquad (A.8.7)$$

9 Logit transformation, modelling and regression

9.1 INTRODUCTION

Up to now, the dependent variables in the economic models we discussed were all measurement variables. But what if the dependent variable we are interested in is categorical in nature? For example, we may be interested in investigating the main determinants of home ownership in an urban setting. Alternatively, our interest may be to find out why some rural labourers succeed in obtaining permanent jobs while others have to depend on temporary work or casual jobs. In both examples the dependent variables are categorical in nature. In fact, they are both dichotomous variables. This chapter looks at dependent categorical variables which are dichotomous in nature and, hence, can be represented by dummy variables. Our focus, therefore, is on regressions in which the dependent variable is a dummy variable.

When dealing with a dichotomous dependent variable our main interest is to assess the probability that one or another characteristic is present. Does a labourer have a permanent job, or not? Does the household own its home, or not? What determines the probability that the answer is yes, or no? It is the latter question which we try to address when dealing with logit regression. This is what makes logit regression, despite many similarities, essentially different from the linear regression models we have discussed so far. In multiple regression, for example, we try to predict the average value of Y for given values of the independent variables with the use of a regression line. In logit regression, however, our interest is to predict the probability that a particular characteristic is present. Hence, we do not predict whether Y equals 1 or 0; what we predict is the probability that $Y = 1$ given the values of the independent variables.

But what are logits anyway? We start this chapter by showing that logits provide a convenient means to transform data consisting of counts of a dichotomous variable. Hence we can show the connection between proportions (or percentages), odds and logits as alternative summaries of observed counts of a dichotomous variable. We argue that the logit transformation is a handy and user-friendly tool for data analysis, independently from its further usefulness in the context of logit model-ling and regression.

Next we turn to logit modelling in the context of multiway contingency tables. You have already come across the concepts of contingency tables and dependence or independence of categorical variables in the previous chapter. In this chapter, we show how this analysis can be extended to investigate the effects of one or more categorical variables (the indepen-dent variables) on a dichotomous response variable (the dependent variable). From here it is a small step to reach logit regression as a flex-ible model to deal with regressions featuring a dummy variable as dependent variable, which is done in the closing sections of this chapter. The final section summarises the main points.

9.2 THE LOGIT TRANSFORMATION

When dealing with a dichotomous categorical variable we count the frequency of a given characteristic in relation to the total number of obser-vations. Table 9.1, for example, depicts the prevalence of high profit enterprises among informal sector enterprises in Tanzania by sector, comparing rural enterprises with those in Dar es Salaam, in 1991.

We can now calculate proportions, odds and logits relating to our dichoto-mous categorical variable. In general, if N is the total number of observa-tions and n is the number of observations which have the required property (e.g. high profit enterprises), the proportion, p, is obtained as follows:

$$p = \frac{n}{N}$$

(9.1)

For example, the proportion of high profit enterprises in the total number of urban small scale manufacturing enterprises is given by

Table 9.1 High profit enterprises in Tanzania's informal sector, 1991

	Number of high profit enterprises		Total number of enterprises	
	Rural	*Dar es Salaam*	*Rural*	*Dar es Salaam*
Agriculture and fishing	4,482	1,116	77,634	11,810
Mining and quarrying	123	0	3,952	0
Manufacture	2,947	2,326	354,529	31,456
Construction	234	684	87,598	10,762
Trade, restaurants and hotels	11,723	10,368	525,730	142,041
Transport	1,143	682	41,508	2,324
C&P services	425	1,182	63,185	12,759

Source: Tanzania: The Informal Sector 1991, Planning Commission and Ministry of Labour, Table ENT25.
Note: High profit enterprises are enterprises with an annual profit of more than Tsh 500,000.

$$P_{man,Dar} = \frac{2326}{31456} = 0.0739$$

or 7.39 per cent of all enterprises. Under conditions of random sampling, a calculated proportion gives us an estimate of the probability of encountering a high profit enterprise in urban informal manufacturing.

The odds, O, is the ratio of the number of observations with the required characteristic to the number of observations which do not have this characteristic:

$$O = \frac{n}{n - N} \tag{9.2}$$

$$= \frac{p}{(1 - p)} \tag{9.3}$$

For example, the odds favouring high profit enterprises in the urban small-scale manufacturing sector in Tanzania are:

$$O_{man,Dar} = \frac{0.0739}{1 - 0.0739} = 0.0798$$

In this case, the odds are very similar in value to the corresponding proportion : 0.0798 as against 0.0739. The reason is easy to understand once we take another look at equation (9.3). For small values of p, the denominator $(1 - p)$ will be approximately 1 and, hence, the odds are approximately equal to the corresponding proportion.

A logit, L, is obtained by taking the logarithm of the odds. Hence:

$$L = \log (O) \tag{9.4}$$
$$= \log p/(1 - p) \tag{9.5}$$
$$= \log p - \log (1 - p) \tag{9.6}$$

In our example, the logit of high profit enterprises in urban informal manufacturing equals:

$$L_{man,Dar} = \ln 0.0798$$
$$= -2.528$$

The difficulty some students have with logits is not to do with the way it is calculated but with the question as to why we should bother computing the logarithm of the odds in the first place. But, as we intend to show, the logit transformation is a convenient way to deal with the analysis of dichotomous categorical variables. Why?

Many people prefer to work with proportions (or, better still, percentages). However, the problem with proportions is that they have clear boundaries – a floor of zero and a ceiling of one – which can cause trouble when working with either very small or very large proportions. In the

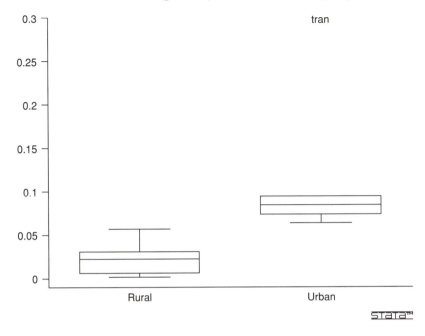

Figure 9.1 Estimated probabilities (proportions)

case of our Tanzanian data, for example, most proportions of high profit enterprises in the total number of enterprises turn out to be very small, particularly in rural-based sectors. This can lead us astray when comparing the variations in these proportions between urban and rural enterprises, as shown in Figure 9.1. The comparative box plots show the variation across sectors in the proportion of high profit enterprises in rural and urban enterprises respectively. With the exception of urban transport as a far-outlier, this figure conveys the impression that the variation across sectors is fairly similar for rural and for urban enterprises. But, in fact, the ratio of the highest to the smallest proportions in rural-based sectors is far in excess of the same ratio for urban-based sector, even if we include the outlier. You can easily verify that this ratio equals 4.6 for urban-based sectors as against 21.6 for rural-based sectors. The comparative box plots shown in Figure 9.1 effectively hide this greater internal variability among rural sectors since all its proportions are small so that the box plot is squashed against the floor.

By contrast, Figure 9.2 shows the comparative box plots of the logits. This plot shows much greater internal variability among rural-based sectors as against urban-based sectors. Why is this? The answer lies in the effects of the logit transformation on proportions. A proportion can range from 0 to 1, that is:

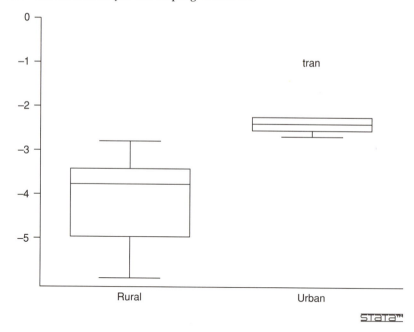

Figure 9.2   Comparing logits

$$0 \leqslant p \leqslant 1 \tag{9.7}$$

but the logit transformation stretches the tails of this distribution, and, hence:

$$-\infty \leqslant L \leqslant +\infty \tag{9.8}$$

where $L = 0$ (i.e. $O = 1$) corresponds to a proportion equal to 0.50. Hence, logits bring out significant variation among small or large proportions far better than can be seen from merely looking at the proportions themselves. Indeed, in our example, the box plot of the logits tells us that, with the exception of urban transport, urban-based sectors are far more homogeneous with respect to the prevalence of high profit enterprise than rural-based sectors.

The logit transformation, therefore, helps us to detect patterns in counts or proportions of dichotomous categorical variables, particularly in cases where the characteristic we are interested in is either very rare or highly prevalent. Fortunately, in the middle range (corresponding to proportions around 0.50), proportions and logits tell a similar story. Consequently, as Tukey (1977: 509) puts it, logits are 'first-aid bandages' when working with counted fractions since, on balance, they allow us to bring out patterns in the data which may be obscured when using proportions or percentages. For this reason, logits are useful exploratory choices for data analysis with counted fractions of categorical variables. But, as we shall see below, logits also improve our capacity to model data when the dependent variable is a dichotomous categorical variable.

Exercise 9.1

Use Table 9.2 to compute the proportion, odds and logits of informal sector enterprises which had existed less than five years by 1991 in both rural and urban areas in Tanzania. Make comparative box plots for each of these cases.

9.3 LOGIT MODELLING WITH CONTINGENCY TABLES

In economic analysis of development issues we prefer statistical models that clearly specify which variable depends on others. Logit modelling allows us to do this in the context of a qualitative dependent variable. In this section we shall show how this can be done in the framework of multiway contingency tables when all variables are categorical in nature. You have already come across contingency tables in Chapter 8. In essence, a contingency table is a cross-tabulation of counts across two or more categorical variables. In the previous chapter we showed how these cross-tabulations can be used to assess the degree of association between categorical variables. We did not make any assumptions, however, about the direction of causation between these variables. This section shows how this can be done explicitly using logit modelling (Demaris, 1992).

Table 9.2 shows the cross-tabulation of counts of Tanzanian informal sector enterprises by urban and rural location, by sector and by the age of the enterprise for the year 1991. The counts for the age of the enterprises are grouped into enterprises less than five years old and those which have existed for five years or more. The reason for grouping the age variable with respect to a cut-off point of five years is that in Tanzania structural adjustment policies were initiated during 1986 and hence, by 1991, had been operative for about five years. Consequently, the cate-

Table 9.2 Tanzanian informal sector enterprises by sector, location and age

| | Urban | | Rural | |
	Less than 5 years	*5 or more years*	*Less than 5 years*	*5 or more years*
Agriculture and fishing	39,788	24,687	34,471	43,163
Mining and quarrying	6,070	7,117	1,802	2,150
Manufacture	51,459	33,448	137,642	212,883
Construction	11,399	17,451	38,613	48,526
Trade, restaurants and hotels	308,312	96,881	341,017	179,995
Transport	5,411	2,460	31,674	9,181
C&P services	20,087	19,648	23,857	38,031

Source: Tanzania: The Informal Sector 1991, Planning Commission and Ministry of Labour and Youth Development, ENT 5 (adapted).

gorical variable of the age of the enterprise (more or less than five years old) divides up the total number of enterprises by the type of policy regime in operation when they were started: roughly, before and after structural adjustment policies were initiated.

Clearly, the data in this table can be used to explore questions about structural changes in the spread of informal sector activities across sectors before and after the implementation of structural adjustment policies and across the rural/urban divide. Note, however, that the table cannot tell you much about the growth in the number of enterprises over time (before and after the era of structural adjustment policies) since the mortality rates of informal sector enterprises at different points in time are unknown. But since there are no clear *a priori* reasons to believe that mortality rates differ markedly across either sectors or the rural/urban divide, a table like this may allow us to make meaningful inferences with respect to structural changes in informal sector activities. One question which springs to mind, among others, is whether there was any inherent bias in favour of trade among informal sector activities as a result of structural adjustment.

Collapsing the data table

To verify this hypothesis it is useful to collapse the data table to function on this particular question. We can therefore introduce a simple trade/non-trade dichotomous variable which will feature as dependent variable in our subsequent analysis. Our main interest is to check whether the period after structural adjustment policies were initiated brought about a shift in favour of trading activities. Furthermore, our interest is to see whether the pattern of change, if any, was similar in both urban and rural areas. Table 9.3 summarises the data organised along three dichotomous categorical variables.

Logit modelling

How do logits come into our analysis? As we have seen, a logit is the logarithm of the odds. In this example, we consider the odds in favour of trading activities since the dichotomous 'trade/non-trade' variable is our dependent variable. We therefore simplify Table 9.3 by introducing the logarithms of the odds in favour of trade explicitly as the dependent variable (Table 9.4).

How do we interpret this table? First start with the logits themselves. For example, the logit in favour of trade for urban enterprises initiated before structural adjustment equals –0.0787. To interpret this value it is useful to work your way back to the corresponding odds and proportion. In general, if L is the logit, the corresponding odds, O, is obtained as follows:

Table 9.3 Informal sector enterprises by trade/non trade, age and location

Age	Trade		Non-trade		Total	
	Urban	Rural	Urban	Rural	Urban	Rural
Less than 5 years	308,312	341,017	134,214	268,059	442,526	609,076
5 or more years	96,881	179,995	104,811	353,934	201,692	533,929
Total	405,193	521,012	239,025	621,993	644,218	1,043,005

Table 9.4 Logits in favour of trade by age and location

Age	Urban	Rural	Difference of logits
Less than 5 years	0.832	0.241	0.591
5 or more years	-0.079	-0.676	0.598
Difference of logits	0.910	0.917	-0.007

$$O = e^L \tag{9.9}$$

which in this example yields:

$$O_{\geq 5, urban} = e^{-0.0787}$$
$$= 0.924$$

To obtain the corresponding proportion, p, we proceed as follows. Since

$$O = \frac{p}{1 - p}$$

it follows that

$$p = \frac{O}{1 + O} \tag{9.10}$$

Substituting (9.9) into (9.10), we obtain:

$$p = \frac{e^L}{1 + e^L}$$

Finally, dividing both the numerator and the denominator by e^L, we obtain the following logistic function:

$$p = \frac{1}{1 + e^{-L}} \tag{9.11}$$

which expresses a proportion as a non-linear function of the value of its corresponding logit. In our example we obtain the following result:

$$p_{\geq 5, urban} = 0.48$$

Exercise 9.2

Calculate the odds and proportions for the three remaining cases in Table 9.4.

Our interest, however, is to analyse how odds differ or change in different circumstances depicted by the explanatory variables in our model. Does rural or urban location matter or not in terms of conditions favouring the prevalence of trading enterprises? Did the change in policy regime favour the development of trading activities within the informal sector? To answer these types of questions explicitly we make use of odds ratios. In general, the odds ratio is a ratio of the odds defined with respect to the dependent variable (a dichotomous variable) at different values of the explanatory variables (which, in this example, are also dichotomous in nature). For example, the odds ratio in favour of trade with respect to urban or rural location of enterprises started before structural adjustment is given by:

$$\Omega_{urban/rural,\geqslant 5} = \frac{O_{urban,\geqslant 5}}{O_{rural,\geqslant 5}} = \frac{96881/104811}{179995/353934} = 1.81$$

which reveals the much stronger prevalence of trading activities in urban as against rural areas for enterprises which are five years old or more. An odds ratio equal to 1 would indicate that the odds are equal in both circumstances. Here this is not the case and, therefore, location clearly matters.

Exercise 9.3

Calculate the odds ratios in favour of trade:

1 with respect to urban and rural location of enterprises initiated after structural adjustment policies;
2 with respect to policy regime (before/after structural adjustment policies) for urban areas; and
3 with respect to policy regime for rural areas.

Now, the important thing to note is that simple differences of logits are in fact logarithms of odds ratios. This result is very convenient since it greatly enhances our ability to make sense of cross-tabulations of logits, as is done, for example, in Table 9.4. To see this, we start with the odds ratio defined as follows:

$$\Omega = \frac{O_1}{O_0} \tag{9.12}$$

where O_1 and O_0 are two odds corresponding to different values of an explanatory variable. Taking logarithms of both sides of equation (9.12) yields:

$$\ln \Omega = \ln \left(\frac{O_1}{O_0}\right) = \ln O_1 - \ln O_0$$

$$= L_1 - L_0 \tag{9.13}$$

Conversely, if we computed both L_1 and L_0, the odds ratio can be obtained by calculating the anti-logarithm of their difference:

$$\Omega = e^{(L_1 - L_0)} \tag{9.14}$$

This simple result now explains why, in Table 9.4, we added a final row and a final column of differences of the logits tabulated across dichotomous explanatory variables. Take, for example, the difference 0.9104 obtained by subtracting the logit in favour of trade for urban enterprises of five years old or more from the logit of similar enterprises less than five years old. The odds ratio for urban areas in favour of trade as a result of the shift in policy regime is then obtained as follows:

$$\Omega_{<5/\geqslant 5, urban} = e^{0.9104} = 2.485$$

which indicates a strong swing in favour of trade in urban areas. In fact, the column difference for rural areas yields a very similar result: an odds ratio equal to 2.50. Consequently, the swing in favour of trade was very similar in terms of changing odds in rural as well as urban areas.

Exercise 9.4

Using Table 9.4, show that the odds ratios between rural and urban location in favour of trade were very similar for enterprises started before and after structural adjustment.

Interaction effect

But what about the computed value in the bottom-right corner of Table 9.4? This value is obtained by taking the difference of differences of logits. Therefore, it involves differencing twice. Note, however, that it does not matter whether we take the difference between row-differences or between column-difference: both yield the same result. But how do we interpret such difference of differences? The interpretation is quite straightforward notwithstanding the apparent complexity of differencing twice. The difference between two logits is the logarithm of an odds ratio; differencing one more time yields the logarithm of the ratio of odds ratios. What this measures is the interaction effect of both explanatory variables on the dependent variable.

In Table 9.4 we already noted that the column differences (respectively, 0.9104 and 0.9169) are very similar in magnitude. Consequently, the odds ratio in favour of trade as a result of a change in policy regime is very similar for both urban and rural areas. In other words, rural and urban location does not interact with the change in policy regime (measured by the age variable) as far as their impact on the prevalence of trading activities within the Tanzanian informal sector is concerned. The interaction effect is measured by the logarithm of the ratio of the odds ratios. To obtain the latter ratio, we only need to take the antilogarithm of the difference of differences between the logits in the table, as follows:

$$\frac{\Omega_{<5/\geqslant 5 , urban}}{\Omega_{<5/\geqslant 5 , rural}} = e^{-0.0065} = 0.994$$

a result which confirms that the changing odds in favour of trade as a result of the change in policy regime was pretty much alike in urban and in rural settings.

Logit regression with a saturated model

The exercise we have just completed was an exercise in logit modelling. It featured a qualitative dependent variable and two explanatory variables, all dichotomous in nature. The distinctive feature of this type of modelling is that we seek to investigate how the probability of a particular characteristic being present (i.e. the enterprise is a trading enterprise) varies with circumstances as depicted by the qualitative explanatory variables. To assess such changes in probabilities we use the logarithms of odds ratios in favour of this particular characteristic. To show both the similarities and differences with the regression models employed in earlier chapters, it is instructive to work our exercise making explicit use of dummy variables. Therefore, let $T = 1$, if the enterprise is in trade, restaurant or hotel sector, $= 0$, otherwise; $U = 1$, if the enterprise is urban-based, $= 0$, otherwise; $A = 1$, if the age of the enterprise is less than five years, $= 0$, otherwise. Table 9.4 can now be rewritten in a single equation which seeks to explain the variation in the logits in favour of trade, L^T, as follows:

$$L^T = -0.68 + 0.60 \; U + 0.92 \; A - 0.01 \; (A \cdot U) \qquad (9.15)$$

where $A \cdot U$ is the interaction dummy obtained by multiplying both explanatory dummy variables. Equation (9.15) is in effect a logit regression in the context of a saturated model (meaning that the number of estimated coefficients is exactly equal to the number of observations). In fact, in this case, the interaction term can conveniently be dropped since, as shown above, its coefficient indicates that the ratio of odd ratios is close to one. A more parsimonious model can thus be obtained by regressing the logits in favour of trade against both dummy variables. But this would lead us to logit regression, a topic we shall now discuss in greater detail.

9.4 THE LINEAR PROBABILITY MODEL VERSUS LOGIT REGRESSION

We saw in previous chapters that linear regression essentially implies averaging Y for given values of the Xs. This makes good sense when the dependent variable, Y, in the analysis is a measurement variable. But what happens when the variable we are interested in is a qualitative dichotomous variable which, as we have seen, can best be depicted by a dummy variable which equals 1 when a particular characteristic is present and zero otherwise? For any given observation, therefore, the characteristic is either present ($Y = 1$) or absent ($Y = 0$). In this case averaging does not seem to make much sense. However, if you average a dummy variable which takes the values one or zero across a sample of observations, the result will give you the proportion of observations in the sample which have the particular characteristic. In the context of random sampling this proportion estimates the probability of encountering this characteristic in the population at large. In other words, averaging in this context does not tell us something about the average value a dummy variable assumes (since it can only be either 1 or zero but nothing in between), but rather it tells something about the probability that the dummy will equal 1. Consequently, when a qualitative dichotomous variable features as the dependent variable in our analysis we seek to find those factors (explanatory variables) which determine the probability that the characteristic this qualitative variable depicts is present in the population.

The linear probability model

Given that averaging a binary dummy variable, Y, gives us an estimator of the probability that Y equals 1, it seems logical to extend the application of linear regression to cases with a qualitative dependent variable. This is indeed what is done in the context of the linear probability model. A simple example may help to illustrate this type of application. In Chapter 8, we investigated the variation in income of Indian workers in relation to age, sex and education. But what if our main interest is to see what determines the prevalence of permanent jobs as against temporary or casual work? In this case we end up with a qualitative dependent variable, F, which equals 1 if a worker has a fixed job and zero otherwise. To keep the analysis simple we shall limit the example to the bivariate case by investigating the effect of age on the prevalence of permanent jobs. The simple regression of F_i on A_i, age, yields the following regression results:

$$F_i = 0.058 + 0.011A_i$$
$$(0.084) \quad (0.0024) \tag{9.16}$$

$$R^2 = 0.075, \text{No. of observations} = 261$$

Perhaps you find the R^2 disappointingly low. Keep in mind, however, that we are dealing with a large sample of cross-section data. Moreover, remember that our dependent variable is a dummy variable which can only take on the values 1 or zero. Now, since the constant term is not significantly different from zero, we can drop it from the equation to obtain the following regression through the origin:

$$F_i = 0.0127 \ A_i \qquad R^2 = 0.46$$
$$(0.0009) \tag{9.17}$$

The slope coefficient did not change very much, but the R^2 is now much higher. Keep in mind, however, that the R^2 in this regression is not comparable to that in the regression with a constant term.

Exercise 9.5

Can you explain why the R^2 of the regression without constant term turns out to be much higher than that of the regression with constant term, although (in fact) the residual sums of squares of both regressions turned out to be very close together? (*Hint*: Keep in mind that in a regression through the origin the total sum of squares of the regression is not the sum of squared deviations from the mean of the dependent variable (as is the case when the regression features a constant term), but the sum of squared values of the dependent variable, which in this case is a dummy variable.)

The scatter plot with this regression line is shown in Figure 9.3. This plot looks quite different from a scatter plot where both variables are measurement variables, since all data points have a Y value 1 or 0. The problem with this plot, however, is that with a large sample it is quite possible that different data points end up being superimposed on one another because many of the workers concerned are likely to have the same age (measured in years). To be able to see the distribution of the data points, therefore, it is advisable to jitter the points a bit so that the thickness of the scatter comes to the fore, as in Figure 9.3. (If your computer package will not do this automatically then add a small random number to your dummy variable for the purpose of drawing the graph.)

The regression line predicts the probabilities that the F_is equal 1 for a given age. Hence, at age 15, our regression line predicts that the probability of encountering a worker with a permanent job is about 0.19, while at age 55 the corresponding probability has risen to 0.70. This is why this type of regression is called the linear probability model: it expresses the probability that the dependent variable equals 1 for different values of the explanatory variable(s). In this case, age clearly matters whether a worker

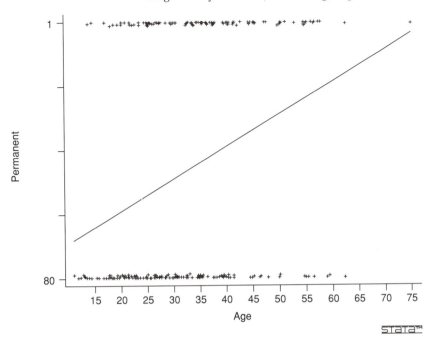

Figure 9.3 Scatter plot of *F* on *A* with regression line

is in permanent employment or not. The importance of the age variable can also be shown by using the more familiar comparative box plots of the age distribution for different values of the dependent variable.

At first sight, it appears that the linear probability model is quite appropriate to deal with a qualitative dependent variable. And, in fact, in this example it does a good job. There are, however, two problems – one minor, one major – with this model. The lesser of the two problems is that the error terms in the model inevitably are heteroscedastics as shown in Box 9.1. This problem can easily be remedied using a two-step procedure involving weighted least squares (see Box 9.1). Using weighted regression, our regression line through the origin now becomes:

$$S_i = 0.013 \, A_i \qquad R^2 = 0.40$$
$$(0.001) \tag{9.21}$$

which yields a similar result as in the case of ordinary least squares.

The second problem inherent in the linear probability model is far more serious. By definition, a probability is bounded between 0 and 1. Consequently, the linear probability model only makes sense if the estimated probabilities for the relevant range of *X* values stay within these boundaries. But nothing guarantees that this will be the case. In our example we were fortunate enough that the estimated probabilities for

Box 9.1   Heteroscedasticity in the linear probability model

Consider the following general bivariate linear probability model:

$$Y_i = \beta_1 + \beta_2 X_i + \epsilon_i \tag{9.18}$$

where Y_i is a dummy variable. Let P_i be the probability that $Y_i = 1$ and, hence, $(1 - P_i)$ is the probability that $Y_i = 0$ since Y is a binary variable. Consequently, $E(Y_i) = 0(1 - P_i) + 1P_i = P_i$ (the mathematical expectation of Y_i equals the probability that Y_i equals 1). Hence:

$$E(Y_i \mid X_i) = P_i = \beta_1 + \beta_2 X_i \tag{9.19}$$

Now, since Y_i can only assume the values 0 or 1, the resulting ϵ_i for given X_i can also only assume two outcomes:

Y_i	ϵ_i	Probability
0	$-\beta_1 - \beta_2 X_i$	$(1 - P_i) = 1 - \beta_1 - \beta_2 X_i$
1	$1 - \beta_1 - \beta_2 X_i$	$P_i = \beta_1 + \beta_2 X_i$

Therefore, ϵ_i is also a binary variable with mean 0 and variance $P_i(1 - P_i)$, the variance of a binomial variable with only one observation. Since P_i depends on the value of X_i it follows that the different error terms corresponding to different values of X_i will have different variances. Consequently, the error terms will be heteroscedastic.

The presence of heteroscedasticity leaves the estimator unbiased but not efficient. It is preferable, therefore, to switch to weighted least squares in order to render the error term homoscedastic, as shown in Chapter 7. The easiest way to do this is by using transformed variables. This involves a two-step procedure, as suggested by Goldberger (1964: 248–50):

Step 1   Estimate equation (9.18) with ordinary least squares and compute the predicted Y_i values to calculate the estimated variances $\hat{Y}_i(1 - \hat{Y}_i)$, the square root of which gives us our weights, w_i.

Step 2   Estimate the regression:

$$\frac{Y_i}{w_i} = \beta_1 \frac{1}{w_i} + \beta_2 \frac{X_i}{w_i} + \frac{\varepsilon_i}{w_i} \tag{9.20}$$

with ordinary least squares without constant term.

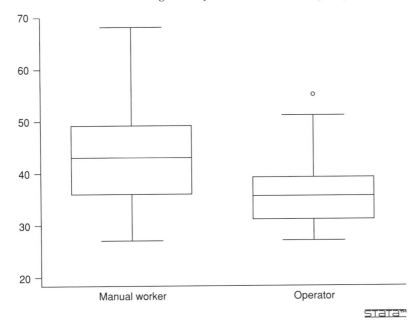

Figure 9.4   Age distribution by worker category

given age within the age range from 10 to 70 years were all less or equal to 1, or more than or equal to 0. But this does not always happen, as can be shown with a similar example taken from another part of the world and in a different context.

This example concerns the selection of machine operators from a pool of casual manual workers in Maputo harbour at the time of independence. The problem emerged when, in Mozambique, many Portuguese settlers who previously occupied most of the skilled jobs left the country in large numbers after independence in 1975. The result was a grave shortage of skilled labour in Maputo harbour, mainly of machine operators. A solution was sought by accelerated training and upgrading of workers selected from a large pool of casual manual labourers. The age of the worker appears to have been an important criterion for selecting trainee operators from among the casual workforce. To verify this hypothesis a stratified random sample was taken of these two groups of workers: newly trained operators and the remaining casual labour force.

As in the previous example, we have a dependent dummy variable, O, which equals 1 if the worker is an operator and 0 otherwise (indicating that the worker is a manual labourer). As before, the explanatory variable in the model is the age of the worker in years. The hypothesis we seek to test is whether selection favoured younger workers. In fact, the comparative box plot of the age of worker by type of work reveals that

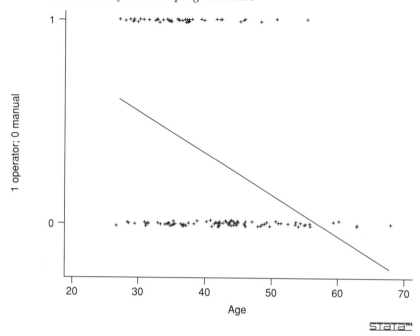

Figure 9.5   Regression of *O* on age: linear probability model

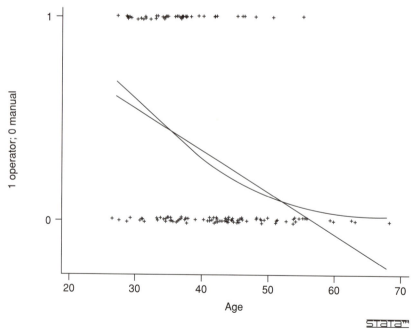

Figure 9.6   Linear probability model and logit regression: Maputo worker data

age matters, as shown in Figure 9.5. However, since age clearly is the explanatory variable in this case we prefer a model which features the type of worker as qualitative dependent variable. Estimating the linear probability model with ordinary least squares yields the following results:

$$O_i = 1.158 - 0.0204 \, A_i$$
$$(0.187) \quad (0.0045) \tag{9.22}$$

$$R^2 = 0.14; \text{ No. of observations} = 129$$

a regression which confirms our hypothesis that the selection procedure for upgrading workers favoured younger workers. But this regression is in fact quite problematic, as can be seen from Figure 9.6 which depicts the scatter plot with the corresponding regression line.

The problem is that our regression predicts negative probabilities from the age of 57 years and above. A worker who was about 25 years old at the time of independence had an estimated probability of 0.65 while a worker of 56.5 years old would not be selected (zero probability). Above the latter age, the probabilities predicted by this regression turn negative. A further problem is that we can no longer apply the two-step procedure of weighted regression to correct for heteroscedasticity either, since some of our weights turn out to be negative.

Comparing logit regression with the linear probability model

How do we cope with this problem? One solution is to truncate the linear probability model by ignoring the regression line whenever it cuts below zero (or above one) and imputing a probability equal to zero (or one) to the X ranges where such applies. Hence, in our example, we could conclude that workers above the age of 56 had zero probability of being selected as operators. This is a reasonable but not particularly elegant solution to the problem. But what if we were to use logits instead of estimated probabilities on the left-hand side of our model? Logits range from minus to plus infinity and can always be reconverted into the corresponding probabilities which will lie within the boundaries zero and one. Logit regression helps us to do this: it features a logit as a dependent variable which is assumed to vary linearly with the explanatory variable(s). The mechanics of logit regression (which can be quite complex since it involves non-linear estimation techniques) will be dealt with in the next section. At this point we want to point out that if logits are linearly related with the explanatory variable(s), it follows that the (estimated) probabilities will be a non-linear function of the explanatory variable(s) since equation (9.11) tells us that probabilities vary non-linearly with logits.

Figure 9.6. compares the regression line obtained with the linear probability model and the logit regression curve along with the scatter plot of observations of the dummy dependent variable on the category of workers

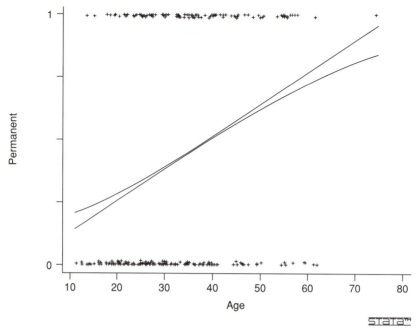

Figure 9.7 Linear probability model and logit regression: Indian worker data

in Maputo harbour. The curve of estimated probabilities obtained through logit regression avoids cutting below 0 and lends itself to easier interpretation for this reason. The graph also shows that logit regression and the linear probability model yield quite different estimates of the probabilities concerned.

By contrast, Figure 9.7 gives us a similar comparison between logit regression and the application of the linear probability model in the case of our first example: the prevalence of permanent jobs as a function of age for Indian workers. Here both models do equally well.

Exercise 9.6

Using the data set INDIA (Indian worker data) estimate the linear probability model between F and the age of worker, respectively, for all data points, for male workers and for female workers. Construct the corresponding scatter plots with regression line.

9.5 ESTIMATION AND HYPOTHESIS TESTING IN LOGIT REGRESSION

In logit regression we are dealing with a qualitative dependent variable, Y_i, which equals 1 when a particular characteristic is present in observation

i ($i = 1 \ldots n$), or zero otherwise. Our interest is to predict the conditional probability, P_i, that Y_i equals 1 for given values of the explanatory variables. We assume that the logit, L_i, is a linear function of the explanatory variables:

$$L_i = \beta_1 + \beta_2 X_{2i} + \ldots + \beta_k X_{ki} \qquad (9.23)$$

and

$$P_i = \frac{1}{1 + 1/e^{Li}} \qquad (9.24)$$

which shows that the conditional probability is a non-linear function of the explanatory variables. Our interest is to estimate the unknown coefficients, β_i ($i = 1 \ldots m$), of the probability model (9.23). Once we obtain such estimates we can calculate the predicted logits from equation (9.23) and use equation (9.24) to obtain the predicted probabilities that $Y_i = 1$ for given X_i values.

At first sight it may appear that logit regression can be done easily with ordinary least squares by regressing a transformed dependent variable, the logit, on the explanatory variables. However, the problem is not as easy as all that. Much depends on the nature of our data: more particularly, on whether they are grouped or not. If our data are not grouped, each observation involves an individual case for which Y_i is either 1 or 0. The estimated probability for this case would thus be equal to 1 or 0 as well. Consequently, the logit transformation will not work since the logits corresponding to probabilities 1 and 0 are respectively plus and minus infinity. It is not possible, therefore, to estimate equation (9.23) with ordinary least squares since we cannot apply the appropriate logit transformation to the individual cases where Y_i is either 1 or 0. With grouped data, however, it is generally possible to apply the logit transformation since each group will normally contain both cases with and without the specific characteristic. This is the reason why we could apply the logit transformation to our examples in sections 9.2 and 9.3.

Logit regression with individual case data

Consider first the case where each observation refers to an individual unit. To estimate the logit model in this case requires more complex non-linear estimation methods which are commonly based on maximum likelihood rather than least squares.

Equations (9.23) and (9.24) show that P_i, the conditional probability that $Y_i = 1$, is a non-linear function of the explanatory variables. Since we are dealing with a binary dependent variable, P_i is the probability that $Y_i = 1$ and, hence, $(1 - P_i)$ is the probability that $Y_i = 0$. To construct the likelihood function, therefore, we note that the contribution of the ith observation can be written as:

$$P_i^{Y_i} (1 - P_i)^{(1-Y_i)}$$

and, in the case of random sampling where all observations are sampled independently, the likelihood function will simply be the product of the individual contributions, as follows:

$$L = \prod_{i=1}^{n} P_i^{Y_i} (1 - P_i)^{1-Y_i} \tag{9.25}$$

The principle of maximum likelihood entails that we choose those values of the parameters of model (9.23) which maximise the likelihood function. In practice, we maximise the logarithm of the likelihood function:

$$\ln L = \sum [Y_i \ln P_i + (1 - Y_i) \ln (1 - P_i)] \tag{9.26}$$

Substituting equation (9.23) into (9.26), and maximising equation (9.26) with respect to the unknown parameters in the model will then yield a system of non-linear normal equations (see, for example, Kmenta, 1986: 550–3) which can only be solved through iteration. Fortunately, nowadays most statistical or econometric computer programs allow us to apply these techniques routinely. What matters is to acquire the skill to interpret the results of logit regressions in applied work.

To do this, take once more our earlier example on the prevalence of permanent jobs among Indian urban workers. To broaden the scope of our analysis we shall also include dummy variables on gender and on educational attainment along with the age variable as possible determinants of the probability that a worker has a permanent job. The results we obtained are listed in Table 9.5.

The variables in Table 9.5 are defined as follows:

F   = qualitative dependent variable, = 1 if worker has permanent (fixed) job, = 0 otherwise A = age of worker in years
DG = 1 for women, = 0 for men
D2 = 1 if educational attainment equals primary school, = 0 otherwise
D3 = 1 if educational attainment equals secondary school, = 0 otherwise

Table 9.5   Logit estimates

F	Coefficient	Standard error	t-statistic
A	0.01	0.01	4.49
DG	0.14	0.35	0.41
D2	0.21	0.38	0.54
D3	1.12	0.35	3.17
D4	3.56	1.06	3.38
Intercept	−2.61	0.49	−5.31

Log likelihood	= −150.9
Number of observations	= 261
$\chi^2_{(5)}$	= 52.91

D4 = 1 if educational attainment equals post-secondary schooling, = 0 otherwise

To interpret the output of this estimation, let us start with the coefficients in the model. Obviously, as with linear regression, each coefficient (apart from the constant term) depicts the change in the predicted logit as a result of a unit change in the corresponding explanatory variable, other things being equal.

The coefficient of the age variable, for example, tells us that the predicted logit (i.e. log odds) in favour of fixed work changes by 0.0549 with every increase in age by one year. However, most people find it hard to interpret changes in logits. A more intuitive interpretation can be obtained by working with odds or odds ratios instead. In fact, the anti-logarithm of each slope coefficient in a logit regression is an odds ratio at two different values, one unit apart, of the corresponding explanatory variable. This interpretation is very useful when dealing with dummy variables. In our example, workers who completed secondary schooling as the highest level of educational attainment face far better odds of having a permanent job than those without schooling; the corresponding odds ratio equals:

$$\Omega_{D3=1/no\ schooling} = e^{1.124}$$
$$= 3.08$$

Exercise 9.7

Show that workers with post-secondary schooling are in an even more advantaged position. To do this, compute the relevant odds ratio.

What is the odds ratio in favour of fixed work between workers with post-secondary schooling and those with secondary schooling as the highest educational attainment? This ratio can be computed as follows:

$$\Omega_{D4=1/D3=1} = \frac{O_{D4=1}}{O_{D3=1}} = \frac{O_{D4=1/O\ no\ schooling}}{O_{D3=1/O\ no\ schooling}} = \frac{e^{3.563}}{e^{1.124}} = 11.46$$

If instead we are dealing with a measurement variable such as our age variable, for example, the antilogarithm of its slope coefficient gives us the odds ratio corresponding to a unit change in the variable. In this case, the odds ratio of a change in age by one year equals the antilogarithm of 0.05, or 1.06. Consequently, with each additional year of age, the odds are again multiplied by this constant odds ratio. The odds ratio corresponding to an age difference of ten years, therefore, will be equal to $(e^{0.0549})^{10}$, which yields 1.73.

Finally, we can always compute the predicted probabilities for given values of the explanatory variables. We can do this using equation (9.11) which tells us how to convert logits into the underlying probabilities. For example, a female worker, 25 years old, with only primary education ($D2 = 1$) has a predicted probability to be in permanent employment equal to:

$$L = -2.608 + 0.0549 \ (25) + 0.143 \ (1)$$
$$+ \ 0.208 \ (1) + 1.124 \ (0) + 3.563 \ (0)$$
$$= -0.885$$

$$p = \frac{1}{1 + 1/e^{-0.885}} = 0.29$$

This type of calculation is quite cumbersome if done on a one-by-one basis, but will prove very useful to design analytical graphs, called conditional effect plots, to help us analyse logit regressions. This we do in the next section.

So much for the interpretation of the coefficients in a logit regression. But how do we handle hypothesis testing and assess the goodness of fit? The *t*-statistics in logit regressions pose no special problems: they can be dealt with much as you would do in linear regressions. In our example we note that the age variable and the educational dummies corresponding to secondary and post-secondary education along with the constant term turn out to be statistically significant at the 5 per cent probability level. The gender dummy and the dummy for completion of primary schooling as highest level of educational attainment turn out to be not statistically significant from 0. Note that a zero coefficient in a logit regression implies an odds ratio equal to $e^0 = 1$, corresponding to a unit change in the variable concerned. An odds ratio equal to 1 means that the change in the variable concerned does not change the odds. As with linear regression, however, two or more insignificant *t*-statistics in a logit regression does not allow us to drop the corresponding variables jointly from the regression. To do this we need a statistic akin to the *F*-test in linear regression. In logit regression we use a chi-square statistic derived from the likelihood ratio between restricted and unrestricted versions of the model.

We illustrate how to do this with reference to Table 9.5, which listed the results of our logit regression. This is the unrestricted version of our model. The estimates for its coefficients were obtained by maximizing the logarithm of the likelihood function (equation (9.26)). In this example the estimated log likelihood equals -150.90. Any restrictions we choose to impose on this model will obviously decrease the estimated log likelihood. However, if these restrictions are reasonably valid in practice we would not expect the estimated log likelihood to decrease significantly. Consequently, the likelihood ratio of the restricted and unrestricted models can serve as a useful indicator of the validity of our restrictions.

Table 9.6 Logit estimates: restricted version of model

	Coefficient	Standard error	t-statistic
A	0.05	0.01	4.48
D3	1.06	0.34	3.15
D4	3.54	1.05	3.37
Intercept	−2.48	0.44	−5.59
Log likelihood	= −151.10491		
Number of observations	= 261		
$\chi^2_{(3)}$	= 52.50		

To test whether we can drop the dummy variables on gender and primary education from the model, we formulate the restricted version of the model subject to the joint hypothesis:

$$H_0 : \beta_{DG} = 0 \text{ and } \beta_{D2} = 0$$

which yields the results listed in Table 9.6.

If we compare the restricted (R) and the unrestricted (U) versions of the model we note that the coefficients of the retained variables did not change much as a result of imposing the restrictions, while the estimated likelihood decreased only slightly. The restricted model therefore appears to be an acceptable, more parsimonious summary of the data. To test more formally whether we can drop both dummy variables from the model we make use of a chi-square statistic with two degrees of freedom (i.e. the number of restrictions) based on the likelihood ratio, L_R/L_U:

$$\chi^2_{(2)} = -2 \ln \frac{L_R}{L_U} = -2 (\ln L_R - \ln L_U)$$

$$= -2 (-151.10 + 150.900)$$

$$= 0.41 \tag{9.29}$$

a value which leads us to accept the null hypothesis that the restricted version of the model can be maintained.

As shown in Tables 9.5 and 9.6, the computer output of a logit regression will generally report a chi-square statistic which tests the hypothesis whether all variables (apart from the constant term) can be dropped from the regression. Consequently, the corresponding number of degrees of freedom equals the number of variables included in the model (respectively, five in the unrestricted version and three in the restricted variant of the model). In both cases the null hypothesis that all variables can be dropped is rejected by the data. Some computer programs may also report a pseudo R^2 for logit regression. Following Aldrich and Nelson (1984, quoted in Hamilton, 1992: 233) this pseudo R^2 is computed as:

$$\text{pseudo } R^2 = \frac{\chi}{\chi + n} \tag{9.30}$$

where the chi-square statistic tests the hypothesis whether all variables but the intercept is zero and n is the sample size. In our example, the pseudo R^2 is equal to 0.17 for the restricted model (and 0.17 for the unrestricted version). Other versions of a pseudo R^2 are also in use but none lends itself to the easy interpretation that can be given to the R^2 in linear regression. For this reason little is gained by reporting a pseudo R^2, but it is useful to know that it is often reported by some statistical computer software.

Logit regression with grouped data

So much for logit regression with 'individual case' data. But it also happens frequently that we work with grouped or replicated data. For example, most published survey data are grouped. Replicated data mean that there are many observations on the dependent (dummy) variable for each given combination of observations of the X variables. This normally occurs when our X variables consist of a few dummy variables only. In both cases (grouped or replicated data) it is possible to calculate observed probabilities (proportions), odds and logits for the range of groupings using equations (9.1), (9.3) and (9.5). Hence, for each group we calculate the proportion of the number of successes (i.e. when the dummy dependent variable equals 1) in the total number of cases and, subsequently, calculate the implied odds and logits as observed in the groups. In case a particular group contains only successes (or only failures), it is not possible to obtain the calculated logit. In such cases, the group of observations is dropped from further analysis. It is important, however, to reflect on whether such cases are purely accidental or could be expected *a priori*.

Given that we can compute the observed logits across the range of groupings (which have mixed successes and failures), it follows that we can use ordinary least squares to estimate the logit regression:

$$L_j^0 = \beta_1 + \beta_2 \, X_j + \ldots + \beta_k \, X_{kj} + \epsilon_j \; (j = 1 \ldots m) \tag{9.31}$$

where, m = number of groupings; L_j^0 = observed (calculated) logit for group j.

For example, Table 9.4 gives us the observed logits in favour of the trading sector for the Tanzanian informal sector in function of rural/urban location and of the age of the enterprise (less than five years/more than or equal to five years). Using dummy variables as defined in section 9.3, the model in equation (9.15) can be estimated without an interaction effect using ordinary least squares:

$$L_j^0 = -0.675 + 0.594 \ U + 0.914 \ A$$
$$(-0.003) \ (0.003) \quad (0.003) \tag{9.32}$$

No. of observations = 4 $R^2 \simeq 1$

a result which is virtually identical to the one obtained with the saturated model in equation (9.15).

There is, however, a problem when using ordinary least squares to estimate a logit regression with grouped data. The problem is that the error term is heteroscedastic. This follows from the fact that, within each group j, the number of successes follows a binomial distribution for which P_j depends on the values of the explanatory variables. Furthermore, group sizes will differ from group to group. It can then be shown (see, for example, Kmenta, 1986: 551–2) that the error term in equation 9.31 has a variance $S_{\epsilon j}^2$ equal to

$$S_{\epsilon_j}^2 = \frac{1}{n_j P_j (l - P_j)} \tag{9.33}$$

where n_j is the number of observations in group j. If n_j is sufficiently large, the binomial distribution can be approximated by a normal distribution, as follows:

$$\epsilon_j - N \left[0, \frac{1}{n_j P_j (1 - P_j)} \right] \tag{9.34}$$

To correct for heteroscedasticity, therefore, we compute the weights, w_j, equal to the estimated group variances:

$$w_j = \frac{1}{n_j P_j^0 (1 - P_j^0)} \tag{9.35}$$

where P_j^0 is the observed (estimated) probability that the dependent dummy variable equals 1 for group j, and re-estimate equation (9.31) using weighted least squares

$$\sqrt{w_j} \ L_j^0 = \beta_1 \sqrt{w_j} + \beta_2 \sqrt{w_j} \ X_{2j} + \ldots + \beta_m \sqrt{w_j} \ X_{mj} \tag{9.36}$$

In doing so, make sure not to introduce an explicit constant term when carrying out regression (9.36).

9.6 GRAPHICS AND RESIDUAL ANALYSIS IN LOGIT REGRESSION

This section is based on Hamilton's (1992: 217–47) excellent discussion of diagnostic graphs in logit regression. As we have repeatedly argued in the context of linear regression, analytical graphs help us to get more mileage out of our data. The same is true of logit regression. This section shows you how to use two different types of graphs in logit regression: conditional effect plots and poorness-of-fit plots. The former help us to understand what logit modelling implies for predicted probabilities while the latter is a diagnostic plot which enables us to spot which data points fit the predicted pattern poorly.

In a bivariate logit regression with an explanatory measurement variable it is always useful to produce a scatter plot of the binary dependent variable against the explanatory variable along with the logistic curve of predicted probabilities. But how do we do this when we are dealing with a multivariate logit regression? In this case, we are often interested in looking at the curve of predicted probabilities in relation to one explanatory measurement variable for given values of the other explanatory variables. The resulting scatter plot and regression curve is a conditional effect plot. Take, for example, the final logit regression arrived at in Table 9.6 after weeding out irrelevant explanatory variables. We may be interested to look at the relation between predicted probabilities of having a permanent job and the age of the worker for given levels of educational attainment. For example, setting $D3 = 0$ and $D4 = 0$, we can calculate the predicted probabilities of getting a permanent job for different ages in the case of workers with educational attainment of primary-level schooling or less. Plotting these predicted probabilities against the age variable gives us a

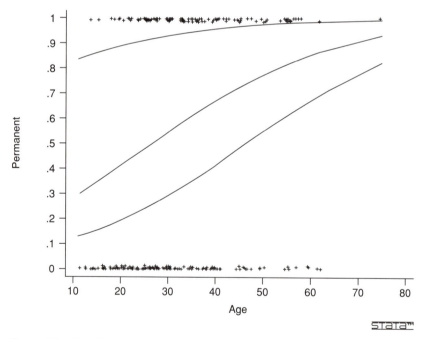

Figure 9.8 Conditional effects plots

conditional effect plot, meaning that the plot is conditional upon both $D3$ and $D4$ being equal to 0. Similarly, we could construct a conditional effect plot for $D3 = 1$ and $D4 = 0$ and another one for $D3 = 0$ and $D4 = 1$.

Figure 9.8 shows these three conditional effect plots all on one graph. Each curve plots the conditional probabilities (given the level of educational attainment) against the age of the worker. Distances between the curve for a given age show the importance of different levels of educational attainment. In this case, a higher level of educational attainment increases the predicted probability of getting a permanent job. Notice, in particular, that post-secondary education strongly boosts the probabilities of getting permanent work.

Logit regressions, like linear regressions, can provide us with useful summaries which give us insight into the data. But they can also mislead us in much the same way as linear regressions do. Problems like multicollinearity, non-linearity, leverage and influence also arise in logit regression. In general, it is a good idea not to attempt logit regression when one or more of the explanatory measurement variables is strongly asymmetric. It is best to transform this variable to avoid the problem of leverage and influence. Furthermore, we should always supplement our logit regressions with residual analysis, for which we may use Pearson residuals.

The Pearson residuals (Hamilton, 1992: 235–8) in logit regression are not calculated with respect to each individual case, but with respect to identical combinations of X values (or X patterns). If J denotes the number of unique X patterns $(J \leqslant n)$ and m_j denotes the number of cases with the jth X pattern, the Pearson residual is defined as:

$$rj = \frac{Y_j - m_j \hat{P}_j}{\sqrt{[m_j \hat{P}_j(1 - \hat{P}_j)]}} \tag{9.37}$$

where $\hat{P}_j$ is the predicted probability of cases with the jth X pattern and Y_j is the sum of observed Y values for cases with the jth X pattern.

At first sight, the Pearson residual may appear forbidding, but its rationale is easy to grasp. In the numerator each group j (which may include only one observation or more) reflects observations on Y, the dependent dummy variable, for identical values on the explanatory variables, X. Hence, $M_j \cdot P_j$ = the predicted number of successes in this group, and Y_j = the actual (observed) number of successes, such that the difference is the unexplained number of successes. The denominator is just the standard deviation of the binomial distribution of the number of successes.

The Pearson chi-square statistic (ibid.: 236) is the sum of squared Pearson residuals:

$$\chi_p^2 = \sum_{j=1}^{J} r_j \tag{9.38}$$

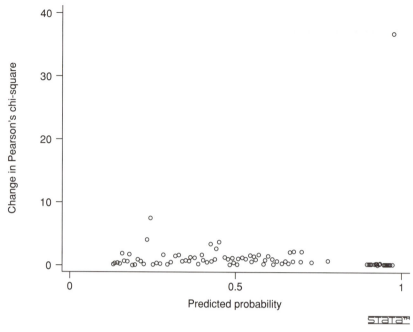

Figure 9.9 Poorness of fit plot for logit regression

The closer Pearson's chi-square is to zero, the better the model fits the data. In fact, in a saturated model Pearson's chi-square statistic will be zero since all residuals equal 0.

We can now obtain a measure of 'poorness-of-fit' of a particular X pattern by calculating the change in Pearson's chi-square that results from deleting all cases with this particular X pattern. Hence:

$$\Delta X^2_{p(j)} = \text{the change in Pearson's chi-square as a result}$$
$$\text{of dropping all cases with the } j\text{th } X \text{ pattern} \qquad (9.39)$$

A 'poorness-of-fit' plot can be obtained by plotting the change in Pearson's chi-square as a result of deleting all cases with X pattern j against the predicted probabilities, P_j. Figure 9.9 provides such a plot for the logit regression in Table 9.6.

When data points are situated near the horizontal axis in this type of plot it means that the predicted probability does not differ much from the observed probability and, hence, Pearson's chi-square will hardly change as a result of deleting those cases which correspond to this particular X pattern. A point which lies far above the horizontal axis fits the model poorly. If it is situated on the right-hand side where the predicted probability equals one, it means that the actual data show that the particular characteristic ($Y = 1$) is not (predominantly) present among cases with this configuration of X values. An outlier on the left-hand side would indicate that the data show that the characteristic is present while the model predicts that it is not.

In fact, the outlier in Figure 9.9 corresponds to only one individual. This was a man, 47 years old, with post-secondary education, who did not have a permanent job. Our model predicts that the corresponding probability of being in a permanent job is very high, which explains the large change in Pearson's chi-square provoked by deleting this observation from the sample. Diagnostic plots such as that in Figure 9.8 allow us to spot the unusual in a large data set. Once more, this illustrates the advantage of using graphical tools in analysis.

Exercise 9.8

Use the data set INDIA (Indian worker data) to redo the estimation of the logit model discussed above along with the conditional effect plots and poorness-of-fit plot.

9.7 SUMMARY OF MAIN POINTS

1   When dealing with counts (frequencies) of a dichotomous qualitative variable we can use proportions, odds and logits as convenient transformations of the data. The logit transformation has the advantage that it shows much better what happens in the tails of a distribution (corresponding to very small or very large proportions), while giving a similar picture as proportions in the middle range.

2   Logit modelling with contingency data allows us to investigate the relation between a dependent dichotomous variable and several explanatory categorical variables. As such we separate the different partial effects of each explanatory variable on the dependent variable by translating the logits back into odds ratios. Similarly, interaction effects can be obtained by twice (or more) differencing logits with respect to two (or more) categorical variables.

3   The linear probability model seeks to model the probability that one or another characteristic depicted by the dependent variable is present. However, the model suffers from two defects: its residuals are heteroscedastic and it may predict negative probabilities as well as probabilities in excess of one.

4   Logit regression always predicts probabilities located between zero and one. Logit regression can either be done with individual case data (which requires an interactive ML estimation technique) or with grouped data, using both dummy and measurement variables as regressors. It extends the reach of regression techniques to deal with the probability of some characteristic being present in the population as depending upon a set of explanatory variables.

5   The interpretation of the regression coefficient of a logit regression is most conveniently done with reference to odds ratios. A zero coefficient implies an odds ratio equal to 1, which indicates that the odds do not change as a result of a unit change in the explanatory variable.

6   Model choice through variable selection is possible in logit regression by using the chi-square statistic in much the same way as we use the *F*-statistic in linear regression.

7   It is advisable to use logit regression results jointly with graphical displays such as the conditional effect plots and the poorness-of-fit plot derived from Pearson's chi-square statistic based on Pearson's residuals. The former plot renders interpretation of the results easier by showing how different values of a particular explanatory variable affect the probability of the characteristic being present along the range of one of the measurement variables included in the model. The latter is a diagnostic plot to spot outliers in logit regressions.

Part IV

Regression with time-series data

10 Trends, spurious regressions and transformations to stationarity

10.1 INTRODUCTION

In Part III we discussed problems specific to cross-section analysis. We now turn our attention to time-series data. In such data the assumption that the error terms from successive observations are uncorrelated is frequently invalid; that is, investigation will find the residuals to be auto-correlated. A likely cause of autocorrelation (which is itself discussed more fully in Chapter 11) is that the series are non-stationary – a concept which is defined in section 10.2.

Non-stationarity is a very serious matter: regression of one non-stationary variable on another is very likely to yield impressive-seeming regression results which are wholly spurious. Section 10.3 illustrates how spurious regression may arise and section 10.4 presents formal tests for stationarity. One possible means of avoiding spurious regression is to transform the data so as to make them stationary – such transformations are discussed in section 10.5. (The other solution to the problem is the application of cointegration techniques which allow the estimation of non-spurious regressions with non-stationary data; these techniques are discussed in Chapter 12.) Section 10.6 summarises the main points from the chapter.

10.2 STATIONARITY AND NON-STATIONARITY

A time series is a set of data connected in time with a definite ordering given by the sequence in which the observations occurred. The time ordering of the data matters a great deal since the moments of the distribution of a time-series variable often change through time. That is, the mean, variance, and so on of the underlying distribution from which an observation is drawn are not constant, but depend on the point in time at which the observation was made.

For example, in a growing economy the level of most macroeconomic aggregates like production, consumption or the volume of trade will increase over time. Figure 10.1 shows the consumer price index for Tanzania for the period 1966–92 and Figure 10.2 the rate of growth of real exports for 1970–88 (the data for these figures are in the data file TANMON). Each figure also shows a horizontal line drawn at the mean level for the period as a whole. But, whilst to say that the average export growth rate over the period as a whole was –5.0 per cent seems a useful summary of the data, it means little to be told that the average CPI was 55.2 Why is this?

Recall that in Chapter 2 we modelled the mean of a variable as:

$$Y_t = \mu + \epsilon_t \tag{10.1}$$

That is, the value of a variable is its mean value plus some random error. Now, it does seem that the model described by equation (10.1) may well fit the data for export growth – the time series does seem to fluctuate around the mean. But equation (10.1) is a wholly inappropriate description of the CPI data – the variation of each observation from the mean does not appear random at all. The lack of randomness of the error term is – as is often the case – the result of the fact that equation (10.1) is not the correct model. An alternative (but not the only alternative) would be:[1]

$$Y_t = \mu t + \epsilon_t \tag{10.2}$$

In equation (10.2) the expected value of Y_t depends on t, in other words the first moment is not time invariant. A variable, such as that given by equation (10.1), whose moments are time invariant is said to be stationary.

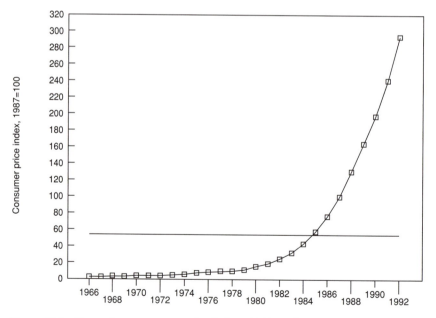

Figure 10.1 Tanzanian consumer price index, 1966–92 (1987=100)

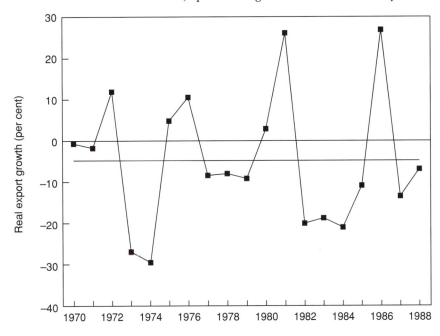

Figure 10.2   Tanzanian real export growth, 1970–88 (%)

If the moments are not time invariant then the variable is non-stationary. The fact that many socioeconomic data are non-stationary has the very serious consequence that regression results calculated with such series may be spurious.

Invariance of series variance

We have just seen that the first moment of the CPI data systematically increases across time. In addition, we often find that variation in the data increases along with their level. Look again at Figure 10.1. Moving along the scatter of points from left to right, the vertical distances between successive points tend to widen. As the level goes up, so does the variance. Hence not only is the level of the CPI not stable over time, neither is the variance. If we wish to transform the data so as to be stationary, then both first and second moments must be rendered time-invariant. We will see below how this may be done.

   Here we have visually inspected for non-stationarity – a method which is often sufficient to allow us to judge if a variable is stationary or not: the Tanzanian CPI series is clearly non-stationary. In practice, formal tests should be applied, and these are also discussed below. First, however, we discuss why non-stationarity is such a problem.

Exercise 10.1

Which of the following time series do you think would be non-stationary: (a) nominal GDP; (b) real GDP; (c) growth of real GDP; (d) nominal interest rates; (e) real interest rates; (f) external current account deficit as a per cent of GDP; (g) life expectancy at birth; and (h) infant mortality rate. Obtain data on each of these for the country of your choice (or use the data in data file PERU) and plot them over time. (You will use these data in several of the exercises in this chapter.) Do the graphs match your expectations?

10.3   RANDOM WALKS AND SPURIOUS REGRESSION

How might we explain the rapid escalation in Tanzanian prices which can be observed in Figure 10.1? One possible explanation is growth in the money supply. As the best-known proponent of monetarism, Milton Friedman, put it: 'inflation is always and everywhere a monetary phenomenon in the sense that it can be produced only be a more rapid increase in the quantity of money than in output' (Friedman, 1970). Figure 10.3 shows the scatter plot of logged CPI against logged money supply (M2). The figure also shows the fitted line from the regression, which is given by the results (figures in parentheses are standard errors; *DW* is the Durbin–Watson statistic to which we will refer below):

$$\ln CPI_t = -5.69 + 0.91\ln M2_t \qquad R^2 = 0.98$$
$$(0.25) \quad (0.03) \qquad DW = 0.20 \qquad (10.3)$$

These results certainly seem to support the argument that monetary growth has fuelled inflation. Yet it is quite possible that this apparent link is wholly spurious. To see why this may be so we have to embark on a digression concerning modelling trends in time series.

Modelling a random walk

The ordering of time series can matter since it contains the 'history' of the variable. That is, the value of the variable in one period is an important factor in determining the variable's value in the following period. This facet of time series may be expressed in a number of time-series models, the simplest of which is the autoregressive model with a single lag, called AR(1). In this model the variable in time t is given by some multiple of its value in period $t - 1$ plus an error term. Algebraically the model is:

$$X_t = \beta_1 + \beta_2 X_{t-1} + \epsilon_t \qquad \epsilon_t \sim N(0,\sigma^2) \ \forall t \qquad (10.4)$$

Spreadsheet simulations of equation (10.4) with different parameter values are the best way to get a feel for the way an AR(1) model works. First we set $\beta_1 = 0$ and examine variations in β_2. If $\beta_2 = 0$ then the series

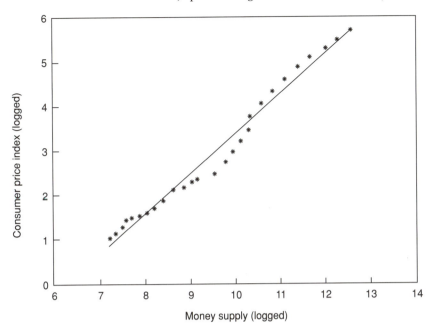

Figure 10.3 Inflation and money supply: scatter plot of CPI against M2, 1966–92

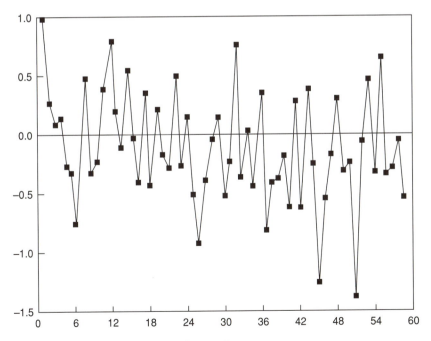

Figure 10.4 AR(1) process: $\beta_1 = 0$; $\beta_2 = 0$

has no memory – the value of X in time t is given only by the error term in that period and preceding values of X are of no relevance. This case is shown in Figure 10.4. This graph therefore shows the 60 error terms which will be used in the following simulations. (The graph contains 61 observations – the first of these, X_0, is given by an assumed initial value, which is taken as 1 in this and subsequent simulations.) For future reference, observe that only eight of the 31 observations from 30 to 60 are positive.

Figure 10.5 shows the simulation of the AR(1) model with $\beta_2 = 0.5$, so that the value of X is half of what it was in the preceding period plus a random error. Compared with Figure 10.4, the series now appears to have some 'memory' – that is, a tendency for the value in one period to be closer to the value of the preceding period. Hence it can be seen that the series takes a while to get away from its initial value of one. The succession of negative error terms in the second half of the series means that X is likely to stay negative – there are only five positive observations from periods 30–60.

The tendency for the series to stay where it was increases as the β_2 coefficient increases towards unity. When $\beta_2 = 1$ we have a special case of the AR(1) process known as a random walk – so called because the value of the variable in one period is equal to its value in the preceding period plus a deviation by a random error. Figure 10.6 shows the simu-

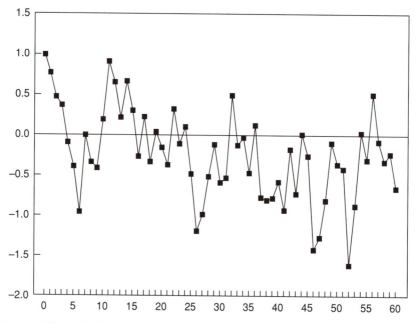

Figure 10.5   AR(1) process: $\beta_1 = 0$; $\beta_2 = 0.5$

lation of the random walk. Despite the fact that a random walk is generated by a succession of unrelated error terms the series displays apparent trends. In this example the disproportionate number of negative errors for observations 30–60 creates an apparent strong downward trend over this period. Even a quite short run of error terms of the same sign will send a random walk off on a seeming trend.

If the β_2 coefficient exceeds unity then this 'trend' factor dominates the series, since the variable in each period is its own past value times some multiple. As may be seen from Figure 10.7, in which $\beta_2 = 1.1$, the resulting escalation in the X value soon drowns out the error term. The similarity between this graph and that of the CPI for Tanzania (Figure 10.1) should be readily apparent. It seems that the AR(1) model with a coefficient of greater than unity would be a good representation of this data series.

A negative value of β_2 results in oscillations, since the negative coefficient will reverse the sign of X in each successive period – though it will sometimes happen that the error term will cancel out this reversal so that two or more X values of the same sign may be observed. This cancelling out effect is more likely if β_2 is relatively small, resulting in a pattern of oscillations which will appear more muted. In Figure 10.8 $\beta_2 = -0.5$ and the 'jagged' nature of the time series is obvious.

What difference is made by non-zero values of β_1? In the case when $\beta_2 = 0$ then X will display random fluctuations around a mean of β_1. If

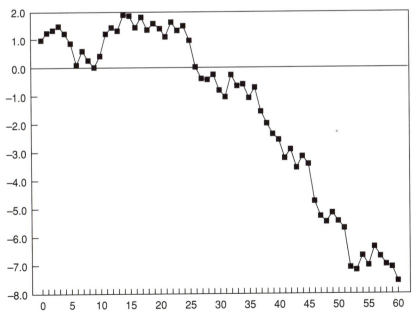

Figure 10.6   AR(1) process: $\beta_1 = 0$; $\beta_2 = 1$ – random walk

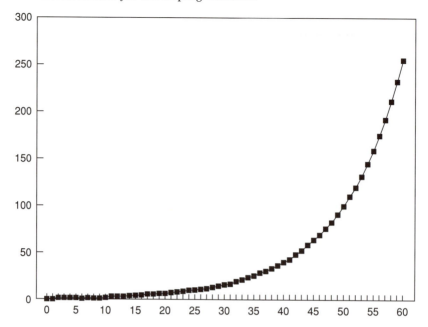

Figure 10.7   AR(1) process: $\beta_1 = 0$; $\beta_2 = 1.1$

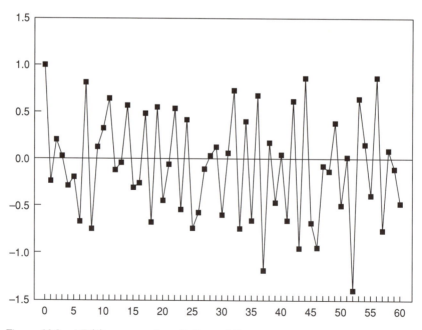

Figure 10.8   AR(1) process: $\beta_1 = 0$; $\beta_2 = -0.5$

β_2 has an absolute value of less than one then the series will fluctuate around a mean of $\beta_1/(1 - \beta_2)$, with apparent runs if $\beta_2 > 0$ and in an oscillatory manner if $\beta_2 < 0$. The former case is shown in Figure 10.9, where the values of β_1 (2) and β_2 (0.3) give an expected value of X of 2.86. The graph of Tanzanian export growth (Figure 10.2) would seem a candidate for being modelled as an AR(1) series with $\beta_1 < 0$ and $0 < \beta_2 < 1$. When $\beta_2 = 1$ the series is known as a random walk with drift, since the apparent trends may be reinforced by the addition of β_1 each period. This case is shown in Figure 10.10. The upward drift goes a long way to cancelling out the strong downward trend that the random walk showed in the later part of the series (Figure 10.6).

The algebra of stationarity

We see that the simple AR(1) model can generate a wide range of different patterns of time series; these are summarised in Table 10.1. We shall now demonstrate that a variable following an AR(1) process is stationary if $|\beta_2| < 1$, but not so otherwise. Repeated substitution into equation (10.4) gives the following expression of X_t:

$$X_t = \beta_2^t X_0 + \beta_1 \sum_{i=0}^{t-1} \beta_2^i + \sum_{i=0}^{t-1} \beta_2^i \epsilon_{t-i} \qquad (10.5)$$

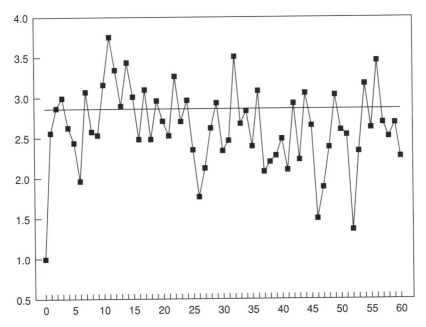

Figure 10.9   AR(1) process: $\beta_1 = 2$; $\beta_2 = 0.3$

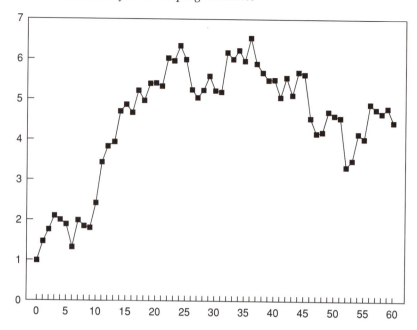

Figure 10.10   AR(1) process: $\beta_1 = 0.2$; $\beta_2 = 1$ – random walk with drift

Interpretation of this expression is easiest by considering the three cases of $|\beta_2| < 1$, $\beta_2 = 1$ and $|\beta_2| > 1$ separately.

First consider the case of a random walk:

$$\beta_2 = 1 : \quad X_t = X_0 + \beta_1 t + \sum_{i=1}^{t} \epsilon_t \tag{10.6}$$

From this expression we can see that the value of X at time t depends on three factors: (a) the initial value, X_0; (b) the amount of drift; and (c) the sum of the current and all past error terms. Hence an error in one period affects the value of X in all future periods: the series has a perfect memory. This feature of a random walk may be contrasted with modelling X as following a deterministic trend, that is:

$$X_t = \beta_1 + \beta_2 t + \epsilon_t \tag{10.7}$$

Superficially equation (10.7) looks very like equation (10.6), but in fact the structure of the error term is wholly different. In the trend, model X follows the trend with random fluctuations about that trend – but it always returns to the trend as an error in one period is immediately 'forgotten' in the subsequent period. By contrast, in a random walk the error is embodied in all future values of X so that the series may stray a long way from its underlying 'trend' value, and is not 'drawn back' to the trend as

Table 10.1 Series resulting from different values of β_1 and β_2 in AR(1) model

	$\beta_1 = 0$	$\beta_1 \neq 0$
$\beta_2 = 0$	X is just random error in each period. No pattern will be discernible	X fluctuates in random manner around mean of β_1
$0 < \beta_2 < 1$	X fluctuates around 0 with 'some memory' resulting in short patterns	X fluctuates around mean of $\beta_1/(1 - \beta_2)$ with some patterns
$0 > \beta_2 > -1$	X fluctuates around 0 in an oscillatory manner	X fluctuates around mean of $\beta_1/(1 - \beta_2)$ in an oscillatory manner
$\beta_2 = 1$	Random walk	Random walk with drift
$\beta_2 > 1$	Explosive (exponential) growth	Explosive (exponential) growth
$\beta_2 < -1$	Ever larger oscillations	Ever larger oscillations

is a series generated by equation (10.7) – a random walk never forgets an error. We saw an example of this in Figure 10.10 – despite the upward drift the series declined in the second half of the period shown – and if we were to run the model for another 1,000 periods we should have no expectation that it would return to 'trend'.

The latter result runs contrary to the general beliefs of many economists, whose theories of long-run behaviour have been based on the notion that variables such as real GDP follow a trend. Moreover the treatment of the fluctuations around this trend (the business cycle) has been treated as an independent area of enquiry. Evidence presented by Sims (1980) that most major macroeconomic aggregates for the USA could be modelled as a random walk – so that the apparent trend and the cyclical behaviour are the result of the same data generation process – struck rather a blow to these traditional views. Subsequent work demonstrating the bias and inconsistency of OLS using non-stationary series therefore cast doubt on much published empirical work.

The expected value of a variable following a random walk is, however, given only by its deterministic component. Taking expectations of equation (10.6) yields:

$$E(X_t) = X_0 + \beta_1 t \tag{10.8}$$

Recall that a non-stationary variable is defined as one whose moments are time-dependent. From equation (10.8) it is clear that a random walk with drift is non-stationary, since its first moment is a function of time. However, the expected value of a random walk without drift ($\beta_1 = 0$) is just the initial value, X_0. This fact does not mean that such a variable is stationary since its second moment is time dependent:

$$E[X_t - E(X_t)]^2 = E\left[\sum_{i=1}^{t} \epsilon_i\right]^2$$

$$= E\left[\sum_{i=1}^{t}\sum_{j=1}^{t} \epsilon_i\,\epsilon_j\right] = t\,\sigma^2 \qquad (10.9)$$

That is, the expected (squared) difference between X and its expected value increases with time, which is to be expected as the 'history of errors' will have a greater cumulative impact, allowing the series to wander away from its underlying trend as time goes by.

Now consider the case of a variable with $|\beta_2| < 1$. In equation (10.5), as t tends to infinity X can be written as:

$$|\beta_2| < 1: \quad X_t \to \frac{\beta_1}{1 - \beta_2} + \sum_{i=0}^{t-1} \beta_2^{\,i}\,\epsilon_{t-1} \quad \text{as } t \to \infty$$

$$(10.10)$$

The initial value is no longer relevant as the series forgets about events too far in the past. Similarly the impact of a specific error term decreases as it moves further into the past. The second component from equation (10.5) is in this case equal to the expected value of $\beta_1/(1 - \beta_2)$. The variance, as $t \to > \infty$, is given by:

$$E[X_t - E(X_t)]^2 = \sum_{i=0}^{t-1}\sum_{j=0}^{t-1} \beta_2^{\,i}\beta_2^{\,j}\, E[\epsilon_{t-i}\,\epsilon_{t-j}]$$

$$= \sigma^2(1 + \beta_2^2 + \beta_2^4 + \ldots)$$

$$= \frac{\sigma^2}{1 - \beta_2^2} \qquad (10.11)$$

where we have used the fact that $E(\epsilon_{ij}) = 0$ for all $i \neq j$ and is equal to σ^2 for all $i = j$. A variable which may be described by an AR(1) series with $|\beta_2| < 1$ is stationary – we have shown that its first and second moments are independent of the time at which the observation occurs.

Finally, equation (10.5) shows the explosive nature of a series in which $\beta_2 > 1$. Since $\beta_2 > 1$ each of the three terms grows larger and larger as t increases. Both first and second moments are time-dependent.

Significant regressions of independently generated random series

We have seen that when $\beta_1 = 0$ and $\beta_2 = 1$ then equation (10.4) describes a random walk. As discussed earlier, a random walk process has 'a perfect memory' so that the current value of X_t is a function of all past disturbances. For this reason a random walk may display apparent trends, such as can be seen in the X series shown in Figure 10.11 which we are to use

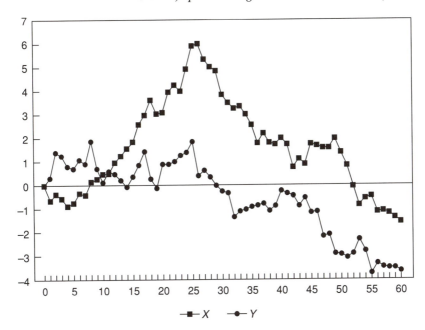

Figure 10.11 Two random walks

in the example below. In fact, a random walk is often called a stochastic trend as distinct from a deterministic trend such as defined in equation (10.7).

Figure 10.11 also shows Y_t which was generated as a random walk:

$$Y_t = Y_{t-1} + \epsilon'_t \qquad \epsilon'_t \sim N(0, \sigma^2) \; \forall t \qquad (10.12)$$

Although the error term for the AR(1) process describing Y_t has the same distribution as the error term for the process for X_t they are not the same variable: the series of ϵ will be different from the series ϵ'.

It should be clear that the two series shown in Figure 10.11 have no relationship with one another. Both are 'hypothetical' series based upon independently generated series of random numbers. Yet if we regress Y_t on X_t we find a significant slope coefficient! The t-statistic is 3.64 (with an $R^2 = 0.18$), compared to the critical value of 2.00 at the 5 per cent level. OLS regression suggests that the independent random variable Y_t is actually a function of X_t – we know this is not true because we made Y_t ourselves, and it had nothing to do with X_t. This is surely a spurious regression. Nor is this a freak result – repeating the experiment with a different set of random numbers (and therefore different X_ts and Y_ts) 120 times gave a significant relationship at the 10 per cent level between the two variables in 96 (80 per cent) of cases – these results are given in the frequency distribution shown in Table 10.2. In nearly two-thirds of cases the relationship was significant at the 1 per cent level.

Table 10.2   Frequency distribution of absolute *t*-statistic from 120 regressions of unrelated random walks

Level (%)	t-statistic	Number of cases	Per cent
	$t \leqslant 1.67$	24	20.0
10	$1.67 < t \leqslant 2.00$	6	5.0
5	$2.00 < t \leqslant 2.67$	11	9.2
1	$t > 2.67$	79	65.8
		120	100.0

The implications of this analysis are profound indeed. Regressing two unrelated series on one another gives apparently significant results. Whilst we have demonstrated the point by empirical example it has been shown theoretically that application of OLS to non-stationary series yields biased and inconsistent results.

Inflation and money supply revisited

So how do we know that the regression results reported in equation (10.3) – showing a strong impact of money supply on the price level – are not spurious? We don't. And they may well be. In fact the results we reported give a strong indication that the regression probably is spurious. Spurious regressions will often display bad residual autocorrelation. We shall deal with this topic in the next chapter, when we shall meet the Durbin–Watson (*DW*) statistic which provides a test for the presence of autocorrelation. For the moment we may note a rule of thumb that if $R^2 > DW$ there is a very strong likelihood that the results are spurious. The regression of the CPI on money supply yielded an R^2 of 0.96, but a *DW* of only 0.23. Hence we should be very wary of accepting the results from equation (10.3) as proof that inflation in Tanzania has been a largely monetary phenomenon.

Before interpreting time series regression results (ideally before conducting any regressions) we must carry out two steps. First, we must check whether the data are stationary or not. If they are not we must usually resort to some technique other than OLS. Tests for stationarity are discussed in section 10.4 and data transformations to stationarity in section 10.5.

Exercise 10.2

Use a spreadsheet to construct an AR(1) model and examine each of the ten possible parameter combinations shown in Table 10.1.

Exercise 10.3

Using the graphs you drew for exercise 10.1, make an assessment of probable parameter values for each series on the assumption that they may be described by an AR(1) process.

Exercise 10.4

Use a spreadsheet to construct two random walks (generated by independent error terms) and regress one on the other. Note down the resulting *t*-statistic. Repeat a further 49 times. In what percentage of cases do you find a significant result? What are the implications of your analysis for OLS regressions using time-series data? (You may also do this exercise using an econometric package with the facility to generate random numbers. If you do use such a package you should also check your regression results to note in which case $R^2 > DW$.)

Exercise 10.5

Can the problem of spurious regression arise in cross-section data? Explain.

10.4 TESTING FOR STATIONARITY

A non-stationary series is one whose moments are not time-invariant. Such a series can be expressed by the following general equation:

$$X_t = \beta_1 + \beta_2 t + \beta_3 X_{t-1} + \epsilon_t \qquad (10.13)$$

The nature of the time series described by equation (10.13) depends on the parameter values – the most important distinction being between cases which are a trend stationary process and those which are a difference stationary process.

Trend stationary process versus difference stationary process

If $\beta_2 \neq 0$ and $|\beta_3| < 1$ then X follows a deterministic trend. The autoregressive component will mean that there may be short-run deviations, but in the end the series will return to trend.[2] An example, with $\beta_1 = 10$, $\beta_2 = 0.5$ and $\beta_3 = 0.9$, is shown in Figure 10.12. A series of this sort is known as a trend stationary process (TSP), as the residuals from the regression of X on a constant and a trend will be stationary. A series is 'detrended' by first regressing the variable on a time series and then using the residuals from that regression in place of the variable.

On the other hand, if $\beta_1 \neq 0$, $\beta_2 = 0$ and $\beta_3 = 1$ the series follows a random walk with drift. The behaviour of such a series is very different from that shown in Figure 10.12, since it displays no tendency to return to trend. A random walk is known as a difference stationary process (DSP), since the first differences will be stationary, where the first difference is given by:

$$\Delta X_t = X_t - X_{t-1}$$
$$= \beta_1 + \epsilon_t \qquad (10.14)$$

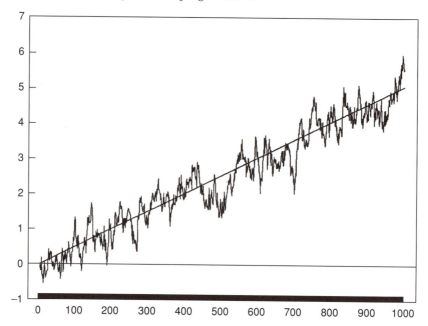

Figure 10.12 Trend with stationary autoregressive component

The fact that many economic series appear to follow a random walk has two important implications. First, there do not exist long-run trend values of these variables, from which they may depart but to which they eventually return – a series of shocks can send the variable off on a wholly different path for the rest of time. Second, as already mentioned, OLS cannot be applied to non-stationary series.

The inapplicability of OLS is equally relevant to trend stationary processes as to difference stationary processes. But if a variable were to be a trend stationary process then OLS would be applicable to the detrended series for that variable. But detrending a difference stationary process, such as a random walk, does not make it stationary – so OLS is still invalid. To apply regression techniques to a DSP, differencing must be applied to make the series stationary. Differencing a TSP will also result in a stationary series. That is, we can treat a TSP as if it were a DSP and achieve valid results. But if we treat a DSP as a TSP we would be led to the invalid application of OLS.

As mentioned, the first difference of a non-stationary variable may well be stationary. Figure 10.13 shows the first differences for the log of the Tanzanian CPI and M2 (as we discuss on p. 360 these variables approximate the rate of inflation and monetary growth respectively). Whereas Figure 10.1 showed the logged CPI to be clearly non-stationary the same is not so obvious of its first differences.

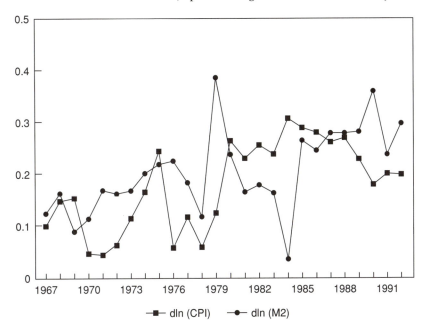

Figure 10.13   First differences in logged Tanzanian CIP and M2, 1967–92

Order of integration (integrated variables)

If the first difference of a non-stationary variable is stationary, that variable is said to be integrated of order one, written as I(1). If second differences are required to achieve stationarity, then the variable is integrated of order two, and so on. Simple regressions should be carried out on variables of the same order of integration.

Saying that any time-series analysis should start by checking the order of integration of each variable is another way of repeating our general exhortation to begin by looking at your data. You will find you can soon make a reasonable guess of the order of integration of a variable by looking at its time path. What you are doing when you do this is to try and match the picture you see against the different graphs generated by the AR(1) process, shown in Figures 10.4–10.10 above.

Testing for non-stationarity (unit roots)

But it is also possible to test formally for stationarity by testing if the variable may be described as a random walk, either with or without drift. This procedure is also commonly called testing for a unit root as an I(1) process has a unit root. If we find we cannot reject the hypothesis that the variable is a unit root (e.g. follows a random walk) then we have found that the variable is non-stationary and must proceed accordingly.

It might seem that the test for stationarity is therefore a parameter test on the AR(1) model given by equation (10.4). Specifically, we can test the hypothesis that $\beta_1 = 0$ and $\beta_2 = 1$, in which case the series is a random walk (i.e. non-stationary) if $\beta_2 = 1$ and with drift if $\beta_1 \neq 0$. Whilst this approach seems intuitively appealing – and indeed is the basis of what we do – it requires modification for the following three reasons:

1   Equation (10.4) is a more restricted version of the general model which includes also a deterministic time trend (equation (10.13)), so we must use the more general model as the basis for our initial testing.
2   It can be shown that if the series is non-stationary then the estimate of β_3 will be downward bias, so we are in danger of finding a series to be stationary when in fact it is not. For this reason we cannot use the standard t- or F-statistics when looking at critical values to conduct significance tests. Alternative critical values have been provided by Dickey and Fuller (and another set provided by MacKinnon).
3   A modified version of equation (10.13) is used, called the augmented Dickey–Fuller (ADF) test, which includes the lagged difference; the inclusion of this term means that the critical values are valid even if there is residual autocorrelation.

The variety of appropriate test statistics are documented elsewhere (e.g. Banerjee *et al.*, 1993: ch. 4). Here we present a modified form of a decision tree process suggested by Holden and Perman (1994) to test for stationarity. This process is rather more complex than the Dickey–Fuller (or augmented Dickey–Fuller) test which the reader will commonly come across. However, this test is made using a restricted version of the general model (usually excluding both trend and drift) without having tested those restrictions. If the restrictions are invalid then the critical values are not applicable (and if they are, then efficiency is lost if the more general model is used). Hence, following the logic of Chapter 6, the testing procedure should begin with the most general model; this is what the decision tree does.

The tree structure, shown in Figure 10.14, allows us to move from a more general to the more specific specifications of the equation, and indicates the appropriate test-statistic at each stage. The critical values are given in the statistical tables on p. 480. Here we work through the decision tree, reporting results for the three Tanzanian series: logged CPI, logged M2 and real export growth (XGROW). Note, however, that these procedures are really only valid for large samples, so that their application to the XGROW series is dubious.

Step 1   The first step is to estimate the most general model:

$$X_t = \beta_1 + \beta_2 t + \beta_3 X_{t-1} + \beta_4 \Delta X_{t-1} + \epsilon_{1,t} \qquad (10.15)$$

Estimate (10.15)

$$y_t = \beta_1 + \beta_2 t + \beta_3 y_{t-1} + \beta_4 \Delta y_{t-1} + \varepsilon_t$$

and test restricted model

$$\Delta y_t = \beta_4 \Delta y_{t-1} + \varepsilon_t'$$

i.e. H_0: $\beta_1 = \beta_2 = 0$ and $\beta_3 = 1$ using calculated F against critical value ϕ_2

- **Accept** — y is a random walk without drift
- **Reject** — Estimate

  $$\Delta y_t = \beta_1 + \beta_4 \Delta y_{t-1} + \varepsilon_t''$$

  and test against (10.15) i.e. H_0: $\beta_2 = 0$ and $\beta_3 = 1$ using calculated F against ϕ_3

  - **Accept** — y is a random walk with drift
  - **Reject** — Test $\beta_3 = 1$ from estimating (10.15) with calculated t-statistic against $N(0,1)$

    - **Accept** — y is random walk with deterministic trend (and perhaps drift): an unlikely outcome for economic series
    - **Reject** — y has not got a unit root, so usual t-statistics are valid to test if β_1 and β_2 are zero. Use t-statistic to test $\beta_2 = 0$ from equation (10.15)

      - **Accept** — y is stationary $t<0$:
      - **Reject** — y is stationary around a deterministic trend $t<0$: y may be I(2), repeat decision tree using first differences

Figure 10.14 Decision tree for testing stationarity

Table 10.3 Application of decision tree for testing stationarity

		ln(CPI) (n = 25)	ln(M2) (n = 25)	XGROW (n = 17)
Unrestricted model	RSS_U	0.0692	0.1041	3,675
$\beta_1 = \beta_2 = 0\ \beta_3 = 1$	RSS_{R1}	0.1018	0.2056	8,426
	F-stat	3.30	6.83	5.60
		Accept	Reject	Reject
$\beta_2 = 0\ \beta_3 = 1$	RSS_{R2}	–	0.1399	8,420
	F-stat		3.61	8.39
			Accept	Reject
$\beta3 = 1$	Estimate	–	–	-0.426
	SE			0.357
	t-stat			-4.10
				Reject
$\beta2 = 0$	Estimate	–	–	0.225
	SE			0.834
	t-stat			0.270
				Accept
Decision		Random walk without drift	Random walk with drift	Stationary

from which the *RSS* is the unrestricted sum of squares RSS_U, shown for each of the three series as the top line of Table 10.3. To examine if the series is a random walk without drift we impose the restrictions $\beta_1 = \beta_2 = 0$ and $\beta_3 = 1$, so that we estimate:

$$\Delta X_t = \beta_4 \Delta X_{t-1} + \epsilon_{2,t} \tag{10.16}$$

and use the resulting *RSS* (RSS_{R1} in Table 10.3) to calculate the usual *F*-test (see Chapter 6). The appropriate critical value is given by the test-statistic Φ_2.

In the case of ln(CPI) and ln(M2) the critical value at the 5 per cent level is 5.68, and is a bit larger than this for XGROW. (The 10 per cent critical value for a sample size of 25 is 4.67.) Hence we accept the null hypothesis in the case of ln(CPI) and reject in the case of ln(M2). The result for XGROW is close to the critical value. Given the weakness of the test in smaller samples it is probably best to reject the null and proceed to the next stage.

Accepting the null hypothesis indicates the variable to be a random walk without drift. Not shown in the decision tree is the suggestion of Holden and Pearson that we may now verify this result by imposing the restriction that $\beta_2 = 0$ in equation (10.15). The *RSS* from this equation is then used to test the joint restriction $\beta_1 = 0$ and $\beta_3 = 1$ (for which the appropriate *RSS* has already been derived, i.e. RSS_{R1}) using the critical values given by Φ_1. In the case of ln(CPI), the *RSS*, once β_2 is dropped from equation (10.15), is 0.082, resulting in a calculated *F*-statistic of 1.77.

This value is below the critical value of 5.18 at the 5 per cent level, so we accept the null hypothesis, thus confirming that ln(CPI) is a random walk without drift.

Step 2   If the null from Step 1 is rejected we test instead whether the series may be a random walk with drift. That is, $\beta_2 = 0$ and $\beta_3 = 1$, so we estimate:

$$\Delta X_t = \beta_1 + \beta_4 \Delta X_{t-1} + \epsilon_{3,t} \tag{10.17}$$

The resulting *RSS* is shown as RSS_{R2} in Table 10.3 (not for ln(CPI) which has been established to be random walk without drift). Relaxing the restriction that the intercept term is zero greatly reduces the *RSS* for the ln(M2) series. Again the *F*-test is used, with the appropriate critical values given by Φ_3, which is 7.24 at the 5 per cent level for a sample size of 25. Clearly we can accept the null for ln(M2), but have to reject for XGROW. Logged money supply is non-stationary, that is, it follows a random walk with drift.

If the null is accepted we may wish to verify the result by calculating the *t*-test for the hypothesis that $\beta_3 = 1$, using the critical value τ_3. Estimation of equation (10.15) for ln(M2) results in an estimate for β_3 of 0.9088 with a standard error of 0.1074. The resulting *t*-statistic is –0.849, compared to the critical value at 5 per cent of –0.80. This result casts some doubt on the conclusion that ln(M2) is a random walk, but given the marginal nature of the result (the null hypothesis is easily acceptable at the 10 per cent level) and the serious consequences of treating a random walk as a non-stationary series, we had best proceed on the assumption that ln(M2) is indeed a random walk with drift.

Step 3   If the null from Step 2 is rejected, the null hypothesis that $\beta_3 = 1$ should now be tested with a *t*-statistic compared to a critical value given by the standard normal tables. The estimated coefficient in the case of XGROW is –0.4626, so the calculated *t*-statistic is –4.10. This value is, in absolute terms, far greater than the $N(0,1)$ critical value of 1.96 at the 5 per cent level, so we reject the null.

Step 4   If the null from Step 3 is rejected we know that the variable does not have a unit root. We can test if it is stationary around a constant mean or around a deterministic trend (i.e. is a trend stationary process, TSP). Since there is no unit root, the usual *t*-tests are valid and we may use the *t*-statistic, compared to the critical value from the usual *t*-tables to test the null hypothesis that $\beta_2 = 0$. The estimated coefficient on the time trend in equation (10.15) for the XGROW series is 0.225, so that the SE of 0.834 results in a calculated *t*-statistic of 0.27. This value is far below the critical value of 3.16 at the 5 per cent level with 13 degrees of freedom, so we accept the null, i.e. there is no deterministic trend.

It therefore seems that XGROW is non-stationary (confirming our initial visual impression), but it should be recalled that the application of these techniques to a sample of less than 25 observations is not strictly valid. The problem of small sample size is one that applied work, especially with developing-country data, continually runs up against. Data quality is poor, and where there are data, there are not many. Modern time-series techniques require large samples, which we do not have, but traditional techniques are simply invalid. There is no ready solution to this dilemma. An important caveat to this procedure is that the variable may be I(2) (most likely with price series), in which cases the restricted model will also be rejected at Steps 1 and 2. However, in this case the *t*-statistic in Step 3 will be positive rather than negative (ie the estimated coefficient is greater than one), so the variable is non-stationary. We may then check the stationarity of the first differences.

Exercise 10.5

Replicate the results shown in Table 10.3.

Exercise 10.6

Test the stationarity of the data series you compiled for exercise 10.1.

Exercise 10.7

Use a spreadsheet to create two series, one following a trend with a stochastic component (a TSP series) and the other a random walk with drift (a DSP series). Alternatively you may use the data given in Appendix 10.1 for this exercise. Carry out an ADF test on: (a) each of the two series; (b) the residuals from regressing each series on a constant and time; and (c) the first differences of each series. Comment on your findings.

10.5   TRANSFORMATIONS TO STATIONARITY

To make a non-stationary series stationary it must be transformed in such a way that its moments are no longer time-dependent. We have already seen that a series which may be described by a random walk may be made stationary by taking first differences; that is, it is a difference stationary process. We pursue this point below, where we re-examine the link between money and prices in Tanzania in the context of a difference equation. But whilst differencing makes the mean (first moment) time invariant, what of the variance? We first examine the problem of stabilising the variance.

Stabilising variances

As just stated, to transform a time series to stationarity we need to stabilise both its mean and its variance over time. This cannot be done with one transformation only. In general, power transformations (using Tukey's ladder of transformations: see section 3.5) are used to stabilise the variance. The reason is that, most commonly, the variance of a time series increases as its mean increases. The examples in Chapter 3 using cross-section data showed that a power transformation can be very effective in dealing with this pattern of covariance between level and spread. As we shall see, the same is true with many time series.

As a rule, always start by stabilising the variance of time series before tackling the problem of its time-varying mean. How is this done in practice?

First of all, it is necessary to check whether or not a time series displays a time-varying variance. Here is a simple method to do this. Slice the time series up into roughly equal sections with between four and twelve observations in each section, depending on the total number of observations available. Take, for example, our time series of Tanzania's consumer price index for the period 1966–92 (a total of 27 years). We divide it up into sub-samples: 1966–74; 1975–83; 1984–92 (hence, three slices of nine observations). Figure 10.15 gives us a comparative display of the box plots for the three sub-periods. This clearly shows that the spread increases as the level goes up; a transformation is undoubtedly called for. But which transformation to use?

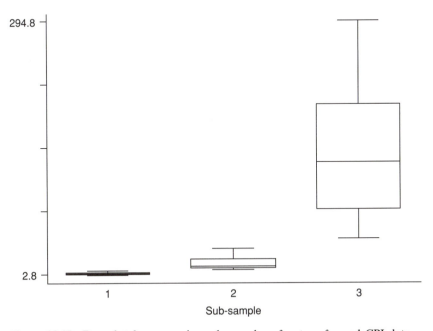

Figure 10.15 Box plot for successive sub-samples of untransformed CPI data

We could proceed by trial and error using the ladder of transformations, but section 7.4 above illustrated an easier way to determine which transformation is likely to do the trick, which may be explained as follows. Equation (7.4) was:

$$\ln\sigma_x = \ln A + k\ln\mu_x \qquad (10.18)$$

where σ_x is the standard deviation of variable x, μ_x its mean and k a constant indicating the data transformation required to stabilise the variance of the series. This equation suggests a practical method to check which transformation is likely to be best. First, plot the logarithm of a measure for spread against the logarithm of a measure for level (average) for successive slices of a time series. Usually we use the interquartile range and the median instead of the standard deviation and the mean because the former are more robust. If the successive points (plotted accordingly to this method) roughly approximate a straight line, the pattern of covariance behaviour level and spread is stable through time: the log-linear model given by equation (10.18) is the appropriate one. Having plotted this line, computing its slope indicates which transformation is likely to do the trick, since this slope corresponds to the variable k.

Figure 10.16 plots the logarithms of the interquartile range for each slice against the logarithm of its corresponding median (see Table 10.4). The scatter of the three points shows a steady increase which can be

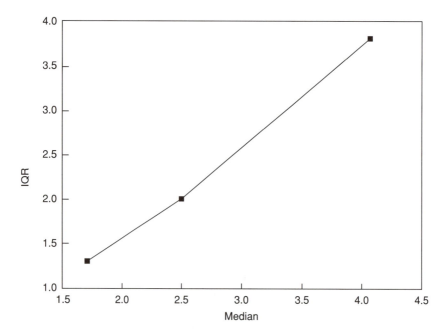

Figure 10.16 Logged IQR against logged median for Tanzanian CPI

Table 10.4 Medians and interquartile ranges

	Median		Interquartile range	
	Value	*Log*	*Value*	*Log*
1966–74	4.40	1.48	1.85	0.62
1975–83	11.90	2.48	13.00	2.56
1984–92	131.10	4.88	152.00	5.02

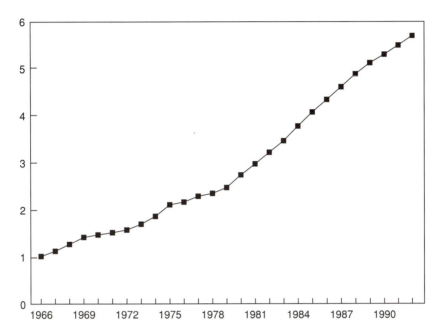

Figure 10.17 Logged Tanzanian CPI, 1970–88

reasonably approximated by a straight line. To calculate its slope we can use the upper and lower points:

$$k = \frac{5.02 - 0.61}{4.88 - 1.43} = 1.29 \tag{10.19}$$

so that $k \approx 1$, suggesting that the logarithmic transformation is the right one to stabilise the variance.

Figure 10.17 plots the logarithm of Tanzania's consumer price index against time. As we can see from this graph, the vertical distances between successive points no longer show the earlier tendency to increase over time (although there is some variation, showing that the transformation has not completely stabilised the variance). In general, in economic analysis it is the case that logarithms stabilise the variance, although, sometimes a series may be encountered for which the square root transformation is appropriate.

Exercise 10.8

Use the procedure outlined above to determine the appropriate transformation to stabilise the variance for each of the series you compiled for
exercise 10.1.

Stabilising the mean

Once we succeed in stabilising the variance through time, we can then
tackle the problem of a time-varying mean. A power transformation used
to stabilise the variance cannot deal with stabilising the mean as well. The
reason is that power transformations alter the shape of the distribution
of the data but, at the same time, preserve their ordering. To stabilise the
mean we need a different type of transformation altogether.

Historically, the detrending of a time series was the common method
to stabilise its mean. A trend line (usually, a polynomial) was fitted to the
data, leaving residuals which, consequently, no longer displayed a time-
varying mean. The practice of detrending implicitly assumes that the series
is a TSP, i.e. follows a deterministic trend to which it will always revert. But
we have found that many series may be described as following a random
walk, and detrending such a series does not remove the problem of non-
stationarity (see exercise 10.7). To do this, differences must be taken.

We saw that both the CPI and M2 are non-stationary, so that regression of one on the other is not generally valid. (As discussed in Chapter
12, it will only be valid if the two variables are cointegrated.) The variances
of each variable can be stabilised by using logs. To stabilise the mean
we must take first differences. The first difference of the natural log of a
variable has the additional advantage of being approximately equal to that
variable's rate of growth, that is, the rate of inflation and monetary growth,
respectively (see Box 10.1).

Suppose a true relationship is given by:

$$Y_t = \beta_1 + \beta_2 X_t + \epsilon_t \tag{10.20}$$

then it follows that:

$$\Delta Y_t = \beta_2 \Delta X_t + \omega_t \tag{10.21}$$

where $\omega = \epsilon_t - \epsilon_{t-1}$. That is, the same slope coefficient should be revealed
in both the levels and difference regressions (and the intercept in the
difference equation should be zero).

Recall that equation (10.3), in which the logged CPI was regressed on
logged M2, showed an apparently strong relationship between the two
variables. Estimation of equation (10.21) with these data gives (standard
error in parentheses):

$$\Delta\ln(\text{CPI}) = 0.79\Delta\ln(\text{M2}) \quad R^2 = -0.26$$
$$(0.08) \qquad\qquad DW = 1.16 \tag{10.22}$$

Box 10.1   Logged differences and rates of growth

For small values of x the following approximation is true:

$$\ln(1 + x) = x$$

Therefore:

$$\ln (X_t) - \ln (X_{t-1}) = \ln \left(\frac{X_t}{X_{t-1}} \right) = \ln (1 + g_x) = g_x$$

where

$$g_x = \frac{X_t - X_{t-1}}{X_{t-1}}$$

That is, the first difference of the log of x is approximately equal to the rate of growth of X.

As an exercise you could use a spreadsheet to examine the range of values of g_x over which this approximation is valid.

Although the t-statistic for the slope coefficient is high, the R^2 of -0.26 clearly indicates that we have invalidly omitted the intercept, which will bias the estimate of the slope coefficient. This fact alone should cast doubt on whether the regression of $\ln(\text{CPI})$ on $\ln(\text{M2})$ is the true model. Including an intercept gives (standard error in parentheses):

$$\Delta\ln(\text{CPI}) = 0.13 + 0.25\Delta\ln(\text{M2}) \quad R^2 \quad = 0.06$$
$$(0.05) \quad (0.21) \qquad\qquad DW = 0.74 \qquad\qquad (10.23)$$

The R^2 remains pitifully low. More importantly, the slope coefficient is now only 0.25, which is far less than the 0.91 obtained in equation (10.3). The growth of the money supply now appears to have no significant effect on the rate of inflation. What happened? The regression between the levels of both variables looks good, but as soon as we switch to regressing changes in these levels on one another the results are disappointing. It appears, therefore, that first differencing took the wind out of our sails. Why?

The problem lies in the regression between the levels of both time series. In regression analysis, the total variation of a dependent variable, Y, around its mean is in part explained by the variation in the independent variable, X, around its mean, leaving the residual variation as the remainder. If, as is the case in our example, both Y and X are stochastic variables, we assume that they are jointly sampled from a bivariate normal distribution. This implies that we assume that each variable (as well as the error term) is distributed normally with a constant mean and a constant variance. The regression line then explains the variation in Y

around its constant mean in terms of the variation in X around its constant mean. Hence, each Y_t (or X_t) is assumed to be sampled from the same distribution with a constant mean and variance. However, in our example this clearly is not the case. The problem is that neither the dependent nor the independent variable has a constant mean through time. Successive observations of either of these variables appear to be drawn from different distributions with progressively higher means.

Take another look at Figure 10.1. It seems far-fetched to assume that this is a sample of observations drawn from a distribution with a constant mean or variance. The log transformation we subsequently applied to this variable in regression allows us to stabilise the variance, but obviously not the level. The reason is that logarithms preserve order although they alter the shape of the data.

Hence, the results we obtained by regressing the levels of both log transformed variables may be as much due to the fact that each variable is constantly on the move in terms of its level as to any real relationship between them. This is what make regressions with time series so prone to the danger of spurious correlations. In Chapter 12, on cointegration, this issue will be taken up again. There we shall show that in some instances it is possible to derive meaningful results by regressing time series which are not stationary over time.

Why did differencing alter the picture so dramatically? The reason is that taking first differences often yields a new time series which no longer manifests a changing mean through time. Consequently, the assumptions of ordinary least squares are more likely to be valid in practice. We can now relate the variation in Y around its constant mean to the variation in X around its constant mean. The regression, therefore, is much less likely to produce spurious results. It follows that with time series it is often useful to transform the original variables in a manner which stabilises their means and variances through time. Regressions with such transformed variables are less likely to fall prey to spurious correlations.

Indeed, we can use the fact that the regression in differences yields different results to levels regression as a test of whether or not a regression is spurious.

An omitted variable version of the Plosser–Schwert–White differencing test

Suppose our model is:

$$Y_t = \beta_1 + \beta_2 X_{2,t} + \beta_3 X_{3,t} + \epsilon_t \tag{10.24}$$

We are interested to test if the regression in differences yields the same parameter estimates of the slope coefficients as the regression in levels. It can be shown that this test is equivalent to testing the joint restriction that $\gamma_1 = \gamma_2 = 0$ in the model:

$$Y_t = \beta_1 + \beta_2 X_{2,t} + \beta_3 X_{3,t} + \gamma_1 Z_{2,t} + \gamma_2 Z_{3,t} + \epsilon'_t \qquad (10.25)$$

where

$$Z_{i,t} = X_{1,t-1} + X_{i,t+1} \qquad (10.26)$$

The null hypothesis is that differencing gives insignificantly different results, so the levels regression is not spurious.

The test can readily be generalised to the case of more right-hand side variables. If one of these variables is the lagged dependent variable then the corresponding Z variable is:

$$Z_{y,t} = Y_{i,t-2} + Y_{i,t+1} \qquad (10.27)$$

with the other Z variables still defined as given by equation (10.26).

As an illustration we apply the test to the regression of logged Tanzanian CPI on the logged money supply. Recall that differenced equation had a negative R^2, suggesting that we should use an intercept – which would not be the case if the parameters of the differenced model corresponded to those from the model in levels. Thus we suspect that the results may well be spurious. We define Z as the sum of lagged and one-period forward logged money supply and regress ln(CPI) on ln(M2) and Z. The results are (t-statistics in parentheses):

$$\ln(\text{CPI}) = -5.79 - 0.28\ln(\text{M2}) + 0.60\,Z \qquad R^2 = 0.98$$
$$(-19.89)\ (-0.26) \qquad\quad (1.22) \qquad\qquad\qquad (10.28)$$

Since we are testing the restriction on only one Z variable a t-test may be applied (as it is equivalent to the F-test – see Chapter 6). The t-statistic is 1.22, so we accept the null hypothesis that Z can be dropped from the regression. That is, we find the results are not spurious. This finding does not match with our expectations, and we should perhaps seek confirmation from another test; this will be done in Chapter 12.

Exercise 10.9

Calculate the series of first differences for each of your series from exercise 10.1, having first applied the appropriate power transformation as determined in exercise 10.8. Conduct the ADF on each of the resulting series. How do your results compare with those obtained in exercise 10.6?

10.6 SUMMARY OF MAIN POINTS

1 Time-series data have special properties deriving from their unique ordering.
2 A non-stationary time series is one whose moments are not time-invariant.
3 A convenient class of models for modelling time series are given by the AR(1) process. With an autoregressive coefficient of one, the

AR(1) model is a random walk (or random walk with drift if there is an intercept term); such series are described as having a unit root. A random walk is a non-stationary process.

4   Regression of one random walk on another is likely to yield a significant result even if the two series are totally unrelated to one another. More generally, application of OLS to non-stationary series yields biased and inconsistent results (except in the special case of the variables being cointegrated – see Chapter 12).

5   If a variable follows a trend stationary process it can be made stationary by detrending. But most economic variables seem better described by a difference stationary process – in which case differences must be taken to stabilise the mean. A power transformation must also first be applied in most cases to stabilise the variance.

6   Testing for a unit root is carried out by estimating an autoregressive model, allowing for the possibility of an intercept and deterministic trend. The procedure tests down to find the appropriate specification and corresponding value of the coefficient on the lagged dependent variable.

ADDITIONAL EXERCISE

Exercise 10.10

Generate 61 observations for a variable following a random walk without drift. Regress the variable on its own lag 200 times, each time noting the value of the estimated slope coefficient and the value of the *t*-statistic for the test of the null that the slope is unity. Plot a histogram of the slope coefficients. How often is the null rejected at the 5 and 10 per cent levels? Why are these results a surprise? What do they tell you about testing for stationarity?

APPENDIX 10.1:
GENERATED DSP AND TSP SERIES FOR EXERCISES

Time	TSP	DSP
0	0.00	0.00
1	5.93	15.61
2	15.58	19.48
3	36.29	31.51
4	41.11	38.13
5	39.00	70.76
6	43.87	100.26
7	52.82	131.19
8	60.31	99.90
9	59.55	96.26
10	73.03	116.62
11	88.84	137.85
12	93.81	144.28
13	106.88	128.05
14	102.19	150.66
15	102.96	119.05
16	111.96	122.41
17	117.91	109.55
18	126.25	121.91
19	131.59	139.14
20	138.90	137.43
21	144.81	118.56
22	157.17	119.76
23	168.70	135.14
24	180.55	137.35
25	176.80	158.92
26	179.94	187.65
27	189.05	170.25
28	198.35	187.97
29	203.92	199.00

NOTES

1 This specification is not appropriate, if only because the relationship between the CPI and time is clearly not a linear one. More importantly, the series may be a difference stationary process rather than a trend stationary process – this distinction is discussed on p. 344–5 and 349–50.

2 The trend is given by the expected value, which is:

$$E(X_t) \rightarrow \frac{\beta_1 + t}{1 - \beta_3} + \frac{\beta_3}{(1 - \beta_3)^2} \quad \text{as } t \rightarrow \infty$$

11 Misspecification and autocorrelation

11.1 INTRODUCTION

Autocorrelation (also called serial correlation) is the violation of the assumption that $E(\epsilon_i\epsilon_j) = 0$. When the error in one period is related to the error in another period then OLS is no longer BLUE. Moreover, the R^2 may be overestimated, standard errors underestimated and t-statistics overestimated. If the regressors include a lagged dependent variable then OLS estimates are biased.

The presence of autocorrelation in the residuals of the estimated model is, however, often a result of model misspecification, rather than 'genuine' autocorrelation of the model error term. Recall that formal tests of the property of the error term are carried out on the residuals. But, whilst the error is a part of the data generation process, the residuals are a product of our model specification. Hence testing for autocorrelation should in the first instance be interpreted as a test for misspecification. A range of techniques are available to detect autocorrelation. Here we will present graphical methods, the runs test and the Durbin–Watson statistic, we also define Durbin's h which should be used in the presence of a lagged dependent variable.

This chapter is organised as follows. section 11.2 explains in more detail what autocorrelation is and why it is a problem and section 11.3 considers the various reasons why autocorrelation may be present. Formal tests for autocorrelation are presented in section 11.4, and section 11.5 discusses how to deal with autocorrelation. Section 11.6 summarises the chapter.

11.2 WHAT IS AUTOCORRELATION AND WHY IS IT A PROBLEM?

The classical linear regression model assumes there is no serial correlation – that is, a zero covariance between the error terms of different observations. Hence, in the model:

$$Y_t = \beta_1 + \beta_2 X_t + \epsilon_t \tag{11.1}$$

we are concerned here with the assumption that $E(\epsilon_t\epsilon_{t-s}) = 0$. (We are now using a t subscript as autocorrelation is a time series problem.) Put more simply, because the error for one observation is large this does not mean that the next one will be. Indeed, the fact that an error term is positive should have no implications for whether the next term is positive or negative.

To understand the implications of autocorrelation for residual plots and the basis for tests for autocorrelation it is useful to spend some time looking at the autoregressive (AR) model, introduced in Chapter 10. The AR model is serially correlated by construction, so it is a good device for seeing what such an autocorrelated error will look like in practice. But you are not required to construct these AR models as a part of testing for autocorrelation in the normal course of events.

Suppose that the error term, ϵ, in the model of equation (11.1) is generated by an AR(1) process with a white noise error (v):

$$\epsilon_t = \rho\,\epsilon_{t-1} + v_t \qquad v \sim N(0, \sigma_v^2)\;\forall t \qquad (11.2)$$

Figure 11.1 shows the case in which $\rho = 0$, so that ϵ is just equal to that period's error term, v.[1] We know here, because we have generated the data, that there is no serial correlation – each error term is indeed independent of the others. How can this fact be seen in the residual plot? If the different terms are independent then we should not see any patterns in the data – for example, there should not be long runs of positives

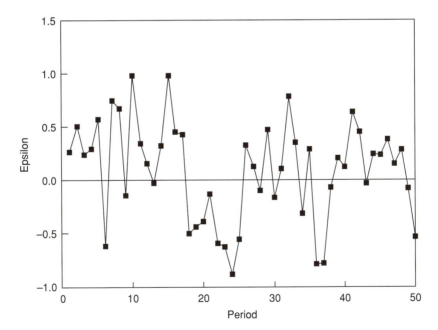

Figure 11.1 No autocorrelation ($\rho = 0$)

followed by long runs of negatives. (A run is defined as successive values of the same sign.) Equally, a positive value in one period should not imply a negative value in the following period, so the plot should not be exceptionally jagged (i.e. have many short runs of positive and negative values).

Figure 11.1 seems to satisfy these conditions. But now look at Figures 11.2, generated using the same set of errors but with ρ = 0.7 and Figure 11.3, again generated with the same errors but with ρ = −0.7. In both of these cases a pattern may be observed. When ρ is positive then the value of ε is equal to some fraction of its previous value plus the error term − so that a positive ε in one period is likely to imply a positive one in the following period (the next period's ε will only be negative if there is a quite large negative error). As can be seen in Figure 11.2, this model produces a number of quite long runs of positive and negative values: there are eight runs in all, four positive and four negative (a single positive or negative observation counts as a run). In Figure 11.3 by contrast there are very many short runs: 32 in all. The deterministic part of the AR(1) model with a negative value of ρ reverses the sign each period − this reversal may sometimes be cancelled out by the error term but is not generally so.

What we see here is that when ε is generated by an AR(1) model with a positive coefficient, the time plot of the variable displays apparently long runs of positive and negatives − this is called positive autocorrelation (because it comes from a data generation process with a positive

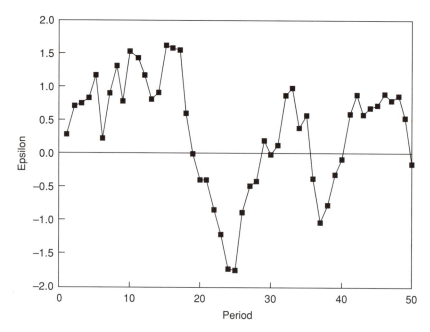

Figure 11.2   Positive autocorrelation (ρ = 0.7)

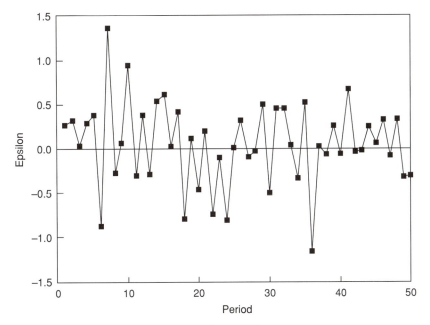

Figure 11.3   Negative autocorrelation ($\rho = -0.7$)

coefficient). With a negative coefficient there is negative autocorrelation, which is shown by very short runs in the data (i.e. a jagged plot). Hence a first test for autocorrelation is to look at the residual plot from the regression to see if there appear to be too few (or too many) runs. A more formal test for autocorrelation is the runs tests, which tests if there are indeed too many or too few runs to be consistent with the null hypothesis that the data are generated in a serially uncorrelated manner. The other test we consider below, the well known Durbin–Watson test, is a test, to see if the residuals are generated from an AR(1) model.

We said above that data generated by the AR model are serially correlated. More formally we may show (see Appendix 11.1) that:

$$E(\varepsilon_i^2) = \frac{\sigma_\nu^2}{1 - \rho^2} \tag{11.3}$$

$$E(\varepsilon_t \, \varepsilon_{t-s}) = \frac{\rho^s \, \sigma_\nu^2}{1 - \rho^2} \tag{11.4}$$

Equation (11.4) shows that the ∈s generated by the AR(1) process are indeed autocorrelated, since the covariance of any pair of ∈s is not zero (though it tends to zero as the ∈s get further apart). However, equation (11.3) shows that the variable is homoscedastic.[2]

Why is autocorrelation a problem?

The proof that LS estimators are BLUE uses the assumption that the error term in the model is not autocorrelated. Violation of this assumption means that the proof is no longer valid, and it is indeed the case that OLS is no longer BLUE.[3] We do not, however, need this assumption of no auto-correlation to prove unbiasedness, so the estimates remain unbiased (except when the model contains a lagged dependent variable, as discussed below).

In addition to the loss of efficiency, the residual variance no longer provides an unbiased estimate of the error variance. Hence the attempt to construct confidence intervals or to test hypotheses about the coefficients is made invalid, since the standard errors are no longer applicable. When there is positive autocorrelation – which is the more common sort in practice – then the estimates of the error variance have a downward bias. Hence our confidence intervals are narrower than they should be and the calculated t-statistics inflated, so that there is a danger that we shall incorrectly reject the null that the variable has no significant impact. Likewise the R^2 and related F-statistic are likely to be over-estimated.

Autocorrelation in the presence of a lagged dependent variable: particularly bad news

If the model contains a lagged dependent variable then the OLS estimators are not only not the most efficient, but they are also biased. Consider the model:

$$Y_t = \beta_1 + \beta_2 X_t + \beta_3 Y_{t-1} + \epsilon_t \tag{11.5}$$

where

$$\epsilon_t = \rho\epsilon_{t-1} + v_t \tag{11.6}$$

Now, the proof of unbiasedness requires that there be no relationship between the model regressors and the error term. In this case we require that $E(Y_{t-1}\epsilon_t) = 0$. But it is easy to show that this requirement is not met. Lagging equation (11.5) by one period we get:

$$Y_{t-1} = \beta_1 + \beta_2 X_{t-1} + \beta_3 Y_{t-2} + \epsilon_{t-1} \tag{11.7}$$

From which it follows that:

$$E(Y_{t-1}\,\varepsilon_t) = E(\varepsilon_t\,\varepsilon_{t-1}) = \frac{\rho\,\sigma_v^2}{1 - \rho^2} \tag{11.8}$$

11.3   WHY DO WE GET AUTOCORRELATION?

It is very important to distinguish between genuine autocorrelation and that which is a product of model specification. The traditional approach emphasises the former (sometimes exclusively so), whereas there are very many cases in which the autocorrelation is in fact a symptom of model misspecification. In this section we discuss these different perspectives.

The traditional view

A common example of autocorrelation is an agricultural production function. Suppose we regress crop output (Q) on the main determinants of output – in this case a relative price variable (P) and fertilizer input (F). The error term captures the random effects excluded from our model. But a negative shock in one period – such as a drought – may well have adverse repercussions on output in the years that follow, resulting in a succession of negative error terms. Hence we may expect that the error term in the model:

$$Q_t = \beta_1 + \beta_2 P_t + \beta_3 F_t + \epsilon_t \tag{11.9}$$

will probably not satisfy the assumption that $E(\epsilon_t \epsilon_{t-s}) = 0$. Figure 11.4 shows the residual plot from estimation of equation (11.9) using a hypothetical data set (given in Table 11.1); there are a number of fairly long runs so the plot suggests that there may be a problem of autocorrelation (a more formal test will be made: p. 384). There are procedures for

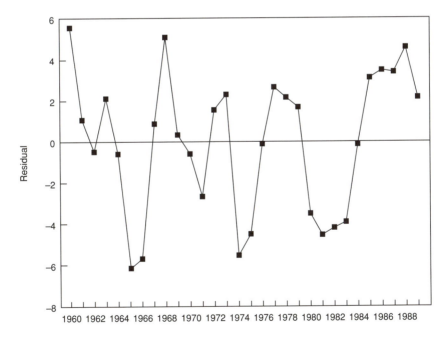

Figure 11.4   Residuals from crop production function

Table 11.1 Hypothetical data set for crop production function

	Output (Q)	Price index (P)	Fertilizer input (F)	Rainfall (R)
1960	n.a.	100.0	100.0	184.2
1961	40.4	106.0	99.4	155.3
1962	36.4	108.1	100.8	107.3
1963	35.4	110.3	102.1	110.1
1964	37.9	110.1	102.9	169.3
1965	34.8	108.6	103.1	81.9
1966	27.9	103.8	104.2	22.0
1967	29.8	109.5	104.6	31.5
1968	34.7	102.6	105.6	198.2
1969	38.4	101.1	106.8	147.5
1970	33.6	100.9	106.7	76.5
1971	33.6	104.7	108.3	90.2
1972	32.2	107.3	108.6	54.3
1973	35.3	103.0	110.4	178.3
1974	39.4	116.4	111.2	70.6
1975	30.6	112.7	111.1	53.0
1976	30.5	108.0	110.7	74.4
1977	33.7	103.2	110.5	136.4
1978	35.8	101.0	112.0	131.1
1979	36.0	103.6	111.6	109.2
1980	37.0	109.6	113.2	112.8
1981	30.7	105.2	114.1	43.0
1982	28.0	98.7	114.8	53.5
1983	28.4	99.2	114.8	20.6
1984	27.6	94.8	114.4	56.4
1985	32.9	100.6	114.6	78.3
1986	37.1	104.5	114.5	151.8
1987	36.0	98.9	114.2	145.2
1988	36.6	101.8	115.5	112.3
1989	38.8	105.6	116.7	161.0
1990	37.1	108.7	118.0	94.5

obtaining valid *t*-statistics under these circumstances, which are discussed below (pp. 387–90). But first we must see how autocorrelation can result from model misspecification.

Exercise 11.1

Use the data given in Table 11.1 to regress output on the price index and fertilizer input. Draw the residual plot and count the number of runs.

Incorrect functional form

The residuals we get are a product of the model we impose on the data. Consider Figure 11.5, which shows the population of Belize for the period

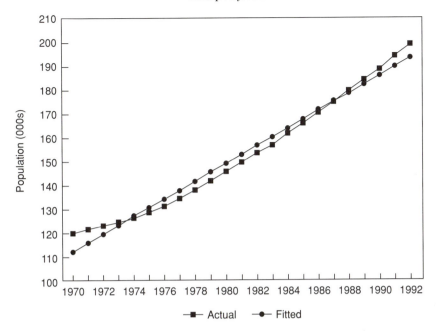

Figure 11.5   Population of Belize and fitted line from linear regression

1970–92 and the fitted line from the linear regression of population on time. Clearly the attempt to fit a straight line to these data is inappropriate – and the result can be clearly seen that the residuals are all positive at first, negative in the middle years, and then positive in the last years. This very clear pattern in the residuals is also displayed in Figure 11.6. This case is one in which the autocorrelation results from the incorrect functional form: the linear regression is not the right one, and this fact affects the residuals so as to induce a pattern of autocorrelation. The autocorrelation is a product of the incorrect functional form and not a property of the error in the true model.

From looking at the graph we might suspect that the true model is to regress the log of population on time.[4] As may be seen from Table 11.2, this data transformation does improve the results. Unfortunately, as Figure 11.6 shows, the residuals from such a specification are a bit lower but still display marked autocorrelation; there are still only three runs and the results don't pass the rule of thumb for spurious correlation ($R^2 > DW$). What is going on here?

If we look at the data it is possible to detect that the rate of increase in population is lower in the earlier period (up to about 1977) than in the later, whereas so far we have assumed the slope coefficient to be constant throughout. To allow for this break in the data we regressed logged population on time and an intercept and slope dummy with the break point

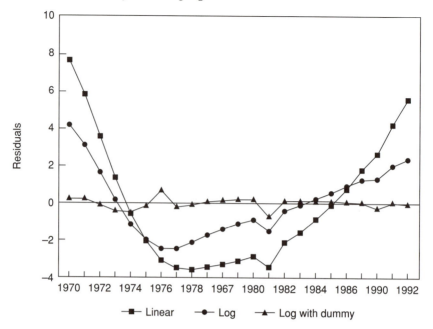

Figure 11.6 Residuals from regressions of population of Belize on time

Table 11.2 Regression results for regression of population of Belize on a trend

Dependent variable	Constant	Trend	Intercept dummy	Slope dummy	R^2	DW
POP	10.85	3.71	–	–	0.98	0.12
	(70.57)	(33.07)				
ln(POP)	4.73	0.024	–	–	0.99	0.16
	(781.25)	(54.71)			0. 99[a]	
ln(POP)	4.77	0.015	-0.075	0.011	0.99	1.81
	(2477.92)	(34.01)	(-17.03)	(25.54)		

Notes:
t-statistics in parentheses
[a] Square of correlation coefficient between exponential of fitted values and actual values.

in 1977. The residuals from this regression are also shown in Figure 11.6. There are now ten runs (compared to the previous three runs) and the danger of having to reject the null hypothesis of no serial correlation is considerably reduced.

A word of caution must be inserted here. The econometric interpretation of our results is that there is a structural break in the regression of

Belize's population on time, with a higher growth rate (slope coefficient) in the later years than the earlier. But in fact we will often find such results with population data. Typically a country's population is enumerated once every ten years in a census; population figures for non-census years are estimates based on the most recent census and observed intra-census trends. When the data from a new census become available there will be a break in the intercept as the actual figure will not equal the estimate made on the basis of the previous census, and a new population growth rate will be used for future estimates as this figure is also revised. The structural break in this case is therefore a product of the way in which the data are produced rather than any sudden change in the proclivity of the people of Belize. None the less, the example serves to illustrate how an inappropriate functional form may result in residual autocorrelation and, also, how adding a further variable to a regression may remove autocorrelation. It is to this latter possibility that we now turn our attention.

Omitted variables as a cause of autocorrelation

We saw in Chapter 6 that the exclusion of relevant variables will bias the estimates of the coefficients of all variables included in the model (unless they happen to be orthogonal to the excluded variable). The normal t-tests and so on. cannot tell us if the model is misspecified on account of omitted variables, since they are calculated on the assumption that the estimated model is the correct one. However, the presence of autocorrelation can be symptomatic of a problem of omitted variables, in which case the least squares estimates are of course biased (Chapter 6).

Let us return to the crop production function discussed above. The residual plot was presented as an example of the traditional view of auto-correlation that it is found because of a genuine relationship between the error term in successive variables. But there may be alternative explanations for the pattern in the residuals in Figure 11.4, one of which is the possibility of an omitted variable. Suppose we had included an indicator of weather conditions in the production function and suppose further that the variable was serially correlated (i.e. a good year is more likely to follow a good year than a bad one – as in the biblical seven years of plenty followed by seven years of drought). Omission of this variable causes the model to underestimate output in years of good rainfall and overestimate in those with poor weather conditions – and since good years are bunched together we would expect to observe runs of positive residuals.

To examine this possibility we re-estimate the crop production function including an index of rainfall (R) in the current period and once lagged amongst our regressors. The resulting residual plot is shown in Figure 11.7. There is far less of a pattern in these residuals than previously (the

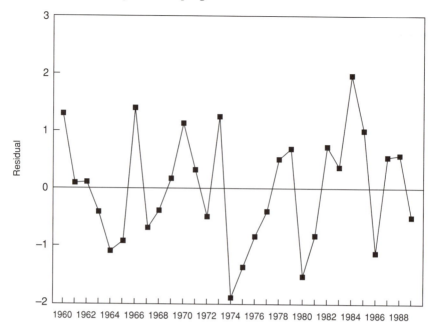

Figure 11.7 Residuals from crop production function from expanded regression

Table 11.3 Results from crop production function regression

| | Regressor | | | | | |
C	P	F	R	R(–1)	R²	DW
10.21	0.26	–0.03	–	–	0.12	0.96
(0.41)	(1.74)	(–0.22)				
–8.07	0.22	0.09	0.05	0.04	0.93	1.78
(–1.07)	(4.95)	(2.24)	(11.46)	(8.84)		

Source: Derived from hypothetical data set given in Table 11.1.

number of runs is increased from 11 to 14), suggesting that the auto-correlation was in fact a symptom of omitted variable bias. (It will also be observed that the significance of the included variables has greatly increased – see Table 11.3 – which also indicates that there was a problem of omitted variable bias.)

Autocorrelation in cross-section data

Many textbooks will tell you that the problem of autocorrelation is partic-ular to time series and consequently it need not be checked for in cross-section data. It is correct that there cannot, literally speaking, be serial correlation of the error in cross-section data, since the data are not a series; that is, there is no natural ordering in the way there is for time-series data. None the less, if the data are ordered then misspecification may show up as autocorrelation. (Genuine autocorrelation in cross section data may also occur and is sometimes called spatial correlation – for example, tastes may show a common pattern in the same street or village. But here we are concerned with serial correlation as a symptom of misspecification.)

Consider the linear regression of life expectancy on income per capita. Figure 11.8 shows the residual plot, where the observations along the axis are ordered alphabetically by country. There is no readily apparent problem in this residual plot. But Figure 11.9 shows the same residuals, but now with the data sorted by income per capita. The autocorrelation is very clear. The cause of the autocorrelation is shown in Figure 11.10, which is the scatter plot for these data, where we are fitting a straight line to an obviously non-linear relationship. The result is that the fitted line lies above most observations for low and high income countries but below those for middle income countries. Another lesson here is that if there is genuine correlation in cross-section data it may be removed simply by reordering the data: but you should be wary of so doing too quickly, as the autocorrelation is most likely the clue to some misspecification. Reordering is not usually an option in time-series data, and certainly not so if the equation includes any lags.

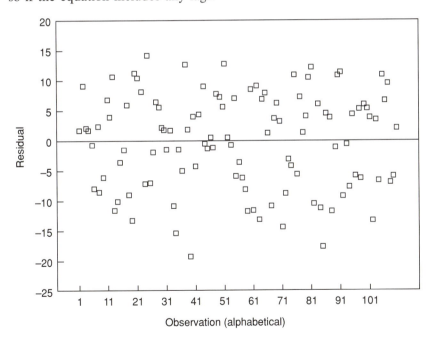

Figure 11.8   Residuals from regression of life expectancy on income per capita, alphabetical ordering

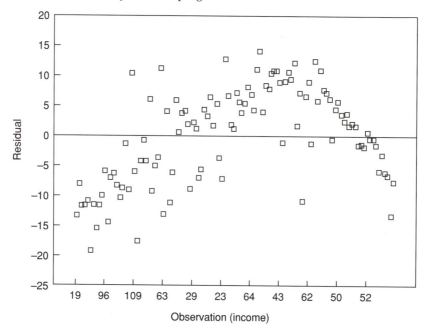

Figure 11.9   Residuals from regression of life expectancy on income per capita, income ordering

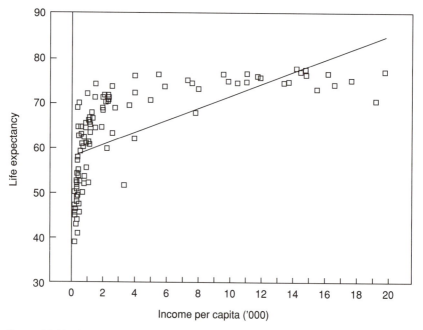

Figure 11.10   Scatter plot and fitted line for regression of life expectancy on income per capita

Exercise 11.2

Compile time-series data for the population of the country of your choice. (The data for Belize are in data file BELPOP and for Peru in PERU.) Regress both population and logged population on time and graph the residuals in each case. How many runs are there in each case? Comment. Can you respecify the equation to increase the number of runs?

Exercise 11.3

Repeat exercise 11.2 using time series data for the country of your choice (or from data file PERU) for: (a) real manufacturing value added; (b) infant mortality rate; and (c) terms of trade. Comment on your results.

Exercise 11.4

Using the results in Table 11.3, use an *F*-test to test the hypothesis that the two rainfall variables may be excluded from the regression. In the light of your results, comment on the apparent problem of autocorrelation in the regression of output on the price index and fertilizer input.

Exercise 11.5

Using data given in data file SOCECON, regress the infant mortality rate on income per capita. Plot the residuals with the observations ordered: (a) alphabetically; and (b) by income per capita. Count the number of runs in each case. Comment on your results.

11.4 DETECTING AUTOCORRELATION

The first check for autocorrelation is to look at the residual plot, which is a vital step after any regression. Another visual device is the correlogram which graphs the covariances calculated from the residuals (standardised by the variance). Correlograms play an important part in identifying the appropriate model to fit to an autocorrelated error term, but this discussion is beyond the scope of this book and we explain them only in passing. We then move to two formal tests for autocorrelation: the runs tests and the Durbin–Watson statistic. Finally, we introduce tests to be used when there is a lagged dependent variable.

Correlograms

The correlogram is the plot of the residual covariances standardised by the residual variance. By plotting the theoretical correlograms from different error generating processes we can learn to spot these processes when confronted with these plots calculated using the residuals from actual regressions. Here we will first consider the correlograms produced by the error term generated using the AR(1) process, presented in Figures 11.1–11.3 above, and then plot those for the residuals from the crop production function data.

Figures 11.11–11.13 show the correlograms for the data generated with the AR(1) process for $\rho = 0$, $\rho = 0.7$ and $\rho = -0.7$. When $\rho = 0$ we expect the 0 term (i.e. the ratio of the error variance to itself) to be unity, as it must always be, and all the others to be zero. In practice, the other terms are not zero, but as Figure 11.11 shows they are comparatively small. The lack of a pattern in Figure 11.11 stands in stark contrast to that shown in Figure 11.12 where, as we would expect from equation (11.4) above, there is a reduction in the covariances as we take errors which are further apart. Equation (11.4) suggests that when $\rho < 0$ then the covariances should alternate between negative (for odd differences) and positive (for even differences) – and this pattern can be clearly seen from Figure 11.13 (for $\rho = -0.7$).

Turning from errors generated by a known model, we now plot the residual correlogram from estimation of the crop production function. Figure 11.14 shows the correlogram for the residuals from the regression of output on the price index and fertilizer input. There is not such a marked pattern as in Figure 11.12, but the high covariance between the residual and

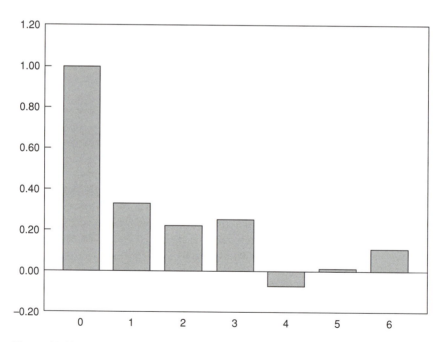

Figure 11.11   Correlogram for AR(1) process with $\rho = 0$

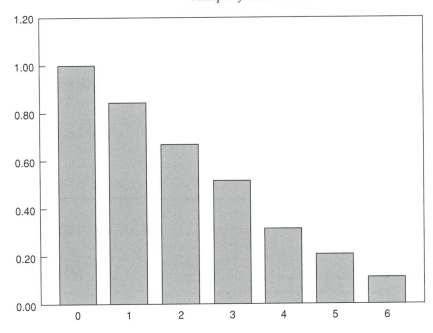

Figure 11.12   Correlogram for AR(1) process with $\rho = 0.7$

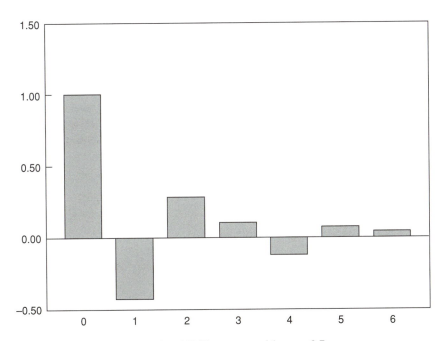

Figure 11.13   Correlogram for AR(1) process with $\rho = -0.7$

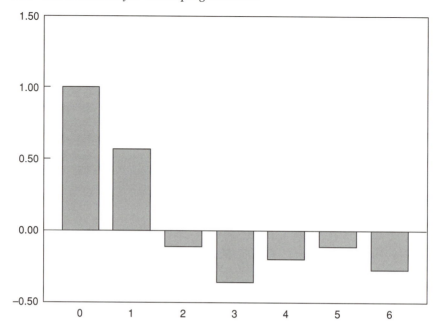

Figure 11.14   Correlogram for crop production function (regression 1)

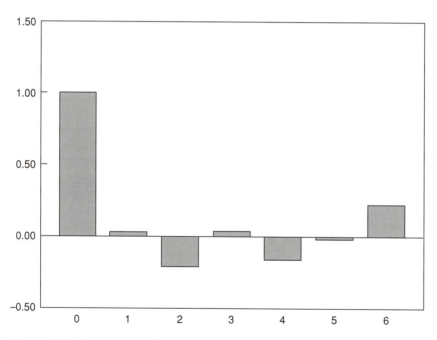

Figure 11.15   Correlogram for crop production function (regression 2)

its first lag are suggestive of positive autocorrelation. But above it was argued that this apparent autocorrelation is not in fact a property of the error term, but rather a symptom of omitted variables. It was found that current and lagged rainfall had been incorrectly excluded from the regression. Figure 11.15 shows the correlogram for the regression including the rainfall variables. The problem of autocorrelation appears to have been removed.

Exercise 11.6

Using the results from your estimation of population against time (exercise 11.2) plot the correlogram for the regression of: (a) population on time; (b) logged population on time; and (c) your improved specification.

Runs test

So far we have been counting the number of runs as an indication of the presence of autocorrelation: if there is positive autocorrelation then there will be rather fewer runs than we would expect from a series with no autocorrelation. On the other hand, if there is negative autocorrelation then there are more runs than with no autocorrelation. But so far we have not said how many runs are 'too many'. In fact it is possible to calculate the expected number of runs from our residuals under the null hypothesis of no autocorrelation and to construct a confidence interval around this number. If the actual number of runs is less than the lower bound we reject the null in favour of positive autocorrelation and if the number of runs is above the upper bound we reject the null in favour of negative autocorrelation.

It can be shown that the expected number of runs is:

$$E(R) = \frac{2N_1N_2}{n} + 1 \tag{11.10}$$

where N_1 is the number of positive residuals, N_2 the number of negative residuals, R the total number of runs, and n the number of observations (so $n = N_1 + N_2$). The expected number of runs has an asymptotically normal distribution with variance:

$$s_R^2 = \frac{2N_1N_2(2N_1N_2 - n)}{n^2(n-1)} \tag{11.11}$$

Hence the 95 per cent confidence interval is given by:

$$E(R) - 1.96s_R \leqslant R \leqslant E(R) + 1.96s_R \tag{11.12}$$

We accept the null hypothesis of no autocorrelation if the observed number of runs falls within this confidence interval. The runs test table on pp. 474–5 gives the confidence intervals for a range of sample sizes. If the required values of N_1 and N_2 are not given in the table then equations (11.10)–(11.12) should be used.

As an illustration we shall apply the runs test to two of the examples given above: the crop production function and the regression of population on a trend. The residuals from the regression of crop output on the price index and fertilizer input have the following data: $N_1 = 16$, $N_2 = 14$ and $R = 11$ (these figures may all be read from Figure 11.4). Using N_1 and N_2 the 95 per cent confidence interval can be read from the runs test table as 10–22. Since the observed number of runs falls within this range we accept the null hypothesis of no autocorrelation.[5] With the crop production function including the rainfall variables, N_1 and N_2 are again 16 and 14 respectively (this fact is a coincidence, it need not be the case) and $R = 14$. The observed number of runs is close to the centre of the confidence interval so we accept the null hypothesis of no autocorrelation at the 5 per cent level.

For the case of Belize's population the simple log regression has $N_1 = 14$, $N_2 = 9$ and $R = 3$, compared to a confidence interval of 7–17 so that we reject the null hypothesis of no autocorrelation. (Since there are fewer runs than expected this is evidence of positive autocorrelation.) When the dummies are added these values become $N_1 = 14$, $N_2 = 9$ and $R = 10$. The confidence interval is 7–17 so that we accept the null hypothesis of no autocorrelation.

Exercise 11.7

Use your population regression results to perform the runs test for autocorrelation for the simple log regression and your preferred specification.

Exercise 11.8

Carry out the runs test on the errors shown in Figures 11.1, 11.2 and 11.3 and comment on your findings.

Durbin–Watson (DW) statistic

The DW statistic (d) is the most commonly reported test for autocorrelation, and is defined as:

$$d = \frac{\sum_{t=2}^{T} (e_t - e_{t-1})^2}{\sum_{t=1}^{T} e_t^2} \tag{11.13}$$

By multiplying out the top of this definition we get:

$$d = \frac{\sum_{t=2}^{T} (e_t^2 + 2e_t e_{t-1} + e_{t-1}^2)}{\sum_{t=1}^{T} e_t^2} \tag{11.14}$$

Making the following approximations:

$$\sum_{t=2}^{T} e_{t-1}^2 \approx \sum_{t=2}^{T} e_t^2 \approx \sum_{t=1}^{T} e_t^2 \tag{11.15}$$

it follows that:

$$d \approx 2(1 - \hat{\rho}) \quad \text{where } \hat{\rho} = \frac{\sum e_t e_{t-1}}{\sum e_{t-1}^2} \tag{11.16}$$

where $\hat{\rho}$ is the slope coefficient from regressing the residuals on their first lag. The Durbin–Watson statistic has thus been shown to be related to the estimation of the AR(1) model, and it is indeed a test for first-order correlation – that is, a non-zero covariance between the error and its first lag. Alternative specifications of the test are required to test for higher orders of autocorrelation, but first order is what we meet most commonly in practice.[6]

From equation (11.16) we can see that if there is no autocorrelation (so that $\rho = 0$) then $d = 2$. As ρ tends to one (positive autocorrelation) d tends to zero, and as ρ tends to –1 (negative autocorrelation) d tends to 4. The Durbin–Watson statistic thus falls in the range 0 to 4, with a value of 2 indicating no autocorrelation; values significantly less than 2 mean we reject the null of no autocorrelation in favour of positive auto-correlation and those significantly above 2 lead us to reject the null in favour of negative autocorrelation.

The critical values for the DW test depend not only on sample size and the number of regressors, but also the particular values of the regressors. Consequently it is not possible to give a single critical value; instead two values are given: an upper and a lower bound. The use of these bounds is shown in Figure 11.16.

If the calculated value of d is less than the lower boundary (d_L) then reject the null hypothesis of no autocorrelation in favour of the positive autocorrelation. If it lies above $4 - d_L$ then reject the null in favour of negative autocorrelation. (Since we more commonly find positive

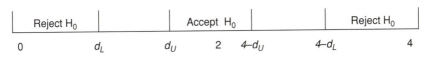

Figure 11.16 Interpretation of the DW statistic

autocorrelation the tables give only the values below 2; if the calculated d is above 2, then you should work out $4 - d_L$ and $4 - d_U$.) If the calculated value lies between d_U and $4 - d_U$ then accept the null hypothesis of no autocorrelation. The problem is if the calculated d lies between d_L and d_U (or $4 - d_U$ and $4 - d_L$); this is the 'zone of indecision'. To be on the safe side we should reject the null, but we may decide not to if the value is close to d_U and we have other evidence (e.g. the runs test) against autocorrelation.

In the case of the crop production function, the calculated DW is 0.96 for the regression of output on prices and fertilizer input. There are 30 observations so with three regressors (including the constant) as $d_L = 1.28$ and $d_U = 1.57$. The calculated value is way below the lower bound critical value (1.28) so we reject the null hypothesis of no autocorrelation in favour of positive autocorrelation. But when we include the rainfall variables the calculated DW is now 1.78. Since the degrees of freedom are reduced by the inclusion of the two extra regressors (R and R_{-1}), the critical values are changed, becoming $d_L = 1.14$ and $d_U = 1.74$. The calculated DW is closer to 2 than is d_U, so we may conclude that it is insignificantly different from 2, reconfirming our argument that the autocorrelation was a product of model misspecification.

Testing for autocorrelation with a lagged dependent variable

We saw above (section 11.2) that when one of the regressors is the lagged dependent variable then OLS estimation is not only inefficient but also biased. Hence detection of autocorrelation in this case is particularly important. Unfortunately, the inclusion of a lagged dependent variable also biases the DW statistic towards 2. Since 2 is the value of the statistic in the absence of autocorrelation, this bias may lead us to accept the null when in fact autocorrelation is present. Therefore the DW statistic may not be used when the regressors include the lagged dependent variable (but the runs test may). Durbin proposed another test, Durbin's h for these circumstances, which is given by:

$$h = \left(1 - \frac{d}{2}\right)\sqrt{\frac{n}{1 - n[\mathrm{Var}\,(b_1)]}} \qquad (11.17)$$

where $\mathrm{Var}(b_1)$ is the square of the standard error of the coefficient on the lagged dependent variable and n is the number of observations. The test may not be used if $n \cdot \mathrm{Var}(b_1)$ is greater than one.

The DW statistic as a test for a unit root

The patterns displayed by a positively autocorrelated residual are the same as those displayed by a non-stationary series around its mean; i.e.

a stationary series would jump randomly around its mean value, whereas a non-stationary one will stay away from it on apparent trends. If we regress a variable on a constant then the estimated intercept from this regression is the variable's mean, and the residuals thus describe the variable's variation around the mean. The DW statistic from this regression is therefore a test for stationarity, using the usual critical values.

11.5 WHAT TO DO ABOUT AUTOCORRELATION

The main message in this chapter has been that autocorrelation may be a symptom of misspecification. The first response to finding a problem of autocorrelation with your regression is to conduct further specification searches. In time-series analysis you should always first check if there is a problem of spurious regression. Detection of spurious regressions was discussed in Chapter 10 and estimation under these circumstances, using an error correction model, is presented in Chapter 12. But in other cases (or in estimating the levels regression for an error correction model) there may be a problem of omitted variables and/or incorrect functional form.

Dealing with 'genuine' autocorrelation

The traditional view of autocorrelation is that in the model:

$$Y_t = \beta_1 + \beta_2 X_t + \epsilon_t \tag{11.18}$$

the assumption that $E(\epsilon_t \epsilon_{t-s}) = 0$ is violated, but the other assumptions hold, including that the model is correctly specified. Throughout this chapter we have stressed that it is very likely that the presence of autocorrelation is in fact a signal that the model is not correctly specified. Further specification searches should thus follow before suppressing the autocorrelation. Suppose you are convinced that the model is the correct one but the autocorrelation remains. Then under these circumstances you may turn to the Cochrane–Orcutt procedure for producing estimates with valid *t*-statistics.

The Cochrane–Orcutt procedure is the BLUE with an autocorrelated error,[7] and is as follows. Suppose that our model has an error which follows an AR(1) process:

$$Y_t = \beta_1 + \beta_2 X_t + \rho\epsilon_{t-1} + v_t \qquad v_t \sim \epsilon(0,\sigma^2) \tag{11.19}$$

If we lag equation (11.19) by one period, multiply through by ρ and subtract the result from equation (11.19) we get:

$$(1 - \rho)Y_t = (1 - \rho)\,\beta_1 + (1 - \rho)\,\beta_2 X_t + v_t \tag{11.20}$$

So if we define new variables $Y^* = Y_t - \rho Y_{t-1}$ and $X_t^* = X_t - \rho X_{t-1}$ to estimate the regression:

$$Y_t^* = \beta_1^* + \beta_2^* X_t^* + v_t \tag{11.21}$$

OLS is now efficient and $\beta_2{}^* = \beta_2$. (Though the intercept must be worked out as $\beta_1 = \beta_1{}^*/(1 - \rho)$.)[8]

Calculation of the transformed variables requires a value of ρ, which may be estimated from the residuals from the original regression or, more simply, by applying the approximation $d \approx 2(1 - \hat{\rho})$, so that $\hat{\rho} \approx 1 - d/2$. If the residuals from estimating equation (11.21) still show auto-correlation the procedure may be repeated (i.e. estimate ρ from the new residuals and define Y^{**} and X^{**} and re-estimate, etc.) until there is no longer any autocorrelation (this is referred to as the Cochrane–Orcutt iterative procedure).

The differencing procedure used to calculate Y^* and X^* reduces the sample size by one, since the first observation is lost. (If the first observation is Y_1, this may be used to calculate $Y_2{}^*$, but it is not possible to apply the C–O correction to calculate $Y_1{}^*$.) The loss of this observation is particularly serious in small samples (though we must also warn that the Cochrane–Orcutt procedure is really only appropriate in larger samples). The Prais–Winsten transformation is a formula for estimating values of these lost initial observations; specifically: $Y_1{}^* = (1 - \rho^2)^{1/2}Y_1$ and $X_1{}^* = (1 - \rho^2)^{1/2}X_1$. Using these estimates allows us to preserve the sample size.[9]

An example: the crop production function

Regression of crop output on the price index and fertilizer input (reported in Table 11.2) was found to be badly autocorrelated: the DW statistic was 0.96 compared to a critical value of d_L of 1.28. We found that the autocorrelation arose from a problem of omitted variable bias. But for illustrative purposes we shall see how the autocorrelation may be removed using the C–O correction. To do this we carry out the following steps:

1   The estimated equation with OLS gives DW = 0.958; thus $\hat{\rho} \approx 1 - d/2$ = 0.521.
2   Calculate $Q_t{}^* = Q_t - 0.521\,Q_{t-1}$, and similarly for P^* and F^* for observations 1962 to 1990. The results are shown in Table 11.4.
3   Apply the Prais–Winsten transformation to get $Q^*_{1961} = (1 - 0.561^2)^{1/2}$ $\cdot Q_{1961}$, and similarly for the 1961 values of P^* and F^*. (Although we do have 1960 values for P and F, though not Q, and so could apply the C–O procedure to the 1960 observations, the fact that we use the Prais–Winsten transformation for one variable means that we must also use it for the others.) The resulting values are shown in Table 11.4.
4   Estimate:

$$Q_t{}^* = \beta_1{}^* + \beta_2{}^*P_t{}^* + \beta_3{}^*F_t{}^* + \epsilon_t{}^* \tag{11.22}$$

Table 11.4 Application of Cochrane–Orcutt correction to crop production function data

	Q	Q*	P	P*	F	F*
1961	40.4	34.5	106.0	90.5	99.4	84.8
1962	36.4	15.4	108.1	52.9	100.8	49.0
1963	35.4	16.5	110.3	54.0	102.1	49.6
1964	37.9	19.4	110.1	52.6	102.9	49.7
1965	34.8	15.1	108.6	51.2	103.1	49.5
1966	27.9	9.8	103.8	47.2	104.2	50.5
1967	29.8	15.3	109.5	55.4	104.6	50.3
1968	34.7	19.1	102.6	45.5	105.6	51.1
1969	38.4	20.3	101.1	47.6	106.8	51.7
1970	33.6	13.6	100.9	48.2	106.7	51.1
1971	33.6	16.1	104.7	52.2	108.3	52.7
1972	32.2	14.7	107.3	52.7	108.6	52.2
1973	35.3	18.5	103.0	47.1	110.4	53.8
1974	39.4	21.1	116.4	62.8	111.2	53.7
1975	30.6	10.1	112.7	52.0	111.1	53.1
1976	30.5	14.5	108.0	49.3	110.7	52.8
1977	33.7	17.8	103.2	46.9	110.5	52.8
1978	35.8	18.2	101.0	47.2	112.0	54.4
1979	36.0	17.3	103.6	51.0	111.6	53.2
1980	37.0	18.3	109.6	55.6	113.2	55.0
1981	30.7	11.4	105.2	48.1	114.1	55.1
1982	28.0	12.0	98.7	43.9	114.8	55.4
1983	28.4	13.8	99.2	47.7	114.8	55.0
1984	27.6	12.8	94.8	43.2	114.4	54.7
1985	32.9	18.5	100.6	51.2	114.6	54.9
1986	37.1	20.0	104.5	52.1	114.5	54.8
1987	36.0	16.7	98.9	44.5	114.2	54.6
1988	36.6	17.9	101.8	50.2	115.5	55.9
1989	38.8	19.7	105.6	52.6	116.7	56.5
1990	37.1	16.9	108.7	53.6	118.0	57.2

Table 11.5 Regression results with Cochrane–Orcutt procedure

		Constant	P	F	R^2	DW
OLS	Coefficient	10.21	0.26	–0.03	0.12	0.96
	(*t*-stat)	(0.41)	(1.74)	(–0.20)		
C–O procedure	Coefficient	–9.57	0.28	0.22	0.62	1.50
	(*t*-stat)	(–2.02)	(2.63)	(1.58)		

The regression results are given in Table 11.5 (which repeats also those for OLS estimation). Calculate the estimate of the intercept $b_1 = b_1^*/(1 - \rho)$, which equals –19.98.

5 Comparing the two regressions, we see that the DW statistic is now 1.50. This value falls towards the upper end of the zone of indecision, so the evidence for autocorrelation is much weaker than in the OLS

regression, though it may be thought worthwhile to repeat the procedure (using a new ρ of 0.25, calculated from the new DW).

Comparison of the slope coefficients from the two regressions shows price to be relatively unaffected. With C–O estimation, the fertiliser variable produces the expected positive sign, though it remains insignificant. The unexpected insignificance of fertiliser is a further indication that we should have treated the initial autocorrelation as a sign of misspecification. In this case, the C–O procedure has suppressed the symptom of misspecification, but cannot provide the cure – which is to include the omitted variables.

11.6 SUMMARY OF MAIN POINTS

1 Autocorrelation is the violation of the classical assumption that the error terms from different observations are unrelated to each other, i.e. $E(\epsilon_i\epsilon_j) = 0$.

2 OLS with autocorrelation estimators is inefficient. Moreover, the residual variance is not an unbiased estimator of the error variance so that the t-statistics used for hypothesis testing are invalid.

3 If one of the regressors is a lagged dependent variable then OLS estimates are also biased if the error is autocorrelated.

4 Traditional econometric practice interprets autocorrelation as a problem of the model's error term. In fact the residuals may well display a pattern of autocorrelation as a result of model misspecification – either of omitted variables or incorrect functional form.

5 Since cross-section data may be reordered, any problem of 'autocorrelation' may readily be removed by reordering the data. None the less, if the data are ordered the presence of autocorrelation may also be symptomatic of misspecification.

6 Various tests are available for autocorrelation. Visual methods include the residual plot and correlogram. We also presented the runs test and Durbin–Watson statistic. The DW may not be used if the model includes the lagged dependent variable; in this case Durbin's h should be used instead.

7 The first response to detecting a problem of autocorrelation in regression results should be to carry out more specification searches.

8 If you believe the model to be correctly specified and there is autocorrelation, then the Cochrane–Orcutt procedure may be used to obtain efficient estimates.

ADDITIONAL EXERCISE

Exercise 11.9

Using the Sri Lankan macroeconomic data set (SRINA), perform the simple regression of I_p on I_g and plot the residuals. Use both runs and DW tests to check for autocorrelation. Add variables to the equation to improve the model specification (see Chapter 6 where this data set was used previously) and repeat the tests for autocorrelation. Use the Cochrane–Orcutt estimation procedure if you feel it is appropriate. Comment on your findings.

APPENDIX 11.1:   DERIVATION OF VARIANCE AND COVARIANCE FOR AR(1) MODEL

The AR(1) process is:

$$\epsilon_t = \rho\epsilon_{t-1} + \nu_t \qquad \nu_t \sim (0,\sigma_\nu^2)\ \forall t \qquad \text{(A.11.1)}$$

Repeated substitution gives:

$$\varepsilon_t = \nu_t + \rho(\rho\varepsilon_{t-2} + \nu_{t-2})$$

$$= \nu_t + \rho\,\nu_{t-1} + \rho(\rho\,\varepsilon_{t-3} + \nu_{t-3})$$

$$= \nu_t + \rho\,\nu_{t-1} + \rho^2\nu_{t-2} + \ldots + \rho^i\,\nu_{t-i} + \ldots$$

$$= \sum_{i=0}^{\infty} \rho^i\,\nu_{t-1} \qquad \text{(A.11.2)}$$

Using equation (A11.2) we may get:

$$\varepsilon_t\,\varepsilon_{t-s} = \rho^{t-s}\sum_{i=0}^{\infty} \rho^{2i}\,\nu^2_{t-s-i} + \text{cross products} \qquad \text{(A.11.3)}$$

Therefore:

$$E(\varepsilon_t\,\varepsilon_{t-s}) = \rho^{t-s}\sum_{i=0}^{\infty} \rho^{2i}\,E(\nu^2_{t-s-i})$$

$$= \frac{\rho^{t-s}\,\sigma_\nu^2}{1 - \rho^2} \qquad \text{(A.11.4)}$$

since the expected value of all the cross products is zero (as ν_t is not serially correlated). From which it follows that:

$$E(\varepsilon_t^2) = \sigma_\varepsilon^2 = \frac{\sigma_\nu^2}{1 - \rho^2} \qquad \text{(A.11.5)}$$

NOTES

1   The data are generated using the Lotus @RAND command. These variables follow a rectangular distribution, but are made approximately normal by averaging over 20 such random numbers. (By the central limit theorem the resulting numbers are approximately normal.)

2   Equation (11.3) is just the special case of equation (11.4) in which $s = 0$.

3   The generalised least squares estimator (GLS) is BLUE, but further discussion is beyond the scope of this text.

4   Such a specification is also desirable because of the interpretation of the slope coefficient as the population growth rate.

5   However, the sample size is not that large and the value near the lower end of the interval so we need to be cautious, perhaps by seeking verification from another test. As we see below, the Durbin–Watson statistic suggests that these residuals do show autocorrelation.

6   The exception worth noting is that quarterly time series data may well have fourth-order autocorrelation.

7   And hence is equivalent to GLS, see note 3.

8   This fact means that we cannot readily use the t-statistic to test the significance of the intercept when applying the Cochrane–Orcutt procedure. The appropriate test is beyond the scope of this book.

9   The C–O procedure is not equivalent to GLS, and therefore not BLUE, unless the Prais–Winsten transformation is applied.

12 Cointegration and the error correction model

12.1 INTRODUCTION

Thus far in Part IV we have discussed problems encountered in time-series analysis: the danger of spurious regression in Chapter 10, and the problem of autocorrelation more generally in Chapter 11. We have emphasised that regression with non-stationary series is generally biased and inconsistent. Transformations to stationarity, notably differencing, create their own problems. In this chapter we will present valid procedures for obtaining regression estimates with non-stationary series. Least square estimates can be used if two non-stationary series are cointegrated, a concept we explain in section 12.2. The test for cointegration, of which examples are given in section 12.3, is to test whether the residuals from the levels regression are stationary. If these residuals are stationary then the series are cointegrated. The levels regression will then provide consistent estimates of the long-run relationship. The full dynamic model is estimated as an error correction model, which is presented in section 12.4. Section 12.5 concludes.

12.2 WHAT IS COINTEGRATION?

In Chapter 10 we saw how the regression of one random walk on another, independently generated, random walk could yield significant results, even though we know for a fact there is no relationship between the two variables. This result indicates the danger of spurious regressions when using time-series data: if two series are non-stationary, then an observed relationship between them may be spurious. We also saw how such spurious relationships collapse when the model is estimated in differences. How can we spot if a regression is spurious or not? The differences test, presented in section 10.5, is one method. More common is to test for the cointegration of a set of variables.

In general, the sum or difference of I(1) variables will also be I(1). Two I(1) variables, X and Y, are said to be cointegrated if there is some linear combination, $Y - bX$, which is I(0).[1] This linear combination may be found by the OLS regression of Y on X, so that the residuals from this regression are equal to $Y - bX$.[2] Thus, simply put, variables are cointegrated with one another if the residuals from the levels regression are stationary.

If variables are cointegrated then the levels regression is not spurious: the OLS estimates are consistent (see Box 13.1 in the next chapter for a discussion of consistency). Indeed, they are 'super-consistent', meaning that the probability distribution converges on the population value more rapidly than with I(0) variables. However, the usual t-tests do not apply. Although the levels regression is consistent, it is usual to proceed to estimation of the error correction model (ECM), which contains information on both the long- and short-run relationship between the variables. We discuss estimation of the ECM in section 12.4, but first we discuss the intuition behind cointegration and how to test for it.

Cointegration: an intuitive approach

Why are stationary residuals indication of a non-spurious relationship? We generated three variables, X, $Y1$ and $Y2$ as follows:

$$X_t = X_{t-1} + \epsilon_{1,t} \tag{12.1}$$

$$Y1_t = Y1_{t-1} + \epsilon_{2,t} \tag{12.2}$$

$$Y2 = -2 + 0.8X_t + \epsilon_{2,t} \tag{12.3}$$

That is, X and $Y1$ are both random walks without drift, and $Y2$ is a function of X. Regression of $Y1$ on X and of $Y2$ on X yields:

$$\hat{Y1}_t = -0.24 + 0.55X_t \quad R^2 = 0.35$$
$$(-0.25) \ (5.18) \quad\quad DW = 0.35 \tag{12.4}$$

$$\hat{Y2}_t = -1.80 + 0.78X_t \quad R^2 = 0.81$$
$$(-3.62) \ (14.46) \quad\quad DW = 1.90 \tag{12.5}$$

Both sets of regression results seem reasonable. But we know for a fact that the results in equation (12.4) are spurious, whereas those in equation (12.5) are a good estimation of the actual data generation process. If we compare Figures 12.1 and 12.2, which show the actual and fitted values from the spurious and true models, we can see (a) why spurious regressions can produce good R^2s; and (b) how a spurious model is distinguished from a true one.

Equation (12.4) shows a reasonable R^2 because X and $Y1$ share the same rough trends. In the first half of the sample period the match between X and $Y1$ is not that close, because neither shows too strong a movement. But from around period 24 both series embark on a downward drift. This downward drift is reversed for $Y1$ after period 40 and for X a few periods later. What of the fitted value of $Y1$? Since $Y1$ is regressed on the single

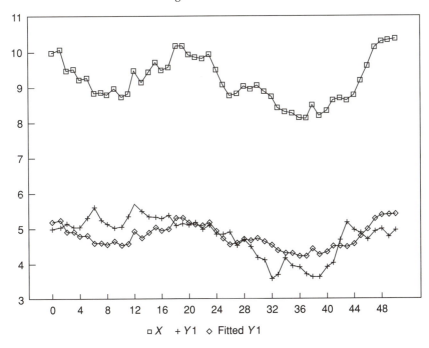

Figure 12.1 Actual and fitted values of spurious regression model

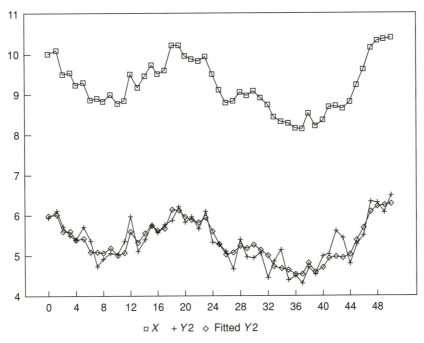

Figure 12.2 Actual and fitted values of true regression model

variable, X, the movements in fitted $Y1$ will precisely match the movement of X, with the intercept term shifting the whole series down so that it lies over the actual $Y1$ series. Since, broadly speaking, X and $Y1$ move roughly the same, by following the trends in X, then fitted $Y1$ follows $Y1$ quite closely, resulting in a reasonable R^2.

Recall that the R^2 is percentage of the total sum of squares 'explained' by the regression model, where the total sum of the squares measures the variance around the mean. As they are non-stationary, both X and $Y1$ deviate from their mean as they have wandered away from it by following a random walk. It is these common general drifts that cause X and $Y1$ to deviate from their means by a similar amount, rather than any causal link between the two variables.

To see this, look more closely at Figure 12.1 and compare it to Figure 12.2. If there is a true relationship between the two variables, then the dependent variable should, in general, move in the same direction as the regressor (i.e. the relationship should also hold for differences) – though this may not be so if there is a large error term in either the current or preceding period. By contrast, if there is no relationship between the two variables then moving in the same direction is a matter of chance. A random walk has an equal probability of going up or down, and so the probability that two random walks will move in the same direction is one-half. Analysis of X and $Y1$ shows the two variables to move in the same direction in 27 of the 50 cases: that is, as expected, approximately half. By contrast, X and $Y2$ move in the same direction in 37 of the 50 cases.

Herein lies the essential difference between a true relationship and a spurious one. A random walk follows an apparent trend, and the resulting deviation from the series' mean explains the largest part of its variation. Hence another random walk, which also follows an apparent trend, will get similarly large deviations from its mean, and so one series may 'explain' the general movements in the other quite well. But whilst the general movements are explained, the actual period-on-period movements will not, except by chance, match. Hence if we look at a graph in levels, the fitted values of $Y1$ will be at the same general level as those of $Y1$, but if we look more closely we see that fitted $Y1$ moves in the same direction as $Y1$ only about half of the time. This fact is why a spurious regression collapses when the model is estimated in differences. The contrast with Figure 12.2, in which the direction of movement matches in 37 cases, is clear.

What are the implications for the residuals? The residual plots from equations (12.4) and (12.5) are shown in Figures 12.3 and 12.4 respectively. The former appears to be clearly autocorrelated, whilst the latter is not. Autocorrelation arises in the spurious regression because the fitted values move only in roughly the same direction as the actual values, but do not match it precisely. To see how this fact results in autocorrelation, consider the other case of the true model. The deterministic part of the model will give fitted values of $Y2$ that almost exactly match the actual series $Y2$ (not exactly, as the regression estimates are close, but not equal, to the true model values). Whether the residual is positive or negative then depends if the error is positive (taking $Y2$ above the fitted value) or negative (taking it below) – and, most importantly, which of these two events occurs is unrelated to what happened in the previous period. Hence the residuals will show no evidence of autocorrelation. In Figure 12.2 the fitted line jumps either side of the actual values in a random manner, as shown by the quite jagged residual plot.

This argument does not apply at all to the case of a spurious regression. Suppose the actual and fitted values of $Y1$ coincide at a particular point in time – as they do in period 28. After period 28 both series embark on a downward drift for four periods – both ϵ_1 and ϵ_2 are negative (except ϵ_2 in period 30). But the drift in $Y1$ is stronger than that in X, so the fitted values of $Y1$ lie above those of actual $Y1$. Moreover, as a random walk remembers where it is, even when the X series is subject to a series of positive shocks, the fitted values of $Y1$ remain above $Y1$ for some time. Hence, as clearly shown in the residual plot, there is a long run of negative residuals from period 28 right through to period 42. Fitted $Y1$ follows X, which is not related to the movements in actual $Y1$, so the fitted values can remain too high or too low for quite lengthy periods, resulting in the pattern of autocorrelation shown in the residual plot from estimating equation (12.4). Thus we see why autocorrelation may well be the symptom of a spurious regression.

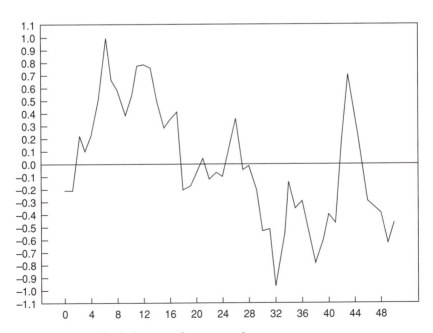

Figure 12.3   Residuals from spurious regression

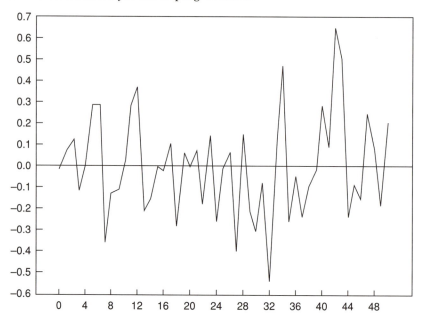

Figure 12.4 Residuals from estimation of true model

The most common test for autocorrelation is the DW statistic, which in its usual form is based on modelling the error as an AR(1) process. Compare the residual plots in Figure 12.3 and 12.4 with the plots of the AR(1) process with different parameter values given in Figures 10.4–10.10. The residuals from estimation of the true model match very closely the plot shown as Figure 10.4: that is, the AR(1) model with a zero autoregressive coefficient. You might think that Figure 12.4 is also similar to Figure 10.5 – which shows an AR(1) process with an autoregressive coefficient of 0.5. In either case, the matching plots suggest that the residuals shown in Figure 12.4 are stationary. The residuals from the spurious regression seem far more like a random walk (Figure 10.6) – displaying the patterns that come from a series remembering where it is. So we find that the residuals from the estimation of a true model are stationary, whereas those from a spurious regression are not. Therein lies the basis of the cointegration test.

Exercise 12.1

Using either the data in data file PERU or data for the country or countries of your choice (be sure to use real macroeconomic data, not nominal), plot (a) the dependent variable, independent variable and fitted values; (b) the residual plot; and (c) the dependent variable and independent variable both expressed in differences, for the following relationships:

1   consumption as a function of income;
2   imports as a function of income;
3   the infant mortality rate as a function of income;
4   real growth as a function of export growth.

In the cases where a significant relationship is found, which of these relationships do you believe to be spurious?

12.3   TESTING FOR COINTEGRATION

There are two approaches to testing for cointegration. The first is an analysis of the stationarity of the residuals from the levels regression, and it is this approach, which is valid for bivariate analysis, that we pursue here. But in multivariate analysis there can be $k - 1$ cointegrating vectors (where k is the number of regressors). The Johansen method is a test for cointegration which also determines the number of vectors. The latter technique is not dealt with here, though the reader is referred to treatments of the topic below.

It was shown in section 12.2 that two variables are cointegrated if the residuals from the levels regression are stationary. Hence the first step in testing for cointegration is to estimate the levels equation:

$$Y = \beta_1 + \beta_2 X_t + \epsilon_t \qquad (12.6)$$

This equation is called the cointegrating regression. We analyse here only the bivariate case. The analysis changes if more variables need be included on the right-hand side, but the technique is beyond the scope of this book. If the residuals from the cointegrating regression are stationary then the variables are said to be cointegrated. We know that the residuals will have a zero mean and no trend by construction, so we do not need to apply the full decision tree presented in Chapter 10. Rather we can proceed directly to the augmented Dickey–Fuller test without a constant or a trend or use the DW-based test. However, when testing for the stationarity of residuals the critical values used in Chapter 10 are no longer valid. The correct ones to use, given below in the statistical tables on p. 480, are slightly larger.

Some examples

The response of Pakistani exports to real devaluation

As a first example, consider the export supply function for Pakistan (data file PAKEXP). Figure 12.5 shows the logged value of real exports. The figure also shows the logged real exchange rate index (RER); that is a weighted average of the index with Pakistan's main trading partners which also allows for differential price movements. The exchange rate is defined as local currency per units of foreign currency, so that an increase in the RER is a devaluation. There was a sharp real devaluation in the early 1970s, which was subsequently eaten away by higher inflation. Since the mid-1980s the government has pursued an adjustment programme which has resulted in a sustained real exchange rate depreciation. It appears from the figure that exports have followed these movements in the RER quite closely, suggesting that there may be a causal link between the two. This view is supported by the scatter plot (Figure 12.6) which shows a close relationship between them, with only one outlier (1972) and no readily discernible influential points.

To analyse this relationship further we regressed log exports on the logged real exchange rate. OLS estimation yields (*t*-statistics in parentheses):

$$\ln(X) = -2.06 + 0.91\ln(RER) \qquad R^2 = 0.71$$
$$(-3.63) \quad (7.89) \qquad\qquad DW = 0.82 \qquad\qquad (12.7)$$

We might be pleased with the result. The price elasticity of supply of exports is 0.91 – a 1 per cent devaluation increases exports by 0.9 per cent. The R^2 is good, though the DW statistic may be a bit of a worry. In fact, more than being a bit of a worry, the low DW is a clue to the fact that these results are wholly spurious.

Before estimating equation (12.7), the first thing we should have done, as with any time-series data, is to check the order of integration of the variables. Table 12.1 reports the results of the relevant tests. These results

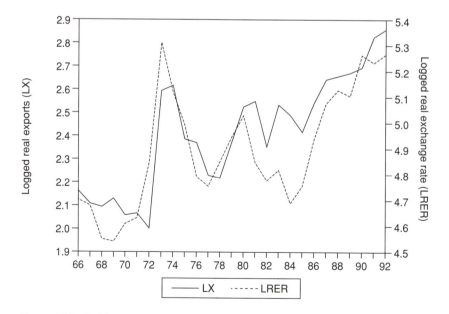

Figure 12.5 Pakistani exports and real exchange rate, 1966–92

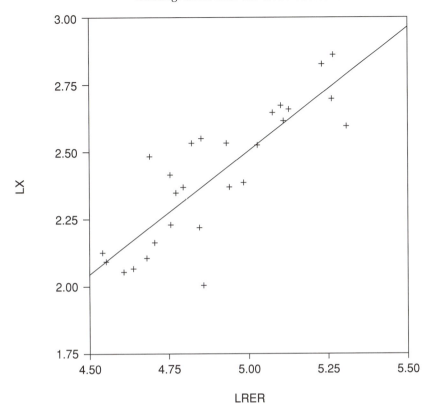

Figure 12.6 Scatter plot of exports and *RER*

are laid out similarly to Table 10.3, where we first met the decision tree for testing for stationarity (except that here we only require the top two rows of the table). Both variables are found to be I(1). Thus there is a danger that OLS estimates using these variables may be spurious. To examine whether or not our results are indeed spurious we must examine the stationarity of the residuals from equation (12.7).

Since the residuals must have zero mean and no time trend we may use the augmented Dickey–Fuller test in which the change in the variable is regressed upon its own lag and a lagged difference term (plus additional lagged differences if they are necessary to remove residual autocorrelation). The null hypothesis that the variable has a unit root is the test of significance of the lagged term, so the normal *t*-statistic is calculated. We first regress the change in the residual on lagged residual and check the DW (this is just the Dickey–Fuller test); if there is autocorrelation we add the lagged difference and re-estimate. In fact the DW without the lag is 2.03, so there is no need to proceed to the augmented version of the test. The *t*-value in this equation is –2.54 (shown in Table 12.1). The critical

Table 12.1   Decision tree applied to exports, RER and residuals from cointegrating regression

	Exports	RER	Residuals
RSS_U	0.352	0.374	–
RSS_{R1}	0.608	0.527	–
(F-stat)	(5.33)	(3.00)	
t-stat	–	–	–2.54
Result	Random walk	Random walk	Random walk

Note: Exports and *RER* are mean deviations of logged values.

values for residuals are not the standard Dickey–Fuller ones but are slightly
larger. At the 5 per cent level the critical value given by Engle and Granger
(1987) is –3.37 for the DF test (and –3.37 for the ADF); Phillips and Ouliaris
(1990) give a slightly lower value of –2.76 (though this value is derived from
much larger samples).[3] Using either value, the null hypothesis is accepted;
that is, the residuals have a unit root so the two series are not cointegrated.

We mentioned in Chapter 11 that an alternative test for non-stationarity
is to regress the series on a constant and look at the DW statistic. When
applying the DW test to a series the result tells whether the variable is stationary or not, but yields no additional information as to the appropriate
dynamic specification. But, as already stated, in the case of residuals we
know there is a zero mean and no time trend and we are, in any case, only
interested to know whether they are stationary or not. The cointegrating
regression DW (CRDW) is simply the DW statistic from the levels regression; in this case the regression of $\ln(X)$ on $\ln(RER)$. Recall that DW = 2(1
– $\hat{\rho}$). Hence the null hypothesis that $\rho = 1$ (i.e. there is a unit root) corresponds to the null DW = 0. Engle and Granger (1987) give the appropriate
critical value at the 5 per cent level to test this hypothesis as being 0.386.
In the example given here the calculated value is 0.824. As the calculated
value is greater than the critical value we should reject the null of a unit
root in the residuals and thus conclude that the series are cointegrated.

The two tests, ADF and CRDW, thus give different results. Engle and
Granger say that the ADF is the recommended test. The critical values
of the DW are in fact very sensitive to parameter values. Hence whilst
CRDW may be a quick and easy test to perform, the ADF (which does
not take much longer anyway) is preferable. Hence we conclude that the
results reported in equation (12.7) are spurious. It would be wrong to
conclude on the basis of these results that exchange rate policy has been
the driving force behind Pakistan's recent export growth.

A consumption function for Costa Rica

Figure 12.7 plots real GDP and real consumption for Costa Rica for the
period 1963–93 (data file CRCON; fitted consumption is also shown, but

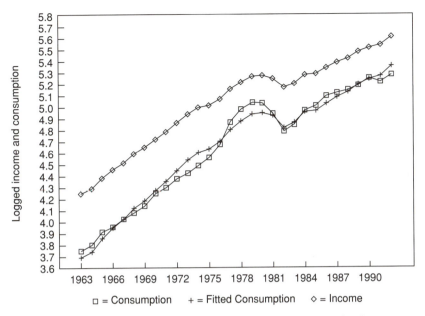

Figure 12.7   Costa Rican consumption function: actual and fitted values

ignore this line for the moment). Even from just looking at this graph we should at least suspect two things. First, regression of consumption on income is going to yield a high R^2 (almost certainly in excess of 0.9). Second, this seemingly good result will probably be spurious, as closer examination shows that, although both series 'trend' upwards, the year-on-year changes in consumption do not in fact match particularly well with the changes in income. That the residuals will be autocorrelated is already clear from this plot, especially for the 20 years to 1982, during which there are only three runs.

Our suspicions should be further aroused by the scatter plot (Figure 12.8), from which the autocorrelation is shown by the pattern of points around the fitted line. This indication of autocorrelation is supported by the regression results, which are (*t*-statistic in parentheses):

$$\ln(C) = -1.53 + 1.23\ln(Y) \qquad R^2 = 0.98$$
$$(-10.42)\ (42.15) \qquad DW = 0.36 \qquad\qquad (12.8)$$

Investigation reveals both logged consumption and income to be random walks without drift. Hence, the estimated consumption function is indeed spurious unless the residuals from the levels regression turn out to be stationary. We see from equation (12.8) that the regression fails the CRDW as the DW is less than the critical value of 0.38. This result is confirmed if we carry out the augmented Dickey–Fuller test. As before the first stage is the Dickey–Fuller test, but the DW statistic from this

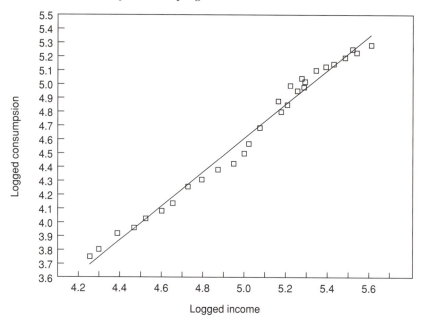

Figure 12.8   Scatter plot for Costa Rican consumption against income

regression is 1.03, suggesting that we need to add some lagged differences to the right hand side. Adding one such term increases the DW to 2.24 and the *t*-statistic from this equation to test the null of no cointegration (i.e. non-stationary residuals) is –2.94. Although in absolute terms this figures is above the critical value of Phillips and Ouliaris it falls below that of Engle and Granger so we are safest to accept the null hypothesis; i.e. the variables are not cointegrated.

In preparing this chapter we estimated consumption functions using annual data for Ecuador, Finland, France, Greece, Pakistan, Philippines, Trinidad and Tobago, and the United Kingdom. All these regressions yielded good fits which turned out to be spurious! This fact underlines the importance of allowing for the effects of non-stationarity in time-series analysis. Our failure to find a non-spurious relationship does not mean that consumption is unrelated to income. Several reasons may explain our result. One important one is likely to be that the real income measure we had available was GDP: whereas, especially for developing countries, it is more appropriate to use GNP (which includes net factor payments) or national disposable income (which includes grant aid received from aid donors and workers' remittances). Another limitation is that we have been using annual data. Quarterly data are rarely available for developing countries (other than for money and prices). But accurate modeling of consumption probably requires quarterly data, the true relationship being drowned out by aggregation to annual figures. Or maybe the data generation process reflects some more complicated relationship between consumption and income, such as the permanent income hypothesis.

A cointegrating consumption function

Using the data for the period 1960–93, in data file COINCON, the following consumption function was estimated (using logged data, *t*-statistics in parentheses):

$$\ln(C) = -0.11 + 0.97\ln(Y) \qquad R^2 = 0.99$$
$$\quad (-0.98) \quad (42.62) \qquad DW = 1.68 \qquad\qquad (12.9)$$

Is this relationship spurious? A look at the actual and fitted values (Figure 12.9) suggests that it may not be so. In Figure 12.9 we see that, although the actual values fluctuate around the fitted ones, they do so in an apparently random manner. This pattern may be contrasted with that shown in Figure 12.7, in which there appears to be a more systematic variation between the actual and fitted values. (This comparison is the same as that made between Figures 12.1 and 12.2, showing the spurious and true regressions.)

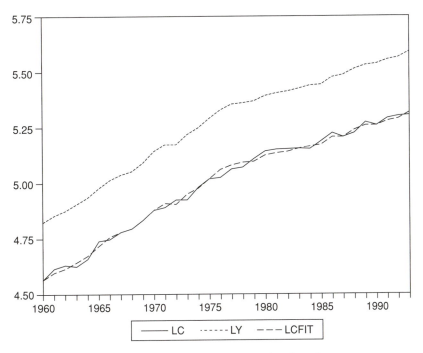

Figure 12.9 Fitted and actual values for consumption function

The residuals from equation (12.8), do indeed turn out to be stationary. The DW is greater than the critical value for the CRDW test. The *t*-statistic from the DF test (the ADF is unnecessary since the DW from this regression is 2.02) is –4.64, thus decisively rejecting the null hypothesis of non-stationary residuals. Hence the two series are cointegrated. The levels regression may thus be interpreted as a consistent estimate of the long-run relationship between the two variables, an interpretation we pursue below in the context of the error correction model.

The coefficient between logged consumption and logged income has been found to be approximately unity. Since the coefficient in a double log function is the elasticity, we have found a unit elasticity of consumption with respect to income; that is, a 1 per cent rise in consumption will, in the long run, result in a 1 per cent rise in consumption. Thus, there is a long-run stable value of the average propensity to consumer (C/Y). We say that there is a long-run relationship, since the estimated equation does not have a lag structure, and we may expect there to be an adjustment period as economic variables adjust to their equilibrium values. The error correction model captures both the long- and short-run relationships between two variables.

A final word on cointegration

We have presented here cointegration analysis for two variables. Turning to multivariate analysis there may be more than one cointegrating vector. Unfortunately, tests for the number of such vectors (of which the Johansen method is the most common) are beyond the scope of this book. The interested reader is referred to Holden and Perman (1994) and papers in the volume edited by Rao (1994). A more comprehensive, but very technical, reference is Hamilton (1994). An important difference between bivariate and multivariate cointegration analysis is that in bivariate analysis two variables must have the same order of integration in order to be cointegrated. This condition need not hold for all the variables in a multiple regression; the set of variables can be cointegrated even though the order of integration varies.

Exercise 12.2

Use the cointegration test to determine if the relationships listed in exercise 12.1 are spurious for your data.

12.4   THE ERROR CORRECTION MODEL (ECM)

Recall the problem we faced. We wish to estimate the relationship between two variables – in this case consumption and income. Yet these two variables are non-stationary, and we know that regression of non-stationary series can give spurious results. What are we to do? Since both variables are I(1) then, by definition, their differences will be stationary and we may regress the change in consumption on the change in income. For some years, the accepted wisdom with time series was therefore that it was best to work with the variables expressed in differences. However, such a regression yields no information on the long-run equilibrium relationship between consumption and income.

Why is this? To solve a dynamic equation for its equilibrium values we set $x^* = x_t = x_{t-1}$, etc. Using this technique all difference terms become equal to zero – there is, after all, no change in equilibrium. If a model contains only differences, then all the variables 'drop out' when we try to solve for equilibrium values! While a model in differences gets round the estimation problem we face, it does so at the cost of not being able to discover the long-run relationship between the variables of interest. Cointegration analysis allows us to avoid paying this price.

The error correction model combines long-run information with a short-run adjustment mechanism. To do this, define an 'error correction term', EC, which is nothing other than the residual from the levels regression. The error correction term is then used to estimate the ECM:

$$\Delta y_t = \beta_1 + \beta_2 \Delta x_t + \beta_3 EC_{t-1} \tag{12.10}$$

Since both difference terms and the error correction term are all I(0) we may estimate equation (12.10) by OLS. (For an alternative view of the ECM, see Box 12.1.)

Estimation using the consumption function data from the last section yields (*t*-statistics in parentheses):

$$\hat{\Delta L C_t} = 0.88\, \Delta\, LY_t - 0.94 EC_{t-1} \qquad R^2 = 0.52$$
$$\qquad\quad (8.81) \qquad\quad (-5.27) \qquad\quad DW = 1.93 \tag{12.11}$$

It is a relief to arrive at an econometrically sound estimate of the relationship between consumption and income. But this is rather far removed from the simple consumption function with which we are familiar. How are we to interpret the result in equation (12.11)? How can we learn from it the marginal and average propensities to consume?

Interpreting the error correction model

We shall discuss interpretation of the ECM in two stages. First, we shall explore the model's dynamics with some simulations. Second, we shall interpret the parameters of the consumption function estimated in equation (12.11).

There are two parts to the dynamics of the ECM: the impact effect and the error correction process. Figure 12.10 shows an exogenous variable X, and the endogenous variable Y. Y has been calculated by a deterministic ECM (i.e. with no stochastic element) in which $\beta_1 = 0$, $\beta_2 = 0.6$ and

---

Box 12.1   The error correction model as a restricted time series model

The error correction model may be arrived at in two ways. The one we are concerned with in the text is as a convenient and valid representation of non-stationary series. But it may also be seen as a specific restriction of a more general model.

The general model (called the autoregressive distributed lag, ADL) is:

$$Y_t = \beta_1 + \beta_2 X_t + \beta_3 X_{t-1} + \beta_4 Y_{t-1} + e_t$$

Spanos (1986: 552) lists eight classes of model which may be derived by various parameter restrictions on this model. The one of interest to us is $\beta_2 + \beta_3 + \beta_4 = 1$.

First, subtract Y_{t-1} from both sides:

$$\Delta Y_t = \beta_1 + \beta_2 X_t + \beta_3 X_{t-1} + (1-\beta_4)\, Y_{t-1}$$

But the restriction implies $\beta_3 = 1 - \beta_2 - \beta_4$. Therefore,

$$\Delta Y_t = \beta_1 + \beta_2 X_t + (1 - \beta_2 - \beta_4)X_{t-1} + (1 - \beta_4)Y_{t-1}$$
$$= \beta_1 + \beta_2 \Delta X_t + (1 - \beta_4)\, (X_{t-1} - Y_{t-1})$$

which is the error correction model.

$\beta_3 = -0.75$. The long-run relationship is $Y^* = 0.9X^*$, so that EC = $Y - 0.9X$. Initially X is constant with a value of 10. Between periods 5 and 6 there is a step increase to 11. The ECM model says that the change in Y in period t equals the change in X in period t plus a correction for the discrepancy between Y and its equilibrium value in period $t - 1$. In period 5 the model was in equilibrium, with Y at 9 (= 0.9 × 10), so the error correction term plays no part in the change in Y in period 6. The coefficient on ΔX_t is 0.6, so that Y increases by 0.6 units (= 0.6 × 1). From period 7 onwards X is constant, so that ΔX is zero, and this term plays no part in the adjustment process.

Since the equilibrium relationship is $Y = 0.9X$, the adjustment in Y of 0.6 units in period 5 is insufficient to restore equilibrium. In period 6, X is 11 but Y is only 9.6, rather than its equilibrium value of 9.9. There is therefore an 'error' of -0.3 (= 9.6 – 9.9.) Since Y is below its equilibrium it needs to increase for the model to converge toward equilibrium. This movement is assured by $\beta_3 < 0$. (Similarly if $Y > Y^*$ then $\beta_3 < 0$ ensures that Y declines toward equilibrium). As we have $\beta_3 = -0.75$, three-quarters of the discrepancy between Y and Y^* is corrected in each period (specifically, $\Delta Y_7 = -0.75 \times -0.3 = 0.225$, so that $Y_7 = 9.825$). Hence, as shown in Figure 12.10, Y converges quite rapidly on to its equilibrium.

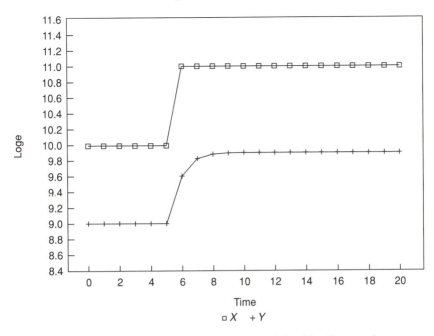

Figure 12.10 Simulation of error correction model (rapid adjustment)

Figure 12.11 shows the same simulation, but now with $\beta_3 = -0.25$, so that only one-quarter of the adjustment process occurs in each period. It now takes rather longer for equilibrium to be restored. If the impact effect is larger than the long-run effect then the model simulations will demonstrate 'overshooting'.

In these simulations we have ignored the intercept, β_1. We should allow the value of this coefficient to be determined by the data. If β_1 is non-zero, then β_1 and β_3 become involved in the equilibrium condition, suggesting that the dependent variable is subject to some drift in addition to the equilibrium relationship and opening a question as to what we mean by equilibrium. Equilibrium as used in the context of the cointegrating regression and the ECM means a statistically observed relationship between the variables over the sample period. This concept does not necessarily correspond to economic equilibrium.

Turning to the estimated values for the consumption function shown in equation (12.11), we can first note that it was valid to exclude the intercept, and that the estimates of β_2 and β_3 have the expected sign. The model converges quickly to equilibrium, with over 90 per cent of the discrepancy corrected in each period. What can we say about the marginal and average propensities to consume?

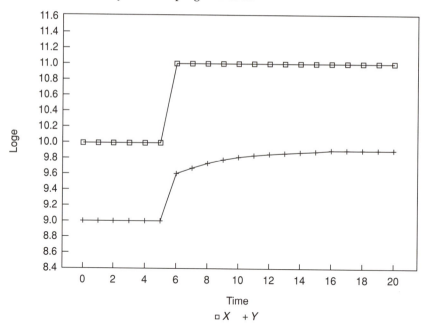

Figure 12.11   Simulation of error correction model (slow adjustment)

When $\beta_1 = 0$, solving equation 12.10 for equilibrium gives:

$$y^* = vx^* \tag{12.12}$$

In this particular case:

$$\ln(C^*) = -0.11 + 0.97\ln(Y^*) \tag{12.13}$$

Suppose that the 0.97 had indeed been 1 (as it may well be for the long-run estimate of the consumption function). Then equation (12.13) could be rearranged as:

$$\frac{C^*}{Y^*} = e^{-0.11} = 0.88 \tag{12.14}$$

As stated above, a unitary elasticity yields a constant APC, and the value of that APC is 0.88. But, in fact, we did not get a unitary elasticity, but a value slightly less than one – suggesting that the APC will fall as income rises (as the percentage increase in consumption is a bit less than that in income). Specifically:

$$\frac{C^*}{Y^*} = e^{-0.11 \, -0.03\ln(Y)} \tag{12.15}$$

So the APC depends on the level of Y. In fact, the variation is slight. As shown in Table 12.2, at the mean level of $\ln(Y)$ the APC is 0.764, and it

Table 12.2 Average and marginal propensities for consumption function

	Y	ln(Y)	APC	MPC (long-run)	C*	dC	MPC (impact)
Minimum	124	4.82	0.775	0.752	96.1	96.8	0.682
Average	198	5.29	0.764	0.741	151.5	152.2	0.672
Maximum	269	5.59	0.757	0.735	203.4	204.1	0.666

Note: Calculated from data and estimates for consumption function; details given in text.

ranges from 0.775 for the lowest value of Y to 0.757 for the highest. The constant APC is therefore not a bad approximation, but to calculate its level we do need to take account of the level of Y (i.e. the APC is not 0.88 as it would appear to be if we ignored the intercept in the calculation).

The marginal propensity to consume will also depend on the value of Y and is best calculated by rearranging the formula that:

$$\text{elasticity} = \frac{MPC}{APC} \tag{12.16}$$

since we know the elasticity to be 0.97. The results of this calculation are shown in Table 12.2. The MPC also varies over a small range: from 0.735 (for the lowest incomes) to 0.752 (for the highest). This MPC is the long-run propensity – that is, an increase in income of 100 units will increase equilibrium consumption by approximately 75 units.

The impact effect of a change in income has to be calculated from the coefficient on the impact term. The percentage change in consumption can be calculated as:

$$\frac{C_t}{C_{t-1}} = e^{b_2 \ln(Y_t/Y_{t-1})} \tag{12.17}$$

Table 12.2 shows the application of this formula. For each of the minimum, mean and maximum values of Y the corresponding equilibrium C was calculated ($= APC \times Y$). The percentage change given by equation (12.17), when income is increased by one unit, is calculated, and this percentage used to calculate the absolute increment in consumption. This increment is the impact MPC. As expected, it is a bit, but not that much, less than the long-run MPC. At the average level of income our results show that an increase in income of one unit will increase consumption by 0.67 units in the year of the rise in income. In the long run, consumption will rise by 0.74 units, with most of the additional 0.07 units coming in the year after the increase in income.

Exercise 12.3

Use a spreadsheet to construct a simulation of the ECM. Experiment with different parameter values.

Exercise 12.4

Using the data of your choice, find a non-spurious regression between two I(1) variables and estimate and interpret an ECM.

12.5 SUMMARY OF MAIN POINTS

Regression of one non-stationary series on another is likely to yield spurious results (i.e. inconsistent estimates). However, cointegration analysis allows us to conduct econometric analysis of non-stationary variables. To do so the following steps should be followed:

1 Test the order of integration of each variable using the decision tree from Chapter 10. Such analysis is often done using log values: this is not always necessary but will usually help stabilise the variance in the series and in many cases is more amenable to economic interpretation.
2 If the series are I(1), conduct the OLS regression as the cointegrating regression.
3 Test the order of integration of the residuals from the cointegrating regression using the Dickey–Fuller (DF) test, or the augmented Dickey–Fuller (ADF) test if the DW from the DF indicates autocorrelation. If the residuals are stationary then the dependent variable and the regressor are cointegrated. The coefficient estimates are super-consistent, but the standard errors invalid.
4 Define the error correction term as the residuals from the cointegrating regression.
5 Estimate the error correction model, by regressing the differenced dependent variable on the differenced regressor and the lagged error correction term. (You should first check that it is valid to exclude the intercept.)
6 The above steps apply to the case of bivariate analysis. They may also be applied in the case of multivariate analysis, although the procedure then assumes that there is only one cointegrating vector, which may not be the case. However, the test for the number of such vectors is beyond the scope of this book.

NOTES

1 This statement is a specific form of cointegration which, more generally defined, encompasses higher orders of integration.
2 As written here we are ignoring the intercept. The addition of a constant to a stationary series will not alter the fact that the series is stationary, so the omission makes no difference to the argument.
3 The critical value depends on the number of regressors in the levels regression, but we are restricting our attention to the bivariate case.

Part V

Simultaneous equation models

13 Misspecification bias from single equation estimation

13.1 INTRODUCTION

Thus far we have considered estimation of single equations. Yet in economics many relationships are a part of a larger system of equations (or model). If we are estimating a supply curve either price or quantity (frequently the former) must be taken as exogenous. Usually, however, economists would consider both variables to be endogenous (see Box 13.1 for a discussion of terminology), the system being completed with a demand curve (and the equilibrium condition that quantity supplied equals quantity demanded). Similarly if we analyse only the goods market in a simple Keynesian model using the IS curve we may consider interest rates as exogenous and the level of income as endogenous. But theory suggests that the interest rate is also endogenous – with a further equation being provided by the money market (the LM curve), in which the interest rate moves to bring money demand – which also depends on income – into line with money supply.

However, suppose that we are only interested in one of the equations in a system. For example, the estimation of agricultural supply schedules is an important issue in the design of macroeconomic policy in developing countries: structural adjustment policies rely on a reasonable degree of price elasticity of supply from this sector. Can we then just ignore the demand side and estimate the supply equation? As we shall demonstrate in sections 13.2 and 13.3, the answer is no. Single-equation estimation of a relationship that is in fact part of a larger system can lead to simultaneity bias. This bias arises since the endogeneity of the regressor(s) in the system as a whole means that these regressors are related to the error term, thus violating one of the assumptions underlying OLS.

Section 13.2 describes a method of assessing the seriousness of this bias, and section 13.3 discusses the underlying theory. Section 13.4 is a slight digression on the Granger and Sims tests for causality and concepts of exogeneity. Section 13.5 moves to a discussion of the identification problem, which must be analysed before a simultaneous system can be analysed. Section 13.6 concludes.

Box 13.1   The terminology of simultaneous systems

Previous chapters have considered single equations, in which the variable on the left-hand side is endogenous (i.e. determined within the system) and those on the right-hand side are exogenous (i.e. given from, or determined, outside of the model). By convention, endogenous variables are denoted as Ys and exogenous ones as Xs. Modern econometrics has adopted a different meaning of exogeneity, which is discussed in section 13.5.

Once we are considering a system containing more than one equation it is quite possible that endogenous variables may appear on the right-hand side of some equations. For example, consider the system:

$$Y_{1,i} = \beta_1 + \beta_2 Y_{2,i} + \beta_3 X_i + \epsilon_{1,i}$$

$$Y_{2,i} = \gamma_1 + \gamma_2 Y_{1,i} + \gamma_3 X_i + \epsilon_{2,i}$$

then both Y_1 and Y_2 are endogenous, even though each appears on the right-hand side of an equation. In general, there must be the same number of equations as there are endogenous variables. And it is good practice to begin your analysis of a model by listing all the variables it contains, and noting which are endogenous and which exogenous.

A time series model may also include the lag of an endogenous variable on the right-hand side. Such terms are said to be pre-determined; this expression is also applied to exogenous variables. Even though they represent an endogenous variable the value of Y_{t-1} is given at time t, i.e. it is not to be determined within the system. As we define them here, the exogenous variables are a sub-set of predetermined variables. More formally, we could say that a predetermined variable is independent of the present and future errors in a given equation, whereas an exogenous variable is independent of the present, future *and* past errors in the equation.

The equations given above are known as the structural equations and their parameters (the βs and γs) are the structural parameters. If we were to solve the system for Y_1 and Y_2, stating each only in terms of predetermined variables, these are the reduced-form equations.

A special class of model is recursive models. A recursive model is a multi-equation model without simultaneity: if, say, Y_1 is a function of Y_2 there will be no equation in which Y_2 is a function of Y_1. For a model to be recursive, at least one of the structural equations must be a reduced form and a model solution must be possible by repeated substitution of one equation into another. In a recursive model the problem of simultaneity bias does not arise as OLS yields consistent estimates (see Chapter 14).

13.2   SIMULTANEITY BIAS IN A
SUPPLY AND DEMAND MODEL

To formalise the discussion in section 13.1, suppose we wish to estimate the supply function:

$$Q_t^s = \beta_1 + \beta_2 P_t + \epsilon_{1,t} \tag{13.1}$$

where Q^s is quantity supplied and P is the price. But the full system has also the demand equation and the equilibrium condition:

$$Q_t^d = \gamma_1 + \gamma_2 P_t + \gamma_3 Y_t + \epsilon_{2,t} \tag{13.2}$$

$$Q = Q_t^s = Q_t^d \tag{13.3}$$

where Q^d is quantity demanded, Q is the market-clearing equilibrium quantity and Y is consumers' income. There are four equations (equation 13.3 is really two equations, $Q = Q^s$ and $Q^s = Q^d$) and four endogenous variables (Q, Q^s, Q^d and P). Let us see what difference it makes to estimate equation (13.1) first as a single equation and then taking into account the whole model. The data used below are contained in data file SIMSIM.[1]

Transforming all variables to logs and estimating by OLS yields:

$$\hat{Q}_t^s = -8.87 + 0.11 P_t \qquad R^2 = 0.15$$
$$(37.93)\ (2.62) \tag{13.4}$$

where figures in brackets are t-statistics; the standard error on the estimate b_2 (which we will need later) is 0.042.

However, as will become clear in the following pages, the fact that price is not an exogenous variable in the system as a whole means that OLS estimation of the supply equation will be biased. In the next section we shall derive this bias formally. Here we illustrate how to test if there is significant simultaneity bias. To do this we have to apply estimation techniques for simultaneous systems. The reader is asked to bear with us in the application of these techniques prior to a full explanation of them, which is given in the next chapter. For the moment, read this section to get the basic point but it would probably pay to come back to it after finishing Chapter 14.

The basic problem for OLS estimation is that since price is not exogenous it will be related to the error term (section 13.3). Instrumental variable (IV) estimation is based on choosing a variable which is exogenous and therefore unrelated to the error term, but which at the same time may serve as a proxy for price. (It must also be an exogenous variable that does not appear in the equation whose parameters we are estimating.) In this case we only have one choice of instrument – that is, income which is the only exogenous variable in our system. The IV estimator of b_2 is:

$$b_2^{IV} = \frac{\sum y_i q_i}{\sum y_i p_i} \tag{13.5}$$

You will find that most econometric packages allow you to select the estimation method – if you choose IV you must specify the instruments to be used.[2] Doing this should yield the result:

$$\hat{Q}_t^s = 8.36 + 0.20P_t$$
$$(30.57) \quad (4.13) \tag{13.6}$$

The price elasticity of supply now appears to be 0.2: compared to 0.1 using OLS, this is quite a difference. Why has this difference occurred?

Here we state a result that we shall prove in the next section. We know that if price is exogenous (and the other OLS assumptions are met) then OLS estimation of equation (13.1) is BLUE. IV estimation will be consistent, but it is not efficient (the standard errors will be larger than if using OLS). But if price is not exogenous – as theory suggests it is not here – then OLS will be biased and inconsistent. By contrast, IV will be consistent even though the price variable is endogenous. Whether single equation estimation is consistent or not therefore rests on the question of whether or not price is exogenous.

The conventional approach has been to determine which variables are exogenous and which endogenous *a priori*. In the supply and demand example, we expect both price and quantity to be endogenous. Yet such an approach conflicts with our data-oriented methodology and recent literature has been concerned to develop tests for exogeneity. But many of these (e.g. Granger causality) do not serve our purpose here (as will be discussed in section 13.4). The test proposed by Hausman (Hausman's specification error test) is suitable, as it directly tackles the question of whether or not simultaneity bias is present in the data.

The estimates obtained by OLS and IV estimation are different. The question (as it usually boils down to in statistics) is: 'is this difference significant?'. In other words, define the difference between the two estimators as u:

$$u = b_2^{IV} - b_2^{OLS} \tag{13.7}$$

We wish to test whether or not u is significantly different from zero: the null hypothesis that $u = 0$ is equivalent to the null hypothesis that the regressor whose coefficient we are testing is exogenous. (Why?) In this case, $u = 0.203 - 0.110 = 0.093$. (Three decimal places are used in the calculation in order to report accurately to two decimal places.)

Recall that for a t-test we deduct the hypothesised value of β (in this case zero) from the observed and divide by the standard error of β. The test statistic for Hausman's is analogously defined, except that the expression is squared:

$$m = \frac{u^2}{\text{Var}(u)} \tag{13.8}$$

which is distributed as a chi-squared with one degree of freedom.

What does it mean if u turns out to be significantly greater than zero? It means that the difference between IV and OLS estimation is significant. Yet if price were exogenous the two estimation techniques should yield the same result; the fact that they do not is symptomatic of the presence of simultaneity bias. Where the difference is significant we have shown that the data reject the hypothesis that price is exogenous, so a simultaneous estimation technique should be used.[3]

To test whether the value of $u = 0.093$ obtained in the above example is significantly different from zero we need to calculate Var(u), which Hausman showed was given by:

$$\text{Var}(u) = \text{Var}(b_2^{IV}) - \text{Var}(b_2^{OLS}) \tag{13.9}$$

where the variances are calculated under the null hypothesis (that price is exogenous). By substituting in the expressions for these variances it can be shown that an alternative formulation for the variance is:

$$\text{Var}(u) = \frac{1 - r^2}{r^2} \text{Var}(b_2^{OLS}) \tag{13.10}$$

where r is the correlation coefficient between the variable whose exogeneity we are testing (price) and the instrument used for the IV estimator (income). For the data here this correlation is 0.908. Var(b_2^{OLS}) is the square of SE(b_2^{OLS}) ($= 0.042^2 = 0.0018$). Substituting equation (13.10) into (13.8) gives:

$$m = \frac{u^2 r^2}{(1 - r^2)\,\text{Var}(b_2^{OLS})} = \frac{0.093^2 \times 0.908^2}{(1 - 0.908^2) \times 0.0018} = 22.57 \tag{13.11}$$

This calculated value of 22.57 compares with a critical value of chi-squared at the 5 per cent level of 3.84, so we reject the null hypothesis that u is insignificantly different from zero, i.e. that price is exogenous. OLS estimation of the supply equation is therefore subject to significant simultaneity bias.

Exercise 13.1

Use the Indonesian national account data contained in data file INDONA to estimate a consumption function for Indonesia using (a) OLS and (b) IV, with investment and the trade balance as a single instrument (i.e. define a new composite exogenous variable, equal to $I + X - M$). Use Hausman's test to see if there is a significant difference between the two estimators. How do you interpret this result?

An omitted-variable version of the Hausman test

Although the above test can be generalised, it becomes cumbersome when there is more than one regressor whose exogeneity needs to be tested, or when we have a choice of instruments. In such cases an alternative form of the test may be used.[4] The test involves two stages:

1   Regress each variable whose exogeneity is to be checked on all exogenous variables in the model (not including any whose exogeneity is being tested).
2   Estimate the expanded regressions, which are the simple regression for each structural equation in turn but with all the fitted values from step 1 included on the right-hand side. The F-test of the joint significance of the coefficients on the fitted values in the expanded regression is equivalent to the Hausman test.

As an example, consider the model of Maltese exports proposed by Gatt (1995; the data are in the data file MALTA):

$$X^s = \beta_1 + \beta_2 P + \beta_3 P^w + \beta_4 Y + \epsilon_1 \tag{13.12}$$

$$X^d = \gamma_1 + \gamma_2 P + \gamma_3 E + \gamma_4 CPI + \gamma_5 I + \epsilon_2 \tag{13.13}$$

$$X^s = X^d = X \tag{13.14}$$

where X^s and X^d are the quantity supplied and demanded of exports and X the observed, market clearing export level; P is the export price index, P^w a world price index, Y an index of real world income, E the nominal exchange rate, CPI the consumer price index and I is investment. All variables are logged for estimation purposes.

There are four equations here, so we should expect there to be four endogenous variables. Desired supply and demand of exports (X^s and X^d) and the market-clearing level of exports (X) are taken to be endogenous – which is why we write equations (13.12) and (13.13) as we have. But one more endogenous variable is required. The selection of this variable is an example of what is known as model closure. We close the model by assuming that price adjusts to equilibrate supply and demand,[5] that is, price is taken as the fourth endogenous variable. It is this assumption we will now test by applying the omitted variable version of the Hausman test to see whether price is exogenous in the demand equation – the null is that price is exogenous though our *a priori* expectation is that we will reject the null.

Table 13.1 shows the regression results. The first column shows those obtained by OLS and the second those from two-stage least squares (TSLS, which must be used rather than IV when there is a choice of instruments. TSLS is described more fully in Chapter 14. The technique involves estimating the reduced form for each endogenous variable and then using the fitted values from these regressions in the structural equations.) The variable we believe to be endogenous is P – and the coefficient of P is very different from the two estimation procedures (as are those on the other variables). Under OLS estimation the coefficient on price in the demand equation is –2.88. But TSLS indicates a much stronger price effect, with a coefficient of –5.07. To test if the difference between these two coefficients is significant we apply the omitted variable version of the Hausman test. First P is regressed on all exogenous variables (P^w, Y, E, CPI and I) (the results of this regression are not shown here) and calculate the fitted values. We next estimate the expanded regression, that is the demand equation with fitted P added as a regressor:[6]

$$X^d = \gamma_1 + \gamma_2 P + \gamma_3 E + \gamma_4 CPI + \gamma_5 I + \delta \hat{P} + \epsilon'_3 \qquad (13.15)$$

The results from this regression are shown in the third column of Table 13.1. The F-test on the restriction that the fitted values may be excluded from the regression ($\delta = 0$). Since there is only one variable under consideration here the t-test may be used (see Chapter 6). The null hypothesis is that the variable is exogenous so there is no simultaneity bias. The t-statistic from the example here is –6.37, so the null hypothesis must be rejected. Hence price is endogenous and a simultaneous estimation technique should be used. The techniques to do so are discussed in Chapter 14; the next section examines why simultaneity bias occurs.

Table 13.1 shows the OLS and TSLS estimates of the supply equation. The coefficients again vary between the two regressions, but it is left as an exercise to apply the Hausman test in this case.

Exercise 13.2

Use the data in the data file MALTA to replicate Table 13.1. Test whether price is exogenous in the supply equation.

Table 13.1 Estimation of supply and demand model for Maltese exports

	Demand			Supply	
	OLS	TSLS	Hausman (OLS)	OLS	TSLS
Constant	–2.41	–2.93	–2.93	3.26	3.50
	(–1.51)	(–1.49)	(–3.01)	(3.48)	(3.65)
P	–2.88	–5.07	–0.02	1.91	2.21
	(–4.44)	(–4.81)	(–0.03)	(5.80)	(6.12)
P^w	3.81	5.62	5.62	–	–
	(6.87)	(6.32)	(12.76)		
Y	0.63	1.01	1.01	–	–
	(1.83)	(2.29)	(4.62)		
E	–	–	–	2.70	3.05
				(5.20)	(5.53)
CPI	–	–	–	–1.12	–1.38
				(–2.90)	(–3.35)
I	–	–	–	0.38	0.32
				(2.65)	(2.16)
Fitted P	–	–	–5.05	–	–
			(–6.37)		
R^2	0.96	0.94	0.99	0.97	0.97

Note: – indicates excluded from regression. See text for explanation of symbols.

Exercise 13.3

Suppose that a fourth equation is added to the model of Maltese export:

$$CPI = \delta_1 + \delta_2 P^w + \delta_3 E + \epsilon_3 \qquad (13.16)$$

Test the exogeneity of P and CPI in the supply and demand equations in this expanded model.

13.3   SIMULTANEITY BIAS: THE THEORY

The supply and demand system given in equations (13.1)–(13.3) may be solved to give the reduced form expression for price:

$$P_t = \frac{\gamma_1 - \beta_1}{\beta_2 - \gamma_2} + \frac{\gamma_3}{\beta_2 - \gamma_2} Y_t + \frac{\epsilon_2 - \epsilon_1}{\beta_2 - \gamma_2} \qquad (13.17)$$

from which it may be seen immediately that price is related to the error term in the supply equation, ϵ_1. More specifically, multiplying equation (13.17) through by ϵ_1 and taking expectations gives:

$$E[(P - E(P))\, \epsilon_1] = -\frac{\sigma^2}{\beta_2 - \gamma_2} \qquad (13.18)$$

where σ^2 is the variance of the error term. Since this latter is positive and we would expect γ_2 to be negative (why?) then the covariance given by equation (13.18) will be negative.

In this example we are regressing quantity (Q) on price (P). Hence as part of the proof of unbiasedness of the OLS estimator for the supply equation we derive the expression (lower case denoting mean deviations):

$$E(b_2) = \beta_2 + E\left(\frac{\sum p\epsilon_1}{\sum p^2}\right) \qquad (13.19)$$

If the regressor (price) is either fixed or independent of the error then the second term on the right-hand side equals zero and the OLS estimator is unbiased. But we have already shown in equation (13.17) that price is neither of these things: it is a random variable that directly depends on the error term. The second term will therefore not disappear and OLS estimation is biased.

To evaluate this bias we must further manipulate equation (13.19). It is not possible to take expectations of the second term. The expectation of the ratio is not the ratio of the expectations. We must resort instead to probability limits (plims; see Box 13.2 for an introduction to this concept), for which (by Slutsky's theorem) we may separate out numerator and denominator:

$$\text{plim}\,(b_2) = \beta_2 + \frac{\text{plim}\,\dfrac{1}{N}\sum p\epsilon_1}{\text{plim}\,\dfrac{1}{N}\sum p^2} \qquad (13.20)$$

so that the numerator will converge on the covariance between price and the error and the denominator on the variance of price (σ_p^2). That is (using equation (13.18)):

$$\text{plim } (b_2) = \beta_2 - \frac{1}{\beta_2 - \gamma_2} \frac{\sigma^2}{\sigma_p^2} \tag{13.21}$$

So that OLS estimation will be biased downwards – it will underestimate the true price elasticity. We saw in section 13.2 that the OLS estimate of the elasticity of supply was indeed lower, that is biased downward, compared to that obtained from the consistent IV estimator. In the case of the demand equation for Maltese exports there is an upward bias; it is left as an exercise to examine why this is so.

Box 13.2   Probability limits (plims)

An estimator is said to be consistent if its distribution converges on the population value as the sample size increases. We write that b is a consistent estimator of β as:

$$\text{plim}(b) = \beta$$

Sufficient conditions for an estimator to be consistent are that (a) it is asymptotically unbiased, that is, its expected value tends to the population value as the sample size tends to infinity; and (b) that the variance of the estimator tends to zero as the sample size increase. Property (b) ensures that the distribution of the estimator converges as the sample size increases and property (a) means that convergence is on the population value.

Hence, if an estimator is consistent it may be used to estimate population values for large samples. But in small samples a consistent estimator may well be biased and so should not be used.

The algebra of plims has an advantage over expectations since the plim of the products is equal to the product of the plims, which is not true for expectations. That is:

$$\text{plim}(xy) = \text{plim}(x) + \text{plim}(y)$$

$$\text{plim}\left(\frac{x}{y}\right) = \frac{\text{plim}(x)}{\text{plim}(y)}$$

This property of plims is known as Slutsky's theorem.

We have just stated again that the IV estimator is consistent, and we are now in a position to illustrate this. From equation (13.5) it follows that:

$$E(b_2^{IV}) = \beta_2 + \frac{\sum y_i e_{1,i}}{\sum y_i p_i} \tag{13.22}$$

We cannot evaluate the final expectation for the same reason as before. But if probability limits are taken, then, since income is independent of the error term, we know that $\text{plim}(1/N)\sum y\epsilon_1 = 0$. Hence $\text{plim}(b_2^{IV}) = \beta_2$, showing that instrumental variables gives a consistent estimator. Note that the estimator is consistent, but not unbiased, as the final expression in equation (13.22) cannot be reduced to zero. Instrumental variable estimation and TSLS are for this reason 'large sample techniques', the distribution of the estimate converges on the population value as the sample size increases – so estimation from a small sample may plausibly give an estimate quite far removed from this population value. 'Large sample' should ideally be taken as at least 50 observations, though we often do not have so many observations for developing countries (notably with time-series data). But the point is an important one, and it would be pointless to apply these techniques to samples of fewer than 25 observations.

The bias in OLS estimation of the supply equation arose because price is not exogenous as OLS assumes. The Hausman test is based on testing whether or not OLS (which will be inconsistent if price is exogenous) gives a significantly different estimate to a technique which is consistent when there is a problem of simultaneity (we used IV, but, as we shall see in Chapter 14, there are other techniques). If we find that, contrary to our theoretical expectation, there is no significant simultaneity bias, then the OLS estimates may be used. Whilst the IV results are the same as (insignificantly different from) those obtained by OLS (both methods are consistent when there is no simultaneity bias), the former are less efficient.

Hausman's test is a test of exogeneity that is directly related to the problem in hand: is OLS estimation appropriate or not? In the next section we discuss other definitions and tests for exogeneity that are common in the literature but which do not have the same intuitive appeal.

Exercise 13.4

The consumption function is often estimated as:

$$C_t = \beta_1 + \beta_2 Y_t + \epsilon_t \tag{13.23}$$

Yet income also depends on consumption through the accounting identity:

$$Y_t = C_t + I_t + (X - M)_t \tag{13.24}$$

where I is investment and $(X - M)$ the balance of trade in goods and services, both of which are taken to be exogenous.[7] Show that single-equation estimation of the consumption function gives a biased estimator of the MPC, with an upward bias of:

$$\text{plim} (b_2) - \beta_2 = \frac{1}{1 - \beta_2} \frac{\sigma^2}{\sigma_y^2} \qquad (13.25)$$

Did your results from exercise 13.1 conform with this expression?

13.4 THE GRANGER AND SIMS TESTS FOR CAUSALITY AND CONCEPTS OF EXOGENEITY

The approach of orthodox econometrics to simultaneous modelling has been to specify the exogenous and endogenous variables *a priori*: the view is that exogeneity cannot be tested and must be assumed. In fact, the Hausman test presented in section 13.2 can tell us if assuming a variable to be exogenous or endogenous makes any significant difference to our regression results – which is what we need to know – and so is a suitable test for determining exogeneity from the data.

Modern econometrics has evolved other definitions of exogeneity, one of which involves the concept of Granger causality. This technique, and the related definitions of exogeneity, are presented here, as the reader is very likely to come across them in applied work. But it is important to realise that Granger causality is not about causality in the normally accepted sense of the word – Leamer has been suggested that 'precedence' would be a more appropriate term to describe what the Granger test captures.

Granger causality

The Granger test that X does not Granger cause Y is the F-test that the Xs may be excluded from the equation:

$$Y_t = \beta_0 + \sum_{i=1}^{k} \beta i \, Y_{t-i} + \sum_{i=1}^{k} \gamma_i X_{t-i} + \epsilon_t \qquad (13.26)$$

Thus applying the test requires three steps:

1 Estimate the unrestricted model given by equation (13.26); the length of the lag used depends on (a) how much data you have available; and (b) examining the data. It is advisable to check that the result is not sensitive to the lag chosen.
2 Estimate the restricted model by regressing Y just on the lagged Ys.
3 Test the restriction with the F-test in the usual way (see Chapter 6). The null hypothesis is that X does not Granger cause Y.

This procedure can then be repeated by 'swapping the variables' to investigate if Y Granger causes X. There are thus four possible outcomes: (a) no causal relationship between the two variables; (b) unidirectional causality from X to Y; (c) unidirectional causality from Y to X; and (c) bidirectional causality (X causes Y and Y causes X). As an example we apply the test to the price and quantity data from the model of Maltese exports used in section 13.2. First, to test if quantity Granger causes price we estimate the unrestricted and restricted models:

$$P_t = \beta_1 + \beta_2 P_{t-1} + \beta_3 P_{t-2} + \gamma_1 Q_{t-1} + \gamma_2 Q_{t-2} + \epsilon_{1,t} \qquad (13.27)$$

$$P_t = \beta_1 + \beta_2 P_{t-1} + \beta_3 P_{t-2} + \epsilon'_{1,t} \qquad (13.28)$$

The results are shown in Table 13.2, where the RSS can be seen to have nearly doubled as a result of imposing the restriction. The calculated F-statistic is 8.55, compared to a critical value of 3.49 at the 5 per cent level, so we reject the null hypothesis. The data suggest that quantity does Granger cause price.

What does this result really tell us? If changes in quantity are to cause changes in price, then the quantity change must come before (precede) the price change – if the quantity change comes after the price change then it cannot be said to have caused it. The Granger test therefore sees if changes in quantity have a significant impact on future prices. However, whilst it is true that if event X follows event Y then X cannot have caused Y, it does not follow that if X precedes Y then X has necessarily caused Y in the normal sense of the term. That X comes before Y is a necessary, but not sufficient, condition for Y to be caused by X.

Table 13.2 also shows the results from testing if price Granger causes quantity. The calculated F-statistic is 0.63, so we accept the null hypothesis that price does not cause quantity. To reject the result would suggest bidirectional causality, which may indicate that a third variable is in fact determining changes in both price and quantity. However, our findings indicate unidirectional causality from quantity to price.

Table 13.2   Granger and Sims test for Maltese export quantity and prices

	Granger				Sims			
	P	P	X	X	P	P	X	X
C	0.41	0.14	0.22	0.42	1.37	1.43	−1.93	−1.65
P_{-2}	−0.65	−0.55	−0.13	–	–	–	0.31	1.06
P_{-1}	1.31	1.52	0.27	–	–	–	0.72	−1.22
P	–	–	–	–	–	–	−0.53	1.77
P_{+1}	–	–	–	–	–	–	0.15	–
P_{+2}	–	–	–	–	–	–	0.99	–
X_{-2}	−0.11	–	−0.10	−0.04	0.11	0.12	–	–
X_{-1}	1.31	–	0.96	0.98	0.30	0.28	–	–
X	–	–	–	–	0.04	0.16	–	–
X_{+1}	–	–	–	–	0.11	–	–	–
X_{+2}	–	–	–	–	0.01	–	–	–
n	25	25	25	25	23	23	23	23
R^2	0.98	0.97	0.98	0.98	0.93	0.93	0.98	0.93
RSS	0.083	0.154	0.253	0.269	0.301	0.305	0.270	0.782

Notes: – indicates excluded from the regression. See text for symbols and explanation.

The Sims test

The test proposed by Sims is differently specified, but has the same intuitive interpretation as the Granger test. The unrestricted equation for the Sims test is:

$$Y_t = \beta_0 + \sum_{j=k1}^{k2} \beta_j X_{t+j} + \epsilon \qquad (13.29)$$

that is, Y is regressed on lagged, current and future values of X (the length of the lag and the lead need not be equal). The restricted equation excludes the lagged values of X:

$$Y_t = \beta_0 + \sum_{j=k1}^{0} \beta_j X_{t+j} + \epsilon \qquad (13.30)$$

Be sure to use the same sample size! So we are testing the null that the coefficients on the lead terms are jointly zero: i.e. future values of X do not affect Y. The null hypothesis is that Y does not cause X. Note the difference between the Sims and Granger tests. Here Y is the dependent variable, but we are checking if Y causes X, which is the opposite of the Granger test. If future X is significant, then Y cannot cause X as it does not precede it.

Table 13.2 reports the results for the Sims test using the price and quantity data. First, price is regressed on past, present and future prices. The omission of the lead terms barely changes the *RSS*, so that the calculated F-statistic is only 0.11. Hence we accept the null hypothesis that price does not cause quantity. By contrast, the calculated F-statistic for the hypothesis that quantity does not cause price is 16.12, so that the null is rejected. We find that quantity does cause price. These findings are, of course, the same as those obtained with the Granger test.

Exercise 13.5

Use the data on money and prices in Tanzania (date file TANMON) to test for Granger causality between the two variables. Carry out also the Sims test and compare your results.

Exogeneity

Three concepts of exogeneity may be identified: weak, strong and super.[8] A variable, X, is weakly exogenous if there is no loss of information by analysing the distribution of Y conditional upon X (which is what OLS regression does) and ignoring the stochastic behaviour of X itself. If our concern is to establish the appropriate estimation technique, then weak exogeneity is all which need concern us. We have already seen that the Hausman test can provide us with this information. Granger causality, on the other hand, is neither necessary nor sufficient to establish weak exogeneity.

Granger causality enters the picture because the definition for X to be strongly exogenous in a model containing X and Y is that X should be weakly exogenous and the X should not be Granger caused by Y. Super-exogeneity is related to the Lucas critique (Lucas, 1976), which is the notion that behaviourial relationships can change in the face of policy changes (i.e. adjustment in 'exogenous' policy variables). A variable, X, is said to be super-exogenous if (a) X is weakly exogenous; and (b) model parameters are invariant to changes in X (formally speaking, the marginal distribution of X). See, for example, Maddala (1992) for a more extended discussion of these concepts. Our main point is to emphasise that the Hausman test comes closest to the conception of exogeneity required in the context of estimating simultaneous equations.

13.5   THE IDENTIFICATION PROBLEM

Sections 13.2 and 13.3 showed that estimation of a single equation by OLS may be inappropriate if the equation is a part of a system of equations. The obvious next step might seem to be to discuss what estimation techniques should be applied in these circumstances. However, before we can do that we must first deal with the identification problem. This is not the digression it might at first appear. The appropriate technique for estimating an equation in a simultaneous system depends on the identification status of that equation: if an equation is not identified then its parameters cannot be estimated.

Identification in the supply and demand model

The supply and demand system presented in section 13.2 (equations (13.1)–(13.3)) may also be presented graphically, as is done in Figure 13.1, where a deterministic form of the model is presented (both error terms are zero). Changes in the endogenous variables are given by movements along the schedules, whereas a change in an exogenous variable shifts the schedules in which it appears. In this case there is only one exogenous variable – income, and the demand schedule will (for a normal good) shift to the right as income increases. Figure 13.1 shows the demand schedule for three different periods in which there are three different levels of income. What can you say about the three resulting equilibria?

The supply schedule is fixed, whereas the demand curve is shifting as income changes. All observed equilibria therefore lie upon the single supply schedule – the schedule is sketched out by the different observations. The same is not true for the demand curve. The observations yield no information as to the slope of the demand curve: there is no estimation technique to estimate the demand curve under these circumstances.

The demand curve is said to be under- or not identified, whereas the supply curve is identified. An equation is identified if it is possible to

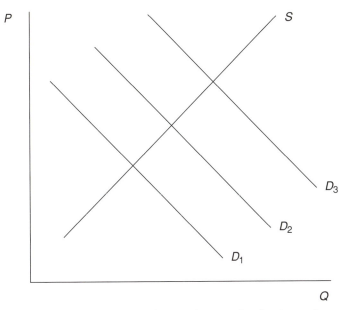

Figure 13.1 The identification of the supply curve by the demand curve

estimate its parameters. If an equation is unidentified the parameters can only be estimated by respecifying the model. (Though we should be wary of model respecifications which are made only to achieve identification!) Even though we cannot estimate the model parameters, if we know the direction of the simultaneity bias then OLS estimation will give us an upper or lower limit – an application of this fact is given in exercise 13.9.

Suppose instead that the supply schedule also contains an exogenous variable, W, which is a proxy for weather conditions:

$$Q_t^s = \beta_1 + \beta_2 P_t + \beta_3 W_t + \epsilon_{1,t} \qquad (13.31)$$

If $\gamma_3 = 0$, the demand curve will be fixed and the shifts in the supply curve will sketch out the demand curve. Now the demand curve will be identified (we can estimate its parameters) and the supply curve will not – this is the case shown in Figure 13.2. Of course, if neither exogenous variable enters the model ($\beta_3 = \gamma_3 = 0$) then neither curve is identified: we cannot estimate any of the parameters in the model. But in the more general case when there is an exogenous variable in each schedule which is excluded from the other schedule, then both equations are identified.

This example suggests what is required for an equation to be identified: it must exclude exogenous variables that appear elsewhere in the model. Though we cannot present this point in the visually appealing manner of the two-equation model above for larger systems, the intuition

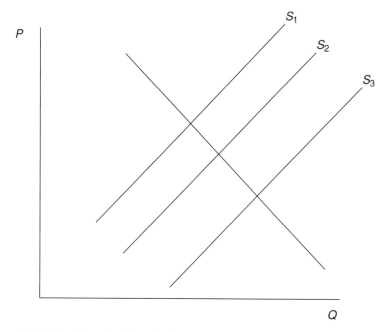

Figure 13.2 The identification of the demand curve by the supply curve

generalises and is formally embodied in the rank and order conditions for identification. These conditions are the subject of the next section.

The rank and order conditions

The rank and order conditions may at first seem complicated. But with some practice their application becomes straightforward. To explain them we must first define:

M: the number of endogenous variables in the system

K: the number of predetermined variables in the system (including the intercept)

m: the number of endogenous variables in the equation under consideration

k: the number of predetermined variables in the equation under consideration

In applying the rank and order conditions the first step is to work out M and K and m and k for each equation we wish to estimate. (As a general rule, whenever working with a simultaneous model under any circumstances this is a useful starting point.)

For the supply and demand model in equations (13.1)–(13.3) we have four endogenous variables, Q^s, Q^d, Q and P, that is, $M = 4$. There are

Table 13.3 Coefficient matrix for supply and demand model

Equation	Constant	Q	Q^s	Q^d	P	Y
Supply	β_1	0	−1	0	β_2	0
Demand	γ_1	0	0	−1	γ_2	γ_3
Equil. 1	0	1	−1	0	0	0
Equil. 2	0	0	−1	1	0	0

two exogenous variables, Y and the intercept; i.e. $K = 2$. We wish to estimate the supply and demand equations:

Supply equation: $m = 2$ and $k = 1$

Demand equation: $m = 2$ and $k = 2$

The two equations $Q = Q^s$ and $Q^s = Q^d$ are identities. We do not have
to test identities to see if they are identified. This is immediately apparent
if we think about why we are looking at the identification problem in the
first place. We are doing so to determine whether or nor we can estimate
the parameters in an equation – yet in an identity there are no parameters to estimate, so there is no problem.

To apply the rank condition we must write out the coefficient matrix
for all the equations in the system (including identities), with all variables
(except the error) on the right-hand side. This is usually done in tabular
form: Table 13.3 shows the coefficients for the supply and demand model
of equations (13.1)–(13.3) (i.e. excluding weather in the supply equation).

The rank condition is as follows: For an equation to be identified it
must be possible to construct at least one $(M - 1) \times (M - 1)$ matrix with
a non-zero determinant from the coefficients of those variables excluded
from that equation but included in other equations in the model.

To apply this condition in practice, cross out the line for the equation under consideration and all the columns which do not have a zero
coefficient in the equation under consideration; then write down the coefficients that are left – these are the coefficients 'of those variables excluded
from that equation but included in other equations in the model'.

For the supply equation we get the matrix:

$$\begin{pmatrix} 0 & -1 & \gamma_3 \\ 1 & 0 & 0 \\ 0 & 1 & 0 \end{pmatrix} \tag{13.32}$$

from which we must form a non-zero determinant of 3×3. In this case
there is only one possible determinant. In general, however, though the
resulting coefficient matrix must have $(M - 1)$ rows (why?) it may have
more (or less) than $M - 1$ columns (why?) and so there will be a choice
of matrices (or none at all) that can be formed. If there is a choice, only
one of the possible combinations need have a non-zero determinant for
the rank condition to be satisfied.

The determinant of the matrix formed by the coefficients of variables excluded from the supply equation is γ_3, so that the supply curve meets the rank condition for identification so long as γ_3 is not zero. This makes intuitive sense, if $\gamma_3 = 0$, then income does not appear in the demand curve and so it will not shift to sketch out the supply curve – which, as we saw in the previous section, means that the equation will not be identified.

When we come to apply the rank condition to the demand equation we find there are only two columns with zeros so the resulting matrix is 2×2 – it is not possible to find any determinant from a 3×3 matrix (let alone see whether it is zero). Therefore the demand equation does not satisfy the rank condition and is not identified – it is not possible to estimate its parameters by any technique. We re-emphasise that we do not analyse identification for identities.

The rank condition is necessary and sufficient for identification, but it does not yield all the information we require – it does not help to choose the appropriate estimation technique. We must also apply the order condition, which may be summarised as follows:

if $K - k < m - 1$ the equation is under-identified

if $K - k = m - 1$ the equation is just identified

if $K - k > m - 1$ the equation is over-identified

For the supply equation $K - k = 1$ and $m - 1 = 1$, so that the equation is just identified. Even though the rank condition is a necessary and sufficient condition for identification (whereas the order condition is only necessary) we use the order condition to find out if an equation in just or over-identified since this affects how the equation is estimated.[9]

As we said at the beginning of this section, this is not all as complicated as it seems at first, as is apparent from doing a few examples. So let us turn to a second example. Consider the Keynesian macro model described in the following five equations:

$$Y = C + I + X - M \tag{13.33}$$

$$C = \beta_1 + \beta_2 Y + \epsilon_1 \tag{13.34}$$

$$M = \gamma_1 + \gamma_2 Y + \epsilon_2 \tag{13.35}$$

$$M^d = \phi_1 + \phi_2 Y + \phi_3 r + \epsilon_4 \tag{13.36}$$

$$I = \delta_1 + \delta_2 r + \epsilon_3 \tag{13.37}$$

$$M^d = M^s = \frac{L}{P} \tag{13.38}$$

where Y is income, C consumption, I investment, X exports, M imports, r the real interest rate, M^s ($= L/P$) real money supply, M^d money demand

Table 13.4 Coefficient matrix and rank and order conditions for Keynesian macro model

Equation	Const.	Y	C	I	X	M	r	L/P	Rank condition satisfied	m − 1	K − k	Identified
Identity	0	1	−1	−1	−1	1	0	0	n.a.	–	–	Identity
Consumption	β_1	β_2	−1	0	0	0	0	0	Yes	1	2	Over
Imports	γ_1	γ_2	0	0	0	−1	0	0	Yes	1	2	Over
Investment	δ_1	0	0	−1	0	0	δ_2	0	Yes	0	1	Over
Money market	Φ_1	Φ_2	0	0	0	0	Φ_3	−1	Yes	0	0	Just

Note: Model values: $M = 5$, $K = 3$

and the ϵ_is are error terms. We combine equations (13.36) and (13.38) so that there are five equations and five endogenous variables (Y, C, I, M and r) and three exogenous variables (L/P, X and the intercept). Table 13.4 gives the coefficient matrix. The final columns also give the information necessary for the order condition, with the last column summarising the identification status of each equation. A table such as this provides systematic means of working through the identification process.

We do not need to discuss the identification of the national accounting identity – we already know all the coefficients are exactly one (or minus one, as the case may be). Let us consider the consumption function. The matrix of coefficients of variables excluded from this equation is the 4 × 5 matrix:

$$\begin{pmatrix} -1 & -1 & 1 & 0 & 0 \\ 0 & 0 & -1 & 0 & 0 \\ -1 & 0 & 0 & \delta_2 & 0 \\ 0 & 0 & 0 & \phi_3 & -1 \end{pmatrix} \tag{13.39}$$

from which we must form one 4 × 4 matrix with a non-zero determinant. Let us try the first the 4 × 4 matrix with no unknown parameters, i.e. no βs, γs, etc., since this will be unambiguously zero or not – that is, its value will not depend on the value of any of the model's parameters):

$$\begin{pmatrix} -1 & -1 & 1 & 0 \\ 0 & 0 & -1 & 0 \\ -1 & 0 & 0 & 0 \\ 0 & 0 & 0 & -1 \end{pmatrix} \tag{13.40}$$

The determinant of this matrix may be calculated as −1, so that the consumption function satisfies the rank condition – we know it to be identified. But we must apply the order condition to see if it is just or over-identified. It turns out to be over-identified ($m − 1 = 1$, $K − k = 2$).

The import and investment functions are similarly over-identified, whereas the money market equilibrium condition is just identified.

Exercise 13.6

Replacing equation (13.1) by equation (13.31) (i.e. use the supply equation with weather), test for identification in the supply and demand model.

13.6   SUMMARY OF MAIN POINTS

1   Most economic models consist of more than one equation. The estimation of single equations from a multi-equation model by OLS can result in simultaneity bias, as right-hand side variables which are endogenous to the model will be correlated with the error term.
2   The Hausman test allows us to test if there is significant simultaneity bias present in the data. If there is, then OLS is not the appropriate estimation technique.
3   Two versions of the Hausman test are presented. The omitted variables version should be applied when there is a choice of instruments or more than one variable whose exogeneity is being tested.
4   Several concepts of exogeneity are used in the econometric literature. One of these, strong exogeneity, is related to Granger causality, which is a test of whether X precedes Y. However, only weak exogeneity, as tested by the Hausman test, need be analysed if the concern is to establish the appropriate estimation technique.
5   If the parameters of an equation may be estimated the equation is said to be identified. If an equation is under-identified then there is no technique by which estimates of the parameters may be obtained; the only option is to respecify the model (though estimates of upper or lower limits may be obtained, which may be useful). Identification of an equation is determined by the rank and order conditions. The rank condition is necessary and sufficient – if it is not satisfied then the equation is under-identified. If the rank condition is met then the order condition is applied to discover if the equation is just or over-identified. This latter step is necessary to determine the appropriate means of estimation, which are the subject of Chapter 15.

ADDITIONAL EXERCISES

Exercise 13.7

Use the Indonesian national accounts data (date file INDONA) to test whether income is exogenous in the consumption and import functions in the simple Keynesian model:

$$C_t = \beta_1 + \beta_2 Y_t + \epsilon_{1,t}$$

$$M_t = \gamma_1 + \gamma_2 Y_t + \epsilon_{2,t}$$

$$Y = C + I + X - M$$

where M is imports, C consumption, Y income, I investment and X exports.

Exercise 13.8

Using equations (13.1) and (13.2) illustrate that the OLS estimate of the coefficient on price suffers from upward bias. (The algebra for this question is a bit messy.) Does this finding agree with the results shown in Table 13.1?

Exercise 13.9

In the demand and supply model in equations (13.1)–(13.3) the demand equation is unidentified, so no simultaneous technique may be applied to estimation of the price elasticity of demand. But of course single-equation estimation by OLS is still possible. Carry out this regression and comment on the information given by the coefficient.

Exercise 13.10

Comment on the estimation procedure for the parameters in the following model:

$$LE_i = \alpha_1 + \alpha_2 y_i + \alpha_3 HEXP_i + \epsilon_{1,i}$$

$$HEXP_i = \beta_1 + \beta_2 y_i + \epsilon_{2,i}$$

where LE is life expectancy at birth, y income per capita and $HEXP$ health expenditure per person.

What different interpretations should be placed on the coefficient of income in the regression for life expectancy as between the structural equation and the reduced form?

NOTES

1 The data have been generated by a simulation of the model specified in equations (13.1)–(13.3).
2 The supply equation actually has two regressors – price and the intercept term. Some packages, e.g. Microfit, require you to specify as many instruments as regressors *including* the intercept term. If this is the case simply include the intercept in your list of instruments – it will act as its own instrument.
3 Subject to comments made in the next section.
4 A version of the omitted-variable Hausman test was used in Chapter 10 as an equivalent form of the Plosser–Schwert–White differencing test.
5 An alternative closure would be quantity adjustment in which the actual level of exports is constrained to the minimum of supply and demand, i.e. $X = \min\{X^s, X^d\}$.

6   If we were testing the exogeneity of more than one variable then the fitted value for each of these variables would be included in the expanded regression.

7   The consumption function is the 'standard text book' example of simultaneity bias. We did not use it as the accounting identity is usually presented in for the case of a closed economy. We have included the trade balance since we use actual data; there are no real economies for which it is true that $Y = C + I$.

8   The reader is warned that exogeneity is a term for which differing definitions abound. We present here those suggested by Engle *et al.* (1983) which have the widest currency.

9   It is perfectly possible to check first the order condition and then the rank. There is no strong argument either way. An equation that fails the order condition *must* fail the rank condition (why?) but not vice versa. Doing the rank condition first may therefore save a small amount of time. In Chapter 14 it will also be seen that it is possible to apply the technique of two- (or three-) stage least squares to both just and over-identified equations: if this is the intention then the order condition is superfluous.

14 Estimating simultaneous equation models

14.1 INTRODUCTION

The previous chapters have shown that OLS estimation may be inappropriate for an equation which is part of a system of equations and that it may not be possible to estimate the parameters of some equations at all (if the equation is unidentified). We also saw that an equation may be just or over-identified and said that this affects how the equation may be estimated. This chapter discusses the appropriate estimation techniques for these different cases.

We begin, however, in section 14.2 with a presentation of recursive systems as a special class of multi-equation model. Section 14.3 discusses the method of indirect least squares (ILS) which may only be used for equations which are just identified. Section 14.4 presents instrumental variables and the related method of two-stage least squares. These techniques are called limited information estimation as they estimate the parameters of one equation at a time. Section 14.5 employs the various techniques to estimate a consumption function for Indonesia.

In section 14.6 we discuss seemingly unrelated regressions (SUR) and three-stage least squares (3SLS) which is a full information technique – all the models' (estimable) parameters are estimated simultaneously. Section 14.7 provides a summary of the chapter's main points.

14.2 RECURSIVE MODELS

A recursive model is a multi-equation model without simultaneity, it may be written in general form as:

$$Y_{1,i} = \alpha_1 + \alpha_2 X_i + \epsilon_{1,i}$$
$$Y_{2,i} = \beta_1 + \beta_2 X_i + \beta_3 Y_{1,i} + \epsilon_{2,i}$$
$$Y_{3,i} = \gamma_1 + \gamma_2 X_i + \gamma_3 Y_{1,i} + \gamma_4 Y_{2,i} + \epsilon_{3,i}$$
$$\vdots \qquad \vdots$$
$$Y_{n,i} = \delta_1 + \delta_2 X_i + \delta_3 Y_{1,i} + \delta_4 Y_{2,i} + \ldots + \delta_{n-3,i} Y_{n-1,i} \qquad (14.1)$$

where the Ys are endogenous and X, which may be a vector, exogenous. The problem of simultaneity bias arises since one of the regressors is correlated with the error term. This problem will not affect X as it is exogenous. But in a simultaneous model – in which say Y_1 depends on Y_2 and Y_2 depends on Y_1 – then a variable which is the dependent variable in one equation will be the regressor in another and simultaneity bias will be present. But this problem does not appear in the recursive model. The expression for Y_1 is equation (14.1) in a reduced form, so clearly OLS can be used. Since Y_1 is a function of only X and its own error ϵ_1, it will not be related to any of the other error terms appearing in the model. The reduced form for Y_2 shows it to be a function of X and ϵ_1 and ϵ_2. So Y_2 will not be correlated to, for example, ϵ_3 when it appears as a regressor in the equation of Y_3, nor ϵ_4 and so on. The same argument carries through for each of the endogenous variables. As there is no simultaneity bias the structural equations from a recursive model apparently may be estimated by OLS.

In fact there is a problem here, which we shall state rather than demonstrate. In a recursive model the order condition is satisfied for only the first equation. However, the other equations may be shown to be identified, provided there is no cross-equation correlation between the error terms, i.e. $E(\epsilon_i \epsilon_j) = 0$ for all $i \neq j$. However, OLS is consistent rather than unbiased, and so only valid for large samples.

There are two important exceptions to the above argument. The first should be apparent from the preceding paragraph, i.e. what happens when the error terms are cross-correlated, e.g. $E(\epsilon_1 \epsilon_2) \neq 0$. In this case multiplying the expression for Y_1 through by ϵ_2 shows that $E(y\epsilon_2)$ is not zero, so that OLS estimation of the equation for Y_2 is now biased and inconsistent. In fact, cross-correlation of the error terms leads us away from OLS even when the equations do not apparently form part of a multi-equation model – that is, they are what is known as seemingly unrelated regressions. The appropriate estimation technique under these circumstances is discussed in section 14.6.

We have discussed here a general form of the recursive model. In economics such models are most likely to arise on account of lags in behaviourial relationships. Examples of this fact are provided in the exercises. But this case is the second exception to our initial description of using OLS for the recursive model. If the first equation contains a lagged endogenous variable, then estimation of this equation by OLS is consistent but not unbiased. This result follows since simple substitution can obtain a reduced form in which Y_1 is a function of its own lag, under which circumstances we know OLS to be biased but consistent.

Exercise 14.1

In a simple two-equation Keynesian model of the closed economy, the accounting identity:

$$Y_t = C_t + I_t \tag{14.2}$$

may be combined either with a contemporaneous consumption function:

$$C_t = \beta_1 + \beta_2 Y_t + \epsilon_t \tag{14.3}$$

or one in which the effect of income on consumption operates with a lag

$$C_t = \beta_1 + \beta_2 Y_{t-1} + \epsilon'_t \tag{14.4}$$

Show that the model with the lagged consumption function is recursive, whereas that with the contemporaneous function is not. Discuss the implications of this finding for estimation of the marginal propensity to consume.

Exercise 14.2

Consider the five-equation IS-LM model given in equations (13.33)–(13.37). Show that a lagged consumption function does not make the model recursive. Show that the model is recursive if the income term is lagged in both the import and consumption functions and that investment depends on the lagged interest rate. In the latter case explain the order of substitution to obtain a recursive solution to the model.

14.3   INDIRECT LEAST SQUARES

We start, once again, with our familiar supply and demand model:

$$Q_t^s = \beta_1 + \beta_2 P_t + \epsilon_{1,t} \tag{14.5}$$

$$Q_t^d = \gamma_1 + \gamma_2 P_t + \gamma_3 Y_t + \epsilon_{2,t} \tag{14.6}$$

$$Q = Q_t^s = Q_t^d \tag{14.7}$$

where P and Q are price and quantity, the s and d superscripts denote supply and demand, and Y is income.

This model may be solved to get the following reduced-form expressions for price and quantity:

$$P_t = \frac{\upsilon_1 - \beta_1}{\beta_2 - \gamma_2} + \frac{\gamma_3}{\beta_2 - \gamma_2} Y_t + \frac{\varepsilon_2 - \varepsilon_1}{\beta_2 - \gamma_2} \tag{14.8}$$

$$Q_t = \frac{\beta_2 \gamma_1 - \beta_1 \gamma_2}{\beta_2 - \gamma_2} + \frac{\beta_2 \gamma_3}{\beta_2 - \gamma_2} Y_t + \frac{\beta_2 \varepsilon_2 - \gamma_2 \varepsilon_1}{\beta_2 - \gamma_2} \tag{14.9}$$

which we may write as:

$$P_t = \pi_1 + \pi_2 Y_t + \omega_{1,t} \tag{14.10}$$

$$Q_t = \pi_3 + \pi_4 Y_t + \omega_{2,t} \tag{14.11}$$

where

$$\pi_1 = \frac{\gamma_1 - \beta_1}{\beta_2 - \gamma_2} \qquad \pi_2 = \frac{\gamma_3}{\beta_2 - \gamma_2}$$

$$\pi_3 = \frac{\beta_2\gamma_1 - \beta_1\gamma_2}{\beta_2 - \gamma_2} \qquad \pi_4 = \frac{\beta_2\gamma_3}{\beta_2 - \gamma_2}$$

$$\omega_1 = \frac{\varepsilon_2 - \varepsilon_1}{\beta_2 - \gamma_2} \qquad \omega_2 = \frac{\beta_2\varepsilon_2 - \gamma_2\varepsilon_1}{\beta_2 - \gamma_2} \qquad (14.12)$$

Since these are reduced-form expressions the variables on the right-hand side are, by definition, exogenous. Equations (14.10) and (14.11) may therefore be estimated by OLS. Then we can work back from the reduced form coefficients (the πs) to the structural coefficients (the βs and γs) – a technique known as indirect least squares, since we obtain the required parameters indirectly by estimating the reduced form equations. But we can see from the expressions gathered under equation (14.12) that we only have four equations (the estimates for π_1, π_2, π_3 and π_4) for five unknowns (γ_1, γ_2, γ_3, γ_4 and γ_5).

This situation of insufficient equations has arisen because the demand equation is unidentified. We have already said that it is not possible to estimate the parameters of an unidentified equation – here we have a concrete example of this impossibility in practice. But we have also said that we should be able to get estimates for equations which are identified, in this case the supply equation. This is indeed the case, since a little manipulation shows that:

$$\beta_2 = \frac{\pi_4}{\pi_2} \qquad \beta_1 = \pi_3 - \beta_2\pi_1 \qquad (14.13)$$

So we can obtain estimates of the parameters of the supply equation, which is just identified, but not for the demand equation, which is unidentified.

Exercise 14.3

In the following model (where W is an index of weather conditions):

$$Q^s = \beta_1 + \beta_2P + \beta_3W + \epsilon_1 \qquad (14.14)$$

$$Q^d = \gamma_1 + \gamma_2P + \epsilon_2 \qquad (14.15)$$

$$Q^s = Q^d = Q \qquad (14.16)$$

which parameters may be estimated using ILS? Derive the algebraic expressions to calculate these parameters. Discuss your answer in the light of the identification of the equations.

To apply ILS to our supply and demand example (equations (14.5)–(14.7)) we first estimate the reduced-form equations. We do this using the data set in data file SIMSIM, where all series have been subject to the log transformation:

$$\hat{P}_t = -1.062 + 1.188 Y_t \qquad (14.17)$$

$$\hat{Q}_t = 8.141 + 0.241 Y_t \qquad (14.18)$$

where we have retained three decimal places for purposes of calculation. Using the formulae in equation 14.13 we have:[1]

$$b_2^{ILS} = \frac{\hat{\pi}_4}{\hat{\pi}_2} = \frac{0.241}{1.188} = 0.204 \qquad (14.19)$$

$$b_1^{ILS} = \hat{\pi}_3 - b_2 \hat{\pi}_1 = 8.141 \div 0.203 \times 1.062 = 8.36$$

If you refer back to Chapter 13, you will see that these are not the same as the results which were obtained by OLS (by which the price elasticity of supply is estimated as 0.11). The latter are biased and inconsistent, whereas the ILS estimates are consistent; but they are not unbiased.[2] That is, in common with all techniques for estimating equations in simultaneous systems, ILS is a large-sample technique. Small-sample bias may be quite serious. Developing-country data sets often do not permit very large samples but a sample size of less than 20 would cast serious doubt on the validity of your results and it is really preferable to work with at least 25 observations.

The above example shows how ILS may be applied to the estimation of an equation which is just identified. What about when an equation is over-identified? We have stated that ILS is then inappropriate, and it is easy to show why this is so. Suppose that our demand equation has an additional exogenous variable, A, which is the real value of advertising expenditure per capita:

$$Q_t^d = \beta_1 + \beta_2 P_t + \beta_3 Y_t + \beta_4 A_t + \epsilon'_{2,t} \qquad (14.20)$$

Checking the identification of the behavioural relationships in this model (which is left as an exercise) shows that, whilst the demand equation remains unidentified, the supply schedule is now over-identified.

The consequences of this over-identification are apparent when we write out the reduced form equations:

$$P_t = \pi_1 + \pi_1 Y_t + \pi_2 A_t + \omega_{1,t} \qquad (14.21)$$

$$Q_t = \pi_4 + \pi_5 Y_t + \pi_6 A_t + \omega_{2,t} \qquad (14.22)$$

We will now get estimates of six πs, but there are only five structural coefficients to be estimated (β_1, β_2, γ_1, γ_2 and γ_3). We have too many equations, so there will be no unique solution. There will be more than one solution for the parameters of the supply curve (the βs) and no means of choosing between them as to the 'right one'. ILS therefore cannot be used when an equation is over-identified.

In practice, ILS is little used even if an equation is just identified. This neglect is because of the algebra (which rapidly becomes tedious in large models) and subsequent substitution required to get the structural coefficients from the reduced-form estimates. The method mainly survives as an introduction to the identification problem in many texts. The preferred method is instrumental variable estimation. In the next section we deal with this technique first for just identified equations and then in its generalised form (for equations which are either just or over-identified), which is equivalent to two-stage least squares.

Exercise 14.4

The Human Development Index may be modelled as a function of income per capita and population growth. But population growth itself is a function of the HDI. Which parameters in this model may be estimated? Derive the algebraic expressions to estimate them by ILS. Calculate these estimates using the data in the data file SOCECON.

14.4 INSTRUMENTAL VARIABLE ESTIMATION AND TWO-STAGE LEAST SQUARES

The method of instrumental variables was briefly introduced in Chapter 13. IV gets around the simultaneity bias caused by the relationship between the regressor and the error by using a proxy which is unrelated to the error but is correlated to the variable whose coefficient we wish to estimate. The choice of proxy is, in practice, circumscribed by the variables in our data set. Recall that the exogenous variable chosen must be one that does not appear in the equation whose parameters we are estimating.

Consider, once again, the demand and supply example, in which supply is a function of price and demand of price and income. We have established that it is not possible to estimate the parameters of the demand function as it is under-identified. We can see that here, by asking what proxy can we use for the endogenous regressor, price, in the demand equation. We cannot use income, since that already appears in the equation. The fact that there are no variables in the model excluded in the demand schedule means that it cannot be estimated (the parallels with the identification conditions should be clear). For the supply schedule, on the other hand, we may proxy price by income. This was done already in Chapter 13 where we obtained the result (*t*-statistics in parentheses in this and subsequent equations in this section):

$$\hat{Q}_t^s = 8.36 + 0.20P_t$$
$$(30.57) \quad (4.13) \tag{14.23}$$

We will not discuss the derivation of the IV estimator here, as it may be calculated by a statistics or econometrics package.[3] More important is to understand its appropriate use and interpretation.[4]

You will have noticed that the results in equation (14.23) are the same as those obtained by ILS, reported in equation (14.19). Provided an equation is just identified (which is when they should be used) then IV and ILS will always yield identical results – they are equivalent. This equivalence is easy to demonstrate:

$$b_2^{ILS} = \frac{\hat{\pi}_4}{\hat{\pi}_2} = \frac{\Sigma yq/\Sigma y^2}{\Sigma py/\Sigma y^2} = \frac{\Sigma yq}{\Sigma py} = b_2^{IV} \tag{14.24}$$

And like ILS, IV estimates are consistent but not unbiased; it is also a large sample estimator. This must obviously be so since it has just been demonstrated that the two estimators are algebraically identical.

The R^2 obtained by OLS will always be greater than that resulting from IV estimation. Indeed, the latter can be negative, which is symptomatic of poor model specification, and perhaps that the equation is not identified at all.

What if we have a choice of instruments. Which should we choose? The answer is that this problem will not arise: if we have a choice of instruments then the equation will be over-, not just, identified and the use of IV with a single instrument is inappropriate. Rather, we should apply 2SLS which utilises the full range of instruments.

The supply and demand model, with advertising included in the demand schedule, is an example of this situation. As before, the demand equation is unidentified. The supply equation is over-identified, and we have a choice of instruments: either income or advertising. Estimating the model using advertising as the instrument gives:

$$\hat{Q}_t^s = 7.32 + 0.39$$
$$(1.19) \quad (0.35) \tag{14.25}$$

which is a rather different answer to that provided by using income (here price is not significant), given in equation (14.23). There is no basis for saying that either equation (14.19) or (14.21) is the 'right answer'. This situation is analogous to that in IV estimation, where we had more reduced form coefficients than structural ones, so there was no unique solution for the latter.

So how can we estimate the supply function when it is over-identified? Since we have no basis for deciding between the exogenous variables in choosing our instrument why not choose both of them? Or, more precisely, a linear combination of them. This sounds promising, but what linear combination should we take (what weight should we give each variable)?

Why not use the coefficient given by regressing the variable we wish to proxy on the instruments (the instruments being all the exogenous variables in the model)? That is, proxy the endogenous regressors by their fitted values from the estimates of their reduced forms. This method is perfectly acceptable, and it will yield identical results to the closely related method of two-stage least squares. But to carry out 2SLS, rather than using the fitted values of the endogenous variables in the formula for the IV estimator, we use the fitted values as the regressors in the original structural equation we are estimating rather than the actual values of these variables.

Thus, the procedure is called two-stage least squares since it involves doing two sets of regressions. First we regress the endogenous regressors from the structural equation we wish to estimate on their reduced forms. Then we estimate the structural equation by OLS, but replacing the endogenous regressors by the fitted values given by the first stage.[5] We now apply the technique to the supply and demand model.

The first stage is to regress the endogenous regressor on its reduced form; this gives:

$$\hat{P}t = -1.14 + 1.19Y_t - 0.03A_t \tag{14.26}$$

which is used to calculate the values of $\hat{P}$ which are then used to estimate the second stage-equation:

$$\hat{Q}_t^s = 8.36 + 0.20\hat{P}_t$$
$$(39.69)\ \ (5.38) \tag{14.27}$$

The standard errors given by this second regression are not the appropriate ones. These are, however, not difficult to calculate, and are given by statistics and econometrics packages.[6] Also it is not necessary to carry out the two stages yourself in practice as this will be done by the package (though it is useful for understanding the technique to do it yourself a few times and, as we shall see, it can yield useful information). The estimated equation given by selecting 2SLS is:

$$\hat{Q}_t^s = 8.36 + 0.20\hat{P}_t \qquad R^2 = 0.04$$
$$(30.57)\ \ (4.14) \tag{14.28}$$

Whilst the coefficients are the same as those reported in equation (14.27), we can see that the correct standard errors are somewhat different to (larger than) those given by the second-stage regression.

The results from 2SLS are not the same as those we obtained by IV and ILS earlier in the chapter – there the supply elasticity was 4.82, now its is 4.43. The difference arises because the 2SLS estimates have been obtained from a different model; that is, one including advertising in the demand equation. Our estimate of the supply elasticity has therefore been shown to be reasonably, but not totally robust, to model specification: what we decide to leave out of the demand equation affects the parameter estimates of the supply equation. For a limited information technique it is only which other variables are included in the model that affects the results, not the precise specification of the other equations; we shall see that this is not the case for full information techniques, for which misspecification bias can also arise for all equations because of misspecification of a single equation.

If we had been estimating the same model, then it would have been the case that 2SLS would be equivalent to IV – so that 2SLS is also consistent but not unbiased: yet again small-sample bias might be a serious problem. The technique also assumes that the errors from the different equations in the system are not correlated with one another – we return to this in section 14.6. Because of the equivalence between 2SLS and IV, it is common just to apply 2SLS to any equation which is identified (whether just or over-identified).[7] Where the equation is just identified 2SLS will yield identical results to IV and therefore also an identical result to using ILS (why?).

The R^2 from the first-stage regression (not available if we execute the whole procedure as a computer package option) can give useful information on the results. If this R^2 is low then the endogenous regressor is poorly explained by the variables in its reduced form – thus the fitted value from this first-stage regression will be a poor proxy for the actual value and the second-stage estimates will not be worth much. On the other hand, if the R^2 from the first stage is high then the fitted and actual values of the endogenous regressor will be very close, so that the 2SLS and OLS results will be very similar. A high R^2 is quite likely to occur in models with a large number of exogenous variables. We showed in Chapter 13 that we can use Hausman's specification test to determine whether or not the difference between the results from OLS and simultaneous techniques is significant or not.[8]

There are two possible definitions of the R^2 for 2SLS: (a) the square of the correlation coefficient between the dependent variable and its fitted value; (b) one minus the ratio of the squared residuals to the total sum of squares. The two are not the same – for our example above we use the second method, the first method yields an R^2 of 0.89 – and different packages report different versions. The resulting R^2 from the second definition may be higher or lower than that from OLS and, like that from IV estimation, can actually be negative: if it is negative (or very low) then (especially if the R^2 from OLS estimation of the structural equation is high) there is a problem in model specification.

14.5   ESTIMATING THE CONSUMPTION FUNCTION IN A SIMULTANEOUS SYSTEM

Here we present a further example using the model and data for the Indonesian consumption function (data file INDONA). The model is:

$$C_t = \beta_1 + \beta_2 Y_t + \epsilon_t \tag{14.29}$$

$$Y_t = C_t + I_t + X_t - M_t \tag{14.30}$$

where I is investment, X exports and M imports of goods and services.

We will first estimate the parameters of the consumption function using IV and ILS, and show their equivalence. If I, X and M are each treated as a separate exogenous variable than it can be shown that the consumption function is over-identified, and we cannot apply either IV or ILS (why not?). Since they are all three exogenous and do not appear in the behaviourial equation to be estimated, we can define a new variable $IXM = I + X - M$, and so rewrite equation (14.29) as:

$$Y = C + IXM \tag{14.31}$$

The consumption function is now just identified. Estimating it using IV with IXM as the instrument yields (t-statistics in parentheses):

$$\hat{C}_t = 1{,}388.83 + 0.65 Y_t \qquad R^2 = 0.99$$
$$\quad (0.91) \quad (42.28) \tag{14.32}$$

which compares with the OLS estimate of:[9]

$$\hat{C}_t = 24.71 + 0.67 PY_t \qquad R^2 = 0.99$$
$$\quad (0.02) \quad (45.43) \qquad DW = 0.33 \tag{14.33}$$

As expected, the OLS estimate has an upward bias.[10] There is also a bias in the estimate of the intercept: although the IV estimator (like that obtained by OLS) is insignificantly different from zero, which conforms with our theoretical expectation.

To estimate by ILS we need to calculate the reduced form for the model. This is:

$$Y = \frac{\beta_1}{1 - \beta_2} + \frac{1}{1 - \beta_2} IXM_t + \frac{\varepsilon_t}{1 - \beta_2} \tag{14.34}$$

$$C = \frac{\beta_1}{1 - \beta_2} + \frac{\beta_2}{1 - \beta_2} IXM_t + \frac{\varepsilon_t}{1 - \beta_2} \tag{14.35}$$

Which we estimate as:

$$Y_t = \pi_1 + \pi_2 IXM_t + \omega_{1,t} \tag{14.36}$$

$$C_t = \pi_3 + \pi_4 IXM_t + \omega_{2,t} \tag{14.37}$$

where:

$$\pi_1 = \frac{\beta_1}{1 - \beta_2} \quad \pi_2 = \frac{1}{1 - \beta_2}$$

$$\pi_3 = \frac{\beta_1}{1 - \beta_2} \quad \pi_4 = \frac{\beta_2}{1 - \beta_2} \tag{14.38}$$

There are only two structural coefficients to be estimated (β_1 and β_2) but four reduced-form estimates. It might appear that we have too many equations, so that the consumption function is over-identified. This is not the case. Applying the order condition shows (subject to the rank condition being satisfied) that the consumption function is just identified. When an equation is just identified but there appear to be multiple solutions (as here), then, in fact, the solutions arrived at by the different channels will turn out to be the same. You should be able to satisfy yourself that this is the case by estimating the $\hat{\pi}$ from equations (14.36) and (14.37) and substituting the results in to equation (14.38).

The reduced form for income is:

$$\hat{Y}t = 4{,}011 + 2.888IXM_t \qquad (14.39)$$

which gives:

$$b_2{}^{ILS} = \frac{\hat{\pi}_2 - 1}{\hat{\pi}_2} = \frac{2.888 - 1}{2.888} = 0.65 \qquad (14.40)$$

$$b_1^{ILS} = (1 - b_2)\,\hat{\pi}_1 = 1{,}388$$

The same answers are arrived at by estimating the reduced form for consumption:

$$\hat{C}_t = 4{,}011 + 1.888IXM_t \qquad (14.41)$$

so:

$$b_2{}^{ILS} = \frac{\hat{\pi}_4}{\hat{\pi}_4 + 1} = \frac{1.888 - 1}{1.888} = 0.65 \qquad (14.42)$$

$$b_1^{ILS} = (1 - b_2)\,\hat{\pi}_3 = 1{,}388$$

thus showing that it does not matter which reduced form is used to derive the results.[11] It can also be seen that, as expected, the ILS estimates are the same as those arrived at by IV.

We can also estimate the model's parameters by two-stage least squares, in which case there is no need to ensure that the consumption function is just identified. Instead I, X and M are treated as three separate exogenous variables.[12] The two stages are therefore to estimate the reduced form for Y, by regressing it on these three variables (and a constant), and then to regress the consumption function, replacing Y by $\hat{Y}$ from the first stage. Both stages have been done in a single step by an econometrics package to get:

$$\hat{C}_t = 232.89 + 0.67Y_t \qquad R^2 = 0.99 \qquad (14.43)$$
$$\quad\;\; (0.16)\;\; (45.09)$$

This gives a slightly better fit than IV using *IXM* as a single instrument. This follows since the fitted value from regressing *Y* on *I*, *X* and *M* separately is sure to be a better proxy for *Y* than is *IXM* (why?).

Exercise 14.5

Use the Indonesian data (data file INDONA) to estimate the model:

$$Y_t = C_t + I_t + X_t - M_t \tag{14.44}$$

$$C_t = \beta_1 + \beta_2 Y_t + \epsilon_{1,t} \tag{14.45}$$

$$M_t = \alpha_1 + \alpha_2 Y_t + \epsilon_{2,t} \tag{14.46}$$

Exercise 14.6

Repeat the procedures followed in the preceding section using the national accounts data for Sri Lanka (data file SRINA) or the country of your choice.

14.6   FULL INFORMATION ESTIMATION TECHNIQUES

The techniques considered so far are limited information: they estimate one equation at a time and only use information pertaining to that equation. Whilst these techniques are consistent, they are not as efficient as full information (or systems) estimation, in which all model parameters are estimated in one go. The inefficiency of limited information estimation arises since the method does not exploit two possible pieces of information: (a) cross-correlation between error terms in different equations; and (b) that the predetermined variable omitted from the equation being estimated may also be omitted from other equations in the system. Seemingly unrelated regression (SUR) takes account of just the first of these, and three-stage least squares (3SLS) takes account of both. These techniques use generalised least squares (GLS) estimation, which is beyond the scope of our text. Hence we focus on an intuitive explanation, so that readers will understand what these methods are and why they are being used, if they should come across them.

Seemingly unrelated regressions

In our discussion of recursive systems in section 14.2, we stated that OLS estimation of each equation is consistent only if there is no cross-correlation between the different error terms. Where such cross-correlation exists then an alternative technique should be used. In fact, if there is cross-correlation then, even if the regressions appear unrelated to one another, it is preferable to utilise this information and hence improve the efficiency of the estimates. A common example of appropriate application of SUR is the demand equations for related products:

$$Q_{1,t} = \alpha_1 + \alpha_2 P_{1,t} + \epsilon_{1,t} \tag{14.47}$$

$$Q_{2,t} = \beta_1 + \beta_2 P_{2,t} + \epsilon_{2,t} \tag{14.48}$$

where P and Q are price and quantity respectively and 1 and 2 are two commodities (e.g. tea and coffee). To apply SUR estimation the samples for the two regressions must be the same (e.g. same period of time or cross-section of households).

SUR estimation combines the two equations into a single equation for estimation purposes, and applies generalised least squares to this equation. Here we state without proof the expressions for the two slope coefficients:

$$a_2^{SUR} = \frac{[\sigma_2^2 \Sigma p_1 q_1 - \sigma_{12} \Sigma p_1 q_2]\sigma_1^2 \Sigma p_2^2 + [\sigma_1^2 \Sigma p_2 q_2 - \sigma_{12} \Sigma p_2 q_1]\sigma_{12} \Sigma p_1 p_2}{\sigma_1^2 \sigma_2^2 \Sigma p_1^2 \Sigma p_2^2 - \sigma_{12}^2 (\Sigma p_1 p_2)^2}$$

$$\tag{14.49}$$

$$b_2^{SUR} = \frac{[\sigma_2^2 \Sigma p_1 q_1 - \sigma_{12} \Sigma p_1 q_2]\sigma_{12} \Sigma p_1 p_2 + [\sigma_1^2 \Sigma p_2 q_2 - \sigma_{12} \Sigma p_2 q_1]\sigma_1^2 \Sigma p_1^2}{\sigma_1^2 \sigma_2^2 \Sigma p_1^2 \Sigma p_2^2 - \sigma_{12}^2 (\Sigma p_1 p_2)^2}$$

$$\tag{14.50}$$

Examination of equations (14.49) and (14.50) shows that if there is no cross-equation error correlation then the estimators are equivalent to OLS. SUR estimators are also equivalent to OLS when the two regressors (P_1 and P_2) are identical.

In order to apply these equations, estimates of the error variance and covariance are required, which are calculated from the residuals:

$$\hat{\sigma}_1^2 = \frac{1}{n-2}\Sigma e_1^2 \quad \hat{\sigma}_2^2 = \frac{1}{n-2}\Sigma e_2^2 \quad \hat{\sigma}_{1,2} = \frac{1}{n-2}\Sigma e_1 e_2 \tag{14.51}$$

Table 14.1 Estimates for two-commodity supply and demand model

	Intercept	*Slope*	*R²*
Ordinary least squares			
Q1	5.78	−1.44	0.90
	(19.6)	(−19.2)	
Q2	3.06	−0.52	0.73
	(16.3)	(−10.8)	
Seemingly unrelated regressions estimation			
Q1	5.87	−1.47	0.89
	(28.9)	(−28.2)	
Q2	3.04	−0.51	0.73
	(23.4)	(−15.5)	

Table 14.2   Cross-products for SUR estimation

	e_1	e_2	p_1	p_2	q_1	q_2
e_1	0.247	0.090	–	–	–	–
e_2	–	0.066	–	–	–	–
p_1	–	–	1.007	–0.074	–1.456	0.056
p_2	–	–	–	0.677	0.097	–0.351
q_1	–	–	–	–	2.351	0.014
q_2	–	–	–	–	–	0.248

where n is the number of observations and e_1 and e_2 are the residuals from OLS estimation of the first and second equations.

To illustrate the technique we apply the data from data file SURE, which contains data simulated using the model in equations (14.47) and (14.48), with the values $\alpha_2 = -1.5$ and $\beta_2 = -0.5$. Table 14.1 shows the results obtained by OLS and SURE, and Table 14.2 the cross-products required to estimate the slope coefficients.[13] The results show not much difference in the coefficient estimates between the two techniques (the SUR estimates are slightly closer to the actual population values). But there is a substantial difference in the *t*-statistics: as we would expect, since SUR estimation is the more efficient technique, it produces lower standard errors and correspondingly larger *t*-statistics.

Exercise 14.7

Using the data in SOCECON estimate the regressions of the birth rate on the square root of infant mortality, and of life expectancy on logged income per capita using (a) OLS and (b) SUR. Comment on your results.

Three-stage least squares

SUR estimation is a two-stage technique in which the residuals are calculated from OLS regression in order to apply generalised least squares. Three-stage least squares (3SLS) is similar to SUR, except that the residuals are obtained from the second-stage regressions of TSLS. Three-stage least squares may be applied to simultaneous models and, like SUR, results in more efficient estimates (usually around 5 per cent more efficient that those produced by TSLS). If there are cross-equation restrictions (i.e. the parameters in one equation are related to those in another) then systems estimation must be applied and 3SLS is the approach to be adopted.

To summarise, the three stages of 3SLS are:

1   Estimate the reduced form equations by OLS.
2   Substitute the fitted values from stage 1 into the structural equations and estimate by OLS (i.e. the second stage regression of TSLS).

Table 14.3 Estimates of simple Keynesian model for Indonesia

	Intercept	*Slope*	R^2
Ordinary least squares			
Consumption	24.71	0.067	0.99
	(0.02)	(45.4)	
Imports	–2862.7	0.24	0.90
	(–1.67)	(14.1)	
Two-stage least squares			
Consumption	–23.5	0.67	0.99
	(-0.2)	(45.2)	
Imports	–3504.5	0.25	0.90
	(-2.0)	(14.4)	
Three-stage least squares			
Consumption	–23.54	0.67	0.99
	(-0.2)	(47.1)	
Imports	–3504.5	0.25	0.90
	(-2.1)	(15.0)	

Source: Calculated from data file INDONA
Note: *t*-statistics in parentheses

3 Calculate the residuals from stage 2 to obtain an estimate of the error variance-covariance matrix and so apply generalised least squares.

Modern econometrics packages will produce 3SLS estimates. Table 14.3 reports the results for the simple Keynesian model for Indonesia with consumption and import functions (see exercise 14.5). The coefficient estimates do not differ greatly between 3SLS and TSLS (though sometimes they do with OLS because the latter is biased). But the 3SLS *t*-statistics are all larger than those obtained from TSLS.

Exercise 14.8

Replicate Table 14.3 using the INDONA data. Reproduce the table also using the data in SRINA or national accounts data for the country of your choice. Comment on your results.

14.7 SUMMARY OF MAIN POINTS

Simultaneous models may be estimated by a range of techniques. Indirect least squares is intuitively appealing, but too cumbersome to use for all but the simplest of models. Two-stage least squares is commonly used, though the equivalent technique of instrumental variables may be used for just identified equations.

ILS, IV and TSLS are single equation estimation techniques, as each equation is estimated in turn. Full information, or systems estimation, produces estimates for all model parameters in one go. Systems estimation can take account of the fact that there may be cross-correlation between the error terms of different equations and so it gives more efficient estimates. Two words of warning are in order. With systems estimation misspecification of a single equation will bias the parameter estimates for all equations. Second, the problem of non-stationarity is more serious than that of simultaneity bias – and a set of cointegrating equations will not suffer from simultaneity bias even if the equations constitute a simultaneous model.

NOTES

1 Standard errors are not reported as there is no simple way of obtaining them from the reduced-form standard errors (which were not reported for the same reason – their significance does not necessarily imply the significance of the structural coefficients). The inability to judge significance from ILS estimation is an additional reason against its use to that given later in the text.
2 The reason being that an attempt to prove unbiasedness runs into the need to take expectations of a ratio of random variables. This is not possible, and we must resort to probability limits.
3 Many packages, for example Microfit, treat the intercept as a variable. Since to estimate an equation by IV we need as many instruments as we have variables, estimation of the supply schedule requires two instruments. But the intercept (or any other exogenous variable appearing in the equation) simply acts as its own instrument.
4 We gave the formula for the slope coefficient (but not the intercept and standard errors) in Chapter 13.
5 We can actually replace *all* the endogenous variables – including that on the left-hand side of the equation – by their fitted values, as using fitted rather than actual values on the left-hand side does *not* affect the parameter estimates. (It does change the standard errors, but these are, as we shall see, the wrong ones anyway.)
6 To get the correct standard errors from the ones given by the second stage it is necessary to multiply by a correction factor. This correction factor is the ratio of the estimated variance of the error in the structural equation being estimated to the variance of the error in the second-stage regression (the structural equation with endogenous regressors replaced by their fitted values from the first stage regression). See Gujarati (1988: 620–1) or Maddala (1988: 311–13) for a derivation.
7 In which case, as stated in Chapter 13, it is unnecessary to check the order condition, since the rank condition is necessary and sufficient.
8 In Chapter 13 we used the IV method to provide a consistent estimator when the regressor is endogenous. It is possible to use 2SLS instead.
9 Note that the DW is substantially less than the R^2, suggesting that there is likely to be spurious correlation here and that cointegration analysis might be appropriate. As stated in Chapter 11, this latter approach should be adopted – using simultaneous techniques does *not* eliminate the inconsistency that results from regressing series that are I(0) on one another.
10 However, the bias is very small. Some suggest simultaneity is never too great a problem – and almost certainly less than the measurement error in the data. We should also note with concern that $R^2 > DW$, suggesting that the regression may well be spurious. It is more important to test for stationarity, and proceed accordingly if the variables prove non-stationary, than to worry about simultaneous estimation.

11 If different results are obtained this tells you there is a problem in the data. This is why we could not use the textbook example of $Y = C + I$, since there is no economy which fits this model. If data are used for which this identity does not hold then different results will be obtained from the two reduced forms. The Y here is GDP at market prices: GNP might be a more appropriate measure to use in the consumption function, in which case net factor payments from abroad should be added as an additional exogenous term in the identity.

12 Endogenising imports through an import function, which may appear an obvious improvement to the model, is left as an exercise.

13 We have not given the formulae for the intercept and standard errors. These estimates were obtained from TSP.

Appendix A
The data sets used in this book

This appendix gives a brief description of each of the sets available on the data diskette and used in the examples and exercises of this book. For your convenience, the data sets are listed in alphabetical order of file name. For each data set, a brief description is given of the nature of the data, its sources, sample size, and a list and definition of the variables. The variables are ordered by columns in each case. For reasons of confidentiality, however, the exact reference to some of the data sets which contain survey data for individual cases is kept vague to avoid identification of case materials.

The order of the variables in each of the data files in ASCII is the same as they appear in the following description of the data files. Since DOS allows only eight characters for the first name of a file, the names KRISH-NAJI and FERTILITY (mentioned in the book) appear as KRISHNAJ and FERTILIT for the data files. The Lotus files include the variable names, but these are excluded in the ASCII files.

AIDSAV (aid and savings)

Cross-country data for 66 developing countries for 1987 taken from the *World Development Report*. The variables are:

1 observation numbers (*OBS*);
2 the savings rate (*S/Y*);
3 aid as a per cent of GDP (*A/Y*); and
4 income per capita in US$ (*Y*).

BELPOP (Belize's population)

Population data for Belize for the years 1970–92 (from the World Bank's *World Tables*). The file contains the following variables:

1 *YEAR* (1970–92); and
2 population (*POP*) in millions.

BIRTH (the birth rate and its determinants)

The file BIRTH contains data (taken from the the World Bank's *World Tables*) for 128 countries in 1985 on the following variables:

1　the crude birth rate (*BIRTH*): the ratio of the number of births in a year over the population in the mid-year, expressed per 1,000 population;
2　the gross national income per capita (*GNPCAP*);
3　infant mortality (*INFMORT*): the number of deaths of infants under age one in a year over the number of live births in that year, expressed per 1,000 live births.

CHINA (household size and income data)

The file contains data sub-sampled from the World Fertility Survey (1975), for 197 rural households, Hebei Province, China. The file contains the following variables:

1　household size (*SIZE*);
2　annual household income (*INCOME*) in US$;
3　number of children (*TPARITY*);
4　number of couples (*COUPLES*);
5　per capita household income (*PI*).

COINCON (a cointegrating consumption function)

Simulated data to estimate a cointegrating consumption function. The data span the period 1960–93 and are in logs. The variables are:

1　*YEAR*;
2　logged consumption (*LC*); and
3　logged income (*LY*).

CRCON (Costa Rican consumption function)

Logged data to estimate a consumption function for Costa Rica for the period 1963–92. Sources are the World Bank's *World Tables* and *International Finance Statistics*. The file contains:

1　*YEAR*;
2　logged consumption (*LC*); and
3　logged income (*LY*).

FERTILIT (the determinants of fertility data)

This file contains comparative cross-section data for 64 countries on fertility and its determinants as given by the following variables:

1　GNP per capita 1980 (*GNP*);

2 the total fertility rate (*TFR*), 1980–85: the average number of children born to a woman, using age-specific fertility rates for a given year;
3 child mortality (*CM*): the number of deaths of children under age five in a year per 1,000 live births;
4 female literacy rate (*FL*), expressed as percentage;
5 an index of family planning effort (*FP*).

With the exception of GNP per capita (taken from the World Bank's *World Tables*), all other data are taken from J. A. Ross *et al.*, *Planning and Child Survival: 100 Developing Countries*, Centre for Population and Family Health, Columbia University, 1988.

INDFOOD (Indian households food data)

This file contains data for a sample of 217 Indian rural households (1994) with the following variables;

1 household expenditures on food (*F*);
2 total expenditures of the household (*T*).

INDIA (industrial worker data, southern India)

This file contains data for a sample of 261 workers collected in a survey of worker households in 1990 in an industrial town in southern India. The file contains the following variables:

1 weekly wage income (*WI*);
2 sex of worker (*SEX*);
3 dummy variable to indicate sex of worker (*DSEX*);
4 education of worker (*EDU*): none, primary, secondary, higher;
5 dummies for education: DE2 (up to primary = 1; 0 otherwise); DE3 (up to secondary =1; 0 otherwise); DE4 (higher education = 1; 0 otherwise);
6 permanent or temporary job (*PT*);
7 dummy for permanent/temporary job (*DPT*) (*DPT* =1 if permanent; 0 otherwise);
8 age of worker in years (*AGE*).

INDONA (Indonesian national accounts data)

Constant price national accounts for Indonesia for the period 1968–92 in billions of Rupiah. (Taken from the World Bank's *World Tables* and the IMF's *International Finance Statistics*.) The variables are:

1 *YEAR*;
2 GDP (*Y*);
3 total consumption (*C*);

4   investment (I);
5   exports (X); and
6   imports (M).

KRISHNAJ (food prices and manufacturing demand)

The data for this file are taken from Krishnaji (1992: 102–3, tables 3 and 4). The data are time series for the period 1960–1 to 1980–1, and include the following variables:

1   disposable income (in Rupees) per capita in current prices (Y);
2   per capita expenditures (in Rs) on manufactured consumer goods at constant 1970–1 prices (M);
3   price index (1970–1 = 100) of cereals and cereal substitutes (P_f);
4   price index (1970–1 = 100) of other foods and beverages (P_{of});
5   price index (1970–1 = 100) of manufactured consumer goods (P_m);
6   price index (1970–1 = 100) of services (P_s).

LEACCESS (determinants of life expectancy)

Data for 87 countries in the late 1980s taken from the UNDP's *Human Development Report*. The variables are:

1   country name (not included in ASCII file);
2   life expectancy at birth (LE);
3   income per capita in US$ (Y); and
4   access to health care $(ACCESS)$.

MALTA (Maltese exports demand and supply)

These data, from Gatt (1995), cover the period 1963–89. The variables are:

1   *YEAR*;
2   exports in US$ (X);
3   a measure of world demand (Y);
4   the export price (P);
5   the world price (PW);
6   the nominal exchange rate (E);
7   consumer price index (CPI); and
8   capital investment (I).

MAPUTO (the demand for and recruitment of casual labour, Maputo harbour)

This file contains data on the daily demand for and recruitment of casual labourers in Maputo harbour for the period from March 1980 to June

1981, a sample of 485 consecutive days (with the exception of a few holidays such as Christmas and New Year). The file contains the following variables:

1   the demand for labour on the day shift (*DEMD*), expressed in number of workers;
2   the demand for labour on the night shift (*DEMN*), expressed in number of workers;
3   the total demand for labour (*DEM*), both day and night shift;
4   the recruitment of labour on the day shift (*RECD*), expressed in number of workers;
5   the recruitment of labour on the night shift (*RECN*), expressed in number of workers;
6   the total recruitment of labour (*REC*), both day and night shift;
7   the trend variable (*t*), indicating successive working days.

PAKEXP (Pakistani export function)

Data for the period 1966–92 from *International Finance Statistics* (and the *Direction of Trade Statistics* to determine weights to calculate the *RER*). The variables are:

1   *YEAR*;
2   real exports (*X*);
3   world demand (*WD*); and
4   the real exchange rate (*RER*).

PERU (data base for Peru)

A database for the period 1967–93 constructed from the World Bank's *World Tables* and *International Financial Statistics*. The variables are *YEAR* and:

1 population (*POP*);
2 nominal GDP (*YC*);
3 real GDP (*Y*);
4 real consumption (*C*);
5 real exports (*X*);
6 real imports (*M*);
7 real manufacturing value added (*MVA*);
8 the external terms of trade (*TOT*);
9 life expectancy at birth (*LE*);
10 infant mortality rate (*IMR*);
11 external current account deficit as a percentage of GDP (*CA*);
12 nominal interest rate (*R*);
13 real interest rate (*r*); and
14 consumer price index (*CPI*).

PRODFUN (production function data)

Data from a business survey in a developing country reporting the data for two manufacturing sectors and covering 109 firms. The following variables are included:

1   *SECTOR* (4 or 9 corresponding to the sector number);
2   logged output (Q)
3   logged capital stock (K); and
4   logged employment (L).

SIMSIM (supply and demand model)

Data simulated (40 observations) from the model in equations 13.1 to 13.3. The variables are:

1   *OBS*;
2   quantity (Q);
3   price (P); and
4   income (Y).
5   advertising (ADV)

SOCECON (world socioeconomic data)

The file SOCECON contains a selection of socioeconomic data, taken from various sources as indicated below, for a total of 125 countries with 1990 as the reference year. The sample size for different exercises or examples will vary due to missing observations for some of the variables involved. Data are from the World Bank's *World Tables* and *Social Indicators of Development* and the UNDP's *Human Development Report*. The data set contains the following variables:

1   GNP per capita, 1990 (data from the World Bank's *World Tables*);
2   *LEX*, 1990: life expectancy at birth (*World Development Report* 1992);
3   *LEXPF*, 1990: life expectancy female (*World Development Report* 1992);
4   *LEXPM*, 1990: life expectancy male (*World Development Report* 1992);
5   *ADULIT*, 1990: adult literacy rate (per cent) (*Human Development Report* 1993);
6   *HDI*, 1990: human development index (*Human Development Report* 1993);
7   *FERTR*, 1990: total fertility rate (*World Development Report* 1992);
8   *BIRTHR*, 1990: crude birth rate per 1,000 population (*World Development Report* 1992);
9   *POP*, 1990: population (World Bank's *World Tables*);
10   POPGTH, 1990: annual population growth rate (per cent) *World Social Indicators* database);

11 *CHILDMF*, 1990: female under 5 mortality rate per 1,000 live births (*World Development Report* 1992);

12 *CHILDMM*, 1990: male under 5 mortality rate per 1,000 live births (*World Development Report* 1992);

13 *INFMOR*, 1990: infant mortality rate per 1,000 live births (*World Development Report* 1992);

14 *URBANPOP*, 1990: urban population as a percentage of total population 1991 (World Bank's *World Tables*);

15 *ENERGCPC*, 1990: energy consumption per capita (World Bank's *World Tables*);

16 *PPPGDP*: per capita gross domestic product in purchasing power party dollars;

17 *HEALTHAC*: per cent of population with access to health services;

18 *WATERAC*: per cent of population with access to clean water;

19 *SANITAT*: per cent of population with access to sanitation facilities;

20 *MVA*: manufacturing value added (as a per cent of GDP);

21 *COUNTRY*, country long name (not included in ASCII file);

22 *CID*, country short name (not included in ASCII file).

SRINA (Sri Lanka macroeconomic data)

A macroeconomic data set for the years 1967–93. All variables are in constant prices. (From the World Bank's *World Tables* and G. Pfefferman and A. Madarassay (various years) *Trends in Private Investment in Developing Countries*, New York: World Bank, for the public/private investment split.) All aggregates are in constant prices. The variables are:

1 *YEAR*;
2 *GDP*;
3 exports (X);
4 imports (M);
5 private consumption (C_p);
6 government consumption (C_g);
7 total consumption (CN);
8 investment (I);
9 private investment (I_p);
10 government investment (I_g);
11 real interest rate (r).

SURE (data for seemingly unrelated regressions)

Data simulated from equations (14.47) and (14.48). The variables are:

1 *YEAR*;
2 quantity for good 1 (Q_1);
3 quantity for good 2 (Q_2);
4 price for good 1 (P_1); and
5 price for good 2 (P_2).

TANMON (money and prices in Tanzania)

Data from the World Bank's *World Tables* and IMF's *International Finance Statistics* for the years 1966–92, covering:

1 *YEAR*;
2 consumer price index (*CPI*);
3 money supply (*M2*); and
4 real export growth (*XGRO*).

TANZANIA (government expenditure and revenue data)

The following data on government finance are taken from the Tanzanian Economic Surveys for the period 1970–90. All data series are deflated by the consumer price index:

1 government recurrent revenue (*REV*);
2 government recurrent expenditures (*REXP*);
3 government development expenditures (*DEXP*);
4 year (*T*): 1970–90.

TOT (developing countries' terms of trade)

The data are the ratio of price indices for non-fuel primary commodities and manufactured goods for the period 1950–86 taken from Grilli and Yang (1988). The file contains:

1 *YEAR*; and
2 terms of trade (*TOT*).

TPEASANT (farm size and household size data, rural Tanzania)

This file contains grouped data (eight classes) based on a sample of 600 peasant households as published by Collier *et al.* (1986: 50, Table 3.12). The data are grouped by classes of farm sizes. The file has the following variables:

1 mean farm size (*F*) in acres;
2 mean household size (*H*): number of persons;
3 per cent of households in each group (percent).

Appendix B   Statistical tables

Note: Tables B.1–B.6 are reproduced, with permission, from D. Gujarati, *Basic Econometrics*, 2nd edn, New York: McGraw-Hill, 1988. The original sources are noted on each table.

Table B.1   Areas under the standardised normal distribution

Example

Pr $(0 \leqslant z \leqslant 1.9607 = 0.4750$

Pr $(z \geqslant 1.96) = 0.5 - 0.4750 = 0.025$

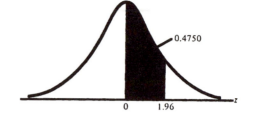

z	0.00	0.01	0.02	0.03	0.04	0.05	0.06	0.07	0.08	0.09
0.0	0.0000	0.0040	0.0080	0.0120	0.0160	0.0199	0.0239	0.0279	0.0319	0.0359
0.1	0.0398	0.0438	0.0478	0.0517	0.0557	0.0596	0.0636	0.0675	0.0714	0.0753
0.2	0.0793	0.0832	0.0871	0.0910	0.0948	0.0987	0.1026	0.1064	0.1103	0.1141
0.3	0.1179	0.1217	0.1255	0.1293	0.1331	0.1368	0.1406	0.1443	0.1480	0.1517
0.4	0.1554	0.1591	0.1628	0.1664	0.1700	0.1736	0.1772	0.1808	0.1844	0.1879
0.5	0.1915	0.1950	0.1985	0.2019	0.2054	0.2088	0.2123	0.2157	0.2190	0.2224
0.6	0.2257	0.2291	0.2324	0.2357	0.2389	0.2422	0.2454	0.2486	0.2517	0.2549
0.7	0.2580	0.2611	0.2642	0.2673	0.2704	0.2734	0.2764	0.2794	0.2823	0.2852
0.8	0.2881	0.2910	0.2939	0.2967	0.2995	0.3023	0.3051	0.3078	0.3106	0.3133
0.9	0.3159	0.3186	0.3212	0.3238	0.3264	0.3289	0.3315	0.3340	0.3365	0.3389
1.0	0.3413	0.3438	0.3461	0.3485	0.3508	0.3531	0.3554	0.3577	0.3599	0.3621
1.1	0.3643	0.3665	0.3686	0.3708	0.3729	0.3749	0.3770	0.3790	0.3810	0.3830
1.2	0.3849	0.3869	0.3888	0.3907	0.3925	0.3944	0.3962	0.3980	0.3997	0.4015
1.3	0.4032	0.4049	0.4066	0.4082	0.4099	0.4115	0.4131	0.4 147	0.4162	0.4177
1.4	0.4192	0.4207	0.4222	0.4236	0.4251	0.4265	0.4279	0.4292	0.4306	0.4319
1.5	0.4332	0.4345	0.4357	0.4370	0.4382	0.4394	0.4406	0.4418	0.4429	0.4441
1.6	0.4452	0.4463	0.4474	0.4484	0.4495	0.4505	0.4515	0.4525	0.4535	0.4545
1.7	0.4554	0.4564	0.4573	0.4582	0.4591	0.4599	0.4608	0.4616	0.4625	0.4633
1.8	0.4641	0.4649	0.4656	0.4664	0.4671	0.4678	0.4686	0.4693	0.4699	0.4706
1.9	0.4713	0.4719	0.4726	0.4732	0.4738	0.4744	0.4750	0.4756	0.4761	0.4767
2.0	0.4772	0.4778	0.4783	0.4788	0.4793	0.4798	0.4803	0.4808	0.4812	0.4817
2.1	0.4821	0.4826	0.4830	0.4834	0.4838	0.4842	0.4846	0.4850	0.4854	0.4857
2.2	0.4861	0.4864	0.4868	0.4871	0.4875	0.4878	0.4881	0.4884	0.4887	0.4890
2.3	0.4893	0.4896	0.4901	0.48901	0.4904	0.4906	0.4909	0.4911	0.4913	0.4916
2.4	0.4918	0.4920	0.4922	0.4925	0.4927	0.4929	0.4931	0.4932	0.4934	0.4936
2.5	0.4938	0.4940	0.4941	0.4943	0.4945	0.4946	0.4948	0.4949	0.4951	0.4952
2.6	0.4953	0.4955	0.4956	0.4957	0.4959	0.4960	0.4961	0.4962	0.4963	0.4964
2.7	0.4965	0.4966	0.4967	0.4968	0.4969	0.4970	0.4971	0.4972	0.4973	0.4974
2.8	0.4974	0.4975	0.4976	0.4977	0.4977	0.4978	0.4979	0.4979	0.4980	0.4981
2.9	0.4981	0.4982	0.4982	0.4983	0.4984	0.4984	0.4985	0.4985	0.4986	0.4986
3.0	0.4987	0.4987	0.4987	0.4988	0.4988	0.4989	0.4989	0.4990	0.4990	0.4990

Note: This table gives the area in the right-hand tail distribution (i.e., $z \geqslant 0$). But since the normal distribution is symmetrical about $z = 0$, the area in the left-hand tail is the same as the area in the corresponding right-hand tail. For example, $P(-1.96 \leqslant z \leqslant 0) = 0.4750$. Therefore, $P(-1.96 \leqslant z \leqslant 1.96) = 2(0.4750) = 0.95$.

Table B.2 Percentage points of the *t* distribution

Example

Pr (*t* > 2.086) = 0.025

Pr (*t* > 1.725) = 0.05 for df = 20

Pr (|*t*| > 1.725) = 0.10

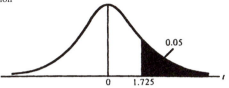

Pr Df	0.025 0.50	0.10 0.20	0.05 0.10	0.025 0.05	0.01 0.02	0.005 0.010	0.001 0.002
1	1.000	3.078	6.314	12.706	31.821	63.657	318.31
2	0.816	1.886	2.920	4.303	6.965	9.925	22.327
3	0.765	1.638	2.353	3.182	4.541	5.841	10.214
4	0.741	1.533	2.132	2.776	3.747	4.604	7.173
5	0.727	1.476	2.015	2.571	3.365	4.032	5.893
6	0.718	1.440	1.943	2.447	3.143	3.707	5.208
7	0.711	1.415	1.895	2.365	2.998	3.499	4.785
8	0.706	1.397	1.860	2.306	2.896	3.350	4.501
9	0.703	1.383	1.833	2.262	2.821	3.250	4.297
10	0.700	1.372	1.812	2.228	2.764	3.169	4.144
11	0.698	1.363	1.796	2.201	2.718	3.106	4.025
12	0.695	1.356	1.782	2.179	2.681	3.055	3.930
13	0.694	1.350	1.771	2.160	2.650	3.012	3.852
14	0.692	1.345	1.761	2.145	2.624	2.977	3.787
15	0.691	1.341	1.753	2.131	2.602	2.947	3.733
16	0.690	1.337	1.746	2.120	2.583	2.921	3.686
17	0.689	1.333	1.740	2.110	2.567	2.898	3.646
18	0.688	1.330	1.734	2.101	2.552	2.878	3.610
19	0.688	1.328	1.729	2.093	2.539	2.861	3.579
20	0.687	1.325	1.725	2.086	2.528	2.845	3.552
21	0.686	1.323	1.721	2.080	2.518	2.831	3.527
22	0.686	1.321	1.717	2.074	2.508	2.819	3.505
23	0.685	1.319	1.714	2.069	2.500	2.807	3.485
24	0.685	1.318	1.711	2.064	2.492	2.797	3.467
25	0.684	1.316	1.708	2.060	2.485	2.787	3.450
26	0.684	1.315	1.706	2.056	2.479	2.779	3.435
27	0.684	1.314	1.703	2.052	2.473	2.771	3.421
28	0.683	1.313	1.701	2.048	2.467	2.763	3.408
29	0.683	1.311	1.699	2.045	2.462	2.756	3.396
30	0.683	1.310	1.697	2.042	2.457	2.750	3.385
40	0.681	1.303	1.684	2.021	2.423	2.704	3.307
60	0.679	1.296	1.671	2.000	2.390	2.660	3.232
120	0.677	1.289	1.658	1.980	2.358	2.167	3.160
∞	0.674	1.282	1.645	1.960	2.326	2.576	3.090

Note: The smaller probability shown at the head of each column is the area in one tail; the larger probability is the area in both tails.

Source: From E.S. Pearson and H.O. Hartley (eds), *Biometrika Tables for Statisticians*, 3rd edn, New York: Cambridge University Press, 1966.

Table B.3   Upper percentage points of the *F* distribution

Example
Pr $(F > 1.59) = 0.25$
Pr $(F > 2.42) = 0.10$ for df $N_1 = 10$
Pr $(F > 3.14) = 0.05$ and $N_2 = 9$
Pr $(F > 5.26) = 0.01$

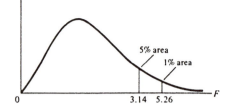

df for denominator N_2	Pr	1	2	3	4	5	6	7	8	9	10	11	12
							df for numerator N_1						
1	0.25	5.83	7.50	8.20	8.58	8.82	8.98	9.10	9.19	9.26	9.32	9.36	9.41
	0.10	39.9	49.5	53.6	55.8	57.2	58.2	58.9	59.4	59.9	60.2	60.5	60.7
	0.05	161	200	216	225	230	234	237	239	241	242	243	244
2	0.25	2.57	3.00	3.15	3.23	3.28	3.31	3.34	3.35	3.37	3.38	3.39	3.39
	0.10	8.53	9.00	9.16	9.24	9.29	9.33	9.35	9.37	9.38	9.39	9.40	9.41
	0.05	18.5	19.0	19.2	19.2	19.3	19.3	19.4	19.4	19.4	19.4	19.4	19.4
	0.01	98.5	99.0	99.2	99.2	99.3	99.3	99.4	99.4	99.4	99.4	99.4	99.4
3	0.25	2.02	2.28	2.36	2.39	2.41	2.42	2.43	2.44	2.44	2.44	2.45	2.45
	0.10	5.54	5.46	5.39	5.34	5.31	5.28	5.27	5.25	5.24	5.23	5.22	5.22
	0.05	10.1	9.55	9.28	9.12	9.01	8.94	8.89	8.85	8.81	8.79	8.76	8.74
	0.01	34.1	30.8	29.5	28.7	28.2	27.9	27.7	27.5	27.3	27.2	27.1	27.0
4	0.25	1.81	2.00	2.05	2.06	2.07	2.08	2.08	2.08	2.08	2.08	2.08	2.08
	0.10	4.54	4.32	4.19	4.11	4.05	4.01	3.98	3.95	3.94	3.92	3.91	3.90
	0.05	7.71	6.94	6.59	6.39	6.26	6.16	6.09	6.04	6.00	5.96	5.94	5.91
	0.01	21.2	18.0	16.7	16.0	15.5	15.2	15.0	14.8	14.7	14.5	14.4	14.4
5	0.25	1.69	1.85	1.88	1.89	1.89	1.89	1.89	1.89	1.89	1.89	1.89	1.89
	0.10	4.06	3.78	3.62	3.52	3.45	3.40	3.37	3.34	3.32	3.30	3.28	3.27
	0.05	6.61	5.79	5.41	5.19	5.05	4.95	4.88	4.82	4.77	4.74	4.71	4.68
	0.01	16.3	13.3	12.1	11.4	11.0	10.7	10.5	10.3	10.2	10.1	9.96	9.89
6	0.25	1.62	1.76	1.78	1.79	1.79	1.78	1.78	1.78	1.77	1.77	1.77	1.77
	0.10	3.78	3.46	3.29	3.18	3.11	3.05	3.01	2.98	2.96	2.94	2.92	2.90
	0.05	5.99	5.14	4.76	4.53	4.39	4.28	4.21	4.15	4.10	4.06	4.03	4.00
	0.01	12.2	10.9	9.78	9.15	8.75	8.47	8.26	8.10	7.89	7.87	7.79	7.72
7	0.25	1.57	1.70	1.72	1.72	1.71	1.71	1.70	1.70	1.69	1.69	1.69	1.68
	0.10	3.59	3.26	3.07	2.96	2.88	2.83	2.78	2.75	2.72	2.70	2.68	2.67
	0.05	5.59	4.74	4.35	4.12	3.97	3.87	3.79	3.73	3.68	3.64	3.60	3.57
	0.01	12.2	9.55	8.45	7.85	7.46	7.19	6.99	6.84	6.72	6.62	6.54	6.47
8	0.25	1.54	1.66	1.67	1.66	1.66	1.65	1.64	1.64	1.63	1.63	1.63	1.62
	0.10	3.46	3.11	2.92	2.81	2.73	2.67	2.62	2.59	2.56	2.54	2.52	2.50
	0.05	5.32	4.46	4.07	3.84	3.69	3.58	3.50	3.44	3.39	3.35	3.31	3.28
	0.01	11.3	8.65	7.59	7.01	6.63	6.37	6.18	6.03	5.91	5.81	5.73	5.67
9	0.25	1.51	1.62	1.63	1.63	1.62	1.61	1.60	1.60	1.59	1.59	1.58	1.58
	0.10	3.36	3.01	2.81	2.69	2.61	2.55	2.51	2.47	2.44	2.42	2.40	2.38
	0.05	5.12	4.26	3.86	3.63	3.48	3.37	3.29	3.23	3.18	3.14	3.10	3.07
	0.01	10.6	8.02	6.99	6.42	6.06	5.80	5.61	5.47	5.35	5.26	5.18	5.11

Table B.3   – *Continued*

15	20	24	30	40	50	60	100	120	200	500	∞	Pr	df for denom- inator N_1
				df for denominator N_1									
9.49	9.58	9.63	9.67	9.71	9.74	9.76	9.78	9.80	9.82	9.84	9.85	0.25	
61.2	61.7	62.0	62.3	62.5	62.7	62.8	63.0	63.1	63.2	63.3	63.3	0.10	1
246	248	249	250	251	252	252	253	253	254	254	254	0.05	
3.41	3.43	3.43	3.44	3.45	3.45	3.46	3.47	3.47	3.48	3.48	3.48	0.25	
9.42	9.44	9.45	9.46	9.47	9.47	9.47	9.48	9.48	9.49	9.49	9.49	0.10	2
19.4	19.4	19.5	19.5	19.5	19.5	19.5	19.5	19.5	19.5	19.5	19.5	0.05	
99.4	99.4	99.5	99.5	99.5	99.5	99.5	99.5	99.5	99.5	99.5	99.5	0.01	
2.46	2.46	2.46	2.47	2.47	2.47	2.47	2.47	2.47	2.47	2.47	2.47	0.25	
5.20	5.18	5.18	5.17	5.16	5.15	5.15	5.14	5.14	5.14	5.14	5.13	0.10	3
8.70	8.66	8.64	8.62	8.59	8.58	8.57	8.55	8.55	8.54	8.53	8.53	0.05	
26.9	26.7	26.6	26.5	26.4	26.4	26.3	26.2	26.2	26.2	26.1	26.1	0.01	
2.08	2.08	2.08	2.08	2.08	2.08	2.08	2.08	2.08	2.08	2.08	2.08	0.25	
3.87	3.84	3.83	3.82	3.80	3.80	3.79	3.78	3.78	3.77	3.76	3.76	0.10	4
5.86	5.80	5.77	5.75	5.72	5.70	5.69	5.66	5.66	5.65	5.64	5.63	0.05	
14.2	14.0	13.9	13.8	13.7	13.7	13.7	13.6	13.6	13.5	13.5	13.5	0.01	
1.89	1.88	1.88	1.88	1.88	1.88	1.87	1.87	1.87	1.87	1.87	1.87	0.25	
3.24	3.21	3.19	3.17	3.16	3.15	3.14	3.13	3.12	3.12	3.11	3.10	0.10	5
4.62	4.56	4.53	4.50	4.46	4.44	4.43	4.41	4.40	4.39	4.37	4.36	0.05	
9.72	9.55	9.47	9.38	9.29	9.24	9.20	9.13	9.11	9.08	9.04	9.02	0.01	
1.76	1.76	1.75	1.75	1.75	1.75	1.74	1.74	1.74	1.74	1.74	1.74	0.25	
2.87	2.84	2.82	2.80	2.78	2.77	2.76	2.75	2.74	2.73	2.73	2.72	0.10	6
3.94	3.87	3.84	3.81	3.77	3.75	3.74	3.71	3.70	3.69	3.68	3.67	0.05	
7.56	7.40	7.31	7.23	7.14	7.09	7.06	6.99	6.97	6.93	6.90	6.88	0.01	
1.68	1.67	1.67	1.66	1.66	1.66	1.65	1.65	1.65	1.65	1.65	1.65	0.25	
2.63	2.59	2.58	2.56	2.54	2.52	2.51	2.50	2.49	2.48	2.48	2.47	0.01	7
3.51	3.44	3.41	3.38	3.34	3.32	3.30	3.27	3.27	3.25	3.24	3.23	0.05	
6.31	6.16	6.07	5.99	5.91	5.86	5.82	5.75	5.74	5.70	5.67	5.65	0.01	
1.62	1.61	1.60	1.60	1.59	1.59	1.59	1.58	1.58	1.58	1.58	1.58	0.25	
2.46	2.42	2.40	2.38	2.36	2.35	2.34	2.32	2.32	2.31	2.30	2.16	0.10	8
3.22	3.15	3.12	3.08	3.04	2.02	3.01	2.97	2.97	2.95	2.94	2.93	0.05	
5.52	5.36	5.28	5.20	5.12	5.07	5.03	4.96	4.95	4.91	4.88	4.86	0.01	
1.57	1.56	1.56	1.55	1.55	1.54	1.54	1.53	1.53	1.53	1.53	1.53	0.25	
2.34	2.30	2.28	2.25	2.23	2.22	2.21	2.19	2.18	2.17	2.17	2.16	0.10	9
3.01	2.94	2.90	2.86	2.83	2.80	2.79	2.76	2.75	2.73	2.72	2.71	0.05	
4.96	4.81	4.73	4.65	4.57	4.52	4.48	4.42	4.40	4.36	4.33	4.31	0.01	

Source: As Table B.2: table 18

Table B.3   Upper percentage points of the F distribution

df for denom-inator N_2	Pr	df for numerator N_1											
		1	2	3	4	5	6	7	8	9	10	11	12
10	0.25	1.49	1.60	1.60	1.59	1.59	1.58	1.57	1.56	1.56	1.55	1.55	1.54
	0.10	3.29	2.92	2.73	2.61	2.52	2.46	2.41	2.38	2.35	2.32	2.30	2.28
	0.05	4.96	4.10	3.71	3.48	3.33	3.22	3.14	3.07	3.02	2.98	2.94	2.91
	0.01	10.0	7.56	6.55	5.99	5.64	5.39	5.20	5.06	4.94	4.85	4.77	4.71
11	0.25	1.47	1.58	1.58	1.57	1.56	1.55	1.54	1.53	1.53	1.52	1.52	1.51
	0.10	3.23	2.86	2.66	2.54	2.45	2.39	2.34	2.30	2.27	2.25	2.23	2.21
	0.05	4.84	3.98	3.59	3.36	3.20	3.09	3.01	2.95	2.90	2.85	2.82	2.79
	0.01	9.65	7.21	6.22	5.67	5.32	5.07	4.89	4.74	4.63	4.54	4.46	4.40
12	0.25	1.46	1.56	1.56	1.55	1.54	1.53	1.52	1.51	1.51	1.50	1.50	1.49
	0.10	3.18	2.81	2.61	2.48	2.39	2.33	2.28	2.24	2.21	2.19	2.17	2.15
	0.05	4.75	3.89	3.49	3.26	3.11	3.00	2.91	2.85	2.80	2.75	2.72	2.69
	0.01	9.33	6.93	5.95	5.41	5.06	4.82	4.64	4.50	4.39	4.30	4.22	4.16
13	0.25	1.45	1.55	1.55	1.53	1.52	1.51	1.50	1.49	1.49	1.48	1.47	1.47
	0.10	3.14	2.76	2.56	2.43	2.35	2.28	2.23	2.20	2.16	2.14	2.12	2.10
	0.05	4.67	3.81	3.41	3.18	3.03	2.92	2.83	2.77	2.71	2.67	2.63	2.60
	0.01	9.07	6.70	5.74	5.21	4.86	4.62	4.44	4.30	4.19	4.10	4.02	3.96
14	0.25	1.44	1.53	1.53	1.52	1.51	1.50	1.49	1.48	1.47	1.46	1.46	1.45
	0.10	3.10	2.73	2.52	2.39	2.31	2.24	2.19	2.15	2.12	2.10	2.08	2.05
	0.05	4.60	3.74	3.34	3.11	2.96	2.85	2.76	2.70	2.65	2.60	2.57	2.53
	0.01	8.86	6.51	5.56	5.04	4.69	4.46	4.28	4.14	4.03	3.94	3.86	3.80
15	0.25	1.43	1.52	1.52	1.51	1.49	1.48	1.47	1.46	1.46	1.45	1.44	1.44
	0.10	3.07	2.70	2.49	2.36	2.27	2.21	2.16	2.12	2.09	2.06	2.04	2.02
	0.05	4.54	3.68	3.29	3.06	2.90	2.79	2.71	2.64	2.59	2.54	2.51	2.48
	0.01	8.86	6.36	5.42	4.89	4.56	4.32	4.14	4.00	3.89	3.80	3.73	3.67
16	0.25	1.42	1.51	1.51	1.50	1.48	1.47	1.46	1.45	1.44	1.44	1.44	1.43
	0.10	3.05	2.67	2.46	2.33	2.24	2.18	2.13	2.09	2.06	2.03	2.01	1.99
	0.05	4.49	3.63	3.24	3.01	2.85	2.74	2.66	2.59	2.54	2.49	2.46	2.42
	0.01	8.53	6.23	5.29	4.77	4.44	4.20	4.03	3.89	3.78	3.69	3.62	3.55
17	0.25	1.42	1.51	1.50	1.49	1.47	1.46	1.45	1.44	1.43	1.43	1.42	1.41
	0.10	3.03	2.64	2.44	2.31	2.22	2.15	2.10	2.06	2.03	2.00	1.98	1.96
	0.05	4.45	3.59	3.20	2.96	2.81	2.70	2.61	2.55	2.49	2.45	2.41	2.38
	0.01	8.40	6.11	5.18	4.67	4.34	4.10	3.93	3.79	3.68	3.59	3.52	3.46
18	0.25	1.41	1.50	1.49	1.48	1.46	1.45	1.44	1.43	1.42	1.42	1.41	1.40
	0.10	3.01	2.62	2.42	2.29	2.20	2.13	2.08	2.04	2.00	1.98	1.96	1.93
	0.05	4.41	3.55	3.16	2.93	2.77	2.66	2.58	2.51	2.46	2.41	2.37	2.34
	0.01	8.29	6.01	5.09	4.58	4.25	4.01	3.84	3.71	3.60	3.51	3.43	3.37
19	0.25	1.41	1.49	1.49	1.47	1.46	1.44	1.43	1.42	1.41	1.41	1.40	1.40
	0.10.	2.99	2.61	2.40	2.27	2.18	2.11	2.06	2.02	1.98	1.96	1.94	1.91
	0.05	4.38	3.52	3.13	2.90	2.74	2.63	2.54	2.48	2.42	2.38	2.34	2.31
	0.01	8.18	5.93	5.01	4.50	4.17	3.94	3.77	3.63	3.52	3.43	3.36	3.30
20	0.25	1.40	1.49	1.48	1.46	1.45	1.44	1.43	1.42	1.41	1.40	1.39	1.39
	0.10	2.97	2.59	2.38	2.25	2.16	2.09	2.04	2.00	1.96	1.94	1.92	1.89
	0.05	4.35	3.49	3.10	2.87	2.71	2.60	2.51	2.45	2.39	2.35	2.31	2.28
	0.01	8.10	5.85	4.94	4.43	4.10	3.87	3.70	3.56	3.46	3.37	3.29	3.23

Table B.3 – Continued

	df for denominator N_1												df for denominator N_2
15	20	24	30	40	50	60	100	120	200	500	∞	Pr	
1.53	1.52	1.52	1.51	1.51	1.50	1.50	1.49	1.49	1.49	1.48	1.48	0.25	
2.24	2.20	2.18	2.16	2.13	2.12	2.11	2.09	2.08	2.07	2.06	2.06	0.10	10
2.85	2.77	2.74	2.70	2.66	2.64	2.62	2.59	2.58	2.56	2.55	2.54	0.05	
4.56	4.41	4.33	4.25	4.17	4.12	4.08	4.01	4.00	3.96	3.93	3.91	0.01	
1.50	1.49	1.49	1.48	1.47	1.47	1.47	1.46	1.46	1.46	1.45	1.45	0.25	
2.17	2.12	2.10	2.08	2.05	2.04	2.03	2.00	2.00	1.99	1.98	1.97	0.10	11
2.72	2.65	2.61	2.57	2.53	2.51	2.49	2.46	2.45	2.43	2.42	2.40	0.05	
4.25	4.10	4.02	3.94	3.86	3.81	3.78	3.71	3.69	3.66	3.62	3.60	0.01	
1.48	1.47	1.46	1.45	1.45	1.44	1.44	1.43	1.43	1.43	1.42	1.42	0.25	
2.10	2.06	2.04	2.01	1.99	1.97	1.96	1.94	1.93	1.92	1.91	1.90	0.10	12
2.62	2.54	2.51	2.47	2.43	2.40	2.38	2.35	2.34	2.32	2.31	2.30	0.05	
4.01	3.86	3.78	3.70	3.62	3.57	3.54	3.47	3.45	3.41	3.38	3.36	0.01	
1.46	1.45	1.44	1.43	1.42	1.42	1.42	1.41	1.41	1.40	1.40	1.40	0.25	
2.05	2.01	1.98	1.96	1.93	1.92	1.90	1.88	1.88	1.86	1.85	1.85	0.10	13
2.53	2.46	2.42	2.38	2.34	2.31	2.30	2.26	2.25	2.23	2.22	2.21	0.05	
3.82	3.66	3.59	3.51	3.43	3.38	3.34	3.27	3.25	3.22	3.19	3.17	0.01	
1.44	1.43	1.42	1.41	1.41	1.40	1.40	1.39	1.39	1.39	1.38	1.38	0.25	
2.01	1.96	1.94	1.91	1.89	1.87	1.86	1.83	1.83	1.82	1.80	1.80	0.10	14
2.46	2.39	2.35	2.31	2.27	2.24	2.22	2.19	2.18	2.16	2.14	2.13	0.05	
3.66	3.51	3.43	3.35	3.27	3.22	3.18	3.11	3.09	3.06	3.03	3.00	0.01	
1.43	1.41	1.41	1.40	1.39	1.39	1.38	1.38	1.37	1.37	1.36	1.36	0.25	
1.97	1.92	1.90	1.87	1.85	1.83	1.82	1.79	1.79	1.77	1.76	1.76	0.10	15
2.40	2.33	2.29	2.25	2.20	2.18	2.16	2.12	2.11	2.10	2.08	2.07	0.05	
3.52	3.37	3.29	3.21	3.13	3.08	3.05	2.98	2.96	2.92	2.89	2.87	0.01	
1.41	1.40	1.39	1.38	1.37	1.37	1.36	1.36	1.35	1.35	1.34	1.34	0.25	
1.94	1.89	1.87	1.84	1.81	1.79	1.78	1.76	1.75	1.74	1.73	1.72	0.10	16
2.35	2.28	2.24	2.19	2.15	2.12	2.11	2.07	2.06	2.04	2.02	2.01	0.05	
3.41	3.26	3.18	3.10	3.02	2.97	2.93	2.86	2.84	2.81	2.78	2.75	0.01	
1.40	1.39	1.38	1.37	1.36	1.35	1.35	1.34	1.34	1.34	1.33	1.33	0.25	
1.91	1.86	1.84	1.81	1.78	1.76	1.75	1.73	1.72	1.71	1.69	1.69	0.10	17
2.31	2.23	2.19	2.15	2.10	2.08	2.06	2.02	2.01	1.99	1.97	1.96	0.05	
3.31	3.16	3.08	3.00	2.92	2.87	2.83	2.76	2.75	2.71	2.68	2.65	0.01	
1.39	1.38	1.37	1.36	1.35	1.34	1.34	1.33	1.33	1.32	1.32	1.32	0.25	
1.89	1.84	1.81	1.78	1.75	1.74	1.72	1.70	1.69	1.68	1.67	1.66	0.10	18
2.27	2.19	2.15	2.11	2.06	2.04	2.02	1.98	1.97	1.95	1.93	1.92	0.05	
3.23	3.08	3.00	2.92	2.84	2.78	2.75	2.68	2.66	2.62	2.59	2.57	0.01	
1.38	1.37	1.36	1.35	1.34	1.33	1.33	1.32	1.32	1.31	1.31	1.30	0.25	
1.86	1.81	1.79	1.76	1.73	1.71	1.70	1.67	1.67	1.65	1.64	1.63	0.10	19
2.23	2.16	2.11	2.07	2.03	2.00	1.98	1.94	1.93	1.91	1.89	1.88	0.05	
3.15	3.00	2.92	2.84	2.76	2.71	2.67	2.60	2.58	2.55	2.51	2.49	0.01	
1.37	1.36	1.35	1.34	1.33	1.33	1.32	1.31	1.31	1.30	1.30	1.29	0.25	
1.84	1.79	1.77	1.74	1.71	1.69	1.68	1.65	1.64	1.63	1.62	1.61	0.10	20
2.20	2.12	2.08	2.04	1.99	1.97	1.95	1.91	1.90	1.88	1.86	1.84	0.05	
3.09	2.94	2.86	2.78	2.69	2.64	2.61	2.54	2.52	2.48	2.44	2.42	0.01	

Table B.3 – Continued

df for denominator N_2	Pr	1	2	3	4	5	6	7	8	9	10	11	12
						df for numerator N_1							
22	0.25	1.40	1.48	1.47	1.45	1.44	1.42	1.41	1.40	1.39	1.39	1.38	1.37
	0.10	2.95	2.56	2.35	2.22	2.13	2.06	2.01	1.97	1.93	1.90	1.88	1.86
	0.05	4.30	3.44	3.05	2.82	2.66	2.55	2.46	2.40	2.34	2.30	2.26	2.23
	0.01	7.95	5.72	4.82	4.31	3.99	3.76	3.59	3.45	3.35	3.26	3.18	3.12
24	0.25	1.39	1.47	1.46	1.44	1.43	1.41	1.40	1.39	1.38	1.38	1.37	1.36
	0.10	2.93	2.54	2.33	2.19	2.10	2.04	1.98	1.94	1.91	1.88	1.85	1.83
	0.05	4.26	3.40	3.01	2.78	2.62	2.51	2.42	2.36	2.30	2.25	2.21	2.18
	0.01	7.82	5.61	4.72	4.22	3.90	3.67	3.50	3.36	3.26	3.17	3.09	3.03
26	0.25	1.38	1.46	1.45	1.44	1.42	1.41	1.39	1.38	1.37	1.37	1.36	1.35
	0.10	2.91	2.52	2.31	2.17	2.08	2.01	1.96	1.92	1.88	1.86	1.84	1.81
	0.05	4.23	3.37	2.98	2.74	2.59	2.47	2.39	2.32	2.27	2.22	2.18	2.15
	0.01	7.72	5.53	4.64	4.14	3.82	3.59	3.42	3.29	3.18	3.09	˙3.02	2.96
28	0.25	1.38	1.46	1.45	1.43	1.41	1.40	1.39	1.38	1.37	1.36	1.35	1.34
	0.10	2.89	2.50	2.29	2.16	2.06	2.00	1.94	1.90	1.87	1.84	1.81	1.79
	0.05	4.20	3.34	2.95	2.71	2.56	2.45	2.36	2.29	2.24	2.19	2.15	2.12
	0.01	7.64	5.45	4.57	4.07	3.75	3.53	3.36	3.23	3.12	3.03	2.96	2.90
30	0.25	1.38	1.45	1.44	1.42	1.41	1.39	1.38	1.37	1.36	1.35	1.35	1.34
	0.10	2.88	2.49	2.28	2.14	2.05	1.98	1.93	1.88	1.85	1.82	1.79	1.77
	0.05	4.17	3.32	2.92	2.69	2.53	2.42	2.33	2.27	2.21	2.16	2.13	2.09
	0.01	7.56	5.39	4.51	4.02	3.70	3.47	3.30	3.17	3.07	2.98	2.91	2.84
40	0.25	1.36	1.44	1.42	1.40	1.39	1.37	1.36	1.35	1.34	1.33	1.32	1.31
	0.10	2.84	2.44	2.23	2.09	2.00	1.93	1.87	1.83	1.79	1.76	1.73	1.71
	0.05	4.08	3.23	2.84	2.61	2.45	2.34	2.25	2.18	2.12	2.08	2.04	2.00
	0.01	7.31	5.18	4.31	3.83	3.51	3.29	3.12	2.99	2.89	2.80	2.73	2.66
60	0.25	1.35	1.42	1.41	1.38	1.37	1.35	1.33	1.32	1.31	1.30	1.29	1.29
	0.10	2.79	2.39	2.18	2.04	1.95	1.87	1.82	1.77	1.74	1.71	1.68	1.66
	0.05	4.00	3.15	2.76	2.53	2.37	2.25	2.17	2.10	2.04	1.99	1.95	1.92
	0.01	7.08	4.98	4.13	3.65	3.34	3.12	2.95	2.82	2.72	2.63	2.56	2.50
120	0.25	1.34	1.40	1.39	1.37	1.35	1.33	1.31	1.30	1.29	1.28	1.27	1.26
	0.10	2.75	2.35	2.13	1.99	1.90	1.82	1.77	1.72	1.68	1.65	1.62	1.60
	0.05	3.92	3.07	2.68	2.45	2.29	2.17	2.09	2.02	1.96	1.91	1.87	1.83
	0.01	6.85	4.79	3.95	3.48	3.17	2.96	2.79	2.66	2.56	2.47	2.40	2.34
200	0.25	1.33	1.39	1.38	1.36	1.34	1.32	1.31	1.29	1.28	1.27	1.26	1.25
	0.10	2.73	2.33	2.11	1.97	1.88	1.80	1.75	1.70	1.66	1.63	1.60	1.57
	0.05	3.89	3.04	2.65	2.42	2.26	2.14	2.06	1.98	1.93	1.88	1.84	1.80
	0.01	6.76	4.71	3.88	3.41	3.11	2.89	2.73	2.60	2.50	2.41	2.34	2.27
∞	0.25	1.32	1.39	1.37	1.35	1.33	1.31	1.29	1.28	1.27	1.25	1.24	1.24
	0.10	2.71	2.30	2.08	1.94	1.85	1.77	1.72	1.67	1.63	1.60	1.57	1.55
	0.05	3.84	3.00	2.60	2.37	2.21	2.10	2.01	1.94	1.88	1.83	1.79	1.75
	0.01	6.63	4.61	3.78	3.32	3.02	2.80	2.64	2.51	2.41	2.32	2.25	2.18

Table B.3 – Continued

					df for denominator N_1								df for denominator N_2
15	20	24	30	40	50	60	100	120	200	500	∞	Pr	
1.36	1.34	1.33	1.32	1.31	1.31	1.30	1.30	1.30	1.29	1.29	1.28	0.25	
1.81	1.76	1.73	1.70	1.67	1.65	1.64	1.61	1.60	1.59	1.58	1.57	0.10	22
2.15	2.07	2.03	1.98	1.94	1.91	1.89	1.85	1.84	1.82	1.80	1.78	0.05	
2.98	2.83	2.75	2.67	2.58	2.53	2.50	2.42	2.40	2.36	2.33	2.31	0.01	
1.35	1.33	1.32	1.31	1.30	1.29	1.29	1.28	1.28	1.27	1.27	1.26	0.25	
1.78	1.73	1.70	1.67	1.64	1.62	1.61	1.58	1.57	1.56	1.54	1.53	0.10	24
2.11	2.03	1.98	1.94	1.89	1.86	1.84	1.80	1.79	1.77	1.75	1.73	0.05	
2.89	2.74	2.66	2.58	2.49	2.44	2.40	2.33	2.31	2.27	2.24	2.21	0.01	
1.34	1.32	1.31	1.30	1.29	1.28	1.28	1.26	1.26	1.26	1.25	1.25	0.25	
1.76	1.71	1.68	1.65	1.61	1.59	1.58	1.55	1.54	1.53	1.51	1.50	0.10	26
2.07	1.99	1.95	1.90	1.85	1.82	1.80	1.76	1.75	1.73	1.71	1.69	0.05	
2.81	2.66	2.58	2.50	2.42	2.36	2.33	2.25	2.23	2.19	2.16	2.13	0.01	
1.33	1.31	1.30	1.29	1.28	1.27	1.27	1.26	1.25	1.25	1.24	1.24	0.25	
1.74	1.69	1.66	1.63	1.59	1.57	1.56	1.53	1.52	1.50	1.49	1.48	0.10	28
2.04	1.96	1.91	1.87	1.82	1.79	1.77	1.73	1.71	1.69	1.67	1.65	0.05	
2.75	2.60	2.52	2.44	2.35	2.30	2.26	2.19	2.17	2.13	2.09	2.06	0.01	
1.32	1.30	1.29	1.28	1.27	1.26	1.26	1.25	1.24	1.24	1.23	1.23	0.25	
1.72	1.67	1.64	1.61	1.57	1.55	1.54	1.51	1.50	1.48	1.47	1.46	0.10	30
2.01	1.93	1.89	1.84	1.79	1.76	1.74	1.70	1.68	1.66	1.64	1.62	0.05	
2.70	2.55	2.47	2.39	2.30	2.25	2.21	2.13	2.11	2.07	2.03	2.01	0.01	
1.30	1.28	1.26	1.25	1.24	1.23	1.22	1.21	1.21	1.20	1.19	1.19	0.25	
1.66	1.61	1.57	1.54	1.51	1.48	1.47	1.43	1.42	1.41	1.39	1.38	0.10	40
1.92	1.84	1.79	1.74	1.69	1.66	1.64	1.59	1.58	1.55	1.53	1.51	0.05	
2.52	2.37	2.29	2.20	2.11	2.06	2.02	1.94	1.92	1.87	1.83	1.80	0.01	
1.27	1.25	1.24	1.22	1.21	1.20	1.19	1.17	1.17	1.16	1.15	1.15	0.25	
1.60	1.54	1.51	1.48	1.44	1.41	1.40	1.36	1.35	1.33	1.31	1.29	0.10	60
1.84	1.75	1.70	1.65	1.59	1.56	1.53	1.48	1.47	1.44	1.41	1.39	0.05	
2.35	2.20	2.12	2.03	1.94	1.88	1.84	1.75	1.73	1.68	1.63	1.60	0.01	
1.24	1.22	1.21	1.19	1.18	1.17	1.16	1.14	1.13	1.12	1.11	1.10	0.25	
1.55	1.48	1.45	1.41	1.37	1.34	1.32	1.27	1.26	1.24	1.21	1.19	0.10	120
1.75	1.66	1.61	1.55	1.50	1.46	1.43	1.37	1.35	1.32	1.28	1.25	0.05	
2.19	2.03	1.95	1.86	1.76	1.70	1.66	1.56	1.53	1.48	1.42	1.38	0.01	
1.23	1.21	1.20	1.18	1.16	1.14	1.12	1.11	1.10	1.09	1.08	1.06	0.25	
1.52	1.46	1.42	1.38	1.34	1.31	1.28	1.24	1.22	1.20	1.17	1.14	0.10	200
1.72	1.62	1.57	1.52	1.46	1.41	1.39	1.32	1.29	1.26	1.22	1.19	0.05	
2.13	1.97	1.89	1.79	1.69	1.63	1.58	1.48	1.44	1.39	1.33	1.28	0.01	
1.22	1.19	1.18	1.16	1.14	1.13	1.12	1.09	1.08	1.07	1.04	1.00	0.25	
1.49	1.42	1.38	1.34	1.30	1.26	1.24	1.18	1.17	1.13	1.08	1.00	0.10	∞
1.67	1.57	1.52	1.46	1.39	1.35	1.32	1.24	1.22	1.17	1.11	1.00	0.05	
2.04	1.88	1.79	1.70	1.59	1.52	1.47	1.36	1.32	1.25	1.15	1.00	0.01	

Source: As Table B.2: table 18

Table B.4   Upper percentage points of the χ^2 distribution

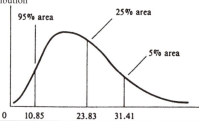

Example
Pr $(\chi^2 > 10.85) = 0.95$
Pr $(\chi^2 > 23.83) = 0.25$ for df $= 20$
Pr $(\chi^2 > 31.41) = 0.05$

Degree of freedom \ Pr	0.995	0.990	0.975	0.950	0.900
1	$392704 \cdot 10^{-10}$	$157088 \cdot 10^{-9}$	$982069 \cdot 10^{-9}$	$393214 \cdot 10^{-8}$	0.157908
2	0.0100251	0.0201007	0.0506356	0.102587	0.210720
3	0.0717212	0.114832	0.2157950	0.351846	0.584375
4	0.206990	0.297110	0.484419	0.710721	1.063623
5	0.411740	0.554300	0.831211	1.145476	1.61031
6	0.675727	0.872085	1.237347	1.63539	2.20413
7	0.989265	1.239043	1.68987	2.16735	2.83311
8	1.344419	1.646482	2.17973	2.73264	3.48954
9	1.734962	2.087912	2.70039	3.32511	4.16816
10	2.15585	2.55821	3.24697	3.94030	4.86518
11	2.60321	3.05347	3.81575	4.57481	5.57779
12	3.07382	3.57056	4.40379	5.22603	6.30380
13	3.56503	4.10691	5.00874	5.89186	7.04150*
14	4.07468	4.66043	5.62872	6.57063	7.78953
15	4.60094	5.22935	6.26214	7.26094	8.54675
16	5.14224	5.81221	6.90766	7.96164	9.31223
17	5.69724	6.40776	7.56418	8.67176	10.08520
18	6.26481	7.01491	8.23075	9.39046	10.86490
19	6.84398	7.63273	8.90655	10.1170	11.6509
20	7.43386	8.26040	9.59083	10.8080	12.4426
21	8.03366	8.89720	10.28293	11.5913	13.2396
22	8.64272	9.54249	10.98230	12.3380	14.0415
23	9.26042	10.19567	11.68850	13.0950	14.8479
24	9.88623	10.8564	12.40110	13.8484	15.6587
25	10.5197	11.5240	13.1197	14.6114	16.4734
26	11.1603	12.1981	13.8439	15.3791	17.2919
27	11.8076	12.8786	14.5733	16.1513	18.1138
28	12.4613	13.5648	15.3079	16.9279	18.9392
29	13.1211	14.2565	16.0471	17.7083	19.7677
30	13.7867	14.9535	16.7908	18.4926	20.5992
40	20.7065	22.1643	24.4331	26.5093	29.0505
50	27.9907	29.7067	32.3574	34.7642	37.6886
60	35.5436	37.4848	40.4817	43.1879	46.4589
70	43.2752	45.4418	48.7576	51.7393	55.3290
80	51.1720	53.5400	57.1532	60.3915	64.2778
90	59.1963	61.7541	65.6466	69.1260	73.2912
100a	67.3276	70.0648	74.2219	77.9295	82.3581

Table B.4 – Continued

Degree of freedom \ Pr	0.750	0.500	0.250	0.100	0.050	0.025	0.010	0.005
1	0.1015308	0.454937	1.32330	2.70554	3.84146	5.02389	6.63490	7.87944
2	0.575364	1.38629	2.77259	4.60517	5.99147	7.37776	9.21034	10.5966
3	1.212534	2.36597	4.10835	6.25139	7.81473	9.34840	11.3449	12.8381
4	1.92255	3.35670	5.38527	7.77944	9.48773	11.1433	13.2767	14.8602
5	2.67460	4.35146	6.62568	9.23635	11.0705	12.8325	15.0863	16.7496
6	3.45460	5.34812	7.84080	10.6446	12.5916	14.4494	16.8119	18.5476
7	4.25485	6.34581	9.03715	12.0170	14.0671	16.0128	18.4753	20.2777
8	5.07064	7.34412	10.2188	13.3616	15.5073	17.5346	20.0902	21.9550
9	5.89883	8.34283	11.3887	14.6837	16.9190	19.0228	21.6660	23.5893
10	6.73720	9.34182	12.5489	15.9871	18.3070	20.4831	23.2093	25.1882
11	7.58412	10.3410	13.7007	17.2750	19.6751	21.9200	24.7250	26.7569
12	8.43842	11.3403	14.8454	18.5494	21.0261	23.3367	26.2170	28.2995
13	9.29906	12.3398	15.9839	19.8119	22.3621	24.7356	27.6883	29.8194
14	10.1653	13.3393	17.1170	21.0642	23.6848	26.1190	29.1413	31.3193
15	11.0365	14.3389	18.2451	22.3072	24.9958	27.4884	30.5779	32.8031
16	11.9122	15.3385	19.3688	23.5418	26.2962	28.8454	31.9999	34.2672
17	12.7919	16.3381	20.4887	24.7690	27.5871	30.1910	33.4087	35.7185
18	13.6753	17.3379	21.6049	25.9894	28.8693	31.5264	34.8053	37.1564
19	14.5620	18.3376	22.7178	27.2036	30.1435	32.8523	36.1908	38.5822
20	15.4518	19.3374	23.8277	28.4120	31.4104	34.1696	37.5662	39.9968
21	16.3444	20.3372	24.9348	29.6151	32.6705	35.4789	38.93210	41.4010
22	17.2396	21.3370	26.0393	30.8133	33.9244	36.7807	40.28940	42.7956
23	18.1373	22.3369	27.1413	32.0069	35.1725	38.0757	41.63840	44.1813
24	19.0372	23.3367	28.2412	33.1963	36.4151	39.3641	42.97980	45.5585
25	19.9393	24.3366	29.3389	34.3816	37.6525	40.6465	44.3141	46.9278
26	20.8434	25.3364	30.4345	35.5631	38.8852	41.9232	45.6417	48.2899
27	21.7494	26.3363	31.5284	36.7412	40.1133	43.1944	46.9630	49.6449
28	22.6572	27.3363	32.6205	37.9159	41.3372	44.4607	48.2782	50.9933
29	23.5666	28.3362	33.7109	39.0875	42.5569	45.7222	49.5879	52.3356
30	24.4776	29.336	34.7998	40.256	43.7729	46.9792	50.8922	53.6720
40	33.6603	39.3354	45.6160	51.8050	55.7585	59.3417	63.6907	66.7659
50	42.9421	49.3349	56.3336	63.1671	67.5048	71.4202	76.1539	79.4900
60	52.2938	59.3347	66.9814	74.3970	79.0819	83.2976	88.3794	91.9517
70	61.6983	69.3344	77.5766	85.5271	90.5312	95.0231	100.425	104.215
80	71.1445	79.3343	88.1303	96.5782	101.879	106.629	112.329	116.321
90	80.6247	89.3342	98.6499	107.565	113.145	118.136	124.116	128.299
100a	90.1332	99.3341	109.141	118.498	124.342	129.561	135.807	140.169

Source: Abridged from same source as Table B.2: table 8

Notes: For df greater than 100 the expansion: $[sqr]2\chi^2 - [sqr](2k-1) = Z$ follows the standardised normal distribution, where k represents the degrees of freedom.

Table B.5 Durbin–Watson *d*statistic: significance points of d_L and d_U at 0.05 level of significance

Example

If $n = 40$ and $k' = 4$, $d_L = 1.285$ and $d_U = 1.721$. If a computed *d* value is less than 1.285, there is evidence of positive first-order serial correlation, if it is greater than 1.721 there is no evidence of positive first-order serial correlation, but if *d* lies between the lower and the upper limit, there is conclusive evidence regarding the presence or absence of positive first-order serial correlation.

n	$k' = 1$ d_L	d_U	$k' = 2$ d_L	d_U	$k' = 3$ d_L	d_U	$k' = 4$ d_L	d_U	$k' = 5$ d_L	d_U
6	0.610	1.400	–	–	–	–	–	–	–	–
7	0.700	1.356	0.467	1.896	–	–	–	–	–	–
8	0.763	1.332	0.559	1.777	0.368	2.287	–	–	–	–
9	0.824	1.320	0.629	1.699	0.455	2.128	0.296	2.588	–	–
10	0.879	1.320	0.697	1.641	0.525	2.016	0.376	2.414	0.243	2.822
11	0.927	1.324	0.658	1.604	0.595	1.928	0.444	2.283	0.316	2.645
12	0.971	1.331	0.812	1.579	0.658	1.864	0.512	2.177	0.379	2.506
13	1.010	1.340	0.861	1.562	0.715	1.816	0.574	2.094	0.445	2.390
14	1.045	1.350	0.905	1.551	0.767	1.779	0.632	2.030	0.505	2.296
15	1.077	1.361	0.946	1.543	0.814	1.750	0.685	1.977	0.562	2.220
16	1.106	1.371	0.982	1.539	0.875	1.728	0.734	1.935	0.615	2.157
17	1.133	1.381	1.015	1.536	0.897	1.710	0.779	1.900	0.664	2.104
18	1.158	1.391	1.046	1.535	0.933	1.696	0.820	1.872	0.710	2.060
19	1.180	1.401	1.074	1.536	0.967	1.685	0.859	1.848	0.752	2.023
20	1.201	1.411	1.100	1.537	0.998	1.676	0.894	1.828	0.792	1.991
21	1.221	1.420	1.125	1.538	1.026	1.669	0.927	1.812	0.829	1.964
22	1.239	1.429	1.147	1.541	1.053	1.664	0.958	1.797	0.863	1.940
23	1.257	1.437	1.168	1.543	1.078	1.660	0.986	1.785	0.895	1.920
24	1.273	1.446	1.188	1.546	1.101	1.656	1.013	1.775	0.925	1.902
25	1.288	1.454	1.206	1.550	1.123	1.654	1.038	1.767	0.953	1.886
26	1.302	1.461	1.224	1.553	1.143	1.652	1.062	1.759	0.979	1.873
27	1.316	1.469	1.240	1.556	1.162	1.651	1.084	1.753	1.004	1.861
28	1.328	1.476	1.255	1.560	1.181	1.650	1.104	1.747	1.028	1.850
29	1.341	1.483	1.270	1.563	1.198	1.650	1.124	1.743	1.050	1.841
30	1.351	1.489	1.284	1.567	1.214	1.650	1.143	1.739	1.071	1.833
31	1.363	1.496	1.297	1.570	1.229	1.650	1.160	1.735	1.090	1.825
32	1.373	1.502	1.309	1.574	1.244	1.650	1.177	1.732	1.109	1.819
33	1.383	1.508	1.321	1.577	1.258	1.651	1.193	1.730	1.127	1.813
34	1.393	1.514	1.333	1.580	1.271	1.652	1.208	1.728	1.144	1.808
35	1.402	1.519	1.343	1.584	1.283	1.653	1.222	1.726	1.160	1.803
36	1.411	1.525	1.354	1.587	1.295	1.654	1.236	1.724	1.175	1.799
37	1.419	1.530	1.364	1.590	1.307	1.655	1.249	1.723	1.190	1.795
38	1.427	1.535	1.373	1.594	1.318	1.656	1.261	1.722	1.204	1.792
39	1.435	1.540	1.382	1.597	1.328	1.658	1.273	1.722	1.218	1.789
40	1.442	1.544	1.391	1.600	1.338	1.659	1.285	1.721	1.230	1.786
45	1.475	1.566	1.430	1.615	1.383	1.666	1.336	1.720	1.287	1.776
50	1.503	1.585	1.462	1.628	1.421	1.674	1.378	1.721	1.335	1.771
55	1.528	1.601	1.490	1.641	1.452	1.681	1.414	1.724	1.374	1.768
60	1.549	1.616	1.514	1.652	1.480	1.689	1.444	1.727	1.408	1.767
65	1.567	1.629	1.536	1.662	1.503	1.696	1.471	1.731	1.438	1.767
70	1.583	1.641	1.556	1.672	1.525	1.703	1.494	1.735	1.464	1.768
75	1.598	1.652	1.571	1.680	1.543	1.709	1.515	1.739	1.487	1.770
80	1.611	1.662	1.586	1.688	1.560	1.715	1.534	1.743	1.507	1.772
85	1.624	1.671	1.600	1.696	1.575	1.721	1.550	1.747	1.525	1.774
90	1.635	1.679	1.612	1.703	1.589	1.726	1.566	1.751	1.542	1.776
95	1.645	1.687	1.623	1.709	1.602	1.732	1.579	1.755	1.557	1.778
100	1.654	1.694	1.634	1.715	1.613	1.736	1.592	1.758	1.571	1.780
150	1.720	1.746	1.706	1.760	1.693	1.774	1.679	1.788	1.665	1.802
200	1.758	1.778	1.748	1.789	1.738	1.799	1.728	1.810	1.718	1.820

Table B.5 – Continued

n	k' = 6		k' = 7		k' = 8		k' = 9		k' = 10	
	d_L	d_U	d_U	d_L	d_U	d_L	d_U	d_L	d_L	d_U
6	–	–	–	–	–	–	–	–	–	–
7	–	–	–	–	–	–	–	–	–	–
8	–	–	–	–	–	–	–	–	–	–
9	–	–	–	–	–	–	–	–	–	–
10	–	–	–	–	–	–	–	–	–	–
11	0.203	3.005	–	–	–	–	–	–	–	–
12	0.268	2.835	0.171	3.149	–	–	–	–	–	–
13	0.328	2.692	0.230	2.985	0.147	3.266	–	–	–	–
14	0.389	2.572	0.286	2.848	0.200	3.111	0.127	3.360	–	–
15	0.447	2.472	0.343	2.727	0.251	2.979	0.175	3.216	0.111	3.438
16	0.502	2.388	0.398	2.624	0.304	2.860	0.222	3.090	0.155	3.304
17	0.554	2.318	0.451	2.537	0.356	2.757	0.272	2.975	0.198	3.184
18	0.603	2.257	0.502	2.461	0.407	2.667	0.321	2.873	0.244	3.073
19	0.649	2.206	0.549	2.396	0.456	2.589	0.369	2.783	0.290	2.974
20	0.692	2.162	0.595	2.339	0.502	2.521	0.416	2.704	0.336	2.885
21	0.732	2.124	0.637	2.290	0.547	2.460	0.461	2.633	0.380	2.806
22	0.769	2.090	0.677	2.246	0.588	2.407	0.504	2.571	0.424	2.734
23	0.804	2.061	0.715	2.208	0.628	2.360	0.545	2.514	0.465	2.670
24	0.837	2.035	0.751	2.174	0.666	2.318	0.584	2.464	0.560	2.613
25	0.868	2.012	0.784	2.144	0.702	2.280	0.621	2.419	0.544	2.560
26	0.897	1.992	0.816	2.117	0.735	2.246	0.657	2.379	0.581	2.513
27	0.925	1.974	0.845	2.093	0.767	2.216	0.691	2.342	0.616	2.470
28	0.951	1.958	0.874	2.071	0.798	2.188	0.723	2.309	0.650	2.431
29	0.975	1.944	0.900	2.052	0.826	2.164	0.753	2.278	0.682	2.396
30	0.998	1.931	0.926	2.034	0.854	2.141	0.782	2.251	0.712	2.363
31	1.020	1.920	0.950	2.018	0.879	2.120	0.810	2.226	0.741	2.333
32	1.041	1.909	0.972	2.004	0.904	2.102	0.836	2.203	0.769	2.306
33	1.061	1.900	0.994	1.991	0.927	2.085	0.861	2.181	0.795	2.281
34	1.080	1.891	1.015	1.979	0.950	2.069	0.885	2.162	0.821	2.257
35	1.097	1.884	1.034	1.967	0.971	2.054	0.908	2.144	0.845	2.236
36	1.114	1.877	1.053	1.957	0.991	2.041	0.930	2.127	0.868	2.216
37	1.131	1.870	1.071	1.948	1.011	2.029	0.951	2.112	0.891	2.198
38	1.146	1.864	1.088	1.939	1.029	2.017	0.970	2.098	0.912	2.180
39	1.161	1.859	1.104	1.932	1.047	2.007	1.990	2.085	0.932	2.164
40	1.175	1.854	1.120	1.924	1.064	1.997	1.008	2.072	0.952	2.149
45	1.238	1.835	1.189	1.895	1.139	1.958	1.089	2.022	1.038	2.088
50	1.291	1.822	1.246	1.875	1.201	1.930	1.156	1.986	1.110	2.044
55	1.334	1.814	1.294	1.861	1.253	1.909	1.212	1.959	1.170	2.010
60	1.372	1.808	1.335	1.850	1.298	1.894	1.260	1.939	1.222	1.984
65	1.404	1.805	1.370	1.843	1.336	1.882	1.301	1.923	1.266	1.964
70	1.433	1.802	1.401	1.837	1.369	1.873	1.337	1.910	1.305	1.948
75	1.458	1.801	1.428	1.834	1.399	1.867	1.369	1.901	1.339	1.935
80	1.480	1.801	1.453	1.831	1.425	1.861	1.397	1.893	1.369	1.925
85	1.500	1.801	1.474	1.829	1.448	1.857	1.422	1.886	1.396	1.916
90	1.518	1.801	1.494	1.827	1.469	1.854	1.445	1.881	1.420	1.909
95	1.535	1.802	1.512	1.827	1.489	1.852	1.465	1.877	1.442	1.903
100	1.550	1.803	1.528	1.826	1.506	1.850	1.484	1.874	1.462	1.898
150	1.651	1.817	1.637	1.832	1.622	1.847	1.608	1.862	1.594	1.877
200	1.707	1.831	1.697	1.841	1.686	1.852	1.675	1.863	1.665	1.874

Table B.5 – Continued

n	k' = 11 dL	k' = 11 dU	k' = 12 dL	k' = 12 dU	k' = 13 dL	k' = 13 dU	k' = 14 dL	k' = 14 dU	k' = 15 dL	k' = 15 dU
6	–	–	–	–	–	–	–	–	–	–
7	–	–	–	–	–	–	–	–	–	–
8	–	–	–	–	–	–	–	–	–	–
9	–	–	–	–	–	–	–	–	–	–
10	–	–	–	–	–	–	–	–	–	–
11	–	–	–	–	–	–	–	–	–	–
12	–	–	–	–	–	–	–	–	–	–
13	–	–	–	–	–	–	–	–	–	–
14	–	–	–	–	–	–	–	–	–	–
15	–	–	–	–	–	–	–	–	–	–
16	0.098	3.503	–	–	–	–	–	–	–	–
17	0.138	3.378	0.087	3.557	–	–	–	–	–	–
18	0.177	3.265	0.123	3.441	0.078	3.603	–	–	–	–
19	0.220	3.159	0.160	3.335	0.111	3.496	0.070	3.642	–	–
20	0.263	3.063	0.200	3.234	0.145	3.395	0.100	3.542	0.063	3.676
21	0.307	2.976	0.240	3.141	0.182	3.300	0.132	3.448	0.091	3.583
22	0.349	2.897	0.281	3.057	0.220	3.211	0.166	3.358	0.120	3.495
23	0.391	2.826	0.322	2.979	0.259	2.128	0.202	3.272	0.153	3.409
24	0.431	2.761	0.362	2.908	0.297	2.053	0.239	3.193	0.186	3.327
25	0.470	2.702	0.400	2.844	0.335	2.983	0.275	3.119	0.221	3.251
26	0.508	2.649	0.438	2.784	0.373	2.919	0.312	3.051	0.256	3.179
27	0.544	2.600	0.475	2.730	0.409	2.859	0.348	2.987	0.291	3.112
28	0.578	2.555	0.510	2.680	0.445	2.805	0.383	2.928	0.325	3.050
29	0.612	2.515	0.544	2.634	0.479	2.755	0.418	2.874	0.359	2.992
30	0.643	2.477	0.577	2.592	0.512	2.708	0.451	2.823	0.392	2.937
31	0.674	2.443	0.608	2.553	0.545	2.665	0.484	2.776	0.425	2.887
32	0.703	2.411	0.638	2.517	0.576	2.625	0.515	2.733	0.457	2.840
33	0.731	2.382	0.668	2.484	0.606	2.588	0.546	2.692	0.488	2.796
34	0.758	2.355	0.695	2.454	0.634	2.554	0.575	2.654	0.518	2.754
35	0.783	2.330	0.722	2.425	0.662	2.521	0.604	2.619	0.547	2.716
36	0.808	2.306	0.748	2.398	0.689	2.492	0.631	2.586	0.575	2.680
37	0.831	2.285	0.772	2.374	0.714	2.464	0.657	2.555	0.602	2.646
38	0.854	2.265	0.796	2.351	0.739	2.438	0.683	2.526	0.628	2.614
39	0.875	2.246	0.819	2.329	0.763	2.413	0.707	2.499	0.653	2.585
40	0.896	2.228	0.840	2.309	0.785	2.391	0.731	2.473	0.678	2.557
45	0.988	2.156	0.938	2.225	0.887	2.296	0.838	2.367	0.788	2.439
50	1.064	2.103	1.019	2.163	0.973	2.225	0.927	2.287	0.882	2.350
55	1.129	2.062	1.087	2.116	1.045	2.170	1.003	2.225	0.961	2.281
60	1.184	2.031	1.145	2.079	1.106	2.127	1.068	2.177	1.029	2.227
65	1.231	2.006	1.195	2.049	1.160	2.093	1.124	2.138	1.088	2.183
70	1.272	1.986	1.239	2.026	1.206	2.066	1.172	2.106	1.139	2.148
75	1.308	1.970	1.277	2.006	1.247	2.043	1.215	2.080	1.184	2.118
80	1.340	1.957	1.311	1.991	1.283	2.024	1.253	2.059	1.224	2.093
85	1.369	1.946	1.342	1.977	1.315	2.009	1.287	2.040	1.260	2.073
90	1.395	1.937	1.369	1.966	1.344	1.995	1.318	2.025	1.292	2.055
95	1.418	1.929	1.394	1.956	1.370	1.984	1.345	2.012	1.321	2.040
100	1.439	1.923	1.416	1.948	1.393	1.974	1.371	2.000	1.347	2.026
150	1.579	1.892	1.564	1.908	1.550	1.924	1.535	1.940	1.519	1.956
200	1.654	1.885	1.643	1.896	1.632	1.908	1.621	1.919	1.610	1.931

Table B.5 – Continued

	k' = 16		k' = 17		k' = 18		k' = 19		k' = 20	
n	d_L	d_U	d_L	d_U	d_L	d_U	d_L	d_U	d_L	d_U
6	–	–	–	–	–	–	–	–	–	
7	–	–	–	–	–	–	–	–	–	
8	–	–	–	–	–	–	–	–	–	
9	–	–	–	–	–	–	–	–	–	
10	–	–	–	–	–	–	–	–	–	
11	–	–	–	–	–	–	–	–	–	–
12	–	–	–	–	–	–	–	–	–	–
13	–	–	–	–	–	–	–	–	–	–
14	–	–	–	–	–	–	–	–	–	–
15	–	–	–	–	–	–	–	–	–	–
16	–	–	–	–	–	–	–	–	–	–
17	–	–	–	–	–	–	–	–	–	–
18	–	–	–	–	–	–	–	–	–	–
19	–	–	–	–	–	–	–	–	–	–
20	–	–	–	–	–	–	–	–	–	–
21	0.058	3.705	–	–	–	–	–	–	–	–
22	0.083	3.619	0.052	3.731	–	–	–	–	–	–
23	0.110	3.535	0.076	3.650	0.048	3.753	–	–	–	–
24	0.141	3.454	0.101	3.572	0.070	3.678	0.044	3.773	–	–
25	0.172	3.376	0.130	3.494	0.094	3.604	0.065	3.702	0.041	3.790
26	0.205	3.303	0.160	3.420	0.210	3.531	0.087	3.632	0.060	3.724
27	0.238	3.233	0.191	3.349	0.149	3.460	0.112	3.563	0.081	3.658
28	0.271	3.168	0.222	3.283	0.178	3.392	0.138	3.495	0.104	3.592
29	0.305	3.107	0.254	3.219	0.208	3.327	0.166	3.431	0.129	3.528
30	0.337	3.050	0.286	3.160	0.238	3.266	0.195	3.368	0.156	3.465
31	0.370	2.996	0.317	3.103	0.269	3.208	0.224	3.309	0.183	3.406
32	0.401	2.946	0.349	3.050	0.299	3.153	0.253	3.252	0.211	3.348
33	0.432	2.899	0.379	3.000	0.329	3.100	0.283	3.198	0.239	3.293
34	0.462	2.854	0.409	2.954	0.359	3.051	0.312	3.147	0.267	3.240
35	0.492	2.813	0.439	2.910	0.388	3.005	0.340	3.099	0.295	3.190
36	0.520	2.774	0.467	2.868	0.417	2.961	0.369	3.053	0.323	3.142
37	0.548	2.738	0.495	2.829	0.445	2.920	0.397	3.009	0.351	3.097
38	0.575	2.703	0.522	2.792	0.472	2.880	0.424	2.968	0.378	3.054
39	0.600	2.671	0.549	2.757	0.499	2.843	0.451	2.929	0.404	3.013
40	0.626	2.641	0.575	2.724	0.525	2.808	0.477	2.892	0.430	2.974
45	0.740	2.512	0.692	2.586	0.644	2.659	0.598	2.733	0.553	2.807
50	0.836	2.414	0.792	2.479	0.747	2.544	0.703	2.610	0.660	2.675
55	0.919	2.338	0.877	2.396	0.836	2.454	0.795	2.512	0.754	2.571
60	0.990	2.278	0.951	2.330	0.913	2.382	0.874	2.434	0.836	2.487
65	1.052	2.229	1.016	2.276	0.980	2.323	0.944	2.371	0.908	2.419
70	1.105	2.189	1.072	2.232	1.038	2.275	1.005	2.318	0.971	2.362
75	1.153	2.156	1.121	2.195	1.090	2.235	1.058	2.275	1.027	2.317
80	1.195	2.129	1.165	2.165	1.136	2.201	1.106	2.238	1.076	2.275
85	1.232	2.105	1.205	2.139	1.177	2.172	1.149	2.206	1.121	2.241
90	1.266	2.085	1.240	2.116	1.213	2.148	1.187	2.179	1.160	2.211
95	1.296	2.068	1.271	2.097	1.247	2.126	1.222	2.156	1.197	2.186
100	1.324	2.053	1.301	2.080	1.277	2.108	1.253	2.135	1.229	2.164
150	1.504	1.972	1.489	1.989	1.474	2.006	1.458	2.023	1.443	2.040
200	1.599	1.943	1.588	1.955	1.576	1.967	1.565	1.979	1.554	1.991

Source: This table is an extension of the original Durbin–Watson table and is reproduced from N.E. Savin and K.J. White 'The Durbin–Watson Test for Serial Correlation with Extreme Small Samples or Many Regressors', *Econometrica*, 45, November 1977, 1989–96 and as corrected by R.W. Farebrother, *Econometrica*, 48, September 1980, 1554.

Notes:

n = number of observations

k' = number of explanatory variables excluding the constant term

Table B.6   Critical values of runs in the runs test

Example

In a sequence of 30 observations consisting of 20 + signs (= N_1) and 10 − signs (= N_2), the critical values of runs at the 0.05 level of significance are 9 and 20, as shown by Table B.6(a) and (b), respectively. Therefore, if in an application it is found that the number of runs is equal to or less than 9 or equal or greater than 20, one can reject (at the 0.05 level of significance) the hypothesis that the observed sequence is random.

(a)

N_1 \ N_2	2	3	4	5	6	7	8	9	10	11	12	13	14	15	16	17	18	19	20
2											2	2	2	2	2	2	2	2	2
3						2	2	2	2	2	2	2	2	2	3	3	3	3	3
4			2	2	2	3	3	3	3	3	3	3	3	3	4	4	4	4	4
5			2	2	3	3	3	3	3	4	4	4	4	4	4	4	5	5	5
6		2	2	3	3	3	3	4	4	4	4	5	5	5	5	5	5	6	6
7		2	2	3	3	3	4	4	5	5	5	5	5	6	6	6	6	6	6
8		2	3	3	3	4	4	5	5	5	6	6	6	6	6	7	7	7	7
9		2	3	3	4	4	5	5	5	6	6	6	7	7	7	7	8	8	8
10		2	3	3	4	5	5	5	6	6	7	7	7	7	8	8	8	8	9
11		2	3	4	4	5	5	6	6	7	7	7	8	8	8	9	9	9	9
12	2	2	3	4	4	5	6	6	7	7	7	8	8	8	9	9	9	10	10
13	2	2	3	4	5	5	6	6	7	7	8	8	9	9	9	10	10	10	10
14	2	2	3	4	5	5	6	7	7	8	8	9	9	9	10	10	10	11	11
15	2	3	3	4	5	6	6	7	7	8	8	9	9	10	10	11	11	11	12
16	2	3	4	4	5	6	6	7	8	8	9	9	10	10	11	11	11	12	12
17	2	3	4	4	5	6	7	7	8	9	9	10	10	11	11	11	12	12	13
18	2	3	4	5	5	6	7	8	8	9	9	10	10	11	11	12	12	13	13
19	2	3	4	5	6	6	7	8	8	9	10	10	11	11	12	12	13	13	13
20	2	3	4	5	6	6	7	8	9	9	10	10	11	12	12	13	13	14	14

(b)

N_1										N_2									
	2	3	4	5	6	7	8	9	10	11	12	13	14	15	16	17	18	19	20
2																			
3																			
4			9	9															
5			9	10	10	11	11												
6			9	10	11	12	12	13	13	13	13								
7				11	12	13	13	14	14	14	14	15	15	15					
8				11	12	13	14	14	15	15	16	16	16	16	17	17	17	17	
9					13	14	14	15	16	16	16	17	17	18	18	18	18	18	18
10					13	14	15	16	16	17	17	18	18	18	19	19	19	20	20
11					13	14	15	16	17	17	18	19	19	19	20	20	20	21	21
12					13	14	16	16	17	18	19	19	20	20	21	21	21	22	22
13						15	16	17	18	19	19	20	20	21	21	22	22	23	23
14						15	16	17	18	19	20	20	21	22	22	23	23	23	24
15						15	16	18	18	19	20	21	22	22	23	23	24	24	25
16							17	18	19	20	21	21	22	23	23	24	25	25	25
17							17	18	19	20	21	22	23	23	24	25	25	26	26
18							17	18	19	20	21	22	23	24	25	25	26	26	27
19							17	18	20	21	22	23	23	24	25	26	26	27	27
20							17	18	20	21	22	23	24	25	25	26	27	27	28

Source: Sidney Siegel, *Nonparametric Statistic for the Behavioral Science*, New York: McGraw-Hill, 1956, table F, pp. 252–3. The table has been adapted by Siegel from the original source: Frieda S. Swed and C. Eisenhart, 'Tables for Testing Randomness of Grouping in a Sequence of Alternatives', *Annals of Mathematical Statistics*, 14, 1943.

Notes: Table B.6(a) and (b) give the critical values of runs n for various values of N_1(+ symbol) and N_2(–symbol). For the one sample runs test, any value of n which is equal to or smaller than that shown in Table B.6(a) or equal to or larger than shown in Table B.6(b) is significant at the 0.05 level.

Table B.7   Critical values for Dickey–Fuller test

Sample size	Probability of a larger value		
	10%	*5%*	*1%*
Φ_1: $(\beta_1,\beta_3) = (0,1)$ in $x_t = \beta_1 + \beta_3\, X_{t-1} + \epsilon_t$			
25	4.12	5.18	7.88
50	3.94	4.86	7.06
100	3.86	4.71	6.70
∞	3.78	4.59	6.43
Φ_2: $(\beta_1,\beta_2,\beta_3) = 0,0,1$ in $x_t = \beta_1 + \beta_2\, t + \beta_3 X_{t-1} + \epsilon_t$			
25	4.67	5.68	8.21
50	4.31	5.13	7.02
100	4.16	4.88	6.50
∞	4.03	4.68	6.09
Φ_3: $(\beta_1,\beta_2,\beta_3) = \beta_1,0,1$ in $x_t = \beta_1 + \beta_2\, t + \beta_3 X_{t-1} + \epsilon_t$			
25	5.91	7.24	10.61
50	5.61	6.73	9.31
100	5.47	6.49	8.73
∞	5.34	6.25	8.27
τ_3: $\beta_3 = 1$ in $x_t = \beta_1 + \beta_2\, t + \beta_3 X_{t-1} + \epsilon_t$			
25	−1.14	−0.80	−0.15
50	−1.19	−0.87	−0.24
100	−1.22	−0.90	−0.28
∞	−1.25	−0.94	−0.33

Source: Fuller (1976) and Dickey and Fuller (1981: 1063)

References

Aldrich, John H. and Nelson, Forrest D. (1984) *Linear Probability, Logit, and Probit Models*, Beverly Hills, CA: Sage.

Banerjee, Anindya, Dolado, Juan J., Galbraith, John J. and Hendry, David F. (1993) *Cointegration, Error Correction, and the Econometric Analysis of Non-stationary Data*, Oxford: Oxford University Press.

Barten, A.P. (1985) 'Het voorgeborchte der econometrie: het parelsnoer van Engel', *Tijdschrift voor economie en management* 30 (3–4): 453–74.

Box, G.E.P. and Jenkins G.M. (1970) *Time Series Analysis, Forecasting and Control*, San Francisco: Holden-Day.

Carr, E.H. ([1961], 1990) *What is History?*, ed. R.W. Davies, Harmondsworth: Penguin Books.

Chambers, John M., Cleveland, William S., Kleiner, Beat and Tukey, Paula S. (1983) *Graphical Methods for Data Analysis*, Pacific Grove, CA: Wadsworth & Brooks/Cole Publishing Company Advanced Books & Software.

Charemza, Wojciech W. and Deadman Derek F. (1992) *New Directions in Econometric Practice: General to Specific Modelling, Cointegration*, Aldershot, Hants.: Edward Elgar.

Chenery, Hollis B. and Strout, William (1966) 'Foreign Assistance and Economic Development', *American Economic Review* 66: 679–733.

Collier, P., Radwan, S. and Wangwe, S. (with Wagner, A.) (1986) *Labour and Poverty in Rural Tanzania: Ujamaa and Rural Development in the United Republic of Tanzania*, Oxford: Clarendon Press.

Dasgupta, P. (1993) *An Inquiry into Well-Being and Destitution*, Oxford: Oxford University Press.

Davies, Richard B. (1994) 'From Cross-sectional to Longitudinal Analysis', in *Analysing Social and Political Change: A Casebook of Methods*, ed. Angela Dale and Richard B. Davies, London: Sage Publications.

Demaris, Alfred (1992) *Logit Modelling: Practical Applications*, Beverly Hills, CA: Sage Publications.

Diaconis, P. (1985) 'Theories of Data Analysis: From Magical Thinking Through Classical Statistics', in David C. Hoaglin, F. Mosteller and J. Tukey (eds), *Exploring Data Tables, Trends and Shapes*, New York: John Wiley.

Dickey, D.A. and Fuller, W.A. (1981) 'Likelihood Ration Statistics for Autoregressive Time Series With a Unit Root', *Econometrica* 49: 12–26.

Emerson, John D. and Hoaglin, David C. (1985) 'Resistant Multiple Regression, One Variable at a Time' in David C. Hoaglin, Frederick Mosteller and John W. Tukey (eds), *Exploring Data Tables, Trends, and Shapes*, New York: John Wiley.

Emerson, John D. and Strenio, Judith (1983) 'Boxplots and Batch Comparison', in David C. Hoaglin Frederick Mosteller and John W. Tukey (eds), *Understanding Robust and Exploratory Data Analysis*, New York: John Wiley.

Engle, Robert F. and Granger, C.W.J. (1987) 'Cointegration and Error Correction: Representation, Estimation and Testing', *Econometrica* 55 (2): 251–76.

Engle, Robert F., Hendry, D.F. and Richard, J.F. (1983) 'Exogeneity', *Econometrica* 55: 277–304.

Friedman, Milton (1970) *The Controversy in Monetary Theory: The First Winicott Memorial Lecture*, 16 September, IEA Occasional Paper no. 33. London: Institute of Economic Affairs.

Fry, M.J. (1988) *Money, Interest, and Banking in Economic Development*, Baltimore, MD: Johns Hopkins University Press.

Fuller, W.A. (1976) *Introduction to Statistical Time Series*, New York: John Wiley.

Gatt, J. (1995) *An Econometric Analysis of the Determinants of the Maltese Exports of Manufacturers*, ISS Working Paper no. 198, The Hague: Institute of Social Studies.

Giere, Ronald N. (1991) *Understanding Scientific Reasoning*, Fort Worth, IL: Holt, Rinehart & Winston.

Gilbert, Christopher (1990) 'Professor Hendry's Econometric Methodology', in C.W.J. Granger (ed.), *Modelling Economic Series*, Oxford: Clerendon Press.

Goldberger, Arthur S. (1964) *Econometric Theory*, New York: John Wiley.

Goldberger, Arthur S. (1991) *A Course in Econometrics*, Cambridge, MA: Harvard University Press.

Gould, S. J. (1996) *Full House: The Spread of Excellence from Plato to Darwin*, New York: Harmony Books.

Granger, C.W.J. (ed.) (1990) *Modelling Economic Series*, Oxford: Clarendon Press.

Granger, C.W.J. and Newbold, P. (1974) 'Spurious Regressions in Econometrics' *Journal of Econometrics* 2: 111–20.

Granger, C.W.J. and Newbold, P. (1977) *Forecasting Economic Time Series*, New York: Academic Press; 2nd edition 1986.

Gregory, C.A. and Altman, J.C. (1989) *Observing the Economy*, London: Routledge.

Griffin, Keith (1970) 'Foreign Capital, Domestic Savings and Economic Development', *Bulletin of the Oxford University Institute of Economics and Statistics* 32: 99–112.

Griffin, Keith (1971) 'Reply', *Bulletin of the Oxford University Institute of Economics and Statistics* 33: 156–61.

Griffin, Keith and Enos, John (1971) 'Foreign Assistance: Objectives and Consequences', *Economics of Development and Cultural Change* 18: 313–27.

Grilli, E. and Yang, M.C. (1988) 'Primary Commodity Prices, Manufactured Goods Prices and the Terms of Trade of Developing Countries: What the Long Run Shows', *World Bank Economic Review* 2: 1–47.

Gujarati, D. (1988), *Basic Econometrics*, 2nd edn, New York: McGraw-Hill.

Hamilton, James D. (1994) *Time Series Analysis*, Princeton, NJ: Princeton University Press.

Hamilton, Lawrence (1990) *Modern Data Analysis: A First Course in Applied Statistics*, Pacific Grove, CA: Brooks Cole.

Hamilton, Lawrence C. (1992) *Regression with Graphics: A Second Course in Applied Statistics*, Pacific Grove, CA: Brooks Cole.

Harriss, B. (1990) 'The Intrafamily Distribution of Hunger in South Asia', in Jean Dreze and Amaryta Sen (eds), *The Political Economy of Hunger*, vol. 1, *Entitlement and Well-being*, Oxford: Clarendon Press.

Heckman, J.J. (1992) 'Haavelmo and the Birth of Modern Econometrics: A Review of *The History of Econometric Ideas* by Mary Morgan', *Journal of Econometric Literature* 30: 876–86.

Helmers, F.L.C.H. (1988) 'Real Exchange Rate Indexes', in R. Dornsbuch and F.L.C.H. Helmers (eds), *The Open Economy: Tools for Policy Makers in Developing Countries*, Oxford: Oxford University Press.

Hoaglin, David C. (1983) 'Letter Values: a Set of Selected Order Statistics', in David C. Hoaglin, F. Mosteller and J. Tukey *Understanding Robust and Exploratory Data Analysis*, New York: John Wiley, pp. 33–57.

Hoaglin, David C. (1985) 'Using Quintiles to Study Shapes', in David C. Hoaglin, F. Mosteller and J. Tukey, *Exploring Data Tables, Trends and Shapes*, New York: John Wiley.

Hoaglin, David C., Mosteller, F. and Tukey, J. (1983) *Understanding Robust and Exploratory Data Analysis*, New York: John Wiley.

Hoaglin, David C., Mosteller F., Tukey J. (1985) *Exploring Data Tables, Trends and Shapes*, New York: John Wiley.

Holden, Darryl and Perman, Roger (1994) 'Unit Roots and Cointegration for the Applied Economist', in B. Bhaskara Rao (ed.) *Cointegration for the Applied Economist*, Oxford: Basil Blackwell.

Hopwood, A. (1984) 'Accounting and the Pursuit of Efficiency', in A. Hopwood and C. Tomkins, *Issues in Public Sector Accounting*, Oxford: Phillip Allan, 167–87.

Huber, Peter J. (1981) *Robust Statistics*, New York: John Wiley.

Kennedy, Peter (1992) *A Guide to Econometrics*, Oxford: Blackwell.

Khan, M.S. and Reinhart, C.M. (1990) 'Private Investment and Economic Growth in Developing Countries', *World Development* 18: 19–28.

Kmenta, Jan (1986) *Elements of Econometrics*, New York: Macmillan.

Krishnaji, N. (1992) 'The Demand Constraint: A Note on the Role of Foodgrain Prices and Income Inequality', in N. Krishnaji, *Pauperising Agriculture: Studies in Agrarian Change and Demographic Structure*, Sameeska Trust, Bombay: Oxford University Press.

Leamer, E.E. (1978) *Specification Searches: Ad hoc Inference with Non-experimental Data*, New York: John Wiley.

Leamer, E.E. (1983) 'Let's Take the Con Out of Econometrics', *American Economic Review*, 23 (1): 31–43.

Levine, J.H. (1993) *Exceptions are the Rule: An Inquiry into Methods in Social Sciences*, Boulder, CO: Westview Press.

Lucas, R.E. (1976) 'Econometric Policy Evaluation: A Critique', in K. Brunner and A.H. Meltzer (eds), *The Phillips Curve and Labour Markets*, supplement to *Journal of Monetary Economics* 1: 19–46.

MacKie-Mason, J.K. (1992) 'Econometric Software: A User's View', *Journal of Economic Perspectives* 6 (4): 165–87.

McKinnon, R.I. (1973) *Money and Capital in a Developing Economy*, Washington, DC: Brookings Institution.

Maddala, G.S. (1988) *Introduction to Econometrics*, Englewood Cliffs: Prentice Hall.

Maddala, G.S. (1992) *Introduction to Econometrics*, New York: Macmillan.

Miller, R.W. (1987) *Fact and Method: Explanation, Confirmation and Reality in the Natural and the Social Sciences*, Princeton, NJ: Princeton University Press.

Moore, D.S. and McCabe, G.P. (1989) *Introduction to the Practice of Statistics*, New York: Freeman.

Morgan, M.S. (1990) *The History of Econometric Ideas*, Cambridge: Cambridge University Press.

Mosley, Paul, Harrigan, Jane and Toye, John (1991) *Aid and Power: The World Bank and Policy-based Lending*, 2 vols, London: Routledge.

Mosteller, Frederick and Tukey, John W. (1977) *Data Analysis and Regression: A Second Course in Statistics*, Reading, MA: Addison-Wesley.

Myers R.H. (1990) *Classical and Modern Regression with Applications*, 2nd edn, Boston, MA: PWS-Kent.

Pelto, Pertti J. and Pelto, Gretel H. (1978) *Anthropological Research: The Structure of Inquiry*, Cambridge: Cambridge University Press.

Phillips, P.C.B. and Ouliaris S. (1990) 'Asymptotic Properties of Residual Based Tests for Cointegration', *Econometrica* 58 (1): 165–93.

Rao, B. Bhaskara (ed.) (1994) *Cointegration for the Applied Economist*, London: Macmillan.

Rawlings, John O. (1988) *Applied Regression Analysis: A Research Tool*, Pacific Grove, CA: Woodsworth & Brooks/Cole.

Riddell, Roger (1987) *Foreign Aid Reconsidered*, London: James Curry.

Rosenberger James L., and Gasko, Miriam (1983) 'Comparing Location Estimators: Trimmed Means, Medians, and Trimean', in David C. Hoaglin, F. Mosteller and J. Tukey *Understanding Robust and Exploratory Data Analysis*, New York: John Wiley, pp. 297–338.

Ross, J.A., Rich, M., Molzan, J.P. and Pensak, M. (1988) *Family Planning and Child Survival, 100 Developing Countries*, Centre for Population and Family Health, New York: Columbia University.

Sapsford, David (1985) 'The Statistical Debate on the Net Barter Terms of Trade Between Primary Commodities and Manufactures: A Comment and Some Additional Evidence', *Economic Journal* 95: 781–8.

Seers, D. (1976) 'The Political Economy of National Accounting', in A. Cairncross and M. Pur (eds), *Employment, Income Distribution and Development Strategy*, London: Macmillan.

Sen, A.K. (1985) 'Women, Technology and Sexual Divisions', *Trade and Development* (UNCTAD), 6.

Sen, A.K. and Sengupta, S. (1983) 'Malnutrition of Rural Indian Children and the Sex Bias', *Economic and Political Weekly* 18.

Sen, Gita (1993) 'Paths of Fertility Decline: A Cross-country Analysis', in Pranab Bardhan, Mrinal Datta-Chauduri and T.N. Krishnan, *Development and Change*, Bombay: Oxford University Press.

Shaw, E. (1973) *Financial Deepening in Economic Development*, New York: Oxford University Press.

Sims, C. (1980) 'Macroeconomics and Reality', *Econometrica* 48: 1–48.

Snedecor, George W. and Cochran, William G. (1989) *Statistical Methods*, New Delhi: Affiliated East–West Press.

Spanos, Aris (1986) *Statistical Foundations of Econometric Modelling*, Cambridge: Cambridge University Press.

Spanos, A. (1990) 'Towards a Unifying Methodological Framework for Econometric Modelling', in C.W.J. Granger (ed.), *Modelling Economic Series*, Oxford: Clarendon Press.

Sproas, J. (1980) 'The Statistical Debate on the Net Barter Terms of Trade Between Primary Commodities and Manufactures', *Economic Journal* 90: 107–28.

Stigler, S.M. (1986) *The History of Statistics: The Measurement of Uncertainty before 1900*, Cambridge MA: Belknap Press.

Tukey, J.W. (1977) *Exploratory Data Analysis*, Reading, MA: Addison-Wesley.

Wheeler, E.F. (1984) 'Intra Household Food Allocation: a Review of Evidence', paper presented at meeting on 'The Sharing of Food', Bad Homborg, London: London School of Hygiene and Tropical Medicine. mimeo.

White, Halbert (1980) 'A Heteroscedasticity Consistent Covariance Matrix Estimator and a Direct Test for Heteroscedasticity', *Econometrica* 48: 817–38.

White, Howard (1992) 'What do we Know About Aid's Macroeconomic Impact?', *Journal of International Development* 4: 121–37.

Working, H. (1943) 'Statistical Laws of Family Expenditure', *Journal of the American Statistical Association* 38: 43–56.

Index